Contemporary Debates in Metaphysics

Contemporary Debates in Philosophy

In teaching and research, philosophy makes progress through argumentation and debate. Contemporary Debates in Philosophy provides a forum for students and their teachers to follow and participate in the debates that animate philosophy today in the western world. Each volume presents pairs of opposing viewpoints on contested themes and topics in the central subfields of philosophy. Each volume is edited and introduced by an expert in the field, and also includes an index, bibliography, and suggestions for further reading. The opposing essays, commissioned especially for the volumes in the series, are thorough but accessible presentations of opposing points of view.

1. Contemporary Debates in Philosophy of Religion *edited by Michael L. Peterson and Raymond J. Vanarragon*
2. Contemporary Debates in Philosophy of Science *edited by Christopher Hitchcock*
3. Contemporary Debates in Epistemology *edited by Matthias Steup and Ernest Sosa*
4. Contemporary Debates in Applied Ethics *edited by Andrew I. Cohen and Christopher Heath Wellman*
5. Contemporary Debates in Aesthetics and the Philosophy of Art *edited by Matthew Kieran*
6. Contemporary Debates in Moral Theory *edited by James Dreier*
7. Contemporary Debates in Cognitive Science *edited by Robert Stainton*
8. Contemporary Debates in Philosophy of Mind *edited by Brian McLaughlin and Jonathan Cohen*
9. Contemporary Debates in Social Philosophy *edited by Laurence Thomas*
10. Contemporary Debates in Metaphysics *edited by Theodore Sider, John Hawthorne, and Dean W. Zimmerman*

Forthcoming Contemporary Debates are in:

Political Philosophy *edited by Thomas Christiano and John Christman*
Philosophy of Biology *edited by Francisco J. Ayala and Robert Arp*
Philosophy of Language *edited by Ernie Lepore*

Contemporary Debates in Metaphysics

Edited by

**Theodore Sider, John Hawthorne,
and Dean W. Zimmerman**

© 2008 by Blackwell Publishing Ltd

BLACKWELL PUBLISHING
350 Main Street, Malden, MA 02148-5020, USA
9600 Garsington Road, Oxford OX4 2DQ, UK
550 Swanston Street, Carlton, Victoria 3053, Australia

The right of Theodore Sider, John Hawthorne, and Dean W. Zimmerman to be identified as the authors of the editorial material in this work has been asserted in accordance with the UK Copyright, Designs, and Patents Act 1988.

First published 2008 by Blackwell Publishing Ltd

6   2013

Library of Congress Cataloging-in-Publication Data

Contemporary debates in metaphysics / edited by Theodore Sider,
John Hawthorne, and Dean W. Zimmerman.
     p. cm. – (Contemporary debates in philosophy)
   Includes bibliographical references and index.
     ISBN 978-1-4051-1228-4 (hardcover : alk. paper) – ISBN 978-1-4051-1229-1
(pbk. : alk. paper)   1. Metaphysics.   I. Sider, Theodore.   II. Hawthorne, John (John P.)
III. Zimmerman, Dean W.

   BD95.C66 2007
   110–dc22   2007019836

A catalogue record for this title is available from the British Library.

Set in 10 on 12.5 pt Rotis Serif
by SNP Best-set Typesetter Ltd., Hong Kong
Printed and bound in Singapore
by Markono Print Media Pte Ltd

The publisher's policy is to use permanent paper from mills that operate a sustainable forestry policy, and which has been manufactured from pulp processed using acid-free and elementary chlorine-free practices. Furthermore, the publisher ensures that the text paper and cover board used have met acceptable environmental accreditation standards.

For further information on
Blackwell Publishing, visit our website at
www.blackwellpublishing.com

Contents

Notes on Contributors

Phillip Bricker is Professor and Head of Philosophy at the University of Massachusetts, Amherst. His interests range broadly over metaphysics, philosophical logic, philosophy of science, and philosophy of mathematics.

John W. Carroll is Professor of Philosophy at NC State University in Raleigh, North Carolina. He works in the areas of metaphysics and the philosophy of science. His interests center on the topics of laws of nature, causation, explanation, and time travel. He is the author of *Laws of Nature* (Cambridge University Press, 1994) and such articles as "Ontology and the Laws of Nature" (*Australasian Journal of Philosophy*, 1987), "The Humean Tradition" (*Philosophical Review*, 1990), "Property-Level Causation?" (*Philosophical Studies*, 1991), and "The Two Dams and that Damned Paresis" (*British Journal for the Philosophy of Science*, 1999). He is the editor of *Readings on Laws of Nature* (Pittsburgh University Press, 2004).

Cian Dorr received his BA from University College Cork, and his PhD from the University of Princeton, where he was a student of the late David Lewis. He is currently Assistant Professor of Philosophy at the University of Pittsburgh.

Matti Eklund is an Associate Professor of Philosophy at Cornell University. He has published articles in metaphysics, philosophy of language, and philosophy of logic.

John Hawthorne is Waynflete Professor of Metaphysical Philosophy at the University of Oxford. He is author of *Metaphysical Essays* (Clarendon Press, 2006), and has published widely in metaphysics, epistemology, philosophy of language, and Leibniz studies.

Eli Hirsch is Professor of Philosophy at Brandeis University. He is the author of a number of works in metaphysics, including *Dividing Reality* (Oxford University Press, 1993).

Robert Kane is University Distinguished Teaching Professor of Philosophy at the University of Texas at Austin. He is author of *The Significance of Free Will* (Oxford University Press, 1996), *Through the Moral Maze* (Paragon House, 1994), *A Contemporary Introduction to Free Will* (Oxford University Press, 2005) and editor of *The Oxford Handbook of Free Will* (2002), among other works in the philosophy of mind and ethics.

Ned Markosian is a philosophy professor at Western Washington University. He grew up in Montclair, New Jersey, graduated from Oberlin College, and received a PhD from the University of Massachusetts. He has worked mainly on issues in the philosophy of time and the mereology of physical objects.

Joseph Melia is a Reader in Metaphysics at the University of Leeds. His main interests are in modality, ontology, and the philosophy of physics. He is currently working on a book on ontology.

Derek Parfit was born in China in 1942 and received an undergraduate degree in Modern History at Oxford in 1964. Since 1967 he has been a Fellow of All Souls College, Oxford. He has often taught in the United States, and is now a regular Visiting Professor to the Departments of Philosophy of Rutgers, New York University, and Harvard. His first book, *Reasons and Persons*, was published by Oxford University Press in 1984. A second book, *Climbing the Mountain*, is nearly completed, and will also be published by Oxford University Press. This book will be about reasons and rationality, Kant's ethics, contractualism, and consequentialism.

Jonathan Schaffer is Professor of Philosophy at the Australian National University. He works mainly in metaphysics and epistemology. Further information about his work may be found on his website: <http://philrss.anu.edu.au/people-defaults/schaffer/index.php3/>.

Theodore Sider is Professor of Philosophy at New York University. He has published articles in metaphysics and philosophy of language, is the author of *Four-Dimensionalism* (Oxford University Press, 2001), and is co-author (with Earl Conee) of *Riddles of Existence: A Guided Tour of Metaphysics* (Oxford University Press, 2005).

J. J. C. Smart is Emeritus Professor, Australian National University, and is now living in Melbourne. He is an honorary in the School of Philosophy and Bioethics at Monash University. His most recent publication is a paper "Metaphysical Illusions" which is pertinent to the chapter in the present volume.

Chris Swoyer is Professor of Philosophy and Affiliated Professor of Cognitive Psychology at the University of Oklahoma. He has published, and continues to work on, the philosophy of logic, metaphysics, philosophy of science, and history of modern philosophy (especially Leibniz).

Judith Jarvis Thomson is Professor of Philosophy at MIT. Her published work is on topics in moral theory, metaethics, and metaphysics.

James Van Cleve taught for many years at Brown University and is now Professor of Philosophy at the University of Southern California. He works in metaphysics, epistemology, and the history of modern philosophy.

Kadri Vihvelin is Associate Professor of Philosophy at the University of Southern California. Her publications include "The Dif" (*Journal of Philosophy*, 2005); "Freedom, Foreknowledge, and the Principle of Alternate Possibilities" (*Canadian Journal of Philosophy*, 2000); "What Time Travelers Cannot Do" (*Philosophical Studies*, 1996); "Causes, Effects, and Counterfactual Dependence" (*Australasian Journal of Philosophy*, 1995); and "Stop Me Before I Kill Again" (*Philosophical Studies*, 1994).

Dean W. Zimmerman is an Associate Professor in the Philosophy Department at Rutgers University. He is editor of *Oxford Studies in Metaphysics* and author of numerous articles in metaphysics and philosophy of religion.

Introduction

Theodore Sider

There is something strange about metaphysics. Two strange things, really, although they are related. Metaphysics asks what the world is like.[1] But the world is a big and varied place. How can one meaningfully ask what apples, planets, galaxies, tables, chairs, air conditioners, computers, works of art, cities, electrons, molecules, people, societies . . . are like? The question is hopelessly general and abstract! One would normally ask first what apples are like, and then ask what planets and the rest are like separately. What meaningful questions are there about such a broad and hetero-geneous subject matter? Furthermore, you'd think that you'd need to ask a biologist what apples are like, an astronomer what planets are like, and so on. What can a philosopher contribute?

Let's have a look.

Consider a certain apple. What is it like? Well, it's red, and it's round. But this information doesn't come to us from *philosophy*. We need to *observe* the apple to learn its color and shape.

Consider another thing, Mars. It has iron oxide on its surface, and it is 6.4185×10^{23} kg in mass. This information about Mars, again, isn't something that philosophy can tell us about; we learn it from astronomers.

So far, we have found no philosophical subject matter. But if we abstract from certain details, we find things in common between our two examples; we find a recurring pattern despite the diverse subject matters. Here are the facts we cited:

The apple is red   Mars has iron oxide on its surface
The apple is round   Mars is 6.4185×10^{23} kg in mass

Notice that in each case, an object is said to have a feature. For example, in the first case, the object is the apple, and the feature is *being red*. Philosophers call objects that have features *particulars*, and they call the features "had" by particulars *properties*. Thus, we have:

$$\underbrace{\text{The apple}}_{\text{particular}} \quad \underbrace{\text{is red}}_{\text{property}} \qquad \underbrace{\text{Mars}}_{\text{particular}} \quad \underbrace{\text{has iron oxide on its surface}}_{\text{property}}$$

$$\underbrace{\text{The apple}}_{\text{particular}} \quad \underbrace{\text{is round}}_{\text{property}} \qquad \underbrace{\text{Mars}}_{\text{particular}} \quad \underbrace{\text{is } 6.4185 \times 10^{23}\,\text{kg in mass}}_{\text{property}}$$

In fact, this pattern is quite general. Think of other facts:

Fact	particular	property
This table is broken	the table	*being broken*
Electron e is negatively charged	electron e	*negative charge*
The stock market crashed	the stock market	*crashing*

The particular-property pattern keeps recurring. It appears that every fact about the world boils down to particulars having properties.[2] So it would seem that the world contains two different sorts of entities: particulars and properties. We have already uncovered a general fact about the world. Just as a scientist establishes generalizations about what the world is like in some limited sphere (for instance that charged particles repel one another or that the planets move in elliptical orbits), we have established a generalization – albeit a much broader and more abstract one – about the world. And we did it without detailed input from the sciences.

Of course, since this is philosophy we are talking about, there is controversy at every turn. The statement that there are two different sorts of objects in the world, particulars and properties, can be challenged. *Nominalists*, for example, believe in particulars, but not in properties. According to a nominalist, there simply is no such thing as the property of being red.

Put that baldly, the statement is misleading. It suggests that nominalists think that there is no such thing as a red object. But nominalists are not *crazy*. They agree that red objects exist; they just deny that *redness* exists.

The nominalist's position can be made clearer by thinking about the sentence 'The apple is red'. The nominalist agrees that the sentence is true. But now, consider the two parts of the sentence: its subject, 'The apple', and its predicate, 'is red'. What the nominalist thinks is that, whereas the subject does stand for an object (namely, the particular in question, the apple), the predicate does *not* stand for an object. The predicate 'is red' is of course *meaningful*; it's just that it doesn't stand for an *object*. Just as a comma is meaningful without standing for an object, predicates can be meaningful without standing for objects. The apple is red, even though there is no such thing as its redness.

We talk *as if* there are lots of things, when really, those things don't exist. We talk, for instance, as if there are such things as holes. We'll say: "Look at the size of that hole in the wall!" "Bring me the piece of cheese with three holes in it." "I can't wear that shirt because there is a hole in it." But surely there aren't *really* such things as holes, are there? What kind of object would a hole be? Surely what really exist are the physical objects that the holes are "in": walls, pieces of cheese, shirts, and so on. When one of these physical objects has an appropriate shape – namely, a perforated shape – we'll sometimes say that "there is a hole in it." But we don't really mean by this that there literally exists an extra entity, a hole, which is somehow made up of nothingness. The nominalist thinks that all subject-predicate sentences are a bit like sentences about holes. It might seem at first that the predicates refer to entities, but they really don't.

Are nominalists right? Do properties exist or don't they? This is no easy question, and Chris Swoyer and Cian Dorr (chapter 1) come to opposite conclusions on this and related matters. But in this brief look at nominalism, we have at least glimpsed what metaphysicians are after: patterns in apparently diverse phenomena, and generalizations that accurately describe these patterns. This book contains chapters in a number of areas of metaphysics; in each area, the goal is to find generalizations about abstract patterns:

Necessity

Scientists tell us of the laws of nature. Physicists tell us of the laws of physics, for example that like-charged particles must repel one another. Chemists tell us of the laws of chemistry, for example that if methane reacts with oxygen, it must produce carbon dioxide and water. Economists tell us of the laws of economics, for example that when demand increases then prices must increase as well. In each case, we have scientists telling us what *must* happen in certain conditions. What exactly are these laws of nature; what is the status of these "musts"? Laws of society exist because governing bodies have legislated them. But there is no governing body that has legislated the laws of nature. Physicists try to *discover* the laws of physics; they do not create them (chapter 2). And if everything happens as these laws of nature specify, human actions must conform to their dictates. How then can we have free will (chapter 7)? Further, there are other cases of "mustness". Every bachelor must be male; every prime number other than two must be odd. In what does the mustness of these facts consist (chapter 3)?

Time

Objects of all sorts, the objects of physics, chemistry, biology, and other sciences, last over time. This raises many philosophical questions. What does it mean for the *same* object to exist over time? A person at age 50, for instance, is the same person as she was as a child, even though nearly all of the matter that made up her body as a child no longer is with her at age 50. What makes a person the same over time? And indeed, what is it for time to pass at all (chapters 4–6)?

Ontology

Different sciences describe different objects. Physics describes subatomic particles, biology describes organisms, and so on. But must we believe that the objects from each science really exist? Consider organisms, for example. Could we not stick with the physicist's objects, and say that the only objects that really exist are subatomic particles? We could still agree that there are distinctively biological *phenomena*, even though there do not exist distinctively biological *objects*. For even if human organisms (for example) do not exist, there are nevertheless certain systems of particles that exhibit biological behavior. These are the systems involving particles that one ordinarily thinks of as being *parts* of a single biological organism. Thus, we have very general *ontological* questions (existence questions) about objects with parts (chapter 8). Other ontological questions include the question discussed above of whether properties exist, the question of whether numbers exist, and even the "metaontological" question of what it *means* to investigate whether objects of a certain sort "really" exist (chapter 9).

Within these and other areas of metaphysics, certain themes recur. For example, metaphysicians tend to fall into two camps: those who go around trying to *reduce* phenomena, and those who prefer instead to "leave the world as they found it." Consider the law of nature saying that like-charged particles repel one another. Of one thing we can be sure: the existence of such a law guarantees a *regularity*: everywhere and at any time, every pair of like-charged particles will indeed repel each other. Jonathan Schaffer (chapter 2.2) is a member of the reductionist camp. He wants to say that, roughly, there is nothing more to this law beyond the regularity. The law reduces to the regularity. What the physicists discover is simply that it is *universally true* that every two charged particles in fact repel each other. John W. Carroll disagrees (chapter 2.1); he is from the anti-reductionist camp. According to him, reductionists like Schaffer leave out something crucial. They leave out the *mustness*, the *necessity*, of laws. It doesn't just *happen* to be the case that charged particles repel one another. When you give two particles the same charge, they *must* repel each other. So there's something more to a law than just the fact that objects everywhere act in accordance with the law; you need to add necessity to a regularity to get a law.

Another example: time's passage. We ordinarily think of time as something that "moves". J. J. C. Smart (chapter 5.2) takes a reductionist approach to time's passage. According to him, time is just another dimension like space. And like space, it is not really correct to describe time as moving. What we ordinarily think of as time's passage just arises from the fact that at any given moment in time, we can only remember what has occurred in one direction through time (the direction we call the "past"). But objects in this direction are not "gone." Just as objects that are spatially distant – for example, objects on Mars – are just as real as objects around *here*, so, objects that are temporally distant – for example, dinosaurs – are just as real as objects around *now*. Dean Zimmerman, on the other hand, resists this reduction (chapter 5.1). Our ordinary belief about the matter is correct: time has passed since the time of the dinosaurs, and the dinosaurs are now gone. And this does not just mean that they are far away in time, just as Mars is far away in space. The dinosaurs simply do not *exist*.

A second (and related) recurring theme in metaphysics is the relationship between a scientific outlook and our ordinary beliefs. What science tells us doesn't always fit neatly with our ordinary beliefs about the world. In cases of conflict, should we revise science so that it doesn't conflict with our ordinary beliefs? Should we revise the ordinary beliefs in light of science? Or is it a mistake to think that they conflicted in the first place?

Time's passage again provides an example. The picture of time we get from physicists, especially from Einstein's theories of relativity, is Smart's picture of space-like time. But where, in this picture, is there room for our ordinary belief that time passes? According to Smart, our ordinary belief must be revised to fit it into the scientific picture, whereas according to Zimmerman, it is the scientific picture that must be revised, or at least augmented.

Or consider the problem of free will and determinism. Science tells us of a world governed by laws of nature. An electron has no choice about where to move; if another charged particle is in its vicinity, it cannot help but be repelled. The laws of nature must be obeyed. But on the face of it, this threatens our ordinary conception of ourselves as having free choices. We *blame* evildoers because we think that their choices were not inevitable; they *freely chose* to do wrong. Robert Kane (chapter 7.1) argues that these two pictures genuinely conflict. If the laws of nature fully determined what each and every object in the world was going to do, then there would be no room for any human freedom. (Fortunately, there is reason to think that the laws of nature that scientists have actually discovered are not quite so restrictive.) Kadri Vihvelin, on the other hand, tries to fit human freedom into the world of science, even a scientific world in which all human behavior is determined (chapter 7.2). But Vihvelin does not think that this calls for a revision of our ordinary beliefs about freedom. (In this way her position is unlike Smart's.) According to Vihvelin, it was a mistake to think that the two world-pictures were in conflict in the first place.

What should we trust when doing metaphysics: science or ordinary beliefs? The question leads some to extremes. At one end, we find those who think that all metaphysics can do is report science. At the other end, we find those who think that metaphysics should ignore science and listen only to ordinary beliefs. Each extreme is questionable.

The first extreme ignores the fact that science does not settle all metaphysical questions, and also the fact that scientists are influenced by their metaphysical presuppositions. We need a metaphysics that goes beyond reporting science in order to address the unsettled questions and evaluate the presuppositions.

The second extreme subdivides. It includes those who think that science and ordinary beliefs can never conflict, because they address "different worlds" (the "world of ordinary life" and the "world of science"). And it includes those dogmatists who think that ordinary beliefs can never seriously be doubted. The problem with each subdivision is that neither ordinary beliefs nor science is intended to be about a *novel* subject matter. Each is about *the world*. Ordinary folks, naturally, have beliefs about the world; but they hope to learn more about it through science. In addition to believing that objects move in space over time, that actions take time, and that objects take up space, ordinary believers also expect science to tell us the underlying nature of space and time. Nor do scientists step into another world when they don their lab coats. The point of science is to understand how the world, the one world, the world in which ordinary folks live, works.

A moderate view of the relation between science and ordinary beliefs seems in order: metaphysics must listen to, but is not exhausted by, science. This, however, leaves the exact nature of the relation wide open. Perhaps ordinary beliefs are *epistemic starting points* – claims with which we are entitled to *begin* our inquiries, but which may later be revised, perhaps because they conflict with science, perhaps because they conflict with one another. Perhaps not all ordinary beliefs should be taken equally seriously. We might, for example, grant more weight to beliefs that are fundamental to the structure of our thought about the world (recall the discussion of particulars and properties above), and grant little (if any) weight to ordinary beliefs about matters more properly addressed by the sciences. Perhaps the mere fact that a belief is an *ordinary* one counts for nothing at all; perhaps we should instead trust *reason*, a faculty capable of guiding both philosophically sophisticated scientists and scientifically informed philosophers.

Any metaphysician is bound, sooner or later, to face the following challenge. Science has been wildly successful. It has led to increasingly successful theories, technological advances, and consensus as to the truth. The history of metaphysics, on the other hand, has been as much one of wild goose chases as progress. Metaphysicians (like all philosophers!) continue to disagree about the same issues for millennia, and have not sent anyone to the moon.

This leads some philosophers to doubt that metaphysics has any value at all. A certain empiricist tradition in epistemology says that the only route to truth is through the senses, and ultimately through science. If you can't do an experiment to settle a question, the question isn't worth asking. At best, it is an idle question whose answer we will never know; at worst, the question is meaningless.

The empiricist is moved by an admirable desire to rid philosophy of undisciplined speculation. But the only empiricism that flatly rules out all metaphysics is one based on a naive view of science. Real scientists do not just "summarize what they see." Scientists must regularly choose between many theories that are consistent with the observed data. Their choices are governed by criteria like simplicity, comprehensiveness, and elegance. This is especially true in very theoretical parts of science, for instance theoretical physics, not to mention mathematics and logic.

A realistic picture of science leaves room for a metaphysics tempered by humility. Just like scientists, metaphysicians begin with observations, albeit quite mundane ones: there are objects, these objects have properties, they last over time, and so on. And just like scientists, metaphysicians go on to construct general theories based on these observations, even though the observations do not logically settle which theory is correct. In doing so, metaphysicians use standards for choosing theories that are like the standards used by scientists (simplicity, comprehensiveness, elegance, and so on).

Emphasizing continuity with science helps to dispel radical pessimism about metaphysics; the humility comes in when we remember the discontinuities. Observation bears on metaphysics in a very indirect way, and it is far less clear how to employ standards of theory choice (like simplicity) in metaphysics than it is in science. But metaphysicians can, and should, acknowledge this. Metaphysics is speculative, and rarely if ever results in certainty. Who would have thought otherwise?

Exactly what one should say about empiricism and metaphysics is a deep philosophical question in its own right, and it's unlikely that anyone will decisively answer it anytime soon. But that shouldn't, on its own, deter you from thinking about metaphysics. Philosophy is the one discipline in which questions about the value of that discipline are central questions within that very discipline. The philosopher must therefore live with uncertainty about whether her life's work is ultimately meaningful – that is the cost of the breadth of reflection demanded by philosophy. Philosophy's reflective nature is generally a good thing, but the down side is that it can lead to paralysis. Don't let it. You don't need to have answers to all meta-questions before you can ask first-order questions (just as you don't need to sort out the philosophy of biology before doing good work in biology). The meta-questions are certainly important. But the history of philosophy is full of sweeping theories saying that this or that bit of philosophy is impossible. Take heart in the knowledge that these have all failed miserably.

Notes

1   As opposed to, for example, what the world *ought* to be like (ethics), what we *know* about the world (epistemology), how we *think of* and *talk about* the world (philosophy of mind and language), and so on.
2   Some facts consist of multiple particulars having a "multi-place" property, also known as a relation. Philadelphia is 100 miles from New York: the particulars Philadelphia and New York have the *100 miles from* relation.

ABSTRACT ENTITIES

"Concrete" entities are the entities with which we are most familiar: tables, chairs, planets, protons, people, animals, and so on. "Abstract" entities are less familiar: numbers (for example, the number seven), properties (for example, the property of *being round*), and propositions (for example, the proposition *that snow is white*). Do abstract entities really exist? No one has ever seen, touched, or heard an abstract entity; but Chris Swoyer argues that they exist nevertheless. Cian Dorr argues that they do not.

Abstract Entities

Chris Swoyer

One of the most puzzling topics for newcomers to metaphysics is the debate about abstract entities, things like numbers (seven), sets (the set of even numbers), properties (triangularity), and so on. The major questions about abstract entities are whether there are any, if so which ones there are, and if any do exist, what they are like.

My aim here is to provide a brief and accessible overview of the debates about abstract entities. I will try to explain what abstract entities are and to say why they are important, not only in contemporary metaphysics but also in other areas of philosophy. Like many significant philosophical debates, those involving abstract entities are especially interesting, and difficult, because there are strong motivations for the views on each side.

In the first section, I discuss what abstract entities are and how they differ from concrete entities and in the second section, I consider the most compelling kinds of arguments for believing that abstract entities exist. In the third section, I consider two examples, focusing on numbers (which will be more familiar to newcomers than other types of abstract objects) and properties (to illustrate a less familiar sort of abstract entity). In the final section, I examine the costs and benefits of philosophical accounts that employ abstract entities.[1]

1 What are Abstract Entities?

Prominent examples of abstract entities (also known as *abstract objects*) include numbers, sets, properties and relations, propositions, facts and states-of-affairs, possible worlds, and merely-possible individuals (we'll see what some of these are in a bit). Such entities are typically contrasted with concrete entities – things like trees, dogs, tables, the Earth, and Hoboken. I won't discuss all of these examples, but will consider a few of the more accessible ones as case studies to help orient the reader.

Numbers and sets

Thought and talk about numbers are extremely familiar. We learn about the natural numbers (like three, four, and four billion), about fractions (rational numbers, like $^2/_3$ and $^7/_8$), and about irrational numbers (like the square root of 2 and e). And we learned a bit about sets in school – for example, the empty set, the set containing just 3 and 4, and the set of even numbers; we even learned to write names of sets using notation like '$\{3,4\}$'.

But what *are* numbers and sets? We cannot see them or point to them; they do not seem to have any location, nor do they interact with us or any of our instruments for detection or measurement in any discernible way. This may lead us to wonder whether there really are any such things as numbers, and whether, when we say things like "there is exactly one prime number between four and six," we are literally and truly asserting that such a number exists (after all, what could it be?). But, as we will see in section 3.1, there are also strong philosophical arguments that numbers do exist. Hence a philosophical problem: do they or don't they?

Properties and relations

The world is full of resemblances, recurrences, repetitions, similarities. Tom and Ann are the same height. Tom is the same height now as John was a year ago. All electrons have a charge of 1.6022×10^{-19} coulomb. The examples are endless. There are also recurrences in relations and patterns and structures. Bob and Carol are married, and so are Ted and Alice; the identity relation is symmetrical, and so is that of similarity. Resemblance and similarity are also central features of our experience and thought; indeed not just classifications, but all the higher cognitive processes involve general concepts. Philosophers call these attributes of qualities or features of things (like their color and shape and electrical charge) *properties*. Properties are the ways things can be; similarly, relations are the ways things can be related.

Assuming for the moment that there are properties and relations, it appears that many things have them. Physical objects: The table weighs six pounds, is brown, is a poor conductor of electricity, and is heavier than the chair. Events: World War I was bloody and was fought mainly in Europe. People: Wilbur is six feet tall, an accountant, irascible, and married to Jane. Numbers: three is odd, prime, and greater than two. All of these ways things can be and ways they can be related are repeatable; two tables can have the same weight, two wars can both be bloody. The two adjacent diamonds in figure 1 are the same size, orientation, and uniform shade of gray.

Champions of properties hold that things like grayness (or being gray) and triangularity (or being triangular) are properties, and that things like being adjacent and being a quarter of an inch apart are relations. Since the goal here is just to give one prominent example of a (putative) sort of abstract object, I will think of properties as universals (as many, but not all, philosophers do). On this construal, there is a single, universal entity, the property of being gray, that is possessed or exemplified by each

a b

Figure 1 Resemblances and Ways Things Can Be

of the two diamonds in our figure. It is wholly present in both *a* and *b*, and will remain so as long as each remains gray.

Philosophers who concur that properties exist may disagree about which properties there are and what they are like, but at least many properties (according to numerous philosophers, all) are abstract entities. Perhaps a property like redness is located in those things that are red, but where is justice, or the property of being a prime number, or the relation of life a century before? Such properties and relations exist outside space and time and the causal order, so they are rather mysterious. But, as we will see, there are also good reasons for thinking that properties and relations can do serious philosophical work, helping explain otherwise puzzling philosophical phenomena. This is a reason to think that they do exist. Another problem.

Propositions

Two people can use different words to say the same thing; indeed, they can even use different languages. When Tom says "Snow is white" and Hans says "Schnee ist weiss," there is an obvious sense in which they say the same thing. So whatever this thing is, it seems to be independent of any particular language. Philosophers call these entities *propositions*. They are abstract objects that exist independently of language and even thought (though of course many of them are expressed in language). Propositions have been said to be the basic things that are true or false, the basic truth-bearers, with the sentences or statements that express them being derivatively true or false.

In addition to saying that snow is white, Tom also believes that snow is white; and Hans, who speaks no English, also believes that snow is white (although he expresses the belief by saying "Schnee ist weiss"). Again, there is an obvious sense in which they believe the same thing. Some philosophers urge that the best way to explain this is to conclude that *there is* some one thing that Tom and Hans both believe. On this view, propositions are said to be the contents or meanings of beliefs, desires, hopes, and the like. They are also said to be the objects of beliefs. Thus the object of Tom's belief that red is a bright color is the proposition that red is a bright color.

On this view propositions are abstract objects that express the meanings of sentences, serve as the bearers of truth values (truth and falsehood), and are the objects of belief. But like numbers, propositions are somewhat mysterious. We can't see them, hear them, point to them. They don't seem to do anything at all. This gives us reason to doubt their existence. But, there are also reasons to think that they exist. Problems, problems, problems.

1.1 What abstract entities are (nearly enough)

Debates about abstract objects play a central role in contemporary metaphysics. There is wide agreement about the paradigm examples of abstract entities, though there is also disagreement about the exact way to characterize what counts as abstractness. Perhaps this shouldn't come as a surprise; if any two things are so dissimilar that their difference is brute and primitive and hard to pin down, abstract entities and concrete entities (*abstracta* and *concreta*) are certainly plausible candidates.

Even so, the philosophically important features of the paradigm examples of abstracta (like those listed above) are pretty clear. They are atemporal, non-spatial, and acausal – i.e., they do not exist in time or space (or space-time), they cannot make anything happen, nothing can affect them, and they are incapable of change. Neither they, their properties, nor events involving them can make anything happen here in the natural world. We don't see them, feel them, taste them, or see their traces in the world around us. Still, according to a familiar metaphor of some philosophers, they exist "out there," independent of human language and thought.

Being atemporal, non-spatial, and acausal are not all necessary for being abstract in the sense many philosophers have in mind. Thus, many things that seem to be abstract also seem to have a beginning (and ending) in time, among them natural languages like Urdu and dance styles like the Charleston. It may seem tempting to say that such things exist in time but not in space, but where exactly? Moreover, this claim can't be literally true in a relativistic world (like ours certainly seems to be), where space and time are (framework-dependent) aspects of a single, more basic thing, namely space-time.

And not all are sufficient. For example, an elementary particle (e.g., an electron) that is not in an eigenstate for a definite spatial location is typically thought to lack any definite position in space. The technicalities don't matter here; the point is just that although such particles may seem odd, they do have causal powers, and so virtually no one would classify them as abstract. Again, according to many religious traditions, God exists outside of space and time, but he brought everything else into existence, and so many would be reluctant to classify him as an abstract object.

All this suggests that the division into concrete and abstract may be too restrictive, or that abstractness may come in degrees. I won't consider such possibilities here, however, because the puzzles about abstract entities that most worry philosophers concern those entities that are, if they exist, atemporal, non-spatial, *and* acausal. And we don't need a sharp bright line between abstracta and concreta to examine these.

A philosopher who believes in the existence of a given sort of abstract entity is called a *realist* about that sort of entity, and a philosopher who disbelieves is called an *anti-realist* about it. Abstract entities are not a package deal; it is quite consistent, and not uncommon, for a philosopher to be a realist about some kinds of abstract entities (e.g., properties) and an anti-realist about others (e.g., numbers).

Not-quite existence

Finally, some champions of abstract entities claim that there are such things, but grant them a lower grade of being than the normal, straightforward sort of existence enjoyed by George Bush and the Eiffel Tower. They often devise esoteric labels for this state; for example, numbers, properties, and the like have been said to *have being*, to *subsist*, to *exist but not be actual*, or partake of one or another of the bewildering varieties of not-quite-full existence contrived by philosophers. Such claims are rarely very clear, but frequently they at least mean that a given sort of entity is real in some sense, but doesn't exist in the spatiotemporal causal order. Which is pretty much just to say it is abstract.

We will not pursue such matters here, however, since many of the same problems arise whether the issue about the status of abstracta is framed in terms of the existence or merely the subsistence or being of such things. Whatever mode of being the number two possesses, we still cannot perceive it, or pick it out in any way, and it seems to make no difference to anything here in the natural world. Because many of the most debated issues arise for all the proposed modes of being of abstract objects, I will focus on existence.

Why questions about abstracta matter

Explicit discussion of abstract entities is a relatively recent philosophical phenomenon. Plato's Forms (his version of universal properties) have many of the features of abstract objects. They exist outside of space and time, but they seem to have some causal efficacy. We can learn about them, perhaps even do something like perceive them, though perhaps only in an earlier life (this is Plato's doctrine of recollection).

Soon after Plato, properties and other candidate abstracta – e.g., merely possible individuals (individual things, e.g., persons, that could have existed but don't) – were reconstrued as ideas in the mind of God. This occurred through the influence of Augustine and others, partly under the influence of Plotinus and partly under that of Christianity. Human beings were thought to have access to these ideas because of divine illumination, wherein God somehow transferred his ideas into our minds. In later accounts like Descartes' we had access to such ideas because God placed them in our minds at birth (they are innate). Such views persisted though medieval philosophy and well into the modern period. In this period, philosophers like Locke began to view what we thought of above as properties (e.g., redness, justice) as ideas or concepts in individual human minds.

It was really only in the nineteenth century, with work on logic and linguistic meaning by figures like Bernard Bolzano and Gottlob Frege, that abstract entities began to come into their own. They emerged with a vengeance around the turn of the twentieth century, with work in logic, the theory of meaning, and the philosophy of mathematics, and, more generally, because of a strongly realist reorientation of much of philosophy at this time in the English- and German-speaking worlds. After a few decades, interest in abstract entities subsided, but by the end of the twentieth century, there was perhaps more discussion of a wider array of abstract objects than ever before.

Although explicit discussion of abstract entities has a fairly recent history, they are central to debates over venerable philosophical issues, including the nature of mathematical truth, the meanings of words and sentences, the features of causation, and the nature of cognitive states like belief and desire. These debates also lie at the center of many perennial disputes over realism and anti-realism, particularly standard flavors of nominalism. Discussions about the existence of abstract objects may also illuminate the nature of human beings and our place in the world. If there are no abstract objects, nothing that transcends the spatiotemporal causal order, then there may well be no transcendent values or standards (e.g., no eternal moral properties) to ground our practices and evaluations. And if there is also no God, it looks like truth and value must instead be somehow rooted here in the natural order. We are more on our own.

2 Why Believe there are Abstract Objects?

The central questions about abstract objects are: Are there any? If at least some kinds of abstract objects exist, can we discover what they are like? How can we decide such issues? (This question is a problem because it seems to be difficult to make contact with abstract objects in order to learn about their nature.) In this section I will offer an answer to the first question that also suggests an answer to the second.

A good way to get a handle on the issues involving abstract entities is to begin by focusing on the *point* of introducing them in the first place. Philosophers who champion one or another type of abstract object almost always do so because they think those objects are needed to solve certain philosophical problems, and their views about the nature of these abstracta are strongly influenced by the problems they think they are needed to solve and the ways in which they (are hoped to) solve them. Hence, our discussion here will be organized around the tasks abstracta have been introduced to perform. These tasks are typically *explanatory*, to explain various features of philosophically interesting phenomena, so to understand such accounts we need to ask about the legitimacy, role, and nature of explanation in metaphysics.

2.1 Philosophical explanations and existence

Ontology is the branch of metaphysics that deals with the most general issues about existence. Of course we know a great deal about what sorts of things exist just from daily life: things like trees, cats, cars, other people, the moon. And science tells us more about what sorts of things there are: electrons, molecules of table salt, genes. But ontology attempts to get at the most general categories or sorts of things there are, e.g., physical objects, persons, numbers, properties, and the like. Some philosophers doubt that the very enterprise of ontology makes sense (see chapter 9), but we will begin by assuming that it does.

For many centuries ontology aspired to be a demonstrative enterprise. On this traditional conception, ontology employs valid arguments to establish conclusions about what the most general and fundamental things in the universe are. It proceeds from obviously secure premises, step by deductively valid step, to obviously secure conclusions. The traditional standards for security were very high, requiring unassailable, necessary, self-evident "first principles." These were supposed to be claims that couldn't possibly be false and that no reasonable person could doubt.

The chief problem with this picture is that when we judge classical arguments in ontology by such standards, most fail, and many fail miserably. There is, among other things, no consensus about which candidates for first principles are even true, much less necessarily so, and, in many cases, demanding valid arguments seems to be asking for too much. By these standards, even the best that the greatest philosophers could devise comes up far short.

Nowadays, many philosophers would gladly settle for premises that are uncontroversially true – or even just fairly plausible. But they still devote a good deal of time distilling arguments for (or against) the existence of one or another sort of abstract object down to a few numbered premises and a conclusion to write on the board; they check for validity, and then (most often) dismiss the arguments. This approach is often invaluable, but it has limitations. For one thing, few philosophical arguments survive long when judged by the pass–fail standards of deductive validity (how likely is it, after all these centuries of inconclusive results, that Jones has just devised an unassailable demonstration that properties exist?). Indeed, it is quite possible that there are no deductively sound arguments beginning from true premises which do not mention abstracta and end with conclusions that abstracta exist ("no abstracta in, no abstracta out"). We often miss things of value if we write arguments off simply because they are not deductively valid. But if traditional and contemporary versions of the demonstrative ideal set the bar too high, how should we think about arguments and disagreements in ontology?

When we turn to the ways philosophers *actually* evaluate views about abstract objects, we typically find things turning on the pluses and minuses of one view compared to those of its competitors. And a very common feature of the (putative) pluses is that they involve explanation. For example, we are told that the existence of numbers would explain mathematical truth or that the existence or properties (like triangularity) would explain why it is that various objects are triangular and that it would also help explain how we recognize newly encountered triangles as triangles.

Moreover, even when the word 'explain' is absent, we frequently hear that some phenomenon holds in virtue of, or because of, this or that property, that a property is the ground or foundation or most enlightening account of some phenomenon, or that a property is (in part) the truthmaker, the *fundamentum in re* (as the medievals would have said) for the phenomenon. For example, it has been urged that the exemplification of a single, common property grounds the fact that our two items in figure 1 (above) are triangular; it makes it true that each is a triangle. The same property also helps to explain how we recognize that they are triangular and why the world 'triangle' applies to them.

Similar claims have been made on behalf of other abstracta. The role of expressions like 'explain' is to give reasons, to answer why-questions, which is a central point of explanation. My suggestion is that we should (re)construe arguments for the existence of abstract entities as inferences to the best overall available ontological explanation (we'll return to this in sections 3 and 4; see also Swoyer 1982, 1983, 1999a).

I will develop this idea in the course of examining the example of numbers, but first let's see what morals we can draw from the view that arguments for the existence of abstract objects are *ampliative* (i.e., deductively invalid but capable of offering good, though not conclusive, support for their conclusions).

First, we should acknowledge at the outset that there will rarely (probably never) be knock-down arguments for (or against) the existence of any type of abstract entity. On this approach, metaphysics (including ontology) is a fallibilistic, ever-revisable enterprise. By way of example, twentieth-century physics presents us with a very surprising picture of physical reality, and it may well call for innovations in ontology. To note just one case, quantum field theory, that branch of physics that deals with things at a very small scale (quarks, electrons, etc.), strongly suggests that there are (at the fundamental level) no individual, particular things; there may be no fact about how many "particles" of a given kind there are in a particular region of space-time. If so, the traditional view that individuals or substances are a fundamental category of reality may be overthrown.

Second, although each specific argument for the existence of a certain kind of abstract entity may not be fully compelling, if there are a number of independent arguments that a given sort of entity exists, the claim that they do could receive *cumulative confirmation* by helping to explain a variety of phenomena.

Third, if some type of abstract entity is postulated to play particular explanatory roles, this *affords a principled way to learn about its nature.* We ask what such an entity would have to be like in order to play the roles it is postulated to fill. What, to take a question considered below, would the existence or identity conditions of properties have to be for them to serve as the meanings of predicates like 'round' or 'red'?

If we are fortunate, we might devise a series of ontological explanations that employ the same entity. This increases information, because different explanations may tell us different things about what that entity is like. It also increases confirmation, because the sequence of explanation may provide cumulative support for the claim that the entity they all invoke actually exists.

Explanatory targets and target ranges

An explanation requires at least two things. First, something to be explained, an *explanation target.* Second, something to explain it. In ontology, it is a philosophical theory (though "theory" is often a bit grandiose) like Plato's theory of forms that does the explaining. We will be concerned with those theories that employ abstract objects in their explanation.

Explanation targets for ontology can come from anywhere. From the everyday world around us (e.g., different objects can be the same color, and a single object can change color over time); from mathematics (e.g., it is necessarily the case that three is a prime number); from natural languages (e.g., the word 'triangle' is true of many different individual figures); from science (e.g., objects attract one another because of their gravitational mass but may repel one another if they are different charges). Explanation targets for ontology can come from almost any area of philosophy (e.g., many moral values seem to be objective, but it's a bit mysterious how this can be so). I will call a more-or-less unified collection of explanation targets a *target domain.*

In the next section I briefly discuss several target domains that have led some philosophers to postulate abstract entities. Although I believe that arguments in ontology are usually best construed as ampliative, much of what follows can be adapted fairly straightforwardly to the view that philosophical arguments should aim to be deductively sound.

3 Examples of Work Abstracta Might Do

When we turn to actual debates about abstract objects, we find few (arguably no) knock-down, iron-clad, settled-once-and-for-all arguments for, or against, the existence of most of the abstract objects that interest philosophers. Instead, the evaluation of the arguments involves the art of making trade-offs, the weighing of philosophical costs and philosophical benefits. I will urge that although there are widely shared, quite sensible criteria for this, they fall short of providing rules or a recipe that forces a uniquely correct answer to the question of which, if any, abstract entities exist. Benefits rarely come without costs, and we will examine some of the costs of abstracta in section 4. In this section we will consider some of their benefits.

There are many candidate abstracta and there is space to discuss only one. I will focus on the natural numbers (0, 1, 2, and so on up forever), because this example will be familiar to readers with little background in philosophy.

3.1 Numbers

Target range for philosophy of mathematics

There is no unanimity about precisely which mathematical phenomena are legitimate targets for philosophical explanation, but in the case of number theory (basic arithmetic), there is widespread agreement about the following.

1 The sentence '7 + 5 = 12' is true, and its truth is independent of our beliefs and opinions. This is also the case for many other sentences of arithmetic. Similarly, many other sentences of arithmetic, like '7 + 5 = 13' are false, and are so independently of what we happen to think. The *truth value* (either truth or falsity) is independent of our beliefs and opinions.

2 Statements of arithmetic *necessarily* have the truth values they do; '7 + 5 = 12' could not have been false under any circumstances and '7 + 5 = 13' could not have been true.

3 Quite apart from questions about language and truth, it is the case that 7 + 5 = 12 but it is not the case that 7 + 5 = 13. And the first is necessarily the case and the second, necessarily, is not.

4 There are infinitely many natural numbers, and necessarily so (there could not have been fewer).

5 The grammatical structure of the sentence '3 is prime' parallels that of 'Sam is tall'. In the later case the subject term, 'Sam', is standardly thought to denote a real object, the person Sam, and the sentence is true because the thing 'Sam' denotes is tall. This suggests that in '3 is prime' the numeral '3' might denote something, and that the sentence is true because the thing it denotes is a prime number.

6 We can employ standard logic in reasoning about arithmetic; the normal, logically valid patterns of inference apply. For example, the step from 'Sam is tall' to 'There is something that is tall' is a valid inference, both intuitively and in standard systems of logic. So too is the step from '3 is prime' to 'there is something that is prime'.

7 The claim 'there is something that is prime' follows from a true sentence ('3 is prime') and seems, quite independently, to be true. But the claim that there is such a thing is just our ordinary, paradigm way of saying that something exists, that it is genuine or really there. Perhaps this is not always the case, but it typically is. So we at least seem to be committed to the view that there is something that is a prime number.

8 It is possible to have reliable justified beliefs and, indeed, knowledge in mathematics.

9 Much of our mathematical knowledge is a priori. This means that we do not need to learn, and almost never justify, our claims in arithmetic by appeal to experience. Once we know what '1' and '2' and '+' and '=' mean, we just see that 1 + 1 = 2.

The list isn't complete, and some of the items (e.g., 1) may be more central than others (e.g., 2). Still, the more of these targets a philosophical account can explain, the better. As we will see, however, the features that enable a theory to explain some of these phenomena sometimes make it difficult for it to explain others.

Sample explanations in mathematics using abstracta

A wide array of philosophical accounts have been developed to explain these targets. I will discuss one of the simplest approaches that employs abstracta.

Here is the metaphysical story. The natural numbers are objects or entities, though ones of a very special kind. They are abstract, existing outside of space and time and the causal order. There are infinitely many of them (what logicians call a denumerable infinity of them). They do not change. They exist necessarily (they could not have failed to exist), and they necessarily have the properties and stand in the relations that they do (it is necessarily the case that 13 is a Fibonacci number and that $13 > 7$).

This metaphysical picture allows us to explain item (3) in a very straightforward way. It's the case that $7 + 5 = 12$ because that it just how things are with these mind-independent, objective entities, the numbers – in particular with 7, 5, and 12. And there are infinitely many natural numbers item (4), because that is just how many of these entities there are (nothing deep here).

The purely metaphysical picture may also seem to explain (1) and (2), but to account for matters involving truth, we have to say something about meaning or semantics. Here, as is often the case with accounts of abstract entities, we need to make one or more additional assumptions, *auxiliary hypotheses*, in order to use those entities to explain the targets we want them to explain.

Here we need some *semantic* auxiliary hypotheses like the following. First, numerals are singular terms, ones that can occupy subject positions in sentences, and they denote the appropriate numbers ('0' denotes 0, '1' denotes 1, and so on out forever). Moreover, numerical terms like these would denote the same things in any possible situation (so they are what philosophers call "rigid designators"). Predicates like 'prime number' stand for the property of being a prime number and relational predicates like '<' stand for the relation of being a smaller natural number (I won't worry here about what these really are). Finally, function expressions like '+' and '×' stand for numerical functions like the addition function (which outputs 5 when you input 2 and 3) and the multiplication function (which outputs 6 when you input 2 and 3). This isn't the entire story, but it is enough for us to see the basic ideas about how the explanations here work.

We then say that a sentence of the form 'n is P', where n is a name of a natural number (e.g., the numeral '3') and P is a predicate (e.g., 'even'), is true just in case n refers to a number that has the property that the predicate P stands for. Similar stories are told for relation and function terms. All of this is a bit loose, but since the work of Alfred Tarski in the 1930s, we know how to make it completely precise. The interested reader can find the details in any good introductory text on symbolic logic, but they aren't needed to appreciate the basic ideas here.

We can now explain why '3 is prime' is true and '4 is prime' is false: '3' stands for an abstract object, the number three; 'prime' stands for the property of being prime, and three has that property. By contrast, '4' stands for an abstract object, the number four, that lacks the property. Similar accounts explain why '5 < 7' and

'7 + 5 = 12' are true and '7 < 5' and '7 + 5 = 13' are false. This explains item (1) on the list. Moreover, since numerical terms necessarily stand for the things that they do, and because the natural numbers necessarily exemplify the properties and stand in the relations that they do, these claims necessarily have the truth values they do (item 2).

Simple sentences of arithmetic appear to have a simple subject-predicate structure (item 5; when relation or function terms are involved there is more than one subject term, with '5' and '7' being the two subject terms of '5 < 7'). We can now explain this because, given the machinery invoked in our explanations thus far, this is exactly the structure such sentences *do* have. And we can apply standard logic in a completely straightforward way to explain why normal logical inference rules are valid when we apply them to arithmetical sentences (item 6). For example, existential generalization (the rule that allows us to infer the conclusion "there is something that is F" from the premise "n is F") works because, if we take a true sentence like '3 is prime', we know that it is true because '3' stands for something (the number three) that is prime. Hence it follows that there is something (three) that is prime. And on this account this sentence does indeed make a true existence claim, telling us that there really is something (once again three) that is prime (item 7).

Items (8) and (9) differ from the preceding seven insofar as they involve notions like justification and knowledge. These are *epistemic notions*, ones studied in the philosophical field known as the theory of knowledge or epistemology (from the Greek *episteme*, 'knowledge', and *logos*, 'theory'). This is the area of philosophy that deals with knowledge and related concepts like justification. Although this is a different field from ontology, claims about ontology meet up with questions in epistemology when we ask whether, and if so how, we can know about abstract entities.

Justification in arithmetic (and in mathematics generally) often proceeds by way of calculations and, at more advanced levels, proofs. These are chains of logically valid patterns of inference. Our previous machinery justifies the application of logic in arithmetic, and so explains some features of mathematical justification. If we are already justified in believing that '3 is odd', we are then also justified in believing 'there is something that is odd'. This is so because existential generalization is a mini-valid argument pattern, so if the first sentence is true, the second must be true as well.

But our reasoning must begin somewhere. How do we justify those of our arithmetical beliefs that we don't prove? How do we justify our belief (assuming we take it as basic) that 1 + 0 = 1? Alas, accounts like the one so far that seem well equipped to explain phenomena (1)–(7) founder when we come to (8) and (9). (The classic discussion of this difficulty is Benacerraf, 1973.)

The basic problem is that since numbers are abstract, they lie completely outside the spatiotemporal order. We seem unable to achieve *any* sort of contact with them. We can't see numbers, touch them, point to them, measure them. Nor do they cause things we can see or touch or point to or measure. So how do we ever learn anything about numbers? Since all of us know that five is an odd number, we do, somehow, know something about them. On the present account, this knowledge is about an abstract object, namely the number five, though of course a person may not think of it as being an abstract object, perhaps never having heard of such things. But how do we acquire this knowledge? The problem is serious enough that we will defer it in order to treat it in some detail below.

There are competing explanatory accounts of our nine phenomena that employ abstracta other than numbers (especially sets, but also properties, categories, and structures). They have many of the same costs and benefits as our simple account using numbers, however, and I will not discuss them here. Finally, we should note that strategies like the one sketched above can be applied in many other parts of mathematics by postulating additional abstract objects, e.g., irrational numbers, complex numbers, and other sorts of mathematical entities (like points, lines, groups, vector spaces).

Lessons the explanations teach us about these abstracta

We know a good deal about numbers before we ever study philosophy, so the present philosophical explanations aren't likely to provide much novel information about their nature (other than telling us that they are abstract). But in the case of less familiar abstracta (like properties or propositions), the explanations might well shed light on the nature of the entity in question. I will say something about what this involves here in the case of numbers to illustrate the sort of thing that is involved in inquires about the nature of any sort of abstract entity.

There are at least four things philosophers often want to know about a given sort of entity: its existence conditions, its identity conditions, its modal status, and its epistemic status.

Existence conditions   There may not seem to be much philosophical interest in the existence conditions of natural numbers, since we already know which numbers there are (0, 1, 2, 3, . . .; anything you can get by starting with 0 and adding 1 as many times as you like). But with less familiar notions, like that of complex numbers or vector spaces, we typically want to know their existence conditions. Under what conditions is something a complex number? Which (putative) items of that sort exist? The aim is to provide necessary and sufficient conditions for something being a complex number. To take another example, in set-theory very elaborate conditions are laid down for telling us which sets exist.

This model is sometimes carried over from mathematics to philosophy, where philosophers ask for the existence conditions for various sorts of non-mathematical abstracta like properties and propositions. It is a matter of debate whether asking for necessary and sufficient conditions of this sort unreasonably assimilates philosophy to mathematics, but obviously the more their proponents can say about which properties or propositions there are, the better. For example, can there be properties that are not exemplified? Again, assuming that being round and being square are properties, are there also "disjunctive" properties like *being round or square*, or "conjunctive" properties like *being round and square*?

Identity conditions   If *x* and *y* are abstract objects, can we provide necessary and sufficient conditions for them being one and the same object (in the way that 2 and the positive square root of 4 are the same, but 2 and the negative square root of 4 are not)? In the case of numbers, we can typically answer specific questions of this sort by calculation or proof, but can we give general identity conditions that apply to *all* natural numbers in one fell swoop? If *x* and *y* have exactly the same numerical properties and stand in exactly the same numerical relations, it then turns out that they must be identical, the self-same number. But we might like conditions that throw more light on what it is to be a natural number. By way of example, if x and y are sets, then x and y are identical just in case they contain exactly the same members. Here we get identity conditions that are specifically geared to sets (in terms of the notion of set membership), and so are more enlightening about their specific nature.

Identity conditions are important in mathematics, and as with existence conditions it is possible to worry that requiring identity conditions for a given sort of abstract object as a precondition to granting its existence (or even to discussing whether it exists or not) is an unreasonable demand. After all, philosophers have thus far not been very successful at spelling out precise identity conditions for physical objects or for persons – but we all know perfectly well that physical objects and persons exist. Of course an account of a given sort of abstract object should tell us as much as possible about that object, so we would like to know as much as possible about when x and y are identical, even if this falls short of full necessary and sufficient conditions for identity.

Modal status   Do the abstract entities invoked in our explanations exist necessarily (they simply couldn't have failed to have existed) or merely contingently (they might not have existed)? Second, we may ask which features of, and relations among, these entities (e.g., being an even number) belong to them necessarily (in any circumstances in which they could exist) and which features only belong to them contingently (they could have existed without having them).

Our hope is that if the answers to questions about the nature of a given sort of abstract entity aren't obvious before developing explanations employing that entity, the explanations themselves will help us answer these questions. In the present case, we hope to see what the modal status of a postulated abstract entity *must be* in order to explain some of the targets it is supposed to explain. In the explanation sketches of the nine phenomena (listed above on page 19), the answer is that the numbers necessarily exist and that they necessarily have the properties and stand in the relations that they do. We must conclude this in order to explain items (2), (3), and (4).

Epistemic status   The most basic epistemological question about an abstract entity we have reason to believe exists is how we can know about it. We can't reasonably expect a detailed scientific answer to such questions at this stage in history, but it would be very useful to be given a general idea. By way of analogy, there is much that we don't currently understand about visual perception. But we have enough of a general idea how visual perception works to see that it is a normal, natural, causal process involving the reflection of light off objects to the backs of our retinas, there stimulating nerves and setting off various electro-chemical reactions that, in turn, trigger processes in the visual cortex and other parts of the brain. Admittedly, we don't understand the conscious aspects of the visual experience itself, but at least they occur in time, surely in space (the brain – besides, you can't really separate time and space), and involve some sorts of natural, neural causal processes. It would be good to have at least a little detail of this general sort in order to shed light on the way we know about abstract objects.

In the process of answering these questions, we may get an answer to the further epistemic question of whether our knowledge about a given sort of entity (here, natural numbers) is a priori or not. We began by assuming it was, as is traditional, though the account we examined didn't yield a very satisfying explanation of how this could be so (there are other accounts that do, but they have trouble explaining earlier items on the list). But in the case of at least some other abstract entities, for example properties, there is some debate as to whether our knowledge about them is a priori, i.e., attainable independently of experience (save for enough experience to acquire the concept of them) or a posteriori (based on experience). We might hope to shed light on this question by examining the kinds of jobs that properties are supposed to do.

Evaluating explanations in ontology

We can rarely explain much with the bald assertions that numbers exist or that properties exist. These claims are typically part of a longer story, a philosophical theory, that tells us something about what the relevant abstract entity is like. The theory also needs to explain how the entity is related to other things, including other abstract entities (theories often invoke more than just one sort of abstract entity, e.g., accounts in semantics often employ both properties and propositions). The account also needs to tell us how its abstracta are related to the phenomena around us that led us to postulate them in the first place.

To take a non-mathematical example, a full account of properties should tell us something about which sorts of things have properties (e.g., can properties themselves exemplify properties?), and should help answer questions like whether there exist such properties as colors, shapes, and masses. How are properties related to those things that have them, i.e., what does exemplification amount to? Answers to such questions help us *apply* the theory of the abstract entity, bridging the gap between the abstract realm and the typically concrete phenomena we want to account for. And an especially important part of an account of abstracta is to tell us at least enough to see that their connection to our cognitive faculties is not hopelessly problematic.

Desiderata

There are various desirable features of ontological explanations, features that, other things being equal, make an explanation more compelling.

Do more with less   This injunction can take various forms. The fewer unexplained (primitive) entities, the better. If two primitive abstract entities will explain the targets in a domain, don't use six to do so. The motivation here is general and somewhat vague, but it is important and has a venerable history. The great Medieval philosopher, William of Ockham (c. 1287–1347), counseled philosophers "not to multiply entities beyond necessity."

This precept has become known as Ockham's Razor, but, as everyone who writes on the matter soon observes, Ockham's exhortation was to avoid multiplying entities beyond necessity. So the relevant question is always whether a given sort of abstract entity is necessary, which typically means: is it *required* in order to *explain* any philosophical targets? The answers to such questions are often controversial, so although we can agree that, *if* a short simple theory works just as well as a long and complicated one, the former is better, in practice, the wielding of Ockham's Razor is often contentious.

Breadth and depth of coverage are important   The more of the nine arithmetical phenomena (and, indeed, the more additional phenomena) a philosophical theory can explain, the better. Similarly, it counts in favor of a theory of meaning based on properties if it can explain the semantic behavior of different constructions of English (e.g., 'Sam is tall' and 'Sam is taller than Jill').

Explain why rival accounts work as well as they do   It is useful if an explanation illuminates why competing accounts work (in those places where they do work) and fail (where they fail).

Explain which things need explaining   It is also good if an account can illuminate what should, and what should not, be on the list of targets it is used to explain. And if it explains a traditional target away (showing that it doesn't really exist), it needs to provide arguments for doing so.

Don't solve one problem only to create another just as bad   It is important to explain a target (e.g., in semantics) without creating new problems elsewhere (e.g., in epistemology).

This list isn't exhaustive, but it illustrates some of the commonly accepted and central desiderata for explanations in ontology. Unfortunately, these desiderata can be in tension. For example, we can sometimes get by with fewer unexplained entities by sacrificing breadth of coverage. Hence, these goals do not add up to rules or recipes that always tell us which of several competing philosophical explanations is best, and this remains the case even if we add further plausible desiderata. But it is important that they often can tell us that certain explanations are not very good.

Constraints

There are also constraints on ontologically satisfactory explanations. Some are nearly universal (e.g., logical consistency, though even that has been challenged lately). Others vary with time or schools of thought, and some reflect quite idiosyncratic philosophical scruples or ideals. Constraints and desiderata fade into one another, but the importance of the former should not be underestimated.

For example, in various periods there have been religious constraints on metaphysical explanations. In medieval disputations about properties, issues involving faith, reason, and the nature of God were never far from view. Indeed, these matters often provided explanatory targets for metaphysicians. Philosophical orientations also provide constraints. For example, many philosophers have argued that knowledge must be grounded in experience. We cannot simply reason out what the world is like from the armchair; we have to go and check. Today, naturalistic world-views are popular, and these are often thought to allow only physical entities, or at most only entities that exist in space-time.

In concrete historical settings, constraints can seem very real, sometimes inevitable, even if at a latter time they seem arbitrary, even quaint. This needn't make metaphysics "subjective" in any debilitating sense (so that whatever a particular culture happens to think about it is "true for them"). But it is a useful reminder that metaphysics, like any other intellectual enterprise, is a human endeavor that takes place in, and is highly colored by, a time, culture, and tradition.

Difficulties with competitors   The best available ontological explanation must meet some minimal threshold of goodness to justify belief in its conclusion. Moreover, the notion of the best available explanation is comparative; a theory doesn't get many points for explaining something if a rival theory explains it much better. Hence, arguments for the existence of a particular sort of abstract entity often need to be bolstered by criticisms of opposing theses. For example, the view that properties are needed to play the role of semantic values of predicates is stronger when accompanied by arguments that other sorts of entities, e.g., sets (of the things to which the predicate applies), cannot play the role nearly as well. Finally, being the best explanation doesn't mean being perfect. Virtually all philosophical accounts have open problems, and trying to solve them is part of the day-to-day work of philosophers.

Quandaries and doubts   I have spoken as though inference to the best ontological explanation were relatively unproblematic, but there are various places where objections to it, and especially to its use in philosophy, can be raised. I have discussed these matters elsewhere (e.g., Swoyer 1983; 1999a; 1999b), however, and will not pursue the matter here.

4 Pluses and Minuses

Metaphysics, like life, often presents us with diverse, not fully compatible, goals that require us to make trade-offs, weigh costs against benefits, make hard decisions. In this section we consider the chief benefits, and costs, of abstract entities.

4.1 Benefits

The primary philosophical attraction of abstract entities is that they seem to offer so much explanatory power. For example, when we encounter words or phrases that look like denoting singular terms (e.g., '3', 'courage') we can explain this very neatly by arguing that they *are* singular terms and that they denote an abstract entity (a number, a property). The realist can often avoid denying the existence of relatively obvious phenomena (like the existence of mathematical truth, which some anti-realists about numbers and sets deny), needn't urge that we have been badly in error about entire realms of discourse (like mathematics), and can avoid resorting to tortured paraphrases to evade ontological commitment. Indeed, the more luxuriant lines of abstracta (e.g., Russell 1903; Zalta 1988; Bealer 1982) contain so much metaphysical machinery that it is almost a foregone conclusion that they can explain any phenomenon that comes their way. All this sounds a little to good to be true. Is it?

4.2 Costs

Ockamist impulses and ontological economy
Few philosophers like ontological bloat. Other things being equal, a good explanation of a philosophical target that doesn't rely on abstracta is preferable to a good expla-

nation that does. But other things are rarely equal. Abstract objects often add enough explanatory power that theories invoking them can give broader and smoother explanations of a target than theories that do not. For example, it is very difficult (though a number of philosophers believe not impossible) to give an account of mathematical truth that does not employ abstracta of any sort. While ontological economy is important, other things are rarely equal, so it is rarely decisive.

Anti-realism: there *are* alternatives

There is always anti-realism, so perhaps we shouldn't feel driven to abstracta as the only game in town. There are many forms that opposition to realism takes nowadays, as new positions (e.g., fictionalism, projectivism, error theories) spill over from the philosophy of mathematics, the philosophy of science, and meta-ethics into philosophy generally. Furthermore, with the demise of behaviorism, philosophy's linguistic turn is beginning to show its age, and the rise of cognitive science, and various flavors of conceptualism, are once again on the menu (e.g., Swoyer 2005). Still, none of these alternatives provides a strong reason for avoiding the need for a given sort of abstract object to explain a legitimate philosophical target unless the anti-realist explanation (or dismissal) of it is spelled out in a reasonably detailed and compelling way. So again, we must consider each approach case by case.

Epistemic access

Epistemology is the Achilles' heel of realism about abstracta. We are biological organisms thoroughly ensconced in the natural, spatiotemporal causal order. Abstract entities, by contrast, are atemporal, non-spatial, and causally inert, so they cannot affect our senses, our brains, or our instruments for measuring and detecting.

A few philosophers have postulated a cognitive faculty of intuition that provides some sort of non-causal access to numbers or other abstracta. The nature of this access has never been explained, however, and many of us find nothing like it in our own perception and thought. Scientists have no inkling where it is located in the brain, and it has yet to turn up in any empirical studies. Empirical investigation of thought that (might) seem to be about abstracta is becoming more common (e.g., Boroditsky and Ramscar 2002), and it may eventually illuminate the issues here. At present, however, it doesn't get at the most basic problems that have worried philosophers about our cognitive access to abstracta.

Perhaps knowledge about abstracta doesn't require contact with them. The only remotely plausible story about this would seem to be that such knowledge is innate. This may well be true of our rudimentary knowledge of arithmetic, but it doesn't scale up well to knowledge about tensor algebra or the semantic values of words for describing the nuances of medieval chivalry.

The epistemic problems here do not stem from any (almost certainly hopeless) causal theory of knowledge, but simply from the fact that our acquisition and justification of beliefs about things lying outside the spatiotemporal causal order is more than a little mysterious. Indeed, even if abstracta did exist, it is difficult to see how they could make any difference to our cognitive processes. Things would seem just the same whether they existed or not, or if they existed up until tomorrow, then suddenly vanished.

Abstract Entities | 27

Reference and non-uniqueness

Nowadays a major reason for postulating abstracta is to use them as semantic values in semantic accounts of natural languages. Unfortunately, the epistemic problems abstracta generate make it difficult to use them for this purpose. We can't make epistemic contact with abstracta, so it is difficult to see how we could get our words to latch onto them. We can't single numbers out, by pointing or in any other obvious way, and say 'that is 0', 'that is 37', and so on. We might try to pick 0 out by saying that '0 is the first of the natural numbers', but this doesn't really help unless we have pinned down the reference or extension of 'natural number' and (less obviously) that of 'first' (as it applies to the sequence of natural numbers). So we are back with the original problem. We can't make identifying reference in language because we can't make identifying reference in thought.

In some cases, particularly in mathematics, we can specify the structure of a given realm of abstract entities. For example, we can pin down the "structure" of the natural numbers with some sophisticated logic (with what is known as a second-order version of Peano's Postulates). The structure is roughly this: there is a first object in the structure (0); there is a second object in the structure (1) with nothing in between it and the first object; there is a third object (2) with nothing in between it and the second object; and so on forever. That is, the structure is that of an infinite, discrete series with a beginning but no end. But if there is one group of things with this structure, then, logicians have demonstrated, there are many, and there is little reason to suppose that any one of them gives the unique metaphysical truth about "What Numbers Really Are" (cf. Benacerraf 1965). Because we lack epistemic contact with numbers, we can only describe the structure of the realm of numbers, and such descriptions underdetermine the denotations of our numerical vocabulary. So, ironically, the apparent success of our earlier explanations for the semantic features of numbers seems undermined by the problems with epistemic phenomena.

5 Conclusion

So . . . are there abstract entities? And if so, which ones? The answers depend on the answers to three prior questions. Is inference to the best available overall ontological explanation ever legitimate? If so, when? And when it is, how do we adjudicate among competing explanations? My answers are more tentative than I would like, but this is a conclusion, so I will end by drawing some.

Is the game optional?

If someone won't play the metaphysical game, there are no knock-down, non-question-begging arguments to show she is wrong. We can cite reasons for, and against, the possibility of inference to the best ontological explanation, but none of them comes close to being conclusive. Indeed, if I am right, differences of beliefs in ontology very often stem from differences of beliefs about the legitimacy and nature of inference to the best explanation in ontology.

Evaluating competing explanations

The gist of the discussion thus far is that evaluation of rival explanations in ontology is a global affair that requires sound philosophical judgment rather than a reliance on hard and fast rules (the problem is that there are no such rules, though there are rough but generally accepted guidelines, so that not just anything goes). The process is global or holistic, in the sense that it depends on the weighing of many different considerations at the same time. And although the decisions that must be made in evaluating competing programs are usually made in light of shared philosophical values, there doesn't seem to be any uniquely correct way to trade such values off against each other. For example, other things being equal, more explanatory power, breadth of coverage, and simplicity are better than less. But then, when are things ever equal? And when they are not, is it better to have a richly detailed explanation of a narrower range of phenomena or a less detailed explanation of a wider range?

Disagreements about simplicity

Arguments over simplicity play a prominent role in debates in ontology, sometimes crowding out consideration of other important explanatory virtues. The verdict of simplicity is rarely unequivocal, however, and judgments about it differ from one philosopher to another. Still, some philosophical disputes actually come down in print to questions about whether two basic, undefined, primitive objects and one basic, undefined, primitive relation are simpler than one primitive object and two primitive relations. Such considerations are surely much too fragile to support conclusions about the "ultimate nature of reality," as if "What There Really Is" could come down to whether an account employs two primitive notions, rather than three.

The fundamental ontological trade-off

There is an even more fundamental trade-off that we face at every turn in philosophy, from ethics to philosophy of science to philosophy of mathematics to metaphysics. I will call it the *fundamental ontological trade-off*. This is the trade-off between explanatory power, on the one hand, and epistemic credibility, on the other; between a rich, lavish ontology that promises a great deal of explanatory punch, and a more modest ontology that promises more epistemological security and believability. How a philosopher strikes a balance in this trade-off goes a long way to determining whether or not she will believe there are abstract entities.

The more machinery (especially abstract machinery) we postulate, the more we might hope to explain – but the harder it is to believe in the existence of all that machinery. Russell makes this sort of point in his famous theft-over-honest-toil passage: "The method of 'postulating' what we want has many advantages; they are the same as the advantages of theft over honest toil. Let us leave them to others and proceed with our honest toil" (Russell 1919: 71). But without at least a little postulation, it is very difficult to even get started.

The upshot

Once ontological explanation is allowed and (rough-and-ready) ground rules are set, there can be winners and losers and perhaps a spectrum of views in between, but it is important that not everyone who plays the metaphysical game gets to win. For example, although Goodman and Quine's (1947) celebrated attempt to provide an account of mathematics that avoided all abstracta remains impressive, it simply cannot account for enough features of mathematics to be judged a success – even by Quine.

But once we eliminate the more unpromising explanations, we may well be left with more than one contender.

In short, if ontological explanations are legitimate, it is unlikely that there will be uniquely correct explanations, and so unlikely that we will arrive at a single picture about which abstracta (if any) there are. Perhaps we can make slow progress to this goal, with a series of explanations zeroing in more and more on the existence and nature of various abstracta. But such a series may instead lead to a fragmentation of entities, with a corresponding fragmentation of our views about them.

If epistemology isn't a problem, then abstracta win

If inferences to the best ontological explanation are legitimate, and if the epistemic problems about cognitive access to abstract entities can be overcome, then the case for at least some abstract entities is very strong. This is so because we can explain much more with them than without them. But the epistemological problems are severe.

A parting thought

Still, would it really be so bad if the best we could do was to rule out some accounts in ontology and learn to live with more than one survivor? Perhaps developing a tolerance for more than one (which need not mean every) ontological framework is the best we can do. If we can do this without falling into some dreadful sort of relativism, maybe that's good enough.

Note

1 Many discussions of abstract objects are rather technical, but in the interests of accessibility I will steer clear of such complexities and avoid logical notation (the interested reader can find many of the more technical matters discussed in some of the works cited here). Because the existence of various sorts of abstract objects, and indeed abstract objects in general, is a matter of contention, prudence suggests constant qualifications like "putative" examples of abstract entities and talk that "seems" to be about them. But this becomes tiresome and I will mostly leave such hedges tacit. I am grateful to David Armstrong, Hugh Benson, Monte Cook, Brian Ellis, Ray Elugardo, Jim Hawthorne, Herbert Hochberg, Chris Menzel, Adam Morton, Sara Sawyer, Ted Sider, Shari Villani, and Ed Zalta for helpful discussions on the topics discussed here.

References

Bealer, George. 1982. *Quality and Concept* (Oxford: Clarendon Press.)
Benacerraf, Paul. 1965. "What Numbers Could Not Be," *Philosophical Review* 74: 47–73.
—. 1973. "Mathematical Truth," *Journal of Philosophy* 70: 661–79.
Boroditsky, Lera, and Ramscar, Michael. 2002. "The Roles of Body and Mind in Abstract Thought," *Psychological Science* 13: 185–9.
Goodman, Nelson, and Quine, W. V. O. 1947. "Steps Toward a Constructive Nominalism," *Journal of Symbolic Logic* 12: 97–122.

Russell, Bertrand. 1903. *Principles of Mathematics* (New York: W. W. Norton & Co).

—. 1919. *Introduction to Mathematical Philosophy.* London: Routledge; repr. 1993.

Swoyer, Chris. 1982. "The Nature of Natural Laws," *Australasian Journal of Philosophy* 60: 203–23. Repr. in *Theory, Evidence and Explanation*, Darthmouth Publishing Co., 1995.

—. 1983. "Realism and Explanation," *Philosophical Inquiry* 5: 14–28.

—. 1999a. "How Metaphysics Might be Possible: Explanation and Inference in Ontology," *Midwest Studies in Philosophy: New Directions in Philosophy* 23: 100–31.

—. 1999b. "Properties," in Edward Zalta, ed., *Stanford Encyclopedia of Philosophy*; available at <http://plato.stanford.edu/entries/properties/>.

—. 2005. "Conceptualism," in P. F. Strawson and A. Chakrabarti, eds., *Universals, Concepts and Qualities* (Aldershot: Ashgate), pp. 127–54.

Zalta, Edward N. 1988. *Intensional Logic and the Metaphysics of Intentionality* (Cambridge, MA: Bradford Books/MIT Press).

There Are No Abstract Objects

Cian Dorr

1 The Thesis

Suppose you start out inclined toward the hard-headed view that *the world of material objects is the whole of reality*. You elaborate: 'Everything there is is a material object: the sort of thing you could bump into; the sort of thing for which it would be sensible to ask how much it weighs, what shape it is, how fast it is moving, and how far it is from other material objects. There is nothing else.' You develop some practice defending your thesis from the expected objections, from believers in ghosts, God, immaterial souls, Absolute Space, and so on.

None of this practice will do you much good the first time you are confronted with the following objection:

> What about *numbers* and *properties*? These are obviously not material objects. It would be crazy to think that you might bump into the number two, or the property of having many legs. One would have to be confused to wonder how much these items weigh, or how far away they are. But obviously there are numbers and properties. Surely even you don't deny that there are four prime numbers between one and ten, or that spiders and insects share many important anatomical properties.[1] These well-known truths evidently imply that there are numbers, and that there are properties. So your thesis is false. Not everything is a material object.

This disconcertingly simple objection is probably quite unlike anything you expected to have to deal with when you first announced your thesis. It is confusing precisely because it is so very simple: if the argument did lead you to give up your initial materialist beliefs, the fact that you ever held those beliefs in the first place should seem profoundly puzzling. How on earth could you have failed to notice the inconsistency between your belief that spiders and insects share many important anatomical properties and your belief that everything is a material object? Seeing this, you will quite naturally wonder whether your disagreement with the objector might not be merely verbal. You may want to begin your reply by making distinctions: 'Of course there is *in a sense* such a thing as the number two; but in another important sense it is still true that material objects are all there are.'

While I have no particular interest in defending the view that the world of material objects is the whole of reality, I think that this reply is right on target. Sentences like

(1)   There are four prime numbers between one and ten.
(2)   Spiders and insects share many important anatomical properties.
(3)   There are numbers.
(4)   There are properties.
(5)   Everything is a material object.

admit of (at least) two systematically different kinds of uses, which I will label "fundamental" and "superficial". Ordinary uses of sentences like (1) and (2) are superficial, and entirely appropriate. When we use these sentences superficially, we assert boring, well-known truths, just as we would have if we had said that spiders and insects both have exoskeletons, or that there are no square prime numbers. On the other hand, anyone who seriously uttered (5) would very likely be using this sentence in the fundamental way. They would be making a claim about "the ultimate furniture of reality": the claim that *in the final analysis*, there are only material objects. This claim is perfectly consistent with the truths that would be expressed by ordinary, superficial uses of sentences like (1) and (2). The appearance of conflict arises from the fact that each of the above sentences can be used in both ways, although the two uses are not always equally natural. (3) and (4) can be used superficially, in which case they would express truths even easier to know than the ones expressed by superficial uses of (1) and (2). Even (5) could in principle have superficial uses, which would express something obviously false. Conversely, (3) and (4), and even (1) and (2), can in principle be used in the fundamental way, in which case they would express claims that are far from obvious, and inconsistent with the claim expressed by fundamental uses of (5). Thus, the arguments from (1) to (3), from (2) to (4), and from (3) or (4) to the negation of (5) are valid in the sense that the conclusions follow from the premises *provided they are used in the same way.*

I hope this all seems too obvious to need arguing for as opposed to pointing out. How strange it would be to think that ordinary people, including those who never give a thought to questions of metaphysics, hold a wide range of beliefs that are incompatible with the thesis that, fundamentally speaking, everything is a material object, and express these beliefs whenever they use sentences like (1) and (2)! But if an argument is wanted, I can offer the following. In ordinary life, we treat arguments such as these as trivially valid:

(6) (a)   There is a planet that is distinct from some planet.
    (b)   So, the number of planets is greater than one.
(7) (a)   The Earth is round.
    (b)   So, the Earth has the property of being round.

Indeed, it is easy to hear the conclusions of these arguments as nothing more than stylistic variants, or "pleonastic equivalents" (Schiffer 2003), of the premises. Surely this can't be an outright mistake. But, taken in the fundamental sense, (6b) and (7b), like (1) and (2), express substantive metaphysical claims – claims that would be false if there were, fundamentally speaking, only material objects. These controversial claims certainly do not follow analytically – just as a matter of meaning – from (6a) or (7a). Whether we take (6a) and (7a) themselves as fundamental or as superficial, there is manifestly nothing in their meaning that could stop them from being true if the world of material objects were the whole of reality.[2]

I conclude that (6b) and (7b) are standardly used non-fundamentally, to express something consistent with the claim that there are, in the fundamental sense, no numbers or properties. But if this is granted for (6b) and (7b), it must also be granted for (1) and (2). Clearly we don't take any more of a metaphysical risk in uttering the latter sentences than we do in uttering the former: in whatever sense our utterances of (1) and (2) commit us to the existence of numbers and properties, our utterances of (6b) and (7b) do the same.

Have I said enough by now to enable me to state my thesis without being misunderstood? Let's give it a try. *There are no numbers. There are no properties.* When I utter these sentences, I mean to be using them in the fundamental way. I mean, if you like, that numbers and properties are not part of the ultimate furniture of reality. I mean that there are, in the final analysis, no such things.

Of course I hold similar views about many of the other putative entities that generally get classified as "abstract". But I don't want to be drawn into a pointless debate about how to define that technical term, so I won't attempt to state any more general thesis from which these claims about numbers and properties could be derived.[3] I will, however, add two more claims at the same level of generality. Just as there are no numbers or properties, there are no relations (like *being heavier than* or *betweenness*), or sets (like the set of people who have read this paper, or the null set). I will provisionally use 'nominalism' for the conjunction of these four claims, but will try to say nothing involving this term that would not also be true of various stronger theses of a similar kind.

'So are sentences like (1), (2), (3), and (4) true or false, according to you?' Well, just as these sentences admit of divergent fundamental and superficial uses, so too do sentences like

(1*) 'There are four prime numbers between one and ten' is true.
(2*) 'Spiders and insects share many important anatomical properties' is true.
(3*) 'There are numbers' is true.
(4*) 'There are properties' is true.

and their negations. Perhaps fundamental uses of (1*) and (2*) and their negations are a bit less unnatural than fundamental uses of (1) and (2). If you heard someone utter (1*) or (2*), you would naturally wonder why they didn't just assert (1) or (2); one reasonable hypothesis is that they did so as a signal that they were speaking fundamentally. But one wouldn't want to rely on hearers to come up with this hypothesis on their own.[4]

'Yes, but which of the above sentences are *literally* true?' Well, I'm certainly not play-acting, or speaking metaphorically, or exaggerating, or being sarcastic, when in the course of doing philosophy I say things like 'there are no properties', or when in the course of doing other things I say things like 'spiders and insects share many important anatomical properties'. So if "literally" is used in the ordinary way to rule out these kinds of verbal maneuvers, I'll happily say in the first kind of context that there are literally no properties, and in the second that spiders and insects literally share many important properties. However, "literal" has come among linguists and philosophers of language to have an extended use, on which it is supposed to stand for some category of deep explanatory importance: the domain of semantics rather than pragmatics. A way of using language might turn out to be non-literal in this sense if it turned out, at some deep explanatory level, to involve the same kinds of capacities or mechanisms that are involved in metaphor, exaggeration, sarcasm, etc. It has occasionally been suggested that what I have been calling the "superficial" uses of sentences like (1)–(5) are non-literal in this sense.[5] But I have no interest in arguing for this surprising empirical claim. Indeed, I wouldn't mind if the *fundamental* use of sentences like (1)–(5) turned out to be non-literal in this sense. Why should it matter, provided I can get my meaning across?

Since I think that the claims expressed by the fundamental uses of sentences like 'there are numbers' and 'there are properties' are of great and enduring philosophical interest, I am naturally disposed to assume that philosophers who utter these sentences mean to be asserting these interesting claims, rather than the trivialities expressed by these sentences on a superficial interpretation. But in some cases, there is other evidence that makes the assumption quite problematic. I am thinking especially of those philosophers who produce these sentences as the conclusions of arguments such as the following:

(6) (a) There is a planet that is distinct from some planet.
    (b) So, the number of planets is greater than one.
    (c) So, there are numbers.
(7) (a) The Earth is round.
    (b) So, the Earth has the property of being round.
    (c) So, there are properties.[6]

As I argued above, these arguments are only valid on a superficial reading. The fact that someone puts forth such an argument as valid is thus weighty evidence in favor of an interpretation on which that person is speaking superficially. On the other hand, why would any philosopher court misunderstanding in this way?

In some cases I suppose the right explanation is that, by failing to be clear about the distinction between the two uses, they have ended up believing that there are numbers or properties in the fundamental sense on the basis of fallacious arguments. But in the more interesting cases, the explanation is, rather, that the philosophers in question *see no alternative* to the superficial way of using sentences like 'there are numbers'. They simply have no idea what the allegedly distinct "fundamental" uses of these sentences are supposed to be. (Or at least, they have convinced themselves that they have no such idea.) Here's how I imagine them responding to my thesis:[7]

> Look, I'd like to interpret you charitably as not expressing that claim – the one *I* would express using the words 'there are no numbers' – which we agree is a trivial analytic

falsehood. But I just don't see what else you could have in mind. The only alternative interpretations of your utterance I can think of are ones on which you are expressing some trivial analytic *truth* (e.g., that numbers are not concrete), or some empirical claim to which your arguments are plainly irrelevant (e.g., that it would be in our interest to adopt a practice in which 'there are no numbers' was used to express a truth – cf. Carnap 1950). I am in a position like the one you would be in if you were faced with someone who maintained that the objects we normally refer to as "chairs", although they do exist, are not really, strictly speaking, in the fundamental sense, chairs. You can't see what could make it appropriate to dignify any variant on our ordinary use of the word 'chair' as especially "strict" or "philosophical" or "fundamental". I am in just the same position with regard to the ordinary use of 'there are' – the one on which 'there are numbers' is used to express a trivial truth.

I would be delighted to be able to argue people out of this position of principled incomprehension, by finding a distinguishing characteristic of the "fundamental" use of expressions like 'there are' that even they would have to recognize. My hope is that this could be done by taking my claim that arguments like (6a)–(6b) and (7a)–(7b) are not valid when understood in the fundamental sense, and the related claim (note 2) that claims of existence are never analytically true in the fundamental sense, as partly definitive of the relevant use of 'in the fundamental sense'. But I won't attempt here to develop this into a workable characterization.[8] For now, let me simply point out that the two anti-nominalist arguments I will spend most of this chapter discussing (sections 3 and 4) purport to show that abstract objects do essential explanatory work of some sort. If these arguments succeed, any way of using language on which 'there are no abstract objects' was used to express a truth (while 'abstract object' continued to mean what it actually means) would be severely explanatorily impoverished. Even those who can make no sense of the claim that such a way of using language is "more fundamental" than our ordinary way of using language might want to resist this claim. They might think that the fact that 'there are abstract objects' is true in ordinary English is just a fact about how we happen to talk, rather than something forced on us by our interest in speaking a language that is not explanatorily impoverished.[9] Those who hold this view have a common interest with me in finding responses to the anti-nominalist arguments I will be discussing.

2 Paraphrase

The superficial way of talking about numbers, properties, relations, and sets is very useful. But it would be wrong to think of it as giving us access to a domain of independent fact from which we would otherwise be completely cut off. Rather, sentences get to be true or false taken superficially in virtue of what there is in the fundamental sense, and what it is like. Thus, each English sentence must have a "paraphrase": a sentence that, when taken in the fundamental sense, says how things would have to be for the original sentence to be true in the superficial sense.[10] For some sentences, appropriate paraphrases are ready to hand. For example, we could take (6a) ('There is a planet that is distinct from some planet') as the paraphrase of (6b) ('The number of planets is greater than one').[11] But there is no obvious way to generalize this assignment beyond these easy cases. If it turned out that no system of paraphrases capturing the apparent logical relations among superficial uses of English sentences was possible, that would undermine my case for the existence of non-equivalent fundamental and superficial interpretations of abstract-object sentences.[12] There would then be no choice but to reject at least one of the premises to which I appealed in arguing for that claim – for example, that we are not making a mistake when we treat arguments like (6a)–(6b) and (7a)–(7b) as valid.[13] If we wanted to continue to be nominalists, we would have to do so in the knowledge that we were disagreeing with something almost everyone has believed. And when we ourselves continued to talk in the usual way about numbers, properties, relations, and sets (as we inevitably would), we would find it hard to explain what we were doing if not expressing beliefs flatly inconsistent with our official doctrine.

Fortunately, the challenge to provide the required system of paraphrases can be met rather easily. We can simply take the paraphrase of any sentence S to be 'If there were abstract objects, it would be the case that S.'[14] Or, if one would prefer the paraphrases to be more explicit and less context-dependent, one could aim to fill in the following schematic analysis:

> If it were the case that [axioms of number-theory] and [axioms of set-theory] and [axioms of property and relation theory] and [axioms for other sorts of abstract objects], and the concrete world were just as it actually is, then it would be the case that S.[15]

One objection to this sort of proposal stems from the widely accepted thesis that counterfactual conditionals with metaphysically impossible antecedents are all vacuously true (Stalnaker 1968, Lewis 1973). Since nominalism seems like the sort of thing that should be metaphysically necessary if true, this thesis would be bad news for my proposal. Fortunately, the thesis is false (see Nolan 1997). Here are some manifestly false counterfactuals whose antecedents seem to be metaphysically impossible:

(8a)   If I were a dolphin, I would have arms and legs.
(8b)   If it were necessary that there be donkeys, it would be impossible that there be cows.
(8c)   If there were unicorns, none of them would have horns.[16]

In fact we seem to be just as good at finding sensible things to say about what would be the case if some impossibility were true as we are at understanding what is the case according to impossible fictions.[17]

3 Abstract Objects in Scientific Explanations

If this reply to the "paraphrase challenge" succeeds, the picture from section 1 stands. There are plenty of short and valid arguments from obvious truths to the conclusion that there are numbers and properties in a superficial sense; but such arguments are irrelevant to the question whether there are any such things in the fundamental sense. It seems clear to me that in that case, Ockham's Razor applies: the burden of proof lies with those who maintain that there are, in the fundamental sense, numbers, properties, relations, or sets. Unless they can show us that their view brings some important explanatory benefit that cannot be had more cheaply, we should be reasonably confident that there are no such things. We should regard it as far more likely that all the things that there really are are material objects, or spirits, or portions of space-time – or at any rate, that they are all causally or spatiotemporally or mentally or physically interrelated as no number, property, relation, or set could ever be.[18]

The disjunctive character of this claim makes it hard to say anything further at this level of generality to justify it. If further justification is demanded, the nominalist's best strategy may involve arguing for some more specific, positive thesis about what reality is like, fundamentally speaking – something strong enough to have explanatory power in its own right, and from which nominalism could be derived as a corollary. I won't try to do this here. Instead, I will spend the remainder of the chapter considering two of the ways in which anti-nominalists have attempted to put abstract objects to work in explanations. I agree with Chris Swoyer (see chapter 1.1) that if it could be shown that the thesis that abstract objects exist (fundamentally speaking) is required by some good explanation of something that couldn't otherwise be explained, or explained so well, that would provide at least some reason to believe it. I will argue, however, that the explanatory benefits abstract objects may seem to bring are in fact illusory.

In this section, I will consider whether the reality of abstract entities might be required for good *scientific* explanations – explanations that answer 'why' questions in the way in which Newton's laws answer the question why the planets move in elliptical orbits. In section 4, I will turn to the question whether the reality of abstract entities might be required for good *philosophical*, or *constitutive*, explanations – explanations that answer 'why' questions in the way in which the claim that a certain object is a four-sided figure with equal sides and angles answers the question why it is a square.[19]

The idea that belief in certain abstract entities is justified by their role in good scientific explanations is called the "indispensability argument", and generally attributed to Quine (1948) and Putnam (1971). At first sight, the case looks strong, especially for mathematical entities. Why would modern science be so full of theories that logically entail 'there are numbers' if everything these theories purport to explain could be explained equally well without positing mathematical entities? But on second thought, it seems quite easy to weaken any ordinary scientific theory so as to make it logically consistent with 'there are no numbers' without affecting the theory's predictions about the concrete world. We already saw one way of doing this in section 2: when T is an ordinary scientific theory incorporating certain mathematical axioms,

> T^* If it were the case that [mathematical axioms] and the concrete world were just as it actually is, it would be the case that T

has exactly the same consequences for the concrete world as T itself. So the proponent of the indispensability argument owes us an argument that T^* provides a worse explanation for these facts about the concrete world than T does. Why would one think this?

Some anti-nominalists appeal at this point to the standards actually accepted by practicing scientists. They point out that one would get short shrift if one were to submit something of the form of T^* to a journal like the *Physical Review* (Burgess and Rosen 1997: 210). Philosophers, they suggest, should defer to the wider scientific community in forming their opinions about what makes for a good explanation. But if I am right that most uses of abstract-object talk, even in the sciences, are superficial uses, this sort of direct appeal to authority is useless in an argument for the existence of mathematical entities in the fundamental sense.[20] True, scientists never pause to consider theories looking like T^*, but that's because the theories they are interested in are *already* of this form, under the surface. Thus, any guidance scientists can give us in our attempt to assess the explanatory goodness of theories like T^* must be indirect: it must depend on some analogy between this case and other cases where scientific practice clearly does take a stand on what is required for a good explanation.

It is not hard to see how such an argument by analogy might go. Putnam (1971) is naturally interpreted as giving an argument of this kind; let me present my own version. If we are "scientific realists" who accept science as a way of finding out about the world, including the unobservable portions of the world, we will presumably think that we have good reason to believe that there are subatomic particles.[21] We will think this even though we recognize that, for any theory T that talks about unobservable entities of some kind, it is possible to find a weaker theory that shares all T's consequences about the observable world without entailing anything at all about those unobservable entities. For example:

$T^\dagger$ All the facts about the positions and motions of atoms are consistent with the hypothesis that T.[22]

(In other words: as far as the positions and motions of atoms are concerned, it is just *as if* T were true.) How can we be justified in believing that there are subatomic particles, rather than cautiously limiting ourselves to beliefs of the form of $T^\dagger$? The standard answer makes use of the notion of explanation. Although $T^\dagger$ has exactly the same observable consequences as T, it does not constitute a good explanation of these consequences. For $T^\dagger$ is the sort of theory which, if true, would itself "cry out" for further explanation. It is extremely unlikely, a priori, that atoms should just happen to move around in exactly the ways predicted by T without this fact having any deeper explanation. T itself is the most obvious possible explanation. There may of course be other explanations inconsistent with T, including some we have not yet thought of. But it would be very surprising if someone were to discover a theory that would, if true, provide a good explanation of $T^\dagger$ without entailing the existence of subatomic particles.

Now, T^* and $T^\dagger$ are similar in some salient respects. There is an obvious sense in which both are "parasitic" theories. Once the original theory T has been written down, it requires no additional effort to formulate the weaker theories T^* and $T^\dagger$; one simply prefaces T with the appropriate complex modal operator, 'If [mathematical axioms] and the concrete world were just as it actually is, it would be the case that...' or 'The facts about the positions and motions of atoms are consistent with the hypothesis that...'. On the basis of this similarity, one might conclude that T^* and $T^\dagger$ must also be similar in respect of being bad as explanations – i.e. in being unlikely to be true without having any deeper explanation.[23]

Once it has been made explicit, this argument by analogy may seem too tenuous to be worth worrying about. T^* and $T^\dagger$ are dissimilar in all sorts of ways. Why should we rest so much on the ways in which they are similar? But on the other hand, what else are we to go on, besides such analogies, in assessing the merits of T^*? It is hard to think of any other way of deciding the status of T^* that would not beg the question by appealing to some premise that only nominalists or anti-nominalists find plausible. For example, many nominalists have seen epistemological significance in the fact that abstract objects, if they existed, would be causally inert (Benacerraf 1973). The number two is not the sort of thing that could, say, move a pointer on some properly designed number-detector. Appealing to this fact, a nominalist might attempt to argue that T^* must be at least as good as an explanation of observed facts about the concrete realm as T itself, since T adds to T^* only in entailing the existence of causally inert entities like numbers. But anti-nominalists are not going to be persuaded by such an argument: they will simply deny that there is any connection between causation and explanatory goodness of the kind the argument needs.[24] Of course, such argumentative deadlocks are the norm across philosophy. But there is something very attractive about the idea that we should try to make progress in philosophy by learning from the disciplines in which progress is most manifest, namely the sciences. More specifically, the proposal is this: in the quest for a theory of good explanatory inference, we should take as our starting point the large and impressive body of case-by-case epistemological judgments shared by all scientific realists. We then decide what we ought to believe about controversial philosophical questions in accordance with whichever epistemological theory does the best job of accounting for and systematizing these data.[25] In this methodological context, at least, the argument by analogy for the badness of T^* is strong enough to be worth taking seriously.

Even if we were to concede that T^* was a bad theory, the debate would by no means be over. Nominalists could still look for alternatives to standard mathematics-laden scientific theories that explain the same data, but don't entail that there are numbers, and are not similar to theories like $T^\dagger$ in any way that would let an argument by analogy get off the ground. This is the strategy favored by Hartry Field. In his book *Science Without Numbers* (1980), Field works out an elegant and clearly non-parasitic version of Newtonian gravitational theory, which entails the existence of nothing besides particles, space-time points, and space-time regions. He shows that, in conjunction with appropriate mathematical axioms and definitions of mixed mathematico-physical predicates, this theory entails the "platonistic" theory it is meant to replace.[26] However, Field's program has yet to be carried out for theories like general relativity and quantum mechanics. At this stage, it is simply too early to say whether it is possible to find nominalistic theories of these matters that are as free as Field's theory is from any taint of similarity to bad theories like $T^\dagger$.[27] So there is a strong motivation for those who think that we can, even now, reasonably believe nominalism – as opposed to merely adopting it as a working hypothesis – to resist the indispensability argument at an earlier stage, by maintaining that T^* is a perfectly good theory as it stands, in spite of the analogies between it and $T^\dagger$.

It is not hard to come up with differences between T^* and $T^\dagger$ that look like they *might* be epistemologically significant. For example, there is the aforementioned fact that the additional strength of T over T^* derives entirely from the postulation of entities that are causally inert. But if we adhere to the "naturalistic" methodology for resolving such questions, we have to do more than merely point to one of these differences and claim it to be relevant. We will need to argue for its relevance by appealing to epistemological judgments common to all scientific realists, nominalists and anti-nominalists alike.

Here's what *I* think is the relevant difference. While both T^* and $T^\dagger$ result from the application of some complex modal operator to the original theory T, the operators in question are of different logical kinds. The one in $T^\dagger$ – 'The facts about the positions and motions of atoms are consistent with the hypothesis that . . .' – is, in essence, a *possibility*-operator. In the often helpful idiom of possible worlds, $T^\dagger$ can be thought of as saying that there is *some* T-world where the facts about the positions and motions of atoms are just as they actually are. By contrast, the operator in T^* – 'If such-and-such mathematical axioms were true, it would be the case that . . .' – has the logical properties of a *necessity*-operator. In possible-worlds terms, it says, in effect, that *every* world where the mathematical axioms are true that is like the actual world in concrete respects is a T-world.[28]

Now to the argument that this is an epistemologically important difference. Surely, if science can tell us about the unobservable at all, one thing it has told us is this: matter is not all alike, but comes in different kinds. Two bits of matter that are alike in respect of shape, size, and motion can still fail to be exactly alike – can fail to be duplicates. For example, they might fail to be duplicates by having different quantities or distributions of mass or charge, or by being composed of different kinds of elementary particles. We have good reason to believe this in spite of the fact that for any theory T that entails that matter comes in different kinds, we can find a weaker theory that makes the same predictions as T about the distribution of matter in space and time, without ruling out the hypothesis that matter is all alike.[29] One way to formulate such a theory is to emulate $T^\dagger$, by saying something like 'The facts about the distribution of matter in space and time are consistent with the hypothesis that T.' But provided that T already contains a little mathematics – enough to entail the existence of sets of particles – there is no need to use the modal notion of consistency: we can achieve the same effect using existential quantifiers. Suppose for the sake of concreteness that T entails that matter is not all alike by virtue of entailing that elementary particles come in different kinds: electrons, photons, quarks, neutrinos. . . . To formulate a new theory T^- consistent with the claim that matter is all alike, we will need to introduce some new variables $v_1, v_2, v_3, v_4, \ldots$, corresponding to T's one-place predicates 'electron', 'photon', 'quark', 'neutrino'. . . . We then proceed in two steps. First, for each one-place atomic formula, like 'x is an electron' or 'x is a photon', in T, we substitute the two-place formula '$x \in v_i$', where v_i is the variable corresponding to the predicate in the original formula. Second, we insert existential quantifiers at the beginning of the resulting formula, to bind all the new variables. The resulting theory T^- says in effect that there is *some* way to assign sets of particles to be the extensions of the predicates 'electron', 'photon', 'quark', 'neutrino' . . . in such a way that T becomes true. This is clearly consistent with the hypothesis that all matter is alike, while having all the same consequences as T as regards the distribution of particles across space and time.[30]

Since the existence of observationally adequate theories like T^- in fact does nothing to undermine our reason to believe that matter comes in different kinds, T^- must be a much worse theory than T. There is a general pattern here. If we want to weaken a theory so as to eliminate its commitment to some sort of hidden structure, we can very often do so by replacing the vocabulary purporting to characterize this structure with variables of an appropriate sort, bound by initial existential quantifiers.[31] So we can draw a general moral: since commitment to hidden structures often plays an essential part in good explanations, such existential quantification must be a source of theoretical badness. When we replace a constant with a variable bound by an initial existential quantifier, the resulting theory will typically be considerably worse than the one we started out with.

Universal quantification doesn't seem to be a source of badness in the same sort of way. Indeed, when it is possible to weaken a theory by replacing one of its constants with a variable bound by an initial (restricted) universal quantifier, the result of doing so is often considerably better than the original theory. Consider for example physical theories formulated in coordinate terms. When we assign 'x', 'y', and 'z' coordinates to particles, we certainly don't mean to suggest that there is a single distinguished, physically privileged coordinate system, concerning which it would make sense to wonder how far we are from the nearest axis. Rather, we are implicitly claiming that such-and-such equations hold in every admissible coordinate system. Similarly, when a theory uses numbers to measure mass or charge, it is often understood that the choice of a scale is arbitrary, so that what's really being said is that the theory holds true for any admissible assignment of numbers.[32] All this seems quite unproblematic. We would make these theories worse, not better, if we eliminated the implicit universal quantification by positing a metaphysically special One True Coordinate System or Privileged Unit of Charge.

The bad theories T^+ and T^- seem to be bad in the very same way. So our explanation of the badness of T^+ should appeal to some factor common to T^+ and T^-. What could this factor be? If T doesn't contain any existential quantifiers of the problematic kind, neither does T^+. But it does contain the possibility-operator 'The facts about the positions and motions of atoms are consistent with the hypothesis that. . . '. And there is a notable logical affinity between possibility-operators and existential quantifiers, one that we exploit when we express claims about possibility in terms of possible worlds. (One need not endorse the unpopular opinion that 'possibly' *means* 'in some possible world' to see this.) Since this is the clearest point of similarity between T^+ and T^- that does not also hold between T^+ and unproblematic theories involving universal quantification over coordinate systems and the like, we can plausibly conclude that it is the basis for the epistemological similarity between the theories. Applying a possibility-operator to a theory, just like changing one of its constants to a variable bound by an initial existential quantifier, generally leaves one with a much worse theory – a theory that, if true, would cry out for further explanation. If so, the example of T^+ gives us no reason to think that applying a necessity-operator to a theory, as we do when we move from T to T^*, need do anything to make it worse. As far as the explanatory status of T^* is concerned, the analogy that turns out to be most important is not the one between T^* and the bad theory $T^\dagger$, but the one between T^* and the good theories with initial universal quantifiers ranging over coordinate systems.

These are, I admit, dialectical baby steps. It's all very well to point out suggestive analogies and disanalogies; the ultimate test for which analogies matter must come when we actually attempt to formulate general epistemological principles and see if we can get them to fit with our intuitions about particular cases. I hope to take some steps in this direction in future work. But I hope that I have already said enough to shift the burden of proof back to those who maintain that belief in the reality of abstract objects can be justified by their role in scientific explanations.

4 Abstract Objects in Philosophical Explanations

Much of philosophy is concerned with questions of the form 'What is it to be F?' or 'What is it for something to R something else?' – requests for analyses, or real definitions. Believers in abstract objects have frequently invoked them in their answers to such questions. They have given analyses on which apparently innocuous claims such as the following turn out to be implicitly about abstract objects:

(9) (a) Necessarily, all dogs are dogs.
    (b) Some people believe that penguins eat fish.
    (c) If I had missed the bus this morning I would have been late for class.

For example, (9a) is often held to be analyzed as 'the proposition that all dogs are dogs is necessary' (Bealer 1993); (9b) as 'some people believe the proposition that penguins eat fish' (Schiffer 2003: ch. 1); (9c) as 'the closest worlds where I miss the bus are worlds in which I am late for class' (Stalnaker 1968; Lewis 1973).

Faced with analyses of this sort, nominalists have three options. First, they can accept the analyses, and conclude that the sentences in question are not true, taken in the fundamental sense. Second, they can suggest alternative analyses. Or, third, they can maintain that the relevant notions are primitive and unanalyzable.

Taking the second option need not always mean a lot of hard philosophical work. A lazy nominalist can simply take an analysis mentioning abstract objects, and insert something like, 'If there were abstract objects, it would be the case that ...' at the beginning.

The hardest cases for nominalism are those where the first of these options, and the lazy version of the second option, can be ruled out. For example, if we want to use counterfactuals in paraphrasing ordinary abstract-object talk, as suggested in section 2, we obviously can't hold that sentences involving the counterfactual conditional are never true in the fundamental sense. And it would be circular to analyze 'If it were the case that P, it would be the case that Q' in general as 'If there were abstract objects, the closest possible worlds in which P would be worlds in which Q.' So we are left with a choice between taking counterfactual conditionals as primitive and maintaining they can be analyzed without bringing in abstract objects.

Despite its importance, I won't have anything more to say here about the difficult task of providing an nominalistically acceptable account of counterfactuals.[33] Instead,

I will consider another hard case, that of *basic physical predicates*. What is it for something to be an electron, for example? Some anti-nominalists, such as David Armstrong (1978a, 1978b), answer as follows:

(10) To be an electron is to instantiate the property *electronhood*.

Surely the first option – accept the analysis, and concede that there aren't, fundamentally speaking, any electrons – is not a real option here. (Not that it is so obvious that there are electrons, fundamentally speaking – but if there aren't, it is not because there are no properties!) Likewise, the lazy version of the second option – claiming that to be an electron is to be something which would instantiate *electronhood* if there were abstract objects – is deeply unattractive. Surely, if this counterfactual is true of an object, it is true because it is an electron, and not the other way round. So we are left with the choice of taking 'electron' as primitive, or finding some analysis quite different in character from (10).

For too long, analyses like (10) were considered only in the context of the claim that all instances of the following schemata are true, no matter what predicates we substitute for '*F*' and '*R*':

(11) To be *F* is to instantiate the property, *F-ness*.
(12) For *x* to *R* *y* is for *x* to bear the relation, *R-ing*, to *y*.

But there are at least two good reasons to reject this sweeping attempt to provide real definitions for all predicates at once.

First, there is Bradley's regress (Bradley 1897: ch.2). If we accept the following instance of (12)

(13) For *x* to instantiate *y* is for *x* to bear the relation, *instantiation*, to *y*

we have taken the first step in a vicious infinite regress. We take the next step when we accept the corresponding analysis of the predicate on the right-hand side of (13):

(14) For *x* to bear *z* to *y* is for *x*, *y*, and *z* to stand in the relation, *bearing*.

And so on. This can't go on forever: analysis must come to an end somewhere.

Second, many predicates already have real definitions not in the form of (11) or (12). For example, we seem to have learned by doing science that

(15) To be a helium atom is to be an atom whose nucleus contains exactly two protons.

If we combined this with the relevant instance of (11)

(16) To be a helium atom is to instantiate the property, *being a helium atom*

we could presumably conclude that

(17) To instantiate the property, *being a helium atom*, is to be an atom whose nucleus contains exactly two protons.

I can see how (17) might be true if we were thinking of the property *being a helium atom* as existing only in a superficial sense, so that truths that appear on the surface to involve it turn out, on deeper analysis, to be truths of a different sort. But how could (17) be true if the property is a fully real thing, existing in the fundamental sense? I can't see how an account of what it is for an object to instantiate a certain real entity could fail to mention that entity at all, any more than an account of what it is for a region of space to contain a certain real particle could fail to mention that particle at all.[34]

So much the worse for (11) and (12) in full generality. But, as Armstrong forcefully argues, it would be a mistake to dismiss the idea that *some* instances of these schemata are true. According to Armstrong, (11) holds only for an elite minority of predicates, which it is up to physics to identify.[35] It is a good question what, if anything, a nominalist should put in place of these analyses.

One might reasonably object that the question what it is to be an electron is one we should not expect to be able to answer from the armchair. Physicists discovered that to be a helium atom is to be an atom whose nucleus contains exactly two protons, and that to be a proton is to be a complex of quarks of certain kinds bound together in certain ways; it would be foolish for metaphysicians to rule out the possibility of some similar discovery about what it is to be an electron.[36] But there is still a challenge: the analysis of "physical" predicates like 'helium atom', 'proton', and 'electron' in terms of other such predicates cannot go on forever. Eventually (since there can't be infinitely regressive or circular real definitions) there must be a *basic* physical predicate that doesn't have a real definition involving other physical predicates – either because it has no definition at all, or because it has a definition that doesn't involve any physical predicates, e.g. a definition of the form of (11). The real challenge for the nominalist is to say something about what happens then. From now on I'll assume for ease of exposition that 'electron' is such a basic physical predicate.

So, why would one think it better to accept (10) rather than taking 'electron' as primitive, or analyzing it in some other way? The appeal of (10) becomes apparent only when we turn to another class of predicates for which analyses in terms of abstract objects are often proposed, namely predicates having to do with resemblance. A good example to focus on is the notion of duplication, or perfect intrinsic resemblance.[37] Suppose that the believer in properties analyzes this as follows:

(18) For *x* to be a duplicate of *y* is for *x* and *y* to instantiate exactly the same things.[38]

Putting this together with (10), we can account for the necessity of the following claim:

(D) Whenever *x* is an electron and *y* is a duplicate of *x*, *y* is an electron.

For, when we replace the predicates 'electron' and 'duplicate' with the analysis given by (10) and (18), (D) reduces to an elementary logical truth:

(D*) Whenever *x* instantiates *electronhood* and *y* and *x* instantiate exactly the same things, *y* instantiates *electronhood*.

This is a significant explanatory achievement. It is not obvious what nominalists should put in its place.

There are three basic options, short of simply denying the necessity of (D).[39] First, we could maintain that the necessity of (D) follows from an analysis of 'duplicate' in which the predicate 'electron' occurs, presumably along with other predicates. Second, we could maintain that it follows from an analysis of 'electron', either alone or in conjunction with some analysis of 'duplicate'. Or, third, we could maintain that the necessity of (D) cannot be explained in terms of the real definitions of its constituent predicates. I will consider each of these strategies in turn.

The physical strategy

Although there have been few explicit defenses of the first strategy, I suspect that it is in fact quite popular.[40] The idea is straightforward: just as we looked to science to provide us with real definitions of predicates like 'water' and 'helium atom', so we must ultimately look to science to provide us with real definitions of 'duplicate' and other predicates of the same general, structural sort. What might such an analysis look like? Bracketing complications raised by duplication amongst complex objects, all we need is a simple conjunction of biconditionals, one for each monadic basic physical predicate:

(19) For x to be a duplicate of y is for it to be the case that x is an electron iff y is an electron, and x is a quark iff y is a quark, and . . .[41]

Since this obviously suffices to entail the necessity of (D), it leaves the nominalist free to take 'electron' as primitive.

The main problem I see for the physical strategy is its inability to accommodate what I will call the Alien Properties Intuition (cf. Lewis 1983: 158ff.). Roughly speaking, this is the intuition that that there might be alien properties, not identical to or constructed from any actual properties.[42] Of course, nominalists can't accept that way of putting it: but we can still think that when believers in properties talk about situations containing alien properties, they are talking about genuine possibilities, even if they are misdescribing them. Typically, these possibilities will contain things that fail to be duplicates even though they are indiscernible as far as the basic predicates of actual-world physics are concerned:

(20) Possibly, there are two simple things x and y that are not duplicates, although x is an electron iff y is an electron, and x is a quark iff y is a quark, and . . .

One special case concerns the possibility that nothing falls under any of the basic predicates of actual-world physics. The proponent of the physical strategy is committed to the claim that if this were the case, the world would be *completely homogeneous*. Any two simple things would be duplicates, and indeed qualitatively indiscernible. But this seems wrong. Intuitively, there could be all kinds of interesting goings-on at possible worlds where nothing falls under any of the basic predicates of actual-world physics: they could be every bit as richly varied in their own ways as the actual world is in its.[43]

If this is right, it shows that 'duplicate' is just not the sort of predicate that could have an analysis in physical terms. (Arguments of the same sort will apply to other predicates with a similarly "structural" or "topic-neutral" character.) That's a lot to rest on intuitions about such remote possibilities. Although I feel the pull of the Alien Properties Intuition quite strongly, I'm not sure that its force would be strong enough to make me reject nominalism, if it turned out that the only way to continue being a nominalist was to give it up. But let's press on and consider the other options.

The structural strategy

The second option for the nominalist is to explain the necessity of (D) as following from a real definition of 'electron', perhaps in conjunction with a real definition of 'duplicate'.

What might the analysis of a basic physical predicate like 'electron' look like? In the first half of the twentieth century, it was widely believed that physical predicates could be analyzed in terms of "observational" predicates: to be an electron is to be something disposed to make white tracks of a certain shape in cloud chambers of a certain design, etc. This sort of view is now deservedly unpopular, for reasons I won't go into. Even if something like this were true, it wouldn't really help us, since observational predicates like 'white' raise the same essential problem for the nominalist as basic physical predicates like 'electron'. Just as any duplicate of an electron must be an electron, so any duplicate of a white object must be white.[44] And as far as the explanation of this necessity is concerned, the analogue of the physical strategy – an analysis of 'duplicate' in terms of observational predicates like 'white' – looks even more problematic than the corresponding explanation of (D). The fact that two objects cannot be distinguished by our observational predicates doesn't entail that they are duplicates.

How could we analyze 'electron' without merely postponing the problem in this way? We might, for example, be Resemblance Nominalists, and attempt – somehow or other – to analyze 'electron' (along with everything else) entirely in terms of *resemblance*. That need not mean that the only non-logical predicate we can use in our analysis is 'x resembles y': most Resemblance Nominalists have allowed themselves more flexible primitives to work with. For example, Price (1953) seems to treat claims of the form 'x_1 resembles x_2 at least as much as y_1 resembles y_2' as primitive. It is not hard to see how one might go about analyzing 'duplicate' in terms of predicates like these. One could say, for example, that for x to be a duplicate of y is for x to resemble exactly the same things as y, or for x to resemble y at least as much as y resembles itself. While we might object to these analyses on other grounds, at least there is no conflict with the Alien Properties Intuition.

There are various other notions with the same abstract, structural character as resemblance – notions which would not look out of place in an analysis of 'duplicate', and hence could occur in an analysis of 'electron' without merely postponing our problem. For example, Natural Class Nominalists take as primitive the notion of a "natural" class – informally speaking, a class of things that all resemble one another in some one respect and resemble nothing else in that respect.[45] Taken at face value, this predicate is of no use to a nominalist in my sense, who denies that there really are any classes (sets). But this is one of those cases where a claim about classes can be regarded as a misleading way of saying something properly expressed using plurals.

That is, instead of saying that *the class of electrons* (singular) is natural, we should really say that *the electrons* (plural) are, collectively, natural.[46] Again, it is not hard to see how this notion might feature in a plausible analysis of 'duplicate'. For example, we could say that for x to be a duplicate of y is for it to be the case that whenever some things are natural, x is one of them iff y is.

Mereological predicates like 'part of' seem to belong in the same "structural" category.[47] Other cases are harder to adjudicate. Perhaps certain causal vocabulary should be allowed. Some (e.g. Campbell 1991) even put *spatiotemporal* predicates in this category – though from my point of view, the inclusion of 'before' or 'between' in a definition of duplication looks only slightly less problematic than the inclusion of 'electron' or 'quark'. But we don't really need to decide these questions: the hard part is seeing how 'electron' could have a definition in terms of *any* of these materials.

It has generally been assumed in discussions of Resemblance Nominalism that the analyses of most ordinary predicates will involve reference to certain "paradigm" particulars. For example, adapting a suggestion of Price's (1953), one might propose the following analysis for 'electron':

(21)   To be an electron is to resemble each of $e_1, e_2, \ldots e_n$ at least as much as any two of them resemble one another.

(There are various possible complications: for example, one might want to have 'anti-paradigms' which one must *fail* to resemble to be an electron.[48]) One initially off-putting fact about analyses like (21) is the arbitrariness of the choice of paradigms. It is not plausible that we are simply ignorant of the identity of the paradigm electrons. But this doesn't seem like a serious problem, since it is open to the proponent of the strategy to claim that there is no determinate fact of the matter as regards the identity of the paradigms: in a sense, 'electron' is vague, though we may know a priori that it has no actual borderline cases.[49]

A second objection to analyses like (21) makes use of the notion of intrinsicness: whether something is an electron is a matter of what that thing is like intrinsically; whether something resembles the paradigm electrons is not; hence, it can't be the case that to be an electron just is to resemble the paradigm electrons.[50] How should a proponent of the structural strategy understand the notion of intrinsicness that features in this argument? On the one hand, an intrinsic characterization of something is supposed to be one that neither explicitly nor implicitly refers to, or quantifies over, anything apart from the thing in question and its parts (and perhaps also the properties and relations they instantiate, and the sets they are members of – but these are things a nominalist doesn't believe in). On this demanding conception, adopting the structural strategy requires one to say that only a very few predicates, like 'resembles itself' or 'has exactly seven duplicate parts', characterize things intrinsically. Clearly, if 'electron' has an analysis in "structural" terms, it will not count as intrinsic in this demanding sense. On the other hand, it is also supposed to be necessary that any two things that have exactly the same intrinsic features are duplicates. But this clearly won't be the case if we adopt the demanding conception. If any form of the structural strategy is correct, it is pretty likely that *any* two simple things are alike in all the respects that count as intrinsic on the demanding conception, whether or not they are duplicates. Given these conflicting desiderata, perhaps the best thing to say is that 'intrinsic' is ambiguous between the demanding sense and some more liberal, but more metaphysically arbitrary, sense on which basic physical predicates do count as characterizing things intrinsically. But whatever we end up saying, we must concede that the structural strategy will be unacceptable to those who think they have a firm grip on a notion of intrinsicness satisfying both desiderata.

There is a third problem for the strategy of mentioning particular objects in the definition of 'electron', which seems to me by far the most serious. Namely: any workable analysis of this sort will entail that it is necessary that at least some of those objects exist, if there are any electrons (Armstrong 1978a: 51–3; Van Cleve 1994: 579). This is seriously implausible. Surely there could still have been electrons even if *no* actual particulars had existed. Let's call this the Alien Particulars Intuition. If we accept it, the idea of using paradigms in the analysis of basic physical predicates must be given up.[51]

The Alien Particulars Intuition rules out just about any structural analysis of 'electron' involving reference to particular objects. That leaves us with *purely general* structural analyses: analyses according to which the facts about the structure of the world are already sufficient to fix which things are electrons, irrespective of which particular objects occupy the positions in the structure.

While this approach is consistent with the Alien Particulars Intuition, it has its own difficulties with modal intuition. Many philosophers (e.g. Lewis 1986, Armstrong 1989a) accept what I will call the Humean Intuitions: they think that there are few, if any, interesting structural conditions something must satisfy in order to fall under a basic physical predicate. Instead of obeying the actual laws of nature, electrons could be distributed in some very different way. For example, there could be exactly seven electrons, evenly spaced in a straight line and motionless in otherwise empty space. Likewise, there could be exactly seven *non*-electrons, evenly spaced in a straight line and motionless in otherwise empty space. But if both of these situations are possible, it cannot be the case that whether something is an electron depends only on its place in the structure of resemblances, natural classes, or whatever: these kinds of structural facts are exactly the same at the world with seven electrons and at the world with seven non-electrons.

But the Humean Intuitions are by no means uncontroversial. Several philosophers have endorsed, for reasons that don't on their face have much to do with nominalism, the "dispositional essentialist" view that it is necessary that the objects falling under a basic physical predicate like 'electron' should play a certain characteristic role in the laws of nature.[52] On this sort of view, many of the truths that would traditionally be classified as laws of nature – "nomological necessities" – will in fact be metaphysically necessary. For example, it might be necessary that if there are any electrons, they repel one another and attract any protons there might be.[53]

If we want to maintain that basic physical predicates have structural definitions, can we at least avoid having to classify as metaphysically necessary any truths we would not otherwise have any reason to classify even as nomologically necessary? Unfortunately the answer seems to be 'no', at least if we hold onto our assumption that 'electron' is a basic physical predicate.[54] The problem is that electrons and positrons play symmetric roles in current physical theories. If one reinterprets 'electron' as standing for positrons, and 'positron' as standing for electrons, while making certain other substitutions of a similar nature, the theory will still be true on the new interpretation. This means that for a purely general structural definition of 'electron' to avoid incorrectly classifying positrons as electrons, it will have to appeal to some distinguishing characteristic of the electrons that a Humean would not even regard as nomologically necessary. For example, if there are in fact many more electrons than positrons, we might say that to be an electron is to be a member of the *largest* natural class playing some characteristic nomological role. If the predominance of electrons over positrons is a merely local phenomenon, we will have to rely on more subtle differences – e.g. the fact that electrons outnumber positrons in the region of space that surrounds a planet that is appropriately similar in structural respects to the planet Earth as it actually is.[55] Clearly it would be unrealistic to expect precision here. If the usual laws of nature don't suffice to do the job of distinguishing electrons from positrons, we're going to have to settle for considerable vagueness as regards just how much of the actual "electron role" some things would have to play to count as electrons.

This is certainly a bit unsettling. But I am inclined to think that if we can reconcile ourselves to giving up the Humean Intuitions, we should not be too concerned to find that some of the truths we end up counting as metaphysically necessary are truths that someone in the grip of those intuitions wouldn't even think of as laws of nature. When the dispositional essentialist idea that objects at a world very unlike the actual world (such as the world with seven static identical particles) could not be electrons starts to seem compelling, it does so precisely because one cannot see what could make objects at a world like that *count* as electrons. Once we start expecting non-trivial answers to questions of this sort, they will seem equally pressing when we consider the putative possibility of electrons and positrons switching roles. We will want to know what could make these things count as the positrons and these as the electrons, rather than vice versa. For a proponent of the Humean Intuitions, this is of course a bad question. But in my experience it is not so hard to get people to feel its force.[56]

Brute necessities

If all this is right, the only way to explain necessities like (D) without giving up the Alien Properties Intuition, the Alien Particulars Intuition, or the Humean Intuitions is to reject nominalism. Before we can evaluate this argument, we must ask why such necessities should *need* explanation. What if a nominalist were to maintain that they are "brute" necessities, which cannot be explained by any analyses of their constituent predicates?

One might object to this view on the grounds that necessities never are brute. The only genuinely necessary truths – one might maintain – are those that reduce, upon analysis, to truths of logic (in some narrowly delimited sense of 'logic').

This is the strongest form a ban on brute necessities might take: various natural weakenings would still work in the argument. I will briefly mention three. (1) If we wanted to allow for facts about the *essences* of objects as a distinct source of necessity (see Fine 1994), we might still hold that all *purely general* necessary truths – all truths that do not either implicitly or explicitly involve reference to any specific entities – reduce to truths of logic. (2) If we were persuaded by Kripke's argument

(1972: 156) for the necessity of sentences like 'there are no unicorns' and 'there is no phlogiston' but despaired of finding appropriate analyses of 'unicorn' and 'phlogiston', we might want to make a special exception for such "semantically defective" predicates.[57] (3) More ambitiously, we might want to make an exception for a category of "non-factual" vocabulary (perhaps including evaluative terms like 'good') whose communicative function is not, strictly speaking, that of expressing our beliefs about reality, but something quite different.[58] Since it is impossible to analyze the non-factual in terms of the factual, most necessary truths essentially involving non-factual vocabulary (e.g., 'love for one's children is good') will not admit of reduction to logical truths. None of these weakenings is of much use to the nominalist faced with the task of explaining the necessity of (D). (1) If we mentioned some particular objects in the analysis of 'electron', we might in principle attempt to explain the necessity of (D) in terms of the essences of these objects; but the Alien Particulars Intuition rules out such analyses. (2) Only an idealist could take seriously the idea that all basic physical predicates are semantically defective; and the idealist would face an exactly parallel problem involving mental predicates. And (3) if the distinction between non-factual and factual vocabulary makes sense at all, 'electron' and 'duplicate' seem to belong on the factual side of the line.

But orthodox anti-nominalists are in no position to accept the claim that there are no brute necessities, even when these qualifications are taken into account. For most anti-nominalists will be committed to the necessity of a wide range of axioms specifying conditions under which numbers, sets, and logically complex properties and relations exist. Since these axioms are existential in form, there is no hope of reducing them to truths of standard logic just by analyzing predicates like 'set' and 'property'. Moreover, if they are true, many of these axioms are purely general, semantically non-defective, and fully factual. Some anti-nominalists (e.g. Bealer 1982) advocate a wider use of 'logic' on which these axioms will count as logical truths. But I can see no *independent* motivation for a principle that would allow such axioms to be necessary while requiring the necessity of (D) to be explained by analyses of 'duplicate' and 'electron'.

In the absence of such a principle, presumably the debate will have to turn on considerations of economy. The question will be which of the available theories makes do with the smallest, simplest set of brute necessities.[59] But it is not at all clear that anti-nominalists will do better by this criterion. And even if it were, it would not be clear how this kind of economy should be weighed against the considerations of ontological economy that favor the nominalist. On the whole, I doubt nominalists have much to fear once the dispute turns into a contest of economy.

However, not all anti-nominalists accept the necessity of all the usual axioms. For example, some of them have denied that it is necessary that for any two properties p and q, there is (in the fundamental sense) a property instantiated by exactly those objects that instantiate either p or q.[60] We can imagine an extreme version of this view, on which the only necessary general principles about properties and instantiation are those that reduce, under analysis, to truths of logic (narrowly conceived). A proponent of this view would have a principled reason for insisting that the necessity of (D) must be explained by analyzing 'electron' or 'duplicate'.

But the prospects for this kind of view seem poor. Consider, first, a version of the view according to which the predicate 'instantiates' is primitive and unanalyzable, so that for sentences whose only piece of non-logical vocabulary is the predicate 'instantiates', metaphysical necessity coincides with strictly logical necessity, and metaphysical possibility with strictly logical possibility. This seems utterly incredible. Not just any old collection of points and arrows connecting them represent a way things might be, if the arrow is interpreted as meaning 'instantiates'. Is there a possible world with just 17 entities, $a_1 \ldots a_{17}$, such that a_1 instantiates a_2, a_2 instantiates $a_3 \ldots$ and a_{17} instantiates a_1? Is there a possible world just like the actual world in respect of the structure of instantiation except that my nose (or its counterpart) instantiates my little finger? Is there a possible world structurally like the actual world except that any two things instantiate one another if they are actually less than a mile apart? Surely not.

Hence, an anti-nominalist who wants to uphold the ban on brute necessities will have to find some analysis of 'instantiates' that can account for these impossibilities. But what might such an analysis look like? I can't see how anything simple or intuitive could do the job. The only way I can see to get the right necessary truths to fall out of a definition of 'instantiates' (without going so far as to make it impossible for anything ever to instantiate anything else) would be to tailor the definition in such a way that exotic situations like those discussed in the previous paragraph get reclassified, in effect, as possibilities in which nothing instantiates anything else. For example, one might begin with a primitive notion of "proto-instantiation," and propose that for x to instantiate y is for x to proto-instantiate y at a world where the facts about proto-instantiation make up the right kind of overall pattern.[61] This feels like cheating to me. If we give ourselves free rein to make up new predicates, conveniently free from any involvement in our pre-existing modal beliefs, it will become a trivial task to find analyses of our old predicates on which all the sentences that intuitively strike us as necessary, and none of the sentences that intuitively strike us as contingent, can be reduced to logical truths.[62] We simply analyze each predicate 'F' as 'proto-F such that P', where P is the conjunction of all the sentences we want to turn out to be necessary, with 'proto-' inserted in front of each predicate.[63] Unfortunately, I am not at all sure how to turn this feeling into an argument against the proposal. I am tempted to protest that the new predicate 'proto-instantiates' is simply unintelligible. But this kind of objection needs to be handled very delicately if it is not to rule out legitimate conceptual innovation. Another tempting line of argument is epistemological: why should we have any confidence that the world has the distinctive kind of structure it would need to have to contain instantiation rather than mere proto-instantiation?[64] But anyone who wields localized skeptical arguments like this one must be prepared for the inevitable response: 'You tell me how you know that you're not a brain in a vat, and I'll tell you how I know this fact you allege I could not know if my account of its nature were correct.' In any case, it is clear that if we do allow "cheating" analyses like this, nominalists have nothing to worry about from the demand for an explanation of necessities like (D), even if they are persuaded by the objections to the physical strategy and the structural strategy discussed above. They can use the very same trick, e.g. by analyzing 'electron' as 'proto-electron that is such that any duplicate of a proto-electron is a proto-electron', or by analyzing 'x is a duplicate of y' as 'x is a proto-duplicate of y, and any proto-duplicate of an electron is an electron'.

Cian Dorr

To sum up: we have not managed to find a stable argument against nominalism based on the use of abstract objects in explaining necessities like (D). Instead, we have stumbled on an argument in favor of nominalism. If there are, in the fundamental sense, numbers, properties, relations, or sets, then there are necessary truths about these things that cannot (assuming we can somehow rule out the trivializing 'proto-instantiation' move) be reduced to truths of logic. Thus, only the nominalist, who denies that there are any such things, can adequately respect the idea that there are no brute necessities.[65]

I think this is quite a powerful argument. To anyone not antecedently convinced of the falsity of nominalism, the idea of a metaphysically necessary truth whose necessity does not flow from real definitions plus logic really should seem quite strange. A notion of necessity that allowed for such necessary truths would seem uncomfortably like nothing more than an extra-strong variety of nomological necessity. But when something strikes us as impossible – say, the hypothesis that some duplicate of an electron is not itself an electron – we don't just think of it as ruled out by a "law of metaphysics": we feel that in some important sense, the idea *just makes no sense at all*. The notion of necessity involved in such intuitions is absolute: it is something that could not be strengthened any further without changing its character in some fundamental way. It is hard to see how any notion of necessity weaker than the notion of reducibility to logical truth could be absolute in this way.[66]

Of course, even for a nominalist, the task of reconciling the ban on brute necessities with the facts about necessity and possibility is not an easy one (assuming we can somehow rule out the trivializing 'proto-electron' move). Resemblance Nominalism, for example, is not an option. All the resemblance-predicates I can think of are involved in manifestly necessary truths that are not logical truths, and contain no other non-logical vocabulary. (A simple example: the necessary truth that any duplicate of a duplicate of an object is a duplicate of that object.) If they are not brute, these necessities must be explained by analysing resemblance-predicates in terms of predicates of some other sort. But the outlook for other nominalist programmes is better. The physical strategy provides one possible approach for foes of brute necessities: it is at least not *obvious* that there are any non-logical necessary truths involving only basic physical predicates.[67] And although Resemblance Nominalism is ruled out, Natural Class Nominalism remains a live option for those who prefer the structural strategy. For there is no clear reason why settling the question whether some given objects are (collectively) natural should entail anything at all about the naturalness of any other objects. Thus, for those who want to uphold a version of the ban on brute necessities strong enough to place a serious constraint on the shape of our metaphysical theorizing, nominalism provides at least two promising research programs, while anti-nominalism provides none.[68]

Notes

1 The latter example is due to van Inwagen (2004).
2 Similarly, our ordinary use of number-talk commits us to treating the argument 'Either there are no planets, or there is a planet; therefore, either the number of planets is zero,

or the number of planets is at least one' as valid. Since the premise of this argument is analytically true (true just in virtue of meaning), the conclusion must be too, on its ordinary use. But it cannot be analytic when taken in the fundamental sense: fundamentally speaking, it is not an analytic truth that there are numbers, since it is not an analytic truth that there is anything at all. As Hume and Kant maintained in criticizing the standard a priori arguments for the existence of God, denials of existence – when taken in the fundamental sense – can never be self-contradictory.

3 On defining 'abstract', see Lewis (1986: 82–6), Burgess and Rosen (1997: 13–25), and section 1 of Chris Swoyer's companion chapter in this volume (1.1).

4 There is a complication here, which arises when we consider a sentence like

(*) 'There are no numbers' is true.

Surely, if there are (fundamentally speaking) no numbers, sets, properties, or relations, there also aren't (fundamentally speaking) any sentences (i.e. sentence types). If so, it is hard to see how (*) could be true in the fundamental sense, given that the term in quotation marks purports to refer to a sentence. And there is certainly *a* superficial use of (*) on which it expresses a falsehood, just as (4*) expresses a truth. Nevertheless, it seems clear that there is some way of using (*) on which I should find it acceptable, given my thesis. (For more details see the discussion in Yablo (2001) of 'The number of numbers is zero.') Indeed, when I make claims about sentences, theories, claims, beliefs, views, hypotheses, and so forth in the course of this chapter, I will often be talking in this way: still superficial, but closer to the fundamental than most ordinary uses of this sort of language.

5 Stanley (2001) and Burgess and Rosen (2005) argue on empirical grounds against this claim, which they attribute to Yablo (2000) – although Yablo's (2001) response to Stanley suggests that he may not in fact accept it.

6 "Something from nothing" arguments along these lines have been defended by, among others, Alston (1963), Wright (1983), and Schiffer (2003). Many other arguments against nominalism seem to embed arguments of this kind at crucial points. For example, Russell (1912: ch. 10) gives a celebrated argument for the existence of relations, which depends on the premise that one thing cannot resemble another thing without bearing the relation of resemblance to it.

7 See also chapter 9 of this volume.

8 I make this attempt in Dorr (2005).

9 This is probably the best way to make sense of the idea that the existence of abstract objects 'is just a matter of linguistic convention.' On its more straightforward interpretations, this slogan is deeply problematic. On one interpretation, it conflicts with the apparently obvious fact that if numbers exist, they would still have existed even if there had never been any human beings. On another interpretation, it is trivial, since every true sentence is true partly in virtue of meaning what it does, and every sentence means what it does partly in virtue of linguistic convention. On a third interpretation, it requires us to make sense of the notoriously difficult idea of a sentence being true *wholly* in virtue of our conventions.

10 The idea of "paraphrase" as a method for reducing one's "ontological commitments" is introduced in Quine (1948). But a warning is in order: given Quine's verificationism and his rejection of the notions of sameness and difference in meaning (1951), any apparent similarities between the project Quine calls 'ontology' and my project of investigating what there is in the fundamental sense are probably quite misleading.

11 These paraphrases will work only if the kind of superficial use of (6b) we are trying to capture is one on which it can be true only if planets exist in the fundamental sense. In

my view, ordinary uses of sentences like (6b) and (6a) do not require planets to exist in the fundamental sense – they are consistent with the claim that, fundamentally speaking, there are no composite objects at all (see Dorr 2005). But in the context of the present discussion, we can harmlessly ignore divergences between the fundamental and superficial ways of talking that have nothing to do with abstract objects.

12 For arguments that an adequate system of nominalistic paraphrases of sentences about abstract objects is impossible, see Pap (1959–60), Jackson (1977), and van Inwagen (1977, 2004).

13 Two qualifications. First, we must distinguish the question whether an adequate system of paraphrases is possible in principle from the question whether we are in a position to *provide* such paraphrases. One can understand two languages without being in a position to translate between them – for example, a bilingual speaker of English and French might understand 'elm' and 'orme' without knowing that they refer to the same kind of tree – and this could be our situation as bilingual speakers of "fundamental English" and "superficial English." Second: it would be enough for the paraphrases to be statable in a version of English supplemented with arbitrarily powerful devices of infinitary conjunction, disjunction, and quantification. It could well be among the benefits of the superficial way of talking that it gives us a finite way of expressing what would otherwise require infinitary resources.

14 For other attempts to paraphrase problematic sentences by embedding them in the scope of some sort of modal operator, see, e.g., Putnam (1967), van Fraassen (1980), Rosen (1990), and Yablo (2000).

15 It is a good question how a nominalist should understand the clause '. . . and the concrete world were just as it actually is.' In section 4, I will consider a question that raises many of the same issues, namely how a nominalist should understand the notion of duplication, or exact intrinsic similarity.

16 Kripke (1972: 156) argues influentially for the claim that it is metaphysically impossible that there should be unicorns.

17 For those who still think that the fact that nominalism is necessary if true poses a problem, the literature on nominalism contains several proposals (e.g. Chihara 1990; Hellman 1989) that aim to get around this supposed problem by finding some metaphysically possible "surrogates" to play the role the impossible axioms about abstract objects play in my paraphrases. I see no problem of principle with these approaches, although they have the practical disadvantage that they can be used to write down paraphrases only for sentences in which all the predicates that apply to abstract objects are ones we already know how to analyze in terms of the predicates that appear in the axioms.

18 Even if there happen to be some "uninvolved" things that have no positive features inconsistent with being a number, etc., it might still be the case that none of them are numbers. Some philosophers (e.g., Lewis 1993) have argued that the meaning of words like 'number' is very undemanding, so that the existence of *sufficiently many* uninvolved objects is all that is required for some of them to count as "numbers." The idea is that provided that there are enough uninvolved objects, names like '0', '1', '2', . . . will refer indeterminately to all of them, so that there is no fact of the matter as regards which of them is 0, which is 1, etc. I see no sound motivation for such a prima facie surprising proposal. If we were determined to interpret ordinary number-talk as fundamental, there would indeed be pressure to interpret 'number' as undemandingly as possible so as to make it as easy as possible for 'there are numbers' to be true. But I have already argued against such an interpretation: to do justice to our ordinary use, 'there are numbers' needs to be interpreted as *analytic*, and it is not analytic that there are infinitely many uninvolved objects. On a more natural interpretation of 'number', the mere existence of infinitely many uninvolved

objects would not be enough for 'there are numbers' to be true in the fundamental sense: certain of these objects would, in addition, have to be structured in the distinctive way captured by the axioms of number theory. Understood in this way, it is clear that even if for some reason we were confident that there were lots of uninvolved objects, we should still, in the absence of positive argument, give little credence to the hypothesis that any of these objects are numbers.

19   I don't mean these labels to suggest that either of these kinds of explanation is the exclusive province of philosophers or scientists.

20   I don't mean to suggest that Burgess and Rosen intend to be arguing for that conclusion. It is clear from their most recent paper (2005) that, to the extent that they have any quarrel with what I call 'nominalism', it is because they think that not enough has been done to explain what it means to ask whether things of a certain kind exist in the fundamental sense.

21   At least in a superficial sense. The claim that subatomic particles exist in the fundamental sense seems much riskier, given the current state of our understanding of quantum field theories.

22   Cf. Field (1988: 260).

23   As far as I know, the most explicit presentation of an argument by analogy along these lines in the literature is Field's (1988: 260–1). However, Field's argument deals in the first instance, not with theories like T^*, but with theories of the form 'All the facts about concrete objects are consistent with the hypothesis that T', which are far more immediately analogous to $T^{\dagger}$. He conjectures that his conclusions about these theories generalize, so that every device by which one might "modalize away" the mathematical content of a theory is immediately analogous to some device by which one might "modalize away" its commitment to subatomic particles. But this conjecture seems to be false: there just isn't any way for an eliminativist about subatomic particles to directly mimic the procedure used by the nominalist in formulating T^*. For what would take the place of the mathematical axioms in the antecedent of the conditional? The obvious candidate would be some claim to the effect that an atom is located at a point iff that point is the centre of mass of some subatomic particles bound together in such-and-such ways. But this won't work. Given any world of atoms, there will be many different worlds where subatomic particles are added in such a way as to make such a claim true while leaving the distribution of atoms unchanged; T will be true at, at most, a few of these worlds. And it is hard to see what, other than the truth of T, could justify the claim that some T-world is closer to actuality than any non-T world.

24   And they are right that if there is any connection here, it is not a very straightforward one. Since we have reason to believe that the world is not about to end, some theories T that entail that it is not about to end must be explanatorily better, in the relevant sense, than any theory of the form 'Up to now, everything has been just as if T' – despite the fact that, since they are located in the future, the additional entities posited by T play no role in causing the observations that constitute our evidence for T.

25   This is my favorite candidate to be the referent of the coveted label 'naturalism' (Burgess and Rosen 1997: 33).

26   The result I have just mentioned holds only for the versions of Field's theory that use logical resources stronger than first-order logic. For debate about whether a commitment to the superiority of theories using first-order logic might revive the indispensability argument, see Shapiro (1983) and Field (1985).

27   And even if the program were fully successful in basic physics, there would be a difficult further question about the role of mathematics in "higher-level" sciences like statistical mechanics and population ecology.

28 Note that if the mathematical axioms are necessarily false, we will need to think of the "worlds" in question as metaphysically impossible worlds.

29 I take it that the hypothesis that matter is all alike is (a priori) consistent with any consistent hypothesis about the distribution of matter in space and time. If the hypothesis that there is some matter shaped in a certain way cannot be ruled out a priori, then neither can the hypothesis that some homogeneous matter is shaped in that way.

30 Provided that the original theory T posits points and regions of flat space-time, we can use an extension of this method to eliminate its commitment to subatomic particles altogether. To begin with, we must supplement T by adding "bridge laws" to make explicit the ways in which the facts about the positions and motions of atoms depend on the facts about subatomic particles. Next, we reconstrue all talk of subatomic particles as talk of regions of space-time: instead of saying that a particle is *present at* a certain space-time point, we say that the point is a *part* of the region that is the particle. Finally, as before, we replace predicates like 'electron' that purport to pick out different kinds of space-time regions with variables ranging over sets of space-time regions, and add initial existential quantifiers to bind these variables. The resulting theory will have the same consequences as the original theory as regards the spatiotemporal distribution of atoms, but will be consistent with the hypothesis that the only concrete things there are, fundamentally speaking, are atoms moving around in a space-time manifold that is otherwise completely homogeneous. But this hypothesis entails that there aren't any subatomic particles, even in a superficial sense. Perhaps subatomic particles could exist, superficially speaking, in a world where there were only space-time points and atoms, fundamentally speaking. But this could happen only in virtue of some asymmetries in the intrinsic character of the space-time, such as electromagnetic fields, or variable curvature.

31 Indeed, once we have enough mathematics on board, we can always use existential quantifiers instead of possibility-operators like the one in $T^{\ddagger}$. Instead of saying that the facts about the positions and motions of atoms are consistent with T, we can say that there is some model of T that accurately represents the facts about the positions and motions of atoms.

32 Gauge theories provide an even more dramatic example. See Belot (1998).

33 For the record, the view I favor is one on which the analyses of counterfactuals will typically be statable only in a language that allows for infinitely long sentences.

34 Cf. Fine (2001).

35 Armstrong also holds that the properties that feature in the analyses of these elite predicates are the only properties there are, fundamentally speaking. But even a believer in "abundant" properties could agree with Armstrong that only a few of these properties feature in true instances of (11).

36 I should note that Armstrong believes in "structural" properties – e.g. a property *being a helium atom* that is necessarily instantiated by any atom whose nucleus contains exactly two protons. And he seems to endorse (11) for the predicates corresponding to such properties. Thus, unlike me, he apparently sees no difficulty in accepting both (15) and (16).

37 Armstrong tends to focus instead on predicates like 'exactly resembles in some respect' (proposed analysis: 'has some property in common with'), and 'is a natural class' (proposed analysis: 'has as members all and only the things that instantiate some property'). But it is not clear that a nominalist should regard these predicates as precise enough to admit of any easily stated analysis.

38 If one rejects Armstrong-style "structural" properties (see note 36), and accepts the existence in the fundamental sense of composite objects (contrary to the position defended in Dorr 2005), one will require a more complicated analysis of 'duplicate' than this. The problem with (18) is that composite objects can fail to be duplicates by having parts that

fail to be duplicates, even though they themselves may not instantiate any real properties. Here is an alternative analysis that avoids this problem: for x and y to be duplicates is for there to be a one-to-one correspondence (bijection) between the parts of x and the parts of y, such that corresponding parts instantiate the same properties and stand in the same relations (cf. Lewis 1986: 61–2),

39 One might refuse to accept that (D) is necessary on the grounds that it might not even be true. If things get to be electrons in virtue of how they stand to other things – e.g. in virtue of being *lower in charge* than other particles (Lewis 1986: 76) – there is nothing to stop a non-electron from being a duplicate of an electron. The easiest way to respond to this worry is to weaken (D) by replacing the notion of duplication with that of *qualitative indiscernibility* (Lewis 1986: 63) – exact resemblance in extrinsic as well as intrinsic respects, of the sort that can occur only if the whole world is perfectly symmetric.

40 Devitt (1980), Field (1992), Van Cleve (1994), and Melia (2005) all defend views that might be interpreted as versions of the physical strategy.

41 As with the analysis of duplication in terms of instantiation (note 38), we will need a more complicated analysis to handle duplication among complex objects. Here is one way we might do it:

> For x to be a duplicate of y is for there to be a bijection f from the parts of x to the parts of y, such that for all parts $z_1, z_2, z_3 \ldots$ of x: z_1 is an electron iff $f(z_1)$ is an electron, $\ldots$ and z_1 is more massive than z_2 iff $f(z_1)$ is more massive than $f(z_2)$, $\ldots$ and z_1 is between z_2 and z_3 iff $f(z_1)$ is between $f(z_2)$ and $f(z_3)$, and $\ldots$

Here the quantified formula has one conjunct for each basic physical predicate. Of course, this will not be acceptable as it stands to a nominalist, given the use of quantification over functions. But we have already seen, in section 2, how such quantification can be paraphrased in such a way as to be acceptable to the nominalist.

42 Ironically, Armstrong (1989a) once argued for the claim that alien properties are impossible. But he later changed his mind about this (1997: section 10.4).

43 Notice that some of the modal intuitions that conflict with an analysis like (19) can be stated without using physical predicates like 'electron' at all. For example, an analysis using exactly 17 basic physical predicates will entail, counterintuitively, that it is impossible for there to be $2^{17} + 1$ simple objects none of which is a duplicate of any of the others. This may be important. Several philosophers (e.g., Bealer 1987; Chalmers 1996) have attempted to draw a principled distinction between words like 'water' which can give rise to the phenomenon of the necessary a posteriori, and other words which cannot. But there is any such distinction to be drawn, it would seem that all the words in the sentence 'it is not the case that there are $2^{17} + 1$ simple objects none of which is a duplicate of any of the others' belong to the latter category. If so, the proposition expressed by this sentence could be necessary only if it were knowable a priori, as it clearly is not.

44 Or at least, anything qualitatively indiscernible from a white thing: see note 39.

45 For discussions of this view see Lewis (1983) and Armstrong (1989b).

46 For arguments, independent of nominalism, against the view that that plural claims of this kind can be analyzed in terms of sets, see Boolos (1984) and Oliver and Smiley (2001).

47 Although it is controversial whether anything that exists in the fundamental sense has any parts – see Dorr (2005).

48 For discussion of some of these complications, see Rodriguez-Pereyra (2002: 131–41).

49 Alternatively, we could allow all electrons to play the role of paradigms: this is the approach favored by Rodriguez-Pereyra (2002).

50 Armstrong (1978a: 50–1) makes essentially this objection.

51 One might attempt to escape this argument by saying something like (21*) To be an electron is to resemble each of e_1, e_2 ... *as they actually are* at least as much as they actually resemble one another. This is unproblematic for modal realists like Lewis (1986) and Rodriguez-Pereyra (2002). But any defense of nominalism that relied on modal realism would be widely, and in my view correctly, regarded as a *reductio*. For a non-modal-realist, "cross-world" similarity can hardly be primitive. One could attempt to analyze it in terms of objects playing similar structural roles at their respective worlds: such an analysis would face the same difficulties as the purely general structural analyses I will be considering in the main text. Ideas along these lines have been considered under the heading of 'counterpart theory for properties': see Hazen (1996), Heller (1998), Black (2000), and Hawthorne (2001).

52 Defenders of dispositional essentialism include Shoemaker (1980, 1998), Swoyer (1982), and Ellis and Lierse (1994). Hawthorne (2001) is an excellent survey of the arguments. For opposition, see Sidelle (2002).

53 Some (e.g., Swoyer 1982) go so far as to hold that all nomologically necessary truths are metaphysically necessary: this requires either rejecting the Alien Properties Intuition, or adopting an unusually restrictive notion of nomological necessity.

54 The problems physical symmetries pose for dispositional essentialism are extensively discussed by Hawthorne (2001).

55 In the unlikely event that the electrons are *structurally indiscernible* from the positrons – if, for example, there is eternal recurrence in both directions, with every second epoch having positrons substituted for electrons – there will be no way to make the necessary distinctions at the purely structural level. But perhaps it wouldn't be so bad to reject the Alien Individuals Intuition in such bizarre circumstances.

56 There is a helpful analogy between the problem the predicates 'electron' and 'positron' pose for the Structural Nominalist and the problem 'left' and 'right' pose for those who think that facts about leftness and rightness are not among the basic geometric facts about the world. We are tempted by the intuition that the other geometric facts don't determine the facts about left and right: for example, that a hand in otherwise empty space could be either right or left. Despite this, the received view is that we need not expand our conception of the basic geometric facts to account for leftness and rightness. 'Left' and 'right' can be analyzed either using paradigms, or by appealing to some initially contingent-seeming asymmetries in the universe, the usual example is the fact that human beings' hearts are on the left side of their bodies. For further discussion, see the papers collected in Van Cleve and Frederick (1991).

57 'Phlogiston' was introduced by eighteenth-century chemists as a name for a hypothetical substance emitted in burning and the calcination of metals. See Dorr (2005: section 16) for a more detailed discussion of the case of semantically defective predicates and its ramifications.

58 Blackburn (1993) and Gibbard (1990) are the most prominent evaluative non-factualists. For a defense of the distinction between the factual and the non-factual and some interesting ideas about how to draw it, see Fine (2001).

59 The appeal to economy of brute necessities is one of Armstrong's characteristic argumentative moves – see, e.g., Armstrong (1978a: 49–50). Lewis (1983) is also explicit about the role of this sort of economy.

60 See Ramsey (1925), Armstrong (1978b: ch. 13), and Mellor (1991).

61 Ramsey (1925) seems to be proposing something like this, but with a symmetric primitive predicate 'x and y constitute a fact' in place of the non-symmetric 'proto-instantiates'.

62 Assuming that the set of sentences that intuitively strike us as necessary is logically consistent with any logically consistent hypothesis according to which nothing falls under any of our old predicates.

63 See Goodman (1951: 86–9).

64 Ramsey (1925: 29), following Wittgenstein (1921), embraces the skeptical response to this objection. Since 'we know and can know nothing whatever about the forms of atomic propositions', we can't know whether the fundamental objects divide into two different kinds that behave in the ways that might justify calling them 'universals' and 'individuals'.

65 Even if nominalism is true, there are still necessary truths having to do with abstract entities whose necessity needs explaining. The most important example is the nominalist thesis itself, if it is taken to be necessary. It is certainly not obvious how to formulate analyses of predicates like 'number' and 'property' that would allow sentences like 'there are no numbers' and 'there are no properties' to be reduced to logical truths. The problem here seems quite similar to that posed by sentences like 'there are no unicorns' and 'there are no phlogiston': it is best dealt with, in my view, by making special allowance for "semantically defective" predicates in formulating the ban on brute necessities.

66 This is of course the merest sketch of an argument; I hope to fill in more of its details in future work. The biggest task in doing so is explaining why the logical truths, narrowly conceived, should be a better place for explanations of necessity to stop than any larger set of truths.

67 The hardest bullet to bite for those who regard basic physical predicates as primitive and unanalyzable while rejecting brute necessities is the contingency of even the most necessary-seeming geometric axioms. See Le Poidevin (2004).

68 Thanks to Hartry Field, Jessica Moss, Kieran Setiya, Ted Sider, and to audiences at Pittsburgh, Texas, and MIT.

References

Alston, William. 1963. "Ontological Commitments," *Philosophical Studies* 14: 1–8.

Armstrong, David M. 1978a. *Nominalism and Realism.* Vol. 1 of *Universals and Scientific Realism* (Cambridge: Cambridge University Press).

—. 1978b. *A Theory of Universals.* Vol. 2 of *Universals and Scientific Realism* (Cambridge: Cambridge University Press).

—. 1989a. *A Combinatorial Theory of Possibility* (Cambridge: Cambridge University Press).

—. 1989b. *Universals: An Opinionated Introduction* (Boulder: Westview Press).

—. 1997. *A World of States of Affairs* (Cambridge: Cambridge University Press).

Bealer, George. 1982. *Quality and Concept* (Oxford: Oxford University Press).

—. 1987. "The Philosophical Limits of Scientific Essentialism," in James Tomberlin, ed., *Philosophical Perspectives 1: Metaphysics* (Atascadero: Ridgewood), pp. 289–365.

—. 1993. "Universals," *Journal of Philosophy* 110: 5–32.

Belot, Gordon. 1998. "Understanding Electromagnetism," *British Journal for the Philosophy of Science* 49: 531–55.

Benacerraf, Paul. 1973. "Mathematical Truth," *Journal of Philosophy* 19: 661–79.

Black, Robert. 2000. "Against Quidditism," *Australasian Journal of Philosophy* 78: 87–104.

Blackburn, Simon. 1993. *Essays in Quasi-Realism* (Oxford: Oxford University Press).

Boolos, George. 1984. "To Be is To Be the Value of a Variable (Or To Be Some Values of Some Variables)," *Journal of Philosophy* 81: 430–449.

Bradley, F. H. 1897. *Appearance and Reality*, 2nd edn. (Oxford: Oxford University Press). Repr. in *Writings on Logic and Metaphysics*, ed. James W. Allard and Guy Stock (Oxford: Oxford University Press), 1994.

Burgess, John P., and Rosen, Gideon. 1997. *A Subject with No Object: Strategies for Nominalistic Interpretation of Mathematics* (Oxford: Oxford University Press).

—. 2005. "Nominalism Reconsidered," in Stewart Shapiro, ed., *The Oxford Handbook of Philosophy of Mathematics and Logic* (Oxford: Oxford University Press), pp. 515–35.

Campbell, Keith. 1991. *Abstract Particulars* (Oxford: Basil Blackwell).

Carnap, Rudolf. 1950. "Empiricism, Semantics and Ontology," *Revue International de Philosophie* 4: 20–40. Repr. in *Meaning and Necessity: A Study in Semantics and Modal Logic*, 2nd edn. (Chicago: University of Chicago Press, 1956).

Chalmers, David. 1996. *The Conscious Mind* (Oxford: Oxford University Press).

Chihara, Charles. 1990. *Constructibility and Mathematical Existence* (Oxford: Oxford University Press).

Devitt, Michael. 1980. "'Ostrich Nominalism' or 'Mirage Realism'?" *Pacific Philosophical Quarterly* 61: 433–49. Repr. in D. H Mellor and Alex Oliver, eds., *Properties* (Oxford: Oxford University Press, 1997), pp. 101–11.

Dorr, Cian. 2005. "What We Disagree About When We Disagree About Ontology," in Mark Kalderon, ed., *Fictionalist Approaches to Metaphysics* (Oxford: Oxford University Press).

Ellis, Brian, and Lierse, Caroline. 1994. "Dispositional Essentialism." *Australasian Journal of Philosophy* 72: 27–45.

Field, Hartry. 1980. *Science Without Numbers* (Oxford: Blackwell).

—. 1985. "On Conservativeness and Incompleteness," *Journal of Philosophy* 81: 239–260. Repr. in *Realism, Mathematics and Modality* (Oxford: Blackwell, 1989), pp. 125–46.

—. 1988. "Realism, Mathematics and Modality," *Philosophical Topics* 19: 57–107. Repr. in *Realism, Mathematics and Modality* (Oxford: Blackwell, 1989), pp. 227–81.

—. 1992. "Physicalism," in John Earman, ed., *Inference, Explanation, and Other Frustrations: Essays in the Philosophy of Science* (Berkeley: University of California Press), pp. 271–91.

Fine, Kit. 1994. "Essence and Modality," in James Tomberlin, ed., *Philosophical Perspectives 8: Logic and Language* (Atascadero: Ridgeview), pp. 1–16.

—. 2001. "The Question of Realism." *Philosopher"s Imprint* 1.

Gibbard, Allan. 1990. *Wise Choices, Apt Feelings*. Cambridge, MA: Harvard University Press.

Goodman, Nelson. 1951. *The Structure of Appearance* (3rd edn., Cambridge, MA: Harvard University Press, 1977).

Hawthorne, John. 2001. "Causal Structuralism," in James Tomberlin, ed., *Philosophical Perspectives 15: Metaphysics* (Cambridge, MA: Blackwell), pp. 361–78.

Hazen, Allen. 1996. "Actualism Again." *Philosophical Studies* 84: 155–181.

Heller, Mark. 1998. "Property Counterparts in Ersatz Worlds." *Journal of Philosophy* 95: 293–316.

Hellman, Geoffrey. 1989. *Mathematics Without Numbers* (Oxford: Oxford University Press).

Jackson, Frank. 1977. "Statements About Universals." *Mind* 86: 427–429. Repr. in D. H Mellor and Alex Oliver, eds., *Properties* (Oxford: Oxford University Press, 1997), pp. 89–92.

Kripke, Saul. 1972. *Naming and Necessity*. Rev. edn., Cambridge, MA: Harvard University Press, 1980.

Le Poidevin, Robin. 2004. "Space, Supervenience and Substantivalism," *Analysis* 64: 191–8.

Lewis, David. 1973. *Counterfactuals* (Oxford: Blackwell).

—. 1983. "New Work for a Theory of Universals," *Australasian Journal of Philosophy* 61: 343–77. Repr. in *Papers in Metaphysics and Epistemology* (Cambridge: Cambridge University Press, 1999), pp. 8–55.

—. 1986. *On the Plurality of Worlds* (Oxford: Blackwell).

——. 1993. "Mathematics is Megethology," *Philosophia Mathematica* 1: 3–23. Repr. in *Papers in Philosophical Logic*. (Cambridge: Cambridge University Press: 1998), pp. 203–29.

Melia, Joseph. 2005. "Truthmaking Without Truthmakers," in Helen Beebee and Julian Dodd, eds., *Truthmakers: The Contemporary Debate* (Oxford: Oxford University Press).

Mellor, D. H. 1991. "Properties and Predicates," in *Matters of Metaphysics* (Cambridge: Cambridge University Press), pp. 170–82.

Nolan, Daniel. 1997. "Impossible Worlds: A Modest Approach," *Notre Dame Journal of Formal Logic* 38: 535–72.

Oliver, Alex, and Smiley, Timothy. 2001. "Strategies for a Logic of Plurals," *Philosophical Quarterly* 51: 289–306.

Pap, Arthur. 1959–60. "Nominalism, Empiricism and Universals," *Philosophical Quarterly* 9–10: 330–40, 44–60.

Price, H. H. 1953. *Thinking and Experience*. 2nd edn., London: Hutchinson, 1969.

Putnam, Hilary. 1967. "Mathematics Without Foundations," *Journal of Philosophy* 64: 5–22. Repr. in *Mathematics, Matter and Method: Philosophical Papers*, vol. 1. (Cambridge: Cambridge University Press), pp. 43–59.

——. 1971. *Philosophy of Logic*. New York: Harper and Row. Repr. in *Mathematics, Matter and Method: Philosophical Papers*, vol. 1. Cambridge: Cambridge University Press, 1975, pp. 323–57.

Quine, Willard van Orman. 1948. "On What There Is," *Review of Metaphysics* 2: 21–38. Repr. with revisions in *From a Logical Point of View* (Cambridge, MA: Harvard University Press, 1953), pp. 1–19.

——. 1951. "Two Dogmas of Empiricism." *Philosophical Review* 60: 20–43. Repr. with revisions in *From a Logical Point of View* (Cambridge, MA: Harvard University Press, 1953), pp. 20–46.

Ramsey, F. P. 1925. "Universals," *Mind* 34: 401–417. Repr. in D. H. Mellor, ed., *Philosophical Papers* (Cambridge: Cambridge University Press, 1990), pp. 8–33.

Rodriguez-Pereyra, Gonzalo. 2002. *Resemblance Nominalism* (Oxford: Oxford University Press).

Rosen, Gideon. 1990. "Modal Fictionalism," *Mind* 99: 327–54.

Russell, Bertrand. 1912. *The Principles of Philosophy* (London: Williams and Norgate).

Schiffer, Stephen. 2003. *The Things We Mean* (Oxford: Oxford University Press).

Shapiro, Stewart. 1983. "Conservativeness and Incompleteness," *Journal of Philosophy* 80: 521–31.

Shoemaker, Sydney. 1980. "Causality and Properties," in Peter van Inwagen, ed., *Time and Cause* (Dordrecht: D. Reidel), pp. 228–54.

——. 1998. "Causal and Metaphysical Necessity." *Pacific Philosophical Quarterly* 79: 59–77.

Sidelle, Alan. 2002. "On the Metaphysical Contingency of the Laws of Nature," in Tamar Gendler and John Hawthorne, eds., *Conceivability and Possibility* (Oxford: Oxford University Press), pp. 309–36.

Stalnaker, Robert. 1968. "A Theory of Conditionals," in *Studies in Logical Theory: American Philosophical Quarterly Monograph Series, No. 2* (Oxford: Blackwell).

Stanley, Jason. 2001. "Hermeneutic Fictionalism," in Peter French and Howard K. Wettstein, eds., *Midwest Studies in Philosophy XXV: Figurative Language* (Oxford: Blackwell), pp. 36–71.

Swoyer, Chris. 1982. "The Nature of Natural Laws," *Australasian Journal of Philosophy* 60: 203–23.

Van Cleve, James. 1994. "Predication Without Universals? A Fling with Ostrich Nominalism," *Philosophy and Phenomenological Research* 54: 577–90.

Van Cleve, James, and Frederick, Robert E., eds. 1991. *The Philosophy of Right and Left: Incongruent Counterparts and the Nature of Space* (Dordrecht: Kluwer Academic Publishers).

van Fraassen, Bas. 1980. *The Scientific Image* (Oxford: Oxford University Press).

van Inwagen, Peter. 1977. "Creatures of Fiction," *American Philosophical Quarterly* 14: 299–308. Repr. in *Ontology, Identity and Modality* (Cambridge: Cambridge University Press, 2001), pp. 37–56.

——. 2004. "A Theory of Properties," in Dean Zimmerman, ed., *Oxford Studies in Metaphysics*, vol. 1 (Oxford: Oxford University Press), pp. 107–38.

Wittgenstein, Ludwig. 1921. *Tractatus Logico-Philosophicus*. English edn., ed. D. F. Pears and B. F. McGuinness. (London: Routledge and Kegan Paul, 1961).

Wright, Crispin. 1983. *Frege's Conception of Numbers as Objects* (Aberdeen: Aberdeen University Press).

Yablo, Stephen. 2000. "A Paradox of Existence," in Anthony Everett and Thomas Hofweber, eds., *Empty Names, Fiction and the Puzzles of Non-Existence* (Stanford: CSLI Press), pp. 275–312.

——. 2001. "Go Figure: A Path Through Fictionalism," in Peter French and Howard K. Wettstein, eds., *Midwest Studies in Philosophy XXV: Figurative Language* (Oxford: Blackwell), pp. 72–102.

CAUSATION AND
LAWS OF NATURE

2.1 "Nailed to Hume's Cross?" John W. Carroll

2.2 "Causation and Laws of Nature: Reductionism,"
     Jonathan Schaffer

It just *happened* to be true, let us suppose, that everyone who ate at the Mar-T Café on April 8, 1990, wore a blue shirt. Other events are not so "accidental." For example, it's no accident that when the cook let go of the French fries, they fell into the fryer. In some sense, the fries *had to fall*, given that the cook let them go. When an event is *caused*, and when there is a law of nature governing its occurrence, it is in some sense *necessary* that the event occurs. Where does this necessity come from? Jonathan Schaffer argues that the necessity boils down to mere regularities. The necessity of the fries' falling boils down to the fact that fries everywhere, and every time, in fact do fall when they are released. John Carroll argues that there is more to it than this; causal and lawful necessity go beyond mere regularity.

CAUSATION AND
LAWS OF NATURE

Nailed to Hume's Cross?

John W. Carroll

1 Lawhood, Causation, and Bearing Hume's Cross

Some scientists try to discover and report laws of nature. And, they do so with success. There are many principles that were for a long time thought to be laws that turned out to be useful approximations, like Newton's gravitational principle. There are others that were thought to be laws and still are considered laws, like Einstein's principle that no signals travel faster than light. Laws of nature are not just important to scientists. They are also of great interest to us philosophers, though primarily in an ancillary way. Qua philosophers, we do not try to discover *what the laws are*. We care about *what it is to be a law*, about *lawhood*, the essential difference between something's being a law and something's not being a law. It is one of our jobs to understand lawhood and convey our understanding to others.

Causation is also central to science and to philosophy. Molecular bonding, planetary orbits, human decisions, and life itself are all causal processes. A scientific explanation of an event will include some mention of the causes of that event – you can't say why something did happen without identifying what made it happen. Just as is the case for lawhood, qua philosophers, one job we have is to understand causation and then to share this understanding with others.

As a result of the work of David Hume, many philosophers are influenced by a metaphysical concern and a skeptical challenge that have shaped what is counted as providing understanding of lawhood and causation. Hume's argument against the idea of necessary connection contains the plausible premise that we lack any direct perceptual or introspective access to the causal relation:

All events seem entirely loose and separate. One event follows another, but we never can observe any tie between them. They seem *conjoined*, but never *connected*. But as we can have no idea of anything which never appeared to our outward sense or inward sentiment, the necessary conclusion *seems* to be that we have no idea of connection or power at all, and that these words are absolutely without any meaning when employed either in philosophical reasonings or common life. (1955: 85; italics in the original)

The skeptical challenge that emerges says that, if lawhood and causation are not analyzable in terms of some more accessible notions, then we would be prevented from having knowledge we ordinarily take ourselves to have. Regarding the metaphysical concern, for various reasons, in trying to say what makes it true that something is a law or that one thing causes another, it can be tempting not to limit oneself to the accessible notions, instead positing necessary connections or other questionable entities as existing in the world. Short of doing so, the concern is that the truthmakers for reports of lawhood and causation would be non-existent, and then the reports couldn't be true; for Hume, they couldn't even have meaning.

To address these worries, philosophers often seek a certain sort of analysis of lawhood. They seek a necessarily true completion of:

(S1)   *P* is a law of nature if and only if . . .

The expectation is that the analysis should make clear that lawhood is suitably accessible for us to have the knowledge of laws we ordinarily take ourselves to have and make clear what it is about the universe that makes true reports of lawhood true. There has been widespread agreement that certain sorts of completions of (S1) are unsatisfactory in this regard. Analyses of lawhood that use the counterfactual conditional (i.e., if *P* were the case, then *Q* would be the case) would do little to address the Hume-inspired worries. Concerns about our knowledge of counterfactuals and their truthmakers are just as prevalent as are the parallel worries about lawhood. The same can be said for completions of (S1) that employ the other nomic concepts: causation, lawhood, explanation, chance, dispositions, and their conceptual kin. As a result, the history of philosophy has shown a preference for what I call a *reduction* of lawhood; philosophers have tried to provide a necessarily true completion of (S1) without using any nomic terms.

The history of philosophy includes many attempts to give a similarly reductive analysis of causation, though, at least recently, the constraints on what counts as a satisfactory analysis of causation have been somewhat less severe. There is still much preoccupation with giving an analysis of causation, with finding some necessarily true completion of:

(S2)   *P* caused *Q* if and only if . . .

And no, not just any necessarily true completion will do; for example, no one would bother with *P* caused *Q* if and only if *P* caused *Q*. But, unlike with lawhood, there has been a lot of attention given to analyzing causation in terms of chance, the counterfactual conditional, lawhood, or some combination of these nomic concepts. That is, in the last 40 years or so, philosophers have not insisted that (S2) be completed non-nomically. This difference in attitude is easy to explain. An underlying belief of the philosophical community has been that lawhood is the best place to get off the nomic bus and squelch the Hume-inspired worries. The thought seems to be that, as a practical matter, it is easier to give a thorough reduction of lawhood. So, we are better off analyzing causation, say, in terms of the counterfactual conditional, maybe analyzing this conditional in terms of lawhood, and then letting a non-nomic analysis of lawhood do the last bit of reductive work.

In *Laws of Nature* (1994), I argue that the history of philosophy has been pretty badly wrong about all of this. I maintain that neither causation nor lawhood can be analyzed non-nomically and, further, that causation even resists any (non-circular) analysis in terms of the counterfactual conditional, chance, or lawhood. What I propose to do in this chapter is defend my brand of anti-reductionism against the Hume-inspired worries. So, after wrapping up this introductory section, I will quickly review in section 2 an example that challenges the prospects of giving a *Humean* reduction of lawhood, a reduction of lawhood that does not require that we posit any mysterious ontology. (This example will at the same time also provide a nice basis for presenting certain other ways of trying to understand what it is to be a law.) In section 3, I take on the metaphysical concern as it applies to my anti-reductionism, offering a sketch of a new non-reductive theory of lawhood. In section 4, I use this analysis to shed light on the skeptical challenge.

In one regrettable way, my defense of anti-reductionism will be limited. I will only directly address the Hume-inspired concerns as they apply to lawhood – defending my anti-reductionism about causation will have to wait. Given the difficulty of the two tasks, I cannot do a good job on both, and it seems to me to be more appropriate to focus on lawhood rather than causation because more attention has been paid in recent years to giving a thoroughly reductive account of lawhood. This is not to say that this chapter is not about causation. As we shall see, my non-reductive theory is non-reductive precisely because it invokes causation (or, strictly speaking, a closely related notion of explanation). I will argue that the laws of nature are exactly those regularities that are caused by nature.

2 Support for Anti-Reductionism and a Glance at Some Alternatives

Suppose that there are exactly 10 different kinds of fundamental particle. So there are 55 possible kinds of two-particle interaction. Suppose also that 54 of these kinds of interaction have been studied and 54 laws have been proposed and thoroughly tested. It just so happens that there are never any interactions between the last two kinds of particle; these are arbitrarily labeled as 'X' and 'Y' particles.

One thing that is ingenious about this example of Michael Tooley's (1977: 669) is that, at least at first glance, it seems that there could be a law about X–Y interactions. After all, in the example, scientists have already discovered laws for all of the other 54 kinds of interaction. Indeed, it is even true that some of these laws are about X particles and that some are about Y particles. Thus, there seems to be some reason to think that there is also a law about what will happen if X and Y particles get together. Another thing that is ingenious about Tooley's case is that it seems that many *different* X–Y interaction laws are perfectly consistent with all the events that might take place during the complete (i.e., past, present, and future) history of the 10-particle world. It seems that the totality of events of this universe could fail to determine what the laws are. Even given the complete history of this universe, there might be a law, L_1, that, when X particles and Y particles interact, the particles are destroyed. But, then again, even given the complete history of this universe, there might be a law, L_2, that, when X particles and Y particles interact, the particles bond. It seems that what the laws are does not supervene on (i.e., is not determined by) the non-nomic facts.

Tooley takes his example to make a case against Humean reductive attempts to solve the problem of laws. To see why, consider what such an account might say about his 10-particle world. For example, a naive Humean might hold that P is a law of nature if and only if P is a true, contingent, universal generalization. This account says about Tooley's example that *both* L_1 and L_2 are laws: it is a law of the 10-particle world that any interaction of X and Y particles results in their annihilation and it is a law of that world that when X and Y particles interact they bond. But that is impossible because such annihilation and bonding events are incompatible; it cannot be true that, if there were an X–Y interaction, then there would be both the bonding and the annihilation. This problem for the simplistic Humean account is a consequence of the fact that the account does not differentiate between L_1 and L_2. Because the two are both true, contingent, generalizations, they both get counted as laws. David Lewis (1973, 1983, and 1986) holds a much more sophisticated Humean account, one that maintains that P is a law of nature if and only if P is a member of all the true deductive systems with a best combination of simplicity and strength. But, at least at first glance, his view is faced with the same problem that faces the naive Humean view. Not only do L_1 and L_2 not differ regarding their logical form, their contingency, or their truth, they also do not differ regarding their simplicity or their strength. Prima facie, either they both would belong to all the best systems or neither would. Humean reductionists must somehow deny that the 10-particle case is genuinely possible.

In contrast, a *universalist* reductive approach of the sort favored by Tooley and also by David Armstrong (1983) and Fred Dretske (1977) seems to be in better shape. Much simplified, universalists hold that:

Fs are Gs is a law of nature if and only if the universal *F*-ness stands in N to the universal *G*-ness.

('N' and sometimes 'necessitation' are names given to the two-placed relation that relates universals. When *F*-ness stands in N to *G*-ness, *F*-ness is said to *necessitate* *G*-ness.) In virtue of its appeal to facts about universals, this is not a Humean reduction of lawhood. Just so, it leaves open the possibility that there is something that grounds the lawhood of exactly one of the generalizations in Tooley's 10-particle case. For all that has been said, it might be the case that being an X–Y interaction necessitates annihilation but not bonding. It could also go the other way: being an X–Y interaction might necessitate bonding but not annihilation.

We need not draw the conclusions drawn by the universalists. Armstrong, Dretske, and Tooley are clearly still very much stuck with the Hume-inspired skeptical challenge. Prima facie, identifying the truthmaker for lawhood reports with a relation (itself taken to be a universal) that holds between universals does nothing to make it clear how observational data could support knowledge of what the laws are. Furthermore, despite *appearing* to have identified a reductive truthmaker for lawhood reports,

John W. Carroll

the metaphysical concern really is still an issue for the universalists. Tooley's example exposes a void in the universalist approach, at least insofar as that view has been presented here. It is awfully convenient that the universals line up so nicely in Plato's Heaven, doling out lawfulness to exactly the regularities that are laws. But, why should we believe that they really do line up so nicely? What do we really know about this necessitation relation, besides its name? What relation is it? Without a specification of the relation, the universalists have not really given a reductive analysis of lawhood. They haven't given an analysis period.

Some philosophers react to the 10-particle case differently from the Humean reductionists and the universalists. At a loss to identify the missing truthmakers, or troubled by the skeptical challenge, they conclude that lawhood sentences do not describe reality. They are *anti-realists* about lawhood. Some anti-realists, e.g., Bas van Fraassen (1989) and Ronald Giere (1999), go so far as to assert *that there are no laws*. Other philosophers, e.g., Simon Blackburn (1984, 1986) and Barry Ward (2002, 2003), adopt a different sort of anti-realism. Though they will utter sentences like, 'It is a law that no signals travel faster than light', they are anti-realists in virtue of thinking that the purpose of such sentences is not to describe the facts. On their view, lawhood sentences convey no information over and above what is conveyed by their contained generalization sentence. Instead, these sentences project a certain non-cognitive attitude about the conveyed generalization. All anti-realists sidestep the Hume-inspired skeptical and metaphysical worries: if lawhood reports are not even meant to describe the way our world is, or do have that purpose but are all false, then we certainly do not need to worry about their truthmakers or how we could know what the laws are.

Certain features of my own view stand out when contrasted with the other standard positions on lawhood. I am an *anti-reductionist* in denying that there are any necessarily true Humean completions of (S1), but also in denying that there is any ontologically rich non-Humean reduction of the sort defended by the universalists. I am also an *anti-supervenience theorist* because I accept Tooley's 10-particle case at face value, and indeed use examples like it in my book *Laws of Nature* as the centerpiece of my arguments for anti-reductionism. So, as I see it, the non-nomic does not determine what the laws are: there are possible worlds that agree on their non-nomic facts and disagree about what the laws are. Yet I am also a *realist*; I do think that there are utterances of lawhood sentences that try (and even sometimes succeed) in describing reality – it is true and I know it is true that it is a law that no signals travel faster than light. Thus, my realist, anti-supervenist, anti-reductionism seems to put me in a horrible position in relation to the Hume-inspired worries. On my view, it is true that there are laws and some of us know what some of the laws are, but there is no reductive analysis of lawhood that could explain how this knowledge of lawhood is attainable or even say what makes it true that the laws are the laws. What can a realist, anti-supervenist, anti-reductionist say to Hume?

3 The Metaphysical Concern

Sometimes the metaphysical concern takes the form of a worry about how uninformative anti-reductionism about lawhood is bound to be. Tooley has this to say about an account of lawhood offered using dispositional terms: "[I]n offering this sort of answer one is not really making any progress with respect to the problem of explaining nomological language in the broad sense" (1987: 68). This lack of progress, however, does nothing to establish even a presumption in favor of reductionism. True, the anti-reductionist denies that there is a reductive answer to the question of what makes something a law. But, failure to provide that sort of answer cannot count against the anti-reductionist and in favor of the reductionist without begging the question. As the anti-reductionist sees it, it is the reductionist that commits the transgression in giving a reductive answer to a question that does not have one.

In any case, questions about informativeness aren't really what scare philosophers away from a realist anti-reductionism. What does that is a demand for truthmakers. When saying why he believes that there needs to be a relation of necessitation between *F*-ness and *G*-ness for *F*s are *G*s to be a law, Armstrong makes such a demand:

> Suppose that one is a Nominalist in the classical sense of the term, one who holds that everything there is is a particular, and a particular only. Because there is nothing identical in the different instantiations of the law, such a Nominalist, it seems, is forced to hold a Regularity theory of law. For if he attempts to hold any sort of necessitation theory, then he can point to no ontological ground for the necessity. He is nailed to Hume's cross. (1983: 78)

If we are unable to say what makes a generalization a law, then, especially given Tooley's 10-particle example, it can appear that *nothing* does. What could it be that makes it true that L_1 is a law rather than L_2? What makes it true that L_2 is a law rather than L_1? What the laws are *floats on nothing* (cf., Armstrong 1983: 31).

It is important to recognize that anti-reductionists about lawhood need not be *primitivists*. The standard arguments for anti-reductionism leave open that there might be some analysis of lawhood in terms of some other nomic concepts. For example, Marc Lange (2000) has analyzed lawhood in terms of membership in a counterfactually stable set of propositions. Lange's idea is that the set of laws is special in that each of its members would still be true under any counterfactual supposition consistent with the set itself. Prima facie, this analysis makes substantive and interesting claims about what lawhood is. We can make enough independent judgments about which counterfactuals are true and about which propositions are laws to test his proposal. If the analysis is correct, it speaks to any leftover concerns stemming from the supposed uninformativeness of anti-reductionism. Obviously, though, Lange's approach will do nothing to convince anyone to set aside Armstrong's float-on-nothing worry. Counterfactuals live too close in logical space to lawhood and behave in all too similar ways. About Tooley's example, what would make it true that, *if some* X *particle were to interact with some* Y *particle, then an annihilation event would occur?* What would make it true that, *if some* X *particle were to interact with some* Y *particle, then a bonding event would occur?* Nothing, it seems, would make either of these counterfactuals true.

I am not endorsing the truthmaker concern. Anyone who has a primitive concept playing some role in their metaphysics (i.e., everyone with a metaphysics) has something that in a certain sense lacks a truthmaker of the sort Armstrong demands regarding lawhood. And, it has always seemed to me, and still does, that the counterfactual conditional is a pretty good candidate to be primitive in a respectable metaphysics. So, I am not moved to abandon my anti-reductionism, and Lange will not be moved to abandon his either. Nevertheless, I will propose an alternative analysis of lawhood, one open to anti-reductionists, that may speak to the metaphysical concern in a way that Lange's non-reductive analysis does not.

It is often alleged, though primarily in informal discussions of our topic, that no laws are *accidentally true*. Such remarks stem from two different sources: their plausibility and the feeling among philosophers that such remarks are no big deal because this is not where any real work will get done. Prima facie, the metaphysical and skeptical worries about lawhood apply in a straightforward way to non-accidentality, and this notion is no better understood than lawhood itself. Investigating accidentality is usually not considered a step in the right direction.

Well, I say that, in this case, we have underestimated the power of an intuitive gloss. Idea: What is an accident equates with what is a coincidence, where a coincidence is something that is unexplained.[1] I run into an old friend at a Durham Bulls game. I did not even know he was in North Carolina; he moved away more than three years ago. Our meeting at the game is a coincidence. What makes it a coincidence? Well, it is a coincidence because it just happened. In other words:

P is a coincidence if and only if there is no *Q* such that *P* because *Q*.

The key notion here is the one expressed by ordinary uses of 'because'. Strictly speaking, it is a kind of explanation. It is, however, different from causation in only uninteresting ways. If *b*'s being *F* caused *c*'s being *G*, then *c* was *G* because *b* was *F*. The other direction is not as straightforward. The number 3 is a square root of 9 because 3^2 is 9, but we are reluctant to say that 3^2's being 9 *caused* 3 to be a square root of 9. In general, we are reluctant to take mathematical explanations, explanations underwritten by definitions, and explanations involving universal generalizations to be causal ones. For some reason, when the explanandum and the explanans are too closely connected, connected in some more-or-less analytic way, and not by some paradigmatically causal process (e.g., colliding), or when the explanandum or explanans themselves are sufficiently unlike paradigmatic causes and effects (e.g., moving billiard balls), philosophers tend not to consider these explanations to be causal. That, however, seems to me to be the extent of the difference. Causation and the relevant notion of explanation amount to pretty much the same thing. So, unofficially, and a bit more stylishly, I like to say that *P* is a coincidence if and only if *P* is uncaused.

One might object that, despite what I said, my seeing my friend at the ball game has an explanation, lots of them even, and that it certainly wasn't uncaused. Wasn't the meeting the result of each of us deciding to take in a ball game over the weekend? Didn't we run into each other at that game because we both like baseball? Fair enough, but also notice how strange it is to pair these explanations with the attribution of coincidentality. For example, notice how odd and even contradictory it is to say all in one breath: *we met because we both like baseball and that we met was a coincidence*. Insofar as our both liking baseball does explain why my friend and I met, the meeting was *not* a coincidence. As I see it, 'because' utterances are context-sensitive and their context sensitivity carries over to 'coincidence' utterances. In an ordinary context, like the one present when I first introduced the baseball example, the sentence 'My friend and I met at the game because we both like baseball' is false. It is a bit of a long story (see my 2005), but such utterances are false because, without a context change, that we both like baseball is not sufficient for my friend and me to meet at the game. In such a context, that we both like baseball, together with what was presupposed or common ground in the context, does not entail that we would meet. Context can shift so that such utterances are true, but then an utterance of 'Our meeting at the ball game was a coincidence' would not be true in the new context.

What about laws? Laws are not coincidences. They are not things that just happen; they are explained.[2] Not being a coincidence, however, is not all there is to being a law. For example, some particular states of affairs, like there being tobacco in North Carolina, are not coincidences but are not suitably general to be laws. Or, for a more interesting case, it might be true that there are no gold spheres greater than a mile in diameter because there is not enough gold. In that case, strictly speaking, it would be true, suitably general and not a coincidence that all gold spheres are less than a mile in diameter. Nevertheless, that still would not be a law; it is not enough to be a law to be general and not coincidental. What seems important about this gold-spheres example is *how* the regularity turns out not to be non-coincidental. What blocks it from being a law is that something *in nature*, or really a certain sort of initial condition of the universe, *an absence of something in nature*, explains the regularity. Contrast this with the law that no signals travel faster than light. With this generalization it seems that it is true because of *nature itself*. Lawhood requires that nature itself – understood as distinct from anything in nature or the absence of something from nature – make the regularity true.

P is a law of nature if and only if *P* is a regularity caused by nature.

While this is a catchy way to put my favored analysis of lawhood, there are certain aspects of my view that require comment. First, we should keep in mind the point made earlier about explanation and causation. My official view is not that laws are *caused* by nature but that they hold *because* of nature. Second, and more important, self-respecting metaphysicians will surely ask what exactly nature is. Think of nature as the universe – not the objects and events in the universe, but whatever *it* is that the objects and events are in. Along this same line, we can think of nature as something like the universe's space-time manifold or the totality of its space and time. Better yet, think of nature as something like an omnipresent and eternal field, a big-as-big-can-be magnetic field that is also as longlasting as longlasting can be whose effects need not have anything to do with magnetism. On my view, a scientist who posits that there are laws of nature is thereby committed to our world being causal/explanatory in exactly this way.

Some will object to the idea that something like nature can stand in the causal/explanatory relation that is being employed in my analysis. Nature is not an event. It is also not a state of affairs (i.e., an object or event having some property). Yet, it is a long-standing opinion of many metaphysicians that only events or states of affairs can cause anything. To some it may even sound like I am taking seriously the idea of substance causation, an idea that is often in disrepute.[3] Nature is not a substance, exactly. It is more like a humongous and ancient field – it contains objects and other substances, but is not itself one. Admittedly, nature is more like a substance than it is like an event or a state of affairs and that will still worry some. But taking it to be causal really should not be any more worrisome than thinking of a magnetic field as causing an electron to move. Furthermore, my account leaves room for properties to play a role. Nature does cause what it does in virtue of being a certain way. On my view, the job of scientists set on discovering what regularities are laws of nature is precisely to describe what these properties are. Roughly, stating that P is a law is science's way of describing how nature is in virtue of which it causes P.

I do not here provide anything like a full defense of my analysis of lawhood. It will suffice for my purposes if I have said enough to make it seem plausible. My analysis is not reductive; a notion of causation/explanation expressed by the word 'because' occurs in the analysans, and that concept is a nomic one. Nevertheless, there is no circularity and the analysis provides understanding. Besides being informative, my analysis also seems to metaphysically ground lawhood in ways that non-reductive analyses normally do not. Of all the nomic concepts, causation seems the most grounded, the one that seems the least to float on nothing. It does not seem to float at all. It is a relation that only holds between existing, occurrent, or obtaining things. Sometimes we can scientifically describe an underlying causal mechanism when the causal relation is instantiated. Some authors have even argued that, despite Hume, causation is directly observable.[4] It certainly seems right that I can see that Nomar hit the ball and it is clear that this fact is causal; Nomar couldn't have hit the ball unless the ball moved because of Nomar. I am less sympathetic to there being some causal percept or an impression of causation in Hume's sense, but I do not see that this matters. We make causal and explanatory judgments easily and without much thought all the time. And, yet, almost all being a law of nature amounts to is holding because of nature.

4 The Skeptical Challenge

To my mind, the most careful and the most confounding formulation of the skeptical challenge comes from John Earman and John Roberts, in their paper "Contact with the Nomic: A Challenge for Deniers of Humean Supervenience about Laws of Nature" (2005). Their paper will be the focus of my reply.

4.1 The challenge from Earman and Roberts

Let T be a theory that posits at least one law. Label one of the laws 'L' and reformulate T as the conjunction that L is a law of nature and X. (So, X is the rest of T aside from the part of T that posits L as a law.) Let T* be the theory that L is true, L is not a law, and X. T and T* cannot both be true because they differ on whether L is a law.

The argument is straightforward:

(1) If HS (Humean Supervenience) is false, then no empirical evidence can favor T or T* over the other.
(2) If no empirical evidence can favor T or T* over the other, then we cannot be epistemically justified in believing on empirical grounds that T is true.

------

(3) If HS is false, we cannot be epistemically justified in believing on empirical grounds that T is true.[5]

HS is defined by Earman and Roberts as the thesis that what is a law and what is not cannot vary between worlds with the same Humean base, where a world's Humean base is the set of non-nomic facts at that world that are detectable by a reliable measurement or observation procedure (p. 253). It follows from the premises that, if HS is false, then we cannot be justified in believing in T. That is an apparent problem for my anti-supervenience, realist, anti-reductionism because Earman and Roberts made no assumptions about T other than that it attributes lawhood to at least one proposition. So, if Earman and Roberts' argument is sound and HS is false, then no one is justified in believing on empirical grounds that any proposition is a law. It is only a short step from there to the conclusion that no one – not us, not the scientists – know what any of the laws are. As Earman and Roberts are averse to skepticism, they ultimately see this as an argument for HS.

4.2 Empirical evidence against cosmic coincidences

To begin my response, I will describe one basic way empirical evidence can support the judgment that something is a law. It is a way suggested by the non-reductive analysis of lawhood given in section 3. But, be warned. Contexts for utterances using the verbs 'to know' and 'to justify' are fragile. Without a lot of work, Earman and Roberts could (and may have already) spoiled the present context in such a way that some of the epistemological claims I am about to make will not ring true. That is why it will be important, in the next subsection, to say something about the context dependence of epistemological terms.

Here is John Foster's insightful description of a hypothetical case of an inference to there being a law. It is in line with the picture I want to sketch:

> The past consistency of gravitational behavior calls for some explanation. For given the infinite variety of ways in which bodies might have behaved non-gravitationally and, more importantly, the innumerable occasions on which some form of non-gravitational behavior might have occurred and been detected, the consistency would be an astonishing coincidence if it were merely accidental – so astonishing as to make the accident-hypothesis quite literally incredible. (1983: 89)

In this spirit, regarding Earman and Roberts' argument, I want to suggest that believing T* sometimes would be to believe implausibly that L does not hold because of nature. Since Earman and Roberts grant that we may have reason to believe L is true, believing T* means believing either that L is caused by nothing (and so is a coincidence) or else that L holds because of something in nature. Sometimes we have good empirical evidence against each of these disjuncts, evidence that thus favors T over T*, and so we may be justified in believing T.

It is not mysterious how we justifiedly judge whether *certain* generalizations are coincidences. This is especially true about some very local regularities. Suppose I come upon a bag of marbles. I open it up, peek in, and see that all the marbles in the bag (right now) are black. I am not likely to take seriously in this situation the possibility that nature explains why the generalization holds. Indeed, I am likely to presuppose that this is not the case. Still, it might be that *there is some explanation* of that generalization. For instance, it might be that the marbles were selected from an urn that contained only black marbles. In contrast, it might also be that *nothing explains* why all the marbles in the bag are black. It might be that the marbles were selected blindly from an urn that contained a mix of black and white marbles, a mix with many more white marbles than black marbles. The important point to notice about these two kinds of possibilities – one kind that includes an explanation for the generalization and the other kind that does not – is that empirical evidence can favor one kind over the other. I might have seen someone picking the balls from an urn containing only black marbles. Then again, I might have seen someone blindly selecting the marbles from an urn with only a small proportion of black marbles. So, on the local scale anyway, there are straightforward ways of gaining evidence that would decide whether a regularity was a coincidence or instead was explained. With cosmic regularities, we are more likely to take seriously the idea that they might be caused by nature. Indeed, I suspect that physicists dealing with fundamental particles and properties are likely to presuppose that, if a generalization of interest to them is true, then it is not a coincidence, and so must be the result of something in nature or nature itself. Consider the principle of the conservation of energy. Years of investigation and careful theorizing reveal that it has no in-nature explanation. The absence of any in-nature explanation supports the hypothesis that this principle holds because of nature, and so is a law.

What is important is that sometimes we find no in-nature explanations of a regularity, but we are also reluctant to conclude that it is a coincidence. We are faced with the choice of its being nature that explains it or its being unexplained. Sometimes the latter fits better with the rest of what we believe. When it does, we are justified in believing a proposition corresponding to Earman and Roberts' T*. With the right sort of empirical evidence, however, the coincidence hypothesis may be much less credible than the lawful one. So, we may be justified in believing a proposition exactly parallel to Earman and Roberts' T. In short, we sometimes have evidence of what nature causes and that is all the evidence we need to distinguish laws from non-laws.

4.3 Contextualism and relevant alternatives

My guess is Earman and Roberts will disagree, and my suspicion is that even you, the reader, will have doubts about my conclusion that scientists sometimes justifiedly infer that a true generalization is caused by nature. Even supposing we know that energy is always conserved, there is no getting around the fact that, on my account, it is consistent with all the evidence that our scientists have that this regularity is uncaused (and so a cosmic coincidence), and it is consistent with all that same evidence that it is caused by nature (and so a law of nature).

There are skeptical arguments that seem to show we don't know much of *anything*. Sometimes these take the form of a skeptical-alternative attack. If I am at the zoo in front of a cage labeled 'Zebra' and see, standing in front of me, a four-legged striped mammal that I take to be a zebra, a friend might give me pause to think by claiming that it might be a mule disguised to look like a zebra. Since such a mule might look just like the animal before me, it can seem that I do not know the animal before me is a zebra. In pointing out that, even given all the observational evidence, if HS is false, then there might be no explanation of why energy is conserved, Earman and Roberts would be raising a possibility like the possibility of a cleverly disguised mule at the zoo.

An epistemological contextualist maintains that the truth-value of an utterance of a sentence containing certain epistemological terms (e.g., the verb 'to know' or the adjective 'justified') may vary depending on the context.[6] So, said in one context, 'I know that animal is a zebra' may be true. For example, this might be the case in a discussion between me and a young child who is insisting that the animal is a gazelle. But, said in another context, say one in which I admit that I do not know that the animal is not a cleverly disguised mule, my utterance of that very same sentence would be false. As contextualism is sometimes described, in the first context, the only *relevant* alternative was that the animal was a gazelle, but, in the second context, there was the relevant alternative that it was a cleverly disguised mule. What is required for a knowledge utterance to be true in a context C is that the cognizer be able to rule out all the alternative hypotheses that are relevant in C. (Keep in mind that in different contexts, different alternatives will be relevant.) This hypothesis about the context sensitivity of epistemological utterances is then used to explain why skeptical arguments of various sorts can seem so convincing and also to mitigate the damage done by those arguments. As the contextualist sees it, even though certain skeptical arguments generate contexts in which many or all knowledge sentences turn out false, this leaves open that there will be lots of important contexts in which utterances of those same sentences will turn out true.

How does all this apply to the skeptical argument advanced by Earman and Roberts in favor of HS? As Earman and Roberts describe it,

> The contextualist maneuver might run as follows: "In contexts where scientists are evaluating a law-positing theory such as T, which is well-supported according to the ordinary standards of scientific inference, alternatives such as T* which differ from T only in that they call one or more laws posited by T* nomologically contingent, are not relevant alternatives. Hence, it is not necessary, in order to be justified in believing T, to have evidence that favors T over T*. So Premise 2 of our epistemological argument for HS is false." (2005: 274)

Now, obviously, Earman and Roberts don't think that this maneuver will work, but we need not delve into their reasons for thinking so. We need not, because the quote just given misrepresents contextualism. Earman and Roberts bill the contextualist way

John W. Carroll

out as a method of objecting to premise 2 of their argument. But, in fact, what is crucial to the contextualist reply is that in certain contexts (maybe all contexts!) an utterance of the sentence expressing premise 2 will be true.

The antecedent of premise 2 and the statement of premise 1, in virtue of including mention of both T and T*, make (or tends to make) T* a relevant alternative to T, and it is one that cannot be ruled out. To argue as Earman and Roberts do is like arguing: (1) For all we know, given all the evidence presently available to us, nothing favors it being a zebra over a disguised mule and nothing favors it being a disguised mule over a zebra. (2) If nothing favors it being a zebra and nothing favors it being a disguised mule then we can't know it is a zebra. When such premise sentences are uttered and taken seriously by the audience, the contextualist wants to "concede" that then the premise sentences are true and that the conclusion sentence is as well. The contextualist gambit is now to argue that, once we properly understand the contextual nature of 'to know', the fact that an utterance of the conclusion sentence is true is hardly worrisome. This does not rule out that there are other much more ordinary contexts in which an utterance of 'I know T' is perfectly true. Science can go on, claims of lawhood are sometimes made, reports of knowledge that such and such is a law sometimes turn out true. The fact that the conclusion sentence of Earman and Roberts' argument is true, perhaps even as uttered by Earman and Roberts, is no more worrisome than is the fact that utterances of 'I don't know the animal is a zebra' are true in contexts in which the disguised-mule hypothesis is a relevant alternative. Regarding laws, there will be contexts where we presuppose that L is not a coincidence. If I have ruled out that there is some in-nature explanation of L, and the presupposition of our conversation is true, then it will be true to say 'I know T'.

Is this enough for science? I think so. According to contextualism, even 'No one has ever known or will ever know that they have hands' is true in some contexts, ones in which the evil-demon hypothesis is a relevant alternative. That there are some contexts arising in philosophical discussions in which the sentence 'No scientist has ever known or will ever know what the laws of nature are' is true seems mild in comparison. As well it should. That there are contexts where an utterance of 'I know that I have hands' is false does not in the least bit undermine the value of my utterance of that sentence in certain contexts in which it is true. The contextualist can concede that Earman and Roberts have generated a context in which 'Scientists know what the laws are' is false. But, as far as I can tell, that does not generate any absurd or undesirable consequences about science or scientists. What contextualism does is allow us to explain why the Hume-inspired skeptical challenge, at least as raised by Earman and Roberts, can seem so utterly convincing. If the context is right, what they say is convincing because the argument they advance is sound.

5 Avoiding the Cross

I hope that the controversial nature of my replies to the foregoing Hume-inspired metaphysical and skeptical worries provide further evidence that anti-reductionism is not any sort of philosophical dead end. Indeed, the position described here puts in special focus some particularly interesting issues that have the benefit of potentially being more manageable than the search for a reductive analysis of lawhood. First, there is the analysis of coincidence. I have offered what I take to be a plausible account, but coincidence is not a notion that has received anywhere near the attention that lawhood has. Second, the analysis of lawhood offered here depends crucially on the possibility of *regularities* holding because of nature. While there has certainly been discussion and awareness that regularities are sometimes explained in science, philosophers of science have seemed much more comfortable when the explanandum is some singular or particular fact. My analysis provides new reason to explore the nature of explanations of regularities. Finally, there is the issue in the philosophy of language and linguistics as to how best to describe and understand the context dependence of 'because' and 'knows'. As is the case with many philosophical problems, attention to the language we use to present and address the philosophical problem of laws is a sensible precaution that may help squelch the lure of reductionism.[7]

Notes

1   Richard Sorabji (1979: 9) attributes this account of coincidence to Aristotle. David Owens (1992: 6) defines a coincidence as an event whose constituents are produced by independent causal processes, but maintains that his definition has the consequence that all coincidences are inexplicable.
2   This may sound a little odd. My claim that all laws have explanations will strike some as counterintuitive. Aren't there any laws that are fundamental or basic? Don't some laws explain though they themselves are unexplained? It is important to keep in mind that what has to be explained in order for *P* to be a law is *P*. It is that generalization that cannot be coincidental if it is also to be a law. This leaves open that the lawhood fact, the fact *that P is a law*, is unexplained; it may be a coincidence. So, for example, it may be a fundamental law that all inertial bodies have no acceleration, even though something explains why all inertial bodies have no acceleration. It would be a fundamental law in virtue of there being no explanation why *it is a law* that all inertial bodies have no acceleration.
3   Randy Clarke (2003: 196–217) in his discussion of agent causation surveys the few arguments actually given against the possibility of substance causation.
4   See Anscombe (1971), Fales (1990) and Armstrong (1997).
5   This is *close* to the exact wording of Earman and Roberts' argument (pp. 257–8). Premise 2 has been simplified by removing words from its antecedent to the effect that realism about lawhood is true. Anti-reductionist anti-realists are not targets of this skeptical attack.
6   There are many versions of contextualism. See, for example, DeRose (1995). My own version is sketched in Carroll (2005).
7   Versions of this paper were presented at Virginia Tech in 2006, at Rutgers University in the spring of 2005 and at NC State University in 2004. Thanks to Troy Cross, Jeff Kasser, Marc Lange, Michael Pendlebury, Jamaal Pitt, Ann Rives, David Robb, John Roberts, and Dean Zimmerman for helpful comments and questions on earlier renditions.

References

Anscombe, G. 1971. *Causality and Determination* (Cambridge: Cambridge University Press).
Armstrong, D. 1983. *What Is a Law of Nature?* (Cambridge: Cambridge University Press).

—. 1997. *A World of States of Affairs* (New York: Cambridge University Press).

Blackburn, S. 1984. *Spreading the Word* (Oxford: Clarendon Press).

—. 1986. "Morals and Modals," in G. Macdonald and C. Wright, eds., *Fact, Science and Morality* (Oxford: Basil Blackwell).

Carroll, J. 1994. *Laws of Nature* (Cambridge: Cambridge University Press).

—. 2005. "Boundary in Context," *Acta Analytica* 20: 43–54.

Clarke, R. 2003. *Libertarian Accounts of Free Will* (New York: Oxford University Press).

DeRose, K. 1995. "Solving the Skeptical Problem," *Philosophical Review* 104: 1–52.

Dretske, F. 1977. "Laws of Nature," *Philosophy of Science* 44: 248–68.

Earman, J., and Roberts, J. 2005. "Contact with the Nomic: A Challenge for Deniers of Humean Supervenience about Laws of Nature (Part II)," *Philosophy and Phenomenological Research* 71: 253–86.

Fales, E. 1990. *Causation and Universals* (London: Routledge).

Foster, J. 1983. "Induction, Explanation and Natural Necessity," *Proceedings of the Aristotelian Society* 83: 87–101.

Giere, R. 1999. *Science Without Laws* (Chicago: University of Chicago Press).

Hume, D. 1955. *An Inquiry Concerning Human Understanding* (Indianapolis: Bobbs-Merrill).

Lange, M. 2000. *Natural Laws in Scientific Practice* (Oxford: Oxford University Press).

Lewis, D. 1973. *Counterfactuals* (Cambridge, MA: Harvard University Press).

—. 1983. "New Work for a Theory of Universals," *Australasian Journal of Philosophy* 61: 343–77.

—. 1986. *Philosophical Papers*, vol. II (New York: Oxford University Press).

Owens, D. 1992. *Causes and Coincidences* (Cambridge: Cambridge University Press).

Sorabji, R. 1979. *Necessity, Cause and Blame* (New York: Cornell University Press).

Tooley, M. 1977. "The Nature of Laws," *Canadian Journal of Philosophy* 7: 667–98.

—. 1987. *Causation* (Oxford: Clarendon Press).

van Fraassen, B. 1989. *Laws and Symmetry* (Oxford: Clarendon Press).

Ward, B. 2002. "Humeanism Without Humean Supervenience: A Projectivist Account of Laws and Possibilities," *Philosophical Studies* 107: 191–218.

—. 2003. "Sometimes the World is not Enough: The Pursuit of Explanatory Laws in a Humean World," *Pacific Philosophical Quarterly* 84: 175–97.

Causation and Laws of Nature: Reductionism

Jonathan Schaffer

Causation and the laws of nature are nothing over and above the pattern of events, just like a movie is nothing over and above the sequence of frames. Or so I will argue. The position I will argue for is broadly inspired by Hume and Lewis, and may be expressed in the slogan: *what must be, must be grounded in what is.*

Roadmap: In sections 1 and 2, I will clarify the reductionist thesis, and connect it to a general thesis about modal and occurrent entities. In section 3, I will argue halfway towards reductionism, by arguing that causation reduces to history plus the laws. In section 4, I will complete the case for reductionism, by arguing that the laws themselves reduce to history.

1 Clarifying the Thesis

The reductionist thesis may be expressed as follows:

R1   Causation and laws reduce to history.

But it is not obvious what R1 means, much less why one should believe in it. In this section I will clarify the notions of causation, lawhood, history, and reduction, to the point where arguments may be considered.

Starting with causation, the intended notion is perhaps best introduced by examples. Causation is present when one billiard ball strikes another (which Hume called 'a perfect instance' of causation), when a person lifts a suitcase, and when a spring uncoils. To a first approximation, one might test for causation by testing for counterfactual dependence: if the cause had not occurred, then the effect would not have occurred.[1] For present purposes, the notion of causation may be left intuitive. To the extent we understand any notion, we understand this one.

Turning to lawhood, what is intended is the sort of thing expressed by the equations of scientists, such as Newton's laws of motion and Schrödinger's law of wavefunction evolution. Laws are generally supposed to be expressed by true universally quantified conditionals, holding in a restricted sphere of possible worlds, encoding how the world evolves through time.[2] For present purposes, this notion may also be left intuitive.

Moving to history, what is intended is the fusion of all events throughout space-time.[3] Each individual event is a concrete particular with an intrinsic nature – what occurs in some region of space-time. History is the whole of this – it is what occurs in all of space-time. History is the total pattern of events. Each event is like a bit of a frame in the movie, and history is the whole picture.

The notion of reduction is intended to be an *ontological* relation, expressing *dependence* between entities. As an ontological relation, the intended notion must be distinguished from theoretical and definitional relations which may also be labeled 'reduction'. Theoretical reduction concerns terms found in theories. Definitional reduction concerns concepts found in the mind. Ontological reduction is independent of how we conceptualize entities, or theorize about them. Ontological reduction is a thesis about mind-and-theory-independent reality.

As a relation of dependence, the intended notion of reduction may be glossed in terms of *grounding*. What reduces is grounded in, based on, existent in virtue of, and nothing over and above, what it reduces to. What does not reduce is basic, fundamental, and brute. By way of parable: to create what reduces, God would only need to create what it reduces to. In general, to create the world, God would only need to create what is basic.[4]

To illustrate, consider the relation between the movie and the frames. Here it is natural to say that the movie depends on the frames. The movie is grounded in, exists in virtue of, and is nothing over and above the frames. To create the movie, the director only needs to arrange the frames. (This is true regardless of how we conceptualize movies, or theorize about them.)

To take a more philosophically interesting illustration, consider the relation between the physical properties, and the mental and moral properties. The physicalist holds that the physical properties are basic, and that the mental and moral properties are grounded in them. According to the physicalist, all God would need to create would be the physical realm.[5]

R1 is thus the thesis that causation and laws are grounded in, based on, and nothing over and above history, in the way that the movie is grounded in the frames, and the mental (by physicalist lights) is grounded in the physical. To make the world, God only needed to create space-time and fill it with intrinsic features. He did not also have to sew the whole thing up with some sort of causal thread. Or so says the friend of R1 – the *reductionist*. The foe of R1 – the *primitivist* – holds that a space-time filled with intrinsic features still needs sewing together.[6]

So understood, R1 has implications for *explanation* and *possibility*. As to explanation, the existence and nature of what reduces is explicable in terms of what it reduces to. What reduces is no further mystery. For instance, the existence and nature of the movie is explicable in terms of the frames.[7] Likewise, R1 entails that the existence and nature of causation and lawhood is explicable in terms of history.

As to possibility, the intended notion of reduction entails that it is impossible for what reduces to differ in any way, without some difference in what it reduces to. In other words, if the reductive grounds are held fixed, then what reduces must hold fixed as well. For instance, if the frames are held fixed, then the movie must hold fixed as well – the movie cannot differ in any way, without some difference in the frames. Likewise, R1 entails that if history is held fixed, then the causes and laws must hold fixed as well.

So here are two *good* ways to try to rebut R1. First, one might argue that history fails to explain causation and laws. Second, one might argue that it is possible for the causes or laws to be different, without any difference in history. If either argument could be substantiated, it would refute R1 – it would prove that causation and the laws fail to reduce, in the intended sense.

And here is a *bad* way to try to rebut R1. One might argue that the concepts of causation and lawhood fail to have conceptual analyses in terms of the concept of history. Because reduction is an ontological relation, and not a relation between concepts in our mind, failure of analysis does not show failure of reduction. There can be reduction without analysis, in the cases where either our concept is insufficiently explicit, or our intuitions are misleading, or the reduction would require an infinite definition.[8]

This matters, since conceptual analyses of natural concepts virtually always fail. If analysis were required for reduction, then one would likely have to be a primitivist about virtually everything, including movies, marching bands, and motor homes, which do not seem like irreducible elements of reality!

So the question of whether causation and the laws of nature reduce to history yields the following questions: (i) are causation and the laws explicable in terms of history? and (ii) is it possible for there to be differences in causation or the laws without any difference in history? Explanation and possibility are reasonably well-understood notions. Thus the question of reduction may prove tractable.

2 Generalizing the Thesis

The reductionist thesis R1 is an instance of a more general thesis about the relation of the modal to the occurrent. Displaying the more general thesis may help to both explicate and motivate R1. The more general thesis is:

R2 Modal entities reduce to occurrent entities.

I will now clarify the notions of the modal and the occurrent, explain how R2 is a generalization of R1, and then provide some motivation for R2.

First the clarifications: the notion of a modal entity is perhaps best introduced by examples. Paradigmatic modal entities include *dispositions, counterfactual properties*, and *powers*. A match, for instance, is disposed to ignite if struck under suitable conditions, has the counterfactual property of being such that if it were struck under suitable conditions it would ignite, and has the power to ignite. These are properties of the match, concerning a *potentiality* the match has (which may not ever be actualized, if the match is never struck). The match also, in contrast, has the property of having a tip made of potassium chlorate and sesquisulfide of phosphorus. These are paradigmatic occurrent properties, which simply concern the way the match actually is.

It is difficult to characterize the distinction between the modal and the occurrent in more precise terms.[9] Sider provides the following characterization: "Categorical [/occurrent] properties involve what objects actually are like, whereas hypothetical [/modal] properties 'point beyond' their instances" (2001: 41). The sense in which modal properties "point beyond" their instances is that they concern *what else must be*, while the sense in which occurrent properties remain self-contained is that they concern just the actual, intrinsic features of the thing itself. This characterization could perhaps use further work, but should be sufficiently clear to work with here.

Causation and the laws are clear cases of modal entities. With causation, if c has the property of causing e, then this property of c "points beyond," adding what else must be the case, namely that e must follow. Causation represents a *necessary connection* between distinct events. Likewise with laws, if c has the property of lawfully entailing e, then this property of c "points beyond," adding what else must be the case, namely that e must follow. Laws represent *necessary connectors* between events. Both causation and laws involve not just the actual event itself, but the modal aspect of what else must be. Both causation and laws concern *natural necessity*.

History, in contrast, is a clear case of an occurrent entity. Each individual event is a particular occurrence. It is what is happening in some region of space-time. History is the sum of all the particular occurrences. It is what is happening in all of space-time.

Indeed, history *exhausts* the occurrences. The occurrent aspect of the world is completely given in the pattern of events. This is the whole picture. No occurrences are left out.[10]

I am now in position to explain how R2 is a generalization of R1. Since causation and the laws are modal entities, R2 entails that causation and the laws reduce to some occurrent entities. Since history exhausts the occurrences, whichever occurrent entities causation and laws reduce to will be found within history. Thus causation and laws reduce to history, as per R1.

Recall (section 1) that the reductionist's general thesis is that God (as it were) only needs to create space-time and fill it with intrinsic features. God does not also have to string the whole thing up with modal hooks. The reduction of causation and lawhood to history is just a special case of this thesis.[11]

It remains to motivate R2. I offer three motivations. First, R2 is intrinsically plausible. Modal entities by themselves seem shadowy and mysterious. It seems they cannot float free – they need grounding in the occurrent. What must be, must be grounded in what is.

Second, R2 fits with a plausible principle about what is possible – *Humean recombination* – which Lewis glosses as: "anything can coexist with anything else, at least provided they occupy distinct spatiotemporal positions" (1986a: 87). Modal entities, insofar as they "point beyond" to what else must be, have implications for what else may exist. Primitive modal entities thus entail implausible limitations on recombination. For instance, if c is accorded the basic property of *causing* e, then the intuitive possibility of c without e is lost.

The third motivation for R2 is that it is theoretically useful, in ruling out certain metaphysical views that are now widely regarded as implausible. One example of such an implausible view is Rylean behaviorism, which invokes behavioral dispositions without any occurrent mental grounds. A second example is the view that counterfactuals are primitive. On this view, it might be true of the match that, if it were struck under suitable circumstances, it would ignite, without there being any intrinsic physical features of the match (having phosphorus on the tip) which grounds this counterfactual. A third example is the view that powers are primitive. On this view, it might be true of the match that it has the power to ignite, without there being any intrinsic physical feature of the match which grounds this power. Since dispositions, counterfactuals, and powers are paradigmatic modal entities, the natural generalization to draw is that primitive modal entities are generally to be shunned.[12]

The denier of R1 thus faces the question of *where to draw the line*. If primitive unreduced causal relations or laws are tolerable, what if anything were wrong with Rylean behaviorism, brute counterfactuals, or ungrounded powers? R2 represents a principled and plausible limit on what can serve as a basic feature of reality, which has R1 as a corollary.

3 Defending the Thesis, Stage One: Causation

In what remains I will return to the reductionist thesis R1, and discuss specific arguments for and against. In this section I will argue halfway towards R1, by arguing that causation reduces to history plus the laws. That is, I will now defend the following half-reductive thesis:

R3   Causation reduces to history plus laws.

I will first reply to the three main arguments in the literature against R3, and then consider three arguments for R3. I will conclude that the reduction of causation is justified on methodological and scientific grounds.

Why bother with the half-reductive thesis R3? First, R3 is an important and contentious thesis in its own right. Second, R3 enables the reductionist to pursue a divide-and-conquer strategy – all that would remain is to argue that the laws themselves reduce to history (see section 4). Third, the reductionist may wish to reserve R3 as a fallback position. The case for R3 will prove stronger than the case for the fully reductive R1, because laws have a more secure place in science than causation does (see section 3.2).

3.1 Three arguments for inflating causation

There are three main arguments in the literature against R3, the first of which is that the concept of causation cannot be analyzed via history plus the laws. An analysis is an attempt at providing finite, non-circular, and intuitively adequate necessary and sufficient conditions. So an analysis of causation via history plus laws will look something like: c causes e iff $--$, where the blank is to be filled in with some finite entry concerning history and laws (and not containing the term 'causation' or any other terms that are themselves to be analyzed via causation), and where the resulting entry will match our intuitive judgments about whether causation obtains in most if not all conceivable cases. So the first argument is that it is impossible (or at least unlikely) that the schema 'c causes e iff −−' can be completed in this way.

The argument from *unanalyzability* might be formulated as follows:

(1) The concept of causation cannot be analyzed in terms of history plus laws.
(2) If the concept of causation cannot be analyzed in terms of history plus laws, then causation does not reduce to history plus laws.
(3) Causation does not reduce to history plus laws.

The argument is valid, so the only question is of the truth of premises 1 and 2.

I would accept (1). There is a long history of attempts to analyze the concept of causation in various terms.[13] All the attempts have been riddled by counterexamples (as have attempts at conceptual analyses for all natural concepts – there is nothing special about causation here). Obviously this does not prove that no analysis is possible. But the prospects seem bleak.

What I would deny is (2). (2) seems to be presupposed by most who have attempted conceptual analyses – this is why they have attempted it.[14] But ontological reduction does not require conceptual analysis (section 1). Perhaps our concept is insufficiently explicit, or our intuitions are misleading, or the analysis would require an infinite definition. From a failure of conceptual analysis, nothing follows about the world.

The philosopher who would uphold the unanalyzability argument must explain (i) how the concept of causation differs from any other natural concept and (ii) why this conceptual difference is relevant to how the world is. The best attempt I know of to maintain that the concept of causation differs from other natural concepts is via the claim that the causal concept is especially central to our conceptual scheme.[15] Perhaps so. But even so, such a conceptual difference does not seem relevant to how the world is. One could imagine a creature wired to think of everything through the concepts of *edible* and *inedible* – what would that prove about the world? So I conclude that the first argument confuses a conceptual with an ontological issue.

The second main argument in the literature against R3 is that events themselves can only be individuated causally. Individuation principles are attempts to describe how to count entities in a given domain, by saying when there is one. So individuation principles for events will look something like: there are no two events $e1$ and $e2$ (where $e1 \neq e2$) such that −−, where the blank is to be filled in by whatever factors would render $e1$ and $e2$ one and the same. So the second argument is that it is impossible to individuate events except in terms of their causes and effects. For instance, one might hold that the relevant individuation condition is: there are no two events $e1$ and $e2$ (where $e1 \neq e2$) such that $e1$ and $e2$ differ in their causes and effects.[16]

The argument from *event individuation* might be formulated as follows:

(4) Events can only be individuated in causal terms.
(5) If events can only be individuated in causal terms, then causation does not reduce to history plus laws.
(6) Causation does not reduce to history plus laws.

The argument is valid, so the only question is of the truth of (4) and (5).

I would accept (5). If events can only be individuated in causal terms, then (onto-logically speaking) there can be no history that is prior to causation. For history itself, as the sum of all actual events, would presuppose some definite number of events in definite relations, which would itself depend on causation. God could not, as it were, simply intone: "Let there be history!" for God would first need to create the causal relations that shape history.

What I would deny is (4). Events can be individuated in purely occurrent terms, by their spatiotemporal locations and intrinsic natures. That is, I would offer the following non-causal individuation principle: there are no two events $e1$ and $e2$ (where $e1 \neq e2$) such that $e1$ and $e2$ occupy the same spatiotemporal region and possess the same intrinsic nature.[17] For instance, if $e1$ is an instance of red here, and $e1 \neq e2$, then $e2$ cannot also be an instance of red here – $e2$ must concern some other property or some other region.

Those who uphold (4) typically argue that the postulation of intrinsic natures is epistemically disastrous. They argue that our only epistemic access to events is through their effects (specifically, their effects on our minds), so to postulate natures is to suffer a skeptical fate. Such natures could never be known save through their effects, so the ontologist should just drop the natures and limit herself to the effects.[18]

My reply to the skeptical concern is that it embodies disastrous epistemic reason-ing. For the same sort of reasoning should lead us to drop the effects and skip straight to the effects *on us* (for our only epistemic access to the effects is through their effects on us). This would be to drop external reality and only recognize the contents of one's own mind – this would be solipsism. Contrapositively, once we countenance an external reality (and who would reject *that*?) we are already dabbling in entities we cannot directly access. Intrinsic natures of events are just more of the same.[19] So I conclude that the second argument makes unsustainable epistemic assumptions.

The third main argument in the literature against R3 is that it is possible for worlds to differ in causation without differing in history or laws. To my mind, this is the most serious argument against causal reduction. Here is a representative example. Imagine that two wizards, Merlin and Morgana, each cast a spell to turn the prince into a frog, and that the prince then transforms into a frog. Imagine that all spells have a 50 percent chance of success, according to the laws of this fantasy world. Now, the argument proceeds, intuitively there are at least *three* distinct possibilities. First, it is possible that Merlin's spell alone caused the transformation. Second, it is possible that Morgana's spell alone caused the transformation. Third, it is possible that both spells causally overdetermined the transformation. These three distinct pos-sibilities involve the same histories and the same laws. So the argument concludes that there can be differences in causation without differences in history or the laws. If correct, this would refute R3.[20]

The argument from *causal differences* might be formulated as follows:

(7) There are worlds that differ in causation without differing in history or laws.
(8) If there are worlds that differ in causation without differing in history or laws, then causation does not reduce to history plus laws.
(9) Causation does not reduce to history plus laws.

The argument is valid. But are (7) and (8) true?

I would accept (8). Ontological reduction has implications for possibility (section 1), such that if there really are two possible worlds that differ in causation without differing in history or the laws, then R3 would stand refuted.

What I would deny is (7). Why believe that there are genuinely distinct possibilities here? To my mind there is only the one possibility (the one in which Merlin and Morgana both cast their spells, and the prince transforms), confusingly described in three different styles. For in what respect are these alleged possibilities said to differ? The alleged causal difference seems to float on nothing – it seems a verbal distinction without any genuine ontological difference.[21]

The philosopher who would uphold (7) would presumably reply that the reason for accepting genuinely distinct possibilities here is *intuitive*, and that this shows that the alleged causal difference need not rest on *anything* – it is a brute and fundamental difference. But this seems a terrible metaphysical price for a relatively flimsy intuition (section 2). Or at least, staying within the realm of intuitions, I would say that I have strong countervailing intuitions that causal facts (and modal facts generally) cannot float free like this. So at most the intuitive argument for (7) has revealed conflicted intuitions, rather than a clear stance against R3.

So the question of whether (7) is true yields the question of how to weigh conflicting intuitions. I do not have a general answer to this question. But it seems to me that the reductionist can explain away the primitivist intuitions, from the conceptual error of *reification*. Reification occurs when a mere concept is mistaken for a thing. We seem generally prone to this sort of error. Our causal vocabulary allows us three different descriptions, and this leaves us prone to positing three different possibilities. So I would conclude with the suggestion that the third and most serious argument against R3 trades on flimsy reifications.[22]

3.2 Three arguments for reducing causation

Here are three main arguments for R3, the first of which is that causal knowledge requires reduction. The idea is that our causal knowledge is ultimately based on our observation of regularities in history, so that if there were more to causation than such regularities, we could have no access to this further feature. Such a feature could not be discovered save through the regularities it engenders, so the ontologist should just drop the further feature and limit herself to the regularities.[23]

The argument from *causal knowledge* might be formulated as follows:

(10)   We possess causal knowledge.
(11)   If we possess causal knowledge, then causation must reduce to history plus laws.
(12)   Causation must reduce to history plus laws.

The argument is valid, and I take it no one would deny (10).[24] So the only serious question is the truth of (11).

Though I favor reduction, I would deny (11). Presumably (11) might be defended as follows:

(11a) If we possess causal knowledge, then causation must be nothing over and
       above what is directly observable.

(11b) All that is directly observable is history.

(11c) If we possess causal knowledge, then causation must be nothing over and
       above history.

Here the idea is that anything beyond the actual pattern of events would escape our direct observation and thus escape our knowledge. As such, this is but another fallacious leap from knowledge to direct access. That is, once we allow that knowledge is possible without direct access (as with knowledge of the external world: section 3.1), then we must either deny (11a) or liberalize what counts as 'directly observable' so as to deny (11b).

The way to deny (11a) would be to allow that we can find indirect theoretical warrant for causation, at least in favorable cases. Here the idea is that (i) causal relations have directly observable consequences, such that (ii) directly observing such consequences furnishes abductive evidence for postulating causal relations. More formally, all that is required is that one might rationally set one's credences such that some bit of evidence E is taken to raise the probability of some hypothesis H. Then discovering E will furnish evidence for H. Here E may be a directly observable fact, and H a causal hypothesis.[25]

The way to deny (11b) would be to allow that we can directly observe some causal relations, in the requisite sense. For instance, one might argue that we can directly observe the causal relation in certain very special cases, such as between willing and action, and/or between pressure on the body and the sensation of it.[26] Or one might argue that we can directly observe the causal relation in a wide range of cases, such as when we see the boulder *flatten* the hut, or when we see the man *pick up* the suitcase and *lift* it on to the rack. Is this not seeing causation?[27]

I take no stand on whether the inflationist should deny (11a) or (11b) (this question involves difficult issues concerning perception). But one way or another, I would deny (11). The epistemic reasoning behind (11) seems to be of a disastrously skeptical sort. If one holds that all that is ultimately directly observable are sense-data, then parallel reasoning will force one to solipsism. If one allows that parts of the external world are directly observable, then no special reason has been given to resist direct causal knowledge. What is interesting here is that the epistemic reasoning behind (11) seems of a piece with the epistemic reasoning behind (4) (which led to the rejection of intrinsic natures for events). So one should conclude that if such epistemic reasoning is acceptable, then both the reductionist and the non-reductionist are in trouble, as the former posits inaccessible causation and the latter posits inaccessible natures. In the other direction, if one thinks that either the reductionist or the non-reductionist is right, one must have equal disdain for both (4) and (11). So I must conclude that the most historically important argument for R3 embodies disastrous epistemic reasoning.[28]

The second main argument for R3 is that sound methodological principles support reduction. To posit an irreducible causal reduction is to offend against (i) theoretical fathomability, and (ii) ontological economy. The argument from theoretical fathomability proceeds by pointing out that necessary connections have an air of the occult, implying inexplicable necessary connections between distinct existents (section 2). The argument from economy proceeds by invoking Ockham's Razor: one should not multiply entities beyond necessity. It is then maintained that it is not necessary to introduce irreducible causal relations. Or at least, none of the arguments canvassed above (section 3.1) show any deep necessity.

The argument from *methodology* might be formulated as follows:

(13)   Sound methodological principles (such as theoretical fathomability and onto-logical economy) support reducing causation to history plus laws.
(14)   If sound methodological principles support reducing causation to history plus laws, then causation must reduce to history plus laws.
(15)   Causation must reduce to history plus laws.

The argument is valid but unsound, since (14) is clearly false. Merely methodological principles can be outweighed (for instance, Ockham's Razor only tells us not to postulate entities *without necessity*). They are merely prima facie constraints.

A more nuanced formulation would replace (14) and (15) with:

(14′)   If sound methodological principles support reducing causation to history plus the laws, then, *unless sufficiently countervailing considerations can be adduced*, causation must reduce to history plus laws.
(15′)   *Unless sufficiently countervailing considerations can be adduced*, causation must reduce to history plus laws.

I take it no one would deny the resulting argument ((13), (14′), and (15′)).[29] But now the conclusion is hedged, and the question of reduction is just the question of whether there are sufficiently countervailing considerations to be adduced. For that is what it would take to move from the uncontentious (15′) back to the contentious (15).

The inflationist must now return to her arguments (c.f. the three main arguments of section 3.1), to identify sufficiently countervailing considerations. I see none. The argument from unanalyzability seems to me to be a mere confusion between conceptual primitiveness and ontological primitiveness. The argument from event individuation seems to me to be a mere invocation of otherwise disastrous epistemic reasoning (which would doom inflationism anyway via the argument for causal knowledge). And the argument from causal differences seems to me to be a mere exercise in reification. But here there is a further point to be made, which is that even if there is some residual intuitiveness to the argument from causal differences, surely it is not sufficiently powerful to overturn the push for a fathomable and economical theory. After all, such a highly questionable intuition hardly seems sufficient to generate the sort of necessity needed to blunt Ockham's Razor. So I conclude that the methodological argument for R3 is *ultima facie* successful, even granting some intuitiveness to the inflationist arguments.

The third main argument for R3 is that *scientific practice* supports reduction. To my mind, this is the best argument for causal reductionism. The idea is that sophisticated science invokes only laws and events. Causation drops out as an imprecise, folk mode of description. So it is concluded that causal relations, if they are real at all, must be nothing over and above the laws and events that serious scientific practice requires.

The argument from scientific practice might be formulated as follows:

(16) Scientific practice only requires history and laws.
(17) If scientific practice only requires history and laws, then causation must reduce to history plus laws.
(18) Causation must reduce to history plus laws.

The argument is valid, so it remains to ask if (16) and (17) are true.

The case for (16) is that causation disappears from sophisticated physics. What one finds instead are differential equations (mathematical formulae expressing laws of temporal evolution). These equations make no mention of causation.[30] Of course, scientists may continue to speak in causal terms when popularizing their results, but the results themselves – the serious business of science – are generated independently.

There are two main ways that the inflationist might oppose (16), the first of which is to maintain that causation is still integral to the practice of the *special sciences*. Here it would be argued that (i) special sciences – especially the social sciences – remain suffused with causal notions, such that (ii) (16) is false when sciences other than physics are considered. (Here the inflationist might rail against special privileges for physics.)

The problem with this first sort of reply is that it would amount to maintaining that there is a brute and fundamental feature of reality that is only accessible to the special sciences. It would mean that physicists could in principle answer every question save for what causes what, at which point they would need to consult the economists. That constitutes a *reductio*.

The second main way that the inflationist might oppose (16) is to maintain that causation is still integral even within physics. Here the most plausible candidate role for causation is in interpreting the relativistic prohibition against superluminal velocities, as a prohibition against superluminal signaling.[31]

The problem with this second sort of reply is that it seems to presuppose reductionism. Invoking causation in the foundations of special relativity is only helpful on the presupposition that certain worldlines (e.g., the billiard ball) are causal processes, while certain worldlines (e.g., Salmon's spot of light) are non-causal pseudo-processes. But if the occurrence of causation is brute, there is no basis for this presupposition. Only the reductionist can render causation fit to play a role in the foundations of special relativity. So I conclude that (16) should stand.

The case for (17) is that science represents out best attempt at a systematic understanding of the world, and if a certain notion proves unneeded in our best attempt at a systematic understanding of the world, this provides strong evidence that what this notion concerns is not ontologically basic.[32]

Of course, one might deny (17) by insisting that there could be more on heaven and earth than is dreamt of in the sciences. Perhaps so. Perhaps there really are witches, vital forces, real simultaneity relations, and other sundries that science has learnt to discard. But I doubt it. Causal relations must either reduce to what is required by science, or else be eliminated.[33] So I conclude that (17) should stand, and that the scientific argument for R3 succeeds. Causation must reduce, or face elimination.

In this vein it is worth returning again to the argument from causal differences (section 3.1). For we can now add that, even if there is some residual intuitiveness to the argument, and even if such intuitiveness were not immediately trumped by methodological considerations, such an intuition should be dismissed as pre-scientific. It is just the afterglow of our ignorance.

3.3 Conclusions on causation

So far I have defended the half-reductive thesis R3. I have examined three arguments against R3 and found them wanting, and examined three arguments for R3 and found the methodological and scientific arguments successful. In short, inflated causation represents an unwarranted reification of a folk concept, which is methodologically and scientifically suspect.

I have not said *how* causation reduces. That is, I have not said what *aspect* of history plus laws grounds causal facts. Here I am partial to Lewis's (1986b) claim that causation has to do with patterns of counterfactual entailments, which are themselves grounded in history. But I am not offering an analysis. I am only treating this as a useful gloss, whose role is to show why there is no further mystery here. (*Compare*: to see that the movie reduces to the sequence of frames – to see that there is no further mystery there – it suffices to have a rough sense of how the sequence of frames comprises the movie. One does not need a conceptual analysis of "movie" for that.)

Of course, R3 is only a half-reductive thesis. The inflationist might accept R3, and simply add that laws are ontologically primitive.[34] So it remains to discuss the second half of the reductive thesis R1, which is that laws reduce to history.

4 Defending the Thesis, Stage Two: Laws

To complete the case for reductionism, it remains to argue that laws reduce to history, as per:

R4   Laws reduce to history.

For given R3 and R4, the fully reductive thesis R1 follows – if causation reduces to history plus laws, and laws themselves reduce to history, then both causation and laws must reduce to history.

In what remains, I will first reply to the three main arguments in the literature against R4, and then consider three arguments for R4. I will conclude that the reduction of laws is justified on methodological and metaphysical grounds.

4.1 Three arguments for inflating laws

There are three main arguments in the literature against R4, the first of which is that the concept of lawhood cannot be analyzed in terms of history. The idea is that the schema: '*L* is a law of nature iff ——' cannot be completed in the requisite way (by finite, non-circular, and intuitively adequate necessary and sufficient conditions concerning history). This argument, which parallels the unanalyzability argument for causation of (1)–(3), might be formulated as follows:

(19) The concept of lawhood cannot be analyzed in terms of history.
(20) If the concept of lawhood cannot be analyzed in terms of history, then laws do not reduce to history.
(21) Laws do not reduce to history.

My reply to (19)–(21) parallels my reply to (1)–(3). I would accept (19), on grounds of the history of failed attempts at a conceptual analysis of lawhood, and also on grounds of the conceptual centrality of lawhood.[35] But I would reject (20), on grounds that a failure of conceptual analysis tells us nothing about the world. I have nothing further to add to what has been said already (section 1), so I will leave the argument here.

The second main argument in the literature against R4 is that events can only be individuated in nomic terms. For instance, one might hold that the relevant individuation condition is: there are no two events $e1$ and $e2$ (where $e1 \neq e2$) such that $e1$ and $e2$ differ in their nomic relations. This argument, which parallels the individuation argument for causation of (4)–(6), might be formulated as follows:

(22) Events can only be individuated in nomic terms.
(23) If events can only be individuated in nomic terms, then laws do not reduce to history.
(24) Laws do not reduce to history.

My reply to (22)–(24) parallels my reply to (4)–(6). I would accept (23), since if events can only be individuated in nomic terms, then (ontologically speaking) there can be no history that is prior to the laws. For the pattern of events that is history would itself presuppose some definite number of events in definite relations, which would itself depend on the laws. But I would reject (22), on grounds that events may be individuated by spatiotemporal locations and intrinsic natures (without untoward skeptical consequences). Here I have nothing further to add to the previous discussion (section 3.1), so I will move forward.

The third main argument in the literature against R4 is that it is possible for worlds to differ in laws without differing in history. To my mind this is the most serious argument against nomic reduction. Here is a representative example. Imagine a relatively simple world with just a single electron moving in a straight line forever. Now, the argument proceeds, there are (infinitely) many distinct possibilities. For instance, there are the possibilities that (i) this world is governed by Newton's three laws; (ii) this world is governed by the single law that all things move in straight lines forever; and (iii) this world is governed by the two laws that all electrons move in straight lines forever, and that all protons spin in mile-radius circles forever. So the argument concludes that there can be differences in lawhood without differences in history. If correct, this would refute R4.[36]

The argument from *nomic differences* might be formulated as follows:

Jonathan Schaffer

(25) There are worlds that differ in lawhood without differing in history.

(26) If there are worlds that differ in lawhood without differing in history, then laws do not reduce to history.

(27) Laws do not reduce to history.

It remains to ask after (25) and (26). I would accept (26), given the implications that ontological reduction has for possibility (section 1).[37] So it remains to ask after (25).

I would, of course, deny (25). Why believe that there are (infinitely many) genuinely distinct possibilities here? To my mind, there is only the one possibility (the one in which a single electron moves in a straight line forever), confusingly described in three different styles. For in what respect are these alleged possibilities said to differ? The alleged nomic difference seems to float on nothing – it seems a verbal distinction without any genuine ontological difference. The case may be even clearer with respect to the empty world, where nothing at all happens. The inflationist, to my mind, faces an embarrassment of riches here, for she is committed to infinitely many empty worlds governed by infinitely many sets of purely vacuous laws. This seems a groundless multiplication.[38]

The philosopher who would uphold (25) might reply in three main ways, the first of which would be that the reason for accepting genuinely distinct possibilities here is *intuitive*, where this shows that the alleged nomic difference need not rest on *anything* – the nomic difference is brute. But this seems a terrible metaphysical price for an especially flimsy intuition (section 2).[39] Or at least, staying within the realm of intuitions, I have strong countervailing intuitions that nomic facts (and modal facts generally) cannot float free like this. So at most the intuitive argument for (25) has revealed conflicted intuitions, rather than a clear stance against R4.

In any case, there are reasons to be skeptical of the intuitions behind (25). For the notion of lawhood in use is a direct descendant of the theological views of Descartes, Newton, and Leibniz, who viewed laws as divine decrees concerning the clockwork of the world.[40] The idea of laws as divine decrees seems to engender the intuitions of distinct possibilities. Here one is intuiting God acting in different ways. But if one rejects the view of laws as divine decrees, it is not clear why one should continue to hold onto the intuitions it engenders. (In particular, if one reinterprets laws as summaries of history (section 4.3) then it is clear one should reject these intuitions as misguided.) So I conclude that there is good reason to reject the intuitions involved, as remnants of a dubious theology.[41]

The second (and perhaps better) defense of (25) would invoke *scientific practice*. Here the idea is that (i) scientists treat, e.g., the empty world as a model of Newtonian mechanics and of other nomic systems, and (ii) what scientists treat as a model of a system of laws should be treated as compossible with those laws.[42] But it is unclear that (i) is essential to scientific practice, and it seems that (ii) is an additional philosophical inference. To reject (ii) is not to reject the practice of modeling, it is only to allow that some models (though they may be useful and interesting) are still models of metaphysically impossible situations. For instance, it might be useful and interesting for a geologist to explore a model in which water is H_2SO_4, even though such is metaphysically impossible (necessarily, water is H_2O). So the scientific practice argument for (25) seems to fall short.[43]

The third (and perhaps best) defense of (25) would involve considerations about *counterfactuals*. Here the idea is to begin with two more complex worlds. For instance, let *w1* be a world in which an electron moves in a straight line forever, and a proton – which comes into existence by chance – does the same. And let *w1* have the law that all things move in straight lines forever. Now let *w2* be a world in which an electron moves in a straight line forever, and a proton – which also comes into existence by chance – spins in a mile-radius circle forever. And let *w2* have the two laws that all electrons move in straight lines forever, and that all protons spin in mile-radius circles forever. What is important about *w1* and *w2* is that these worlds beg no questions against the reductionist. For the nomic difference between *w1* and *w2* seems suitably grounded in the different histories at these worlds.[44] Now we add the following principle about laws under counterfactuals:

> LUC   If it is nomologically possible that *p*, and nomologically necessary that *q*, then had *p* been the case, then it would (still) be nomologically necessary that *q*.

Now from *w1* and LUC (given that the existence of the proton is chancy and so might not have obtained) we get the possibility of a single electron world *w3* that still has the single straight-line law, while from *w2* and LUC we get the distinct possibility of a single electron world *w4* that still has the dual electron-line and proton-circle laws.[45]

But it is unclear why LUC should be endorsed. Whether LUC is valid depends on the correct modal logic for lawhood. In particular, LUC is only valid in K4 or stronger modal systems with transitive accessibility.[46] Here is an argument against transitive accessibility for lawhood. Transitive accessibility would function as a meta-law generator. Transitivity entails that if it is a law that *p*, then it is a law that it is a law that *p*. Repeated applications entail an infinite hierarchy of meta-laws: $\Box\Box p$, $\Box\Box\Box p$, $\Box\Box\Box\Box p$, etc. This would mean that the existence of laws entails the existence of laws of laws, laws of the laws of laws, etc. But clearly there is no reason to believe that laws *require* laws of laws, much less that laws require an infinite hierarchy of meta-laws. It seems enough just to have the laws. Meta-laws are strange entities, scientific practice does not require them, and philosophers have hitherto not dreamt of them. So there is good reason to reject the counterfactual argument for (25), as presupposing a poor modal logic for lawhood.[47] And thus I conclude that the third and most serious argument against R4 fails.

4.2 Three arguments for reducing laws

Here are three main arguments for R4, the first of which is that nomic knowledge requires reduction. The idea is that our nomic knowledge is ultimately based on our observation of regularities in history, so that if laws were more than such regularities, we could have no access to this further feature. So the ontologist should just drop the further feature and limit herself to the regularities.[48]

The argument from *nomic knowledge* might be formulated as follows:

Jonathan Schaffer

(28)   We possess nomic knowledge.

(29)   If we possess nomic knowledge, then laws reduce to history.

(30)   Laws reduce to history.

I would reject (29), however, for reasons parallel to my rejection of (4) and (11). There is some difference between the causal and nomic cases, in that it is much less plausible that nomic knowledge can be attained by direct observation. Or at least, the sorts of cases in which one might argue that causation is directly observable (such as operations of the will, seeing the boulder flatten the hut: section 3.2), do not seem like cases in which the relevant laws (psychological laws and laws of motion, presumably) are themselves directly observable. But this is only to show that lawhood seems more towards the theoretical side of the blurry line between observation and theory. It remains perfectly appropriate, as far as I can see, for the inflationist to argue that we can directly observe certain sequence of events, that provide *evidence* for theoretical claims about the laws. So I will not press the argument further.

The second main argument for R4 is that sound methodological principles support reduction. To posit an irreducible nomic relation is to offend against theoretical fathomability and ontological economy. The argument from theoretical fathomability proceeds by pointing out that necessary connections have an air of the occult, in the sense that they imply inexplicable necessary connections between distinct existents (section 2).[49] The argument from economy proceeds by invoking Ockham's Razor: one should not multiply entities beyond necessity. It is then maintained that it is not necessary to introduce irreducible nomic relations. Or at least, none of the arguments canvassed above (section 4.1) shows any real necessity for irreducible laws.

The argument from *methodology* (nuanced to allow for methodological concerns to be overridden, as per section 3.2) might be formulated as follows:

(31)   Sound methodological principles (such as theoretical fathomability and ontological economy) support reducing laws to history.

(32)   If sound methodological principles support reducing lawhood to history, then, unless sufficiently countervailing considerations can be adduced, laws reduce to history.

(33)   Unless sufficiently countervailing considerations can be adduced, laws reduce to history.

Here the main question is whether sufficiently countervailing considerations can be adduced, to discharge the "unless..." qualification on (33).

The inflationist must now return to her arguments (section 4.1), to identify sufficiently countervailing considerations. I see none. The argument from unanalyzability seems to confuse conceptual primitiveness and ontological primitiveness (an instance of reification). The argument from event individuation seems to me to embody disastrous epistemic assumptions (which would doom inflationism anyway via the argument for nomic knowledge). And the argument from nomic differences seems to me steeped in dubious theology. But here there is a further point to be made, which is that even if there is some residual intuitiveness to the argument from nomic differences, surely it is not sufficiently powerful to overturn the push for a fathomable and economical theory. Such a highly questionable intuition hardly seems sufficient to generate the sort of necessity needed to blunt Ockham's Razor. So I conclude that the methodological argument for R4 is *ultima facie* successful, even granting some intuitiveness to the inflationist arguments.

There is some difference between the methodological arguments for causal reduction (section 3.2) and for nomic reduction, in that irreducible laws seem far less fathomable than irreducible causation. This may be due to the more theoretical, less observable nature of lawhood. In any case, it renders the nomic inflationist in the perilous position of presenting a completely unfathomable theory, that *for us* could contain little more than theistic metaphors.[50]

The third main argument for R4 returns to the need to ground modal entities in occurrent entities, as per R2 (section 2). To my mind this is the best argument for nomic reductionism. Here the idea is that laws are modal, history exhausts occurrent existence, and as such the laws need to be grounded in history.

The *argument from grounding* might be formulated as follows:

(34)   Modal existents reduce to occurrent existents.
(35)   If modal existents reduce to occurrent existents, then laws reduce to history.
(36)   Laws reduce to history.

But is the argument sound? Are (34) and (35) true?

(34) has been defended above (section 2), as intuitively plausible, consistent with modal recombination, and useful in ruling out some bad metaphysics. Laws require grounding. Here the inflationist must identify some sort of error driving the arguments for (34) (beyond complaining that (34) conflicts with her theory). Pending such a response, I conclude that (34) should stand.

The case for (35) has two parts. The first part is the claim that laws are modal existents (section 2). This should be uncontroversial. The second part is the claim that the pattern of events exhausts occurrent existence (for then whatever occurrent existents the laws reduce to will be present in the pattern of events). It is this second part of (35) that proves controversial, for there is a certain sort of inflationist who would reject it.

The sort of inflationist who would reject the second part of (35) would expand the realm of occurrent existence to include *further occurrences* alongside history. She would accept the reduction of laws to the occurrent, while denying the reduction of laws to history alone.[51] As such, this occurrent inflationist might seem to respect both the intuition of nomic differences in 25, and the intuition of grounding in (34). This seems like the best of both worlds. So the occurrent inflationist might claim victory, at this late hour.

But the occurrent inflationist faces an underlying dilemma. The underlying dilemma concerns the modal status of the link between her extra occurrents and the regularities. Never mind what the nature of this link is. Instead, ask of this mysterious link whether it holds *necessarily* or *contingently*. For instance, does N(F,G) necessarily entail $(\forall x) (Fx \rightarrow Gx)$, or does N(F,G) only contingently entail $(\forall x) (Fx \rightarrow Gx)$? In other words, are *all* the worlds in which N(F,G) exists worlds in which $(\forall x) (Fx \rightarrow Gx)$ holds, or only *some*?

If the link is said to hold necessarily, then the allegedly "occurrent" lawmaker is revealed as modal after all. For it will concern what else must be the case, namely the regularity. In other words, it will limit how things may be combined. The state Fa and the lawmaker N(F,G) cannot be combined with the absence of Ga. So on this horn, the grounding intuition remains unsatisfied. On this horn, the occurrent inflationist fares no better than the nomic primitivist with respect to grounding modal entities in occurrent entities.

On the other horn of the dilemma, if the link is said to hold contingently, then the alleged "lawmaker" is revealed as insufficient. It will not govern the events. There will be worlds in which the lawmaker exists but the events pay it no heed. For instance, there will be worlds in which N(F,G) exists and Fa obtains, but Ga does not. Further, the nomic differences intuition will remain unsatisfied. For there will be worlds that agree on both history and the "lawmakers," but differ on their linkage. For instance, there will be a world $w1$ in which N(F,G) exists, $(\forall x)$ (F$x \rightarrow$ Gx) holds, and these are linked; and there will be a world $w2$ in which these are unlinked. So on this horn, the occurrent inflationist fares worse than the reductionist with respect to the platitude that the laws cannot be violated, while faring no better than the reductionist with respect to nomic differences.[52] Thus (35) should stand. Thus lawhood must reduce, or lose grounding.

In this vein it is worth returning again to the argument from nomic differences (section 4.1). For we can now add that, even if there is some residual intuitiveness to the argument, and even if such intuitiveness were not immediately trumped by methodological considerations, such an intuition should be dismissed for groundlessness.

4.3 Conclusions on laws

I have now defended the second stage of the reductionist thesis R1 by defending the reduction of laws to history as per R4. I have examined the arguments against R4 and found them wanting, and examined the arguments for R4 and found the methodological and metaphysical arguments successful. In short, inflated lawhood is a methodologically and metaphysically suspect vestige of dubious theology.

I have not said *how* lawhood reduces. That is, I have not said what *aspect* of history grounds nomic facts. Here I am partial to Lewis's (1973) suggestion that the laws represent the theorems of the best deductive systematization of the occurrent facts.[53] The suggestion is vague (what makes a system "best"?), and I am not interested in providing an analysis. I am only treating this as a useful gloss, whose role is to show why there is no further mystery in lawhood, given the pattern of events.

The reduction of lawhood via R4, together with the reduction of causation via R3, entails the reductionist thesis R1. So I am now in a position to conclude that causation and laws reduce to the pattern of events, just like a movie reduces to the sequence of frames. Each event is like a bit of a frame of the movie. There are causes and laws in the movie, but only, as it were, as themes of the plot, present in virtue of what is in the frames.

Interesting philosophical disputes arise from conflicted intuitions. The dispute over whether causation and laws reduce arises for this reason. On the one hand, we have inflationist intuitions about possible causal and nomic differences given the same history; while, on the other, we have reductionist intuitions about ontological economy and the metaphysical need for occurrent grounding. Something must give. I have cast aspersions on the inflationist intuitions, arguing that our intuitions about possible causal differences are due to reifications of a folk concept, and that our intuitions about possible nomic differences are due to vestiges of a theological world-view. Perhaps the inflationist can cast similar aspersions on ontological economy and metaphysical grounding. That is what it would take to counter the line of argument here. Pending such a response, I must conclude that the reductionist view is overall best. To summarize, the reductionist offers a more fathomable and economical theory that respects the need for grounding, while the inflationist relies on dubious folk and theological intuitions to attempt to convince us that more things exist than we may fathom or need.[54]

Notes

1 For a sophisticated development of this idea, see Lewis (1986b). Note that I am *not* suggesting that causation may be analyzed in terms of counterfactual dependence, or even suggesting that causation may be analyzed at all. As I will explain below, part of my purpose is to *separate* the question of ontological reduction from the question of conceptual analyzability.

2 See Armstrong (1983) for a sophisticated (though anti-reductionist) view of laws along these lines. Note that I am *not* offering an analysis of lawhood, but only trying to convey the intended notion.

3 Point of clarification: as I use the notion, history includes past, present, and future. It is not limited to the past, to the environs of the earth, or any proper part of the actual world. Though it is limited to the actual world.

4 Here I am following Fine, who suggests: "Reduction is to be understood in terms of fundamental reality" (2001: 26). For further discussion of ontological dependence and basicness, see Fine (1994), Lowe (2005), and Schaffer (forthcoming).

5 Thus Loewer expresses the physicalist credo as follows: "The fundamental properties and facts are physical and everything else obtains *in virtue of* them" (2001: 39).

6 There is a second sort of foe of R1 – the *eliminativist* – who denies that there is any causation or lawhood in the world at all. See Russell (1992) for a defense of eliminativism for causation, and van Fraassen (1989) for eliminativism about laws (or at least for "a programme for epistemology and for philosophy of science which will allow them to flourish in the absence of laws or belief therein" (1989: 130)). In the main text I will simply be *presupposing* that causation and lawhood are real. The prospects for eliminativism will not be considered further here.

7 This is not to suppose that the explanation can be written in finite terms, or grasped by human minds. If there could be an endless and patternless movie, for instance, we might never succeed in saying how the movie is grounded in its infinite frames. But it would still be the case that the endless and patternless movie harbors no further mystery (beyond its infinity of frames).

8 There can also be analysis without reduction, in the cases where either our concept is overly deflated, or the terms in the definition denote entities that actually reduce to those denoted by the target concept, rather than the other way around. The moral of all this is that one must be careful to distinguish *the conceptual order*, which is an ordering of concepts in our minds by the relations "figures in the definition of," from *the ontological*

Jonathan Schaffer

order, which is an ordering of entities in the world by the reductive relation. Even if there is a conceptual order in the intended sense, it need not track the ontological order in any way. There is no guarantee that our minds match the world here.

9   This is one of those cases (such as with the question of what is art, or what is pornography) where I am more confident about my judgment in particular cases than I am with any general formula that purports to cover every possible case.

10 This claim of exhaustivity will prove contentious. Some inflationists (for instance, Armstrong 1983) would expand the realm of occurrent existence to include entities beyond history, and would go on to ground the laws in these additional occurrent entities. For further discussion see section 3.2.

11 It is worth distinguishing the reductionist's general thesis, as I am explicating it, from the thesis that Lewis labels 'Humean supervenience' (1986b: ix–x). The reductionist thesis is both stronger and weaker than Humean supervenience. The reductionist thesis is stronger in that it is supposed to hold with metaphysical necessity, whereas Humean supervenience is only supposed to hold at a restricted region of logical space. But the reductionist thesis is weaker in that it makes no claims to locality or to reduction of whole to part, whereas Humean supervenience adds that the whole is grounded in its parts (thus the Humean would add that history itself reduces to the arrangement of the little point events).

12 Sider draws a similar moral: "What seems common to all the cheats is that irreducibly hypothetical [/modal] properties are postulated, whereas a proper ontology should invoke only *categorical*, or occurrent, properties and relations" (2001: 41; see also Armstrong 1997: 80–3).

13 Some of the more important attempts at a conceptual analysis of causation include Mackie (1974), Lewis (1986b), and Mellor (1995). For a discussion of some systematic counterexamples (as well as a failed attempt at further analysis), see Schaffer (2001a).

14 Premise 2 is also explicitly invoked by the inflationist Tooley: "If causal facts are logically supervenient upon non-causal facts, then it would seem that it must be in principle possible to analyze causal concepts in non-causal terms" (1987: 177). Though no further argument is given.

15 This claim of conceptual centrality is explicit in Hume, who spoke of the concepts of causation, resemblance, and contiguity as "the only ties of our thoughts, . . . *to us* the cement of the universe . . ." (1978: 662) The centrality claim resurfaces in Carroll's inflationism: "With regard to our total conceptual apparatus, causation is the center of the center" (1994: 118; see also pp. 81–5).

16 This proposal is defended in Davidson (1969).

17 See Schaffer (2001b) for a defense of this individuation principle for *tropes* (particular properties), which may be identified with events. The hardest case for this principle is the seeming possibility of multiple tropes/events with the same intrinsic natures *piled* in one place (Daly 1997: 154). I reply that the alleged piling either makes for an intensive difference or not. If not, I see no reason to believe that more than one trope/event is present. If so, I see no reason to believe that a pile of low-intensity tropes/events is present, rather than one high-intensity trope/event. In any case, the causal individuation principle surely does worse with respect to piling intuitions. Why can't there be a world containing the following closed causal sequence: (i) *e1* causes *e2a* and *e2b*, and (ii) *e2a* and *e2b* cause *e3*? Here *e2a* and *e2b* are causally piled – they have the exact same causes (*e1*) and effects (*e3*). Still they may be located in different places and have distinct natures: *e2a* might be a flash of green over here, while *e2b* might be a thunderous boom over there. This is excellent reason to think that more than one event is present, or so it seems to me.

18 Thus Shoemaker has argued:

> [I]f the properties and causal potentialities of a thing can vary independently of one another, then it is impossible for us to know (or have any good reason for believing) that something has retained a property over time, or that something has undergone a change with respect to the properties that underlie its causal powers. (1980: 215)

19 For further discussion, see Schaffer 2004 (esp. §3). There I consider the leading accounts of our knowledge of the external world, and conclude that "[knowledge of intrinsic natures] is possible in the same way that knowledge of the external world is possible, whatever that may be." (p. 228)

20 Armstrong (1983: 133), Tooley (1987: 199–202), and Carroll (1994: 134–41) all provide examples of this sort.

21 So what does cause the prince to transform into a frog? Given the case as described, I would answer that both spells caused the prince to transform (both spells independently raised the chance of the transformation, after all). Though the case may be modified to rule out the 'both' answer, by making it such that (i) when two spells both work the effect is enhanced (the prince would become extra-green with an extra-long tongue, say), and (ii) the enhanced effect does not obtain. In such a case I would answer that one of the spells caused the prince to transform, though it is ontologically indeterminate as to which. In some cases there is simply no fact of the matter. That is OK. Fundamental reality remains perfectly determinate.

22 The defender of (7) might offer the counterargument that (i) the three distinct scenarios are each conceivable, (ii) conceivability entails (or at least provides strong evidence for) possibility, so (iii) the three distinct scenarios are each possible (or at least there is strong evidence for such). To this I would reply that we must distinguish *off-hand* from *ideal* conceivability. Many things are off-hand conceivable that turn out to be impossible, such as trisecting an angle with ruler and compass. The only plausible link from conceivability to possibility is via ideal conceivability (Chalmers 2002). So I would grant that the three distinct scenarios are off-hand conceivable, but draw no conclusions from that. And I would deny that the three distinct scenarios are ideally conceivable – I am claiming that they are the result of conceptual error.

23 Something like this argument is present in Hume's skeptical reflection on the notion of necessary connection: "One event follows another; but we never can observe any tie between them. They seem *conjoined* but never *connected*" (1975:). Indeed, something like this argument seems to be the main impetus to reduction in the literature, both for causation and for lawhood (see section 3.1).

24 Or at least, only the person who is skeptical of knowledge generally would deny (10). But such a skeptic should already be accustomed to postulating entities she claims no knowledge of, so she should not find causal inflationism any worse.

25 See Tooley (1987) for a sophisticated inferential account of causal knowledge.

26 See Fales (1990: esp. ch. 1) and Armstrong (1997: esp. 211–16) for a defense of this idea, though see Hume (1975: 352–9) for anticipatory criticism.

27 These examples are from Strawson (1985: 123). See Anscombe (1993: esp. 92–3) for further defense of this idea.

28 Point of clarification: I am *not* opposing the use of epistemological arguments in metaphysics, but only the use of *bad* epistemological arguments. If (11) were true, then causal reductionism would follow by *modus ponens*. The occurrence of epistemic terminology does not invalidate *modus ponens*!

29 Or at least, I take it no one would deny the ontological economy aspect of (13). The theoretical fathomability aspect might be more contested. But this will not matter for the argument of the main text.

102 **Jonathan Schaffer**

30 In this vein, Russell dismissed causation as a relic of 'Stone Age metaphysics', since: "In the motions of mutually gravitating bodies, there is nothing that can be called a cause, and nothing that can be called an effect; there is merely a formula." (1992: 202) See Quine (1966) for a similar claim.

31 See Reichenbach (1956: 147–9) and Salmon (1984: esp. 141–4) for the relevant arguments. The core idea is that there are some worldlines (which Reichenbach calls "unreal sequences" and which Salmon calls "pseudo processes") that can move faster than light. Salmon gives the example of a rotating beacon in the center of a very large dome – if the beacon spins fast enough, and the wall of the dome is distant enough, then the spot of light moving around the wall can move at superluminal velocities. The reconciliation with special relativity is that such worldlines are not capable of being used for *signaling*, which is a causally loaded notion. (It is worth noting here, in anticipation of the argument of the next paragraph, that both Reichenbach and Salmon advocate reductive accounts of causation.)

32 Note that the converse does not hold. If a certain notion proves needed in our best attempt at a systematic understanding of the world, this may be because what this notion concerns is ontologically basic, *or* it may be because this notion constitutes an irreplaceable conceptual shortcut for us. The latter represents the position I will take on laws (see section 4.3).

33 Point of clarification: Russell argued for the elimination of causation, calling it "a relic of a bygone age, surviving, like the monarchy, only because it is erroneously supposed to do no harm" (1992: 193). I am not embracing Russell's eliminativism (after all, I am defending reductionism here). Rather, I am arguing that *if* the inflationist could establish a failure of reduction, *then* she would face Russell's rejoinder that such an irreducible and scientifically irrelevant relation deserves to be eliminated.

34 An example of such an inflationist is Maudlin (2004 and manuscript). When I mentioned reserving R3 as a fallback position (section 2), this was the sort of view I had in mind.

35 The conceptual centrality of lawhood is emphasized by Carroll: "Lawhood is conceptually intertwined with many other blatantly modal concepts that all have a massive role to play in our habitual ways of thinking and speaking" (1994: 3).

36 Tooley (1977: 669–72), van Fraassen (1989: 46–7), and Carroll (1990: 215–18; 1994: ch. 3.1) are among the many who have provided examples of this sort.

37 Earman (1984: 195) provides the following "empiricist loyalty test on laws": (E1) For any $w1$ and $w2$, if $w1$ and $w2$ agree on all occurrent facts, then $w1$ and $w2$ agree on laws. Earman's E1 is a consequence of reductionism and the further claim (section 2) that history exhausts occurrent existence.

38 It is contentious whether the empty world is a genuine possibility. But the "embarrassment of riches" problem arises for the inflationist either way – the empty world is just the most dramatic case.

39 The intuition about lawhood seems even flimsier than the analogous intuition about causation that arises in the causal differences argument of (7)–(9). Lawhood is not quite as central a notion as causality. Indeed (as will be discussed shortly), our concept of lawhood is a relatively recent introduction by seventeenth century natural philosophers, involving the dubious idea of divine decrees for how the world should work.

40 See van Fraassen (1989: 5–7), and for a more extended historical discussion, Milton (1998). Here is what Milton concludes: "By the end of the sixteenth century the idea of God ordaining laws of nature had become sufficiently familiar. . . . It was Descartes who more than anyone created the modern idea of a law of nature" (1998: 699)

41 Here I am following Beebee, who argues that the intuitive argument for 25 is simply question-begging: "[S]uch thought experiments do not succeed in finishing off the Humean conception of laws, because they presuppose a conception of laws which Humeans do not

share: a conception according to which the laws *govern* what goes on in the universe" (2000: 573). Beebee goes on to trace the idea of *governing* to the theological conception of laws (pp. 580–1)

42 This argument is provided by Maudlin (manuscript, pp. 25–6).

43 There is the further worry that this aspect of scientific practice might have historical roots in the theological conception of laws, where the implicit idea is of modeling different acts of creation (this suspicion is voiced in Beebee [2000: 581]). Loewer (1996, pp. 116–17) provides the further suggestion that this portion of scientific practice may be explained away (without great loss to science) as a hasty generalization from acceptable ways of applying the actual laws to *subsystems* of the actual world.

44 Strictly speaking, the inflationist should require that the electron and proton be embedded in a bigger world where enough is going on to ground the attribution of chance to the proton. But I take it that this should not raise any problems. Perhaps the easiest embedding strategy is to move to worlds with lots of electrons moving in straight lines, some random portion of which are accompanied by protons popping into existence and moving as they are wont.

45 This mode of argument is due to Carroll (1990: 215–18) who later develops it in detail (1994: ch. 3.1 and app. B). My principle LUC corresponds to Carroll's SC*. Carroll mainly focuses on the principle he labels SC (If it is nomologically possible that p and nomologically necessary that [if p then q], then had p been the case then q would have been the case), claiming that SC*(=LUC) is a consequence of SC sufficient to trouble the reductionist. But the derivation of SC* from SC requires the following inference: "Since Q is a law, Q is a law in every possible world with the same laws as the actual world, and so it is physically necessary that Q is a law" (Carroll 1994: 59). This is an inference from $\Box q$ (q is a law) to $\Box\Box q$ (it is physically necessary that q is a law). That inference is only valid in modal systems that include the K4 axiom $\Box p \to \Box\Box p$. See the next footnote for further discussion.

46 K4 is a normal modal system (meaning that it includes as theorems all the tautologies and distribution axioms, and is closed under modus ponens, substitution, and necessitation) augmented with the axiom $\Box p \to \Box\Box p$. This axiom functions to make accessibility transitive, which is what validates LUC. One can generate countermodels to LUC in normal modal systems without the transitivity-generating K4 axiom. For instance, here is a countermodel in T (a normal modal system augmented with the reflexivity-generating axiom $\Box p \to p$, which I think is the best modal logic for modeling lawhood). Set the model $<W, R, V>$ to $W = \{w1, w2, w3\}$ – these are the worlds under consideration, $R = \{<w1, w1>, <w1, w2>, <w2, w2>, <w2, w3>, <w3, w3>\}$ – this is the accessibility relation set to be reflexive but intransitive, and $V = \{<w1, \sim p, q>, <w2, p, q>, <w3, \sim p, \sim q>\}$ – this sets the truth-values of p and q at the worlds under consideration. Now at $w1$ the following will hold: (i) $\Diamond p$ (since p holds at some world that $w1$ accesses, namely $w2$), (ii) $\Box q$ (since q holds at all the worlds $w1$ accesses, which are $w1$ and $w2$), and (iii) $\sim(p > \Box q)$ (the nearest (and only) p world is $w2$, and $\Box q$ does not hold at $w2$, since q does not hold at some world that $w2$ accesses, that being $w3$). This proves the invalidity of LUC in T.

47 The argument against meta-laws also serves as an argument against the symmetry-generating B axiom $p \to \Box\Diamond p$. For iterations of this axiom will produce an infinite hierarchy of meta-laws of the form $\Box\Diamond p$, $\Box\Diamond\Box\Diamond p$, $\Box\Diamond\Box\Diamond\Box\Diamond p$, ... which comprise laws about what the laws allow, laws about what those laws allow, and so on. In contrast, the reflexivity-generating T axiom $\Box p \to p$ (if it is a law that p, then p) seems obviously correct and not in danger of forcing us to meta-laws. Thus I conclude that nomic accessibility should be reflexive, but neither symmetric nor transitive, as per the modal system T.

Jonathan Schaffer

48   Something like this argument is present in Earman and Roberts' (2005) argument for nomic reductionism, where the inflationist is challenged to discriminate the case where a certain systematic regularity holds as a matter of law, from the case where that regularity holds as a matter of accident.

49   This style of argument has been developed by van Fraassen (1989: esp. 38–9), who asks what prevents (i) Fa from holding, (ii) it being a law that all Fs are Gs, but (iii) $\sim Ga$ from holding. Van Fraassen extends this argument into an underlying dilemma for accounts of laws, between (i) having 'it is a law that p' entail 'p' (*the problem of inference*) and (ii) having 'it is a law that p' entail 'necessarily p' (*the problem of identification*). According to van Fraassen, reductionist accounts of lawhood have trouble with (ii), mainly due to the nomic differences argument (which I have replied to in section 4.1); while non-reductionist accounts of lawhood have trouble with (i), since there is no explanation of how the nomic entity could 'govern' the regularities.

50   This worry surfaces in Armstrong's postulation of second-order necessitation relations N between universals as lawmakers. Armstrong tells us that we should accept the inference from the second-order $N(F,G)$ to the regularity $(\forall x)\,(Fx \rightarrow Gx)$ as an inexplicable sort of 'bringing along' which we must admit "in the spirit of natural piety" (1983: 92). Lewis (1983: 366) replies that calling the second-order universal 'necessitation' no more renders it capable of bringing anything along, than does calling a man 'Armstrong' render him capable of impressive bicep curls. (To Armstrong's credit, he has since attempted a substantive explanation as to how $N(F,G)$ engenders the regularity $(\forall x)\,(Fx \rightarrow Gx)$ (1997, pp. 227–30), though it is not obvious that he is successful.)

51   Dretske (1977), Tooley (1977, 1987), and Armstrong (1983, 1997) are examples of inflationists of this stripe. For them, the further occurrent entities are the second-order necessitation universals of the form $N(F,G)$, which serve as the lawmakers.

52   So why might it have seemed as if the occurrent inflationist could achieve the best of both worlds? Perhaps the appearance was created when the occurrent inflationist called her extra occurrent entity 'necessitation'. What emerges from the dilemma above is that if the name is apt then the entity is not occurrent; while if the name is not apt then the entity is no lawmaker. See Carroll 1994 (App. A) for further arguments against the occurrent form of inflationism.

53   Lewis suggests this view (1973: 72–7; see also Lewis 1994: §§3–4), tracing its ancestry to Mill and Ramsey. The Lewisian view is further developed and defended in Earman (1984) and Loewer (1996), *inter alia*.

54   Thanks to John Carroll and John Hawthorne for helpful comments. My greatest debt is to my teacher, David Lewis.

References

Anscombe, G. E. M. 1993. "Causality and Determination," in E. Sosa and M. Tooley, eds., *Causation* (Oxford: Oxford University Press), pp. 88–104.

—. 1983. *What is a Law of Nature?* (Cambridge: Cambridge University Press).

—. 1997. *A World of States of Affairs* (Cambridge: Cambridge University Press).

Beebee, H. 2000. "The Non-Governing Conception of Laws of Nature," *Philosophy and Phenomenological Research* 81: 571–94.

Carroll, J. 1990. "The Humean Tradition," *Philosophical Review* 99: 185–219.

—. 1994. *Laws of Nature* (Cambridge: Cambridge University Press).

Chalmers, D. 2002. "Does Conceivability Entail Possibility?" in T. Szabó Gendler and J. Hawthorne, eds., *Conceivability and Possibility* (Oxford: Oxford University Press), pp. 145–200.

Daly, Chris. 1997. "Tropes," in D. H. Mellor and A. Oliver, eds., *Properties* (Oxford: Oxford University Press), pp. 125–39.

Davidson, D. 1969. "The Individuation of Events," in *Essays on Actions and Events* (Oxford: Oxford University Press), pp. 163–80.

Dretske, F. 1977. "Laws of Nature," *Philosophy of Science* 44: 248–68.

Earman, J. 1984. "Laws of Nature: The Empiricist Challenge," in R. J. Bogdan, ed., *D. M. Armstrong* (Dordrecht: Reidel Publishing), pp. 191–223.

Earman, J. and Roberts, J. 2005. "Contact with the Nomic: A Challenge for Deniers of Humean Supervenience about Laws of Nature. Part II: The Epistemological Argument for Humean Supervenience," *Philosophy and Phenomenological Research* 71: 253–86.

Fales, E. 1990. *Causation and Universals* (London: Routledge & Kegan Paul).

Fine, K. 1994. "Ontological Dependence," *Proceedings of the Aristotelian Society* 95: 269–90.

—. 2001. "The Question of Realism," *Philosophers Imprint* 1: 1–30.

Hume, D. 1975 *An Enquiry Concerning Human Understanding* (Oxford: Oxford University Press).

—. 1978. *A Treatise of Human Nature* (Oxford: Oxford University Press).

Lewis, D. 1973. *Counterfactuals* (Cambridge, MA: Harvard University Press).

—. 1983. "New Work for a Theory of Universals," *Australasian Journal of Philosophy* 61: 343–77.

—. 1986a. *On the Plurality of Worlds* (Oxford: Basil Blackwell).

—. 1986b. *Philosophical Papers*, vol. 2 (Oxford: Basil Blackwell).

—. 1994. "Humean Supervenience Debugged," *Mind* 103: 473–490.

Loewer, B. 1996. "Humean Supervenience," *Philosophical Topics* 24: 101–27.

—. 2001. "From Physics to Physicalism," in C. Gillet and B. Loewer, eds., *Physicalism and its Discontents* (Cambridge: Cambridge University Press), pp. 37–56.

Lowe, E. J. 2005. "Ontological Dependence." *Stanford Encyclopedia of Philosophy.* <http://plato.stanford.edu/entries/dependence-ontological/>.

Mackie, J. L. 1974. *The Cement of the Universe* (Oxford: Oxford University Press).

Maudlin, T. 2004. "Causation, Counterfactuals, and the Third Factor," in J. Collins, N. Hall, and L. A. Paul, eds., *Causation and Counterfactuals* (Boston: MIT Press), pp. 419–43.

Maudlin, T. *manuscript.* Why be Humean?

Mellor, D. H. 1995. *The Facts of Causation* (London: Routledge & Kegan Paul).

Milton, J. R. 1998. "Laws of Nature," in D. Garber and M. Ayers, eds., *The Cambridge History of Seventeenth Century Philosophy*, vol. 1 (Cambridge: Cambridge University Press), pp. 680–701.

Quine, W. V. O. 1966. *The Ways of Paradox* (London: Random House).

Reichenbach, H. 1956. *The Direction of Time* (Berkeley: University of California Press).

Russell, B. 1992. "On the Notion of Cause," in J. Slater, ed., *The Collected Papers of Bertrand Russell v6: Logical and Philosophical Papers 1909–1913* (London: Routledge & Kegan Paul), pp. 193–210.

Salmon, W. 1984. *Scientific Explanation and the Causal Structure of the World* (Princeton: Princeton University Press).

Schaffer, J. 2001a. "Causes as Probability-Raisers of Processes," *Journal of Philosophy* 98: 75–92.

—. 2001b. "The Individuation of Tropes," *Australasian Journal of Philosophy* 79: 247–57.

—. 2004. "Quiddistic Knowledge," in F. Jackson and G. Priest, eds., *Lewisian Themes: The Philosophy of David K. Lewis* (Oxford: Oxford University Press), pp. 210–30.

—. *Forthcoming* "On What Grounds What," in David Chalners, David Manley, and Ryan Wasserman, eds., *Metametaphysics* (Oxford: Oxford University Press).

Shoemaker, S. 1980. "Causality and Properties," in P. van Inwagen, ed., *Time and Cause: Essays Presented to Richard Taylor* (Dordrecht: Reidel Publishing), pp. 109–35.

Sider, T. 2001. *Four-Dimensionalism: An Ontology of Persistence and Time* (Oxford: Oxford University Press).

Strawson, P. F. 1985. "Causality and Explanation," in B. Vermazen and M. Hintikka, eds., *Essays on Davidson: Actions and Events* (Oxford: Oxford University Press), pp. 115–36.

Tooley, M. 1977. "The Nature of Laws," *Canadian Journal of Philosophy* 7: 667–98.

——. 1987. *Causation: A Realist Approach* (Oxford: Oxford University Press).

Van Fraassen, B. 1989. *Laws and Symmetry* (Oxford: Oxford University Press).

MODALITY AND POSSIBLE WORLDS

3.1   "Concrete Possible Worlds," Phillip Bricker

3.2   "Ersatz Possible Worlds," Joseph Melia

The twentieth-century writer Rex Stout wrote detective fiction, but he might have become a real detective instead. In some other possible world, he really does become a detective. In yet another world, Stout has yet another occupation: he is a salesman. For every occupation that Stout *could have had*, there is a possible world in which Stout *has* that occupation. Many things vary between different possible worlds: Stout has different occupations, different clothes, different hair color, different friends, and so on. The only things that hold constant in all possible worlds are the *necessary truths*: in every possible world, Stout is either a salesman or he isn't. Philosophers have found it convenient to speak in this way of "possible worlds," but what are possible worlds, really? Phillip Bricker argues that we should take possible worlds talk at face value. Other possible worlds, containing other Rex Stouts with their different occupations, clothes, and friends, really exist. Joseph Melia disagrees; we should instead regard talk of possible worlds as really being talk of more mundane entities; for example, *stories* that describe the alternate occupations of Rex Stout and other non-actual matters.

Concrete Possible Worlds

Phillip Bricker

1 Introduction

Open a book or article of contemporary analytic philosophy, and you are likely to find talk of possible worlds therein. This applies not only to analytic metaphysics, but also to areas as diverse as philosophy of language, philosophy of science, epistemology, and ethics. Philosophers agree, for the most part, that possible worlds talk is extremely useful for explicating concepts and formulating theories. They disagree, however, over its proper interpretation. In this chapter, I discuss the view, championed by David Lewis, that philosophers' talk of possible worlds is the literal truth.[1] There exists a plurality of worlds. One of these is *our* world, the *actual* world, the physical universe that contains us and all our surroundings. The others are *merely possible* worlds containing *merely possible* beings, such as flying pigs and talking donkeys. But the other worlds are no less real or concrete for being merely possible. Fantastic? Yes! What could motivate a philosopher to believe such a tale?

I start, as is customary, with modality.[2] Truths about the world divide into two sorts: *categorical* and *modal*. Categorical truths describe how things are, what is actually the case. Modal truths describe how things could or must be, what is possibly or necessarily so. Consider, for example, the table at which I am writing. The table has numerous categorical properties: its color, perhaps, and its material composition. To say that the table is brown or that it is made of wood is to express a categorical truth about the world. The table also has numerous modal properties. The table *could have been* red (had it, for example, been painted red at the factory), but it could not, it seems, have been made of glass, not *this very table*; it is *essentially* made of wood. Just where to draw the line between the categorical and the modal is often disputed. But surely (I say) there is some level – perhaps fundamental physics – at which the world can be described categorically, with no admixture of modality. Now, suppose one knew the actual truth or falsity of every categorical statement. One might nonetheless not know which truths are necessary or which falsehoods are possible. One might be lacking, that is, in *modal* knowledge. In some sense, then, the modal transcends the categorical.

And that's trouble; for modal statements are problematic in a way that categorical statements are not. I see that the table is brown, but I do not see that it is *possibly* red. I can do empirical tests to determine that it is made of wood, but no empirical test tells me that it is *essentially* made of wood. By observation, I discover only the categorical properties of objects, not their modal properties. That makes special trouble for the empiricist, who holds that all knowledge of the world must be based on observation. But empiricist or not, modal properties are mysterious: they do not seem to be among the basic or fundamental ingredients that make up our world. What to do? Should we turn eliminativist about modality, holding that modal statements are unintelligible, or, at any rate, that their communicative purpose is not descriptive?[3] That would be implausible. We assign truth and falsity to modal statements in principled ways; we reason with modal statements according to their own peculiar logic. No, we must hold that modal statements are descriptively meaningful, but not fundamental. Thus begins the search for an *analysis* of modal statements, the attempt to provide illuminating truth conditions for modal statements without just invoking more modality.

Consider this. Modal statements can be naturally paraphrased in terms of possible worlds. For example, instead of saying "It is possible that there be blue swans," say "In some possible world there are blue swans." Instead of saying "It is necessary that all swans be birds," say "In every possible world all swans are birds." When paraphrased in this way, the modal operators 'it is possible that' and 'it is necessary that' become *quantifiers* over possible worlds. Intuitively, these paraphrases are merely a *façon de parler*, and not to be taken with ontological seriousness. But perhaps the ease with which we can produce and understand these possible worlds paraphrases suggests something different: the paraphrases provide the sought-after *analyses* of the modal statements; they are what our modal talk has been (implicitly) about all along.[4] And if that is so, then we have a reduction of the modal to the categorical after all: although the modal properties of this world transcend the categorical properties *of this world*, they are determined by the categorical properties of this world, *and other possible worlds*. But the introduction of possible worlds may seem to raise more questions than it answers. What are these so-called worlds? What is their nature, and how are they related to our world?

Philosophers who believe in possible worlds divide over whether worlds are *abstract* or *concrete*. I use the terms 'abstract' and 'concrete' advisedly: there are (at least) four different ways of characterizing the abstract/concrete distinction, making the terms 'abstract' and 'concrete' (at least) four ways ambiguous.[5] Fortunately, however, on the Lewisian approach to modality I am considering, the worlds turn out (with some minor qualifications) to be "concrete" on all four ways of drawing the distinction.

(C1) Worlds (typically) have parts that are paradigmatically concrete, such as donkeys, and protons, and stars.

(C2) Worlds are particulars, not universals; they are individuals, not sets.

(C3) Worlds (typically) have parts that stand in spatiotemporal and causal relations to one another.

Phillip Bricker

(C4)   Worlds are fully determinate;[6] they are not abstractions from anything else.

It is convenient, then, and harmless, to call worlds "concrete" if they satisfy all four conditions listed above. The concrete worlds taken altogether I call the *modal realm*, or, following custom, *logical space*.[7] The denizens of logical space – the worlds and their concrete parts – are called *possibilia*.

In one sense, concrete possible worlds are like big planets within the actual world: two concrete worlds do not have any (concrete) objects in common; they do not overlap. Thus, you do not literally exist both in the actual world and in other merely possible worlds, any more than you literally exist both on Earth and on other planets in our galaxy. Instead, you have *counterparts* in other possible worlds, people qualitatively similar to you, and who play a role in their world similar to the role you play in the actual world. This constrains the analysis of modality *de re* – statements ascribing modal properties to objects. When we ask, for example, whether you could have been a plumber, we are not asking whether there is a possible world in which *you* are a plumber – that is trivially false (supposing you are not in fact a plumber), since you inhabit only the actual world. Rather, we are asking whether there is a possible world in which a *counterpart* of you is a plumber.[8] (More on this in section 5 below.)

In another sense, however, concrete worlds are quite unlike big planets within the actual world. Each possible world is spatiotemporally and causally isolated from every other world: one cannot travel between possible worlds in a spaceship; one cannot view one world from another with a telescope. But although this makes other possible worlds *empirically* inaccessible to us in the actual world, it does not make them *cognitively* inaccessible: we access other worlds through our linguistic and mental representations of ways things might have been, through the descriptions we formulate that the worlds satisfy.

I say that merely possible concrete worlds, no less than planets within the actual world, *exist*. I do not thereby attribute any special ontological status to the worlds (or planets): whatever has any sort of being "exists," as I use the term; 'existence' is coextensive with 'being'. Of course, merely possible concrete worlds do not *actually* exist. For the realist about concrete worlds, existence and actual existence do not coincide. In most ordinary contexts, no doubt, the term 'exists' is implicitly restricted to actual things – as, for that matter, is the term 'is'. The phenomenon of implicit contextual restriction allows us to truly say, in an ordinary context, "flying pigs do not exist" or "there are no flying pigs," without thereby denying the existence of concrete non-actual worlds teeming with flying pigs. It is the same phenomenon that allows us to truly say, when there is no beer in our fridge, "there is no beer," without denying that there are other fridges in the world packed with beer. Ordinary assertions of non-existence, then, do not count against realism about concrete worlds.

Call approaches to modality that analyze modality in terms of concrete possible worlds and their parts *Lewisian approaches*. I take the following four theses to be characteristic of Lewisian approaches to modality:

1   There is no primitive modality.
2   There exists a plurality of concrete possible worlds.

3 Actuality is an indexical concept.[9]
4 Modality *de re* is to be analyzed in terms of counterparts, not transworld identity.

In what follows, I devote one section to each of these theses. I write as an advocate for Lewisian approaches, and feel under no obligation to give opposing views equal time. For each thesis, I take Lewis's interpretation and defense as my starting point. I then consider and endorse alternative ways of accepting the thesis, some of which disagree substantially with Lewis's interpretation or defense. There is more than one way to be a Lewisian about modality.

2 No Primitive Modality

The rejection of primitive modality is a central tenet of Lewisian approaches. It motivates the introduction of possible worlds, the most promising avenue of analysis. And it motivates taking possible worlds to be concrete: Lewis's most persistent complaint against accounts of worlds as abstract is that they must invoke primitive modality in one form or another. But for all the talk of rejecting primitive modality by Lewis and others, there is no clear agreement as to just what this means. Indeed, I think three different and independent theses have been taken to fall under the "no primitive modality" banner. Although Lewis accepts all three theses, only one of them is truly central to the Lewisian approach. Before turning to discuss that central thesis, I will briefly mention the other two.

First off, it is natural to interpret 'no primitive modality' as a supervenience thesis: the modal *supervenes* on the categorical. To say that modal statements *supervene* on categorical statements is to say that there can be no difference as to how things are modally without some difference as to how they are categorically. Or, cashed out in terms of possible worlds: whenever two possible worlds differ in their modal features, they differ in their categorical features as well. Thus, for example, no two possible worlds differ just with respect to brute dispositional properties, or primitive causal relations. This supervenience thesis is central to Lewis's (broadly) Humean analyses of laws, causation, and counterfactuals, of the physical and causal modalities (see chapter 2.2). But the thesis is not directed at the metaphysical (or logical) modality that is the target of our current analytic endeavor. I therefore set it aside.

A second way one might understand the 'no primitive modality' thesis is as what Lewis calls a *principle of recombination*. His initial formulation of the principle is: "[A]nything can coexist with anything else, and anything can fail to coexist with anything else" (1986: 88). The first half, when spelled out, says that any two (or more) things, possibly from different worlds, can be patched together in a single world. To illustrate: if there could be a unicorn, and there could be a dragon, then there could be a unicorn and a dragon side by side. Since worlds do not overlap, a unicorn from one world and a dragon from another cannot *themselves* exist side by side. So the principle is to be interpreted in terms of *intrinsic duplicates*: at some world, a duplicate of the unicorn and a duplicate of the dragon exist side by side. The second half of the principle of recombination, spelled out in terms of worlds and duplicates, says

Phillip Bricker

this: whenever two (non-overlapping) things coexist at a world, neither of which is a duplicate of a part of the other, there is another world at which a duplicate of one exists without a duplicate of the other. To illustrate: since a talking head exists contiguous to a living human body, there could exist an unattached talking head, separate from any living body. More precisely: there is a world at which a duplicate of the talking head exists but at which no duplicate of the rest of the living body exists.

According to Lewis, the principle of recombination expresses "the Humean denial of necessary connections between distinct existents" (Lewis 1986: 87). But two caveats are needed. First, only the second half, strictly speaking, embodies a denial of necessary *connections*; the first half embodies instead a denial of necessary *exclusions*. And, second, the thesis that the modal supervenes on the categorical is an alternative way to capture the denial of necessary connections, one that may be closer to Hume's intent; it denies that there are necessary connections *in the world*, ontological interlopers somehow existing over and above the mere succession of events, and somehow serving as ground for modal truths about powers or laws or causation.

Lewis sometimes charges those who reject principles of recombination with being committed to primitive modality.[10] But I do not think that a principle of recombination is the right way to capture the 'no primitive modality' thesis. Violations of recombination impose a modal structure on logical space, allowing that the existence of some *possibilia* necessarily entail or exclude the existence of other *possibilia*; but the structure imposed need not be *primitive* modal structure. It may be that the violations can all be accounted for in non-modal terms, that necessary connections and exclusions only occur when some non-modal condition is satisfied. Thus, *contra* what Lewis suggests, violations of recombination are not – or at least not by themselves – primitive modality.

The first two interpretations of the 'no primitive modality' thesis each put constraints on logical space, though in opposite ways. The supervenience thesis demands that there not be *too many* worlds, that there never be two worlds that differ modally without differing non-modally. Principles of recombination demand that there not be *too few* worlds, that there always be enough worlds to represent all the different ways of recombining. The third interpretation – the one we' re after – is different: it puts constraints on our *theorizing* about logical space, not (directly) on logical space itself. It demands that our *total theory*, our best account of the whole of reality, can be stated without recourse to modal notions, that the (primitive) *ideology* of our total theory be non-modal.[11]

Can the Lewisian meet this demand? First, we need to know what terms of our total theory count as non-modal. Here I will suppose this includes the Boolean connectives ('and', 'or', 'not') and unrestricted quantifiers ('every', 'some') of logic, the 'is a part of' relation of mereology, the 'is a member of' relation of set-theory, the 'is an instance of' relation of property theory, and a (second-order) predicate applying to just those properties and relations that are fundamental, or *perfectly natural*.[12] I will also suppose that the notion of a spatiotemporal relation is non-modal; perhaps it can be given a structural analysis in terms of the above.[13] Now, let us suppose that the Lewisian has succeeded in providing possible worlds paraphrases for the vast panoply of modal locutions. That still leaves the notion of a possible world itself, an ostensibly modal notion. It won't do simply to take this notion as primitive. At best, that would reduce the number of modal notions to one. If primitive modality is to be eliminated, the Lewisian must provide an analysis of 'possible world' in non-modal terms.

It might appear that analyzing 'possible world' involves two separate tasks: first, analyzing the notion of world; then, distinguishing those worlds that are possible from those that are not. This second task, however, would appear to land the Lewisian in vicious circularity: possibility is to be analyzed in terms of possible worlds, which in turn is to be analyzed in terms of possibility, and round and round and round.[14] But the threat of circularity is bogus because there is no second task to perform. On a conception of possible worlds as concrete, there are no impossible worlds. For suppose there were a concrete world at which both *p* and *not-p*, for some proposition *p*. Then there would be a property corresponding to *p* such that the world both had and didn't have the property. Contradictions could not be confined to impossible worlds; they would infect what is true *simpliciter*, thereby making our total theory contradictory.[15] The law of non-contradiction, then, demands that the Lewisian reject impossible worlds. But if there are no impossible worlds, the 'possible' in 'possible world' is redundant, and no separate analysis is needed to pick out the worlds that are possible from the rest.

Let us, then, focus on the one and only task: analyzing the notion of world. To accomplish this task, it suffices to provide necessary and sufficient conditions for when two individuals are *worldmates*, are part of one and the same world. Lewis's proposal is this: individuals are *worldmates* if and only if they are spatiotemporally related to one another, that is, if and only if every part of one stands in some distance (or interval) relation – spatial, temporal, spatiotemporal – to every part of the other (Lewis 1986: 71). This leads immediately to the following analysis of the notion of world: a *world* is any maximal spatiotemporally interrelated individual – an individual all of whose parts are spatiotemporally related to one another, and that is not included in a larger individual all of whose parts are spatiotemporally related to one another. On this account, a world is *unified* by the spatiotemporal relations among its parts. If one further assumes with Lewis that being spatiotemporally related is an equivalence relation (reflexive, symmetric, and transitive), it follows that each individual belongs to exactly one world: the sum (or aggregate) of all those individuals that are spatio-temporally related to it. Now, the point to emphasize for present purposes is this: if Lewis's analysis is accepted, the notion of world has been characterized in non-modal terms, and the claim to eschew primitive modality has been vindicated.

The acceptability of Lewis's analysis of world hinges on the acceptability of his analysis of the worldmate relation. One direction of the analysis (sufficiency) is uncontroversial. Whatever stands at some spatiotemporal distance from us is part of our world; or, contrapositively, non-actual individuals stand at no spatiotemporal distance from us, or from anything actual. In general: every world is *spatiotemporally isolated* from every other world. According to the other direction of the analysis (necessity), worlds are unified *only* by spatiotemporal relations; every part of a world is spatiotemporally related to every other part of that world. This direction is more problematic, for at least three reasons. Although I believe Lewis's account needs to be modified to solve these problems, in each case the modification I would suggest does not require introducing primitive modality.

Phillip Bricker

First, couldn't there be worlds that are unified by relations that are not spatiotemporal? Indeed, it is controversial, even with respect to the actual world, whether entities in the quantum domain stand in anything like spatiotemporal relations to one another; the classic account of space-time may simply break down. I have defended elsewhere a solution that Lewis considered but (tentatively) rejected: individuals are *worldmates* if and only if they are *externally related* to one another, that is, if and only if there is a chain of perfectly natural relations (of any sort) extending from any part of one to any part of the other (Bricker 1996). This analysis quantifies over all perfectly natural relations rather than just the spatiotemporal relations, but it is none the worse for that with respect to primitive modality.

Second, isn't it possible for there to be disconnected space-times, so-called "island universes"? Couldn't there be a part of actuality spatiotemporally and causally isolated from the part we inhabit? Lewis must answer "no." When Lewis's analysis of world is combined with the standard analysis of possibility as truth at some world, island universes turn out to be impossible: at no world are there two disconnected space-times. But although Lewis rejects the possibility of island universes, he is uneasy, and for good reason: principles of recombination that Lewis seems to accept entail that island universes are possible after all.[16] Of course, if one took the worldmate relation to be primitive, one could simply posit as part of the theory that some worlds are composed of disconnected space-times. But that's no good. A primitive worldmate relation is primitive modality: what is possible – for example, the possibility of island universes – depends on how the worldmate relation is laid out in logical space. Is there a way to allow for the possibility of island universes without invoking primitive modality?

This time, I think, the best strategy is to amend the analysis of modality instead of the analysis of world. The modal operators should be taken to quantify over worlds *and pluralities of worlds.* For example, to be possible is to be true at some world, *or some plurality of worlds.* What is true at a plurality of worlds is, intuitively, what would be true if all the worlds in the plurality were actualized. If a plurality of two or more worlds were actualized, then actuality would include two or more disconnected parts; and so, on the amended analysis, island universes turn out to be possible.[17]

A third problem afflicts Lewisians who are also Platonists of a certain kind, namely, those who believe that in addition to the modal realm consisting of the isolated concrete worlds there is a mathematical realm consisting of isolated mathematical systems of abstract entities. Most Platonists (although not Lewis) believe in at least one such system: the pure sets, externally related to one another in virtue of the structure imposed by the membership relation. But I, for one, believe also in *sui generis* numbers, externally related to one another in virtue of the structure imposed by the successor relation, in *sui generis* Euclidean space, and much, much more. But, then, on the (amended) analysis of world being considered, the pure sets comprise a world, the natural numbers comprise a world, and so on for all the mathematical systems one believes in. That makes metaphysical possibility, which is analyzed as a quantifier over worlds, depend on what mathematical systems there are, and that seems wrong.[18] The Lewisian, then, needs to find a way to demarcate modal reality from mathematical reality, a way that that does not invoke primitive modality.

It might seem that the conditions (C1)–(C4) used to characterize what makes a world concrete could do the job. For the mathematical systems, one might hold, are abstract in virtue of violating (C4): they are not fully determinate; it is neither true nor false of numbers, for example, that they are red, or weigh ten grams. But that is not how I see it. Indeed, the pure sets, or *sui generis* numbers, or Euclidean points have no intrinsic qualitative nature, but not because they are somehow abstractions from something else.[19] Rather, they determinately fail to instantiate every qualitative property.[20] Their nature is purely relational, but it is no less determinate for that. But perhaps there is a simple fix. I think there is a fifth way in which entities can be said to be concrete: concrete entities have an intrinsic qualitative nature in virtue of instantiating, or having parts that instantiate, perfectly natural properties. This provides a fifth condition to be satisfied by the concrete worlds:

(C5)   A world is a sum of individuals, each of which instantiates at least one perfectly natural property.[21]

Incorporating (C5) into the analysis of world provides the needed distinction between the modal and the mathematical realm. And since the notion of a perfectly natural property is non-modal, we have not had to invoke primitive modality to do the job.

The elimination of primitive modality is a central goal of Lewisian approaches. To achieve this goal, the Lewisian must make a case for the following controversial claims. First, there is the claim that there exists a plurality of concrete worlds; that claim will be the focus of section 3. Second, there is the claim that the analysis of modality in terms of concrete worlds is materially and conceptually adequate; that claim will be put to the test in section 4 with respect to the analysis of actuality, and in section 5 with respect to the analysis of modality *de re*. Finally, there is the claim, noted above, that there are no impossible concrete worlds. That claim rests ultimately on a defense of classical logic, a topic too far afield to pursue further here.

3 Concrete Worlds Exist

Why believe in concrete worlds other than the actual world? Throughout his career, Lewis held to a broadly Quinean methodology for deciding questions of existence. Roughly, we are committed to the existence of those entities that are *quantified over* by the statements we take to be true.[22] And we should take those statements to be true that belong to the *best total theory*, where being "best" is in part a matter of being fruitful, simple, unified, economical, and of serving the needs of common sense, science, and systematic philosophy itself. What we should take to exist, then, is determined by criteria both holistic and pragmatic.

Early on, Lewis applied the Quinean methodology directly to statements we accept in ordinary language (Lewis 1973: 84). We accept, for example, not only that "things might be otherwise than they are," but also that "there are many ways things could have been besides the way they actually are." This latter statement quantifies explicitly over entities called "ways things could have been," entities that Lewis identifies with concrete possible worlds. But that identification is far from innocent. It was soon pointed out (in Stalnaker (1976)) that the phrase 'ways things could have been' seems to refer, if at all, to abstract entities – perhaps uninstantiated properties – not to concrete worlds. Indeed, it is doubtful that any statements we ordinarily accept quantify explicitly over concrete worlds.

In *On the Plurality of Worlds*, Lewis abandoned any attempt to apply the Quinean methodology directly to ordinary language, and applied it instead to systematic philosophy. Concrete worlds, if accepted, improve the unity and economy of philosophical theories by reducing the number of notions that must be taken as primitive. Moreover, concrete worlds provide, according to Lewis, a "paradise for philosophers" analogous to the way that *sets* have been said to provide a paradise for mathematicians (because, given the realm of sets, one has the wherewithal to provide true and adequate interpretations for all mathematical theories). Here Lewis has in mind not just the use of possible worlds to analyze modality, but also their use in constructing entities to play various theoretical roles, for example, the meanings of words and sentences in semantics and the contents of thought in cognitive psychology.[23] So, when asked "why believe in a plurality of worlds?" Lewis responds: "because the hypothesis is serviceable, and that is a reason to think that it is true" (Lewis 1986: 3).

Lewis does not claim, of course, that usefulness by itself is a decisive reason to believe: there may be hidden costs to accepting concrete worlds; there may be alternatives to concrete worlds that provide the same benefits without the costs. Lewis's defense of realism about concrete worlds, therefore, involves an extensive cost-benefit analysis. His conclusion is that, on balance, his realism defeats its rivals: rival theories that can provide the same benefits all have more serious costs. I will not attempt here to summarize Lewis's lengthy and intricate discussion.[24] But I will say something about the general idea that belief in concrete worlds can be given a pragmatic foundation, and I will ask whether an alternative foundation is feasible.

Lewis's argument for belief in concrete worlds depends on the assumption that we should believe pragmatically virtuous theories, theories that, on balance, are more fruitful, simple, unified, or economical than their rivals. Although this assumption is orthodoxy among contemporary analytic philosophers, I find it no less troubling for that. It is one thing for a theory to be pragmatically virtuous, to meet certain of our needs and desires; it seems quite another thing for the theory to be true. On what grounds are the pragmatic virtues taken to be a mark of the true? It is easy to see why we would desire our theories to be pragmatically virtuous: the virtues make for theories that are useful, productive, easy to comprehend and apply. But why think that reality conforms to *our* desire for simplicity, unity, and the other pragmatic virtues? Believing a theory true because it is pragmatically virtuous leads to *parochialism*, and seems scarcely more justified than, say, believing Ptolemaic astronomy true because it conforms to our desire to be located at the center of the universe. Such wishful thinking is no more rational in metaphysics than in science or everyday life.

But if we reject a pragmatic foundation for belief in concrete worlds, what is there to put in its place? My hope is that there are general metaphysical principles that support the existence of concrete worlds, and that we can just *see*, on reflection, that these principles are true. This "seeing" is done not with our eyes, of course, but with our mind, with a Cartesian faculty of rational insight. This faculty is fallible, to be sure, as are all human faculties. (*Contra* Descartes, I do not take the faculty to be invested with the imprimatur of an almighty deity.) But fallible or not, some such faculty is needed lest our claim to have a priori knowledge be bankrupt. Now, what general principles could play a foundational role for belief in a plurality of concrete worlds? I will consider, briefly, two lines of argument.

One way to argue for controversial ontology is to invoke a *truthmaker principle*: for every (positive) truth, there exists something that makes it true, some entity whose existence entails that truth.[25] Truths don't float free above the ontological fray. They must be grounded in some portion of reality. For example, *that Fido is a dog*, if true, has Fido himself as a truthmaker. (Assuming, as is customary, that an animal belongs to its species essentially.) *That some animals are dogs* has multiple truthmakers: each and every animal that is a dog. (On the other hand, a negative truth, such as *that no dog is a bird*, is made true by the lack of false-makers, by the non-existence of any dog that is a bird.) A more controversial case: *that there are infinitely many prime numbers*, I claim, is made true by the existence of the system of natural numbers. Mathematical truths have mathematical entities as truthmakers.

Consider now a (positive) modal truth such as *it is possible that there be unicorns*. What could be a truthmaker for this truth? Not any actual unicorn: there aren't any. Not actual ideas of unicorns, or other actual mental entities; for the possibility of unicorns doesn't depend on whether any mind has ever conceived of unicorns, or even whether any mind has ever existed. What then? To find the truthmakers for a statement, it helps to ask what the statement is *about*. *That unicorns are possible* appears to be about unicorns, if about anything at all. And, by the truthmaker principle, it is about *something*. But since there are no *actual* unicorns, that leaves only *merely possible* unicorns for it to be about: it has each and every possible unicorn as a truthmaker.

Thus baldly presented, the truthmaker argument for concrete *possibilia* may fail to convince. Indeed, the argument would need to be supplemented in at least two ways. First, even if one grants that modal truths require *possibilia* for truthmakers, why hold that the *possibilia* in question must be *concrete*? Perhaps abstract *possibilia* can meet the demand for truthmakers. Filling this gap in the argument, it seems, must wait on a decisive critique of all abstract accounts of *possibilia* – a tall order. Second, the truthmaker principle is often restricted to *contingent* truths, and for good reason. A *truthmaker* for a statement is an entity whose existence *entails* that statement. As entailment is ordinarily understood in terms of possible worlds, one statement *entails* a second just in case every world at which the first is true is a world at which the second is true. Thus understood, any statement entails a necessary truth, and so truthmaking for necessary truths becomes a trivial affair, devoid of ontological consequence. But the thesis that concrete worlds exist (with "exists" unrestricted) *is* a necessary truth. If the truthmaker principle is to apply to this thesis, truthmaking must be based on a more discriminating notion of entailment. It won't do to take this discriminating notion of entailment as primitive, lest the "no primitive modality" thesis be violated. So, some non-standard account of truthmaking in terms of worlds will need to be developed – no easy task.

Given these difficulties with the truthmaker argument for concrete *possibilia*, I find a different line of argument more promising, one that focuses on the nature of *intentionality.* Intentionality, in the relevant philosophical sense, refers to a feature of certain mental states such as belief and desire: these states are always "directed" toward some object or objects; one doesn't *just* believe or desire, one always believes or desires *something.*[26] That some of our mental states have this feature is something we know a priori by introspection. We know, that is, a general principle to the effect that mental states with this feature – "intentional states" – are *genuinely relational.* The second line of argument, then, is that this general principle can serve as foundation for belief in concrete possible objects and possible worlds. Concrete *possibilia* are needed to provide the objects of our intentional states, to provide an ontological framework for the content of our thought.

To illustrate how the argument might go, consider the intentional state of *thinking about* some object or objects. Suppose, for example, that I am now thinking about a dodecahedron made of solid gold. I can do this, of course, whether or not any such object actually exists. If there is, unbeknownst to me, an actual gold dodecahedron, then I am related to it in virtue of being in my current intentional state; it is an object of my thought. But what if there is no actual gold dodecahedron? Does that somehow prevent me from thinking about one? Of course not. In either case, I claim, *thinking about* is relational, and relations require *relata.* In the latter case, only merely possible gold dodecahedrons are available to be objects of my thought; I am related to possible but non-actual objects.

However, if the relationality of intentional states is to serve as a foundation for a Lewisian account of worlds, at least three further claims require support. First, the objects of thought, even when merely possible, must instantiate the same qualitative properties as actual objects of thought. Suppose again that a merely possible gold dodecahedron is an object of my thought. Does this object *instantiate* the property of being gold? Or is it an abstract object that somehow *represents* the property of being gold? I say the former. It is one thing to think about a gold dodecahedron, another thing to think about some abstract simulacrum thereof. If I am thinking about a gold dodecahedron and *thinking about* is genuinely relational, then there is a gold dodeca-hedron that I am thinking about. That it is made of gold and shaped like a dodeca-hedron is independent of whether it is actual or merely possible. Indeed, nothing prevents actual and merely possible objects from being perfect qualitative duplicates of one another.

But, second, more is needed if the objects of my thought are to count as concrete: they must not only instantiate qualitative properties, they must be fully determinate in all qualitative respects. How can that be? Intentional states such as *thinking about* do not seem to be determinate with respect to their objects. In thinking about a gold dodecahedron, I wasn't thinking about a gold dodecahedron of any particular size. Should I say, then, that I was related by my thought to an object that has no definite size? No. It is one thing to think indeterminately about a gold dodecahedron, another thing to think about an indeterminate object. The indeterminacy is in the thinking, not the object of thought. I am related by my thought to a multitude of possible gold dodecahedrons with a multitude of different, but fully determinate, sizes.[27]

But still more is needed if the argument is to support a Lewisian account: each concrete object of thought must be part of a fully determinate concrete world. In thinking about a gold dodecahedron, I wasn't thinking about how it is situated with respect to other objects. But that is just another aspect of the indeterminacy of my thought. Each possible gold dodecahedron has a determinate *extrinsic* nature; my thought doesn't discriminate between differently situated gold dodecahedra, and it therefore ranges indeterminately over them all. Perhaps, as I believe, there exists in logical space a solitary gold dodecahedron that is a world all by itself. But then distinguish: it is one thing to think about a *solitary* gold dodecahedron, another thing to think about a gold dodecahedron without considering how it relates to other objects. In the former case, what I am thinking about stands in no spatial or temporal relations to other objects; in the latter case, it is indeterminate whether what I am thinking about stands in spatial or temporal relations to other objects. In either case, the possible gold dodecahedra that are objects of my thought belong to fully determinate concrete worlds.

That, in barest outline, is how the relationality of thought could serve as foundation for a Lewisian account of concrete worlds. A thoroughgoing Quinean pragmatist would say, of course, that the thesis of the relationality of thought – or the truthmaker principle of the preceding argument, or any fundamental metaphysical principle – can support belief in concrete worlds only to the extent that *its* acceptance confers benefits on our total theory. But if I am right that the pragmatic virtues are never, in and of themselves, a mark of the true, then a "pragmatic foundation" is not to be had; indeed, it is a contradiction in terms. *Contra* what Lewis claims, that a belief is "serviceable" for the project of systematic philosophy provides no reason at all to hold it. Founding belief in concrete worlds instead on a (fallible) faculty of rational insight into matters metaphysical is controversial, to be sure, and in need of much development. But better a shaky foundation, I say, than no foundation at all.

4 Actuality is Indexical

Thus far, I have said very little about the notion of actuality. But some of the commitments of a Lewisian account are already clear. Since the Lewisian believes that merely possible worlds exist, she rejects the thesis that whatever exists is actual; that is to say, the Lewisian is a *possibilist*, not an *actualist*. Moreover, since the Lewisian believes that merely possible *concrete* worlds exist, she rejects any identification of the actual with the concrete. Furthermore, since the Lewisian holds that actual things have qualitative duplicates in merely possible worlds, actuality cannot itself be any sort of qualitative property. What, then, is it? In virtue of what do actual things differ from their merely possible counterparts? The Lewisian needs a positive account of actuality.

Lewis responds by proposing a deflationary account of actuality. The actual world and the merely possible worlds are ontologically all on a par; there is no fundamental, absolute property that actual things have and merely possible things lack. Nonetheless, I speak truly when I call my world and my worldmates "actual" because 'actual' just means 'thisworldly', or 'is part of my world'. For Lewis, 'actual' is an *indexical* term, like 'I' or 'here' or 'now'. What 'actual' applies to on a given use depends on features of the context of utterance, in particular, on the speaker, and the speaker's world. When I say of something that it is "actual," I say simply that it is part of *my* world;

when my otherworldly counterpart says of something that it is "actual," he says simply (if he is speaking English) that it is part of *his* world. I call my worldmates "actual" and my otherworldly counterparts "merely possible"; my counterpart calls his world-mates "actual" and me "merely possible." And we all speak truly, just as many people in different locations all speak truly when each says, "I am here." For Lewis, being actual or merely possible does not mark any ontological distinction between me and my counterparts because – as with being here or being there – there is no ontological distinction to be marked.

What sort of property is expressed by a given use of 'actual' on Lewis's account? When Lewis's indexical analysis of actuality is combined with his analysis of world, we get that, in any context, 'actual' expresses the property of being spatiotemporally related to the speaker in that context. Thus, in any context, the property expressed by 'actual' is a *relative* property, a property things have in virtue of their relations to things, not in virtue of how they are in themselves. That makes actuality, on Lewis's account, *doubly* relative: what property is expressed by a given use of 'actual' is relative to the speaker; and the property thus expressed is itself a relative property.

Lewis's indexical account conflicts rather severely with our ordinary way of thinking about actuality. As Robert Adams vividly put it: "We do not think the difference in respect of actuality between Henry Kissinger and the Wizard of Oz is just a difference in their relations to us" (Adams 1974: 215). According to Lewis, however, a believer in concrete worlds has no choice but to accept an indexical analysis of actuality according to which actuality is doubly relative. For, Lewis argues, if my use of 'actual' instead expressed an absolute property that I have and my otherworldly counterparts lack, then no account could be given of how I know that I am actual. I have counterparts in other worlds that are epistemically situated exactly as I am; whatever evidence I have for believing that *I* have the supposed absolute property of actuality, they have exactly similar evidence for believing that *they* have the property. But if no evidence distinguishes my predicament from theirs, then I don't really *know* that I am not in their predicament: for all I know, I am a merely possible person falsely believing myself to be absolutely actual. Thus, Lewis concludes, accepting concrete worlds together with absolute actuality leads to skepticism about whether one is actual. Since such skepticism is absurd, a believer in concrete worlds should reject absolute actuality.[28]

Lewis's indexical account makes short work of the skeptical problem, and that is an argument in its favor. On Lewis's analysis, 'I am actual' is a trivial analytic truth analogous to 'I am here'. Just as it makes no sense for me to wonder whether I am here (because 'here' just means 'the place I am at'), so it makes no sense for me to wonder whether I am actual (because 'actual' just means, according to Lewis, 'part of the world I am part of'). Moreover, my otherworldly counterparts have no more trouble knowing whether they are actual than I do. When one of my counterparts says, "I am actual," he speaks truly (if he is speaking English), and he knows this simply in virtue of knowing that he is part of the world he is part of. Thus, Lewis can explain why it strikes us as absurd for someone to wonder whether or not she is actual.

Is Lewis correct, however, that a believer in concrete worlds has no choice but to reject absolute actuality? I hope not. I, for one, could not endorse the thesis of a plurality of concrete worlds if I did not hold that there was a fundamental ontological distinction between the actual and the merely possible. A Lewisian approach to modality that rejects absolute actuality does not seem to me to be tenable. Actuality, I claim, is a *categorial* notion: whatever belongs to the same fundamental ontological category as something actual is itself actual. When Lewis insists, then, that all worlds are ontologically on a par, this can only be understood as saying that all worlds are equally actual – his denials notwithstanding. But that undercuts Lewis's defense of concrete worlds: an analysis of modality as quantification over concrete parts of actuality, no matter how extensive actuality may be, is surely mistaken.[29]

A way to test whether actuality is absolute or merely relative is to ask whether it is coherent to suppose that actuality is composed of island universes: parts that stand in no spatiotemporal (or other external) relations to one another. If actuality is absolute, the hypothesis of island universes is coherent: something could be actual even though entirely disconnected from the part of actuality we inhabit. But if actuality is merely relative, as Lewis supposes, then the hypothesis of island universes is analytically false – and that seems wrong. Nor would it help for Lewis to switch to the amended analysis of possibility suggested in section 2: that analysis would make the hypothesis of island universes metaphysically possible – true at some plurality of worlds; but the hypothesis would remain analytically false of (what Lewis calls) actuality. Accepting that combination compounds the problem, rather than solving it.

Fortunately, I think a Lewisian can accept absolute actuality without falling victim to the skeptical problem. To see how, we first need to distinguish, for any predicate, the *concept* associated with the predicate from the *property* expressed by a given use of that predicate. The concept associated with a predicate is naturally identified with its meaning. It embodies a rule that determines, for each context of use, what property is expressed by the predicate in that context. A predicate is *indexical* if it expresses different properties relative to different contexts of use; in that case, the associated concept can also be called indexical. Indexicality is one kind of relativity: relativity to features of context. But that sort of relativity must be distinguished from the relativity of the property expressed. Lewis's argument against absolute actuality presupposes that these two sorts of relativity must go together, that any indexical analysis of actuality will be *doubly* relative. But that assumption, I think, is mistaken. Indexical concepts can be associated with predicates that express either relative or absolute properties.

For example, consider the indexical predicate 'is a neighbor'. On different occasions of use, it expresses different properties. When I use the predicate, it expresses the property of being one of *my* neighbors; when you use the predicate, it expresses the property of being one of *your* neighbors. On any use, the property expressed is a *relative* property: whether a person has the property expressed depends on that person's relations to the speaker. Other indexical predicates, however, express absolute properties on each occasion of use. For example, the indexical predicate 'is nutritious' expresses different properties relative to different speakers (depending on age, or state of health). But, on each use, the property expressed is absolute, not relative: something is nutritious (for the speaker) in virtue of its chemical nature, not in virtue of its relative properties; if two things are chemical duplicates of one another, then either both or neither are nutritious (for the speaker).

Now, on Lewis's analysis of actuality, the concept associated with the predicate 'is actual' is indexical, and the property expressed by the predicate, on each context of use, is relative. It is the indexicality of the concept that allows for a solution to the skeptical problem. It is the relativity of the property that leads, I have claimed, to an untenable position. Is there a way of analyzing actuality so that the concept is indexical but the property is absolute? Consider this: 'is actual' in my mouth expresses the property, "belonging to the same fundamental ontological category as me." That builds the categorial nature of actuality directly into the analysis. But, thanks to the indexical component, it makes short work of the skeptical problem. On this analysis, I know that I am actual simply in virtue of knowing that I belong to the same ontological category as myself. Knowledge that I am actual is just as trivial as on Lewis's analysis of actuality, as it should be, but the property of actuality remains ontologically robust.[30]

Lewis would no doubt object that a theory of concrete worlds with absolute actuality is less parsimonious than his own. Granted. What matters, however, is which theory gets it right. If actuality is a categorial notion, as I believe, then Lewis's indexical theory must be rejected. Lewis would also, I suspect, object that the notion of absolute actuality is mysterious. Perhaps. (It is not, however, the mystery of primitive modality: absolute actuality is no more primitive modality than is absolute truth.) It does not help our understanding, for example, to say that merely possible entities are "less real" than actual entities: both merely possible and actual entities *exist*, and I do not understand how existence could be a matter of degree. Nor does it help to say that actual and merely possible entities exist *in different ways*, that there are two *modes* of existence: if that means anything at all, it just means that there are two fundamental ontological categories. The best inroad to understanding the distinction between the actual and the merely possible, I would say, comes from considering how we and our surroundings differ from what exists merely as an object of our thought.

Lewis himself allows that there are entities of distinct ontological categories: individuals and sets. The distinction between an individual and its singleton is arguably no less mysterious than the distinction between an actual thing and its merely possible qualitative duplicates. In the case of sets, Lewis embraces the mystery.[31] Why not also, in the case of *possibilia*, embrace the mystery of absolute actuality? The answer turns on whether concrete talking donkeys and flying pigs are any easier to believe in if they belong to a different ontological category than actual donkeys and pigs. I leave that to the reader to ponder.

5 Modality *De Re* and Counterparts

It is traditional to divide modal statements into two sorts: *de dicto* and *de re*. A modal statement is *de dicto*, it is sometimes said, if the modal operator applies to a *proposition* (Latin: *dictum*); it is *de re* if the modal operator applies to a property to form a modal property, which is then attributed to some *thing* (Latin: *res*). Thus, 'necessarily, all birds are feathered' is *de dicto*; 'Polly is necessarily feathered' is *de re*. The traditional characterization, however, is defective in a number of ways. For one thing, equivalent statements are not always classified alike. Indeed, any *de dicto* modal statement is equivalent to a statement attributing a modal property to the (actual) world. Thus, 'necessarily, all birds are feathered' is equivalent to 'the world is necessarily such that all birds are feathered', which the above criterion classifies as *de re*. Moreover, a *de re* modal statement such as, 'Polly is necessarily feathered' is equivalent to 'necessarily, Polly is feathered' (or, perhaps, 'necessarily, if Polly exists, Polly is feathered'), which the above criterion classifies as *de dicto*. Another defect of the traditional characterization is that it fails to provide an exhaustive classification of modal statements: modal statements with a complicated structure will not be classified either as *de dicto* or *de re*.

A better way to characterize the *de dicto/de re* distinction looks to the *content* of modal statements, rather than their *form*. Here is the rough idea, neutrally expressed so as to apply to Lewisians and non-Lewisians alike. All possible worlds theorists will have to provide an account of how *truth at* a world is to be determined, how a world *represents* that things are one way or another. Part of any such account will involve providing for each world a *domain* of entities – the entities that in some primary sense "inhabit" the world – and saying, for each entity in a world's domain, what properties it has at the world. Any such account will also have to say how it is determined, when an entity is picked out as belonging to the domain of one world, whether the entity exists at some *other* world, and what properties it has at this other world. Call this "crossworld representation *de re*." Now, what makes a modal statement *de re* is that in the course of evaluating its truth or falsity, one must have recourse to facts about crossworld representation *de re*. A modal statement is *de dicto*, on the other hand, if no recourse to crossworld representation *de re* is needed to evaluate its truth or falsity. To illustrate with a standard example: compare the *de re* 'everything is necessarily material' with the *de dicto* 'necessarily, everything is material'. The former statement depends on crossworld representation *de re*: it says that every entity in the domain of the actual world is material, not only at the actual world, but at every possible world (better: at every possible world *at which it exists*). The latter statement does not depend on crossworld representation *de re*: it says that at every possible world, everything in the domain of *that world* is material. These two statements are not equivalent. The *de dicto* statement is made false by a possible world whose domain contains a non-material object; but if that possible world doesn't represent *de re* concerning any actual object that it is non-material, then the *de re* statement may still be true.

How is crossworld representation *de re* determined? The simplest answer, of course, would be this: an entity picked out as belonging to the domain of one world exists at some other world just in case it also belongs to the domain of that other world. On this account, the domains of different worlds overlap, and all facts about what properties an entity has at a world are given directly by how that world represents that entity to be. To *exist* at a world is just to belong to the domain of that world. I will say, following standard though somewhat misleading usage, that such an account endorses "transworld identity." To illustrate, consider George W. Bush. On the transworld identity theory, Bush belongs not only to the actual domain, but also to the domain of many merely possible worlds. Some of these worlds represent him as having properties he doesn't actually have, such as losing the presidential election in 2004, or being a plumber.

The Lewisian, however, needs a different account of crossworld representation *de re*. For the Lewisian, each world has as its domain just the entities that are part of the world. Bush is part of the actual world, and is in the actual domain. But since worlds do not overlap, Bush is not in the domain of any merely possible world. How, then, does a merely possible world represent Bush as existing and having properties he doesn't actually have? Lewis responds: by having in its domain a *counterpart* of Bush. A merely possible world represents *de re* concerning Bush that he exists and, say, is a plumber by containing a counterpart of Bush that is a plumber. So, for the Lewisian, *existing at a world* must be distinguished from *being in the domain of a world*: Bush exists at many worlds, although he is in the domain of – is part of – only one. Because Bush exists at many worlds, the Lewisian can be said to accept "transworld identity" in a weak, uncontroversial sense; but not in the stronger sense that requires overlapping domains.

What makes an entity in one world a counterpart of an entity in another? According to Lewis, the counterpart relation is a relation of qualitative similarity. He writes:

> Something has for *counterparts* at a given world those things existing there that resemble it closely enough in important respects of intrinsic quality and extrinsic relations, and that resemble it no less closely than do other things existing there. Ordinarily something will have one counterpart or none at a world, but ties in similarity may give it multiple counterparts. (Lewis 1973: 39)

With a counterpart relation in place, *de re* modal statements can be analyzed in terms of concrete worlds and their parts. For example, to consider the simplest cases: 'Bush is possibly a plumber' is true just in case at some world some counterpart of Bush is a plumber; 'Bush is necessarily (or essentially) human' is true just in case at every world every counterpart of Bush is human.[32] For the Lewisian, we have a simple way of distinguishing *de re* from *de dicto*: *de re* modal statements depend for their evaluation on the counterpart relation; *de dicto* modal statements do not.

Whether one is a Lewisian or not, there are good reasons to prefer counterpart relations to transworld identity as an account of representation *de re*. I have space here to consider just one such reason, namely, that only counterpart relations can allow for essences that are moderately, without being excessively, tolerant.[33] Let me explain. Modality *de re* is the realm of essence and accident. A property had by an individual is *essential* to the individual if that individual couldn't exist without the property; it is *accidental* if it is not essential. An individual's *essence* is the sum of all its essential properties. These notions will be translated into the framework of the counterpart theorist and the transworld identity theorist in different ways. For the counterpart theorist, an essential property of an individual is a property had by the individual and all of its counterparts. For the transworld identity theorist, an essential property of an individual is a property had by the individual itself at every world at which it exists. These two accounts come apart if the counterpart relation does not have the logical properties of identity, such as transitivity.[34] When they come apart, the counterpart theorist enjoys a flexibility that the transworld identity theorist cannot match. In particular, only a counterpart theorist can allow that an individual could have been *somewhat* different, say, with respect to its material composition or its origins, but could not have been *wildly* different. The transworld identity theorist will have to hold that essential properties are either not tolerant at all (with respect to material composition, or origins) or excessively tolerant; moderation will have to be abandoned. And that, in many cases, will lead to the wrong truth conditions for *de re* modal statements.

To illustrate the problem of moderately tolerant essences, consider the following simple, though somewhat implausible, example. Suppose that it is essential to any person to have *at least one* of the (biological) parents he or she in fact has, but that it is not essential to have *both*. Thus, I could have had a different mother, and I could have had a different father, but I couldn't have had *both* a different mother *and* a different father. My essence, then, is moderately tolerant with respect to my origins. Now, if representation *de re* works by transworld identity, an essence such as this leads to contradiction. Call my mother *m* and my father *f*. Since my essence is (moderately) tolerant, I could have had a different father and the same mother. So there is a world *w* and a person *p* existing at *w* such that $p = $ me and *p* has father f' ($\neq f$) and *p* has mother *m*. But now, since *p*'s essence is (moderately) tolerant, *p* could have had a different *mother* and the same *father*. So there is a world w' and a person p' existing at w' such that $p' = p$ and p' has mother m' ($\neq m$) and p' has father f'. But if $p' = p$ and $p = $ me, then $p' = $ me (by the transitivity of identity). So, at w' I exist and my father is f' and my mother is m'. I could have had both a different father and a different mother after all, which contradicts the supposition that my essence is *moderately* tolerant.

What to do? It would not be plausible, I think, to deny that individual essences can be moderately tolerant. A better solution is to switch to counterpart theory. If representation *de re* works by counterpart relations instead of transworld identity, then moderately tolerant essences are unassailable. A counterpart relation is based (at least in part) on qualitative similarity, and relations of similarity are not in general transitive. For the example at hand, the counterpart theorist will simply say that although *p* is a counterpart of me and p' is a counterpart of *p*, p' is not a counterpart of me. Thus, the counterpart theorist is not driven to assert that I could have had both a different mother and a different father, and no contradiction can be derived.[35]

So much in favor of counterpart theory; now for something on the other side. Many philosophers have argued, the theoretical benefits of counterpart theory notwithstanding, that counterpart theory provides unacceptable truth conditions for *de re* modal statements. If Lewisian realism is committed to counterpart theory, they say, so much the worse for Lewisian realism. I will briefly consider two of the most common lines of attack, both of which can be traced to Saul Kripke's influential discussion of counterpart theory in *Naming and Necessity*.[36] For the first line of attack, consider Kripke's complaint that according to counterpart theory:

> [I]f we say "Humphrey might have won the election (if only he had done such-and-such)," we are not talking about something that might have happened to *Humphrey*, but to someone else, a 'counterpart'. Probably, however, Humphrey could not care less whether someone *else*, no matter how much resembling him, would have been victorious in another possible world. (Kripke 1980: 45)

Kripke's objection naturally falls into two parts. The first part is that, on the analysis of modality *de re* provided by counterpart theory, the modal property, *might have won the election*, is attributed to Humphrey's *counterpart* rather than to Humphrey himself.

But surely, the objection continues, when we say that "Humphrey might have won," we mean to say something about *Humphrey*. This part of the objection, however, is easily answered. According to counterpart theory, Humphrey himself has the modal property, *might have won the election*, in virtue of his counterpart having the (non-modal) property, *won the election*. Moreover, that Humphrey has a winning counterpart is a matter of the qualitative character of Humphrey and his surroundings; so on the counterpart theoretic analysis, the modal statement is indeed a claim about Humphrey.

The second part of Kripke's objection is more troublesome. We have a strong intuition, not only that the modal statement, "Humphrey might have won the election," is about Humphrey, but that it is *only* about Humphrey (and his surroundings). On counterpart theory, however, the modal statement is also about a merely possible person in some merely possible world; and that, Kripke might say, is simply not what we take the modal statement to mean. The first thing to say in response is that the charge of unintuitiveness would apply equally to any theory that uses abstract worlds to provide truth conditions for modal statements; for our intuitive understanding of modal statements such as "Humphrey might have won the election" does not *seem* to invoke abstract worlds any more than counterparts of Humphrey. The objection, then, if it is good, would seem to cut equally against all possible worlds approaches to modality; if anything, it would favor a non-realist approach that rejects possible worlds, concrete or abstract. But is the objection good? Should our pre-theoretic intuitions as to what our statements are and are not *about* carry much, or even any, weight? I think not. A philosophical analysis of our ordinary modal statements must assign the right truth values and validate the right inferences; moreover, it must be able to withstand mature philosophical reflection. But requiring that philosophical analyses match all our pre-theoretic intuitions would make systematic philosophy all but impossible.

The second line of attack on counterpart theory I want to consider also has its origin in Kripke's *Naming and Necessity*; but I will present the argument in the way I find most effective, even though it may not coincide with Kripke's intentions. The argument begins with the observation that we often simply *stipulate* that we are considering a possibility for some given actual individual. For example, we can simply say: consider a possible world at which Bush lost the election in 2004. In doing so, we consider a possible world that represents *de re* concerning Bush that he lost. Of course, such stipulation cannot run afoul of Bush's essential properties: we cannot stipulate that a world represents *de re* concerning Bush that he is a poached egg if Bush is essentially human. The point, rather, is that such stipulation may be legitimate even if no loser at the world in question can be singled out as qualitatively most similar to Bush. But then, the argument concludes, representation *de re* cannot be based (entirely) on relations of qualitative similarity. If counterpart relations are relations of qualitative similarity, as Lewis asserts, then counterpart theory must be rejected.

To illustrate the argument, consider the possibility that I have an identical twin. It seems coherent to suppose that, in the possibility being considered, neither I nor my twin is qualitatively more similar to the way I actually am than is the other. Nonetheless, in the possibility being considered, I am one of the twins and not the other; indeed, we can stipulate that I am the first-born twin. How can the Lewisian account for such a possibility? It seems that the Lewisian has to hold that there is a possible world that represents *de re* concerning me that I am the first-born twin without representing *de re* concerning me that I am the second-born twin. But if representation *de re* works by counterpart relations, that would seem to be impossible. Both twins are equally good candidates to be my counterpart, if the counterpart relation is a relation of qualitative similarity.

A Lewisian has the following perfectly adequate response. If counterpart relations are relations of qualitative similarity, then indeed each twin is a counterpart of me at the world in question. Given that, the world can only represent *de re* concerning me that I am the first-born twin if it *also* represents *de re* concerning me that I am the second-born twin, lest representation *de re* not be determined by counterpart relations. But the Lewisian can allow that the one world represents two distinct possibilities for me: it represents *de re* concerning me that I am the first born of two identical twins in virtue of containing a counterpart of me that is a first-born identical twin; but it *also* represents *de re* concerning me that I am the second born of two identical twins in virtue of containing a counterpart of me that is the second born. In this way, all the facts of crossworld representation *de re* still depend only on the one qualitative counterpart relation; but when there are multiple counterparts at a world, multiple possibilities are represented within a single world.[37]

There is another sort of example involving stipulation *de re*, however, that the above response does nothing to accommodate. Not only can we stipulate that we are considering a possibility that involves a given individual, we can also stipulate that we are considering a possibility that *does not* involve a given individual. And, with this sort of stipulation, there do not seem to be any qualitative constraints. Indeed, it is perfectly legitimate to say: consider a possibility qualitatively indiscernible from actuality but in which I do not exist. In the possibility envisaged, I have a doppelganger, a person exactly like me in every qualitative respect, intrinsic and extrinsic; but that person isn't *me*. I find this intuition compelling, and think that any account of modality *de re* must find a way to accommodate it. But now the counterpart theorist is in trouble if counterpart relations are relations of qualitative similarity. If the possibility in question is represented by some non-actual world qualitatively indiscernible from the actual world, then an inhabitant of that non-actual world is qualitatively indiscernible from me without being my counterpart. If the possibility in question is instead somehow represented by the actual world, then there would have to be a counterpart relation under which I am not a counterpart of myself. Either way, the Lewisian would have to reject the idea that counterpart relations are (always) relations of qualitative similarity. So be it. That is a retreat from Lewis's original understanding of counterpart theory, but it is by no means a defeat for the Lewisian. Counterpart theory, first and foremost, is a semantic theory for providing truth conditions for *de re* modal statements. As such, it should adapt to those *de re* modal statements we take to be true. As long as this is accomplished in a way that doesn't compromise the metaphysics of Lewisian realism, nothing of value is lost.[38]

6 Conclusion

When Lewis first began advocating the thesis that there exists a plurality of concrete worlds, he received in response mostly "incredulous stares." That soon changed. Over the ensuing years, arguments for and against Lewisian realism have filled philosophical books and journals. Lewisians have had to develop and revise their position in the light of powerful criticism; non-Lewisian alternatives have sprouted like weeds in the philosophical landscape. The debate goes on; as with other metaphysical debates, a decisive outcome is not to be expected. And through it all, the incredulous stares remain: Lewisian realism does disagree sharply, as Lewis himself concedes (Lewis 1986: 133), with common-sense opinion as to what there is. There seems to be a fundamental rift – unbridgeable by argument – between ontologically conservative philosophers who have, what Bertrand Russell called, "a robust sense of reality," and ontologically liberal philosophers who respond, echoing Hamlet: "there is more on heaven and earth than is dreamt of in your philosophy." No doubt, the Lewisian approach to modality will always be a minority view. But the power and elegance of the Lewisian approach has been widely appreciated by philosophers of all stripes. The bar is set high for the assessment of alternative views.

Notes

1 The fullest statement of Lewis's theory of possible worlds is contained in his *magnum opus*, *On the Plurality of Worlds* (1986). Lewis's view is sometimes called "modal realism."

2 Historically, it was the attempt to provide semantics for modal logic that catapulted possible worlds to the forefront of analytic philosophy. The *locus classicus* is Kripke (1963).

3 The *locus classicus* of the eliminative approach to modality is "Reference and Modality" in Quine (1953).

4 Of course, there is much more to modality than statements of (metaphysical) possibility and necessity. But the project of paraphrasing more complex modal locutions in terms of possible worlds has also met with considerable success.

5 For a discussion of the four ways, see Lewis (1986: 81–6).

6 An object is *fully determinate* if and only if, for any property, either the property or its negation holds of the object. In the case of worlds, this is equivalent to: for any proposition, either the proposition or its negation is true at the world.

7 Because logical relations between propositions can be represented by relations between classes of worlds; for example, one proposition *logically implies* another just in case the class of worlds at which the one is true is included in the class of worlds at which the other is true. But see note 18.

8 The analysis of modality *de re* in terms of counterpart relations was first introduced in Lewis (1968).

9 What it means for the *concept* of actuality to be indexical, and how that relates to whether the *property* of actuality is relative or absolute, is discussed in section 4.

10 See Lewis's discussion of "magical ersatzism" (1986: 174–82).

11 I use 'ideology' roughly in Quine's sense; see Quine (1953: 130–2). But I do not suppose our total theory is couched in first-order predicate logic. Thus, all primitive terms of the language contribute to the ideology, not just the primitive predicates.

12 The perfectly natural properties make for intrinsic qualitative character; the perfectly natural relations are the fundamental ties that bind together the parts of worlds. (See also note 20.) For discussion of the notion of a perfectly natural property, and a defense of its legitimacy, see Lewis (1986: 59–69).

13 Lewis (1986: 75–6) sketches such an analysis. (He calls them the "analogical spatiotemporal relations," but I drop the 'analogical'.)

14 For (a version of) the argument that Lewisian analyses of modality are circular, see McGinn (2000: 69–74). For a response, see Bricker (2004).

15 Lewis's brief argument for this occurs in a footnote in Lewis (1986: 7). For further discussion, see Stalnaker (1996). Of course, the argument presupposes classical logic, that our total theory satisfies the law of non-contradiction. For a non-classical approach to contradictions, see Priest (1998).

16 For example, according to one such principle, for any individual, simple or composite, it is possible that a duplicate of that individual exist all by itself. Applying this principle to a disconnected sum leads to the possibility of island universes. See Bricker (2001: 35–7) for detailed argument. Lewis (1986) does not explicitly accept any principle this strong; but Langton and Lewis (1998: 341) accept such a principle, and claim that it is part of the combinatorial theory put forth in Lewis (1986).

17 This view is presented and defended in Bricker (2001). Note that, on this approach, if island universes *actually* exist, then there is more than one actual world. But I will continue to speak of *the* actual world for ease of presentation.

18 Note that on a view that accepts mathematical systems alongside the concrete worlds, it is natural to distinguish between logical, metaphysical, and mathematical modality. Logical modality is absolute modality: it quantifies over concrete worlds and abstract systems both. Metaphysical and mathematical modality are both restricted modality, quantifying over just the concrete worlds or just the mathematical systems, respectively. The term 'logical space' is now best used to refer to mathematical and modal reality together, not just modal reality.

19 I do not accept that there are any entities that are abstract in virtue of violating (C4). There is a mental operation of abstraction, which involves ignoring some features and attending to others; and we can represent the results of this mental procedure, if we want, by using set-theoretic constructions in ways made familiar by mathematicians. But, in my view, there are no "indeterminate objects."

20 A property is *qualitative* (in the narrow sense) if its instantiation does not depend on the existence of any particular object, but does depend on the instantiation of some perfectly natural property. (The broad sense drops the second clause.) Every object *a* instantiates the non-qualitative property: *being identical with a*. Every natural number other than zero instantiates the non-qualitative (structural) property: *being the successor of something*. I suppose that the perfectly natural properties are all qualitative, and that the qualitative properties supervene on the perfectly natural properties and relations. All qualitative properties are categorical, but not conversely.

21 This "simple fix" presupposes that material objects can be *identified* with regions of space-time. That is, it presupposes that worlds do not divide into two distinct domains: an immaterial space-time, and material objects that occupy regions of space-time. On the "dualist" view, the immaterial space-time regions, arguably, would not instantiate any perfectly natural properties.

22 Or, in Quine's slogan: "To be is to be the value of a variable." That is to say, we are ontologically committed to those entities that belong to the domain over which the variables of our quantifiers range. See Quine (1953: 13).

23 Lewis (1986: 5–69) surveys some of the uses to which possible worlds have been put in systematic philosophy. Lewis's *oeuvre* taken altogether provides a monumental testament to the fruitfulness of possible worlds.

24 Chapter 2 of Lewis (1986) argues that the cost of accepting concrete worlds is manageable by responding to eight objections from the literature; chapter 3 argues that rival views that take worlds to be abstract entities all have serious objections. For summaries of some of these arguments, see Bricker (2006a).

25   For an introduction to truthmaking, see Armstrong (2004). For reasons to accept only a weak truthmaker principle that applies to positive truths, see Lewis (2001).

26   For an introduction to the logical and metaphysical issues raised by this notion of intentionality, see Priest (2005).

27   We can call on the method of *supervaluations* to explain why I can truly say that there is one thing that I am thinking about: a dodecahedron made of solid gold. See Lewis (1993).

28   Lewis (1970) first introduced his indexical theory of actuality and invoked the skeptical argument to support it. See also Lewis (1986: 92–6).

29   As Lewis himself concedes: "if the other worlds would be just parts of actuality, modal realism [Lewis's brand of realism about possible worlds] is kaput" (1986: 112).

30   For a detailed attempt to develop an alternative indexical analysis of actuality on which actuality is absolute, see Bricker (2006b).

31   See Lewis (1991), especially pp. 29–35 on "mysterious singletons."

32   Not all *de re* modal attribution follows this pattern. For example, 'Bush necessarily exists' should be analyzed as the falsehood, 'at every world there is some counterpart of Bush', not the trivial truth, 'at every world every counterpart of Bush exists'. For discussion, see Lewis (1986: 8–13).

33   Two other important arguments supporting counterpart theory are the following. (1) *Contingent Identity Statements*. Only counterpart theory allows one to hold, for example, that a statue is identical with the lump of clay from which it is made, even though one can truly say: "that statue might have existed and not been identical with that lump of clay." (2) *Inconstancy of Representation De Re*. Only counterpart theory allows one to hold, in accordance with ordinary practice, that attributions of essential properties may vary from context to context. In both of these cases, the counterpart theorist introduces multiple counterpart relations to achieve the desired result. See Lewis (1986: 248–59).

34   A relation is *transitive* if and only if whenever one thing bears the relation to a second, and the second bears the relation to a third, then the first bears the relation to the third.

35   The problem of moderately tolerant essences was first introduced in Chisholm (1967). The counterpart-theoretic solution is discussed in Lewis (1986: 227–35).

36   See Kripke (1980: 44–53). For other well-known objections to counterpart theory, see Plantinga (1973).

37   Lewis (1986: 243–8) presents and defends this response.

38   Anti-Haecceitism – the view that representation *de re* supervenes on qualitative features of worlds (in the broad sense) – is arguably an essential component of the metaphysics of Lewisian realism. But the Lewisian need not abandon anti-Haecceitism to accommodate the possibility that things could be qualitatively the same as they actually are and yet nothing actual exist. The Lewisian can say that the actual world represents this possibility with respect to a counterpart relation under which nothing is a counterpart of anything. Although, *contra* Lewis, this counterpart relation is not a relation of qualitative *similarity*, it is nonetheless *qualitative* (in the broad sense): it does not distinguish between qualitative indiscernibles. See Lewis (1986: 220–35) for his characterization and defense of anti-Haecceitism.

References

Adams, Robert. 1974. "Theories of Actuality," *Nous* 8: 211–31. Repr. in Loux (1979).

Armstrong, D. M. 2004. *Truth and Truthmakers* (Cambridge: Cambridge University Press).

Bricker, Phillip. 1996. "Isolation and Unification: The Realist Analysis of Possible Worlds," *Philosophical Studies* 84: 225–38.

—. 2001. "Island Universes and the Analysis of Modality," in Gerhard Preyer and Frank Siebelt, eds., *Reality and Humean Supervenience: Essays on the Philosophy of David Lewis* (Lanham, MD: Rowman and Littlefield).

—. 2004. "McGinn on Non-Existent Objects and Reducing Modality," *Philosophical Studies* 118: 439-51.

—. 2006a. "David Lewis: On the Plurality of Worlds," in John Shand, ed., *Central Works of Philosophy.* Volume 5: *The Twentieth Century: Quine and After* (Chesham: Acumen).

—. 2006b. "Absolute Actuality and the Plurality of Worlds," in John Hawthorne, ed., *Philosophical Perspectives 2006, Metaphysics* (Oxford: Blackwell).

Chisholm, Roderick. 1967. "Identity Through Possible Worlds: Some Questions," *Nous* 1: 1-8. Repr. in Loux (1979).

Kripke, Saul. 1963. "Semantical Considerations on Modal Logic," *Acta Philosophical Fennica* 16: 83-93.

—. 1980. *Naming and Necessity* (Cambridge, MA: Harvard University Press).

Langton, Rae, and Lewis, David. 1998. "Defining 'Intrinsic'," *Philosophy and Phenomenological Research* 58: 333-45.

Lewis, David. 1968. "Counterpart Theory and Quantified Modal Logic," *Journal of Philosophy* 65: 113-26. Repr. in Loux (1979).

—. 1970. "Anselm and Actuality," *Nous* 4: 175-88.

—. 1973. *Counterfactuals* (Oxford: Basil Blackwell).

—. 1986. *On the Plurality of Worlds* (Oxford: Basil Blackwell).

—. 1991. *Parts of Classes* (Oxford: Basil Blackwell).

—. 1993. "Many, But Almost One," in Keith Campbell, John Bacon, and Lloyd Reinhardt, eds., *Ontology, Causality, and Mind: Essays on the Philosophy of D. M. Armstrong* (Cambridge: Cambridge University Press).

—. 2001. "Truthmaking and Difference-Making," *Nous* 35: 602-15.

Loux, Michael. ed. 1979. *The Possible and the Actual: Readings in the Metaphysics of Modality* (Ithaca, NY: Cornell University Press).

McGinn, Colin. 2000. *Logical Properties: Identity, Existence, Predication, Necessity, Truth* (Oxford: Oxford University Press).

Plantinga, Alvin. 1973. "Transworld Identity or Worldbound Individuals?" in Milton Munitz, ed., *Logic and Ontology* (New York: New York University Press). Repr. in Loux (1979).

Priest, Graham. 1998. "What is So Bad About Contradictions?" *Journal of Philosophy* 95: 410-26.

—. 2005. *Towards Non-Being: The Logic and Metaphysics of Intentionality* (Oxford: Oxford University Press).

Quine, Willard Van Orman. 1953. *From a Logical Point of View* (Cambridge, MA: Harvard University Press).

Stalnaker, Robert. 1976. "Possible Worlds," *Nous* 10: 65-75. Repr. in Loux (1979).

—. 1996. "Impossibilities," *Philosophical Topics* 24: 193-204.

Ersatz Possible Worlds

Joseph Melia

1 Introduction

The philosophical benefits that possible worlds offer are rich indeed. Everyday modal statements such as 'there are many different ways the world could have been' can be taken at face value, as talking about possible worlds other than the actual one. A wide range of modal concepts can be analyzed in terms of possible worlds in a logic that is familiar and well understood. Problematic and capricious *de re* modal statements can be tamed and understood. Physical necessity, deontic obligation, and other strengths of modality can be given unifying analyses in terms of possible worlds. Previously unanswerable questions about modal validity can be resolved. Once obscure intensional logics can be given a possible worlds model theory, and completeness and soundness results will have genuine philosophical significance.[1] Unifying ontological reductions – *propositions* as sets of possible worlds, *properties* as sets of possible individuals – become available once we help ourselves to possible worlds.

Though not conclusive, the fact that possible worlds enable us to unify and simplify our theories in such ways speaks in their favor. True, one can wonder whether the simplification and systematization that result are reason for thinking the resultant theory more likely to be true; harshly stated, such criteria can appear to be aesthetic rather than rationally compelling. But appeals to simplicity and unification are not restricted to philosophical theories; they appear in the theoretical sciences and in certain parts of common sense. When one doubts whether such theoretical virtues are worth having, one runs the risk of thereby being skeptical about a great deal more than just possible worlds.

For all this, it is hard to accept David Lewis's view of possible worlds. On Lewis's view, merely possible worlds are like the actual one, concrete island universes containing – well, just about anything you care to think of, really. If it's possible, it'll literally be part of one of Lewis's possible worlds. The view that there is an infinite number of concrete island universes containing talking donkeys and stalking centaurs sits uneasily with common sense. The view that *every* possible object exists is an appalling violation. Though the kinds of simplicity and unification that possible worlds bring to our theories may be theoretical virtues worth having, simplicity of ontology, of the *entities* that a theory postulates, is a theoretical virtue too. Here, Lewis's theory of possible worlds scores very badly.[2] One could grant the entire case for possible worlds' theoretical utility, grant that the theoretical benefits are great, yet still rationally believe that they are simply not worth the massive ontological costs.

If only there were a way of getting all, or most, of the theoretical benefits that possible worlds have to offer without the excessive ontological costs and appalling violation of our common-sense beliefs, the case for possible worlds might be restored. Enter the *ersatzer*. Like Lewis, the ersatzer is a realist about possible worlds: possible worlds exist, can be referred to and quantified over in our theories and analyses. But the ersatz possible worlds have quite a different *nature* from Lewis's possible worlds. There may be no ontological free lunch – perhaps the ersatzer will have to invoke unreduced propositions, or states of affairs, or properties – but the ersatzer hopes his theory will be ontologically a lot cheaper than Lewis's and a whole load easier to believe in. The ersatzer's theory may not yield *all* the benefits that Lewis's theory offers (primitive modal concepts, for example, are hard to eliminate altogether on the ersatzer's scheme) but the ersatzer's laudable aim is to construct an ontologically parsimonious theory of possible worlds capable of getting as many of the theoretical benefits as possible.

It is essentially this goal, rather than any particular thesis about the nature of possible worlds, that unifies the ersatzers. We cannot characterize the ersatzer as one who believes that worlds are *abstract* rather than concrete, as there are versions of ersatzism where possible worlds come out concrete. We cannot characterize the ersatzer as one who rejects mere *possibilia* – things that don't actually exist but that could have – for there's no reason why the ersatzer couldn't have ersatz *possibilia* along with his ersatz possible worlds. Ersatzism is better seen as a *program* rather than a particular unified position in the philosophy of possible worlds, and there are a number of different versions on the market.

2 The Ersatzer's Zoo

Even if modality cannot be analyzed non-circularly, all ersatzers agree on the following:

$\Diamond P$ iff there is a possible world according to which P

As a realist about worlds, the ersatzer takes the right-hand side literally. This requires him to provide (a) an account of possible worlds and (b) an account of 'according to'. It is (b) (which is essentially an account of how it is that possible worlds represent that P is the case) as much as (a) that distinguishes the different ersatzisms. In sections 2.1 and 2.2, we examine two versions that are distinguished by the fact that the ersatzer tries to give an account of the *according to* relation. Many versions of ersatzism, however, are quiet or neutral about how exactly this is to be done. In section 2.3 we will examine a quiet version of ersatzism.

2.1 Linguistic ersatzism

For the linguistic ersatzer, worlds are a kind of *book*: they represent by containing sentences of an interpreted language.

Concrete books, unlike concrete worlds, are part of a safe and sane ontology. Few doubt the existence of the familiar concrete books we find in bookshops or that we put on our shelves. But such books are ill-suited to play the theoretical role we require of possible worlds, for there are not enough of them. The number of possible worlds is infinite: for every finite n, it is possible that there be exactly n atoms. So, for every number n, we'll need a book that contains the sentence 'there are exactly n atoms', which implies that an infinite number of books is needed to cover all these possibilities.

Fortunately, the ersatzer can get around this problem by taking advantage of the fact that the language in which the books are written (henceforth, the 'world-making language') is not something that has to be written or spoken. It doesn't much matter *what* the ersatzer takes sentences to be. Nothing relevant to the representational power of language hangs on the particular notation that he uses, whether he takes the words of his world-making language to be marks of black ink or pixels on a screen. Provided merely that the atomic parts of the language can be interpreted and that these parts can be syntactically structured to form complex formulas, the ersatzer is free to take his words and sentences to be whatever he likes. By letting each individual and property be its own name, the linguistic ersatzer has at his disposal a powerful world-making language.[3] Atomic sentences of the language can be identified with ordered n-tuples, such as $<F, a>$, where F is a property, such as *being red*, or *having charge*, and a is an individual. Naturally, $<F, a>$ is interpreted as saying that the object a has the property of F-ness. Worlds themselves can be identified with sets of sentences.

In this way, the linguistic ersatzer can give an account of the *according to* relation: P is true according to the set of sentences w if and only if w contains a sentence that expresses P, or a set of sentences that jointly entail that P.

Unfortunately, there remain possibilities about individuals and properties that outstrip this language's descriptive power. For instance, it is possible that there be something which doesn't actually exist. But on the scheme above, the only things which have names are the actual objects. There is no world described by the ersatzer containing something that doesn't actually exist.[4]

There is a similar problem for properties. The fact that a property is not actually instantiated doesn't immediately imply that it is beyond the reach of the linguistic ersatzer's language. For instance, as far as we know, the property *being a talking donkey* is not actually instantiated. But since this can be analyzed in terms of properties that *are* actually instantiated – *being a donkey* and *talking* – the linguistic ersatzer can describe worlds containing such objects. However, there is a problem describing worlds containing things that instantiate *alien* properties, properties which are neither instantiated by anything in the actual world nor which can be analyzed in terms of such properties. It seems plausible that there could have been things that instantiated properties that are alien to actuality, but the current world-making language cannot describe them.

Solution: supplement the language with quantifiers, variables, the identity symbol, and give it the wherewithal to say that there exists an entity which is distinct from a, distinct from b, distinct from $c \ldots$, plus further clauses that may characterize this non-actual object. (This may seem outrageous. Since when were infinitary sentences ever part of a respectable language? But remember: the ersatzer's world-making language is not something that has to be spoken or written.) Such a sentence describes a world containing something which is not identical to any actual object – in other words, a world containing something which doesn't actually exist. A similar trick should also allow the ersatzer to describe worlds containing alien properties.

Is *this* world-making language strong enough? It has been argued that, at least in the case of alien properties, the linguistic ersatzer ends up conflating intuitively distinct possibilities (Lewis 1986: 158–65; Bricker 1987). The trouble here is that there are many ways in which a sentence describing such possibilities can come true, and so the ersatzer is unable to distinguish intuitively distinct possibilities. Consider a world where a and b instantiate alien property P and c instantiates alien property Q. Isn't it a further possibility that a and b instantiate Q whilst c instantiates P? Certainly, our intuitions support the idea that there can be distinct worlds which differ only over which actual properties play which roles: a world containing two round things and one square thing is not the same as one containing two square things and one round thing. Shouldn't the same be true of alien properties? Unfortunately, with his current resources, the only story the ersatzer can tell goes something as follows: "There are two alien properties, one of which is instantiated by a and b, the other of which is instantiated by c." That story equally well describes the situation when the objects swap their properties. If we have many possibilities corresponding to the single story, the linguistic ersatzer's identification of worlds with books is in trouble.

The ersatzer might just bite the bullet, deny the modal intuition for alien properties and say there is just one possibility after all (Skyrms 1981). This may not be too big a price to pay, for it's not as if such modal intuitions about alien properties are sacrosanct. Or it may be that, to accommodate these intuitions, the ersatzer merely needs a way of representing the transworld identity of alien properties, and that such a way is available to the ersatzer.[5] Nevertheless, the worry remains that, no matter how powerful his language, the possibilities outrun the ersatzer's means of expressing them.

Besides the problem of finding words to describe *all* the possibilities, the linguistic ersatzer also has a problem of consistency. Possible worlds can't be identified with *any* set of sentences: a book according to which an object is red and green all over doesn't describe a possibility. Only the *consistent* books count as the possible worlds. But *consistency* is a modal notion: a set of sentences is consistent if the members of the set *could* all be true together. In defining which sets of sentences are the possible worlds, primitive modality enters the ersatzer's theory. Unless this can be remedied, the analytic ambitions of ersatzism are curtailed.

It may be that the linguistic ersatzer can find a way of distinguishing the consistent stories from the inconsistent ones that doesn't use primitive modality. Suppose, for instance, that he limits the properties that explicitly appear in his stories to the most fundamental or basic ones. Suppose he also limits the particulars to the simples. Possible worlds are still sets of *n*-tuples, but now they are *n*-tuples of the simple properties and particulars. Now maybe, as Wittgenstein believed, any rearrangement of the most fundamental individuals and properties results in a *possible* world. So any set of *n*-tuples of the simple properties and individuals does indeed describe a possible world, and there's no need to employ a primitively modal restriction.[6]

Unfortunately, primitive modality remains. Recall what the linguistic ersatzer has to say about *according to*: *P* is true according to the set of sentences w if and only if *w* contains a sentence that expresses *P*, or a set of sentences that jointly entail that *P*. The trouble is that *entails* is a modal notion. If the world-making language were rich, if it contained a sentence that expressed every proposition, the ersatzer could drop all talk of entailment without loss. But on the current proposal, his worlds contain only sentences for simple objects and simple properties. Merely saying that P is true according to *w* if and only if *w* contains a sentence that expresses *P* is insufficient: Since *being a donkey* and *talking* are both complex properties, the ersatzer's theory would fail to generate worlds according to which a donkey talks. Of course, a particular description of the fundamental properties and relations of the fundamental object may *entail* the truth of 'a donkey talks' so, providing he keeps the extra disjunct, everything is alright. But it seems the entailment used here can only be modal.

2.2 Structural ersatzism

Maps and pictures represent. Representation occurs because the representing objects have properties that mirror or reflect what they represent; the spatial relations between the parts of a map, for example, reflect the spatial relations between the parts of the terrain. What's doing the work here is a kind of isomorphism between the picture and the pictured. The structural ersatzer's possible worlds represent that *P* is the case by isomorphism rather than language.

It would be nice if we could say that such ersatz worlds represent simply by being isomorphic to that which they represent. But this can't always work; there are no talking donkeys and so there is no isomorphism between the talking donkey and the structure that is isomorphic to it. Instead it seems that the ersatzer must say that his world *would* have been isomorphic to a talking donkey, and that it *couldn't* be isomorphic to anything that isn't a talking donkey. So primitive modality again rears its head on this view.

Lewis considers the proposal that worlds represent by isomorphism (1986: 165–74), but focuses on one version of this idea: that ersatz worlds are idealized pictures that represent by being *similar* to what they represent. Though similarity is a form of isomorphism, the idea quickly leads to an ontology too similar to Lewis's for comfort. With ordinary pictures, we have only a limited similarity between the representations and the represented. Flat pictures have a problem representing three-dimensional scenarios: a picture represents a (distant) big boy chasing a (nearby) tiny ant, rather than a (nearby) tiny boy being chased by a (distant) giant ant not solely by isomorphism, but because background assumptions held by the community of viewers enable them to 'read' the picture correctly. Three-dimensional waxwork dummies arranged appropriately would do a better job. But then, one of the dummies represents the fact that the boy is flesh and blood again only because of background assumptions held by the community of viewers. This difficulty could be patched over by taking the representations to be themselves made out of flesh and blood.

It's clear where this is going and it's clear that the ersatzer shouldn't like it. The ontology we are going to end up with is going to be just as bad as Lewis's. For pictures to picture the world as being a certain way, they have to have so much in common with the things that they are supposed to represent that they end up being duplicates of the represented object. Lewis allows that the ersatzer might maintain that, despite the properties the pictures instantiate, the ersatzer's worlds might still be abstract rather than concrete, but I cannot see how this could be so. If a picture, in order to represent a cat perfectly, has to have fur, has to be made of flesh and blood, has to have four legs, and so on, then it just *is* a cat. And, if in order to represent a unicorn, a picture has to have all the properties that a unicorn would have, then it *is* a unicorn. Ersatzism was supposed to avoid Lewis's ontology, not embrace it.

All this shows, however, is that *similarity* was the wrong isomorphism for the structural ersatzer to choose. Two things do not have to share the same properties in order to be isomorphic to each other: sharing the same properties is one way in which two complex things can be isomorphic, but it is not the only way. A scale drawing may perfectly represent the size of some two-dimensional physical object without it being the very same size. Isomorphisms require merely that the picture and the pictured share a particular *structure* – not that they be duplicates of each other.

There's no reason why the ersatzer can't take the isomorphism to hold between the concrete and the abstract. As the case of applied mathematics shows, the abstract can be isomorphic to the concrete. For example, assuming that space is continuous, the abstract real numbers under the *greater than* relation are isomorphic to the points on a spatial line ordered by the *left of* relation. Similarly, the powerset of a pure set of cardinality n minus the empty set is, under the *is a subset of* relation, isomorphic to the mereological sums of a collection of – simples under the *is a part of* relation. Logically, an isomorphism is treated as a 1–1 mapping from the elements of one domain to the elements of another, such that the properties and relations of the objects in the first domain are mapped onto properties and relations of the objects of the second domain. Let domain 1 be the set of objects that actually exist. Domain 2 can be any set of elements that one likes, abstract or concrete. With only this much structure in place, the ersatzer can generate worlds that represent the cardinality of possible worlds: a model containing n elements represents the world as containing n elements – for the only way in which the world can be isomorphic to a set containing n elements is if it too has n elements. Similarly, the properties and relations possessed by domain 1 must be mapped onto the properties and relations possessed by domain 2. In the above examples, we saw how the isomorphism mapped the relation *is a subset of* to the relation *is a mereological sum of*. If this, rather than similarity, were the isomorphism the ersatzer chose to deploy, then his abstract structures could represent various facts about parthood.

One might worry about the role of convention on this structuralist view. If we are presented with a map and told that it has been done perfectly to scale, this will allow us to draw conclusions about the shape of the object, but not about its size. This information isn't even enough to infer whether the represented object is supposed to be smaller or larger than the picture. Only when the scale of the drawing is given, when we are told which distances in the map correspond to which distances in the

Joseph Melia

terrain, can we say what the map represents. But, so the worry goes, the choice of scale is arbitrary, a matter of convention. Against this, the ersatzer may counter that we don't *make* or *create* the isomorphism – the shared structure is there independently of our thought and talk. It is true that the map represents different things depending upon the choice of scale, but choice of scale is a matter of the *selection* of a particular structure-preserving mapping, not a matter of the *creation* of one. The structure preserving mappings are there independently of our thought and talk, and pictures have their representational properties in virtue of these mappings – but a particular structure preserving mapping has to be chosen to fix the representational properties of the pictures, or to fix upon a particular interpretation of 'according to'.

This structural account of representation gives us another, perhaps more natural, way of interpreting the view that worlds are sets of n-tuples of properties and particulars – the same entities that the Lagadonian linguistic ersatzer took possible worlds to be. Just as the object a instantiates F-ness at a world, so the pair $<F, a>$ may appear within a particular combination. Just as the pair $<a, b>$ may instantiate the R relation at a world, so the pair $<R, <a, b>>$ may be a member of a particular combination. The mathematical relations between the elements appearing in the ordered pairs mirrors or reflects the instantiation relations that hold (or would hold) between particulars and properties. Representation occurs in virtue of the abstract, mathematical structure such sets of n-tuples display.

The strengths and weaknesses of this proposal are similar to those found for linguistic ersatzism. Primitive modality is used in explaining how these structures represent. A safe and sane ontology is offered, and the representation relation is not mysterious. What is less clear is how this version of ersatzism can generate worlds that represent the existence of non-actual objects, but it may be that by choosing the appropriate isomorphism, the structural ersatzer can find a way of doing this. It's not clear that it offers any definite advantages over linguistic ersatzism, but structural ersatzism is worth further exploration.

2.3 Quiet ersatzers

The linguistic and structural ersatzers aim high. Ontologically, they offer an account of worlds which identifies them with set-theoretic constructions of elements of the concrete natural world. They also offer an account of how it is that their possible worlds represent. But perhaps a satisfactory ersatzism doesn't have to be so ambitious. Perhaps it is not necessary for the ersatzer to give an account – linguistic, structural, or otherwise – of the nature of the *according to* relation. Perhaps it can appear simply as a primitive of his system, something which is basic and undefined.

The world-making language of the linguistic ersatzer was restricted by human limitations. The linguistic ersatzer focuses on the details of his world-making language and has problems finding a language capable of describing all the possible worlds. But it's not the details of the language that matter so much as what the sentences *mean*. Why not avoid the linguistic ersatzer's problems by constructing the possible worlds out of *meanings* – or, more precisely, out of *propositions*? Although, at first sight, *propositions* may not be the elements of a safe and sane ontology, one might try to sweeten the pill by pointing out that our everyday thought and talk does in fact commit us to such things. After all, it is a commonplace that there are sentences from different languages that express the same thing; that there are many things that people from the same religion all believe; that there are as yet undiscovered truths that transcend our current means of expression. In these cases and others, the natural candidate for the object we are quantifying over is the *proposition*. Moreover, just as mathematical entities earn their spurs through the role they play in the empirical sciences, so defenders of propositions argue that they earn theirs through the role they play in the science of mind.

Possible worlds cannot be identified with any old set of propositions. Certain propositions ascribing incompatible properties to an object describe *impossibilities*. Most propositions do not describe a complete world. But worlds are typically taken to be both *possible* and *complete* entities: nothing, no matter how small or seemingly trivial, is overlooked by a possible world. Fortunately, propositions have certain modal properties and stand in certain modal relations to each other. Some propositions, such as *there exists a talking donkey* and *there exists a stalking centaur*, are propositions which *could* have been true. Some propositions, such as *Andy is angry* and *Andy is happy*, are incompatible. And some propositions entail others. Use these modal features to define the *maximally consistent sets* of propositions. A set of propositions is consistent if all the propositions in the set could be true together. A set of propositions is maximal if every set of propositions that properly includes it is inconsistent. With this machinery in place, we recover the desired biconditional:

$\Diamond$P if and only if P is true at some possible world.

Were propositions identified with ordered *n*-tuples of properties and propositions, we would reach the same ontological view of worlds as is found in linguistic ersatzism, Lagadonian style. Were a linguistic or structural theory of representation also adopted, then this version of ersatzism would seem to collapse into one of the two previous versions. But the ersatzer may resist such a collapse by digging in his heels at this point and refusing to give an informative account of propositions or how they manage to represent things about the concrete world. *Proposition* may be a primitive of his theory. One proposition, *a donkey talks*, is such that, necessarily, the concrete world contains a talking donkey if and only if this proposition is *made true* by the actual world. An informative account of how propositions are *made true* is not to be had here – it's another primitive of the theory.

Effectively, this view appears in many different guises. *Propositions* that may or may not be true can be replaced by *states of affairs* (Plantinga 1974, 1976) that may or may not obtain, or *world-natures* (Forrest 1986) that may or may not be instantiated. It's not clear whether such substitutions result in brand new theories, or are just the same old theory presented under a different name.

3 Actualism and Possibilism

Many ersatzers stress that they are *actualists*: everything that exists is *actual*. In other words, there are no merely possible objects. But it's *possibilia* as much as possible worlds that play a useful theoretical role. For instance, possible worlds models for predicate modal logic are taken to be tuples of the form $<W, R, D, d, val, w^*>$. W is a set which represents the set of worlds and R is the accessibility relation between worlds. No problems here: the ersatzer has his set of ersatz worlds and so has something straightforward to say about the relation between semantics and modal reality. But D represents the set of *possibilia* and $d(w)$ represents the *possibilia* which exist at world w. Some account needs to be given of how these elements of the model correspond to modal reality. Those who accept *possibilia* have an easy answer. Those who do not have work to do.

Actualism is independent of ersatzism. As we shall see, there's nothing in the spirit of ersatzism that is incompatible with the postulation of ersatz *possibilia* on top of ersatz worlds.

3.1 Actualist ersatzisms

It would be odd to accept possible worlds but to reject possible worlds semantics. But without *possibilia*, how is the actualist ersatzer to account for the D and $d(w)$ that appear in such semantics? Since the ersatzer does believe in actual individuals, he might try identifying D with the set of actual individuals. But that would imply that $d(w)$ is a subset of the actual individuals for every w – in other words, that there are no worlds at which there exist non-actual objects. If the ersatzer wants to allow that there could have been things that don't actually exist, he had better think again.

But perhaps D and $d(w)$ don't have to be interpreted so literally in order to justify the workings of possible worlds semantics. The issue is delicate for it is contentious exactly what has to be done before a formal semantics for modal logic can be said to be more than a mere mathematical game and something which gives us information about particular modal concepts. Although actualist ersatzers can't interpret D and $d(w)$ as literally corresponding to sets of *possibilia*, they nevertheless still might be able to tell a story. Perhaps the representational properties of the worlds the ersatzer has postulated will suffice. We have seen that the linguistic ersatzer is able to generate a world w according to which there are things that don't actually exist. Perhaps the actualist ersatzer can say that $d(w)$ just represents what exists according to the ersatz world w, and D just represents what exists according to all the ersatz worlds w. Unfortunately, certain aspects of the logical behavior of D and $d(w)$ in the possible worlds semantics are not explained by this story. Consider the sentence: 'Fred could have had a brother who doesn't actually exist, who could have been an astronaut.'[7] On a possible worlds approach, this requires a world w and some object o from D such that o is not in $d(w^*)$, where w^* represents the actual world, o is in the domain of $d(w)$, o is a brother of Fred at w *and* there is another world $w\#$ such that o is in $d(w\#)$ and, at $w\#$, o is an astronaut. The trouble here is that sense needs to be made of the idea of one and the same non-actual object existing according to different worlds, and one and the same object having various properties according to these different worlds. The linguistic ersatzer has given no story about how this aspect of D and $d(w)$ is rooted in the representational properties of his books. Books talk of non-actual objects merely by quantification. Nothing that the ersatzer has said so far grounds the fact that an object that exists according to one story and which is merely spoken of by existential quantification is identical or different to a non-actual object that exists according to a different story. This is trouble. Without such an account, how is the ersatzer to explain this aspect of D and $d(w)$?

This problem for the linguistic ersatzer is tied directly to the way the ersatzer represents possibilities containing non-actuals. Can actualist ersatzers of the quiet persuasion do better? Perhaps they can say that their ersatz worlds, be they propositions or properties, are capable of representing not just that merely possible objects exist, but of representing the *identity* of a merely possible object. For instance, the proposition *Andy is happy* represents a particular object, Andy, as being a certain way. *Andy is calm* represents that very same thing, Andy, as being a different way. Now, though Andy might not have existed, the ersatzer takes the proposition *Andy is happy* as a necessary existent that would exist even if Andy did not. Consider an impoverished world, one in which Andy never existed. Although a philosopher who lived at such a world could never have named Andy, propositions about this very actual Andy would still have existed at this world. Facts about the transworld identity of Andy are thus represented in exactly the same way as facts about him actually are. As it is for the impoverished philosopher, the story goes, so it is for us: there exist propositions which represent particular individuals being a certain way even if the individual does not exist. Some maximal set of propositions represents the existence of a particular non-actual individual Fred's brother, and another maximal set of propositions represents that very same individual being an astronaut. The ersatzer can thereby account for the function of D and $d(w)$ in the possible worlds semantics.

The worry with such a proposal is that it postulates very strong representational properties of the ersatz worlds. The very idea that representations can represent the existence of a *particular* non-actual object is questionable. Normally, such *de re* representation happens because of an intimate relation between the representation and the represented. In natural language, a name denotes an object because, in part, of the causal relations between the name and its denotation; in the case of the linguistic ersatzer's language, a name represented an object by simply *being* that object. But when the represented does not even exist, how can 'that particular object' be represented?

Perhaps the quiet ersatzer is better off following Plantinga's (1976) suggestion that, as well as ersatz worlds, there also exist *essences*, and use these essences to provide an actualist conception of D. An object's essence is a property which (a) that object has essentially; and (b) *only* that object can instantiate. So, for instance, *being identical to Andy* is an essence; it satisfies (a) as Andy could not exist without being identical to Andy, and it satisfies (b) as, necessarily, anything which instantiates this property is identical to Andy. Now, the story goes, not only are there essences corresponding to *actual* individuals, but so too are there essences corresponding to *non-actual* individuals: not all essences are actually instantiated. But although these essences are not actually instantiated they *might* have been, and had any of these essences been instantiated, then there would have been something that didn't actually exist. Accordingly, these essences give us a way of understanding sentences such as 'there could have been things that do not actually exist' in a way which does not require us to posit merely possible objects that do not exist: it holds precisely when there is some (actually existing) essence that is not instantiated, but that could have been. Unlike typical properties, such as *being a unicorn* and *being a talking donkey*, which are qualitative and repeatable, the very point of essences is that they are necessarily unique to one thing. Accordingly, no actual object can instantiate an uninstantiated essence. The only way that it could be instantiated is if something non-actual were to exist. Essences also give us a way of tracking the identity of possible objects across worlds, and thus a way of justifying the way in which D and $d(w)$ function in possible worlds semantics.

Nevertheless, worries remain. If it is hard to see how a representation of a particular individual could exist without that individual existing, it is just as hard to see how an individual's essence could exist without that individual existing. And traditionally, although some forms of primitive modality have not been too worrying, the notion of *essence* has been one that has caused particular concerns. If possible worlds were unable to analyze all modal notions, there was still the hope that it might provide an illuminating analysis of the more problematic ones. But on this proposal, it appears that the notion of an essence is built into the heart of the theory. And even amongst those who think that the notion of an essence makes sense, there will be many who will hesitate to accept that there are essences of things that do not exist.

3.2 Possibilist ersatzism

Why shouldn't the ersatzer take possible objects as seriously as he takes possible worlds? Certainly, the ersatzer doesn't want his ersatz *possibilia* to be like Lewis's, as the old ontological problems would just raise their head all over again. In the case of possible worlds, the various theories of ersatz worlds were made available by the fact that the operator *according to* could be interpreted in various ways. Nothing similar seems to be available in the case of quantification over *possibilia* (we do not say 'there is a possible object according to which *P*'). But maybe the ersatzer can use the representational properties of his ersatz worlds to do all the hard work. Perhaps what the *possibilia* are like in and of themselves is wholly irrelevant; all that matters is what they're like *according to possible world w*. What's required is not a non-actual talking donkey, but merely a non-actual object which some world represents as being a talking donkey. Now, if the intrinsic properties the non-actual object possesses are irrelevant here, then the ersatzer is free to say pretty much anything he likes about the nature of the *possibilia*. There need to be a lot of them, of course, but they can all be exactly alike. In fact, they don't need to have any qualitative properties at all. They can all be mere featureless blips, if the ersatzer likes, outside space and time. Or they could be identified with mathematical objects. On this view, even if a large *number* of *possibilia* are accepted into our ontology, there would be no real decrease in the *qualitative* parsimony of our theory. From an ontological point of view, then, a failure of actualism construed this way is no big deal.

The drawback to this view is that it forces us to accept the idea that there are things that don't actually exist. But if, as argued above, the denial of actualism is not ontologically profligate, then it's not clear why actualism is particularly desirable. The big problem with Lewis's view was its profligate and implausible ontology – not the fact that this ontology is classified as non-actual. Imagine a philosopher who held exactly Lewis's ontological views but rejected his views about the analysis of modal statements. His position would be no more attractive if he told us that everything in his ontology was *actual*. Conversely, it seems to me that an ontology is no worse for some objects being labeled *non-actual*. Using the word 'actually' to restrict quantifiers to the things that existed only in the solar system, or to only the concrete objects, or to only the things that are spatiotemporally related to me may be a strange use of the word 'actually' – but it doesn't change the attractiveness of the ontology.

True, if we took the *possibilia* to be elements of the set-theoretic hierarchy, then, if we'd been minded to call these cardinals 'actual' beforehand, this is a practice we would have to renounce – once the identification has been made, they are the merely possible objects. But it's not clear that this would be a big blow against ordinary practice, or that there's anything much in ordinary thought or language that thinks that inaccessible cardinals must be actual. Non-actualism can be entirely consistent with a conservative ontology, one that doesn't even damage common sense: instead of treating non-actualism as the proposal that our quantifiers range over more than we previously thought to exist, it can equally well be treated as the view that the actual objects are a *subset* of what we previously thought existed. Only one pretheoretic thought has to be given up – the thought that everything is actual. Even here, it might be questioned whether this is such a central tenet of common sense. We have a tendency implicitly to restrict our quantifiers to things that actually exist anyway. Perhaps the view that everything is actual only seems so certain because the quantifier is typically restricted to actual objects anyway.

There is an objection to the view that non-actual objects are abstract. Suppose the ersatzer accepts ersatz *possibilia* and that he takes them to be abstract, for example. Since there are worlds which represent these *possibilia* as unicorns, and since unicorns are concrete, it then follows that these possible objects could have been concrete. This in turn seems to imply that there are objects that, though abstract, are only abstract *contingently*, that they fall under their particular ontological category merely contingently. But this is absurd.[8]

The ersatzer has the resources to resist this argument. On his analysis, an object has property *F* contingently if it has *F* at some worlds and lacks *F* at others. Let *o* be one of the abstract *possibilia*. There is a world according to which *o* is concrete. But is there a world where *o* fails to be concrete? It's natural to think so: after all, *o* is abstract. But, under the proposal currently under consideration, we cannot conclude from this that it is *actually* true that *o* is abstract, that *o* is abstract at the actual world. Object *o* doesn't even exist in the actual world – it is a merely possible object and so outside the range of the quantifier – and so, at the actual world, it isn't concrete. As long as the ersatzer postulates no world which describes this object as abstract, there is no reason to say that it is contingently abstract. This move is surprising, but this might be only because we typically tend to think that the properties an object has *simpliciter* are the properties it has at the actual world. But once we have given up actualism, it is no longer the case that the truth of a proposition implies its actual truth.[9]

Accepting *possibilia* solves certain problems for the ersatzer. He can give a straightforward account of the role D and $d(w)$ play in possible worlds semantics, and can give a straightforward account of the problematic sentence $\Diamond \exists x (\neg AEx \ \& \ Bax \ \& \ \Diamond Fx)$. He can have worlds according to which there are non-actual objects. On the linguistic

Joseph Melia

account, for example, these are just books that contain names for non-actual objects.

Non-actualist ersatzism is an intriguing option for the ersatzer. It does require him to give up on the natural idea that everything is actual. But if the ersatzer can give this up, then he has a natural and straightforward way of dealing with the applications of *possibilia* considered in this section.

4 Ersatz Ontology, Ersatz Ideology

4.1 Shaky foundations?

The ontology and ideology of the linguistic and structural ersatzers look to be in relatively good standing. It's true that worlds are identified with certain set-theoretic constructions and the ideology and ontology of set-theory is not entirely unproblematic, but many philosophers have come to accept it (see chapters 1.1 and 1.2). True, these ersatzisms must also use properties in their constructions, but the ersatzer needs only *instantiated* properties. Moreover, the world-making language of the linguistic ersatzer is no weaker if it contains predicates for only the most fundamental properties and relations, so he really only needs to reify these. This allows him to buy into an attractive sparse theory of properties, such as Armstrong's (1978) theory of universals. Indeed, when fundamental physics is completed, we will find ourselves with a language containing predicates for all these basic properties. With this supply of predicates, the linguistic ersatzer will be able to construct just as strong a world-making language without even having to reify fundamental properties and relations.

All the ersatz theories take modality as primitive. But this is no terrible thing. While some have complained that the modal is mysterious because we have no empirical access to it, even Lewis's reduction of the modal to the non-modal doesn't solve that problem: as concrete as they may be, Lewis's worlds are not empirically accessible. It's true that, when weighing the pros and cons of different theories, Lewis's theory may score an extra point for the number of distinct concepts it can analyze.[10] But the ersatzer can fairly claim that he scores far better on the ontology front.

It's also true that Lewis effects a kind of reduction of the modal to the non-modal. On Lewis's view, when you've fixed what there is, what things are categorically like and how they are categorically arranged, then you've fixed the modal facts also. Ersatzers seem unable to effect such a reduction – the consistency of certain sets of sentences or of certain propositions is not reduced or explained in categorical terms. In certain respects, then, Lewis's world-view seems simpler. But, at least for those who are realists about modality, the thought that the primitively modal should enter into our most fundamental description of the world is not an unnatural one. Indeed, there are those who find it positively counterintuitive that the modal should be grounded in the non-modal, as they are on Lewis's system. What, they ask, has the existence of island universes cut off from the actual world got to do with what we think is *possible* (van Inwagen 1985)? Why should the fact that concrete island universes of such and such a sort exist imply anything about the impossibility or otherwise of talking donkeys?

The ontology and the ideology of the quiet ersatzers are more problematic. The notion of a proposition is itself one that cries out for a proper analysis and ontological definition. The identification of possible worlds with complete sets of propositions may not be coherent: a complete 'collection' of propositions may be too big to form a set (see Grim 1984). What good are possible worlds analyses of our concepts if the foundations of possible worlds is built on sand? And until we possess a worked out theory of propositions, it will be unclear whether they are suited to play the theoretical roles we want of them.

4.2 Grasping the primitives

Unlike the linguistic and structural ersatzers, who offered a substantive account of the *according to* relation, the quiet ersatzers said very little about how their abstract propositions and properties manage to represent things about the way the concrete world is. Perhaps there isn't much to be said. Necessarily, when, and only when, the concrete world contains a talking donkey, the abstract proposition *a donkey talks* is made true. There's no analysis to be given of the concept of a proposition, nor any analysis of 'makes true'. Without analyses, these notions will have to be taken as primitive. But then, every theory has its primitives.

Lewis thinks that the ersatzer's primitives are particularly problematic: it is a mystery how the ersatzer can ever grasp them. His argument runs as follows. Since whether the world *makes true* a particular proposition depends upon the goings on of the concrete actual world, we can treat this as a relation between the concrete world and propositions. Lewis thinks that it is a mystery how the ersatzer could have picked out a particular relation by his primitive 'makes true'. The ersatzer refuses to analyze this in terms of anything else. Nor can he say that 'makes true' gets its meaning through acquaintance with pairs of things that stand in the relevant relation: since the propositions are outside space and time and acausal, we can never be acquainted with the *relata*. It is a mystery how the ersatzer ever came by a word for this relation (Lewis 1986: §3.4).

Unfortunately, as Lewis concedes (1991: §2.2), this argument proves too much: the primitives of the set-theorist are subject to analogous worries (van Inwagen 1986). Since we have no way of pinning down the meaning of 'x is a member of y' relation by analysis or by acquaintance, the set-theorist is at a loss to explain how he has ever managed to pick out a particular relation with this predicate. Lewis seems to accept that it's a mystery how the set-theorist ever manages to pick out a particular relation by 'is a member of'.

However, a move *is* available to the set-theorist, a move outlined by Lewis himself (1991: §2.6). One way to define theoretical terms that requires neither explicit definition nor acquaintance is via the Ramsey-Carnap method. Take the total theory involving the problematic predicates, replace the problematic predicates with variables, and let the relevant predicates stand for whatever properties and relations satisfy the relevant open formula. There's a danger: what happens if the properties and relations are multiply realized? The predicates of the theory then fail to designate uniquely. But maybe that doesn't matter. Perhaps a kind of structuralist approach is acceptable here, and set-theoretic claims can be understood as being about *any* of the relations that satisfy the relevant claims. Moreover, in the case of set-theory, we have a theory which, when formulated using plural quantifiers and clever coding devices, essentially captures its models up to isomorphism[11] without having to take the concept of *membership* as primitive.[12] The set-theorist can therefore *Ramseyfy* out the *membership* relation, and say that a set-theoretical statement *S* involving '*x* is a member of *y*' is true if, for *any* relation *R* satisfying the axioms of set-theory,[13] if *S* is true when '*x* is a member' is interpreted by *R*.

Lewis himself is not happy with this. It's not that set-theory so construed is unable to play its familiar useful pragmatic and theoretical roles – the fact that the *membership* relation has been so tightly characterized by the powerful axioms sees to that. It's true that, even in its Ramseyfied version, set-theory commits us to a vast number of entities, more than the concrete world around us can contain. But since the relation may be taken to be external, the intrinsic properties of the propositions are irrelevant – propositions may be taken to be all alike, and thus, though the theory may not be quantitatively parsimonious, the cost in terms of qualitative parsimony is low. Worse, for Lewis, is that this way of construing set-theory is a kind of rejection of mathematics as it is currently practiced: 'If we want to understand set theory as we find it now, we have to concede that it claims a primitive understanding of membership' (1991: 54). But I don't know where in set-theory anything about the primitiveness or otherwise of membership occurs. Besides, if the justification for believing in set-theory really lies in the theoretical utility that sets bring, then the Ramseyfied theory scores just as well. Since it does not commit us to a mystery about how we can come by a name for the membership relation, that is a good reason for adopting it.

Can the ersatzer similarly Ramseyfy away the predicates '*x* makes true *y*' and '*x* is a proposition'? It seems not. There's no ersatz analogue of second order set-theory. All it seems the ersatzer can do is to write down a few axioms:

Necessarily, there is a proposition *e*, *A donkey talks* that the world makes true if and only if a donkey talks.
Necessarily, there is a proposition *e*, *A centaur stalks* that the world makes true if and only if a centaur stalks.
  etc.

If the ersatzer could write down every one of these biconditionals, then he could say that any relation satisfying the theory will do. But there's no known way of doing this. The problem will be especially acute generating biconditionals for those states of affairs that are about alien individuals and properties; explicit clauses like those above cannot, since we don't have words for the particular alien properties. Until the ersatzer puts forward a theory that is plausibly capable of implicitly capturing the relevant relation, the question how the ersatzer can grasp his own primitives remains unanswered.

5 Conclusion

Between the ersatzisms, the linguistic variety is the most promising. Its ontology and ideology are both reasonably safe and sane and there are no worries about how we can grasp the primitives of the theory. And yet, I cannot recommend it wholeheartedly. The ersatzer's aim is to get a theory of possible worlds which has most or all the advantages of Lewis's theory, but without the costs. A safe and sane ontology and ideology shows that it doesn't have the costs – but what remains to be seen is whether it has the advantages. We've already seen the ersatzer give up on an analysis of modality – but what the ersatzer still owes us is a thorough account of how his ersatz possible worlds, perhaps aided by ersatz *possibilia*, are capable of delivering the benefits. Until a thorough account is forthcoming, we may find that the costs of ersatzism, like with Lewis's theory, are still not worth the benefits – not because the costs are too high but because the benefits are too low.

Notes

1   Of course, the set-theoretic semantics alone doesn't require a belief in possible worlds, just a belief in sets. But unless the semantics faithfully represents the kinds of states of affairs that make the sentences of the intensional language true, there's no reason to think that the set-theoretic semantics is anything more than a formal game.
2   See Melia (1992).
3   Such a language is frequently called *Lagadonian*.
4   Some think it better to readjust our modal intuitions and deny the possibility of non-actual objects. Although this goes against our pre-theoretic intuitions, saving an attractive theory of worlds might be make it worthwhile. An ingenious way of making this proposal less damaging to common sense is found in Linsky and Zalta (1994).
5   See Roy (1995) and Melia (2001).
6   And *combinatorialist* theories of possible worlds are still popular today. See Armstrong (1989).
7   More formally, so it's clear what modal proposition is being expressed here: '◊ ∃x(¬AEx & Bax & ◊ Fx)', where 'Fx' is 'x is an astronaut', and 'Bxy' is 'y is the brother of x' and 'a' is a name for Fred.
8   Though Linsky and Zalta defend this idea (1994).
9   The same is true on Lewis's view. It is true *simpliciter* that there are many possible worlds, but it is not actually true that there are.
10 And even this is not agreed by all; there are those who think that Lewis too must use primitive modality in his theory. See, for instance, Shalkwoski (1994), Lycan (1988), and Divers and Melia (2002).
11 Certain questions about the "height" of the set-theoretic hierarchy are left open, even in a second-order formulation.
12 Hazen and Burgess have shown how this can be done. See the appendix of Lewis (1991) for details.
13 Plus perhaps some informal axioms.

References

Armstrong, D. M. 1978. *Universals and Scientific Realism*, 2 vols. (Cambridge: Cambridge University Press).
—. 1989. *A Combinatorial Theory of Possibility* (Cambridge: Cambridge University Press).

Bricker, P. 1987. "Reducing Possible Worlds to Language," *Philosophical Studies* 52: 331–55.

Divers, J., and Melia, J. 2002. "The Analytic Limits of Genuine Modal Realism," *Mind* 111: 15–36.

Forrest, P. 1986. "Ways Worlds Could Be," *Australasian Journal of Philosophy* 64: 15–24.

Grim, P. 1984. "There is no Set of All Truths," *Analysis* 44: 206–8.

Jeffrey, R. 1965. *The Logic of Decision* (Chicago: McGraw-Hill).

Lewis, D. 1986. *On the Plurality of Worlds* (Oxford: Blackwell).

—. 1991. *Parts of Classes* (Oxford: Blackwell).

Linsky, B., and Zalta, E. 1994. "In Defence of the Contingently Nonconcrete," *Philosophical Studies* 84: 283–94.

Lycan, W. 1988. Review of D. Lewis, 'On the Plurality of Worlds', *Journal of Philosophy* 85: 42–7.

Melia, J. 1992. "A Note on Lewis's Ontology," Analysis 52: 191–2.

—. 2001. "Reducing Possibilities to Language," *Analysis* 61: 19–29.

Plantinga, A. 1974. *The Nature of Necessity*, (Oxford: Clarendon).

—. 1976. "Actualism and Possible Worlds," *Theoria* 42: 139–60. Repr. in M. J. Loux, ed., *The Possible and the Actual* (Ithaca: Cornell University Press, 1979), pp. 253–73.

Roy, T. 1995. "In Defence of Linguistic Ersatzism," *Philosophical Studies* 80: 217–42.

Shalkowski, S. 1994. "The Ontological Ground of the Alethic Modality," *Philosophical Review* 103: 669–88.

Skyrms, B. 1981. "Tractarian Nominalism," *Philosophical Studies* 40: 190–206.

van Inwagen, P. 1985. "Plantinga on Transworld Identity," in James Tomberlin and P. van Inwagen. eds., *Alvin Plantinga: A Profile* (Dordrecht: Reidel).

—. 1986. "Two Concepts of Possible Worlds," *Midwest Studies in Philosophy* 11: 185–213.

PERSONAL IDENTITY

You were once a young child. *You*, not someone else, did the things that you remember doing many years ago. But the person you are now is very different from the person you were then. Your experiences have changed you psychologically, and you have changed physically as well. What makes a person the same over time? What sorts of changes to a person count as changes to the *same person*? After all, there are some alterations that *destroy* a person, for example melting a person down into a kind of person soup. Judith Jarvis Thomson argues that a person remains the same so long as her physical body continues intact. Derek Parfit argues instead for a more psychological criterion for being the same person.

PERSONAL IDENTITY

People and their Bodies

Judith Jarvis Thomson

I

The simplest view of what people are is that they are their bodies. That view has other attractions besides its simplicity. I feel inclined to think that this fleshy object (my body is what I refer to) isn't something I merely currently inhabit: I feel inclined to think that it *is* me. This bony object (my left hand is what I refer to) – isn't it literally part of me? Certainly we all, at least at times, feel inclined to think that we are not merely embodied, but that we just, all simply, *are* our bodies.

What stands in the way of adopting this simple and attractive view?

Some people would say that the manner in which death ordinarily comes on us stands in the way of adopting it. Some people's deaths issue from total destruction of the body, as in an explosion, but that is not the ordinary case. Suppose Alfred and Bert are people who died of a disease, in their beds. Their bodies did not go out of existence at that time. So if Alfred and Bert went out of existence at that time, then they are not their bodies.

But did Alfred and Bert go out of existence at that time? Don't people who die in bed just become dead people at the time of their deaths? Cats who die in bed become dead cats at the time of their deaths; why should it be thought otherwise in the case of people? Can't there be some dead people as well as some dead cats in a house after the roof falls in? The answer surely is that there can be.

You might have wondered why I have been talking in the plural, of *people*. I did so because the only available candidate in the singular for the plural 'people' is 'person', and philosophers do not use 'person' as a mere innocuous singular for 'people': 'person' in the hands of a philosopher trails clouds of philosophy. 'Dead people', like 'dead cats', causes no one any discomfort; but 'dead person', unlike 'dead cat', causes a philosopher (though not, I think, a non-philosopher) to feel at best anxious.

Judith Jarvis Thomson, "People and their Bodies," pp. 202–29 in *Reading Parfit*, ed. Jonathan Dancy (Oxford: Blackwell Publishing, 1997). Reprinted by permission Blackwell Publishing.

Locke said that a person is 'a thinking intelligent being', and I think he meant that a thing is a person at a time t only if it is a thinking intelligent being at t, so if we agree with him, we must of course conclude that nothing is, at t, both dead and a person. I think he meant us to conclude also that a thing is a thinking intelligent being at t only if it is thinking at t, and since he said that consciousness is essential to thinking, I think he meant us to conclude also that a thing is a thinking intelligent being at t only if it is conscious at t. So if we agree with him here too, we must of course also conclude that nothing is, at t, both unconscious and a person. Thus nothing is at any time both a person and dreamlessly asleep. But then what on earth could persons *be*? Consciousnesses? Are there such entities as consciousnesses?

Did Locke believe that persons are people? That persons are ordinary men or women, children or infants? Locke said: "if it be possible for the same Man to have distinct incommunicable consciousnesses at different times" – and he plainly did believe this possible – "it is past doubt the same Man would at different times make different Persons." Now one way of interpreting this passage is to take Locke to be relativizing identity – that is, to take him to be saying that the following can be the case: x and y are the same man, and each is a person, but x and y are not the same person. Interpreted in this way, Locke does believe that some persons are men. But I think it best to take him to believe that no person is a man, though a man may "make" a person, and indeed a different person at different times.[1]

Whatever is to be said about how we should interpret Locke, it will in any case be just plain people – ordinary men, women, children and infants – that I will be concerned with throughout. And a thing can certainly be, at t, both a man and unconscious. Even a man in a coma. (Isn't it perfectly clear that that is Nancy Cruzan, the very woman herself, lying in that hospital bed?) A thing can even be, at t, both a man and dead. ('Dead men tell no tales' is true, but that is not because nothing is both dead and a man.)

Some philosophers may say "Okay, I give you people. They're just their bodies. What interests me is instead persons, persons not being people." But I suspect that most philosophers who write on these matters would not give me people in this easy-going way; I think it *is* people whom they mean to be writing about. Most of them do take seriously some theories about the entities they are writing about that are incompatible with the view that those entities are their bodies. But that is not, I think, because they are writing about something other than people; it is rather because they take seriously the idea that people are not their bodies. We will have to look at what inclines them to do so.

I will myself, for brevity, often use the word 'person'; but when I do, I mean it to be understood merely as the singular of 'people'. I hope no confusion will result from this practice.

II

I asked what stands in the way of adopting the following simple and attractive view:

Physical Thesis: People are their bodies.

And I suggested that the manner in which death normally comes on us (in bed) does not stand in the way of adopting it. The most familiar of the other objections to it are objections to it by virtue of being objections to something it entails, namely,

Physical Criterion: $x = y$ if and only if x's body = y's body.

(I here and throughout let x, y and z range only over people.)

But before looking at those objections, let us first stop over a point of interest. What I have in mind is that much of the current literature on personal identity focuses on personal *identity*, attending to what we might call personal *ontology*, if at all, only as something of an afterthought.

Physical Thesis is a thesis about personal ontology. It entails a criterion for personal identity: namely, Physical Criterion. But these two theses are not equivalent, since Physical Criterion does not entail Physical Thesis. On the face of it, at any rate, there seems to be no contradiction in supposing that $x = y$ if and only if x's body = y's body and that x is nevertheless not identical with x's body. (For example, let a and b range over sets with one member. Then $a = b$ if and only if a's member = b's member. But a is nevertheless not identical with a's member.) If this is right, then Physical Criterion does not entail Physical Thesis, and the two theses are therefore not equivalent.

I should imagine, however, that anyone who accepts Physical Criterion is very likely to accept Physical Thesis as well; I should imagine, in fact, that anyone who accepts Physical Criterion accepts it precisely because he or she accepts Physical Thesis.

There seems to be no analogue of this intuitively tight connection between identity criterion and ontological thesis in the case of the other identity criteria familiar to us from the literature on this issue. I have in mind in particular the identity criteria that (very roughly) take something mental, or psychological, to be the mark of personal identity. Is there an ontological thesis you are very likely to accept if you accept a psychological identity criterion? Is there an ontological thesis such that you accept a psychological identity criterion precisely because you accept *it*? Not, anyway, the ontological thesis that people are mental substances: that is a very unpopular view nowadays. A contemporary philosopher is not at all likely to accept that people are mental substances on the ground of accepting a psychological identity criterion, and is also not at all likely to accept a psychological identity criterion because of having accepted that people are mental substances.

I do think this point worth taking note of. More generally, when philosophers tell us their views about personal identity, we should keep in mind that there is a further question to be answered: namely, what people *are*. And if the identity criterion a philosopher offers us is such that if that criterion were true, then it is obscure what people could possibly be, then isn't that a count against his or her criterion? Or might it turn out that there's no saying what people are, the best we can do being to find an account of their identity conditions? (Most philosophers think that this is our situation in the case of sets. But then some of them worry about whether there are such things as sets for that very reason.) In any case, the ontological question is waiting there in the wings, whenever a philosopher is on-stage answering the identity question.

III

To return to the question whether there is something else, besides the manner in which death ordinarily comes on us, that stands in the way of adopting the simple and attractive view that people are their bodies.

The most striking kind of objection issues from cases that descend from Locke's case of the prince and the cobbler. Here are two people, Brown and Robinson, and let us give the names 'Brown-body' and 'Robinson-body' to their bodies.[2] If

Physical Criterion: $x = y$ if and only if x's body = y's body

is true, then it is not the case that Robinson = Brown, since it is not the case that Robinson-body = Brown-body, and that is exactly as it should be. If Physical Criterion is true, then, quite generally, x = Brown if and only if x's body = Brown-body. So far, so good. Now for the trouble. We transplant the brain of Brown-body into Robinson-body, destroying the rest of Brown-body. Let us suppose that the operation succeeds, and that the survivor thinks he is Brown, wants much of what Brown wanted, seems to remember a good bit of what Brown experienced, and so on. It strikes many people as intuitively right therefore to say (i) that the survivor = Brown. It also seems intuitively right to say (ii) that it is not the case that the survivor's body = Brown-body. For isn't the survivor's body Robinson-body? Robinson-body with a new brain? (Compare transplanting someone else's liver into your body. Isn't the result your body? Your body with a new liver?) But if we accept (i) and (ii), then we think that Brown has switched bodies, and we must therefore give up Physical Criterion and therefore also Physical Thesis.

But intuitions in this area are merely openings for discussion, not closings. Let us go back to why people are inclined to opt for (i). As I said, the survivor thinks he is Brown, wants much of what Brown wanted, and so on. What if there had been a slip-up in the process of transplanting the brain of Brown-body into Robinson-body? Let us call the original story Brown-Case-One. In what we might call Brown-Case-Two, the drugs we injected into Robinson-body to prevent rejection of the new brain had the effect of altering the new brain in such a way as to make its configuration resemble that of the brain formerly in Robinson-body, so that the survivor thinks he is Robinson, wants much of what Robinson wanted, and so on. *Here* the only reason to think that the survivor is Brown is the fact that the survivor's body's (new) brain was formerly in Brown-body. But is that of interest from the point of view of the question who the survivor is? Is it of any more interest from that point of view than the fact of your getting a new liver is from the point of view of the question who gets off the operating table after the liver transplant? Everyone, I think, would say that the survivor is not Brown in Brown-Case-Two.

But then it seems plausible to think that the role of the brain transplant in Brown-Case-One – the force which its being the brain that was transplanted has on people's intuitions about that case – lies wholly in the fact that the brain is normally, and slip-ups apart, the 'carrier of a person's psychology'. For where we imagine, as in Brown-Case-Two, that the transplanted brain does not carry Brown's psychology, we are not in the slightest inclined to think that the survivor is Brown.

So what if we imagine that we transplant merely Brown's psychology, without transplanting his brain? In Brown-Case-Three we reconfigure the Robinson-body brain: we reprogram it with Brown's psychology and destroy *all* of Brown-body. The survivor thinks he is Brown here too, and no part of Brown-body was transplanted at all. Many people therefore feel inclined to say of the survivor in Brown-Case-Three, as of the survivor in Brown-Case-One, that he is Brown. They think that transplanting Brown's psychology is necessary for Brown to switch bodies (for Brown does not switch bodies in Brown-Case-Two), and that transplanting Brown's psychology is sufficient for Brown to switch bodies (for Brown switches bodies in Brown-Case-Three as well as in Brown-Case-One). On their view, the force which its being the brain that is transplanted in Brown-Case-One has on people's intuitions about that case really does lie wholly in the fact that the brain is normally, slip-ups apart, the carrier of a person's psychology.

But others would deny these things. On their view, the survivor is not Brown in Brown-Case-Three. They think that transplanting Brown's psychology is necessary for Brown to switch bodies (for Brown does not switch bodies in Brown-Case-Two); but they think that transplanting Brown's brain is also necessary for Brown to switch bodies (for Brown switches bodies in Brown-Case-One, but not in Brown-Case-Three) – they think that the transplanting of Brown's psychology must have been caused by the transplanting of his brain. On their view,[3] the force which its being the brain that is transplanted in Brown-Case-One has on people's intuitions about that case does not lie wholly in the fact that the brain is normally, slip-ups apart, the carrier of a person's psychology.

What to make of all this? Let us call the view that transplanting a person's psychology is both necessary and sufficient for that person to shift bodies *the pure psychological criterion for body-switching.* On this view, Brown switches bodies in Brown-Case-Three as well as in Brown-Case-One. Let us call the view according to which transplanting a person's psychology, and doing so by way of transplanting that person's brain, is both necessary and sufficient for that person to switch bodies *the impure psychological criterion for body-switching.* For my own part, I find it hard to get a grip on why anyone would prefer the impure to the pure criterion. Why is it to be thought that body-switching requires that the transplanting of psychology have been caused by transplanting the brain? Suppose a psychology-transplanting was caused by transplanting a liver. (The drugs injected in the donor to anaesthetize him before the operation caused his brain to imprint on his liver in such a way that, when transplanted, the liver caused reprogramming of the recipient's brain.) Was that good enough? So that what is required for body-switching is really that the psychology-transplanting be caused by the transplanting of just any old body-part the transplanting of which *in fact* causes psychology-transplanting? (Why must some transplanted body-part play this causal role?) Or was it not good enough on the ground that transplanting a liver doesn't *normally* cause psychology-transplanting? (Why should that matter?) So I will concentrate on the pure psychological criterion,

People and their Bodies 159

making occasional comments on the impure psychological criterion only in footnotes.

Those who think Brown switches bodies in both Brown-Case-One and Brown-Case-Three, and therefore accept the pure psychological criterion, think that body-switching is possible, and they therefore reject Physical Criterion. What do they opt for instead? Well, why do they think that the survivor is Brown in those two cases? As I said, the fact that the survivor in those two cases thinks he is Brown, wants much of what Brown wanted, and so on. That is, the fact that the survivor is in some appropriate sense psychologically connected with Brown. They are therefore likely to conclude that psychological connectedness is the mark of personal identity – in some appropriate sense of 'psychological connectedness', and in some appropriate way of being 'the mark of'.

What sense of 'psychological connectedness'? Let us say that y is at t' psychologically connected with x at t if and only if t' is later than t, and y believes at t' a good bit of what x believed at t, y wants at t' a good bit of what x wanted at t, y seems to remember at t' a good bit of what x experienced at t, and so on. If you think that psychological connectedness is the mark of personal identity, you might well think that something like this is the appropriate sense.[4]

What way of being 'the mark of'? Here there are several possibilities, among which is the following:

> Psychological Criterion (Connectedness): $x = y$ if and only if there are times t and t' such that y is at t' psychologically connected with x at t.

If you think that Brown switches bodies in Brown-Case-One and Brown-Case-Three, and therefore conclude that psychological connectedness is the mark of personal identity, then you might well opt for Psychological Criterion (Connectedness): for in Brown-Case-One and Brown-Case-Three, the survivor is at the survivor's waking-time psychologically connected with Brown at Brown's becoming-unconscious-time, and that is exactly why, on your view, the survivor *is* Brown in those two cases – by contrast, of course, with the survivor in Brown-Case-Two.

I stress that if you think that psychological connectedness is the mark of personal identity, you probably have a variety of theses in mind, of which Psychological Criterion (Connectedness) is only one possibility. Another is not itself an identity criterion but instead a thesis about people, to the effect that there are no sudden, dramatic alterations across time in a person's psychology. (Very roughly: a person's psychology is connected throughout time.[5]) Indeed, this is a thesis you are very likely to have in mind if you think that psychological connectedness is the mark of personal identity. It is, of course, entirely consistent with Psychological Criterion (Connectedness).

IV

We should stop to take a closer look at what we have so far.

If you think that Brown switches bodies in Brown-Case-One and Brown-Case-Three, what do you think people *are*?[6] You certainly cannot think that Brown switches bodies in those cases compatibly with thinking that people are their bodies.

Judith Jarvis Thomson

I said that if you think Brown switches bodies in Brown-Case-One and Brown-Case-Three, you are likely to conclude that psychological connectedness is the mark of personal identity. It is of interest that one *can* accept the latter cluster of ideas compatibly with thinking that people are their bodies. For example, one can accept Psychological Criterion (Connectedness) compatibly with thinking that people are their bodies. How so? Let us call Bloggs's body Bloggs-body. Psychological Criterion (Connectedness) says that Bloggs is Bloggs-body if and only if there are times t and t' such that Bloggs-body is at t' psychologically connected with Bloggs at t; and couldn't that be true? But do *bodies* believe things, want things, and so on? If we think that people do, and that people are their bodies, we will certainly think that bodies do. And why shouldn't we?[7]

I will call the view that psychological connectedness is the mark of personal identity, and that people nevertheless are their bodies, *the hybrid view of personal identity*.

Since hybridists think that people are their bodies, they must deny that Brown switches bodies in Brown-Case-One and Brown-Case-Three. (*A fortiori*, they must reject the pure psychological criterion for body-switching.) What do they say happens to Brown in those cases? Let us for simplicity focus on Brown-Case-Three, in which no body parts are transplanted: we merely do a brain-reprogramming. Hybridists think that psychological connectedness is the mark of personal identity, so they accept (i) that the survivor = Brown. If they also accept (ii) that it is not the case that the survivor's body = Brown-body, then they must give up Physical Criterion. It follows that they must also give up the thesis that people are their bodies. Hybridists must therefore deny (ii): they must say that the survivor's body really is Brown-body.

There is only one way in which they can make this out: they must accept the metaphysic of temporal parts.

Suppose we say that for every physical object O and every time point and time stretch T through which O exists there is an entity E such that E exists only throughout T, and E occupies every place throughout T that O occupies throughout T, and E is part of O – indeed, O is just the fusion of such entities E. Then in particular, a person's body is the fusion of such entities E, which are its temporal parts.

Now I said at the outset of my description of the case of Brown: here are two people, Brown and Robinson, and let us give the names 'Brown-body' and 'Robinson-body' to their bodies. But which bodies exactly are their bodies? There are what the vulgar think are Brown's body and Robinson's body, but the hybridist can say that the vulgar are just mistaken.

Suppose that the brain-reprogramming is performed at t. Then if psychological connectedness is the mark of personal identity, Brown does, at t, what the vulgar would say is body-switching. The hybridist can instead say that Brown's body is *really* the fusion of (a) the beginning-to-t temporal part of what the vulgar would call Brown's body and (b) the t-to-ending temporal part of what the vulgar would call Robinson's body. If that is what Brown's body really is, then Brown does not switch bodies at t: he has the same body throughout. And if 'Brown-body' is the name of Brown's body – Brown's *real* body – then it follows that the survivor's body = Brown-body.

It was not the metaphysic of temporal parts itself that yielded this conclusion about what Brown's real body is: accepting the metaphysic of temporal parts does not by itself commit one to any view at all about personal identity, and *a fortiori* does not by itself commit one to hybridism. If you accept the metaphysic of temporal parts, you believe that every human body is the fusion of its temporal parts; but that leaves open which temporal body-parts you will believe are parts of a given human body – which temporal body-parts you will believe are, as we may put it, co-bodily.

Suppose you accept the metaphysic of temporal parts. If you also accept hybridism, then you think that people are their bodies, so you think that the relation of co-bodiliness and the relation of co-personality are one and the same. Moreover, you think that psychological connectedness is the mark of personal identity, so you think that the relation of co-personality is definable in terms of psychological connectedness. Perhaps you think it definable in three steps, (roughly) as follows. Let A and B range over temporal body-parts. First, you define 'psychological connectedness': B is psychologically connected with A if and only if B believes a good bit of what A believed, wants a good bit of what A wanted, and so on. Second, you define 'psychological continuity': B is psychologically continuous with A if and only if B has the ancestral of psychological connectedness to A. Third, you define 'co-personality': B is co-personal with A if and only if B is psychologically continuous with A. This *is* rough, but the underlying idea is plain enough. And its puzzlingness is also plain enough. Notice in particular that the relation of psychological connectedness that I defined earlier is a four-place relation on people and times, whereas the relation of psychological connectedness defined here is a two-place relation on temporal body-parts, and that makes for trouble. For example, can one really think that point-duration temporal slices of bodies believe things or want things? (Temporal chunks are one thing; temporal slices seem to be quite another.) Again, how is a hybridist to secure that an unconscious or postdeath temporal slice or chunk of a body is psychologically connected with a conscious, pre-death temporal slice or chunk of a body? On the other hand, I see no deep theoretical difficulty standing in the way of defining a relation of psychological connectedness on temporal body-parts in a way that bypasses this and other difficulties. And we may assume in any case that a hybridist will so define psychological connectedness, and thereby co-personality, that the *t*-to-ending temporal part of what the vulgar would call Robinson's body is co-personal with the beginning-to-*t* temporal part of what the vulgar would call Brown's body, the fusion of the two being Brown's body.

Should we accept the metaphysic of temporal parts? I think we should not. I will not argue for that here, however; I throughout leave it open.[8]

Many philosophers who write about personal identity help themselves to the terminology of temporal parts in laying out psychological identity criteria; a certain simplicity is gained in this way. But it should be noticed that this terminology can usually be regarded as mere *façon de parler*: it can be translated out. Even if you positively like, or anyway see nothing objectionable in, the metaphysic of temporal parts, you might find it of interest to see at what place in a discussion of personal identity the terminology has to be interpreted literally and not as mere *façon de parler*. (At exactly what place does getting a plausible account of people really require making reference to temporally bounded proper parts of people and their bodies?) One place is here. You need that metaphysic to be a literal truth if you want to have both that psychological connectedness is the mark of personal identity and that people nevertheless are their bodies.

V

The more important question for our purposes is whether we should accept that psychological connectedness is the mark of personal identity. *Is* there good reason to suppose that the survivor in Brown-Case-Three really is Brown? To suppose that the survivor in that case is Brown is to suppose that the reprogramming done on Robinson's brain produced the state of affairs that consists in

The survivor is Brown,

instead of the state of affairs that consists in

The survivor is Robinson,

Robinson being horrendously confused in that he (wrongly) thinks he is Brown. Why should we agree to this?

I drew attention earlier to the fact that if you think that psychological connectedness is the mark of personal identity, you probably have a variety of different things in mind; and I said that among them, very likely, is a thesis about people, to the effect that there are no sudden, dramatic alterations across time in a person's psychology. Thus, where there is such an alteration across time, a new person has replaced the old one.[9] Why should we agree to this? Isn't it really an odd idea that tinkering with someone's brain – or feeding a person a drug – might result in a new person? A new personality, perhaps. A new consciousness, perhaps. (Remember Locke.) But a new man or woman, child or infant? If I just took LSD and the person now sitting at my desk therefore has beliefs, wants and so on that are dramatically different from those I had an hour ago, shouldn't we say, not that here is a new woman, but rather that here is the same old woman, poor Thomson, who has gone off the deep end?

Suppose that the LSD I just took brought about not merely that the person now sitting at my desk has beliefs, wants and so on that are dramatically different from those I had an hour ago, but, more, that those beliefs, wants and so on are very like those Queen Victoria had shortly before her death. (It was a special British LSD, designed to have this effect.) Can anyone really think it within reason to suppose that the person now sitting at my desk is Queen Victoria – or even to wonder whether it is? Maybe Queen Victoria's consciousness is back with us again; but Queen Victoria, the very woman herself, surely isn't.[10] And if she isn't, then psychological connectedness is not the mark of personal identity.

VI

And then there is the unfortunate possibility of duplication. If we can reprogram Robinson's brain with Brown's psychology, we can also concurrently be reprogramming Dickenson's. Suppose we do; let us call this Brown-Case-Four. There are two survivors in Brown-Case-Four, both of whom are, at their waking-time, psychologically connected with Brown at his becoming-unconscious-time. But the two survivors cannot both be Brown since they are not identical with each other.

Two consequences follow. First, the pure psychological criterion for body-switching is false. According to that criterion, transplanting a person's psychology is both necessary and sufficient for that person to switch bodies; according to that view, therefore, Brown has switched to both Robinson's and Dickenson's bodies in Brown-Case-Four. But Brown cannot be both survivors since they are two.[11] Those who think that Brown switched bodies in Brown-Case-One and Brown-Case-Three must therefore find some other way of explaining what marks him as having done so.

Second, Psychological Criterion (Connectedness) is also false, for both survivors being at waking-time psychologically connected with Brown at becoming-unconscious-time, Psychological Criterion (Connectedness) yields that Brown is both. I said in section III that if you think that psychological connectedness is the mark of personal identity, you probably have a variety of different theses in mind, of which Psychological Criterion (Connectedness) is only one possibility. Brown-Case-Four brings out that Psychological Criterion (Connectedness) had better not be among the theses you have in mind.

What to do? Well, the first question to be answered is what happens in Brown-Case-Four. It seems to me of great interest that most (all?) of those who think that psychological connectedness is the mark of personal identity would say that the result of the double reprogramming in Brown-Case-Four is the state of affairs that consists in

Neither survivor is Brown.

It pays to ask why, however, since they do have other options. In particular, they could instead say that the result of the double reprogramming in Brown-Case-Four is the state of affairs that consists in

Either Brown is the survivor who has what was formerly Robinson's body, or Brown is the survivor who has what was formerly Dickenson's body, and it is indeterminate which,

or the state of affairs that consists in

Either Brown is the survivor who has what was formerly Robinson's body, or Brown is the survivor who has what was formerly Dickenson's body, or neither survivor is Brown, and it is indeterminate which.

I cannot think of anyone who chooses one of these indeterminacy options, and we will return in section X to what this shows.

Meanwhile, however, most of those who think that psychological connectedness is the mark of personal identity would say that the result of the double reprogramming in Brown-Case-Four is that neither survivor is Brown. Suppose *we* take that view. Then, if we think that body-switching is possible, we will want to insert what might be called a no-competitors (or no-branching) clause in the pure psychological

Judith Jarvis Thomson

criterion for body-switching; and we will then say that it is because there is only one survivor in Brown-Case-One and Brown-Case-Three that Brown switches bodies in those cases, the presence of the second (competing) survivor in Brown-Case-Four being why Brown does not switch bodies in that case. If we are hybridists, we think that body-switching is not possible, and we will therefore reject the result of inserting a no-competitors-clause in the pure psychological criterion for body-switching, just as we originally rejected the pure psychological criterion for body-switching itself. But all of us, hybridist or not, will agree on the need to insert a no-competitors-clause in Psychological Criterion (Connectedness). Here is one way of doing so:

Psychological Criterion (Connectedness without Competitors): $x = y$ if and only if
(a) there are times t and t' such that y is a t' psychologically connected with x at t, and
(b) there is no z of which the following is the case: Not-$(z = y)$ and there are times t and t' such that z is at t' psychologically connected with x at t.

And all of us, hybridist or not, will say that, strictly speaking, it is not mere psychological connectedness, but rather *psychological connectedness without competitors* that is the mark of personal identity.

There is a difficulty here which I think has not been adequately appreciated. What I have in mind is the fact that a no-competitors-clause is going to have to contain a non-identity-clause. For example, the no-competitors-clause (b) in Psychological Criterion (Connectedness without Competitors) contains the clause

Not-$(z = y)$.

But if we are in search of criteria which tell us under what conditions x is identical with y, we should surely not be satisfied with one that requires that we know independently under what conditions z is not identical with y.

How are we to analyse that non-identity-clause out? If we are hybridists, we have room to manoeuvre: we can appeal to bodily non-identity. (I will come back to this in the following section.) If we are not hybridists, however, we have a real problem on our hands.[12] Whichever we are, however, we must take a stand on the matter. Airy hand-waving about the presence or absence of competitors (or branches) just isn't good enough.

A second difficulty here is familiar. One who thinks that psychological connectedness without competitors is the mark of personal identity thinks that a question about personal identity can be settled by appeal to a fact that should surely be irrelevant to it. On this view, neither survivor is Brown if both reprogrammings succeed; but if only one succeeds, then the survivor of that one is Brown. So a small, chance slip-up in the procedures, which fixes that only one reprogramming goes through, fixes that Brown survives. This sounds very implausible.

In short, we have been led by these ideas to some very implausible conclusions: namely, that tinkering with someone's brain, or feeding a person a drug, could result in a new person (section V), and that the question whether it does turns on what should surely be the irrelevant question whether two brains were tinkered with, or two people fed the drug (this section).

VII

I asked in the preceding section what those who think that psychological connectedness is the mark of personal identity are to do in face of the possibility of duplication, as in Brown-Case-Four, for example. And I said that most of them would say that the result in that case is that neither survivor is Brown. I then drew attention to two difficulties which they face. What if they instead say that the result in that case is indeterminacy? Suppose they do. They still face the first of the two difficulties, for they still stand in need of an account of what marks the case as one in which there *are* two survivors; after all, it is only because there are two that the result is indeterminacy. And they face an analogue of the second, for they are committed to the idea that determinateness in surviving, and in who one is, can be settled by appeal to a fact that should surely be irrelevant to it. On their view, indeterminacy results if both reprogrammings succeed; a small, chance slip-up in the procedures, which fixes that only one reprogramming goes through, fixes that Brown determinately survives, and is, determinately, the sole survivor. This sounds very implausible.

As I said in the preceding section, hybridists do not face the first of those difficulties, for they can appeal to bodily non-identity as sufficient for personal non-identity. Let us have a look at what hybridists would say about Brown-Case-Four. Suppose that the double reprogramming in Brown-Case-Four is carried out at *t*, and consider the following three entities:

(a) the beginning-to-*t* temporal part of what the vulgar would call Brown's body,

(b) the *t*-to-ending temporal part of what the vulgar would call Robinson's body,

and

(c) the *t*-to-ending temporal part of what the vulgar would call Dickenson's body.

Hybridists can say that Brown's body, and thus Brown himself, just is (a); if they do, they are saying that Brown goes out of existence at *t*, and *a fortiori* that neither survivor is Brown in Brown-Case-Four.[13] And *they* have no trouble saying what marks the two survivors off from each other, for (b) is one survivor, and (c) is one survivor, and (b) and (c) are physical objects which occupy different places. On the other hand, the second difficulty remains; for on this view a small, chance slip-up in the procedures – which fixes that only one reprogramming goes through, the Robinson reprogramming as it might be – fixes that Brown's body is the fusion of (a) and (b), instead of merely being (a) alone, and thus fixes that Brown survives. This sounds very implausible.

Judith Jarvis Thomson

It is worth noticing that hybridists have yet another option in respect of Brown-Case-Four; they can instead say the following. The fusion of (a) and (b) is *a* body, and thus *a* person; call it Brown–Robinson. The fusion of (a) and (c) is *a* body, and thus *a* person; call it Brown–Dickenson. Since (b) is not identical with (c), Brown-Robinson is not identical with Brown-Dickenson. But Brown-Robinson and Brown-Dickenson overlap, for they share (a). Then, although neither survivor is Brown, this is not because Brown goes out of existence at *t*, but rather because there was no (one) person Brown – there always were two people called 'Brown'.[14]

However an analogue of the second difficulty faces this option. One who takes this line is thereby committed to the idea that how many people there are at a given time and place can be settled by appeal to a fact that should surely be irrelevant to it. On this view, there were two people sitting at Brown's desk prior to *t* if both reprogrammings were going to succeed; a small, chance slip-up in the procedures, which fixes that only one reprogramming goes through, fixes that there was only one. This again sounds very implausible.

In short, if you think that the survivor is Brown in Brown-Case-One and Brown-Case-Three, and therefore think that psychological connectedness is the mark of personal identity, then you have no plausible options in respect of Brown-Case-Four.

VIII

So there is serious trouble for those who think that psychological connectedness is the mark of personal identity. On the one hand, they are committed to its being the case that tinkering with someone's brain, or feeding a person a drug, could result in a new person, and that is very implausible (section V). On the other hand, they are committed to its being the case that a question about personal identity (section VI), or about determinacy in personal identity, or about how many people there are at a given time or place (section VII), can turn on a fact that should surely be irrelevant to it. Why, then, do so many philosophers nevertheless think that psychological connectedness *must* be the mark of personal identity – in some appropriate sense of 'psychological connectedness', and in some appropriate way of being 'the mark of'? There seem to be three reasons.

In the first place, it seems to many philosophers that body-switching – or anyway, doing what is body-switching if the metaphysic of temporal parts is false – really must be possible, for they think we can imagine it. Suppose it is possible. What could be thought to mark the person *x* who now has body A as the person *y* who formerly had body B, and who has thus switched from body B to body A? All that is available by way of mark that this has happened is the connectedness of *x*'s psychology with *y*'s. So it must be that psychological connectedness really is the mark of personal identity.

Can we imagine body-switching? Many people have described states of affairs in which, as they say, body-switching would really be going on – or perhaps, more modestly, social arrangements in which, as they say, the participants would themselves say that what was going on is body-switching.[15] But I do not think that those descriptions are themselves what bear the weight: I doubt that people would be moved by those descriptions to conclude that body-switching is possible if they did not think they could imagine body-switching from inside, as it were. It is *that*, I think – the idea that one can imagine oneself switching bodies – that bears the weight, and thereby makes the descriptions seem to be more convincing than they would otherwise be.

Can we imagine body-switching from inside? One is initially inclined to think it's easy. I close my eyes, and form a mental picture of Mary's lap as it would look to her if she were looking down at it, and of Mary's hands on the keyboard of her typewriter as they would look if she were looking down on them, and so on; and I think to myself, "Now I am imagining my having switched to Mary's body." But how does my having formed that mental picture warrant my saying that what I am imagining is my having switched to Mary's body? There is nothing in the picture itself which could be thought to make it a picture of my having switched to Mary's body: the picture is merely a picture of Mary's body. (Compare a drawing or photograph of Mary's lap and hands.)

With what reason do I describe myself, having formed the picture, as 'imagining my having switched to Mary's body'? Why not instead as 'imagining how things would look to Mary if she were at her typewriter now'? Or as 'imagining myself under a delusion as to how my own lap and hands look'? It cannot be said that I am master of what I am imagining, on pain of making my being able to imagine something be no ground at all for thinking it possible, for if I am master of what I am imagining, then it is up to me whether I am imagining round squares all over my desk. Moreover, if I am master of what I am imagining, then why did I bother to form the mental picture in the first place? It is of interest that my forming a picture of Mary's lap and hands did seem to play a role in making me feel it right to describe myself as 'imagining my having switched to Mary's body'.

But my forming that picture cannot really have played any more of a role than this: the picture shows how my body would now look to me *if* I had switched to Mary's body and were at her typewriter now. If that is right, then the picture does nothing at all to support the possibility of body-switching, for it shows what I take it to show only on the supposition that I have switched to Mary's body. (Compare my drawing a picture of a banana and saying "This is how tigers would look *if* tigers were bananas." Have I now imagined tigers being bananas?)

There is a deep and quite general difficulty in the offing here: namely, what is involved in imagining something from inside, for oneself, and I bypass it. Meanwhile, however, I think it clear that the kind of exercise in picture-forming I have drawn attention to does not bear the weight that needs bearing if we are to conclude that body-switching is possible, or even that we can imagine it.

A second reason why it seems to many philosophers that psychological connectedness must be the mark of personal identity is that it seems to them that people could exist without bodies at all. Suppose that is possible. What could be thought to mark a certain bodiless person x as a certain bodiless person y? All that seems to be available by way of a mark of this identity is the connectedness of x's psychology with y's. So it must be that psychological connectedness really is the mark of personal identity.

Why do we think that people could exist without bodies at all? Something similar goes on. I close my eyes (it is of interest that we close our eyes in engaging in these exercises), and I attend to my toothache and my general feeling of fatigue. 'There', I think; 'that could exist without any physical objects existing, and *a fortiori* without my body existing. So *I* could exist without my body existing.' Well, these are things I am inclined to think. The thoughts bubble up so naturally that they seem obvious truths. But they are not. The difficulties here are familiar enough, however, and have a long history, so I set this second reason aside.

A third reason is more direct. Here is David Lewis:

> I find that what I mostly want in wanting survival is that my mental life should flow on. My present experiences, thoughts, beliefs, desires, and traits of character should have appropriate future successors. My total present mental state should be but one momentary stage in a continuing succession of mental states.[16]

And he takes his intuitively finding that what he mostly wants is that his mental life flow on to give him a reason for believing, and thus for trying to show, that *its* flowing on fixes that *he* does. I am sure that Lewis is not alone in taking this route to the idea that psychological connectedness is the mark of personal identity.

On the other hand, he grants that if his mental life's flowing on turned out on analysis not to fix that he does, then he would give up his intuitive finding that what he mostly wants in wanting survival is that his mental life flow on. ("Else it would be difficult to believe one's own philosophy!", he says.) People must of course speak for themselves on these matters, but it is surely true for most of us that if we were told that we will die this afternoon, it would be small consolation to be told also that there will be someone else alive tomorrow who will then be psychologically connected with us today. There are, of course, things we want done in future, many of them such that the more likely it is that there will be someone tomorrow who will then be psychologically connected with us today, the more likely it is that the things will actually get done. (I want my cat to be cared for, for example, and who but someone psychologically connected with me could love so scrawny a creature?) But that those things will actually get done would be, for most of us, thin gruel as consolation. Furthermore, there are also things we want done in future that we do not *just* want done: I have in mind things we want done in future by us, among them being things we want done in future only by us. (Someone psychologically connected with me is going to want to wear my wedding-ring, and that prospect is anything but consoling.)

Parfit thinks that the attitude I express here, and attribute to most of us, is irrational. He argues that, given that there will be someone alive tomorrow who will be, tomorrow, psychologically connected with me today, it is irrational for me to care whether that person will be *me*. His argument appeals to duplication, and can be reconstructed as follows. He invites us to accept

(i)   The survivor in the single reprogramming Brown-Case-Three is Brown,

and

(ii)   Neither survivor in the double reprogramming Brown-Case-Four is Brown.

Given (i), Brown survives single reprogramming: he lives. Given (ii), Brown does not survive double reprogramming: he dies. So, given that there will be at least one reprogramming at *t*, Brown will live after *t* if and only if there is no more than one. So if Brown cares about survival, what he is caring about – given that there will be at least one reprogramming – is whether there will be more than one. But Brown can hardly be thought to get less if there is more than one reprogramming than he gets if there is only one: after all, the relation in which he stands to the survivor in the single reprogramming case is the very relation in which he stands to each of the two survivors in the double reprogramming case, but for the sheer fact that double repro-gramming is single reprogramming twice over, and hence results in two survivors. It is therefore irrational for Brown to care whether there will be more than one repro-gramming. Therefore, given that there will be at least one reprogramming at *t*, it is irrational for Brown to care whether he himself will survive what happens at *t*.[17]

Parfit does not spell out how this conclusion about Brown is to be generalized to the rest of us, but I suppose his thought is this. Suppose there will be someone in existence tomorrow who will then be psychologically connected with me today – *whatever* is going to cause this phenomenon. Given analogues of (i) and (ii) for me, I will live tomorrow if and only if there is no more than one. It is irrational for me to care whether there will be more than one. Therefore, given that there will be at least one, it is irrational for me to care whether I survive tomorrow.

The argument rests, of course, on its premises (i) and (ii); should we accept them? Those who believe that psychological connectedness is the mark of personal identity will of course accept (i); but I have been arguing that that idea leads to serious trouble. And that most of us do not in fact accept (i) comes out in this way: if a doctor tells us we will die this afternoon, but that someone else, exactly one, will be alive tomor-row who will then be psychologically connected with us today, most of us do not reply "You're suffering from metaphysical confusion, for if there'll be exactly one it'll be me," but instead, "Well, I suppose that isn't nothing, but it isn't much." Parfit's argument does nothing at all to show that we are mistaken, since accepting its first premiss (i) requires just assuming that we are mistaken.

And what of (ii)? As I said in section VI, most people who think that psychological connectedness is the mark of personal identity do choose to say that neither survivor is Brown in Brown-Case-Four, but I drew attention to the implausibility of saying (ii), having said (i).[18]

In short, accepting Parfit's premises (i) and (ii) requires supposing that psychologi-cal connectedness without competitors is both necessary and sufficient for personal identity. To the extent to which we are right to be suspicious of this idea, we are right to remain unmoved by Parfit's argument for the conclusion that, as he puts it, personal identity is not what matters.

IX

Suppose we reject the idea that psychological connectedness is the mark of personal identity. Suppose we accept the simple and attractive idea that people are their bodies, and therefore take bodily identity to be the mark of personal identity – *and* agree

Judith Jarvis Thomson

with the vulgar about which body is Brown's body or yours or mine. (We can, if we like, also accept the metaphysic of temporal parts, but our views about personal identity do not require us to do so.) Then we conclude that Brown dies in all four of the cases we have looked at. In the single and double reprogramming cases, Brown-Case-Three and Brown-Case-Four, Brown's body is wholly destroyed at the relevant time t, and so, we conclude, is Brown. In the brain transplant cases Brown-Case-One and Brown-Case-Two, Brown's body is not wholly destroyed at t, for his brain is preserved and transplanted into Robinson's head; but while a part of Brown's body, and so of Brown, does therefore survive in those cases, his body does not, and we say the same of Brown himself.

I will call this 'the ordinary view' of people and their identity conditions, because it does seem to be the view that we would take if we had not gone wandering into the clouds of philosophy trailed by the word 'person'.

In particular, the duplication in Brown-Case-Four makes no trouble for the ordinary view. Both survivors think they are Brown in that case; but if we accept the ordinary view, we think they are mistaken, just as we think the one survivor who thinks he is Brown in Brown-Case-One and Brown-Case-Three is mistaken.

What of duplication of another kind? In a fifth case, Brown's body is split down the middle, and the resulting bits of flesh and bone are refashioned into two smaller living bodies. If we accept the ordinary view, we will say that neither survivor is Brown in this case too. Compare, after all, what happens when an amoeba splits: neither of the resulting two amoebae is the original. No matter if both say 'Me, me, I'm the original!' – neither is.

Does our concern for survival shed doubt on the ordinary view? Would I care about survival if I really thought that for me to survive is merely for this mass of flesh and blood to survive? What is so special about *it* that I should want it to survive? The short, and I think entirely adequate, answer is that it *is* me, so that if it does not survive, I do not.

But a longer answer is available. It is not the mere continued existence of this human body that so concerns me. For example, I think at the moment that I would prefer being buried to being cremated after death, but my preference is not a firm one, and I might later decide otherwise. What I want in wanting to survive is not merely that this body should continue to exist, but that it should continue to function in the ways in which living human bodies function. And not merely that it should continue to function in just any of the ways in which living human bodies function, for the prospect of coma ending only in death is no more attractive than death is. (Nancy Cruzan would surely not have welcomed the prospect of being in the condition she is now in.) What I want in wanting to survive is that this body should continue to function in the ways in which living human bodies function when they support consciousness, and, for preference, in which they function when they also support perception and make action of a wide variety of kinds possible. Mere consciousness wouldn't be nothing: I could still ruminate on the nature of the universe. But the enterprise would pall after a while. What I want is to go on leading a more or less full human life, and for that, this more or less well-functioning human body is exactly what I do need. If I could switch to another – a younger and healthier one – that would be splendid. But since I can't, I do need this one.

X

The difficulty that stands in the way of adopting the ordinary view is not anything that supports a psychological criterion for personal identity: quite to the contrary, it stands in the way of adopting psychological criteria too. What I have in mind is what inclines us to think that Descartes must be right, and that people must really be mental substances. What I have in mind, in short, is what inclines us to reject indeterminacy for people.

Let us go back. I drew attention in section VI to the interesting fact that most people who think that psychological connectedness is the mark of personal identity say that when we reprogram both Robinson's and Dickenson's brains, the result is the state of affairs that consists in

Neither survivor is Brown.

They do not say that the result is the state of affairs that consists in

Either Brown is the survivor who has what was formerly Robinson's body, or Brown is the survivor who has what was formerly Dickenson's body, and it is indeterminate which,

or

Either Brown is the survivor who has what was formerly Robinson's body, or Brown is the survivor who has what was formerly Dickenson's body, or neither survivor is Brown, and it is indeterminate which.

Why do they reject the indeterminacy options? Because they are inclined to think that it just cannot be indeterminate which of two people a given person is, or whether a person survives. Why are they inclined to think this?

What Parfit's Psychological Spectrum (*RP*, p. 231) brings home to us is that even if you reject indeterminacy about which of two people a given person is, you are going to be committed to indeterminacy about whether a person survives – if you accept a criterion of identity whose central piece of conceptual machinery is psychological connectedness. Parfit invites us to imagine a series of possible operations on a person's brain, Green's, let us say. In the first operation, just a little tinkering is done on Green's brain: the survivor wakes having a belief which Green did not have prior to the operation. Here we are all inclined to say that it is Green who wakes, thus that the survivor is Green. In the second operation, a bit more tinkering is done on Green's brain. And so on. In the last operation of the series, massive tinkering is done on Green's brain, and the survivor wakes thinking he is Napoleon. If you think that psychological connectedness is the mark of personal identity, you will of course say that the survivor of the last operation is not Green. But what of operations somewhere in the middle of this series? Is the survivor Green? There's no saying whether he is.[19] Even if you have avoided indeterminacy as to which of the two survivors is Brown in Brown-Case-Four – by fiat, thus by simply declaring that neither survivor is Brown in that case – you will have to allow for indeterminacy as to whether a person survives at all. After all, the central piece of conceptual machinery in your

Judith Jarvis Thomson

account of personal identity is psychological connectedness, and that relation is vague. But if you must accept indeterminacy about whether a person survives, why not also about which survivor Brown is? I can see no reason to think that indeterminacy about which is worse than indeterminacy about whether.

If you accept Physical Criterion, then you are not committed to indeterminacy as to which of two survivors a person is in the case I mentioned in the preceding section, in which Brown's body is split down the middle and the resulting bits of flesh and bone are refashioned into two smaller living bodies. What of a case in which we successively removed and then replaced parts of (what we took to be) Brown's body, and then someone else constructed a second body out of the parts that we had removed?[20] Is one of the two resulting bodies Brown's? And if so, which? Compare our successively removing and replacing planks in (what we took to be) the ship of Theseus, and then someone else's constructing a second ship out of the planks that we had removed. Is one of the two resulting ships the ship of Theseus? And if so, which? I am inclined to think that 'One is, but it's indeterminate which' is as good an answer as any, for the ship of Theseus, as for Brown's body.

In any case, Parfit's Physical Spectrum (*RP*, p. 234) brings home to us that anyone who accepts Physical Criterion is going to be committed to indeterminacy as to whether a person survives. Parfit invites us to imagine a series of operations on a person Blue, in which Blue's cells are replaced: in the first operation, one cell of Blue's body is replaced, in the second, two are replaced, . . . , in the last, all cells but one are replaced. If you accept Physical Criterion, you will say that Blue's body, and thus Blue himself, survives the first operation, and does not survive the last; but what of operations in the middle of the series?[21] There is no saying whether Blue's body, and thus Blue himself, survives them. That this outcome confronts those who are attracted by Physical Criterion should be no surprise: it is a familiar enough fact that the question whether what we have before us today is the same body (ship, shoe, computer) as the one we had before us yesterday may have no determinate answer.

But we are inclined to think that there cannot be indeterminacy *either* as to which of two people a given person is *or* as to whether a person survives. If that thought is right, then Physical Criterion, and *a fortiori*, Physical Thesis, must be rejected – along with all psychological criteria in which psychological connectedness supplies the central piece of conceptual machinery. And the thought that there cannot be either kind of indeterminacy is intimately connected with the thought that a person must really be a mental substance – a mental monad, in fact. For if there cannot be either kind of indeterminacy, then doesn't that mean that people have to be indivisible? (If people have parts, as bodies do, then indeterminacy in respect of them would surely be possible.)

Why are we inclined to think that there cannot be either kind of indeterminacy? This inclination is very strong in us,[22] and I think it has not been taken seriously enough in the contemporary literature on personal identity: people do not ask exactly why it has such a grip on us.

Consider Blue, and imagine he has been subjected to a middle-of-the-series operation, so that it is indeterminate whether the resulting body is Blue's. Physical Criterion says that it is indeterminate whether the survivor is Blue. But we think that it just cannot be indeterminate whether Blue survived, and I suggest that this is because we want to ask what Blue is now experiencing if it is supposed to be indeterminate whether he survived, and that nothing we will count as an answer could possibly *be* the answer. We reject 'Either the recovery room or nothing' as not an answer at all. And what we would count as an answer – as it might be, 'A flickering between the recovery room and nothing' – cannot be the answer if (as let us suppose) the survivor is not experiencing a flickering; for if Blue is experiencing a flickering and the survivor is not, then Blue is determinately not the survivor.

Similarly, I think, with indeterminacy as to which person a given person is. Suppose someone were to say that in Brown-Case-Four the result is that Brown determinately survived, but that it is indeterminate which of the two survivors he is. We think it just cannot be indeterminate which of the two survivors Brown is, and I suggest that this is because we want to ask what Brown is now experiencing if it is supposed to be indeterminate which survivor he is, and that nothing we will count as an answer could possibly *be* the answer. Suppose one survivor is looking at Boston, the other at Worcester. We reject 'Either Boston or Worcester' as not an answer at all. And what we would count as an answer – as it might be, 'A flickering between Boston and Worcester' – cannot be the answer if (as let us suppose) neither survivor is experiencing a flickering; for if Brown is experiencing a flickering, and neither survivor is, then Brown is determinately neither survivor.

But why do we feel that the question what a person is now experiencing *has* to have a non-disjunctive answer? If it can be indeterminate whether a person survives, or which survivor he is, then the question what a person is now experiencing really can lack a non-disjunctive answer. Why do we feel so tempted to proceed from there, not by *modus ponens*, but instead by *modus tollens*? That feeling must surely have some interesting source, and it probably lies in our overestimating what goes on in determinate survival. In any case, I suspect that no account of personal identity will entirely satisfy us in the absence of an understanding of it.[23]

Notes

1 I here follow Vere Chappell, "Locke on the Ontology of Matter, Living Things and Persons," *Philosophical Studies* 60/1–2 (Sept.–Oct. 1990). pp. 19–32. Chappell rebuts the attribution of relativized identity to Locke in "Locke and Relative Identity," *History of Philosophy Quarterly* 6/1 (Jan. 1989), pp. 69–83.

2 The case I begin with comes from Sydney Shoemaker, *Self-knowledge and Self-identity* (Ithaca, NY: Cornell University Press, 1963).

3 I take this to be Mark Johnston's view. I take him to believe that we cannot switch bodies without the continuing of our 'mental life', and he says that 'we cannot switch bodies without brain transplantation'. See his "Human Beings," *Journal of Philosophy* 84/2 (Feb. 1987), pp. 79–80.

4 I adapt this account of psychological connectedness from Derek Parfit, *Reasons and Persons* (Oxford: Oxford University Press, 1984), pp. 205–6 [hereafter *RP*].

5 We could state this thesis more precisely if we introduced a relation 'psychological continuity' – defined in terms of the relation 'psychological connectedness' that I set out in the text above – in the manner of Parfit, *RP*, pp. 206–7. I will not take space to do so, however, since actually laying out the definition is a rather messier enterprise than is usually

thought. (One way of supplying the details may be found in my "Ruminations on an Account of Personal Identity," in *On Being and Saying, Essays for Richard Cartwright*, ed. J. J. Thomson (Cambridge, MA: MIT Press, 1987), pp. 215–40.) For it must be remembered that the relation of psychological connectedness that I set out in the text above is a four-place relation on people and times. In section IV we take note of two-place psychological connectedness and continuity relations.

6   It is worth stress that this question is no less pressing if you think that Brown switches bodies only in Brown-Case-One.

7   We do not *say* 'My body believes that today is Thursday' or 'My body wants a banana'; we instead say 'I believe that today is Thursday' or 'I want a banana'. Does this fact of usage refute Physical Thesis? Anyone who thinks so will have to explain why we also do not say 'My body weighs 250 pounds', preferring instead, 'I weigh 250 pounds', and why, by contrast, 'My body is all over red splotches' and 'I am all over red splotches' are quite on a par. It seems to me an interesting question what lies behind these facts of usage, but I see nothing in them on which to rest a rejection of Physical Thesis.

8   I argue for it in "Parthood and Identity across Time," *Journal of Philosophy* 80 (1983), pp. 201–20. See also Sally Haslanger, "Persistence, Change, and Explanation," *Philosophical Studies* 56 (1989), pp. 1–28.

9   Some of those who think that psychological connectedness is the mark of personal identity think that even a gradual alteration in a person's psychology may result in a new person, and does result in a new person if the change is sufficiently deep and extensive. Why should we agree to this? If my Uncle Alfred gradually, over the years, comes to suffer from a severe case of Alzheimer's disease, then isn't the outcome just poor Uncle Alfred, the very man himself, who has undergone this terrible change? (Compare Nancy Cruzan.)

10 Suppose that Queen Victoria's brain had been carefully preserved and was just transplanted into my head, and that it was *that* which caused the current beliefs, wants and so on of the person now sitting at my desk to be those of Queen Victoria. Can anyone really think it is Queen Victoria who sits there now?

11 Instead of reprogramming both Robinson's and Dickenson's brains, we could have split Brown's brain, transplanting half into Robinson's body and the other half into Dickenson's. As many people have pointed out, a person can survive with only half a brain, so we might have two survivors here too, both of them psychologically connected with Brown. I characterized the impure psychological view as follows: transplanting a person's psychology, and doing so by way of transplanting that person's brain, is both necessary and sufficient for that person to switch bodies. So those who accept the impure psychological view are safe against the possibility of duplication only if they insist that body-switching requires that the transplanting of psychology be caused by the transplanting of all of the brain (or anyway, of enough of the brain so that transplanting what is left into someone else does not cause a second transplanting of psychology). Is there supposed to be good reason for this further bit of digging in of heels?

12 Consider a pair of identical twins who die shortly after birth, and whose psychologies, we can suppose, never come to differ. We can hardly fancy the idea that only one baby was born, though it had two bodies; we had better allow that two babies were born. It follows that there isn't going to be any *purely* psychological conceptual machinery that will enable non-hybridists to analyse the non-identity-clause out. What else is available to a non-hybridist? (I need hardly add that those twins make quite general trouble for the ideas we are looking at.)

13 A hybridist who chooses this account of what happens in Brown-Case-Four would of course have to adopt a rather more complicated account of co-personality than I pointed at in section IV.

14 This account of what goes on in Brown-Case-Four comes from David Lewis, "Survival and Identity," in *The Identities of Persons*, ed. Amelie O. Rorty (Berkeley: University of California Press, 1976), pp. 17–40. Lewis says that persons are aggregates of psychologically related person-stages, but does not declare himself on what those things are. If we construe his person-stages as temporal body-parts, then we are construing Lewis as a hybridist.

15 See e.g. Sydney Shoemaker and Richard Swinburne, *Personal Identity* (Oxford: Blackwell, 1984), pp. 108–11.

16 Lewis, 'Survival and Identity', p. 17.

17 This is a reconstruction, not a mere summary, of Parfit's argument, which appears on pp. 255–66 of *Reasons and Persons*, for Parfit's single and double survivor cases there involve half-brain transplants, and not (as I have it here) reprogrammings. But I take the transplants not to be essential to Parfit's argument, and he says, in fact, that for his part, the psychological connectedness between survivor(s) and original could have had any cause at all (p. 262). Indeed, it is hard to see how Parfit's argument could be generalized so as to bear on the rest of us, who will not be undergoing transplantation, if the transplantation really were essential to it.

18 Parfit himself expresses discomfort about (ii): he asks, 'How could a double success be a failure?' (*RP* p. 256). He nevertheless goes on to say that 'the best description' of a duplication case is that neither of the survivors is the original (*RP* p. 260), and that 'we can best describe the case by saying that neither' is the original (*RP* p. 262); that is because he regards 'It's indeterminate' as an unacceptable answer to the question of which survivor is the original.

19 I say there's no saying whether he is, but do not mean to commit myself thereby to any particular way of squaring indeterminacy with logic. Suppose we have a pair of options p and not-p, and it is indeterminate which. On some views, we should conclude that p and not-p lack truth-values. On other views, we should instead conclude that p and not-p do have truth-values, though it is indeterminate which truth-values they have. (For a recent argument for the latter choice, see Paul Horwich, *Truth* (Oxford: Blackwell, 1990), pp. 80–7.) I take no stand on this matter. If psychological connectedness is the mark of personal identity, then it is indeterminate whether the survivor of a middle-of-the-series operation in Psychological Spectrum is Green, just as it is indeterminate whether a colour mid-way between red and orange is red; I leave open whether we should conclude that 'He is Green' and 'It is red' lack truth-values.

20 I am grateful to Barbara Von Eckardt and Joseph Mendola for reminding me of this possibility.

21 Sheer quantity of matter replaced is surely not what counts, however, I imagine that we would be inclined to say 'same body' even if more than half the matter in it had been replaced, so long as the replacement had been made at places not important to the continued functioning of the body. For example, contrast replacing body fat with replacing the head and chest. (An analogous point holds of ships, shoes and computers.)

22 Discussing a case of future fission on himself, Chisholm says: 'I see the following . . . clearly and distinctly to be true . . . that if Lefty and Righty clearly *are* persons, as we are imagining, then the questions "Will I be Lefty?" and "Will I be Righty?" have entirely definite answers.' Determinate answers, I take him to mean. (That 'I will be Lefty' and 'I will be Righty' have truth-values, it being indeterminate which – see n. 19 – would not satisfy him.) Doesn't he here express a feeling we share? See Roderick M. Chisholm, "Reply to Strawson's Comments," in *Language, Belief, and Metaphysics*, ed. H. E. Kiefer and Milton K. Munitz (Albany, NY: State University of New York Press, 1970).

23 I am indebted to George Boolos and Paul Horwich for comments on an earlier draft of this essay.

Persons, Bodies, and Human Beings

Derek Parfit

Of the possible criteria of personal identity, there were three that I took seriously in the book that Judith Thomson discusses.[1] On the *Wide Psychological Criterion*, for some future person to be me, we must be psychologically continuous. On the *Physical Criterion*, which I shall here rename the *Brain Criterion*, we must have the same brain. On the *Narrow Psychological Criterion*, we must both be psychologically continuous and have the same brain.[2]

My discussion of these criteria was confused. At one point, I endorsed the Wide Psychological Criterion (*RP* 208). That was a mistake. As I later claimed, we should not try to decide between these criteria.[3] In the so-called "problem cases," where these criteria conflict, questions about personal identity would be indeterminate, and empty. If we knew the facts about both physical and psychological continuity, there would be nothing further to discover.

According to some writers, even if there is nothing to discover, we should at least consider how we can best refine our concept of a person, by adopting one of these criteria. But that, I believe, is not worth doing. First, as I shall argue again below, personal identity is not what matters. Nor should we try to find some criterion that would make identity coincide with what matters. Such coincidence could not be complete. Unlike what matters, for example, numerical identity cannot hold to different degrees. And, if we try to preserve the coincidence between identity and what matters, it will be harder fully to shake off the view that identity is what matters.

Though I believe that we need not choose between my three criteria, we cannot discuss persons without making some assumptions about personal identity. And, in some of my arguments, I assumed

(1) If there will be a single future person who will have enough of my brain to be psychologically continuous with me, that person will be me.

(2) If some future person will neither be psychologically continuous with me, nor have enough of my brain, that person will not be me.

These claims I shall call *my view*. This view seemed to me uncontroversial, since it is the shared or common element in my three criteria.

Judith Thomson rejects my view. She accepts a fourth criterion, which I dismissed, too lazily, in a single sentence.

1 Thomson's View

Thomson accepts:

The Bodily Criterion:
(1) We continue to exist if and only if our bodies continue to exist.
(2) Our bodies would continue to exist even if our brains were replaced.

On Thomson's view, if her brain were destroyed, and my brain were successfully transplanted into her empty skull, it would be she who would wake up, mistakenly believing that she was me.

Thomson sees little need to defend her view. She calls it "the ordinary view," and she asks: Can anyone think otherwise?

The answer is Yes. I know many people who have considered this question, and most think otherwise.[4]

Even if we all thought otherwise, Thomson's view might still be true. But, before considering Thomson's arguments, it is worth suggesting why hers is *not* the ordinary view.

To apply Thomson's view, we must decide what would count as the continued existence of the same body. We, and our bodies, would survive the loss of certain limbs and organs. But how far could this process go? Thomson says that she wants her body to continue to "support consciousness." Even if she could not act, she writes, "Mere consciousness wouldn't be nothing: I could still ruminate on the nature of the universe."[5] What would be required for someone's body still to support consciousness?

Suppose that I became paralyzed, and lost sensation in all of my body below the neck. Suppose also that, because of damage to my heart and lungs, my brain was connected to a heart-lung machine. If these things happened, both I and my body would continue to exist. I could still see, and hear, and speak, and do philosophy.

Suppose next that, in a second operation, my head was disconnected from the rest of my numb and paralyzed body.[6] Would I then cease to exist? On Thomson's view, the answer depends on whether, if my head continued to exist and to support consciousness, that would amount to my body's continuing to exist.

Assume, first, that it would not. Thomson's view then implies that I would have ceased to exist. If we accept this view, we must decide how we should regard my surviving head. Even if I had ceased to exist, my head would be that of a conscious being, with many of the properties of an ordinary person. This being would have a mental life like the one that I had before my head was disconnected from the rest of my body. It could admire the sunrise, talk to my friends, and dictate the rest of my unfinished book. Given these facts, it would be hard not to regard my head as a living

Derek Parfit

person's head. But, on this version of Thomson's view, this person cannot be me. My head must now be the head of a new person.

If we accept that conclusion, this case challenges the view that identity is what matters. Suppose that I knew in advance that, if my head were disconnected from the rest of my body, my brain would function rather better, and would no longer be subject to migraine attacks. On that assumption, as I shall argue later, I ought to accept this operation. It would be irrelevant whether, after my head was disconnected, it would become the head, not of me, but of a new person.

Thomson might give a different answer. She might claim that, if my head continued to exist, after the rest of my body was destroyed, this would amount to my body's continuing to exist, though in a diminished state. On this version of Thomson's view, even after this operation, I would still exist.

Our story might continue. Suppose that, after another operation, the blood going to my head came, not from a heart-lung machine, but from someone else's heart and lungs. And suppose that my head was then grafted onto the rest of that other person's body. That other person we can assume to be Thomson, whose head had earlier been destroyed in some accident.

Would these further operations make it true that I would cease to exist? Thomson's answer must be Yes. She believes that, if her body was given a new brain, it would still be the same body, and she would therefore still exist. It could not affect the identity of Thomson's body if its new brain retained its covering of bone and skin. Thomson's view thus implies that, at the end of our story, it would be she who would have my head.

If we accept this view, our story again suggests that identity is not what matters. Thomson may think that no objection. As she remarks, so far as the metaphysics is concerned, whether personal identity matters is not what matters. Our story also, however, challenges Thomson's view. We have now imagined four operations. My head would first be connected to a heart-lung machine, then disconnected from the rest of my body, then reconnected to Thomson's heart and lungs, then grafted onto Thomson's headless body. On Thomson's view, I would not survive all these operations; by the end of this story, my head would have become hers. It is hard to accept this view. In each of these operations, my head would be unharmed. We could even suppose that, throughout our story, there would be no interruption in the stream of thoughts and experiences that would be directly related to my brain. It is hard to believe that, of this continuous stream of experiences, the first would be had by me, and the last by Thomson.

It may be objected that I am appealing here to a Sorites argument, of a kind we know to be unsound. I may seem to be claiming only that, in this series of operations, there could not be a point at which I would cease to exist. And that may seem no better than the claim that, if I kept losing single hairs, there could not be a point at which I would become bald. But my claim is not of this kind. There could, I agree, be a sequence of events in which what starts as one person's body ends as the body of someone else. And, in claiming that such a sequence might occur, we need not suppose that there would have to be some point at which the first person ceased to exist. We could claim that, in the middle of this sequence, it would be indeterminate which person existed.

Persons, Bodies, and Human Beings | 179

My claim is different. I believe that, when we consider my imagined story, most of us would be confident that I would survive. Given what we know about physiology, most of us believe that, if our heads will continue to receive the blood that our brains need, and our brains will continue to function in a normal way, we ourselves will continue to exist. What happens below our necks, though it may affect the content of the experiences that are directly related to our brains, cannot, we assume, make it true that these experiences will not be ours.

2 Cases and Intuitions

Thomson's view is, I have claimed, implausible. It may be objected that, in supporting that claim, I have appealed only to one example. Might there not be cases where it is *my* view that is implausible?

It will help to classify the cases where I and Thomson disagree. We are asking when it is true that some future person will be me. On Thomson's view, that person will be me if and only if we have the same body. On my view, that person will be me if we have the same brain, and are uniquely psychologically continuous. If we have different brains, and are not psychologically continuous, that person will not be me. In other cases, on my view, there is indeterminacy, or no answer to the question whether that person will be me.[7]

We can next distinguish two kinds of disagreement. Thomson and I *strongly* disagree when there is some claim that she thinks true, and I think false. We *weakly* disagree when there is some claim that she thinks true, and I think indeterminate, or neither true nor false.

If some future person will be psychologically continuous with me, let us say, for short, that this person will have *my psychology*. Thomson and I strongly disagree in any case where

(A) some future person would have my brain and psychology, but a different body,

or

(B) some future person would have my body, but a different brain and psychology.

There are six kinds of case. (A) would be true when some future person would have my brain and psychology, but either (1) someone else's body, or (2) a new body. (B) would be true when some future person would have my body, but either (3) a new brain and psychology, or (4) someone else's brain and a third person's psychology, or (5) someone else's brain and a new psychology, or (6) a new brain and someone else's psychology.[8]

These imagined cases would involve three kinds of operation. One we have already described: the transplanting of some part of one body into another. I shall assume this part to be, not just a brain, but a whole head. That puts more

Derek Parfit

pressure on Thomson's view, but in a way that is not unfair. I shall also assume that, if a different head were grafted onto the rest of some headless body, that would not make this a different body. Whether we must accept that assumption I shall reconsider later.

The second kind of operation is the creation of new heads, or bodies. In some cases, these would be exact copies of some existing person's head or body, as in my imagined case of Teletransportation (*RP*: 199–201). Such cases may always be technically impossible. But they are not deeply impossible, or against the laws of nature. And they are easy to understand. We know what it would be for some head, or body, to be exactly copied.

The third kind of operation, which is less straightforward, is the remodeling of some existing person's brain, in a way that destroys all psychological continuity. In some cases, this remodeling would make this brain functionally equivalent to the now destroyed brain of some previously existing person. The resulting person would then be psychologically continuous with that previously existing person. In other cases, this remodeling would not copy any other brain, and the resulting person would be psychologically continuous with no one. Since it is unclear what would be involved in such brain remodeling, these examples are harder to assess.

Let us now consider our six kinds of case:

Case (1), or *Head Transplant*: Thomson's head is destroyed, and my head is grafted onto the rest of Thomson's body. The resulting person is psychologically continuous with me.

This is the case discussed above. On my view, I survive, but with a different body below the neck. On Thomson's view, she survives, but with my head. Most people's intuitions, I have claimed, here support my view.

Case (2): My head is grafted onto the rest of a newly created body. The resulting person is psychologically continuous with me.

In one version of this case, the newly created torso and limbs are exact copies of mine. As before, on my view, I survive. On Thomson's view, I die, and the person with my head is someone new. Most people's intuitions, I believe, again support me.

Case (3): My head is destroyed, and a newly created head, which is unlike mine, is grafted onto the rest of my body. The resulting person is psychologically continuous with no one.

On my view, I die, and a new person has what is left of my body. On Thomson's view, I survive, but with a new head. It may make some difference, here, that this head had no previous owner. But I believe that our intuitions still support me. If we knew that our heads will be destroyed, and that the rest of our bodies will then be connected to dissimilar heads, few of us would expect to wake up again.

The remaining cases can be discussed together:

Persons, Bodies, and Human Beings | 181

If some future person will have:	Thomson's Bodily Criterion	My view	The Brain Criterion	The Narrow Psychological Criterion	The Wide Psychological Criterion
			This person is, according to:		
(1) My brain and psychology, but Thomson's body	Thomson	Me	Me	Me	Me
(2) My brain and psychology, but a new body	A new person	Me	Me	Me	Me
(3) My body, but a new brain and psychology	Me	A new person	A new person	A new person	A new person
(4) My body, but Thomson's brain and Williams's psychology	Me	Not Me	Thomson	A new person	Williams
(5) My body, but Thomson's brain and a new psychology	Me	Not Me	Thomson	A new person	A new person
(6) My body, but a new brain and Thomson's psychology	Me	Not Me	A new person	A new person	Thomson
(7) A new body, but my brain and Thomson's psychology	A new person	–	Me	A new person	Thomson
(8) My body and brain, but Thomson's psychology	Me	–	Me	A new person	Thomson
(9) My body and brain, but a new psychology	Me	–	Me	A new person	A new person
(10) A new body and brain, but my psychology	A new person	–	A new person	A new person	Me
(11) My brain, but Thomson's body and psychology	Thomson	–	Me	A new person	Thomson
(12) My brain, but a new body and psychology	A new person	–	Me	A new person	A new person
(13) A new brain, but my body and psychology	Me	–	A new person	A new person	Me

Figure 1

Case (4): My head is destroyed, and Thomson's head is grafted onto the rest of my body. Thomson's brain has been remodeled, in a way that copies the brain of some other previously existing person, whom we can suppose to be Bernard Williams. The resulting person is psychologically continuous with Williams.

Case (5): As in (4), Thomson's head is grafted onto my headless body. Thomson's brain has again been remodeled, but in a way that does not copy anyone else's brain. The resulting person is psychologically continuous with no one.

Case (6): My head is destroyed, and a new head is grafted onto the rest of my body. Since this new head contains a replica of Thomson's brain, the resulting person is psychologically continuous with her.

In all three cases, on Thomson's view, I survive, but with her head. On my view, since my head has been destroyed, and the resulting person is not psychologically continuous with me, that person is not me. In all these cases, as in (3), I die. Our intuitions, I believe, still favor this view.

I conclude that, in all the cases where my view and Thomson's strongly disagree, her view is less plausible.

There are also cases where our views weakly disagree. It is worth listing both kinds of case. And we can include, in this list, what is implied by our other three criteria (see figure 1).

This list can be explained as follows. The views we are considering appeal to three elements: body, brain, and psychology.[9] In the cases in Group B, all three elements have different origins. In Case (4), these elements come from three existing people. In the other cases in this group, one element is newly created: the psychology in (5), the brain in (6), and the rest of the body in (7). In the remaining cases, two elements stay together, but the third has a different origin. In Group A, this third element is the body; in Group C, it is psychology; in Group D, it is the brain.

We can next compare the implications of our five views. In Cases (1) to (3), things are simple. In all three cases, Thomson's view gives one answer to our question, and the other views agree on a different answer.

In Cases (4) to (6), Thomson again gives an answer which the other views reject. Thomson claims that, in each case, the future person would be me. On every other view, that person would *not* be me. But, while the other views agree in rejecting Thomson's claim, they do not agree on who this person would be.

Case (4) is the one where there is most disagreement. In this case, which might be called the *Neapolitan Sandwich*, the resulting person would have Thomson's head, the rest of my body, and be psychologically continuous with Williams. Our views give five different answers. On Thomson's view, the resulting person would be me. On the Brain Criterion, he would be Thomson. On the Narrow Psychological Criterion, he would be a new person. On the Wide Criterion, he would be Williams.[10] On my view, this person would not be me, but it would be indeterminate whether he would be Thomson, Williams, or a new person.

Though I believe that, in Case (4), there is indeterminacy, Thomson and I still strongly disagree. On my view, while none of the other answers is determinately true, Thomson's answer is determinately false.

My view may seem inconsistent. Why do I treat Thomson's answer in a different way? Since I believe that there is indeterminacy, and I claim that we should not try to choose between the other views, why do I reject Thomson's view?

There is no inconsistency. Indeterminacy is always limited. Even if we should not choose between some views, we should reject others. Suppose it were claimed that, if some future person will have my heart, that person will be me. We should reject that view. If my heart were transplanted, we could insist that the resulting person would not be me. Thomson claims more plausibly that, if some future person will have my whole body below the neck, that person will be me. But I am also inclined to reject this view. I am inclined to insist that, if my head were destroyed, and Thomson's head were grafted onto the rest of my body, the person with Thomson's head tomorrow would not be me.

My rejection of Thomson's view might be misunderstood. When Thomson claims that it would be I who would have her head, and I deny that claim, I am not making a different prediction about what, in such a case, I could expect to happen. On my view, if I knew that someone would wake up tomorrow with Thomson's head and the rest of my body, that description tells me what would happen. I can truly claim that this person would not be me. But, in stating that fact, I am not giving further information about what would happen. I am merely giving an acceptable redescription.[11]

That I can truly give this redescription is, I have claimed, a *conceptual* fact. But that claim could also be misunderstood. I do not mean that, when Thomson rejects my redescription, she shows ignorance of our concept of a person. What I mean is, roughly, this. When we consider this imagined case, most of us would accept my redescription; and Thomson's arguments do not, I believe, show that we are mistaken.

I am, I have said, *inclined* to reject Thomson's view. But I might be persuaded that, here too, there is indeterminacy. On my view, the "problem cases" raise no problem, since there is nothing to discover, nor is it important how, given our concept of a person, these cases can be redescribed. So I might be persuaded that Thomson's is among the views between which we need not choose. Indeed, as I shall argue later, even if Thomson's view was determinately true, that should not affect our conclusions about what matters. But, since most of us assume that our identity is what matters, it is worth discussing whether, as I am inclined to believe, we can reject Thomson's view.

I have discussed the cases where Thomson's view seems to me determinately false. In the remaining cases, her view is not, I believe, determinately true.

In

Case (10): My body is destroyed, and a replica created. The resulting person is psychologically continuous with me.

On my view, it would be indeterminate whether the resulting person would be me, or be a new person. But this is one of the cases where, though there is indeterminacy, one description would be most convenient. It would be best, I suggested, to call my Replica a new person (*RP*: 205). On Thomson's view, that is not merely the best description; it is straightforwardly true. I suspect that, in this case, many people would find Thomson's view more plausible than mine. But the intuitive difference is, I think, much less than in Cases (1) to (6).

Derek Parfit

In the similar

Case (13): My head is replaced with an exact replica. The resulting person is psychologically continuous with me.

On Thomson's view, the resulting person would here be me. On my view, it would again be indeterminate whether this person would be me, or someone new.

Here, I believe, our intuitions slightly favor my view. Suppose we accept Thomson's claim about Case (10). We believe that, if my whole body is destroyed, I cease to exist. On this view, for me to continue to exist, it is not enough that there will be a replica of my body. If we accept that claim, we may doubt that Case (13) is, as Thomson claims, quite different. If my head will be destroyed, it may not seem enough that there will be a replica of my head. True, this head will be grafted onto the rest of my body. But that may not seem decisive. After all, if this head were Thomson's, most of us doubt that I would survive. And, if I would not survive either if my whole body were destroyed and copied, or if my head were replaced by a head that is not a copy, why should we be confident that I *would* survive if my head were replaced by a copy?

Consider next

Case (9): My brain is remodeled, in a way that removes all of my psychological features. The resulting person is psychologically continuous with no one.

On Thomson's view, the resulting person would be me. On my view, it is indeterminate whether this person would be me, or someone new. Thomson's claim may again seem more plausible than mine. When he considers such a case, Williams (1970) argues forcefully that, however much my brain is interfered with, I would continue to exist. This, I conceded, might be the best description. But that concession may again seem inadequate.

Our assessment of this case turns upon the view we take of such brain remodeling. As Shoemaker points out, the required brain surgery might have to be extreme (Shoemaker and Swinburne 1984: 87). In considering a case like (9), we cannot appeal to what we believe about ordinary cases of psychological discontinuity, such as those involving amnesia, or severe brain damage. In those cases, many psychological features are retained. And, even when, at the conscious level, such features have been lost, their underlying neurophysiology is largely undisturbed. If we wanted wholly to remove all psychological connections, we would have to destroy very many of the links between the nerve cells of the brain. And, to create a new psychology, we would have to create new links, in different patterns. It is not intuitively obvious that, if my brain were *zapped* in such a way, and the resulting person was wholly unlike me, I would still exist. Those who make that claim need to appeal, as Williams does, to some argument.

Consider next the similar

Case (12): As in (9), my brain is remodeled, in a way that removes all psychological features. My head is then grafted onto the rest of a new body.

Persons, Bodies, and Human Beings | 185

On my view, as in (9), it is indeterminate whether I survive. On Thomson's view, (9) and (12) are quite different. She believes that, if my remodeled brain stays in my body, I survive; but, if my head is transplanted, my brain becomes the brain of someone new. As before, we may doubt that this makes all the difference. Our intuitions may be closer to my view.

Of the remaining cases, (8) and (11) are like (9) and (12); and, in (7), Thomson's view is close to mine. I conclude that, in three of these cases – (8), (9), and (10) – Thomson's view may better fit most people's intuitions. But these are cases where our views only weakly disagree; and, in some of the other cases of weak disagreement, our intuitions may favor me. In the more important cases, where I and Thomson strongly disagree, Thomson's view conflicts sharply with most people's intuitions.

Our intuitions may be mistaken. So we must now consider Thomson's arguments.

3 Thomson's Arguments

Thomson argues by elimination, or by rejecting other views. She does not directly discuss my view; but, in rejecting other views, she may give sufficient grounds for rejecting mine.

Consider first her remarks about the Brain Criterion. Thomson appeals to a version of

Case (11): My brain is remodeled so that it becomes like Thomson's brain, and is then transplanted into Thomson's empty skull.

On the Brain Criterion, I survive, though with Thomson's body, and psychologically continuous with her. Thomson says that, in such a case, we would all agree that I do *not* survive. If that is so, sameness of the brain cannot be sufficient for personal identity. Thomson might also appeal to Case (13), in which my brain is replaced with an exact replica. On the Brain Criterion, in such a case, I do not survive. On Thomson's view, I *do* survive, though with a different brain. If that is so, sameness of the brain cannot be necessary for identity.

I agree that, in these cases, the Brain Criterion gives the wrong answers.[12] Where Thomson claims these answers to be determinately false, I claim only that they are not determinately true. Suppose that we accept Thomson's stronger claim. Should we then conclude, as Thomson seems to do, that the sameness of the brain is not even *relevant* to personal identity?[13]

That conclusion does not follow. Our examples involve three elements: sameness of the brain, sameness of the body, and psychological continuity. On what I shall call the *Majoritarian View*, none of these elements is either sufficient for personal identity, or necessary. But all three elements are relevant, since any *two* elements are sufficient. If some future person will have either my brain and body, or my brain and psychology, or my body and psychology, that person will be me. In all other cases, that person will not be me.

Compared with Thomson's, this Majoritarian View better fits most people's intuitions. These views differ only in Cases (1) to (6), and these are precisely the cases where Thomson's view is least plausible. The Majoritarian View, in these cases, gives the same answers as the Narrow Psychological Criterion. And, compared with Thomson's, these answers are easier to believe. So, whenever these views differ, Thomson's view is harder to believe.

Despite its intuitive appeal, the Majoritarian view faces theoretical objections. Majority voting, though an excellent procedure, is seldom more than that. My present point is only this. On the Majoritarian View, the sameness of the brain is always relevant to personal identity. That claim cannot be challenged by appeals to cases like (11) or (13), since the Majoritarian View, in those cases, coincides with Thomson's view. And, in the six cases where that claim *is* challenged, because these views conflict, that claim is supported by most people's intuitions.

Consider next the Narrow Psychological Criterion. On this view, one of our three elements, the sameness of the body, never matters. The other two elements are each necessary for identity, and together sufficient. For some future person to be me, we must both be psychologically continuous, and have the same brain.[14]

Though Thomson rejects the Narrow Criterion, she says little to explain why. She may assume that, since we should reject the Brain Criterion, we can also reject all views that take the sameness of the brain to be relevant to identity. I have just explained why that does not follow.

Thomson might reply that, on the Narrow Criterion, the sameness of the brain is claimed to be, not merely relevant to identity, but necessary. And that stronger claim may seem to be refuted by a case like (13), in which my brain is replaced by a replica. This example does, I agree, cast some doubt on the Narrow Criterion. We may find it hard to believe that, as this criterion implies, if my brain were destroyed and a replica were grafted in its place, I would cease to exist. But this example cannot, I think, refute this criterion. Every view may have some counterintuitive implications. One example is Thomson's claim that, if my brain were destroyed and her brain were successfully grafted into its place, I would continue to exist. We may find that just as hard to believe.

Thomson suggests a different ground for rejecting the Narrow Criterion. She believes that, if we accept some version of Psychological Criterion, we should prefer the Wide Version. Both criteria agree that, for some future person to be me, we must be psychologically continuous. But, on the Wide Criterion, this continuity could have any cause. On the Narrow Criterion, it must have its normal cause: the continued existence of enough of the same brain. Thomson suggests that it cannot be important how such continuity is caused. If the cause is abnormal, why, she asks, is that "not good enough"?

I agree that, in an account of what matters – what has rational or moral significance – it is irrelevant how such continuity is caused. But it could still be true that, in stating a criterion of identity, we should require that such continuity should have its normal cause, the continued existence of the same brain.[15] Thomson says that she cannot understand why we might prefer the Narrow Criterion, which makes that requirement. But the rest of her paper provides one answer. She advances arguments against the Wide Criterion, and some of these arguments do not apply to the Narrow Criterion. If Thomson's arguments are good, they give us reason to prefer that view.

Thomson also appeals to

Case (14): I take some drug which causes my brain to "imprint" on my liver. After the rest of my body is destroyed, my liver is transplanted into Thomson's body, where it causes the remodeling of Thomson's brain. The resulting person is psychologically continuous with me.

Such a case, Thomson suggests, challenges the Narrow Criterion. Suppose we believe that, if my brain were transplanted into Thomson's body, and carried with it my psychology, I would continue to exist. Thomson suggests that, if the transplanting of my liver had the same effects, we should take the same view. We should believe that, here too, I would continue to exist. We should therefore drop the requirement that, to constitute identity, psychological continuity must have its normal cause. Nor could we plausibly require that, even if the causal story is abnormal, it must involve the continued existence of *some* part of the body. Why, she asks, should *that* be required? We should move to the Wide Criterion, which allows such continuity to have any cause.

Thomson's example does not, I think, support these claims. As Thomson remarks elsewhere, on any plausible criterion of identity, there could be borderline cases, where our questions would have no clear answer.

On Thomson's own view, for me to continue to exist, my body must continue to exist. Consider the cases in my Physical Spectrum, in which different proportions of my body would be destroyed and replaced. In some of these cases, on Thomson's view, it would be indeterminate whether I continue to exist. But, as Thomson would agree, such cases do not cast doubt on her view. Thomson's imagined Case (14) is of this kind. If we accept the Narrow Criterion, we reject Thomson's claim that, for me to continue to exist, my body must continue to exist. It is enough, on our view, that there should continue to exist one part of my body: the part which supports consciousness, and carries with it psychological continuity. We believe that part to be my brain. Thomson asks us to imagine that my liver, amazingly, acquires some of the properties of a brain. If we accept the Narrow Criterion, we may be puzzled by this example. But, as before, such a case casts no doubt on our view. Life can be distinct from death, though there are some cases in between.

We can now turn to Thomson's main arguments, which are directed at the Wide Criterion. I shall ask whether, if these arguments were redirected, they would have force against my view.

Supporters of the Wide Criterion, Thomson says, sometimes appeal to the claim that we can imagine switching bodies, or surviving without a body. Thomson challenges these appeals to what we think we can imagine. She may be right. But these remarks do not apply to my view.

Thomson also appeals to our intuitions. She discusses a case like (8), in which, by remodeling Robinson's brain, surgeons make the resulting person psychologically continuous with Brown, whose whole body has been destroyed. According to the Wide Criterion, the person with Robinson's body would now be Brown. Thomson calls it "odd idea" that "tinkering" with Robinson's brain could have that result. To apply this objection to my view, we must change the example. We must suppose that, rather than remodeling Robinson's brain, surgeons destroy this brain, and transplant Brown's brain into Robinson's empty skull. On my view, the resulting person would be Brown. That is not an odd idea. It is what most of us, on reflection, believe. If that idea is wrong, we need some other ground for thinking so.[16]

4 The Extrinsicness Objection

Thomson then appeals to what Williams calls the "reduplication problem." If we accept the Psychological Criterion, we cannot exclude the possibility that there might be psychological continuity between a single person at one time and two different people at some other time. But one person cannot be the same as each of two different people. So our criterion must be stated in a way that avoids that implication. My original statement was:

> X today is one and the same person as Y at some past time if and only if X is psychologically continuous with Y . . . and there does not exist a different person who is also psychologically continuous with Y. (*RP*: 207)

Thomson objects that, in this formulation, our criterion is circular, since it assumes that we can tell whether Y is continuous with some person *different* from X. A criterion of identity should explain what makes people the same or different; so it should not assume an answer to this very question.

One reply would be to claim that, in describing personal identity *over* time, we are entitled to assume that we can distinguish people who exist at the *same* time. But my reply was to revise this criterion, so that its final clause becomes "and this continuity does not take a *branching* form." Such branching can be described without assuming answers to questions about personal identity.

Thomson's main objection is that, however we revise this clause, the Psychological Criterion makes identity depend, implausibly, on accidental and extrinsic facts. On this criterion, whether some future person will be me does not depend only on the intrinsic nature of the relation between us. It also depends on whether that relation holds *elsewhere*. Judgments of identity, Thomson claims, should not depend on such extrinsic facts. Let us call this the *Extrinsicness Objection*.

This objection has been advanced by several writers; and several others have suggested answers. Since these answers seem to me sufficient, my comments will be brief.

First, I believe that we should reject this objection's premise. Truths about identity can depend on extrinsic facts. And, when we see why that is so, it should not seem puzzling.

To illustrate this objection, let us consider two of my imagined cases. In the *One-Sided Case*, the right half of my brain would be destroyed, and the left half would be transplanted into the empty skull of another similar body. In the *Two-Sided Case*, or *My Division*, both halves would be transplanted. In both cases, someone would wake up with the left half of my brain. Let us talk of the *left-brained person*, where that phrase is not a name, but only a description. On the Psychological Criterion, in the

One-Sided Case, the left-brained person would be me. In the Two-Sided Case, the left-brained person would not be me. He would be a new person, who can be named *Lefty*.

Assume that what actually happens is the Two-Sided Case. And suppose that you are Lefty. On the Psychological Criterion, if what had happened was the One-Sided Case, you, Lefty, would never have existed.[17] Several writers think that absurd.

We should state more precisely what these people think absurd. There is a similar-sounding claim which we would all accept. If things had gone differently elsewhere, that might have caused things to go differently here, in a way that affected you, or even prevented your existence. But that is not the claim that we are now considering. We can suppose that, if what had happened was the One-Sided Case, in which the right half of my brain was destroyed, this would have had *no* effects on what happens to, or in, the left half of my brain. In both cases, this half-brain would be transplanted into the very same body, and the resulting left-brained person would have the very same, or at least exactly similar, thoughts and experiences. What is thought to be absurd is the view that, in the One-Sided Case, that person would be me, while, in the Two-Sided Case, he would *not* be me, but Lefty. If the history of the left-brained person is, in both cases, just the same, how could events elsewhere make a difference to who this person is?

Properly understood, this conclusion is not, I think, absurd. It will help to consider a simpler pair of cases: those involving Hobbes's famous *Ship of Theseus*. In *Case One*, this ship is dismantled, plank by plank, and is later reconstructed by antiquarians. In *Case Two*, when each plank is removed, it is replaced, so that a working ship continues to exist, though it becomes entirely made of new planks. On what Nozick calls the *Closest Continuer* view, in Case One, the antiquarian's ship *is* the original ship, which has been reconstructed. In Case Two, since the continuously working ship is a closer continuer, it is claimed to be the original ship, and the antiquarian's ship, though made of the original planks, is here claimed to be a different ship.

Wiggins objects that such a view

> licenses the following as a possibility: we could walk up to the antiquarian's relic, seen as a candidate to be Theseus' ship, and say that, but for the existence of its rival [the continuously working ship] it would have veritably coincided as a ship with Theseus' original ship. But the idea that in *that* case it would have been Theseus' very ship seems to be absurd.

This view is absurd, Wiggins suggests, because it implies that "anything might have been a numerically different entity from the entity it actually is" (1980: 95).[18]

Such a view need not have that implication. On this view, we need not claim that this *very ship*, though in fact different from the original ship, might have been identical to that ship. Our claim could be re-expressed as follows. Though this set of planks actually constitutes a different ship, if there had not been the continuously working rival ship, this *very set of planks* could have been correctly claimed to be constituting, here and now, the reconstructed original ship.

Similar remarks apply to the One-Sided and Two-Sided Cases. In both cases, there would exist the very same left half-brain, in the same body, and there would occur what would be, in one sense, the very same thoughts and experiences. On the

Derek Parfit

Psychological Criterion, our claims are these. If my right half-brain is destroyed, this left half-brain and body, and these thoughts and experiences, can be correctly called mine. If my right half-brain is not destroyed, this left half-brain and body, and these thoughts and experiences, cannot be called mine, but must be described as those of a new person. What happens elsewhere does not, mysteriously, affect what happens here. In the most straightforward sense, the very same things happen here. What events elsewhere affect is only the *label* that we can apply to what happens here. That is no more puzzling than the fact that, if my father has another child, though in a way that has no effects on me, that could make it true that I am not my father's only child. Whether I am my father's only child is partly an extrinsic fact: it does not depend only on my father's relation to me. Why should not the same be true of our identity over time?

Some would reply that, while such a claim can be true of a genuine *relation*, like being the only child of, it cannot be true of numerical identity. That is not a genuine relation, since it does not hold between *two* items. Or at least, if identity is regarded as a relation, it must be wholly internal. That *I am me* must be a truth that is wholly about me.

If these remarks fail to convince, there is a different reply. Thomson takes the Extrinsicness Objection to count in favor of her own view. But that is not so.

We can first consider how, if we accept the Narrow Criterion, we might try to avoid this objection. On this view, for some future person to be me, that person must have enough of my brain. Wiggins once suggested that, by "enough," we could mean *more than half*. That would avoid the reduplication problem, since there could not be two future people who each met that requirement. But, with that revision, the Narrow Criterion would be unacceptable. People could survive, as Thomson notes, even if they lost the use of half their brains.[19]

Similar remarks apply to Thomson's Bodily Criterion. For Thomson's view to avoid the reduplication problem, it must similarly claim that, for some future person to be me, that person must have more than half my body. But that requirement is also unacceptable. If half my brain and body were destroyed, but the remaining half continued to function and to support consciousness, what was left would still be the same body, and we cannot plausibly deny that I would still exist. Thomson herself claims that a body might continue to exist if it retained its more important organs, even if *less* than half this body continued to exist, because more than half had been replaced. We are now supposing that a full half continues to exist, and that there is no replacement. Nor does a body need to retain all of its more important organs. Just as we need only half a brain, we need only one lung, or kidney, and only half a liver. In the case of some vital organs, such as the heart or stomach, someone with only half a body would need reconstructive surgery, and some artificial aids.[20] But Thomson should agree that, if half this person's body continued to exist, and function, this person would still exist.[21]

I conclude that, even on Thomson's view, personal identity could depend on extrinsic facts. If my body was divided, and only one half survived, the resulting person would be me.[22] If both halves survived, the two resulting people could not each be me. So, when we ask whether each is me, the answer depends upon what happens to the other.

Since Thomson's own view faces the Extrinsicness Objection, this objection cannot support her view. Thomson might reply that, when applied to the Bodily Criterion, this objection has less force. She might repeat Williams's remark that, when bodily continuity takes a branching form, that fact is not, in the same objectionable sense, extrinsic. But the same could be said in defense of the Narrow Criterion, or the Brain Criterion, or my view. If the dividing of the body is not an extrinsic fact, nor is the dividing of the brain.

Every plausible criterion, it seems, faces the Extrinsicness Objection. That supports my earlier claim that this objection is mistaken.

5 Thomson's Ontological Argument

Thomson also argues:

(1)   People are their bodies,

therefore

(2)   X and Y are the same person if and only if they have the same body.

I shall call this Thomson's *Ontological Argument.*

It may seem that, if this argument is sound, we must accept Thomson's view, and reject mine. But that does not follow. (2) is only the first part of Thomson's Bodily Criterion. Thomson adds

(3)   If we put one person's brain into another person's body, that would not make this a different body.

Even if we accept (2), we might question (3).

Reconsider our first case, in which my head is grafted onto the rest of Thomson's body. The resulting body, Thomson assumes, would still be hers. In my earlier discussion of this case, I accepted that assumption. I claimed that, despite having Thomson's body, the resulting person would be me. If people *are* their bodies, that claim would be undermined. If we wish to defend my view about this case, we would have to claim, instead, that the resulting person would have *my* body. Nor would it be enough to claim that, since this person would be me, what used to be Thomson's body would have *become* mine. If I am my body, our claim would have to be that, if my head were grafted onto the rest of Thomson's body, the resulting body would be the one that has *always* been mine.

To defend that conclusion, we would have to claim

(4)   X and Y have the same body if and only if they have the same brain.

Williams calls (4) absurd (1973: 77). That dismissal is, I think, too quick. In trying to defend (4), we might appeal to my original version of this case. I supposed that, after my head is disconnected from the rest of my body, it is supported by a heart-lung machine, and my brain continues to function. It is natural to believe that, if that happened, I would continue to exist. And, if we believe that people are their bodies, we might claim that the survival of my head amounts to the survival of my body, though in a severely diminished state. We might then claim that, when what is left of my body is attached to what is left of Thomson's body, my body continues to exist, though it now reassumes an expanded form. My body would now contain what were once parts of Thomson's body, just as it might in a more ordinary operation, in which I was merely given Thomson's heart and lungs. In this imagined case, much more of my expanded body would be new. But, as Thomson agrees, mere mass is not decisive. A human body continues to exist, she writes, if its most important parts continue to exist, and function. On the view we are now considering, there is one such part: the brain.

This view is not, I think, absurd. But I would agree with Williams that it can be reasonably denied. So it cannot provide a wholly satisfactory reply to Thomson's argument.

6 Are We Our Bodies?

How else might we reply? According to Thomson's argument,

(1)   People are their bodies,

therefore

(2)   X and Y are the same person if and only if they have the same body.

I have now agreed that, if we accept (2), we cannot convincingly reject the rest of Thomson's view. Since this argument is valid, our only other possible reply is to question (1).

Thomson says little to defend (1). She mentions only one other possibility: that we are immaterial substances, such as Cartesian Egos. Her assumption seems to be that, if we are not immaterial substances, we must be our bodies, since there is nothing else for us to be.

There are several other possibilities. Nagel suggests that what we are, essentially, is our brains (1986: 37–43). Like the view that a body's identity depends on that of its brain, Nagel's view is, I believe, plausible. We could explain how, even if we are essentially our brains, the rest of our bodies could also be regarded as parts of us. A similar view is well defended by McMahan (2002: 3–94). I shall here consider other possibilities.

If we are not our bodies, or our brains, what else could we be? I defended the unexciting view that we are persons, or human beings: entities that *have* bodies, and *have* brains. On this view, we are distinct from our bodies and our brains, though we are not separately existing entities, such as immaterial substances.

This view, I claimed, stays closer to our actual concept of a person. We often distinguish between ourselves and our bodies. If we thought we *were* our bodies, we would not claim that we *have* bodies, since bodies cannot have themselves. And there are many other properties that we ascribe to ourselves, rather than our bodies. Thus we do not regard our bodies as being witty, or solving crossword puzzles, or remembering our childhood.

After mentioning such "facts of usage," Thomson replies that, in other ways, we seem not to distinguish between ourselves and our bodies. For example, rather than saying that our bodies weigh some amount, we say that *we* weigh that amount. This reply is not, I think, sufficient. There is an asymmetry here. Even if we distinguish between ourselves and our bodies, it is easy to explain our claim that we weigh what our bodies weigh. That could be like our claim, when our coat has been splashed with mud, that *we* have been splashed with mud. If something is true of X when and because it is true of Y, that need not be because X *is* Y. X may own Y, or consist in Y, or be related to Y in some other way. If instead we believe that we *are* our bodies, it is hard to explain why we deny that our bodies have all our properties. If we believe that Einstein was a genius, and that Einstein was his body, why do we deny that Einstein's body was a genius?

Our question, however, is not what we do believe, but what we should believe. Even if we do distinguish between ourselves and our bodies, Thomson may be right to reject that distinction.

In asking whether she is right, it will help to return to a similar but simpler question. What is the relation between a statue and the lump of matter of which it is composed? According to some writers, if we claim that Cellini's Venus *is* a lump of gold, we would not be using the "is" of identity. We would mean only that this statue consists in this lump, or that the statue and the lump are made up of the same matter. On this view, though this statue and this lump are very closely related, they are distinct entities.

As an account of what we mean, this view may be too precise. But the distinction which it draws is, I believe, defensible. If that is so, we can also defensibly distinguish between ourselves and our bodies.

To defend the first of these distinctions, I appealed to a standard argument. If X and Y were one and the same entity, we could not destroy X without destroying Y. But, if we melted down Cellini's Venus, we could destroy this statue without destroying this lump of gold. So these cannot be the same.

Some reply that, though we can destroy the statue without destroying the lump, that is not because the statue is a distinct entity. On their view, the concept of a statue is like the concepts of a child, or tadpole, or butterfly. It is what Wiggins calls a *phased sortal*, a term which applies to some persisting entity, in the present tense, only during part of its history, while it has certain properties. The statue *is* the lump of gold, but this lump is only a statue *while it is shaped like Venus.*

One problem for this view is what, when we use a phased sortal, we refer to an entity that may continue to exist even after it loses the properties that our term ascribes to it. Thus, when children grow up, they do not cease to exist; they merely cease to be children. The parallel claim would be that, when we melt down our statue into a shapeless lump, it continues to exist, and merely ceases to be a statue. But most of us would claim that, even though the lump continues, the statue ceases to exist. If the statue *is* the lump, as the phased-sortal view maintains, that would be a contradiction.

There is a greater problem for this view. Suppose that we do not melt down the whole statue. We heat the statue from within, and thereby manage to extract, in a single malleable lump, almost all the gold. This process does not affect our statue's surface, which amounts to 1 percent of the gold. When we have removed the statue's core, we give it a cheaper iron core instead. If our original lump continues to exist, it must be the gold core which we have removed, after detaching its outer layer.[23] We might now destroy this lump, by turning it into coins. But our statue still exists. With the same shape, and visible surface, the statue has not suffered at all. So the statue cannot be the lump, as the phased-sortal view maintains. Since it might continue to exist even after the lump was destroyed, it must be a distinct entity.

This argument appeals to what Wiggins calls

The Life Histories Principle: X cannot be the same as Y if they could have different histories.

To apply this principle, we must produce a convincing case in which the histories of X and Y diverge. We began by claiming that the lump's history might be longer than the statue's. It was objected that the statue is merely the lump while-Venus-shaped. We therefore claimed that the statue's history might be longer than the lump's. These two examples, I believe, refute the phased-sortal view. X and Y cannot be the same if either might continue to exist after the other has been destroyed.

Our distinction might be challenged in another way. Some writers appeal to

The Exclusion Principle: There cannot be two objects that are wholly composed, at the same time, of the same matter.

When applied to objects of the same kind, this principle can seem compelling. Suppose our statue left Cellini's workshop as a 50-pound lump of gold. It would be hard to defend the view that we should regard this gold as *two* 50-pound lumps. What could make these *different* lumps? Nor could a single mass of gold be easily regarded as two different statues.

What we are defending, though, is a different view. On this view, though these 50 pounds of gold constitute two different objects, there is only one lump, and one statue. And, since these are objects of different kinds, we can explain why they are distinct. They have different criteria of identity. As our second example shows, the statue and the lump might cease to share all the same matter. The statue might survive, with a new iron core, after the lump has been extracted, and sold off for turning into coins.

This example gives us, I believe, sufficient reason to reject the Exclusion Principle. When two objects are of different kinds, they can remain distinct, in a quite unpuzzling way, even while they are wholly composed of the same matter.

It is sometimes claimed that, if we reject the Exclusion Principle, we can be led to absurd conclusions. If our statue is distinct from our lump of gold, and each weighs 50 pounds, why do they not *together* weigh 100 pounds? If we scratch the statue, why are there not *two* scratches, one on the statue, and one on the lump of gold? But such objections can be answered. As Williams says, when two objects share the same matter, we should not count that matter twice. That is why the statue and the lump do not, together, weigh more. And, if we scratch the statue, we thereby scratch the lump, and vice versa. Just as they share their matter, and their surface, they share this scratch.

Though there are other arguments for the Exclusion Principle, none, I believe, succeeds. The most that can be claimed is that, for certain purposes, it is worth using a conceptual scheme which obeys that principle. But we are asking whether, within our ordinary scheme, we can defensibly distinguish between statues and the lumps of which they are composed. And the answer, I believe, is Yes.

In the same way, I believe, we can defensibly distinguish between ourselves and our bodies. And we can thereby answer Thomson's argument. Though we and our bodies share the same matter, we are not the same as them; and that is partly because we and they might have different histories. Just as our statue might continue to exist, with a new core, after the original lump had been destroyed, we might continue to exist, with a body below the neck, after the rest of our old body had been destroyed. That is what, when we consider such a case, most of us are inclined to believe. And Thomson's argument does not, I believe, show that we are wrong.[24]

7 Persons and Human Beings

Let us now take stock. Thomson argued:

(1) People are their bodies,
(2) If we transplant a brain from one body to another, that would not affect the identity of this second body,

Therefore

(3) If we transplant my brain into Thomson's body, the resulting person would be Thomson.

If we find it hard to believe Thomson's conclusion, we must reject one of her premises. Though we might question (2), it is enough that, as I have argued, we can defensibly reject (1).

Consider next a similar argument:

(4) People are animals of a certain kind: human beings,
(5) If we transplant a brain from one animal to another, that would not affect the identity of this second animal,

Therefore

(3) If we transplant my brain into Thomson's body, the resulting person would be Thomson.

This, which I shall call the *Animalist Argument*, has been advanced by several recent writers. If this argument is sound, it provides a different route to Thomson's conclusion.

Derek Parfit

Some writers would reject this argument's first premise. Following Locke, they distinguish between persons and human beings. These Lockeans need not claim that this distinction is already part of our conceptual scheme. They can propose their distinction as a refinement of that scheme. On their proposed view, persons are human beings only in the constitutive sense in which our statue is a lump of gold. According to these Lockeans, while the identity of human beings may depend on that of their bodies, the identity of persons, when regarded as distinct from human beings, depends instead on psychological continuity, with the right kind of cause. To adapt one of Locke's examples, if a prince's head were grafted onto the rest of a cobbler's body, even if the resulting human would still be the cobbler, the resulting person would be the prince.

Animalists, however, have a powerful response. Human beings are conscious animals, who can have thoughts and other experiences. When a person has some experience, Lockeans must admit that a human being has that very same experience. So, if Lockeans distinguish persons from human beings, they must admit that, on their view, our thoughts and other experiences are each had *both* by a person *and* by a human being. And that may seem absurd. As McDowell writes: "surely there are not *two* lives being led here, the life of the human being . . . and the life of the person" (1997: 237).

To assess this *Two Lives Objection*, it is essential to be clear about the kind of question that we are discussing. If Lockeans distinguish persons from human beings, they may have to claim that there are twice as many lives being lived. But, in making that claim, they should not be thought to be advancing a different *hypothesis*. They are not *disagreeing* with those who do not draw their distinction. The question is only which concepts we should use. If we do not distinguish persons from human beings, we can truly claim

(6) In each human body, only one life is lived.

Since the Lockeans do draw this distinction, they claim

(7) In each human body, two lives are lived.

If we wish to reject (7), we cannot simply appeal to (6). It may seem that, if (6) is true, (7) must be false. But that is not so. Unlike us, Lockeans distinguish persons from human beings. Since they use these concepts in a different way, their claim does not conflict with ours.

To reject (7), we must challenge the Lockean proposal. Thus we might argue that, even if statues are distinct from lumps of gold, and persons are distinct from bodies, it is incoherent to distinguish persons from human beings. Or we might argue that, when Lockeans make their proposal, they do not provide, for the entities which they call persons, an adequate criterion of identity. Or we might argue that, in some other way, the Lockean distinction is defective.

In making these remarks, I assume

(8) If the concept of an X is coherent, and the conditions for its application are fulfilled, we cannot deny that there are Xs.

According to some writers, (8) implies absurdly that objects can be caused to exist by mere stipulation. But that is not so. We may invent the concept of an X; but, except in very special cases, that does not ensure that there are any Xs. Mere stipulation cannot cause reality to be a certain way.

Other writers object that, if we accept (8), our ontology will become incredible. Suppose that I define a squigillion as the combination of any bull frog and the planet Jupiter. According to (8), we cannot deny that squigillions exist. That, they claim, is wildly implausible.

This objection is, I think, misguided. There may be some defect in my suggested definition. And the concept that I define cannot have a serious use. But our objection cannot be that, when I say that squigillions exist, my claim is incredible. As defined, squigillions are not strange, separately existing entities, like ghosts, or flying saucers. When I claim that squigillions exist, I do not revise our view about reality. My proposed concept merely allows us to redescribe some ordinary facts. If there can be constellations, or archipelagos, or metropolitan areas, there can be squigillions.

Return now to the Lockean proposal. If Lockeans distinguish persons from human beings, does that lead to incoherence, or some other defect in their conceptual scheme?

One charge of incoherence might be this. Locke defines a person as a rational and conscious being that is aware of its own identity. Snowdon objects that, on this definition, human beings qualify as persons (1990: 90). So, if Lockeans try to distinguish persons from human beings, they must admit that, on their view, every adult human body is shared by two *persons*, the one which is also the human being, and the one which isn't. That seems to undermine the whole point of this Lockean distinction. Some would add that, with this admission, this distinction violates the more compelling form of the Exclusion Principle. As Locke himself declared, two objects of the *same* kind cannot be simultaneously composed of the same matter.

Part of this objection can be answered. Even if human beings are also persons, they must be persons of a *different* kind from the ones who are not human beings. These two kinds of person have different criteria of identity. Though each pair of persons usually share one body, either might continue to exist after the other was destroyed. Thus, on our present assumptions, if my head were grafted onto the rest of Thomson's body, the surviving *animal-person* would be Thomson, but the surviving *pure-person* would be me.

The rest of this objection stands, however, and does count against the Lockean proposal.

There are other objections. As the case of a statue shows, it is not a problem that, on the Lockean proposal, each pure-person shares its body with a human being. But can these beings be claimed to share all of their experiences? How can a single mental event have two subjects? "In the same way," the Lockeans might say, "in which a single scratch can be a scratch on both a statue and a lump of gold." But this analogy may seem insufficient. And suppose these beings jointly think, "I am a human being." On the Lockean proposal, there must be two thoughts here, one of which is false. How can a single mental event be regarded as the thinking of two different thoughts? In the same way, Johnston suggests, in which the raising of a banner, by two people, might be regarded as two assertions of the sentence written on that banner. But this analogy may again seem insufficient.

It is not clear that, with such objections, we can show the Lockean proposal to be incoherent. Though McDowell raises the Two Lives Objection, he himself suggests that, in the actual split-brain cases, single experiences are shared by two subjects.[25] It is tempting to protest that, even if not incoherent, such claims are wildly implausible. But, as I have said, plausibility is not the issue.

For different reasons, though, I reject the Lockean proposal. This conceptual revision would be both difficult and confusing; and it would serve, I think, no useful purpose.

One obvious question is: Who should we take *ourselves* to be, the pure-persons, or the human beings? It may seem that, without an answer to this question, we cannot even think about ourselves. And suppose that, as a Lockean, I claim to be the pure-person. Olson objects that I might be mistaken. How do I know that I am not the human being? My chance of being right, Olson claims, is only one in two (1997: 107–7).

These objections can be partly met. In some cases, if some statement is ambiguous but would be true on either of its meanings, it can be counted true. Suppose I point to Cellini's Venus, and say merely "That weighs 50 pounds." My use of "that" might refer to either the statue, or the lump of gold. But, since both weigh 50 pounds, my claim is true. If we draw the Lockean distinction, most of our thoughts about ourselves could have the same harmless ambiguity. They would have the same truth value whether applied to the pure-person or the human being.

The Lockean distinction cannot be useful, though, except in the cases where it makes a difference. And, in these cases, it is no use. Return to my question whether I am the pure-person or the human being. The problem is not that, if I try to guess, I might get the answer wrong. I could not get the answer right. For my question to have an answer, my use of "I" must be unambiguous. It must refer only to the pure-person, or only to the human being. And, on the Lockean proposal, that condition is not fulfilled.

It may seem that, if my question has no answer, I could decide to *give* it an answer. I could decide to which of these two entities I intend to refer. That would indeed be possible in most cases of this kind. I could decide, for example, whether to refer to the statue or the lump of gold. But, when I think about *myself*, this is no solution. Even if I accept the Lockean proposal, I am not free to decide whether, when I use "I," I intend to refer to the pure-person, or the human being. Any use of "I" must refer to its user. And, on this proposal, any use of "I" has two users. Whenever I use "I," both the pure-person and the human being thereby refer to themselves. So, when I ask "Who am I?" that is not a single question, whose ambiguity might be removed. I – or we – have asked two questions, with two answers. As Snowdon rightly says, when we try to think about ourselves, the Lockean proposal induces vertigo (1990: 95).

8 The Identity of Animals

Return, now, to our motive for considering this proposal. The Animalists argue:

(1) Persons are animals of a certain kind, human beings,
(2) If we transplant a brain from one animal to another, that would not affect the identity of this second animal,

Therefore

(3) If we transplant my brain into Thomson's body, the resulting person would be Thomson.

If we find (3) implausible, as most of us would, Lockeans tell us to question (1). We do better, I believe, to question (2).

Compared with Thomson's, the Animalist Argument is, in one way, stronger. Its first premise is harder to reject. We are already inclined to deny that people are their bodies; and, to defend that distinction, we need only claim that two different objects could share the same matter. We are less inclined to distinguish between persons and human beings; and, to defend that distinction, we would have to claim that two different conscious beings could share all of their thoughts and experiences. That is much more questionable, even if offered as a conceptual revision.

The Animalists' second premise is, in contrast, weaker than Thomson's. Thomson claims that, if we destroy some body's brain, and replace this with a different brain, the result would still be the same body. The Animalists claim that, in such a case, the result would still be the same animal. This claim is easier to reject.

We can start by imagining animals whose bodies mostly consist of their brains. Consider *the Mekon*, the imagined ruler, in *Dan Dare*, of a Martian species. The Mekon's head is about nine-tenths of its whole body. Must we believe that, if we replaced the remaining tenth, the Mekon would cease to exist?

As before, mere quantity is not decisive. But, by inverting the normal proportions, we can see more clearly what the Animalists might claim. Why might the Mekon's identity go with the small fraction of its body that lies below its neck? The Animalist answer would, I think, be this. In that part of the Mekon's body, there are many organs. The Mekon's brain, however large, is only a single organ. When we replace other single organs – such as a heart or kidney – no one doubts that the same animal continues to exist. Why believe that, in this respect, the brain is different?

Before we discuss this Animalist claim, we can make some general remarks. We are asking whether, if some part of an animal's body were destroyed and replaced, the resulting animal should be counted as one and the same. This is not a scientific question. Our imagined cases would not involve some natural process, which might follow discoverable laws. These cases would all be artificially produced. Ours is a purely conceptual question.

Of the possible answers to this question, the simplest would appeal only to *how much* of the animal's body is replaced. But this, we have said, cannot be right. Some parts of the body, though smaller, are more important. Another answer might appeal only to *how many organs* are replaced. But that would also be too crude. Just as some parts of the body matter more than others, so do some organs. What kind of importance, though, should we be considering?

Organs are important, we might say, if they are *vital*: if, without them, the animal could not survive. The appendix, for example, hardly counts. But this suggestion is not much better. First, we are not asking whether, after our imagined operations, the resulting animal could survive. Since all removed organs would be replaced, the resulting animal would be just as able to survive. We are asking the different question of *which* animal this would be. Second, we can imagine organs that were vital, but had little relevance to a judgment of identity. These organs might be like the kind of removable device, intended to prevent theft, without which the engines of some cars cannot function. The identity of these engines would hardly be affected by the replacement of such a simple mechanism. The same seems true of many vital organs, such as the wind-pipe. It seems true, indeed, even of such organs as the heart.

We need, then, some further measure of importance. In asking what this might be, we face another general question. When they discuss animal identity, some writers assume that it should make no difference what kind of animal we consider. Olson reminds us that, as animals, we are more like oysters than angels. According to these writers, our proposed criterion should be universal. But this assumption is too simple. We are indeed, in certain ways, strikingly like oysters. For example, they and we have much chemistry and many genes in common. But, if the identity of animals partly depends on the importance of their different organs, our criterion must be sensitive to the kind of animal that we are considering. Not all animals have the same organs. And, in different kinds of animal, the same organ can have different importance.

Return now to our main question. When compared with other organs, can the brain be claimed to be overridingly important? In the case of certain animals, that claim could be reasonably denied. Many animals have hardly any brain, and some have none. But, in the case of animals like us, the brain is not merely one of several vital organs. Though it is only a single organ, it *is* special. It is the controlling organ: governing, in several ways, most of the body. Its relation to the body is like that of a nucleus to a cell. For animals like us, it might be the individuating organ, which determines our identity.

In asking whether that is so, it may help to reconsider our first case. At the start of my story, my head continues to function after the rest of my body is destroyed. When discussing Thomson's view, we asked whether that would amount to my body's continuing to exist. In considering the Animalist view, we have a different question. My surviving head is that of a conscious being, whose mental life is much like mine. Is this being an animal?

Suppose, first, that the Animalists say "No." They will then face a problem like the one with which they embarrass Lockeans. On the Lockean proposal, a person starts to exist during the early infancy of a human animal. It would be easier for Lockeans if, at that stage, the animal retired from the scene, leaving its body for sole occupancy by the person. If Lockeans could make that claim, they would avoid the Two Lives Objection. But, as the Animalists object, we have no reason to accept that claim. When the animal starts to be rational, and aware of its own identity, why should it, conveniently, cease to exist?

We are now supposing that, on the Animalist view, my surviving head is that of a conscious being, which is not an animal. Similar remarks apply. When my head is grafted onto the rest of Thomson's body, there will again be a living animal. What then happens to this conscious being? It would be easier for the Animalists if, at that stage, this being retired from the scene. But why should we think that? Why should this being cease to exist, leaving the animal as the new and sole possessor of my head? But, if this being continues to exist, the animal will have to share her thoughts with it. So, like the Lockeans, the Animalists face the Two Lives Objection.

Persons, Bodies, and Human Beings | 201

Suppose next that, according to these Animalists, my disconnected head continues to be that of a living animal. This animal must still be me. Do I then cease to exist when my head is grafted onto the rest of Thomson's body? The answer should in part depend on the view we take of the rest of Thomson's body. We can suppose that, after Thomson's head has been destroyed, the rest of her body has its functioning maintained by artificial means. Would this headless body still be a living animal?

Animalists, I believe, should answer "No." As Van Inwagen claims, there is an important difference between the head and the rest of the body (1990: ch. 15). For my head to continue to function, all that it needs is a fairly simple pump, keeping it supplied with blood. There would then be a conscious being, who could see, hear, talk, and finish my book. For a headless body to continue to function, more assistance would be needed. There must be an artificial surrogate for a lower brain, sending down the spinal column much highly complex electrical information. This torso and these limbs are very far from being a self-sustaining, unified organism. They cannot, on their own initiative, do anything. As Animalists should agree, they do not constitute a living animal.

If Animalists accept these claims, they should change their view about the rest of our story. In the intermediate stage, we are now assuming, I survive as a living animal, though all that I have left is my head. Thomson does *not* survive in her headless body. So why believe that, when we connect my head to the rest of Thomson's ventilated corpse, the living animal dies, and the dead animal comes to life again? When my brain is attached to Thomson's heart and lungs, why should I, conveniently, cease to exist? But, if I survive, and Thomson comes to life again, the Animalists again face the Two Lives Objection. On their view, I and Thomson will both have to share all of our thoughts and other experiences. While such a claim might not be incoherent, there is a simpler, better view. We can claim that, when Thomson's brain is destroyed, that, for her, is the end.

The Animalist Argument, I conclude, does not undermine the view defended in my book. On that view, if our brains will continue to exist and function, we shall continue to exist. What happens below our necks, though it may affect the experiences that will be directly related to our brains, cannot cause these experiences not to be ours. That is what, on reflection, most of us are inclined to believe. And Animalists can believe this too.

9 Empty Questions

This defense of my view is, in a way, misleading. It suggests that, in this imagined story, there are different possibilities, any of which might be what really happens. But that, I believe, is not so. We have asked six questions:

1   If my head continued to exist and function, after it was disconnected from the rest of my body, would that amount to the continued existence of my body?
2   Would my surviving head still be the head of a living animal, or would it be the head of a conscious being that was not an animal?

3   If the latter, what would happen to this conscious being when my head is grafted onto the rest of Thomson's body?

4   After this second operation, would the resulting body be the same as my original body, or the same as Thomson's original body, or neither?

5   Would the resulting animal be the one that originally had my body, or the one that originally had Thomson's body, or neither?

6   What would happen to Thomson, and to me? Could either, or both, or neither expect to wake up again?

These questions, I believe, are all empty. None describes different possibilities. In trying to answer these questions, we learn nothing more about what, in such a case, would really happen. There is nothing more to learn.

Here is what would happen. My head would be disconnected from the rest of my body, and would then be grafted onto the rest of Thomson's body. There would be a series of thoughts and experiences, directly related to each other, and to my brain. If I had to decide whether to accept these operations, that is all I would need to know. What matters is reality, not how it is described.[26]

If that is so, it would be irrelevant whether, for me too, this would be the end. That would be merely another redescription. But, if you were in my position, and you cared what things were called, you could tell yourself that this would *not* be the end. As I have argued here, if your head were successfully transplanted, it would be correct to call the resulting person you. So you could expect to wake up again.

We may think that, in expecting that, you would be expecting something different to happen. But, if we do not have souls, what could the difference be?

10 Does Our Essence Matter?

It is worth adding some remarks about the Lockean proposal. I have argued that, to defend our view about such imagined cases, we need not try to distinguish between persons and human beings. But Lockeans have other grounds for drawing that distinction. They would claim, for example, that even if a fetus is a human being, it is not a person. Or consider someone who, because of brain damage, is irreversibly unconscious. Lockeans claim that, in such a case, even if the human being is still alive, the person has died.

Suppose that, to avoid the Two Lives Objection, Lockeans concede that persons are human beings. They must then withdraw the second of these claims. They must admit that, since the brain-damaged human being is still alive, so is the person. But they might appeal instead to a less ambitious form of the Lockean proposal. They might use "person" as a phased sortal: a term which applies to us, in the present tense, only while we have certain properties. On this use, just as we are children only while we are immature, we are persons only while we are rational and self-conscious. These Lockeans could then claim that, when a person has become irreversibly unconscious, though this person is still alive, he or she has ceased to be a person. That is not a contradiction, since it is merely like the claim that, when children have grown up, they have ceased to be children. Similar remarks apply to the Lockeans' other claim.

They could say that, just as some human beings are *no longer* persons, fetuses are *not yet* persons.

Compared with the bolder Lockean distinction between persons and human beings, this proposal stays closer to our actual use of the word "person." But these Lockeans might now insist that, though persons are human beings, they have a special moral status only while they are persons. As a claim about moral agents, that is uncontroversial. Only persons can have obligations, or be morally responsible. But, in some of its other implications, the Lockean claim is controversial. Consider, for example, the morality of killing. On this neo-Lockean view, while it is nearly always wrong to kill persons, there is much less objection to the killing of those human beings who, at the time, are not persons. Such a view could support some kinds of euthanasia, and most abortions. And, since this view implies that newborn babies are not yet persons, it could support infanticide as well.

Many of us would reject this view. In explaining where it goes wrong, we might say that, if "person" is used as a phased sortal, this concept must be of secondary importance. While we are persons for much of our lives, that is not what we *are*. As these Lockeans admit, we are human beings. Perhaps, as a newborn baby, I was not yet a person; but, in killing that baby, we would have been killing *me*. That, we may claim, is what counts.

If we make these claims, however, we must answer further questions. Consider a fertilized ovum, or a zygote. Are *these* human beings?

Given the vagueness of the term "human being," these questions are indeterminate. But we are free to adopt a tighter definition. Suppose, first, that we decide to use "human being" so that it applies to any organism of our species. On this *biological* use, a fertilized human ovum – or at least an early brainless embryo – is a human being.

If we adopt this definition, we may need to reconsider some of our moral principles. Suppose that, when rejecting infanticide, we appeal to the principle that it is seriously wrong to kill innocent human beings. On the biological definition, this principle implies that the killing of a human ovum is seriously wrong. Most of us would not accept that implication. And we cannot be forced to do so merely by our adoption of this definition. Or suppose we believe that, if we could save from death one human being, or many, we have more reason to save the many. What if the single human were an adult, and the many were one-celled organisms in a Petrie dish? Would it then be better to save the many? Most of us would answer "No."

If we give these answers, our concept of a human being will lose much of its significance. We shall no longer believe that all human beings have the same moral status. We shall give a special status to those human beings who are sufficiently developed to have brains, and other organs. To express these beliefs, it would help to use some term as a phased sortal, so that it applies to human beings only while they do have brains, or other organs. That is how some people already use the term "human being." But, if we have adopted the biological definition, we shall need some other phrase. We might say "*fully developed* human being." That would be the term which, on our view, has most moral significance. On this view, it is not wrong to kill those human beings who have not yet have developed brains.

Suppose, next, that we reject the biological definition. We adopt the other use just mentioned, which treats "human being" as a phased sortal. On this use, just as acorns are not oak trees, and eggs are not chickens, fertilized ova are not human beings. We agree that, as human beings, we are organisms of a certain species. But just as a child is not yet an adult, and an acorn is not yet an oak tree, a fertilized ovum is not yet a human being. Given this use of "human being," we need not revise our moral principles. We can still claim it to be seriously wrong to kill any innocent human being, while it is a human being.

The two views just described are, in substance, the same. The difference is only that, where one says "human being," the other says "*fully developed* human being."

Neo-Lockeans may now smile. These views are, in their structure, just like the neo-Lockean proposal. On all three views, though we are essentially organisms of a certain species, that is not what counts. These organisms have a special status only *while* they have certain properties. The difference between these views is only in the properties they single out.

On the two views just sketched, these properties are having a brain, and other organs. Human organisms acquire these properties by about the fourth month of pregnancy; and, once acquired, these properties are hard to lose. According to the neo-Lockeans, the relevant properties are those of being rational and self-conscious. These properties are more restrictive, and are easier to lose. They are not had either by newborn babies, or by some brain-damaged human beings.

In choosing between these views, we should distinguish different moral questions. Thus, if we are considering the infliction or relief of suffering, we may think it irrelevant whether the sufferer is now a person, or even a human being. But in other contexts, such as those involving autonomy, or responsibility, it is personhood which counts. Questions of life and death are harder to decide. If some animal is not a person, or not yet a person, it is not, in a strong sense, living a life, so it may seem less important whether its life is cut short. But, in the presence of a newborn baby, that may be hard to believe.

I am not concerned, here, with the choice between these views. My point is only that, as I have said, they are views of the same kind. On the neo-Lockean proposal, though what we *are* is human beings, we have a special moral status only while we are persons. If we take either of the views just sketched, we cannot reject this proposal in the way described above. We cannot claim that, since we are essentially human beings, the concept of a person must have only secondary importance. On these other views, though what we *are* is human organisms, we have a special status only while we are human beings, or full human beings. As on the neo-Lockean proposal, what matters is not what we are, but whether, at the time, we have certain properties.

This provides a different sense in which our identity is not what matters. On all three views, I was once a fertilized ovum. If doctors had destroyed that ovum, they would have been killing *me*. But that, we believe, is not what counts.[27]

Notes

1   Derek Parfit, *Reasons and Persons*, henceforth *RP* (Oxford: Oxford University Press, 1984), Part III.

2 I also took seriously a Cartesian Criterion, which appeals to the continued existence of the same soul. But I shall assume here that we can reject that view, if only for lack of evidence.

3 I corrected this and related mistakes in the reprinted versions of *RP* (as noted on page x).

4 Those who don't think otherwise include, however, some other excellent philosophers, such as Bernard Williams, Paul Snowdon, Quassim Cassam, and Michael Ayers.

5 See this vol., p. 171. Thomson says that she wants her body to "continue to function in the ways in which living human bodies function when they support consciousness."

6 For answers to some objections here, see Unger (1990: ch. 8).

7 There may be some exceptions. For example, if there would be two such future people, it may be determinate that neither would be me.

8 Or, in a mirror-image of (1), which need not be separately listed, my body, but someone else's brain and psychology.

9 We are now considering five criteria. Three we can call *pure*, since they appeal to only one of our three elements. These are Thomson's Bodily Criterion, the Brain Criterion, and the Wide Psychological Criterion (which can be taken to include the widest version). The Narrow Psychological Criterion and what I have called my view both appeal to a pair of elements: psychological continuity with, as its cause, sameness of brain.

10 For this to be implied, we must assume that there is no other living person who is also psychologically continuous with Williams.

11 This part of my view is *not* supported by our intuitions. But that is irrelevant here.

12 On my view, it is not determinate that, in (11), the resulting person is me, nor determinate that, in (13), this person is not me.

13 Except as one element in our judgment about the sameness of the body.

14 On this view, if some future person will have both my brain and psychology, that person will be me; and, if that person will have either a different brain, or a different psychology, that person will not be me.

15 In defending her claim that the method of causation cannot matter, Thomson imagines a case where transplanting a liver carries psychological continuity. "Was it not good enough on the ground that transplanting a liver doesn't *normally* cause psychology-transplanting. (Why should that matter?)" (this vol., p. 159). To assess Thomson's imagined case, we must know what kind of causal story she has in mind. She supposes that the drugs injected in the donor caused his brain to imprint on his liver in such a way that, when transplanted, the liver caused reprogramming of the recipient's brain. That makes the liver the equivalent of my Scanner and my Replicator.

16 In Thomson's example, my view implies that it is indeterminate whether the resulting person would be Brown, or Robinson, or a new person. Thomson might call that an "odd idea." But, as I have said, given how extreme such remodeling would have to be, it is not intuitively odd that there is indeterminacy here. (I abstract from the fact that, intuitively, indeterminacy is hard to accept. Thomson and I agree that, however counterintuitive this may be, personal identity could be indeterminate.)

17 That does not follow directly from the Sufficient Condition. We need the further claim that, in the Two-Sided Case, it cannot be true that each of the resulting people would be me, nor can we plausibly suppose that one of them might be me. It doesn't quite follow that neither would be me, since we might claim that this is a case of indeterminacy: that there is no answer to the question whether, in the Two-Sided Case, either person would be me.

18 Wiggins also talks of "the impossibility of conceiving of an entity's not being identical with that which it *is* in fact identical."

19 This vol., p. 175 (n. 11).

20 The most contentious detail here is that the lower brain stem may not be straightforwardly divisible. But that is not deeply impossible, as would be needed to challenge the relevance of this imagined case.

21 If, as she claims, I could survive with only half my brain, and I could survive with less than half my body, why could I not survive with half my brain and half my body? I am not appealing to transitivity here, in a questionable way. I am merely putting together the claims that, for me to survive, I only need half my brain, and I don't even need half my body.

22 For some needed refinements here, again see Unger (1990: ch. 8).

23 When some lump has been unevenly divided, we might claim that the larger part is the original lump, or we might claim that neither part is that lump. If the larger part is 99 percent of the original lump, the first of these claims would be more plausible. But we could not claim that the smaller part, which is a mere 1 percent, is the original lump.

24 As this analogy also shows, in order to distinguish between ourselves and our bodies, we need not reject Physicalism. Even if we had no purely mental properties, we could still be distinct from our bodies. Cellini's Venus, though distinct from the lump of gold, is wholly physical.

25 In such cases, McDowell believes, a single person has two series of thoughts and experiences, in each of which there is no awareness of the other series. But McDowell suggests that, in such a case, there are three different subjects of experience. There is the person, who has the thoughts in both streams. But there are also two subjects of experience, each of which has the thoughts in one of the streams. So each of these thoughts, on McDowell's view, is thought by two thinkers: one of these sub-personal subjects, and the person. (See McDowell 1990.)

26 For a brief defense of that slogan, see my paper "The Unimportance of Identity" (in Harris 1995).

27 Though published here for the first time, this paper was written in around 1990, and was intended to be a response to Judith Thomson's contribution to *Reading Parfit* (ed. Jonathan Dancy, Blackwell, 1997), reprinted in this volume as chapter 4.3. I apologize to Thomson for the way in which my writing of this and other responses held up the original publication of her paper. I have not revised this paper to take into account any later publications (though I have added a few references.).

References

Harris, Henry, ed. 1995. *Identity* (Oxford: Oxford University Press).

McDowell, John. 1990. "Peacocke and Evans on Demonstrative Content," *Mind* 99: 255–66.

—. 1997. "Reductionism and the First Person," in Jonathan Dancy, ed., *Reading Parfit* (Oxford: Blackwell Publishing).

McMahan, Jeff. 2002. *The Ethics of Killing* (Oxford: Oxford University Press).

Nagel, Thomas. 1986. *The View from Nowhere* (Oxford: Oxford University Press).

Olson, Eric. 1997. *The Human Animal* (Oxford: Oxford University Press).

Shoemaker, Sydney, and Swinburne, Richard. 1984. *Personal Identity* (Oxford: Blackwell Publishing).

Snowdon, Paul. 1990. "Persons, Animals, and Ourselves," in Christopher Gill, ed., *The Person and the Human Mind* (Oxford: Oxford University Press).

Unger, Peter. 1990. *Identity, Consciousness, and Value* (Oxford: Oxford University Press).

van Inwagen, Peter. 1990. *Material Beings* (Ithaca: Cornell University Press).

Wiggins, David. 1980. *Sameness and Substance* (Oxford: Blackwell Publishing).

Williams, Bernard. 1970. "The Self and the Future," *Philosophical Review* 79(2); repr. in, *Problems of the Self* (Cambridge: Cambridge University Press, 1973).

—. 1973. "Are Persons Bodies?," in *Problems of the Self* (Cambridge: Cambridge University Press).

CHAPTER FIVE

TIME

5.1 "The Privileged Present: Defending an 'A-Theory' of Time," Dean Zimmerman

5.2 "The Tenseless Theory of Time," J. J. C. Smart

Time and space are analogous in various ways. Objects exist in both time and space; events can be separated by distances in both time and space; matter moves continuously through space and time. In recognition of the analogies, physicists lump the two together under the heading of "space-time." How far does this analogy go? Very far indeed, answers J. J. C. Smart. Just as *objects that are distant in space are real* (for instance, Mars), objects that are distant in time are real (for instance, dinosaurs). Just as there is nothing special about *here* (beyond the fact that it is the place where *I* am), there is nothing special about *now* (beyond the fact that it is the time when I am). Dean Zimmerman rejects these alleged analogies. The present is special; it is the only time whose events and objects are truly real.

The Privileged Present: Defending an "A-Theory" of Time

Dean Zimmerman

1 Introduction

The following questions go to the heart of the deepest metaphysical disagreement about the nature of time: (1) Are there objective differences between what is past, present, and future? (2) Are present events and things somehow more "real" than those wholly in the past or future? I should like to respond, "Yes," to both questions. Affirmative answers sound obvious and commonsensical, at least to me. Indeed, I suspect that, for many of us, belief in a deep distinction between past, present, and future can be given up briefly, if at all; and then only by a mighty effort of will! Over the course of the twentieth century, however, more and more philosophers have argued for negative answers to these questions. In many quarters, the impulse to posit a deep difference between past, present, and future is now taken to be no better grounded than the impulse to suppose that there is an objective "downward" direction, the same everywhere in the universe; or that the earth is stationary, while the sun, moon, and stars are not.

There are two parts to my defense of affirmative answers to (1) and (2). First, I describe a number of theories of time that answer "Yes" to (1), and raise a worry about the ones that do not also answer "Yes" to (2). Then I assess reasons to reject or accept a metaphysics of time that answers (1) and (2) affirmatively. I consider some metaphysical and scientific arguments against affirmative answers, and find them wanting. More positively, I argue that belief in a real difference between past, present, and future has a certain positive status: it is "innocent until proven guilty," and guilt remains unproven.

2 A-Theories and B-Theories

At the beginning of the twentieth century, J. McT. E. McTaggart introduced some (arbitrarily chosen and rather bland) terminology that has been used ever since. He gave the name "A-series" to "that series of positions which runs from the far past through the near past to the present, and then from the present through the near future to the far future, or conversely"; and the name "B-series" to "[t]he series of positions which runs from earlier to later, or conversely" (1998: 68)[1] McTaggart's labels have stuck, and been put to further use. The properties *being past*, *being present*, and *being future* are generally called the "A-properties." The relations of *being earlier than*, *being later than*, and *being simultaneous with* are the "B-relations."

Metaphysicians who argue about time are divided by their attitude toward the A-properties and B-relations. Some regard A-properties as fundamental, and B-relations as derivative – they are "A-theorists" – while others regard the B-relations as fundamental, and the A-properties as derivative – they are the "B-theorists." To be an A-theorist is to believe in some sort of objective distinction between what is present and what is past and what is future. A-theorists answer question (1), above, in the affirmative: the present is distinguished from past and future in a way that is not relative to any other temporal thing, such as a conversation, a time, or a frame of reference. To be a B-theorist, on the other hand, is to deny the objectivity of our talk about past, present, and future. When we say that certain events and times are past, present, or future, we are not describing the world "as it is in itself"; we are merely describing the temporal locations of things relative to one particular (but not at all special) temporal location – the point in time at which the description is being given.

A-theorists disagree about the exact nature of the objective differences they posit between past, present, and future. But most of them would give an affirmative answer to (2), as well: The difference between present events and things, as opposed to those in the past or future, is that the present events and things are in some sense "more real." The future is "open," a realm of "mere possibilities." The past is a realm of things that have "faded away."

3 Competing Versions of the A-Theory

Consider some event that is happening, right now – for example, your reading the words in this very sentence. Too late! That event is over; it is already past. Consider some individual that exists now but soon will not – for example, a positron within the sun. Too late again! It collided with an electron, and both were annihilated in a violent explosion that left behind only a neutrino. The neutrino, with its tiny mass, could hardly be composed of the electron and positron that went into the reaction. So our poor positron is no more; it has utterly ceased to be. I expect that most of my readers would happily agree to the following claim about the two short-lived things I described: because they are entirely in the past, both the event that was your reading of the sentence, and the positron, *do not exist*. Another sensible-sounding claim: the event of your reading the final sentence in this paper does not exist; nor do the positrons that will be created by proton fusion within the sun later today. And that is

Dean Zimmerman

just what it is for an event or thing to "move" from the future into the present, and from the present into the past: It is to come into existence and then go out of existence. "Presentism" is the usual name given to a version of the A-theory that accepts, at face value, this account of the differences among past, present, and future things.

Suppose that a moment of time (say, the instant at which you finish reading this parenthetical clause) is just the sum of all the events going on right then – a popular view, and surely *one* thing that could be meant by the phrase "moment of time." In that case, past and future times would have to be composed of events that, according to the presentist, don't exist. Saint Augustine drew the logical presentist conclusion: "[I]t is abundantly clear that neither the future nor the past exist, and therefore it is not strictly correct to say that there are three times, past, present, and future."[2] Presentists, then, maintain that there exist only *present* events, individuals, and times – assuming times are sums or collections of simultaneous events.

Some A-theorists are not presentists. Augustine imagines the following sort of objection to presentism. We can, after all, foresee that certain things will happen or come into existence, and we can remember things that did happen or did exist. And so past and future things must have *some* kind of reality, in order for us to stand in these relations to them. "Otherwise, how do prophets see the future, if there is not yet a future to be seen? It is impossible to see what does not exist. In the same way people who describe the past could not describe it correctly unless they saw it in their minds, and if the past did not exist it would be impossible for them to see it at all." Accepting this conclusion would lead to a very different sort of A-theory: the view "that past and future do exist, but that time emerges from some secret refuge when it passes from the future to the present, and goes back into hiding when it moves from the present to the past."[3]

If an A-theorist follows this line of reasoning, she must admit that past and future things, events, and times all exist. Reality consists of the events of many times, in something like a four-dimensional array. But the A-theory implies that only some events are genuinely present. So the present becomes a kind of "moving spotlight" playing over a four-dimensional universe.

The image of the spotlight was introduced by C. D. Broad in 1923, in the form of a "policeman's bull's-eye" – a lamp that focuses a beam of light:

> We are naturally tempted to regard the history of the world as existing eternally in a certain order of events. Along this, and in a fixed direction, we imagine the characteristic of presentness as moving, somewhat like the spot of light from a policeman's bull's-eye traversing the fronts of the houses in a street. What is illuminated is the present, what has been illuminated is the past, and what has not yet been illuminated is the future. (1923: 59)

On the moving-spotlight A-theory (which, incidentally, Broad did not endorse), future and past events and things are just as much a part of "the furniture of the world" as present events and things. But there is something special about the ones that are present – they are "lit up" in some way. Before and after being illuminated, they reside in darkness – in a "secret refuge," to return to Augustine's metaphor.

Defending an "A-Theory" of Time

An intermediate form of the A-theory accepts the existence of past and present events, things, and times; but denies the reality of the future. This is the "growing block" view of time defended by Broad: Although both past and present things and events exist, present events differ from past ones in that there are (ever so briefly!) no events later than them. "[T]he essence of a present event is, not that it precedes future events, but that there is quite literally *nothing* to which it has the relation of precedence" (1923: 66).[4]

What makes present things special, according to the moving-spotlight or growing-block A-theories? How do things change as they cease to be present? In his arguments against the reality of time, McTaggart took a moving-spotlight theory as his primary target; and he describes the moving spotlight of "presentness" as a property that events gain or lose without undergoing any other significant changes; and a moving-spotlighter *might* conceive of the passage of presentness in this extremely thin way. Broad's growing-block A-theory is similar to a thin spotlighter's view; it implies that things and events do not change significantly when they cease to be present. For Broad, being present is simply a matter of being on the "cutting edge" of a growing universe spread out in four dimensions; ceasing to be present, and becoming past, involves no intrinsic change whatsoever: "Nothing has happened to the present by becoming past except that fresh slices of existence have been added to the total history of the world" (1923: 66).

These two "thin" conceptions of the nature of the present are A-theories, to be sure; they give an affirmative answer to (1), the first of the two questions with which I began. They do not, however, give an unqualified "Yes" to the second question. The moving-spotlighter, as imagined by McTaggart, answers (2) negatively: past and future things are in no meaningful sense "less real" than present things. They lack a peculiar property called "presentness"; but, as they acquire and lose this property, they undergo no interesting changes of any other kind. Unlike McTaggart's moving-spotlighter, Broad grants that *future* events and things are less real – for, on the growing block theory, they do not exist at all. But Broad gives a negative answer to *part* of question (2): past things and events are in no sense "less real" than present ones; they undergo no intrinsic changes, but only relational ones, as "fresh slices of existence" are added to the four-dimensional block of which they are parts.

Neither of these is a version of the A-theory I should care to defend. When I notice that a headache, or some other painful episode, has become part of the past, I am relieved that this is so; and when a pleasant experience becomes past, I am often disappointed. If a theory of time makes such changes in attitude utterly mysterious, we should have grave doubts about its adequacy. And neither of the two versions of the A-theory under consideration can explain why we care so much about whether things are present or past.[5] If a pain is just as intrinsically painful when it has the spotlight upon it, or when it is on the cutting edge, why should the passage of the spotlight or the adding of slices change our attitude toward it? And even if we *did* care about these rather obscure changes, how could we ever know when they have occurred? If either view is right, the mental and physical states that now char-acterize me will continue, intrinsically just the same, for the rest of time. If my state of mind does not change intrinsically when it becomes past, then, even if I am now correct in my beliefs about what is presently happening, won't these beliefs quickly become mostly false, and go right on being mostly false for all eternity?[6] The A-theory certainly loses much of its appeal, if it induces such skepticism.

Some recent defenders of the moving-spotlight or growing-block have ready answers to the questions: "Why should we care whether things are present?" and "How could we know what time is present?" They maintain that at least *some* objects and events, when they are present, are intrinsically different from the way they are when not present; some things change, drastically, when they cease to be "lit up" by presentness or when they become embedded within the growing block.

Today's spotlighters and moving-blockers generally agree that when an object ceases to be present, it loses a great many of its most interesting properties. Quentin Smith and Timothy Williamson, for example, believe that the entire block of past, present, and future individuals and events *exists*; but that, when objects and events pass from being future to present to past, they change in much more than just their A-properties – i.e., their presentness, or their degree of pastness or futurity. For example, they think that future things and events are not located anywhere in space until they are present; and, when past, they again become non-spatial – though of course it remains true that they once occupied space. These spotlighters strip past and future objects and events of all their interesting *intrinsic* properties, too. A table yet-to-be-made has no shape or mass or color; and when it is destroyed, it will lack these properties as well. On Williamson's view, things even cease to belong to (what one would ordinarily have thought to be) their essential *kinds*: "A past table is not a table that no longer exists; it is no longer a table" (1999: 195). Robert M. Adams and Peter Forrest are growing-blockers with broadly similar views about the way in which objects and events change when they cease to be on the "cutting edge," and thereby become past.

These versions of the A-theory seem to be able to do justice to the feeling that what's in the past is over and done with, and that what's in the future only matters because it will eventually be present. They can also plausibly explain how we know what time is present. But if past headaches are to be much better than present ones, these A-theorists must say things like: a headache is only *truly* painful when it is present; yesterday's headache, although it exists, is no longer painful. It has a past-oriented property, *having been painful* – a sort of backwards-looking relation to the property *being painful*. But actually being painful is a matter of simply having the property itself, not standing in some other relation to it; and that's why it no longer concerns us. Similar things can be said about someone's past observation that the present time (i.e., the spotlit time, or the cutting edge) is exactly noon. If this judgment about what time is present continues to exist even though it is past, then either it is almost always false, or else the observation of an event (such as the coincidence of watch hands) by a person only *actually* occurs when the observation is present. The wise A-theorist should take the latter alternative: once the person's observation has ceased to be present, it is no longer in any sense occurring. And the strategy can be extended to all the interesting properties of events and objects; to be *truly* loud, tall, hungry, etc. is to be *presently* loud, tall, hungry, etc.

Although this view makes sense of our relief when pain is past, and of our knowledge of what time is present, it has less appealing consequences as well. Headaches can exist but not be truly painful; a horse can exist although it is not actually alive or even spatially located. What's left of these past things and events is extremely thin: a physical object can survive a change in which it ceases to have any shape or size; an explosion can continue to exist when all its energy has dissipated. If the spotlighter or growing-blocker tries to tone down her claims about the thinness of past things – if she says, for instance, that past headaches are still "sort of painful" and that we remain "sort of aware" of what we observe even when our observations are no longer present – then it once again becomes difficult to answer the questions, "Why care that the headache is past?" and "How do we know what time is present?"

For the presentist, answering these questions is easy. Past headaches do not exist; consequently, they have no properties whatsoever, including being painful. And we can be sure that *we* are present, and not buried deep in the past of a four-dimensional block; for, as Braddon-Mitchell points out, "according to the presentist all that exists is the present, so the fact that we know we exist guarantees that we are in the present" (2004: 199). The presentist need not posit "some secret refuge" where past things hide (and, for the spotlighter, future things as well) – no realm of ghostly individuals lacking form and substance. Of course the presentist has other sins to answer for, as shall appear when objections to the A-theory are considered, below; and some of the objections might be easier to answer if one is a growing-blocker or moving-spotlighter. But, when all is said and done, I believe presentism remains the best version of the A-theory going.

4 Yes, But Is It True?

So far, I have distinguished a range of versions of the A-theory; and argued that, if you want to be an A-theorist, you should be a presentist. But that begs the most important question of all: is the A-theory true? In the remainder of this chapter, I defend the truth of the A-theory by criticizing two influential arguments for the B-theory, and then explaining why it is that I accept the A-theory.

An introductory essay of this kind can barely scratch the surface of a debate that has gone on for 100 years or more, with no signs of stopping. B-theorists have developed an impressive array of arguments against the A-theory in general and presentism in particular. Some of them are, I believe, simply specious.[7] But others are quite challenging. Here, I can do little more than mention a couple of the more important objections, and point in the general direction of an appropriate A-theorist response.

Arguments against the various versions of the A-theory fall fairly neatly into two categories: those that could just as easily have been given *before* Einstein's Special or General Theory of Relativity was formulated, and those that could not. I will consider one of each.

Arguments of the first sort generally appeal to metaphysical principles that are independent of the results of the scientific study of time. These principles tend to be controversial, and I usually find the arguments based upon them to be no harder to resist than the arguments against many other philosophical views that are widely admitted to be tenable. One of the most popular of these purely metaphysical arguments against presentist versions of the A-theory is based on something called "truthmaking."

5 An Objection to Presentism Based on the Need for "Truthmakers"

It is fairly natural to suppose that, whenever someone says something, and what they said was *true*, then there must be something "in the world" – some real object, thing, event, state of affairs, or fact – that "makes" what they said true. Philosophers have developed this idea by spelling out various "truthmaker principles." One plausible way to affirm the need for truthmakers would go like this: for every true proposition – where a "proposition" is the sort of thing that can be believed and doubted, the sort of thing that can be true or false – there must exist something that *requires* that the proposition be true – in other words, a thing that could not possibly exist, unless the proposition in question is true.

Frequently, the opponents of a philosophical theory will attack it by alleging that it violates this sort of truthmaker principle. Defenders of the theory are said to posit truths of some kind for which they cannot provide adequate grounding. Here's an example of a truthmaker objection in action. Some philosophers believe that laws of nature are really just ways of summing up the facts about the powers and liabilities of the fundamental particles and fields; and that these powers and liabilities – e.g., the tendency of massive objects to attract one another, of similarly charged things to repel one another, etc. – are "brute"; they are basic to causal explanations of why things behave the way they do, and there is no more to say about these powers other than to describe their causes and effects in various circumstances. Other philosophers are appalled by the idea of "ungrounded" powers, dispositions, or liabilities. Such properties are too "spooky," too "hypothetical," not sufficiently "categorical," etc. And these philosophers are likely to raise a truthmaker complaint against the defenders of basic powers: "Point to something in the world," they will say, "that *makes it true* that this particle has the power to repel that one, when in fact it is not doing any repelling and may never do any repelling."[8]

But truthmaker objections are rather blunt instruments with which to attack someone else's theory. For the defender of the theory may always respond by positing "brute facts" involving the problematic notion, and insist that these facts make the problematic propositions true. So, for example, the defender of brute powers and dispositions can simply say: "A disposition or power is a real feature or property of the things that have it; and just as there exist facts about the non-dispositional properties of things in virtue of which it is true to say that they have those properties, there are facts about the dispositional properties of things in virtue of which it is true to say that they have these dispositions. Where's the problem? You want truthmakers, there are your truthmakers." Unless the opponent can say a good deal more, specifically, about why it is wrong to take dispositions as primitive or brute features of things, the truthmaker objection amounts to little more than dissatisfied grumbling. And once those deeper objections to the very idea of primitive dispositions are on the table, one has an argument that ordinary talk about dispositions requires analysis or replacement in non-dispositional terms (or that such talk simply never conveys anything *true*); and there is no need to drag in the business about "truthmakers."[9]

The truthmaker objection to presentism is similar to the complaint about ungrounded powers. When dinosaurs roamed the earth, they passed many places without leaving much of a trace; most footprints were washed away or never allowed to petrify into solid rock, for example. An opponent of presentism could make the following demand about any one of these places: "Point to something in the world," the objector says, "that *makes it true* that a dinosaur walked past this place 150,000,000 years ago. It *is* true, but there is nothing about the way the world is now that *requires* that it be true or that *makes* it true; and according to you presentists, there is nothing more to the world than the way it is now. So you have no truthmakers for such straightforward truths about the past."

One presentist response mirrors the response of the defender of brute powers: "There are 'backward-looking' properties that objects *really have*, properties like *having been occupied by a dinosaur 150,000,000 years ago*; and there are real facts about which objects have these properties, facts that make propositions about the past true. What's the problem?" The opponents of presentism have attempted to answer this challenge; but, by my lights, they are still in the dissatisfied grumbling stage.

6 Objections to the A-Theory Based on Relativity

Many B-theorists have alleged that the A-theory is in conflict with Einstein's Special and General Theories of Relativity. If there is real conflict, A-theorists should be very worried. Philosophers have often given arguments to the effect that space or time *must* have a certain structure; for instance, that the geometrical structure of space must be Euclidean. Working scientists, meanwhile, have often ignored the philosophers and simply gone about their business, eventually proving conclusively that the philosophers were wrong. The canny A-theorist should be very reluctant to go down this road, banking on the falsity of extremely successful scientific theories.

But what exactly is the nature of the supposed conflict? Why is it harder to combine the A-theory with relativity than with a Newtonian conception of time, say? I cannot begin to do justice to this question here; it demands a detailed comparison of Newton's theory of "absolute" space and time with the radically different conception found in Einsteinian relativity. Since ostensible conflict with relativity is too important to ignore altogether, I simply sketch three objections that seem to me to be the grounds for most allegations of conflict between relativity and the A-theory; and gesture towards the replies I defend at greater length elsewhere.

The first apparent conflict is primarily between relativity and presentism. Relativity is formulated in terms of a four-dimensional manifold of space-time points. Taken at face value, the theory attributes important spatiotemporal structure to this manifold. One of the most important kinds of structure is exhibited by sets of points that constitute a "straight line" running in a time-like direction. Relativity uses this structure to explain why objects take the paths they do within space-time; a straight line is the path a particle will take if it is not experiencing any forces. Now, the A-theorist must think that one instantaneous, three-dimensional "slice" of the four-dimensional universe corresponds to the *real* present moment. And the *presentist* A-theorist is committed to the view that only that slice of the block *exists*. But these lines are composed of points that must come from different instantaneous slices; so, according to the presentist, when one of them exists, none of the others does. This leaves nothing to exhibit the important spatiotemporal structure of a straight line in a time-like direction.

But why must a presentist be committed to the non-existence of all but one slice of this four-dimensional manifold? My commitment to presentism stems from the difficulty I have in believing in the existence of such entities as Bucephalus (Alexander the Great's horse) and the Peloponnesian War, my first grandchild and the inauguration of the first female US president. It is past and future *objects* and *events* that stick in my craw. The four-dimensional manifold of space-time points, on the other hand, is a theoretical entity posited by a scientific theory; it is something we would not have believed in, were it not for its role in this theory; and we should let the theory tell us what it needs to be like. As a presentist, I believe that only one slice of this manifold is filled with events and objects. The future is determined by the character of these events and objects together with the structure of the manifold in their neighborhood. The fact that a given point lies along a straight-line in a time-like direction amounts to this: those other points are the ones from which a particle could get to this point, and the ones to which a particle would go from this point, if it were undergoing no accelerations or decelerations. The fundamental relations that give the manifold its causally interesting structure can be thought of as relations of "accessibility." Some parts of the manifold are accessible from a given location; others are not. Take the parts of the manifold that like along a straight line with a time-like (positive) length: the later parts of the line are accessible to a particle located at the earlier parts. The straightness of the line tells a particle "where to go next" if it is located at a series of points on the line, and no other forces are at work.

A second objection to the A-theory is that the structure relativity attributes to space-time does not single out just one set of points as "the time" of a given event within the block. There are many different angles at which the block can be sliced into sets of points that look for all the world like instantaneous, three-dimensional states of the universe – or "times." No one of these ways of slicing it into a series of times is better than any other; which angle will seem most natural to a given person will depend upon her state of motion. But the A-theorist must suppose that there is now, has always been, and will always be a fact of the matter about which parts of space-time are really "present" all together; and these facts will privilege one way of dividing the four-dimensional block into a series of *truly* "co-present" slices. Since the A-theory posits structure within space-time that is not countenanced by relativity, it contradicts the theory – which is taken to say that there is a certain amount of structure, *and no more*.

This objector is saying, in essence, "If fundamental physics can't see a distinction between two classes of things, there is no distinction to be made." But we all believe in lots of distinctions physics "can't see." Arguably, fundamental physics does not require the existence of composite objects; all it needs to describe the events with which it concerns itself are things like tiny particles, gigantic fields, and space-time. Is there no difference, then, between groups of particles that make up larger wholes, and groups that do not? Should we conclude that, since physics does not mention things like dogs, there is no reason to believe in such things – as opposed to mere swarms of particles arranged in various canine shapes? (For more on this question, see chapter 8 in this volume.) The modal realist (represented in this volume by Phillip Bricker; see chapter 3) provides a different sort of example. He believes in all sorts of space-time universes, spatially and temporally unrelated to this one. We can all certainly contemplate such "other universes" as abstract possibilities. But physics alone will not tell us what they are like; at least, I can see no argument from statements in the language of physics, describing the contents of our universe and its laws, to the conclusion that merely possible worlds are *not* universes much like ours that happen to be spatially and temporally disconnected from us. Still, am I not perfectly justified in maintaining my conviction that *this* universe is special – that it is radically unlike the merely possible ones, if there are any such things? The fact that my belief finds no support from physics, and is not fundamentally a distinction between two physical kinds, is quite irrelevant.

Here is an example even closer to the current controversy, and more telling. Would anyone want to say that, if space-time were *Newtonian* – and therefore divisible into a privileged series of instantaneous slices – then our best theory of motion would be in conflict with the A-theory? No.[10] Yet, if the objection from relativity is just the positing of a distinction not found in the physics, Newtonian physics should also provide an objection to the A-theory. Suppose the complete physical description of a Newtonian world is taken to consist in just Newton's timeless laws plus a "tenseless" description of the locations of particles and associated forces. Newtonian physics, so understood, would not "tell us" which time is present; and so the Newtonian B-theorist could mount a similar argument against the A-theory: physics cannot "see a difference" between the time that is present and the ones that are not, so there is no difference to be seen. Of course, if the description of the particles contained statements about where they are *now*, Newton's picture of the physical world *would* include a privileged present. But the same could be said about the relativistic four-dimensional block: If a description of the *present* distribution of matter were added to relativity (along with information concerning which distributions of matter were or will be present), then a privileged slicing of the manifold would reappear.

What should one conclude from the parity of Newton's theory and relativity on this score? At the very least, it appears that a simple "physics-doesn't-see-it" objection to the A-theory is not a radically new kind of objection that only became available after Einstein. If relativity is to provide a powerful new argument against the A-theory, the A-theorist must be convicted of something worse than merely positing a layer of space-time structure that relativity fails to mention. If that is the extent of the A-theorist's crimes, she cannot be convicted of the wholesale rejection of a perfectly good physical theory on metaphysical grounds.

But many have thought the conflict between relativity and the A-theory is much worse. The A-theorist does not just posit more space-time structure than is strictly needed to do physics; she is forced to reject relativity altogether, retreating to a theory of motion like Lorentz's. If this were what the A-theory requires, it would be deeply revisionary indeed. Lorentzian space-time is not just relativistic space-time plus some extra facts about a privileged slicing. A Lorentzian space-time manifold has Newtonian, not relativistic, structure. It includes absolute simultaneity and absolute sameness of position, neither of which has a place in relativity. And Lorentz's theory makes no use of the space-time distance relations that are fundamental to the relativistic manifold. I do not believe the A-theory automatically requires a return to Lorentz; and I try to explain why elsewhere.[11] Granted, the A-theorist attributes a special status to one way of slicing the manifold. But this structure can be added without thereby undermining relativity's account of the way space-time works; the causal role assigned to space-time by relativity is consistent with a privileged slicing. The A-theorist's additional fundamental structure can, in principle, leave the web of relativistic space-time distance relations intact – still doing its intended job in explanations of why things move in the ways they do.

7 Why Think the A-Theory Is True?

My reason for believing the A-theory is utterly banal (some philosophers reading this essay will want to say "insipid"): it is simply *part of commonsense* that the past and future are less real than the present; that the difference between events and things that exist at present, and ones that do not, goes much deeper than the difference between events and things near where I am and ones that are spatially far away – in Australia, for example. These platitudes about past, present, and future may not immediately imply one particular version of the A-theory; perhaps no very specific metaphysical theory deserves to be called "the" common-sense view about time. But the various versions of the A-theory – at least, presentism and the most plausible versions of the growing-block and moving-spotlight theories – are metaphysical pictures that preserve this commonsense conviction. And the B-theory does not.

J. J. C. Smart is a B-theorist who is particularly forthright in his rejection of the platitudinous beliefs that imply the A-theory. The source of these beliefs is, he thinks, a kind of misguided "anthropocentrism" – though perhaps "egocentrism" would be just as appropriate a label for what Smart has in mind.[12] At each moment, I am, quite naturally, especially interested in the place in time that I happen to occupy right then; and, from this special interest, I slide into the false conviction that my place in time is also *objectively* more important than the others. According to Smart, when you become a B-theorist, you adopt a more accurate perspective: you come to recognize that this particular time is no different than any other – it merely happens to be more important to you while you are located at it.

In this final section, I first explain what I mean by saying that the A-theorist's favorite platitudes about the deep difference between past, present, and future are "part of commonsense." And then I say why their having this status should be thought to count in their favor.

It would be a mistake to think of "commonsense" as a *faculty*, in the full sense of the word. It is not a special source of human knowledge – a distinctive and innate method by means of which we human beings gather information about the world, like sight or hearing. What it is for some statement to be commonsensical is just for it to seem obviously true to most sane human beings; for it to be part of the stock of things we all – or at least almost all of us – take for granted. Is the A-theory part of commonsense? I think so. *Everybody knows* that when events and things "recede into the past" they are very different from the way they are when present; and that the future is a "realm of mere possibilities, not realities." These are truisms denied by a relatively small group of people – basically, people who have become accustomed to using spatial metaphors to understand temporal notions (as one does when drawing space-time diagrams or reading the more consistent science fiction stories about time travel).

Still, how does the ubiquity of belief in the A-theory constitute serious support for the view? Haven't we discovered that, at various times in our history, the vast majority of us have taken things to be obvious that turned out to be provably false – for instance, that the sun rotates around the earth? Why think the A-theory is any better?

Of course it is true that a great many things that have seemed obviously true to most people have turned out, upon inspection, to be false. All I insist upon, however, is that something's being commonsensical must be allowed to count very strongly in its favor, other things being equal. Those who deny this relatively modest role to commonsense are courting extreme skepticism about much more than just the A-theory.

Epistemology is the philosophical examination of knowledge and related notions, such as evidence and rationality. One task of epistemology is to explore the question each of us can put by asking, "What is it *reasonable* for me to believe?" Epistemologists have learned something from the failure of modern attempts, from Descartes onward, to find absolute certainties and infallible chains of reasoning that take us from these certainties to the rest of the things we think it is reasonable for us to believe. The moral is this: unless we are willing to become extreme skeptics, we must allow that it is reasonable to believe things that seem obviously true, in the absence of special reasons to doubt them; and we must allow this even if the beliefs are admittedly not certainties, and cannot be "proven" in any interesting sense of the word. This conclusion privileges commonsensical beliefs. To be part of commonsense, a thing must seem obvious to almost everyone. So, for almost everyone, it is reasonable to believe it – in the absence of serious objections. It is "innocent until proven guilty." Now, one reason to doubt the truth of some seemingly obvious statement would be the fact that it is disbelieved by many other people whom one takes to be equally well placed to have an opinion on the matter. But if some particular example of an obvious truism is part of commonsense, then it is *widely held*; and so, assuming most people are well placed to have an opinion about its subject matter, it has passed a further test of reasonableness. For a belief to be part of commonsense is, then, a considerable "epistemic boon" or "plus."

Those who accept the commonsensical platitudes about the past, present, and future, are, therefore, *at least* justified in regarding the A-theory as "innocent until proven guilty." I take it to be as innocent, at least on first pass, as many other commonsensical beliefs that skeptical philosophers have tried to undermine: for example, the belief that there is a world of objects "outside" my mind, not dependent upon anyone's awareness of them for their existence; the belief that others have experiences much like mine and are not mere "zombies"; and the belief that we can reach justified conclusions by relying upon induction (an example of "relying upon induction" is postulating laws of nature that are universally true on the basis of a limited number of observations confirming the laws). All these commonsensical beliefs (and many more besides) have been challenged by skeptics; and their arguments often have a

Dean Zimmerman

certain plausibility – that is, their weakest premises are philosophical statements that sound at least moderately reasonable. Most intelligent adults, when confronted by the cleverest skeptical arguments for the first time, do not immediately see the best way to resist them. (Indeed, in some cases, there is considerable disagreement about how to resist them even *among philosophers*; and widespread agreement only that, one way or another, the skeptical arguments must be unsound.) When typical skeptical arguments are brought to bear upon beliefs as innocent as these targets, it is more sensible to conclude that there is something wrong with the premises (even if one cannot quite put one's finger on it) than to accept their conclusions. And it is more reasonable to reject the least plausible premise of these skeptical arguments on the basis of the falsehood of the conclusion – even if that premise seemed true, when one first heard it – than to become a skeptic. Why? Because the conclusion is the rejection of something that is part of commonsense – something that all but a few of us take to be utterly obvious.

So, unless we are prepared to become serious skeptics, we should admit that being part of commonsense gives a belief a *non-negligible* positive status. Such beliefs are not something that skeptical philosophers should expect us to give up at the merest hint of controversy, or in the face of anything but a powerful case against them. Everything turns, then, on positive arguments against the A-theory. I was not much impressed with the truthmaker objection against presentism; and I can here only report that other metaphysical arguments against the A-theory in general and presentism in particular leave me unperturbed, though sometimes not sure *exactly* what to say. Skepticism on the basis of these arguments seems to me to be no more warranted than in many other cases in which we side with commonsense, while not being entirely certain what is wrong with the skeptic's argument.

Objections to the A-theory based on relativity are more troubling – mainly because the progress of science has taught us to be extremely wary of putting much stock in the details of our untutored judgments about how causes operate, and what the laws of nature are like. We have ample evidence that, in these matters, not everyone is equally well placed to know the truth; and in that case, we should trust the experts, not the deliverances of commonsense. Now, the scientific experts support relativity (though not unequivocally, given the difficulty of unifying relativity and quantum mechanics). Fair enough. But, if I am right, the arguments that are supposed to lead from relativity to the falsehood of the A-theory are not very impressive.

To sum up: I find that – like most people throughout history – I believe things that imply the A-theory. Indeed, affirmative answers to (1) and (2), the questions with which we began, seem obviously right. It is, I claim, reasonable to believe something that seems obvious, unless there are significant reasons to doubt it; the commonsensical is "innocent until proven guilty." If I have correctly assessed the collective force of the arguments against the A-theory – those from metaphysical principles and relativity – then the innocence of the A-theory remains relatively unsullied. I would not claim to *know* that that the A-theory is true; but, in my view, few philosophers should claim to *know* the substantive philosophical doctrines they defend against their equally intelligent and well-informed philosophical opponents. I do insist, however, that it remains *reasonable* for me to *believe* it. And that is often the best one can say for a metaphysical theory.[13]

Notes

1 The terms "A series" and "B series" were introduced in McTaggart (1908).
2 Augustine, p. 269 (Book XI, §20).
3 Augustine, p. 267 (Book XI, §18).
4 Broad's defense of the growing block view is reprinted as ch. 12 of van Inwagen and Zimmerman 2007.
5 Arthur Prior is famous for lodging a similar objection against the B-theory of time, under the slogan "Thank goodness that's over!" See Prior (1996: 50).
6 The question is asked by Braddon-Mitchell (2004) and Merricks (2006).
7 Those based upon McTaggart's argument against the reality of time are singularly unimpressive. For criticism of McTaggart, see Broad (1998).
8 Chapter 2 of this volume continues the long-running debate about laws of nature.
9 For an in-depth discussion of "truthmaker objections," see Merricks (2007).
10 This is not strictly true! My colleague Frank Arntzenius would say this (and did). But he is gutsier than most; not many will be prepared to go so far.
11 See Zimmerman (forthcoming). Other A-theorists – e.g. Craig (2001) – argue that Lorentzian space-time is not so bad, after all.
12 See Smart (1963: 132–42).
13 This paper benefited from comments I received in conferences or colloquia at the University of Texas (Austin), Leeds, Geneva, and Oxford. In addition, I am grateful to Frank Arntzenius, John Hawthorne, Franklin Mason, Tim Maudlin, Ted Sider, and Jason Turner for discussions in which I learned (or tried to learn) a great deal about relativity and the ways it might conflict with presentism. None of them should be held responsible for whatever confusions remain in this paper – with the possible exceptions of Ted and Frank, who went above and beyond the call of collegial duty, providing comments and suggestions on late drafts . . . and this is the thanks they get!

References

Adams, Robert M. 1986. "Time and Thisness," in Peter A. French, Theodore E. Uehling, and Howard K. Wettstein, eds., *Midwest Studies in Philosophy: Volume 11* (Minneapolis: University of Minnesota), pp. 315–29.
Augustine. 1961. *Confessions*, trans. R. S. Pine-Coffin (Harmondsworth: Penguin).
Braddon-Mitchell, David. 2004. "How Do We Know it is Now Now?" *Analysis* 64: 199–203.
Broad, C. D. 1923. *Scientific Thought* (London: Routledge & Kegan Paul).
—. 1998. "McTaggart's Arguments Against the Reality of Time: An Excerpt From *Examination of McTaggart's Philosophy*," in van Inwagen and Zimmerman, eds. (1998), pp. 74–9 (also to appear as ch. 10 in van Inwagen and Zimmerman, eds. (2007).
Craig, William Lane. 2001. *Time and the Metaphysics of Relativity* (Dordrecht: Kluwer Academic Publishers).
Forrest, Peter. 2006. "General Facts, Physical Necessity, and the Metaphysics of Time," in Zimmerman, ed. (2006), pp. 137–52.
McTaggart, J. McT. E. 1908. "The Unreality of Time," *Mind* 17: 457–74.
—. 1998. "Time: An Excerpt From *The Nature of Existence*," in van Inwagen and Zimmerman, eds. (1998), pp. 67–74 (also to appear as ch. 9 in van Inwagen and Zimmerman, eds. (2007)).

Merricks, Trenton. 2006. "Goodbye Growing Block," in Zimmerman, ed. (2006). pp. 103–10.

—. 2007. *Truth and Ontology* (Oxford: Clarendon Press).

Prior, Arthur. 1996. "Some Free Thinking About Time," in Jack Copeland, ed., *Logic and Reality* (Oxford: Clarendon Press), pp. 47–51; repr. as Ch. 14 in van Inwagen and Zimmerman (2007).

Smart, J. J. C. 1963. *Philosophy and Scientific Realism* (London: Routledge & Kegan Paul).

Smith, Quentin. 1993. *Language and Time* (New York: Oxford University Press).

van Inwagen, Peter and Dean Zimmerman, eds. 1998. *Metaphysics: The Big Questions* (Malden, MA: Blackwell).

—, eds. 2007. *Metaphysics: The Big Questions*, 2nd edn. (Malden, MA: Blackwell).

Williamson, Timothy. 1999. "Existence and Contingency," *Proceedings of the Aristotelian Society*, suppl. vol. 73: 181–203.

Zimmerman, Dean, ed. 2006. *Oxford Studies in Metaphysics*, vol. 2 (Oxford: Oxford University Press).

—. Forthcoming. "Presentism and Other A-theories," in Craig Callendar, ed., *The Oxford Handbook of Time* (Oxford: Oxford University Press).

The Tenseless Theory of Time

J. J. C. Smart

1 Attractions of the Tenseless Theory of Time

Strictly speaking, the tenseless theory of time is not a theory of time (or space-time) in the way in which, for example, the special theory of relativity is. It has to do with the unimportance for ontology of words such as 'past', 'present', 'future', 'now', and the temporal inflections of verbs, and the tensed 'is', 'will be', 'was', etc. I shall include 'past', 'present', 'future', and 'now' as tenses, no less than the inflections of verbs. I shall distinguish the tenseless 'is' as in '7 plus 5 equals 12'. Some philosophers say that 7 plus 5 always was, is, and always will be equal to 12. It seems to me a pity to sully the purity of mathematics by bringing in time references, even trivial ones. I shall also contend that a tenseless idiom is most appropriate for physical theory. A tensed locution could avoid the tensed inflections of verbs but would say 'is future', 'is present', and 'is past' with tenseless 'is'. I have been told that Chinese is like this in eschewing tense inflections on verbs. Opponents of the tenseless theory tend to be influenced by the phenomenology of our immediate experience of time, whereas I distrust phenomenology. I hope that such phenomenology can be explained away. There can be metaphysical illusions (Armstrong 1968 and Smart 2006.) Note that I am using the word 'phenomenology' in a relatively sensible way, not as used obscurely by a certain school of German philosophy.

Opponents of the tenseless theory do not treat tenses and words such as 'past' as indexicals, as are 'I' and 'you' and 'here' whose reference depends on who utters them and the time of utterance. The opponents of the tenseless theory generally treat such inflections and words as referring to intrinsic properties in respect of which events change. Thus a person's marriage may be said to have the property of futurity, then of presentness, and then of pastness. The tenseless theorist sees this as, at the very least, highly misleading. All this is sketchy and merely preliminary to details in subsequent sections. I shall use the term 'A-theory' to refer to opponents of the tenseless theory, which I shall call the B-theory. This is by analogy with McTaggart's (1927) two ways of ordering events in time, the former in respect of their greater or lesser pastness or futurity, and the latter in respect of being earlier or later than one another. I must add that I do not really believe in the existence of time but only of space-time, unless one gives the name 'time' to a particular 'world line' in space-time. However this will not greatly affect most of the argument.

I hope that this gives the flavor of the difference between those who accept the B-theory and those who accept the A-theory. Perhaps we should use the term 'A-theory' as referring to a syndrome, rather than as having a very tight definition. What, then, are the attractions of the B-theory?

The first thing of consequence to note is that mathematical and physical theories are properly expressed tenselessly. Their truths are, in a sense, eternal truths, not sempiternal ones as the A-theorist will contend. Now if, like me, you want to see the world *sub specie aeternitatis* (to echo Spinoza), or "from the point of view of the universe" (Sidgwick 1981: 382), you should want a tenseless language for metaphysics (Smart 1987). Tenses and other indexicals make us see the world from a particular and egocentric perspective, at least if we take them with ontological significance. Of course we can never see the world other than from the perspective of our place and time, but we should aspire to doing so as approximately as we can. Of course there are other, less metaphysical, reasons for wanting a tenseless theory of time, in that we may think that it would give a better understanding of how tensed language functions, for example by giving the truth conditions for tensed language in a tenseless metalanguage. I appreciate this interest in linguistic theory, but as a metaphysician I see the linguistic theory, though intrinsically interesting, as also a means. I wish to suggest also that plausibility in the light of total science is an important indicator of metaphysical truth.

Biology, in contrast to physics and chemistry, is cosmically parochial. It is concerned with terrestrial organisms and generalizations about them. It uses the laws of physics and chemistry to explain these generalizations of natural history. The natural history may be highly sophisticated, using fairly high technology to make observations, but it issues in mere generalizations, the holding of which, even with exceptions, get explained (we hope) by the physical and chemical laws. A scientist need not be surprised by such anomalies. Organisms are complex mechanisms, and motorcars, even though they obey the laws of mechanics, electromagnetism, and petroleum chemistry, often unsurprisingly break down. Thus we may say that, though there are speculations about exobiology, biology is concerned with terrestrial matters and is cosmically parochial. Metaphysics should not be cosmically parochial. It should eschew tensed language. Tenses in their own way can tempt us to a cosmically parochial, anthropocentric, or even egocentric perspective on the world. Of course, this is not to deny that intelligent beings elsewhere in the universe could have their own cosmically parochial perspectives from tensed language.

This desire for a non-parochial and non-anthropocentric view of the universe provides reasons for liking a tenseless view of time. It must be conceded that some A-theorists try to mitigate cosmic parochialism by (despite the special theory of relativity) holding that at any instant there is a cosmic "now" or simultaneity. I shall indeed shortly make a little bit of an irenic suggestion to the A-theorist on this matter. This, however, is by the way. As I have said, my motivation is metaphysical, but this does not mean that pure linguistics is not relevant to philosophical concerns. I hold that tenses are indexicals and the semantics of tenses and indexicals generally is important for the ontology of temporal discourse. Compare the case of the word 'I', which in any occasion of normal use refers to the speaker or act of writing. It does not carry any interesting metaphysical baggage. There have indeed been misguided people who talk about the 'I' or who say 'the ego', thus slightly covering up their absurdity with the respectability of a learned language. Some have used the expression 'the Self', though 'self' has its natural habitat in 'myself', 'himself', 'yourself', etc. You kick yourself but it does not make sense to say that you kick your Self (Flew 1949).

2 Two Ways of Treating of Tenses as Indexicals

There are two ways of dealing with tenses and indexicals in general, which I will present as containing no objectionable consequences for the metaphysics of time. These are (1) the token-reflexive approach due to Reichenbach (1947: sects. 50–1), and (2) the approach due to Donald Davidson's "Truth and Meaning" (1984).

Reichenbach called an utterance of a word or phrase a "token" of the word or phrase, whereas a word type is an abstract object. Indeed we can have different senses of 'type word', since if a lad sends 'love and love' to his sweetheart, there is one sense in which he has used three (token) words and another sense in which he has used only two (type) words. If I shout "Fire" I utter a token of the type 'fire'. We can talk in the same way of type and token sentences. In the case of written words these persist but we can identify the token with the act of writing it. After all if we find in an old manuscript letter "Queen Anne is dead," we take the present tense 'is' to refer to the time or the act of writing the letter, and certainly not to the time of our reading it. With this proviso I shall regard inscriptions as momentary events and shall count them as utterances.

According to Reichenbach words such as 'I', 'you', 'here', 'now', and also tense inflections are token reflexive: they refer to their own utterances. An obviously token reflexive expression is 'this utterance'. In theory we could get by with this single token reflexive, though as I shall indicate shortly there could be some difficulty with compound tenses such as pluperfects. Thus 'I' could be replaced by 'the maker of this utterance', 'you' by 'the hearer or reader of this utterance', 'here' by 'near this utterance', 'past' by 'earlier than this utterance', and so on. 'This utterance' does not have as much context dependence as many indexicals, but the extra context dependence of 'here', for example, can be picked up by the context-dependence of 'near' in 'near this utterance'.

Thus we can translate 'The battle of Waterloo is past' by 'The battle of Waterloo *is* earlier than this utterance', and the (nowadays false) statements 'The battle of Waterloo is present' and 'The battle of Waterloo is future' respectively by 'The battle of Waterloo *is* simultaneous with this utterance' and 'The battle of Waterloo *is* later than this utterance'. (Here I indicate tenseless 'is' and other verbs by italics.) Similarly 'was', tensed 'is', and 'will be' can be treated in the same way. 'Joe was a coal miner' can be rendered 'Joe *is* a coal miner earlier than this utterance'. Indeed the difference between perfect and pluperfect can be accommodated, following Reichenbach, by referring also, definitely or indefinitely, to a contextually agreed reference point. Thus 'Joe will have come before the lecture begins', is to say 'Joe *comes* at some time later than this utterance and before the lecture begins'. With imperfects we need to refer to stretches of time.

So 'past' is just 'earlier than this utterance', 'present' is just 'simultaneous with this utterance', and 'future' is just 'later than this utterance'. There are indeed things that the A-theorist wants to say, such as "The battle is future, will be present and then will be past" and "Thank goodness that's over" (Prior 1959). At first sight, these curious remarks seem to support the A-theorist, who does not think that 'past', 'present', 'future', and in this context perhaps 'over' are indexical, but thinks that they refer to intrinsic properties of events. I shall consider a B-theorist reply when I come to discuss the A-theory.

I now consider the second, also essentially B-theory, way of dealing with tenses and 'past', 'present', 'future', etc., and which I now prefer to the 'token reflexive' way. It is due to Donald Davidson (1984) who gives the semantics for tenses in a tenseless metalanguage. This seems to me to avoid the questionable metaphysics of the A-theory just as well as the token reflexive approach, and I think that it has significant advantages. I shall also consider possible disadvantages noted by Heather Dyke (2002). Dyke usefully refers to the second and metalinguistic approach as "the date theory." Davidson suggests that a semantics for sentences containing tenses or other indexicals should relativize truth of a sentence to a person and a time. Thus, he says, the theory will entail sentences such as '"I am tired" *is* true as (potentially) spoken by person P at time t if and only if P *is* tired at t' and '"I was tired' *is* true as (potentially) spoken by person P at time t if and only if P *is* tired at a time earlier than t' (I have used italics for the relevant occurrences of 'is' and 'was' to emphasize the tenselessness of the metalanguage.) Other tenses can be treated analogously though with obvious complications for compound tenses. This seems to have the advantage over the token reflexive approach in that it deals with sentences, not utterances. There is only a finite number of (say) English sentences that ever get uttered, and yet the language contains an infinite number of sentences as abstract objects. Tarski's semantics for formalized languages with the structure of first-order logic gives a finite axiomatization of the truth conditions for such an infinity of sentences. Davidson's program was to show the underlying structure of natural languages as that of first-order logic. It was an exciting program for whose success I would hope, but we do not need to accept the full program in order to accept the semantics for tenses.

I feel slight unease on account of the word 'potentially' in the suggestion as stated above, and I do not suppose that Davidson really liked the modal word 'potentially' here.[1]

Consider the sentence 'The sun's becoming a supernova is future, will be present and then will be past'. On the token reflexive approach we might try: 'The sun's becoming a supernova *is* later than this utterance, simultaneous with some utterance later than this utterance, and earlier than some utterance later that utterance'. This is at best false, since presumably there are no persons or utterances at the time in question (assuming there are no extraterrestrials and we do not colonize other solar systems). The date theory fares little better, for lack of appropriate utterances at that distant time. We might take the B-theorist's inability to make much sense of sentences of the form 'Event E is future, will be present and then will be past' as simply the trouble which arises when we treat 'past', 'present', and 'future' as signifying properties in which events change (Smart 1949). We might say that events happen, things and processes change. The B-theorist of course has her own way of dealing with the fact of change. 'The traffic light *changes* from red to green' is just to say that a red temporal stage of the traffic light *is* red and an immediately later temporal stage *is* green.

The A-theorist of course will aver that sentences such as 'E was future, is present and will be past' are perfectly intelligible because 'past', 'present', and 'future' (or rather the corresponding abstract nouns) refer to intrinsic properties of events in respect of which events change and so the (in my view pathological) sort of sentence discussed in the last paragraph is perfectly in order and even platitudinous. Perhaps this is a minor advantage of the A-theory, and I will consider what to say about it in the next section. I now think that in metaphysics we tend to get into a trade-off or comparison of plausibilities, and only in some cases is it a matter of knock-down proof or, as Wittgenstein said, showing the fly the way out of the fly bottle.

3 B-Theorist Critique of the A-Theory

The A-theory is doubtless protean, with various minor differences between different practitioners, but, as I indicated in the last section, I take the essential nature of the A-theory to be the assertion that the words 'past', 'present', and 'future' correspond to intrinsic properties of events. However, I also consider Arthur Prior to be in the A-theorist camp because of his stress on the metaphysical importance of tenses. He had what he called a 'no present' theory, in which the work done by 'past', 'present', and 'future' is done by tense operators. His is not a tenseless theory of time but quite the opposite. Prior was a great man but (influenced by Davidson) I regard him as wrong in his proliferation of sentential operators as in 'Joe believes that', 'Joe desires that', 'It is necessary that', 'Joe says that'. Prior's approach really needs a semantics for 'past', 'present', and 'future', and this would be difficult for him since he holds that the indexicality – or, as he calls it, 'egocentricity' – of these words is spurious ("A Spurious Egocentricity," in Prior 1968). I think that his semantics would be metaphysically in the camp of the A-theorists.

To put it roughly, and acknowledging that there may be need for qualifications, Prior was perhaps the last of important logicians who thought of interesting axiom systems and then fitted interpretations to them (as resulted in his "tense logic"), whereas the semantic approach has been to fit axioms to a model or interpretation. Neither the token-reflexive way of dealing with tenses nor the date theory treats tenses as operators. Prior suggests a "no present" theory analogous to F. P. Ramsey's "no truth" theory that to say that grass is green is true is just to say that grass is green. Similarly to say that something is going on now is just to say that something is going on. However, this is because for Prior verbs are always tensed. Even the tenseless 'is' of mathematics gets thought of as 'always was, is, and always will be', thus sullying the purity of mathematics with temporal reference. Now, if 'is' is tensed, then if something is going on now (or at present), it is going on – and vice versa. To have both the tensed 'is' and 'now' or 'present' is like wearing both belt and braces. Either keeps one's trousers up, and tensed verbs do the same job as could be done with tenseless verbs and 'past', 'present', or 'future'. Unless one recognizes the indexicality, the operators of Prior's tense logic do not save us from the A-theorist's ontology. At any rate, I shall take it that the A-theorist's assertion that events change in respect of past, present, and future cannot be avoided by representing it in terms of changes of the tenses of verbs we use to describe them. The stronger medicine of the B-theory is needed.

McTaggart claimed that time involves change and that the B-theory denies change. If event E is before event F, then according to him it always was and always will be that it is so. Here he is inappropriately foisting tensed 'is' on the B-theorist. The B-theorist should say that E *is* (tenseless) earlier than F. As I mentioned earlier, the B-theorist does not want to say that instantaneous events change (for example, the beginning of the war does not change unless by 'beginning of' one means 'early part of'). As mentioned above, the B-theorist accommodates the facts of change by tenselessly saying that one temporal stage of a thing or process can differ in certain respects from an adjacent temporal stage. Partly by not recognizing this fact, McTaggart finds a contradiction in both his A-series and his B-series and comes up with a mysterious C-series, but this need not detain us here.

The word 'event' is etymologically cognate to 'outcome' and generally works like 'result' (patently, in its archaic use, as in 'the event of the tournament' in Sir Walter Scott's *Ivanhoe*). Similarly with 'beginning'. Beginnings and endings do not have beginnings and endings, except that I concede that sometimes the words 'beginning' and 'ending' are used with the sense of 'early part' and 'final part', in which case they are process words and not event words. Things and processes can change, events happen. The B-theorist elucidates change as immediately adjacent temporal stages of a thing or process having different properties. McTaggart went the other way, since he held that change, if it exists, pertains to events, not to things and processes. Of course he goes on to argue that there is a contradiction in supposing that events change, by an argument generally held to be fallacious and which I shall not consider here. The matter of interest here is his belief that the B-theory denies change in processes and things and his own locating change wrongly in events. He says that this would be in respect of being past, present, or future. This would be regarded by a B-theorist to be highly misleading to say the least. If 'past', 'present', 'future', and 'now' are indexical, they cannot refer to intrinsic properties. Such intrinsic properties would be 'spooky' and they are not mentioned in physical theory. In physical theory there is no past and future, only earlier and later. Consider the Minkowski space-time of special relativity. It is true that the light cones at a point O in Minkowski space-time are sometimes described as 'past' and 'future', but all that is meant is 'earlier than O' and 'later than O'. Indeed, the mechanics and electromagnetism of special relativity are time-symmetrical and the difference between earlier and later has to be brought in from thermodynamics and cosmology.

Actually physics is not quite time-symmetrical but CPT-symmetrical, where C is charge, P is parity, and T is time. One can think of an anti-particle as the particle lying backwards in time. Time-symmetry can be thought of as reflection in a time mirror and so it seems very natural to reverse parity (reflection in a space mirror). So one might think of CPT-symmetry as time-symmetry only more so (just as Lord Tweedsmuir, when Governor-General of Canada, said that Canada was like Scotland but more so). It was the great theoretical physicist Richard Feynman who thought of a positron as an electron moving backwards in time, but with philosophical pedantry (necessary for the concerns of this article) I must stress that one cannot move either backwards or forwards through time. Time is already in the Minkowski picture. As a B-theorist I do not really believe in space and time but only in space-time. Of course I do believe in the special relativity distinction between time-like and space-like world lines, and so I am not really being disingenuous in writing this essay on theories of time. This distinction is seen in the minus signs in the expression for the metric of Minkowski space-time. In special relativity there is no absolute space-time and there is no cosmic present. This is a worry to some A-theorists. However, I shall shortly offer a small olive branch to the A-theorist on this matter.

Some A-theorists take a rather pragmatic view of space-time. Thus Peter Geach, in his subtle but I think wrong-headed paper 'Some Problems about Time' (1966), speaks of the four-dimensional and semi-Euclidean space of special relativity as merely "a graph." This strikes me as instrumentalist. I view Minkowski space-time as a real physical entity and the postulation of it, as I think that Minkowski did, as explanatory. Of course in the light of general relativity it is only an approximation, valid only approximately in the absence of very strong gravitational forces. Nor in being realist about space-time do I want to pre-empt the question of whether Minkowski's or Einstein's space-time is to be thought of as absolute or merely a system of relations between physical entities, though there is much to be said in favor of the absolute theory (Nerlich 1994a, 1994b).

Of course it is possible to state the special theory of relativity in commonsense language. Einstein pretty well did it in 1905. There would be a problem, in that commonsense does not recognize that the applicability of the notion of 'now' is local only. For communication with fast (near the speed of light) spaceships, new conventions would be needed. For example, 'now' could refer to simultaneity in the frame of reference in which the message sender was at rest. (The receiver would have to do some very quick calculations!) Minkowski showed the matter in a much clearer and more explanatory light. The Lorentz transformations correspond to a rotation of axes in space-time. The familiar Newtonian transformation amounted to a rotation of time axis *without* a rotation of a space axis. As Minkowski pointed out, this looks arbitrary in a way that the Lorentz transformations do not. Minkowski's way of looking at special relativity helped to pave the way for Einstein's general theory with its space-time of variable curvature. The main insight of Einstein's 1905 paper, which he stated, unfortunately, in rather operationist language, was in connection with the question of how to reconcile Newton's mechanics with Maxwell's electromagnetism. Maxwell's equations are Lorentz invariant, whereas Newton's are not, being the Galilean transformations of commonsense. Should Newton's or Maxwell's equations be modified? Einstein modified Newton's equations that had worked well where velocities that are low compared with the velocity of light are concerned. The modified mechanics has been amply confirmed by observations of fast particles in cyclotrons and indeed in the very design of a cyclotron. Minkowski's geometrical approach makes time-dilation and the supposed twin paradox almost obvious because it is a matter of Pythagoras's theorem modified by the minus signs which occur in the metric for Minkowski space. Consilience with Minkowski and with Einstein's later general theory is an important motive for liking the B-theory.

I have remarked that special relativity may be felt as a problem for the A-theorist, who believes in an objective and universal present, and even more if she believes in a cosmic advance through time. Here I shall briefly offer a very small olive branch to the A-theorist. Though special relativity does not determine a preferred frame of reference, it does not rule out the possibility of some such preferred frame being determined from outside the theory. We might suppose that we should consider a locally preferred frame in which the cosmic background radiation is equal in all directions. Because of the expansion of the universe, in each cluster of galaxies the preferred time dimension would be at an angle to that of others. This would point to the idea of a cosmic simultaneity given by the surface of a curved hyperspace.

However, though cosmology might give comfort to the A-theorist, it raises other worries for her. There are speculations that universes may be spawned from the backs of black holes, thus arising from new big bangs (Smolin 1997). At any rate it does suggest that the A-theorist's usual idea of a single ordering of past, present, and future may need revising. I surmise that the B-theorist will quite happily allow for a mere partial ordering of earlier and later, even though a very complicated one.

The main objections to the A-theory, as discussed above, are due to the metaphysical mysteriousness of the A-theory ideas of past, present, and future, and also tenses, and to the greater plausibility of analyzing them as indexicals. Tensed discourse also facilitates (though it is not the sole cause of) the supposed intuition of the passage of time in immediate experience. As I mentioned earlier in this chapter, Arthur Prior laid stress on the feeling, after a period of suffering that has come to an end, 'Thank goodness that's over'. The A-theorist thinks that this sort of consideration and an appeal to immediate experience more than compensate for the ontological economy and scientific plausibility of the B-theory. The B-theorist thinks that these considerations do not really support the A-theory.

4 "Thank Goodness That's Over"

Suppose that we interpret your utterance "Thank goodness that's over" as expressing relief that the utterance of it is later and not simultaneous with or earlier than the pain referred to by the 'that'. But are we really rejoicing that the pain is earlier than a certain utterance? As Arthur Prior remarks in his article "Thank Goodness That's Over" (1959), why should anyone thank goodness for *that*? Certainly it is not just a matter of your thanking goodness that something is earlier than your utterance. It is an expression of relief. On the other hand, if you said to a physician "My pain has stopped," your intent might be to give him useful diagnostic information. And though not very idiomatic, "My pain *is* earlier than this utterance" would serve the physician equally well. (As far as avoidance of the unidiomatic is concerned, the date account of tenses and related indexicals may have a small advantage.)

Now why are we pleased that a pain has stopped and not that it is about to begin? This is a question whose answer may seem obvious to commonsense and yet it raises deep questions about the temporal asymmetry of the universe and about the theory of evolution. We are future oriented because we need to plan or at least take quick action. Why we need to plan for the future and not the past, or why planning for the past does not even seem to have clear sense, is nothing to do with A-theory fantasies, such as that the future is not real or that the supposed passage of time is one way. The question has often been seen as that of the so-called direction of time. I prefer to describe it as the problem of the temporal asymmetry of the universe or at least of our cosmic era. As physicists and philosophers such as Boltzmann, Reichenbach, and Grünbaum have argued, the problem is largely to do with statistical mechanics and cosmic thermodynamics.[2] If, contrary to what is on the whole believed, the universe went after expansion to contraction and big crunch and if the thermodynamic asymmetry was reversed too, then denizens of that era would have their past toward our future – that is, memory traces would be of later events by our reckoning, but they would think of the causes of the traces as earlier. In between the two eras, at a time of heat death, there would be traces in neither direction. Indeed, I doubt if it is possible to imagine a mental state in which we had memories in both directions. I suspect that it is also this thermodynamic (statistical) asymmetry that makes us think of causality as one way (oppositely in the two eras).

It is this asymmetry between earlier and later that makes us care about the future in a way in which we do not care about the past (though we may rejoice in or regret the past). Animals may plan for the future or have instincts that cause them to behave rather as if they had planned. A humanoid ancestor confronted by a tiger knows that he was safe in the previous hour but is not sure whether or not the next hour will contain a tiger with his body dead and perhaps partly in the tiger's stomach. It is no wonder that our anxious worries are future-oriented. (Note that my use of 'past' and 'future' here is not the indexical one I was concerned with in criticizing the A-theory. With a little more attendant verbiage, I could have used 'earlier' and 'later'.) No wonder that we say "Thank goodness that's over" when pain or unpleasantness is no longer something about which we need to plan and make decisions. Evolution by natural selection has seen to it that our minds are turned predominantly to thinking about what will, or will be likely to, happen later (Maclaurin and Dyke 2002). A prisoner who has served nine years of a ten-year sentence is relatively happy that he has only one year left to serve, whereas if he has served one year of a ten-year sentence, even though he is just as temporally near freedom, he will be less happy. The past is not in the time direction in which our planning and emotions are usefully oriented.[3] It comes down in the end to the temporal asymmetry of the universe, not to temporal flow or coming to be. If the prisoner thinks that his release is coming or that his consciousness is advancing toward the time of his release, he is in a perhaps happy state of confusion. We do not need this idea to explain why he feels happier a year before the end of his long sentence than he was a year after its beginning.

5 The Supposed Passage of Time

The myth of passage, as Donald Williams called it in a fine article (1951), the idea that time passes by us, is cognate with what I regard as the equally absurd idea that we advance through time. A politician will pontificate "as we move into the twenty-first century" and a hymn goes "Time like an ever-rolling stream bears all its sons away." We can feel that we are adrift on a river and being borne inexorably toward the big waterfall that is our death. Or, more pleasurably, that one's wedding day is coming toward one, though all too slowly. I hold that all these ideas and feelings are born of confusion. A first move against this confusion is to ask: 'How fast is this flow of time or our advance through it?' Does a meter bar flow toward the 100-centimeter mark at 1 centimeter per centimeter? In mathematics, of course, we do have $dt/dt = 1$ and $dx/dx = 1$, but neither is informative.

Notice how motion looks if we represent it in Minkowski space-time. To say that two particles are at rest with respect to one another is to say that they (or tangents to them) are parallel, and motion is a matter of them or their tangents being inclined to one another. I am supposing that particles have no dimensions as in Newtonian dynamics, and so in Minkowski space they *lie* along a line, their 'world line'. Even sizable objects are thin space-time worms. Taking the units of space and time such that the velocity of light is unity (thus avoiding an arbitrary-looking constant in the expression for the metric) one second is equivalent to 300 million meters, so that even a star is a very thin space-time worm and approximates to its world line. So in space-time, rest and motion are a matter of parallelism and inclination of world lines. Now if motion is just relative inclination of world lines, there is no room in Minkowski (or Einstein's Riemannian) space-time for us to represent motion of time (flow of time) or motion through time (advance through time). Thus, if we take Minkowski's dictum at the beginning of his famous 1908 paper seriously, that "Henceforth space by itself and time by itself are doomed to fade away into mere shadows, and only a kind of union of the two will preserve an independent reality," and still want to talk of the flow of time or of our advance through time, we would need to think of ourselves extending into this hypertime and we would have to have four-dimensional hypertime slices much like our instantaneous three-dimensional time slices of our four-dimensional selves. If we think of Minkowski space as a playing-card, the world of hyperspace would be like a pack of cards. Then if it was felt that there would have to be motion through hyperspace, we would need there to be a hyper-hyperspace –and so on without end. Some philosophers have thought of Minkowski space as "static," but that is a crude mistake. Not all world lines of particles are parallel. The supposedly flowing world of the A-theorist is often described as "dynamic" and the Minkowski world as "static." This is a strange use of the words 'dynamic' and 'static'. In mechanics, 'dynamics' is about forces. Perhaps 'kinetics' would better express what the A-theorist who makes this objection has in mind, but the Minkowski world captures mechanics and a fortiori kinetics. It is not static. Not all tangents to world lines are parallel. Moreover, anyone who thought that time flowed would be likely to call the hyper-hypertimes 'static' too. Confusion proliferates.

If it is said that time flows, it seems, then, that the question "How fast does it flow?" is a devastating one for the A-theorist. However, Ned Markosian (1993) has challenged the rate of passage argument against the notion of time flow or passage argument. Now, I have conceded that the rate of passage argument is not knock-down or apodeictic. For example, it is logically possible that the hypertime is constituted by a mere ordering of instants, but that (unlike normal time segments) its segments would not constitute magnitudes. As Markosian points out, we define rates of change by comparison of spatial changes, such as the distance walked and the change in the angle of the sun in the sky. A measure of time is better if it keeps the laws of nature simple and not cosmically parochial. So the rate of rotation of the earth will not do because we want to say that, because of tidal friction, the rate of the earth's rotation is decreasing. The best measure of time is the frequency of vibrations of a cesium atom. Nevertheless, the (in my opinion confused) phenomenology that makes us feel that we are aware of a continuous passage of time, analogous to the flow of a river, has done much to make the A-theory seem attractive. To expose the seductiveness of the metaphor is not necessarily to assert that all changes have rates of change. There could be instantaneous changes (though quantum mechanics suggests that the positions of such changes might be indeterminate). There may not be any step functions in fundamental physics, though there are functions that approximate to them. To explain the seductiveness of the phenomenology, I have conjectured that we confuse the flow of information through our short-term memories with a flow of time itself (Smart 1980). I am of course more convinced that the flow of time is a metaphysical illusion than I am of the suggested explanation of it. However, for a plausible explanation of it, see Hartle (2005).

Markosian demands that the B-theorist should be able to analyze tensed sentences in terms of tenseless ones. The B-theorist could follow Reichenbach and Dyke and say that tensed utterances contain a token-reflexive expression. Obviously it is unfair to expect the B-theorist to translate a token reflexive into a non-indexical sentence. If we take the Davidsonian way of giving the truth conditions of indexical sentences in terms of a non-indexical metalanguage, this also does not constitute translation and it is unfair to demand it.

It is often said by A-theorists that the four-dimensional world is "static" where the A-theorist's world is "dynamic." (Of course, dynamics has to do with forces and so perhaps they should say 'kinetic'.) But, of course, relative motion is represented in the Minkowski picture by relative inclinations of world lines and acceleration by curvature of world lines. No fact of motion is lost!

6 Presentism and Fatalism

There is a bizarre form of A-theory called presentism. Of course I reject it. Both past and future are real. It is said that we cannot change the past. Equally we cannot change the future. Suppose that I say to you that I am going to change the future by lifting my left arm or by lifting my right arm. I lift my left arm. Have I changed the future? No, lifting my left arm was the future. The historical past is earlier than us in Minkowski space and the future is up ahead of us. Both are real. Our actions are caused by our beliefs and desires and in part cause future events. There is not room for the silly sort of fatalism that implies that our decisions do not matter.[4] If belief in the reality of the future is fatalism, it is not the silly sort of fatalism.[5]

Notes

1   "'Julius Caesar crossed the Rubicon' is true if it *is* spoken by *P* at *t* and *t* *is* later than the time at which Caesar *crosses* the Rubicon." Well, lots of people have spoken this particular sentence but what about the sentences that never get uttered? Heather Dyke makes the pertinent objection that by truth functional logic, if the clause after the 'if' is false, then the whole sentence is trivially true and so useless as a statement of truth conditions. She therefore prefers the token-reflexive approach. A semantics for indexicals based on utterances not sentences must give up the idea of a recursive semantics, but as has just been noted, the date approach fares no better. Perhaps the best that we can do for the date approach is to aspire to a recursive semantics for non-indexical sentences and give a non-recursive (except in the trivial sense in which a finite set is recursive) semantics for the set of triples <*S*, *P*, *t*> where *S* is actually uttered by a *P* at a *t*. On this view we might propose a recursive semantics for the non-indexical part of language and no recursive surface rules for the indexical and indeed other contextually dependent sentences. It still remains the case that when we know that a particular tensed sentence *S* has been uttered (or indeed will be uttered) by a particular person *P* at a particular time *t*, we can go on to give its truth conditions non-trivially by a tenseless sentence in the metalanguage. So perhaps I can come to some compromise with Dyke. In any case there is no metaphysical difference between the token-reflexive approach and the date approach. Each, if correct, removes the mystery that arises from the A-theorist's supposed properties of pastness, presentness, and futurity.

2   See Reichenbach (1956) and Grünbaum (1973). For an outstanding recent philosophical treatment of this issue, see Huw Price (1996). For a useful treatise for physics students, see Paul Davies (1974).

3   I hope that this answers the example of the prisoner put up by George Schlesinger (1983: 109–10).

4   See Smart (1981). Peter Geach has called this a laughable argument, which puzzled me until I recollected that he had a strong tensed view of truth.

5   For reasons of space, I omit a comparison of the commonsense language of substance and change with the four-dimensional idiom. (It is my belief that four-dimensionalism together with mereology, the theory of part and whole, makes many philosophical problems as easy as shelling peas. A case in point is the philosophical problem of personal identity, though here there remain psychiatric, juristic, and perhaps theological ones.) On this matter, see Sider's contribution to this volume (chapter 6.1) and Sider (2001).

References

Armstrong, D. M. 1968. "The Headless Woman Illusion and the Defence of Materialism," *Analysis* 29: 48–9.

Davidson, D. 1984. *Inquiries into Truth and Interpretation* (Oxford: Blackwell).

Davies, P. C. W. 1974. *The Physics of Time Asymmetry* (Leighton Buzzard: Surrey University Press).

Dyke, H. 2002. "Tokens, Dates and Tenseless Truth Conditions," *Synthese* 131: 329–51.

Flew, A. G. N. 1949. "Selves," *Mind* 58: 353–8.

Geach, P. T. 1966. "Some Problems about Time," *Proceedings of the British Academy* 51: 321–36.

Grünbaum, A. 1973. *Philosophical Problems of Space and Time*, 2nd edn. (Dordrecht: D. Reidel).

Hartle, J. B. 2005. "The Physics of Now," *American Journal of Physics* 73: 101–9.

Maclaurin, J., and Dyke, H. 2002. "Thank Goodness That's Over: The Evolutionary Story," *Ratio* 15: 276–92.

Markosian, Ned. 1993: "How Fast Does Time Pass?" *Philosophy and Phenomenological Research* 53: 829–44.

McTaggart, J. McT. E. 1927. *The Nature of Existence*, vol. 2 (Cambridge: Cambridge University Press).

Nerlich, G. C. 1994a. *The Shape of Space*, 2nd edn. (Cambridge: Cambridge University Press).

—. 1994b. *What Spacetime Explains* (Cambridge: Cambridge University Press).

Price, H. 1996. *Time's Arrow and Archimedes' Point* (New York: Oxford University Press).

Prior A. N. 1959. "Thank Goodness That's Over," *Philosophy* 34: 78–84.

Prior, A. N. 1968. *Papers on Time and Tense* (Oxford: Clarendon Press).

Reichenbach, H. 1947. *Elements of Symbolic Logic* (New York: The Macmillan Company).

—. 1956. *The Direction of Time* (Berkeley: University of California Press).

Schlesinger, G. 1983. *Metaphysics* (Oxford: Blackwell).

Sider, Ted. 2001. *Four-Dimensionalism: an Ontology of Persistence and Time* (Oxford: Clarendon Press).

Sidgwick, H. 1981. *The Methods of Ethics*, 7th edn. (Indianapolis: Hackett).

Smart, J. J. C. 1949. "The River Of Time," *Mind* 58: 483–94.

—. 1980. "Time and Becoming," in van Inwagen. ed. (1980).

—. 1981. "The Reality of the Future," *Philosophia* 10: 141–50; repr. in Smart (1987).

—. 1987. *Essays Metaphysical and Moral* (Oxford: Blackwell).

—. 2006. "Metaphysical Illusions,"*Australasian Journal of Philoosophy* 84: 167–75.

Smolin, L. 1997. *The Life of the Cosmos* (London: Weidenfeld and Nicholson).

van Inwagen, P., ed. 1980. *Time and Cause* (Dordrecht: D. Reidel).

van Inwagen, P., and D. W. Zimmerman, eds. 1998. *Metaphysics: The Big Questions* (Oxford: Blackwell).

Williams, D. C. 1951. "The Myth of Passage," *Journal of Philosophy* 48: 457–72.

PERSISTENCE

Chapter 5 dealt with certain facets of the analogy between time and space; this chapter deals with a further facet. Objects that take up space are *spread out in space*. An office building, for example, is spread out over a certain region of space. If you look at a part of this region, the upper half, say, you will find a mere part of the building: the part consisting of the upper floors. Lower parts of the region contain other parts of the building, namely, the lower floors. Furthermore, if the building is dirty *at* the top and clean *at* the bottom, this is because of features of the parts: the upper parts are dirty and the lower parts are clean. According to Theodore Sider, objects that last over time are analogous; they are *spread out in time*. If the building was built in 1900 and torn down in 2000, it was only a mere part of the building – a *temporal part* – that existed in 1900. Separate temporal parts existed in 1901, 1902, and so on, just as separate parts of the building (the floors) are located in different regions of space. And if the building was originally built white but later painted red, the building was initially white because its earlier temporal part was white, and it was later red because its later temporal part was red. Some philosophers wholly reject the idea that objects are spread out in time; they claim that temporal parts do not exist. John Hawthorne rejects only part of the idea. While he agrees that temporal parts exist, he does not agree that the building was first white and later red because of the colors of its temporal parts. Instead, its temporal parts had its colors because of the colors had by the building itself. Hawthorne goes on to deny other components of the picture that objects are "spread out in time."

CHAPTER 6.1

Temporal Parts

Theodore Sider

1 What Are Temporal Parts?

I will argue that temporal parts theory is true, but first we need to get clear on what exactly this theory says. Let's start with the idea that *time is like space.*[1]

Everyone has seen timelines, in magazines and encyclopedias:

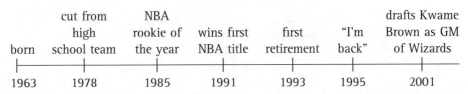

Michael Jordan's life

	cut from high school team	NBA rookie of the year	wins first NBA title	first retirement	"I'm back"	drafts Kwame Brown as GM of Wizards
born						
1963	1978	1985	1991	1993	1995	2001

For some reason, time is easier to comprehend when represented by a spatial diagram. A timeline is such a diagram. The spatial line on this page represents a stretch of time – Jordan's life.

Diagrams of motion from high school physics take this a step further, by representing one dimension of space in addition to time. Figure 1 represents a moving particle. The horizontal axis represents time; the vertical axis, space. Since the diagram contains only a single spatial axis, it can represent only one spatial dimension of the particle's motion (motion in the x direction). The curved line on the diagram represents the motion of the particle, which begins at spatial location $x = 1$ at time $t = 0$, moves to location $x = 2$ by time $t = 1$, then moves back to location $x = 1$ by time $t = 2$.

Space-time diagrams take this a step further, by representing more spatial dimensions alongside time. The space-time diagram in figure 2 includes two spatial dimensions in its depiction of a dinosaur from the Jurassic period and a person born in 2000 AD.

All these diagrams represent time as just another dimension, alongside the spatial dimensions. Given how convenient this method of representation is, many philosophers

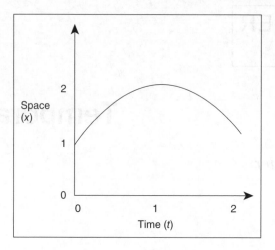

Figure 1

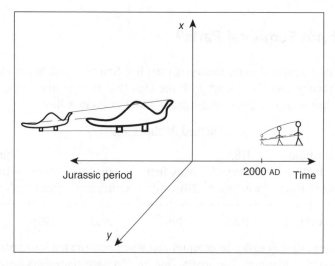

Figure 2   Space-time diagram

and scientists have wondered whether time itself is in some sense just another dimension. The question amounts to whether, and to what extent, time is like space.

Temporal parts theory is the claim that time is like space in one particular respect, namely, with respect to *parts*. First think about parts in space. A spatially extended object such as a person has *spatial parts*: her head, arms, etc. Likewise, according to temporal parts theory, a temporally extended object has *temporal parts*. Following the analogy, since spatial parts are smaller than the whole object in spatial dimensions, temporal parts are smaller than the whole object in the temporal dimension. They are shorter-lived. The space-time diagram makes this clear. The whole person is the following object: ⚇⚇. He is spread out from left to right because

Theodore Sider

he lasts over time; he begins to exist in 2000 AD, and lasts for a number of years beyond that. The parts of the diagram, 𝟃, 𝟃, and 𝟃, represent some of his temporal parts.

A person's temporal part at a time is exactly the same, spatially, as the person at that time, but it exists only for a moment. Thus, the early temporal part 𝟃 looks, feels, and smells like a baby, but it lasts only for an instant. If you watch the baby for a while, you will first be looking at one temporal part, then another much like it, then another much like the last one, and so on. If you watch long enough, you will notice that the later temporal parts are slightly bigger than the earlier ones. This is because the baby is growing. Accordingly, the leftmost temporal parts represented on the diagram are smaller than the rightmost temporal parts. For comparison, imagine looking at a person's wrist. Now move your gaze slowly up the person's arm, toward the shoulder. The arm in your field of vision "grows," from wrist-size to shoulder-size, since your eyes pass over different spatial parts of the person, first smaller parts (the wrist), then larger parts (the shoulder).

Temporal parts have spatial parts, and spatial parts have temporal parts. Consider the head of the person in the diagram: ⌀⊸o. This representation of the head extends from left to right because heads, like people, last over time. The head – a spatial part of the person – thus has temporal parts: ∘, ∘, and o. Like the person, the head grows; its earlier temporal parts are smaller than its later ones. Now, consider one of these temporal parts of the head, the last one for example: o. It is part of the last pictured temporal part of the person: 𝟃. In fact, it is a spatial part of this temporal part of the person. (Notice that the very same object, namely o, is both a temporal part of a spatial part and also a spatial part of a temporal part.)

The existence of temporal parts is just one way that I believe time to be like space. Here are two others (the nature of time is discussed more fully in chapter 5). (1) Time is like space regarding the *reality of distant objects*. Spatially distant objects, such as objects on Mars, are just as real as objects here on Earth. The fact that Mars is far away doesn't make it any less real; it just makes it harder to learn facts about it (we need a telescope). Likewise, I think, temporally distant objects, such as dinosaurs, are just as real as objects we experience now. The fact that a dinosaur is far away in time doesn't make it any less real; it just makes it harder to learn facts about it (we need to examine fossils). The belief that temporally distant objects are real is sometimes called 'eternalism.' (The main opposing view, 'presentism,' says that only objects in the present time exist.) (2) Time is like space regarding the *relativity of here and now*. When speaking to my brother in Chicago, if I say "here it is sunny" and he says "here it is raining," we do not really disagree. What is called 'here' changes depending on who is speaking: I mean New Jersey, he means Chicago. There is no one true *here*. I think that the word 'now' works analogously. Imagine the dinosaur in the space-time diagram above (figure 2) saying "It is now the Jurassic Period." I, on the other hand, say "It is now 2006." According to the relativity of 'now,' the dinosaur and I do not really disagree. There is no one true *now*. What is called 'now' changes depending on who is speaking: I mean 2006, the dinosaur means the Jurassic Period. The combination of this theory of the function of 'now' and eternalism is often called the 'B-theory of time.'

It is important to distinguish between the different facets of the space-time analogy, since some philosophers accept some facets while rejecting others.[2] Some accept the B-theory while denying the existence of temporal parts; and some embrace temporal parts while denying that time is like space in one or more ways. What I will defend here, however, is the 'B-theory' version of temporal parts theory.

So: is temporal parts theory true? Do temporal parts *really exist* – do persons and other physical objects really have parts that last only for an instant? Temporal parts theory is a very general and speculative theory about the world, about what objects exist and what they are like. It is speculative because the question of its truth is hard to settle by observation or experiment.[3] Crudely put, objects look the same, whether or not they are made of temporal parts. Experiment and observation would be unnecessary if all rival theories were internally inconsistent; then we could deduce temporal parts theory from pure logic alone. Unfortunately, this is not the case; there are internally consistent opposing theories.

We cannot prove temporal parts theory, but never fear! I believe that assessing the philosophical case for temporal parts allows one to make a decent educated guess. I will consider the following arguments for temporal parts: (1) the problem of change, (2) the paradoxes of material constitution, and (3) the argument from vagueness and anthropocentrism.

2 Change and Temporary Intrinsics

The oldest argument for temporal parts starts with the mundane fact that things change. Suppose that I am first standing, so that I am straight-shaped. Then I sit down, so I am bent-shaped. The standing person, call him Ted_1, seems to have different properties from the sitting person, call him Ted_2; only Ted_1 has the property *being straight-shaped*. But everyone agrees that *Leibniz's Law* is correct:

> Leibniz's Law: Objects x and y are identical only if they have exactly the same properties.

For if x and y are identical, then when we talk about x and y, we are talking about a single object, in which case it makes no sense to say that x has different properties from y. Leibniz's Law seems to tell us that Ted_1 and Ted_2 are not identical, since they have different properties. So, the argument concludes, Ted_1 and Ted_2 are distinct temporal parts of me.

This is a bad argument. Its flaw can be seen by viewing the situation from the perspective of a space-time diagram (figure 3). A space-time diagram depicts the entirety of an object all at once. It is as if we take the perspective of God and look in on time from the outside; we take the "timeless perspective" on reality. From the timeless perspective, what properties do I – in my entirety – have? What am I like? The argument above spoke of properties such as 'being straight-shaped' and 'being bent-shaped,' but in light of the space-time diagram, it isn't right to describe me as simply being straight-shaped *or* as simply being bent-shaped, since I am straight-shaped at some times and bent-shaped at others. From the timeless perspective, it

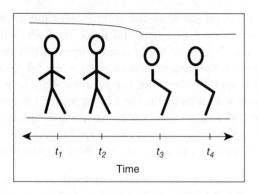

Figure 3

makes no sense to speak of properties like 'being straight-shaped'. Instead, we must speak of my shape *at various times*. Here, then, are the properties that I have from the timeless perspective:

(P) being straight-shaped at time t_1
being straight-shaped at time t_2
being bent-shaped at time t_3
being bent-shaped at time t_4

Moreover, *both* Ted_1 and Ted_2 have all the properties (P), for Ted_1 and Ted_2 are the very same object, namely, the person depicted in the diagram! The names 'Ted_1' and 'Ted_2' were introduced as names for "the standing person" and "the sitting person," respectively. But the standing person and the sitting person are the very same person, namely, the person depicted in the diagram; namely, *me*. I am a person who was straight-shaped at times t_1 and t_2, and who was bent-shaped at times t_3 and t_4. So the argument goes wrong when it claims that Ted_1 and Ted_2 have different properties.

The argument fails. But some people think that further reflection on the subject of change leads to a new argument for temporal parts. Let's look more closely at the reply to the argument from change that was given in the previous paragraph.

The crucial move came when I said that the properties an object has are those it has from the timeless perspective. These properties, as we saw, are properties like *being straight-shaped at time t_1*. Call these *indexed* properties, since they involving "indexing" (or "relativizing") temporary properties (in this case, *being straight-shaped*) to times (in this case, t_1). Now, in addition to making the crucial move of saying that objects have indexed properties, a temporal parts theorist will want to go one step further, and say something about what having indexed properties amounts to. He will want to give the following temporal parts theory of (at least some) indexed properties: a person is straight-shaped *at* time t_1 because that person's temporal part at t_1 is straight-shaped, period. A temporal part, unlike a continuing person, can be said to "have a straight shape, period" (as opposed to having a straight shape *at* one time or another), because a temporal part exists at only a single time. Temporal parts, unlike continuing objects, can have *non-indexed* properties.

Temporal Parts | 245

An opponent of temporal parts, on the other hand, cannot take this further step, since the further step assumes that temporal parts exist. She will instead stop with the claim that Ted$_1$ and Ted$_2$ have the indexed properties (P); she will not go on to say that objects have indexed properties because of temporal parts with non-indexed properties.[4] For her, properties like shape are *fundamentally indexed*.

Now for the new argument from change for temporal parts, put forward by David Lewis (1986: 202–4). The new argument is in essence a complaint against fundamentally indexed properties. According to Lewis, certain properties – including shape properties – *must* be explained in terms of non-indexed properties:

> [According to the indexer,] shapes are not genuine intrinsic properties. They are disguised relations, which an enduring thing may bear to times. One and the same enduring thing may bear the bent-shape relation to some times, and the straight-shape relation to others. In itself, considered apart from its relations to other things, it has no shape at all. . . . This is simply incredible. . . . If we know what shape is, we know that it is a property, not a relation. (1986: 204)

If fundamental indexing is no good, then shape properties must be explained in terms of non-indexed properties of temporal parts. Therefore, Lewis concluded, temporal parts must exist. This argument for temporal parts is known as the *argument from temporary intrinsics*.

Lewis's argument has been discussed extensively, especially his reason for claiming that shape properties must be explained in terms of non-indexed properties. Why is he so sure that "If we know what shape is, we know that it is a property, not a relation"? On one way of reading Lewis, the reason is that properties like shape are *intrinsic*. Intrinsic properties are those that are had by an object just in virtue of the way that object is, regardless of what other objects are like. Shapes are, Lewis thinks, paradigm examples. Extrinsic properties, on the other hand, depend on what other objects are like. *Being an uncle* is a paradigm example: whether you are an uncle constitutively depends not just on you, but also on other people; namely, on whether you have a niece or nephew. That is, it depends on whether you bear the *is an uncle of* relation to someone. (Extrinsic properties are sometimes called "relational.") Now, if shapes are indexed, so the argument goes, then shapes become just as extrinsic as *being an uncle*, for I have the properties in (P) in virtue of being related to other objects. Which other objects? *Times*. I have the property *being straight-shaped at time t_1*, for example, in virtue of bearing the *is bent-shaped at* relation to the time t_1.

This reason is not very convincing. Even if all properties turn out extrinsic in a sense, there may yet be an important difference between properties like shapes and properties like *being an uncle*. Only properties like the latter involve other *particular objects*, as opposed to times.[5]

Lewis might instead appeal to a fairly abstract metaphysical intuition. Late in the nineteenth century, British idealists like F. H. Bradley claimed that the world is a single interconnected whole. According to Bradley, to describe a single object, for instance a certain eight-ball, one must bring the entire world into the description. In addition to saying that the eight-ball is black, has a certain mass, and so on, one must also mention the eight-ball's distance from the cue ball. Not only that; one must

Theodore Sider

also mention what is going on in the house next door, occurrences in other countries and other times . . . All these facts pertain equally to the eight-ball. We cannot separate the facts about the eight-ball into the facts about the eight-ball's intrinsic features and the facts about its relations to other things. Subsequent philosophers, notably G. E. Moore and Bertrand Russell, rejected this view emphatically. Against Bradley's holism, Moore and Russell advanced an opposing picture of a world of many separate little bits. Each bit can be described intrinsically without bringing in the rest. There are, of course, relations between the bits. A description of the world that characterizes the eight-ball perfectly, down to the last detail, and likewise for the cue ball, is not complete until it specifies the distance relation holding between the balls. Moore and Russell's complaint was not that Bradley accepted relational facts, for they accepted them too. It was rather that Bradley did away with intrinsic properties.[6]

Lewis's complaint about indexing is like Moore and Russell's complaint about Bradley. The indexer claims that all of reality is relational. No object is just plain straight, or just plain black, or just plain 50 grams. Objects are straight, black, or 50 grams, with respect to, or relative to, other objects (times). That, Lewis says, is implausible.

There may be something to this complaint, but it is nowhere near as forceful as Moore and Russell's complaint against Bradley, for the indexer's world is nowhere near as holistic as Bradley's. An indexer is free to agree that the eight-ball can be completely described without bringing in the cue ball, let alone the house next door. The description must indeed bring in a time, but that is all.

Lewis's argument that shape properties are not indexed to times is based on the brute metaphysical intuition that *shape doesn't work that way*. Shapes are instantiated, period (not relative to a time); at the most fundamental level they are Moorean/Russellian non-relational properties. Unfortunately, Lewis's opponent is likely to flatly reject the alleged intuition. Of course, the fact that an opponent can reject the premises of an argument doesn't on its own show that the argument is no good, for it may be irrational to reject the premises. But in this case, it is hard to convict Lewis's opponent of irrationality. It is unclear how powerful Lewis's metaphysical intuition is.

3 The Paradoxes of Material Constitution

Let us consider next a number of fascinating puzzles known collectively as the paradoxes of material constitution. Each consists of an argument for the apparently outrageous conclusion that two distinct objects can be made up of, or constituted by, the same matter. Call this conclusion 'cohabitation,' for it says that the same matter can be "inhabited" by two objects. The philosophical task is to say where the flaw in the argument lies, or, alternatively, to say why cohabitation is not as outrageous as it appears. Either approach requires developing a general theory of the nature of material objects. The argument for temporal parts lurking here is that the best approach to the paradoxes appeals to temporal parts. To show that this approach is the *best*, we must examine alternate approaches; that is the plan for this section and sections 3.1–3.5.

The paradoxes come in many forms. I will consider two: *the statue and the clay*, and *undetached parts*.

The statue and the clay: a sculptor begins on Monday with an unformed piece of clay, which she shapes on Tuesday into the form of a statue. We now argue as follows:

P1: The piece of clay that existed Monday continues to exist on Tuesday after being given statue shape.

P2: The sculptor *creates* a statue, which exists on Tuesday but not on Monday.

P3: If P1 and P2 are correct, then the statue and the piece of clay are two different material objects that on Tuesday are made up of exactly the same matter. They are not the same object because of Leibniz's Law: the piece of clay, but not the statue, exists on Monday.

C: Therefore, different material objects can be made up of the same matter at a single time.

The argument is logically valid, and its premises seem correct, yet its conclusion seems false. That is the paradox.

Suppose the sculptor tires of the statue on Wednesday, and squashes it, seemingly destroying it. We can then form a parallel argument for the same conclusion:

P1′: The piece of clay that composes the statue on Tuesday is not destroyed when it is squashed, so it continues to exist after Wednesday.

P2′: The statue that exists on Tuesday is destroyed when it is squashed, and so does not exist after Wednesday.

P3′: If P1′ and P2′ are correct, then the statue and the piece of clay are two different material objects that on Tuesday are made up of exactly the same matter. They are not the same object because of Leibniz's Law: the piece of clay, but not the statue, exists after Wednesday.

C: Therefore, different material objects can be made up of the same matter at a single time.

Undetached parts: in addition to its tail, legs, head, and so on, a cat also has larger parts, for instance its *torso*: all of the cat except for the tail. Consider now a certain cat, Tibbles, and its torso, Tib. Unfortunately for Tibbles, on Tuesday its tail is chopped off and the tail's matter is destroyed. We now argue as follows:

P4: Tibbles exists on Tuesday, since a cat can survive the destruction of its tail.

P5: Tib exists on Tuesday, since chopping off the tail did not affect Tib at all; it merely removed an external object that was once attached to Tib.

P6: If P4 and P5 are correct, then on Tuesday, Tibbles and Tib are two different material objects made of the same matter. They are not the same object because of Leibniz's Law: Tibbles, but not Tib, had a tail as a part before Tuesday.

C: Therefore, different material objects can be made up of the same matter at a single time.

Again, the argument's premises seem correct, yet its conclusion seems false.

To get an intuitive handle on what is going on with these arguments, the concept of "tracing" is helpful. Suppose you are given the task of tracing a certain object through time. This, you are told, means ascertaining where this very object has been in the past, and where it will be in the future. What information will you need to accomplish the task?

One thing you will need to know is what *sort* of thing your object is. We ordinarily think of the world as involving objects of various sorts: pieces of clay, statues, cats, and so on. These objects persist over time, through various changes. Cats age; pieces of clay change their shape. But a cat or a piece of clay cannot survive just any change: some changes *destroy* a thing. Dismembering a cat destroys it; we do not think of the resultant body parts as being the same object as the cat. Furthermore, other changes *create* a new thing. Sculpting a piece of clay, we ordinarily think, creates a statue. Finally – and here is the crucial bit – whether a given change destroys a thing, or creates a new thing, depends on what sort of object that thing is. Sculpting the clay creates a statue; it does not create a new piece of clay. Being squashed flat destroys a statue but not a piece of clay. At least, that is what we ordinarily think. So, since tracing an object requires ascertaining when it was created, and which changes it survives (since we must ascertain whether *the very same object* is present at different times) tracing an object requires knowing what sort of thing it is.

The paradoxes of constitution are based on this fact, that different sorts of objects are associated with different criteria for tracing. Each argument shows that two paths of tracing can intersect at a location that appears to contain only a single object. In the statue/clay case, for instance, *piece of clay* tracing begins before Monday, leads to the clay in statue form on Tuesday, then extends beyond Wednesday to the clay in squashed form. *Statue* tracing has a different starting point: it begins on Tuesday when the sculptor's work is done, but also leads to the clay in statue form; it then ends on Wednesday when the statue is squashed. Our ordinary beliefs associate an object with each way of tracing, and so lead to two objects made up on Tuesday of the same clay, at the point where the paths of tracing intersect.

We have, then, three arguments for the apparently absurd conclusion of cohabitation. The challenge is to find a reason to think that cohabitation is not as outrageous as it seems, or a reason to reject a premise from each argument. Either sort of reason requires articulating a general theory of material objects. As we will see at the end, temporal parts theory is one such theory, but first let us examine some rivals.

3.1 The constitution view

One of the most popular responses to the arguments is simply to accept cohabitation. This response has the advantage of taking all of our beliefs about tracing seriously. We want to trace pieces of clay as well as statues, and torsos as well as cats. As the arguments show, this leads to admitting the possibility of two different objects sharing exactly the same matter. The *constitution view* simply embraces this conclusion (without admitting the existence of temporal parts).

Since the statue and the piece of clay share the same matter, they are *extremely* similar. Obviously, the piece of clay is exactly the same mass, shape, size, and smell as the statue. Now, a perfect replica of a statue, made by a master forger, would also share these qualities. But the piece of clay is far more similar to the statue, for it is made of the very same matter. It is in exactly the same place as the statue. How, then, can it be a different object?

Defenders of the constitution view say that the statue and the piece of clay can be different objects despite being so similar because each is *constituted* by the same matter. Constitution is the relationship that holds between a thing and the quantity of matter that makes it up. But speaking of "constitution" does not *explain* how cohabitation is possible; it merely places a label on a problem.

And there is indeed a problem. Let me mention two arguments that have been put forward against the constitution view. First: according to the constitution view, squashing the statue destroys the statue, but does not destroy the piece of clay from which it is made. Thus, the statue is vulnerable to destruction in a way that the piece of clay is not. But how can that be? The vulnerability of a thing to destruction, one might have thought, is a function of what that thing is made of; but the piece of clay and the statue are made up of the same matter.

The second argument appeals to abstract considerations about parts and wholes. The constitution view says that two wholes can be made up of the very same parts. It therefore implies that a whole object is something "over and above its parts," for if wholes were nothing over and above their parts, you could never get two wholes out of the same parts. But in fact, wholes are not extra entities, over and above their parts. Subtract a thing's parts, and there is nothing left. Would it make sense to paint every part of a house red, but claim that the house itself had not changed color one bit? Of course not! – the house just *is* its parts; that is why its parts cannot change while it remains the same (Sider 2007).

These arguments have detractors as well as proponents. But, for these or other reasons, many philosophers remain suspicious of simply accepting cohabitation. How else might we respond to the paradoxes?

3.2 Mereological essentialism

Upon completing her work, the sculptor holds her handiwork aloft. If we reject cohabitation, we must say that only one object is in her hands. That apparently means choosing a *single* method of tracing. But how can we choose? Does she hold a statue or a piece of clay? Or something else? *Mereological essentialism* provides a way of choosing a single method of tracing in every case. That method of tracing is: always trace under the sort *quantity of matter.*

Mereological essentialism is the claim that the part is essential to the whole ('mereological' means pertaining to parts and wholes).[7] It says that the only objects that exist are *quantities of matter*, which are things that are defined by their parts. The only way to create one is to create some new matter. Changing or rearranging old matter alters pre-existing quantities of matter, but does not bring new quantities of matter into existence. And the only way to destroy one is to destroy some of its matter. Rearranging or changing that matter just alters the features of the quantity of matter, but does not destroy it. Thus, whenever we want to trace an object, we simply trace according to its matter. As we will now see, this lets us reject the arguments for cohabitation.

Theodore Sider

According to mereological essentialists, the mistaken steps in the statue/clay arguments are P2 and P2'. P2 says that shaping the piece of clay into statue form *creates* something, namely the statue. That is false, according to mereological essentialism, because shaping the piece of clay into statue form does not create any new matter. It merely alters the shape of a certain quantity of matter (the piece of clay), from lumpy to statue-shaped. Likewise, P2' is false: squashing the statue does not destroy it, for what we call "the statue" is just a quantity of matter, and squashing it does not destroy any of its matter. In the undetached parts argument, P4 implies that Tibbles exists even after the matter in its tail is destroyed; that premise is false, according to mereological essentialism, because no object can survive the destruction of any of its matter.

Mereological essentialism does indeed avoid the paradoxical conclusion of the arguments, but it does so by claiming that most of our ordinary beliefs about tracing objects are badly mistaken. Our ordinary beliefs say that dismembering a cat destroys the cat. But not according to mereological essentialism! – dismemberment destroys none of the cat's matter. The mereological essentialist may respond that, once dismembered, the object we formerly called "the cat" can no longer be called a cat. This is correct, but nevertheless, the original *object* – a quantity of matter, according to the mereological essentialist – still exists. Moreover, our ordinary beliefs for tracing cats say that a cat changes its matter over time. My cat Sada was 16 years' old when she died in 2005. If asked to trace her back in time, I would trace her back to a small black kitten living in Rochester, NY in 1989. But the matter making her up when she died was completely different from the matter that made up that kitten. The quantity of matter, M, that made up Sada in 2005 was scattered across the surface of the Earth in 1989; it did not then make up a kitten. If Sada *is* the quantity of matter M, as mereological essentialists say, then tracing Sada back to the small black kitten in Rochester is incorrect; one must instead trace her back to a quantity of matter scattered over the surface of the Earth. Indeed, we could trace Sada back even further, hundreds of years back in time, back to any time at which all the matter in quantity M existed.

Thus, mereological essentialism says that our ordinary beliefs about tracing cats are incorrect. For similar reasons, mereological essentialists must reject our ordinary beliefs about tracing most other sorts of objects as well. The only sort we trace correctly is *quantity of matter*.

Perhaps we really are drastically mistaken in this way. If there is no better way to answer the paradoxes of constitution, our only recourse would be to grit our teeth and accept mereological essentialism. But first, let's see whether there is a better choice.

3.3 Dominant sorts

Avoiding cohabitation requires choosing a single method of tracing in any given case. Mereological essentialism told us always to trace according to a single sort, namely the sort *quantity of matter*, but that led to an unappealing result. Perhaps we should instead choose different sorts in different cases. We could trace statues under the sort *statue*, cats under the sort *cat*, and so on.

If an object falls under just one sort, then of course we trace under that sort. But in most cases, objects fall under more than one sort. Our clay statue falls under both *statue* and *piece of clay*. Under which sort should we trace? Tracing it under the sort *statue* leads to saying that it began existing on Tuesday, when the sculptor formed the clay into statue shape, and ceases to exist when flattened on Wednesday. Tracing it under *piece of clay* leads to saying that it existed already on Monday, and continues to exist after Wednesday. Which answer is correct?

According to Michael Burke (1994), we must always trace under an object's *dominant* sort. A clay statue's dominant sort is *statue*, Burke says. Thus, the statue did not exist on Monday. The statue, therefore, is not the same object as the unformed piece of clay with which the sculptor began on Monday. Now, Burke rejects cohabitation, and so agrees that the statue is the *only* object present on Tuesday. And the unformed piece of clay is not identical to the statue, since the statue does not exist on Monday whereas the unformed piece of clay obviously does. That means that the unformed piece of clay does not exist on Tuesday. Thus, that unformed piece of clay is destroyed when kneaded into statue shape. The premise in the first statue/clay argument that Burke rejects, therefore, is P1.

For parallel reasons, Burke rejects P1′ in the second statue/clay argument. The dominant sort of the piece of clay which constitutes the statue on Tuesday (i.e., the statue itself) is *statue*. We trace its future, therefore, under the sort *statue*, and so it ceases to exist when squashed.

What of Tibbles and Tib? Burke rejects P5. On Monday, Tib is a large part of Tibbles. Its dominant sort is *torso*. It does *not* fall under the sort *cat*, because it is a mere part of a cat. On Tuesday, however, after the tail is destroyed, a single object falls under both *cat* and *torso*. Of these two sorts, the first is dominant, so we trace the past of the one and only object on Tuesday back to Tibbles the cat, not Tib the torso. The Tuesday object, therefore, is identified with Tibbles, not Tib. There is no other object on Tuesday for Tib to be. Tib, therefore, stops existing when the tail is destroyed, even though the tail was merely attached to Tib, not part of it.

Burke's solution to the paradoxes is ingenious but problematic. There is first the problem of saying what makes a given sort dominant. The problem is particularly pressing in certain cases. Imagine a statue made from a single living tree that has been pruned and constrained to grow into a desired form. Is that object's dominant sort *statue* or *tree*?[8]

There is also a problem of anthropocentrism. Imagine a tribe of alien creatures who trace objects over time very differently. They have no sorts like *statue* and *piece of clay*; instead they trace under the following sorts:

outpiece: piece of clay located outdoors, no matter how shaped
inpiece: piece of clay located indoors, no matter how shaped[9]

According to the members of this tribe, pieces of clay and statues do not exist. There exist instead inpieces and outpieces. When an inpiece or an outpiece changes shape, that is irrelevant to its continued existence, and does not cause any new thing to exist. What *does* cause a new thing to exist is taking an outpiece indoors. When that happens, according to the members of this tribe, the original outpiece stops existing and a new object, an inpiece, comes into existence. This inpiece exists so long as it stays indoors. But if it is taken outdoors, it stops existing and is replaced by a new outpiece.

Burke is committed to saying that the members of this tribe are *wrong* in what they say about persisting objects. Think of our statue/clay case. Burke rejects cohabitation, and claims that the one and only object that exists Tuesday (a statue) did not exist Monday, even though it was then indoors. But the members of the tribe say that the one and only object that exists Tuesday (an inpiece) *did* exist Monday (because the formation of an inpiece into statue shape is irrelevant to its continued existence.) Thus, according to Burke, the world contains statues and pieces of clay; and it does not contain inpieces and outpieces. But shouldn't Burke be worried that it is he, rather than the members of the tribe, that is mistaken? It feels suspiciously convenient that the objects in the world just happen to exactly match the sorts that *we* have words for, rather than the sorts that the members of the tribe have words for. Our decision to have a word for, and trace under, *statue* rather than *inpiece* feels like an arbitrary decision; but for Burke, it is one of vital ontological importance. Burke's world-view is anthropocentric: it elevates arbitrary human decisions into serious ontology.

Finally, Burke's claims clash with our ordinary practices of tracing. No one other than a philosopher would dream of saying that an unformed piece of clay can be destroyed simply by kneading it into a more interesting shape! The slogan with which I introduced the theory sounded plausible: "always trace an object by its dominant sort." But in fact, Burke cannot really adhere to this slogan. If he did, he would have to admit that the unformed piece of clay survives the sculptor's kneading after all. For the unformed piece of clay's dominant sort is *piece of clay*, and tracing under that sort yields the conclusion that it survives the kneading. There is no way to hold onto everything we want, by tracing every object under its dominant sort (assuming we want to deny cohabitation). The dominant sort of the unformed piece of clay on Monday is *piece of clay*, which leads us to identify the piece of clay with the statue on Tuesday, but the dominant sort of the statue on Tuesday is *statue*, which leads us to reject the identification.

3.4 Nihilism

In any given case, under which of the available sorts must we trace? Burke and the mereological essentialists say: *one*. (For Burke, the sort varies from case to case; for mereological essentialists the sort is always *quantity of matter*.) That leads to the right *number* of objects in every case – one – but, as we saw, it leads to some unappealing conclusions about what those objects are like. Constitution theorists say *all*. That leads to cohabitation – too many objects. A remaining logical possibility is to trace under *no* sorts at all. That would lead to saying that there are no objects involved in the puzzle cases, for if there were objects involved, we would have to trace them in some way or other. *Nihilists* claim just this. None of the objects in our puzzle cases – statues, pieces of clay, cats, torsos – exist at all, and so the puzzles never arise.[10]

Nihilists do not quite deny the existence of *everything*. They believe in *mereological simples* – things with no smaller parts. If current physics is on the right track, these are subatomic particles like quarks and electrons. According to nihilists, the quarks and electrons are fine; it is mereologically complex things, larger things with smaller parts, that cause all the trouble. Complex things can be traced over time in different ways, which leads to the paradoxes of constitution. Mereologically simple things are more theoretically tractable. They can be traced over time in only one way, and therefore do not lead to paradoxes.

"Of *course* statues exist!" one wants to say, but matters are not so clear. Though the nihilist says that the statue does not exist, he accepts the existence of (an immense number of) simples, which are "arranged statuewise." "Arranged statuewise" does not mean *arranged so as to compose a statue*; rather, it means something like: *arranged in a way that would lead then to compose a statue if nihilism were false.* Though nihilists do not believe in cats, or torsos (or planets, or people), they do believe in all the subatomic particles that the rest of us believe in, some of which are arranged catwise, others torsowise, others planetwise, others personwise. One cannot tell simply by looking that statues exist, for the visual sensations most of us attribute to statues could just as easily be caused by mere simples arranged statuewise.

Then again, none of the views we have been considering can be refuted just by looking. You cannot tell, just by looking, whether cohabitation is true: since the allegedly distinct statue and piece of clay would be made up of exactly the same matter, they would look exactly like a single object. You cannot tell, just by looking, whether the mereological essentialist is right that the dismembered cat keeps existing, since you cannot tell, just by looking, whether objects at different times are identical. Objects do not have name tags.

If you cannot tell which metaphysical theory is true just by looking, then how *do* you tell? That is a very hard question, and not one that I will try to answer in any general way. But thus far we have been holding the other views up to the following standard: a good view of constitution must not clash too much with our ordinary beliefs about objects and persistence. Judged by this standard, nihilism looks pretty bad.

Nihilism also rests on a substantial empirical hypothesis, which may, for all we know, be false. The nihilist avoids utter absurdity only because he follows up his denial of the existence of statues by saying: "Still, there *do* exist simples arranged statuewise." But is it clear that there exist any simples at all? Scientists initially thought that the atoms of chemistry had no smaller parts. Then electrons were discovered, then protons and neutrons. Protons and neutrons were later discovered to be composed of yet smaller particles, quarks. Perhaps this process will continue forever; perhaps absolutely *every* object has smaller parts. If so, then there is no escape from complex objects, and the puzzles of constitution to which they give rise.

3.5 Temporal parts to the rescue

As we will now see, temporal parts theory resolves the paradoxes of constitution. Together with the previous four sections, which found the competing accounts wanting, this completes the constitution argument for temporal parts.

The paradoxes arise from the multiplicity of methods of tracing: we want to trace both statues and pieces of clay, and both cats and torsos. In different ways, mereological essentialists, Burke, and nihilists deny the multiplicity. That leads to trouble, as we saw. What we really want is to accept the multiplicity. That leads to cohabitation, which initially seems absurd. What we really need, then, is a way to accept

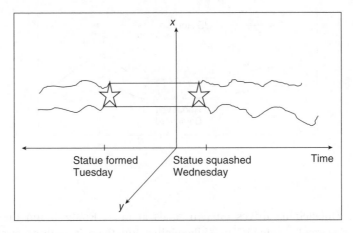

Figure 4 Space-time diagram of the statue and the clay

cohabitation and dispel the impression of absurdity. The constitution view attempted this, but failed (section 3.1). Temporal parts theory gives a better explanation of why cohabitation is not absurd after all, and therefore gives us a satisfying way to embrace the conclusion of the paradoxical arguments for cohabitation.

Figure 4 shows a space-time diagram of the statue and the piece of clay. The piece of clay first has a lumpy shape, then is formed into a statue of a star, then is squashed back into a lumpy shape again. According to temporal parts theory, statues and pieces of clay are aggregates of temporal parts – "spacetime worms" as they are sometimes called.

Thus, the statue is the following object: ☆_____☆. It is an aggregate of of temporal parts, each of which has a statue shape. The piece of clay is a larger

aggregate of temporal parts: 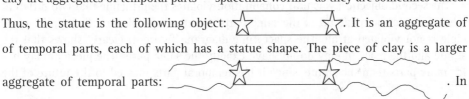 . In

addition to the temporal parts that make up the statue, the piece of clay contains earlier and later temporal parts that do not have statue shape. Now, these two space-time worms are not the same object; the piece of clay is longer in time. Thus, the space-time diagram depicts the truth of cohabitation – both space-time worms are represented as being present between Tuesday and Wednesday, when the piece of clay has statue shape. But the worms are intimately related: the statue worm is *part* of the piece of clay worm. Thus understood, cohabitation does not seem strange at all! When the sculptor holds the statue in her hand, she holds a single temporal part, which is part of both the statue and the piece of clay: ☆. That temporal part is the only object she directly holds. She *indirectly* holds both the piece of clay and the statue in her hands, for the temporal part is part of each, just as you indirectly touch a person when you directly touch his nose.

The case of the statue and the piece of clay may be illuminated by a spatial analogy. A portion of US Route 1 in Philadelphia is called the Roosevelt Boulevard (figure 5). The Boulevard is not the same road as Route 1, since it is much shorter. Thus, a

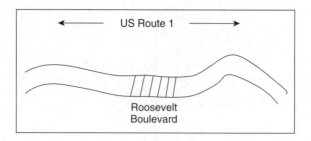

Figure 5

motorist in Philadelphia drives on two roads at once, Route 1 and the Roosevelt Boulevard. The roads "cohabit" in Philadelphia. But there is nothing strange about this; the Boulevard is *part* of Route 1.

A space-time diagram of Tibbles and Tib reveals a similar moral. Tib, the torso, _____ , is a part of the entire cat Tibbles: ----------/_____ (the tail, ---------->, is initially present but is then destroyed.) Consider again a spatial analogy: a four-lane road traveling left to right in which the fourth lane on the bottom merges into the road and disappears.

Pictures are not enough; the temporal parts theorist must answer the objections to cohabitation from section 3.1. The objections undermined the constitution view, but they have no force against temporal parts theory. Let's take them in reverse.

The second objection was that cohabitation violates the principle that two different wholes cannot be made up of the same parts. Given temporal parts theory, the principle is not violated at all. The space-time diagram (figure 4) clearly shows that the statue and the piece of clay do *not* have exactly the same parts. The piece of clay has far more parts than the statue, since it has temporal parts located to the future of the

statue: 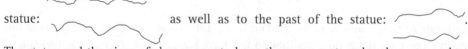 as well as to the past of the statue: .

The statue and the piece of clay appear to have the same parts only when we neglect the fourth dimension of time. Likewise for Tibbles and Tib.

The first objection asked how the statue could be so vulnerable to destruction when it is made of exactly the same material as the piece of clay. But no one wonders why the Roosevelt Boulevard stops existing at the city limits of Philadelphia, despite being made of the same asphalt as Route 1, which continues north into New Jersey. Like any road, Route 1 has many parts. Some extend beyond Philadelphia, and some do not. The good people of Philadelphia saw fit to apply the words 'The Roosevelt Boulevard' to one of the stretches that ends at the city limits. Similarly, according to temporal parts theory, any piece of clay has temporal parts. Some of these are statue-shaped throughout their temporal length, others are not. We speakers of English have decided to use the word 'statue' only for the temporal parts of pieces of clay that are statue-shaped.

The first objection is puzzling because of a mistaken picture of the statue and the piece of clay as both being "directly" present on Tuesday. The correct picture is that only a single object – the Tuesday temporal part, common to each – is directly present. The statue and the piece of clay are indirectly present on Tuesday by containing that temporal part. If both the statue and the piece of clay were directly present, perhaps their survival or destruction would depend on their Tuesday qualities, in which case we would indeed face the question of how the statue could be so fragile when the piece of clay is so robust. But since the only thing directly present is the current temporal slice of both the statue and the piece of clay, what happens afterward is just a function of the qualities of the slice, and what the sculptor does to it. If she squashes it, then future clay temporal parts will have lumpy shapes; if she leaves it alone, then those temporal parts will continue to be statue-shaped. There is then the question of what we will *call* various aggregates of temporal parts. We reserve the word 'statue' for aggregates of statue-shaped temporal parts. So if the sculptor squashes the statue and the further temporal parts have lumpy shapes, only the aggregate terminating at the squashing counts as a 'statue.'

4 The Argument from Vagueness and Anthropocentrism

The final argument for temporal parts that I want to give employs the concept of *tracing* that figured so prominently in the last section.[11] Tracing is charting the histories of objects. If I know how to trace statues over time, then if you give me appropriate information about what happens at various times (for instance, facts about pieces of clay and how they are shaped), then I will be able to tell you when statues begin to exist, and when they cease to exist. More generally, if I know how to trace *all* objects, that means I can tell you when *any* object begins to exist, and when it stops existing, provided you give me appropriate information about what happens at various times.

So far we have been using the concept of tracing informally, but since it will be the focus of this section's argument, let's make the concept more rigorous by carefully defining some terms. By a *tracing scenario*, I will mean (i) a series of times, the *tracing times*, and (ii) various objects at each of those times, the *tracing objects*. To illustrate, consider two examples of tracing scenarios. Scenario 1: the tracing times are all and only the times when our piece of clay from the previous section is shaped into statue form; the tracing objects at each moment are the parts of the clay. Scenario 2: the tracing times are all and only the times at which Tibbles the cat exists; at each moment, the tracing objects are the particles that make up Tibbles at that moment. Notice that in scenario 2, the tracing objects vary from one tracing time to another, since Tibbles, like all cats, has different parts at different times.

Let's focus on scenario 2, and in particular on how it relates to Tibbles. The tracing scenario is the *entire life history* of Tibbles. For:

(i) The tracing scenario contains *exactly* the moments at which Tibbles exists. (If we had chosen one of the tracing moments hundreds of years beforehand, or if we had included only a part of Tibbles's life, this would not have been the case.)

(ii)   At each moment of the tracing scenario, Tibbles is exactly composed of the tracing objects, no more, no less. (If we had left out Tibbles's whiskers, or had included extra objects, for example one of Tibbles's toys, this would not have been the case.)

In light of this, let's introduce another concept. Let's call Tibbles the *tracing target* of scenario 2. An object x is the tracing target of scenario S if and only if (i) S contains exactly the moments at which x exists, and (ii) at each moment of S, x is exactly composed of the tracing objects for that moment. As another example of how this concept functions, notice that the statue is the tracing target of scenario 1. Scenario 1 contains exactly the moments at which the statue exists, and at each such moment, the statue is exactly composed of the tracing objects – the parts of the piece of clay.

More cautiously: the statue and Tibbles are the tracing targets of scenarios 1 and 2 *according to our ordinary beliefs about tracing*. A mereological essentialist, for example, would deny each of these claims. In fact, a mereological essentialist would say that neither tracing scenario has any tracing target at all. A tracing target for scenario 2 by definition must be composed of different objects at different times, since the tracing objects of that scenario vary between its tracing times. Mereological essentialism prohibits the existence of any such object, because mereological essentialism says that the only objects that exist are quantities of matter, which have the same parts at all times. Thus, scenario 2 has no tracing target whatsoever, if mereological essentialism is correct. The mereological essentialist would also deny the existence of a tracing target for scenario 1, but for a different reason. Scenario 1 contains tracing times only when the piece of clay is statue-shaped. But a tracing target of a scenario exists *only* at the scenario's tracing times. Thus, a tracing target of scenario 1 would have to come into existence when the piece of clay is statue-shaped, and go out of existence after it ceases to be statue-shaped – i.e., when the "statue" is squashed. According to mereological essentialism, no such object exists, for a quantity of matter continues to exist so long as its matter does; the shape of the matter is irrelevant.

Thus, the question of which tracing scenarios have targets and which do not is precisely the question of how to trace objects over time. Let's look at one more example. Suppose we define scenario 3 as a part of the case of the statue and the piece of clay: the tracing times are the times in the history of the piece of clay *before* the clay is sculpted into statue shape; the tracing objects are, at each moment, the parts of the piece of clay then. Does this scenario have a tracing target? Since we included only times before the piece of clay was formed into statue shape, a tracing target of scenario 3 would go out of existence when the clay is sculpted. Now, Michael Burke, as we saw in section 3.3, thinks that such an object exists, for, according to him, sculpting the clay into statue form destroys the original piece of clay. (It goes out of existence to "make room for" the statue.) Many others disagree that any such object exists. Again, the question of which tracing scenarios have targets is exactly the question of how to trace objects over time.

Thus, all the theories of constitution from the last section make claims about which tracing scenarios have tracing targets. Burke would say that scenarios have targets depending on how dominant sorts apply. Mereological essentialists would say that a scenario has a target when and only when it is the entire history of some portion of matter, no matter how arranged. Nihilists would say that scenarios almost never have targets, since a target must be made up of the tracing objects at the tracing times. (The exceptions are scenarios with just one tracing object, a particle, and tracing times matching the particle's career; then the target object is that particle.) Defenders of the constitution view would say that "overlapping" tracing scenarios – scenarios with a common time and set of tracing objects for that time – can both have target objects. Let scenario 4 consist of all the times when the piece of clay exists; let the tracing objects be the parts of the piece of clay at each moment. Notice that scenario 4 overlaps with scenario 1 during the times when the clay is statue-shaped, for each scenario contains these times, and contains as tracing objects then the parts of the piece of clay. Scenario 4 differs from scenario 1 by containing some additional times, namely, times at which the clay is not statueshaped. The defender of the constitution view would say that *both* scenarios 1 and 4 have targets. The target of scenario 1 is the statue; the target of scenario 4 is the piece of clay. At the times common to both scenarios, the statue and the piece of clay both exist, and are made up of exactly the same parts.

What theory of tracing is implicit in temporal parts theory? A fairly extreme one, as it turns out: *all* tracing scenarios have targets.[12] The target for any scenario is just a space-time worm consisting of temporal parts for each of the tracing times in the scenario. The target of scenario 1 is the aggregate of all the temporal parts of the piece of clay while it has statue form; the target of scenario 4 is the aggregate of all the piece of clay's temporal parts, whether or not those temporal parts have statue form. (That is, the target of scenario 4 is the piece of clay itself.) Even if a scenario contains times scattered from different periods in history, there will still be a target. Let scenario 5 consist of times in the Jurassic period when the dinosaur pictured in section 1 (figure 2) exists, plus the times in the present when the statue we have been discussing exists. The tracing objects for the first times are the parts of the dinosaur; the tracing objects for the second times are the parts of the piece of clay. What would a tracing target for this scenario look like? It would need to be an object that started existing in the Jurassic period shaped as a dinosaur, which stopped existing until the present time, and which then resumed existing in the present time shaped as a statue. A strange object? Not at all – it is simply the space-time worm consisting of the dinosaur's temporal parts, plus the statue's temporal parts. This dinosaur + statue is the target of scenario 5.

Thus, if temporal parts theory is correct, all scenarios have targets. In fact, the converse is also true: if all scenarios have targets then temporal parts theory is correct. For there exist scenarios concerning only one time. Let scenario 6 consist of just one tracing time, the present moment, and let the tracing objects be my current parts. If all scenarios have targets, then scenario 6 must have a target. A target, by definition, exists only at the tracing times. That means that a target of scenario 6 exists only at the present moment, and is currently composed of the same parts as me. This object must be my current temporal part! We can repeat the argument for any chosen object at any time: simply choose a scenario consisting of that object's parts at that time, and infer the existence of a temporal part then from the fact that all scenarios have targets. This means that, in order to argue for temporal parts theory, all we must do is argue that all scenarios have targets.

Some scenarios have targets, since some objects exist. So anyone who denies that *all* scenarios have targets must draw a line somewhere, between the scenarios that have targets and those that do not. But such a line turns out to be very difficult to draw, for two reasons. First, the line must not be *anthropocentric*, and second, it must not be *vague*.

Our natural inclination is to trace objects over time according to our ordinary beliefs about tracing. We want to accept ordinary objects like statues and pieces of clay, people and planets, and so on, whereas many of us do not want to accept strange objects such as inpieces and outpieces, or temporal parts (not initially, anyway). But keeping just the ordinary objects while rejecting the strange objects requires drawing an anthropocentric line between tracing scenarios. We seem to be choosing statues and pieces of clay over inpieces and outpieces just because we humans have words for the former. Burke ran into this trouble in section 3.3: he had to say that the members of the alien tribe, who believe in inpieces and outpieces, were simply wrong, even though they seem merely to have a different language from ours. Temporal parts theory avoids this problem by saying that inpieces and outpieces exist in addition to statues and pieces of clay. An inpiece or an outpiece is just another space-time worm, just as good an aggregate of temporal parts as any other.

In addition to requiring an anthropocentric line between tracing scenarios that have targets and those that do not, accepting just the ordinary objects would also require a *vague* line. An example of a vague concept is *baldness*. Some people are clearly bald; others are clearly non-bald. But some people cannot be classified as either bald or non-bald; they are *vague*, or *borderline*, or *blurry* cases. They are just sort-of-bald-and-sort-of-non-bald. *Existence*, on the other hand, is not vague. It makes no sense to speak of an object that "just sort-of exists". No matter how small you shrink a thing, no matter how insignificant you make it, it is still there, definitely existing – unless you shrink it down to nothing at all, in which case it definitely does not exist! But if we wanted to say that only the ordinary objects exist, we would need to admit that existence can be vague after all, for our ordinary beliefs do not define precise conditions, down to the tiniest detail, governing when a tracing scenario has a target that is a *statue*, *piece of clay*, *person* or *planet*. For any of these concepts – *statue*, *piece of clay*, *person* or *planet* – we can define a tracing scenario in which it is vague whether there exists any ordinary object that is its target. Simply begin with a scenario that definitely *does* have an ordinary object as its target, a statue, say. Now, a tiny bit at a time, change the scenario; change the properties and configuration of its tracing objects and tracing times, gradually making it less like the scenario of a statue. If you continue in this way, you will eventually reach a scenario that definitely does not have a statue as a target, but long before that you will reach cases where the existence of a statue is simply indeterminate, unclear, blurry. If the only tracing scenarios that have targets are those corresponding to ordinary objects, then we will need to say that what *exists* is likewise indeterminate, unclear, blurry. But as we saw, this makes no sense. Temporal parts theory avoids this problem by not limiting the things that exist to those that satisfy vague ordinary concepts.

So, suppose you think that not all tracing scenarios have targets. You then have to draw a line – between those tracing scenarios that have targets and those that do not. And you face a choice of what kind of line to draw. On the one hand, you could draw a *moderate* line: a line that fits our ordinary beliefs about tracing. But as we have seen, this line would need to be vague and anthropocentric; and I argued against drawing such a line. On the other hand you could draw a *drastic* line: a line with no basis in our ordinary beliefs about tracing, but which is neither anthropocentric nor vague. Nihilism and mereological essentialism would do this, but I have already said why I think those views are mistaken. I think you have backed yourself into a corner. And here's how to get out: *draw no line at all*, say that all scenarios have targets, and so embrace temporal parts.[13]

Notes

1   Parts of this chapter are based on chapter 3 of Conee and Sider (2005). Thanks to Cian Dorr for the idea of introducing space-time diagrams with timelines, and to Eliza Block, John Hawthorne, Irem Kurtsal Steen, and Dean Zimmerman for helpful comments.
2   The task of keeping the facets clearly distinguished is made more difficult by badly chosen terminology: some philosophers use the term 'four-dimensionalism' for the doctrine of temporal parts alone, even though the term suggests the stronger claim that time and space are analogous in more ways. Another (better) bit of jargon is the following. To say that objects *perdure* is to say that they have temporal parts; to say that objects *endure* is to say that they do *not* have temporal parts.
3   I do not say "impossible to settle"; science sometimes bears on metaphysical questions in unforeseen ways.
4   A complication: certain opponents of the B-theory can make a different reply to the argument from change than I made above, and so never need to appeal to indexed properties, and so escape Lewis's argument. See Zimmerman (2006).
5   See Haslanger (1989).
6   This is merely a caricature; see Hylton (1990) for a historically responsible discussion.
7   See Chisholm (1976: ch. 3).
8   See Rea (2000).
9   Compare Eli Hirsch's (1982: 32) "incars" and "outcars."
10   See Merricks (2001: chs. 1, 2) for a nihilistic solution to the puzzle of the statue and the clay. (Merricks is not a true nihilist, however: he believes that living things exist.)
11   I discuss this argument in more detail in Sider (2001, sect. 4.9). It is based on an argument given by David Lewis (1986: 212–13).
12   Given the doctrine of unrestricted composition, anyway, which I have been assuming throughout this chapter. See chapter 8 in this volume.
13   For further reading on the topics in this chapter, see Haslanger (2003), Hawley (2001), Heller (1990), and Sider (2001).

References

Burke, Michael. 1994. "Preserving the Principle of One Object to a Place: A Novel Account of the Relations Among Objects, Sorts, Sortals, and Persistence Conditions," *Philosophy and*

Phenomenological Research 54: 591–624. Repr. in Michael Rea, ed., *Material Constitution* (Lanham, MD: Rowman and Littlefield Publishers, 1997), pp. 236–69.

Chisholm, Roderick. 1976. *Person and Object* (La Salle, ILL: Open Court).

Conee, Earl, and Sider, Theodore. 2005. *Riddles of Existence: A Guided Tour of Metaphysics* (Oxford: Oxford University Press).

Haslanger, Sally. 1989. "Endurance and Temporary Intrinsics," *Analysis* 49: 119–25.

Haslanger, Sally. 2003. "Persistence Through Time," in Michael J. Loux and Dean W. Zimmerman, eds., *The Oxford Handbook of Metaphysics* (Oxford: Oxford University Press), pp. 315–54.

Hawley, Katherine. 2001. *How Things Persist* (Oxford: Oxford University Press).

Heller, Mark. 1990. *The Ontology of Physical Objects: Four Dimensional Hunks of Matter* (Cambridge: Cambridge University Press).

Hirsch, Eli. 1982. *The Concept of Identity* (Oxford: Oxford University Press.)

Hylton, Peter. 1990. *Russell, Idealism and the Emergence of Analytic Philosophy* (Oxford: Oxford University Press).

Lewis, David. 1986. *On the Plurality of Worlds* (Oxford: Basil Blackwell).

Merricks, Trenton. 2001. *Objects and Persons* (Oxford: Clarendon Press).

Rea, Michael. 2000. "Constitution and Kind Membership," *Philosophical Studies* 97: 169–93.

Sider, Theodore. 2001. *Four-Dimensionalism* (Oxford: Clarendon Press).

Sider, Theodore. 2007. "Parthood," *Philosophical Review* 116: 51–91.

Zimmerman, Dean W. 2006. "Temporary Intrinsics and Presentism," in Sally Haslanger and Roxanne Marie Kurtz, eds., *Persistence: Contemporary Readings* (Cambridge, MA: MIT Press), pp. 393–424.

Three-Dimensionalism vs. Four-Dimensionalism

John Hawthorne

In debates about the nature of persisting material objects, philosophers tend to cluster into two groups, often labeled "three-dimensionalists" and "four-dimensionalists". While no single idea sharply defines either group, some rough and ready characterizations are possible. Four-dimensionalists contend that there is a deep analogy between the structure of ordinary material objects and the structure of the space-time of modern physics; three-dimensionalists question this analogy. Three-dimensionalists tend to embrace the slogan "persisting things are wholly present at each time that they exist"; four-dimensionalists tend to reject it. In what follows, I will clarify what is meant by each of these contentions, and explore some promising strategies for making good on the three-dimensionalist picture. One theme of note will be that some versions of three-dimensionalism are compatible with temporal parts theory, as outlined by Sider (this volume, chapter 6.1).[1]

1 Space-time

In order to get a clearer sense of the four-dimensionalists' picture, it will be helpful to begin with some widely accepted ideas about space-time that form the backdrop for many contemporary metaphysical discussions. On the now-standard physical picture, *space-time* is conceived of as a multi-dimensional object, where one of the dimensions is temporal and the others are spatial. (So, for example, in a world with only one spatial dimension where everything lived on a single spatial line, space-time would be two-dimensional; in a world with three spatial dimensions, space-time is four-dimensional.) Space-time itself is made up of ultimate constituents – *space-time points* – that are not extended along any dimension and have no smaller parts. Any collection of space-time points makes up exactly one *space-time region*: for any given collection of points, there is a region made up of those points, and if two space-time regions are different, there is some difference in the space-time points that make them up. Each region will have parts corresponding to subsets of the points that make up the original region. Certain of those parts will be temporal parts (in Sider's sense) of the original region, where a temporal part is a part that is temporally smaller than the original but which has the same spatial dimensions as the original during the period that the temporal part exists.

For the sake of further discussion, it will be useful to note three theses that are central to the picture at hand: (i) *Pointiness*: Every space-time region is composed of point-sized parts. (ii) *Universality*: Every collection of space-time points composes something. (iii) *Uniqueness*: For every collection of space-time points there is exactly one thing that is composed of the space-time points in that collection.[2] (It goes without saying that contemporary science has a great deal more to say about space-time, in its topological, geometric, and metrical aspects, but these details need not concern us here.)

Two supplementary theses about space-time will also be relevant to our discussions below. A bit of background will make clear what the theses are maintaining. Metaphysicians frequently try to distinguish between fundamental and less fundamental objects, and, between fundamental and less fundamental facts. The basic idea is that (in a sense that we shall not undertake to make fully clear here) the less fundamental objects exist in virtue of the fundamental objects (and not vice versa), and the less fundamental facts obtain in virtue of the fundamental facts (and not vice versa). In antiquity it was common for philosophers to admit the existence of points only as derivative entities and, relatedly, to think of facts about points as derivative from more fundamental facts about extended objects. On this conception, points exist only derivatively, as limits of lines, and surfaces without thickness exist only derivatively as limits of bulky objects. Nowadays, however, it is common for metaphysicians to hold both that space-time regions are less fundamental than the space-time points that compose them and that facts about the intrinsic character[3] of space-time regions are less fundamental than the facts about the intrinsic character of space-time points and facts about how the space-time points are arranged.[4] On this picture, a line exists in virtue of the points that make it up (and not vice versa), and the character of a line – facts about how the line is qualitatively – obtains in virtue of facts about the points in the line and the relations between them. (Obviously, these ideas about a line can be generalized to arbitrarily many spatial dimensions.)

These last reflections provide us with two further theses for consideration: (iv) *Pointy Object Fundamentality*: Points are ontologically more fundamental than extended regions. (v) *Pointy Fact Fundamentality*: Facts about points and the relations between them are more fundamental than facts about extended regions.

So-called four-dimensionalists embrace most or all of theses (i)–(v) above and maintain a similar set of theses concerning persisting material objects. In what follows, we shall look at a few versions of four-dimensionalism.

1.2 Spatiotemporalism

In this section we shall look at a particularly bold version of four-dimensionalism, one which holds that material objects are in fact identical with space-time regions.[5] According to such a view – call it *spatiotemporalism* – the relation between, say, a poached egg and the spatiotemporal region that it occupies is one of identity. (Since the contours of the spatiotemporal region exactly match the contours of the life history of the poached egg, why not go ahead and identify the region with the egg? Why bother having two objects with exactly the same boundary?)[6]

How might one object to such a view? We will first consider three arguments from ordinary language and commonsense intuition, and then turn briefly to an objection from physics.

One objection we might make against spatiotemporalism would be to point out that its identity claims – say, that a certain poached egg is identical to a region of space-time – seem directly to violate commonsense. More subtly, we might offer an objection based on modal considerations that runs as follows. It is natural to think of space-time regions as having their spatiotemporal profile essentially, but of their occupants as having their spatiotemporal profile only accidentally. For example, it seems obvious that the space-time region I occupy could not have been shorter in temporal extent, but that I could. If so, and if we accept the principle concerning identity known as Leibniz's Law (that if x has some characteristic that y lacks, then x is not identical to y), then I am not identical to the space-time region that I occupy.

A third style of argument turns on non-modal properties. Many of the adjective and verb constructions (hereafter 'predicates') that seem true of me sound very odd when combined with noun phrases that explicitly pick out space-time regions that I occupy. For example:

(1) The space-time region that I occupy walked to the fish and chip shop last night.

Here the problem is not so much that the claim conflicts with a previous explicit commitment about the nature of space-time regions (say, that space-time regions do not walk to fish and chip shops); rather, it's that predicates like 'walk' sound very odd in combination with noun phrases that are explicitly about space-time regions, whereas they don't sound odd at all in combination with noun phrases concerning their occupants.

In response to the first objection, the spatiotemporalist would do well to point out that, while ordinary people often deploy the concept of a three-dimensional spatial region, it is not clear that they ordinarily deploy the concept of a four-dimensional space-time region. Hence it is not clear that commonsense offers any direct verdict at all about the relevant identity claims.

The second and third style of objections are more pressing. Each relies on predicates that (a) seem to yield true sentences when combined with various noun phrases that pick out certain material objects, but (b) do not seem true when combined with noun phrases that pick out the regions that the aforementioned material objects occupy. If some such predicate picks out the same characteristic in both contexts of use, then, on pain of denying Leibniz's Law, the spatiotemporalist will have no choice but to (a) deny that the predicate was true of the material object, or (b) claim that the predication is, after all, true of the space-time region, even though it sounds odd. In the case of various non-modal predications, (b) would seem to be the less radical tack.[7] After all, it seems less radical to affirm that space-time regions walk to fish and chip shops than to deny that people do. The task of the spatiotemporalist will be then to show that the oddity to our ears of (1) is not very good evidence of its falsity. This is certainly a significant challenge (though I doubt that it is a devastating one).

A defensive strategy that may be especially tempting in connection with the modal arguments makes appeal to the notion of context-dependence. We are familiar enough with the idea that some predicates are context-dependent and involve reference to an unarticulated standard. For example, 'I am tall' may express a truth where tallness-for-a-human is the key standard, but express a falsehood in a context where tallness-for-a-basketball-player is the key standard. Furthermore, some noun phrases may strongly encourage us to use one standard rather than another. Thus it is quite hard to hear "The new power forward for the Denver Nuggets is tall" as being uttered with 'tall-for-a-human' as the operative standard. Further, it is well known that certain modal predications are context-dependent. Consider the ordinary 'can' of ability statements. If I am in the garden without a spade, one person can say "He can't dig a hole. He hasn't got a spade" and intuitively make a true speech, while another says "He can dig a hole. Just give him a spade" and also, intuitively, made a true speech. The former use of 'can' holds fixed the unavailability of spades, but the latter does not.[8] How far does this context-dependence for modal predicates extend? Some philosophers have suggested that all modal predications are context-dependent – and turn similarly on what, in context, one is obliged to hold fixed. According to such philosophers, there are some contexts in which it is held fixed that I am human, and so 'I could not have been a non-human' is true, but others where it is not, and so 'I could by now have been a heap of rotting flesh' is also, in context, strictly and literally true. Such philosophers will naturally think of some noun phrases as encouraging some standards rather than others, as encouraging one to hold some rather than other facts fixed. And it is not hard to see how such a package of views could be used to explain why 'That space-time region could have been shorter in temporal extent' generally expresses a falsehood (on the grounds that the use of 'That space-time region' encouraged a context where the dimensions of the object talked about are 'held fixed') but 'That person could have lived less long' generally expresses a truth.

The objector will argue that the phenomenon of context-sensitivity does not provide a plausible resolution of the philosophical arguments at hand. From a more orthodox perspective, predicates such as 'could have existed for a shorter period of time', *as they figure in philosophical discussions*, always mean the same thing. Orthodoxy recognizes a certain type of question – whether it is metaphysically possible or necessary or impossible for a thing to be F – and takes modal predicates, as they occur in the relevant discussions, to constitute expressions of metaphysical possibility and necessity, ones that do not themselves need to be tied to some further standard in order to be evaluated.

Orthodoxy is certainly on strong ground in at least the following respect: it does not seem very plausible that the joint attractiveness of, say

(2) I could have lived for significantly less long

and

(3) The spatiotemporal region that I occupy could not have been significantly less long in temporal extent

can plausibly be explained using the model of familiar context-sensitive predicates. One significant point of disanalogy in this.[9] In the case of an ordinary context-sensitive predicate, a single occurrence of that predicate cannot be simultaneously tied to two different standards by two noun phrases that pick out the same object. Thus 'The new power forward for the Denver Nuggets is not tall but my best friend is' cannot be used felicitously in a case where my best friend is also the new power forward and is tall for a person but not tall for a basketball player. Consider, similarly, the context-sensitive expression 'nearby'. 'My best friend is going to a nearby bar,' as uttered by me, might mean that my best friend is going to a bar nearby to me, or else nearby to him, or else nearby to some other location salient in the conversation. But this kind of flexibility still does not permit me ever to say 'My best friend but not the lord mayor is going to a nearby bar' in a case where 'my best friend' and 'the lord mayor' pick out the same object. Now if the individual acceptability of 'The spatiotemporal region that I occupy could not have been significantly less long in temporal extent' and 'I could have been significantly less long in temporal extent' were the product of ordinary context-dependence, then the sentence 'I, but not the spatiotemporal region that I occupy, could have been significantly less long in temporal extent' should be unacceptable. But it is perfectly acceptable.

The best strategy for the spatiotemporalist, I suggest, would be to concede that the joint acceptability of (2) and (3) is no run-of-the-mill case of context-dependence. She should urge that we distinguish those kinds of context-dependence that are tacitly recognized by ordinary, competent users of natural language from context-dependence that results from a mismatch between ordinary ways of talking and the structure of the world. Where there is a failure of fit of this latter sort, the best construal of what is going on semantically may involve appeal to context-dependence that is not tacitly recognized by ordinary speakers. Consider temporal discourse and relativity theory. We do not, even tacitly, think of our use of 'happened at the same time' as somehow relative to a frame of reference or relative to a somewhat arbitrary slicing ('foliation') of space-time. But supposing there is no absolutely simultaneity, it may be that the best way of salvaging ordinary ways of talking about simultaneity is to construe speakers as – without their knowing it – expressing different relations by 'happened at the same time' on different occasions. Here, context-dependence is posited as a way of making some sense of ordinary talk from a God's-eye perspective in the face a mismatch between ordinary ways of talking and the ultimate structure of the world. The spatiotemporalist had better construe his project in the same vein. But, at the very least, that puts a considerable burden on him to justify his deviant perspective on the world. In the case of relativity theory, the new perspective has an array of powerful considerations in its favor. In the case of spatiotemporalism, we should expect more than, say, vague appeals to the virtues of simplicity or desert landscapes if we are to reorient our conception of the world in such significant ways.

The objections we have considered so far have largely relied on, broadly, commonsense intuition. Other objections may flow from the internal structure of physics itself. Notably, contemporary physics seems to wish to allow for cases where two particles have the same location, even cases where the particles have the same location for the entirety of their careers.[10] Identifying each particle with the space-time region that it occupies will, in the latter case (owing to the transitivity of identity), have the result of identifying the particles with each other, contrary to the description of the case integral to the physical theory. The spatiotemporalist might hope that this would require only a modest rewriting to physical theory, but it is hard to speculate about this. After all, it might interfere with certain laws if, for example, one could no longer distinguish the probability that one particle take a certain trajectory from the probability that the other (spatiotemporally coincident) particle does.[11] And it might deprive the theory of certain kinds of natural explanations grounded in the physical possibility of certain, but not other, combinations of spatiotemporally coincident particles. Of course, those philosophers who think that they can know from the armchair that it is impossible that two bits of matter cannot be in the same place at the same time will not worry about this objection. I do not recommend physics from the armchair.

1.2 Four-dimensionalism without spatiotemporalism

Many four-dimensionalists do not identify ordinary physical objects with space-time regions. On their account, the relation of physical objects to their parts is strongly analogous to the relation between spatiotemporal regions and their parts, where the points of analogy are captured by analogues of Pointiness, Universality, Uniqueness, Pointy Object Fundamentality, and Pointy Fact Fundamentality.

Begin with the analogues of Pointiness, Universality, and Uniqueness. Physical objects are thought to be built out of simple material parts that have zero spatial and temporal extent, and any collection of such simples is held to make up one and only one material object. On such a picture, the last of the worries mentioned for spatiotemporalism no longer arises: since point-sized material objects are not identified with points, then there is no principled difficulty in allowing two of them to occupy the same spatiotemporal point. (Here we must take care to distinguish spatiotemporal coincidence – which is a matter of occupying the same region – with mereological coincidence – which is a matter of having the same parts. In the conjectured circumstance, there would be spatiotemporal but not mereological coincidence between the point-sized bits of matter.)

However, certain of the worries that we raised for the spatiotemporalist re-emerge. In a case where a quantity of steel and a ship come in and out of existence at the same time (we could consider instead a more far-fetched but possible case where both eternally exist), it would seem that the quantity of steel and the ship will have to be identified. (They have the same point-sized material constituents.) Similarly for the popular example of a statue and a lump of clay that come in and out of existence at the same time. Now it is no argument for the acceptability of such an identity claim that in such a case we are willing to say: "The statue is a lump of clay." After all, we are willing to say that even in a case where we know that the statue was created long after the lump of clay and hence we know they are not identical.[12] Moreover, there are well-known arguments against such an identity thesis, ones that replay earlier concerns. One takes the form of Leibniz Law arguments that appeal to modal predications. A second turns on Leibniz Law arguments involving non-modal predicates.

The Leibniz Law arguments involving non-modal predicates are seldom regarded as very conclusive. Granted, 'That statue is reminiscent of Rodin' sounds fine, while 'That lump of clay is reminiscent of Rodin' does not. But the infelicity of 'That lump of clay is reminiscent of Rodin' does not appear to be deep and general. If a sculptor announced "By the time I am done, this lump of marble will be reminiscent of Rodin," that sentence would not sound odd to my ear. Thus it is far from clear that the relevant data point to some property possessed by the statue and not the lump. Turning to an example from the literature, it is true that 'That statue is well made' sounds acceptable, while 'That lump is well made' sounds awkward (even in a case where the statue and lump come into existence at the same time). But notice that there is a similar contrast between 'That actress is well trained' and 'That person is well trained', but we hardly wish to infer from this that the actress is not identical to the person.[13]

The Leibniz Law arguments from modal predication are much more powerful. Here we seem to have positive and conflicting modal intuitions about the statue/lump and ship/quantity of steel pairs, even in a case where their paths actually coincide. (Notice that while such sentences as 'The statue but not the lump is well made' and 'The statue but not the lump is reminscent of Rodin' merely sound awkward and strange, the sentence 'The lump but not the statue could have survived crushing' sounds straightforwardly true. This is essentially why the Leibniz Law arguments from modal predication are more promising.) And as with spatiotemporalism, an attempt to explain away the data used the methodology of ordinary linguistics will likely prove inadequate. The sentence 'The ship but not the quantity of steel could have existed even if some of the steel had been annihilated and replaced with some other steel (or indeed, some other material)' sounds true, but (for reasons given above) ordinary models of context-dependence cannot account for this. Here again, the most promising four-dimensionalist strategy will be to concede a kind of mismatch between ordinary ways of thinking and her favored package, presenting that package as a kind of salvage of ordinary ways of talking in the face of the mismatch. But once this concession is explicitly made, one wonders again exactly what the motivation is supposed to be for the recommended departures from ordinary, natural ways of thinking. The burden certainly seems to be squarely on the proponent of the package to find a powerful motivation for it.

2 The "Three-Dimensional Picture"

We turn next to theses that are more or less inspired by the three-dimensional picture.

2.1 Dropping uniqueness

The objections that we have considered so far disappear once Uniqueness is dropped. Leaving fundamentality issues to one side for now, what should we make of a position that embraces Pointiness and Universality for material objects (call this combination 'Plenitude'), but drops Uniqueness? This defender of Plenitude holds that everything is made of point-sized things, and that every collection of point sized things makes up something, but allows that there may be a number of things made of the very same point-sized things. She is therefore well placed to maintain that even when a quantity of steel and a ship made of the steel have exactly the same point-sized parts, they are not identical.[14]

Regarding Pointiness: we do not find it immediately intuitive or natural to posit material objects that are the size of spatiotemporal points. Even if we learn enough physics to become open to the existence of point-particles as the ultimate constituents of all further being, this does not take us to the desired conclusion, since point particles have temporal duration. Now some may be sympathetic to Descartes' maxim that whatever can be divided in thought can be divided in a corresponding way in reality.[15] Descartes thought, for that reason, that it was unintelligible that there should be a thing that takes up space that has no smaller parts, since we can always divide it up into smaller parts in thought. Supposing that we can divide anything 'in thought' into instantaneous and point-sized pieces,[16] the proponent of Descartes' maxim would hope for some rationalist guarantee of a corresponding division in reality. However, not many of us today share Descartes' rationalist ambitions and, relatedly, are unwilling to posit a deep correspondence in principle between the divisions we may construct in thought and those that actually occur in reality. Turning to Universality: here again, we do not find it immediately compelling to posit some scattered material object whenever we find a plurality of objects, especially if the plurality is scattered across time. Commonsense is not familiar with an object that was once materially coincident with the *Titanic* and is now materially coincident with my socks.

The proponent of Plenitude has a good reply. Suppose one is willing already to countenance the objects that commonsense recognizes: rabbits, statues, quantities of steel, corporations, record collections, archipelagos, and so on. It seems very arbitrary to then disallow the other myriad objects posited by the combination of Pointiness and Universality. Better to be metaphysically even-handed than radically anthropo-centric in one's ontology. In being willing to countenance archipelagos, one embraces scattered objects. Why not then also embrace the "archipelago" of my car and the Eiffel Tower? (After all, if it turned out that an actual archipelago was in part an overturned ancient ship, in part the remnants of an ancient monument, that would not lead us to say that the archipelago did not exist.) In being willing to countenance record collections that used to consist entirely of jazz albums and now consists entirely of heavy metal albums, and ships that undergo entire slow material replacement of all its parts, one is willing to countenance objects that are materially constituted by one collection of atoms at one time and an entirely different collection of atoms at another time. Some of these objects are recognized by commonsense because of their practical significance or our hands-on engagement with them, but others for more frivolous reasons. I may speak of a circle of clouds or the parade of clouds of all shapes and sizes during an interval of time, without any ontological qualms about whether the relevant parade or circle really exists. Nor is there any temporal limit on how short the objects of commonsense are. Having allowed corporations, we could imagine that to satisfy a legal requirement, documents were drawn up so that a cor-poration was formed at noon and dissolved immediately thereafter. We could imagine a circle of clouds existing for only an instant. We could imagine a person only exist-ing for an instant – just imagine him destroyed right after the first moment of exis-tence. With the general tendency toward liberalism in place, it will be not easy to find a reasonable stopping point short of Pointiness and Universalism that is not unduly anthropocentric.[17,18]

These motivations for a liberal ontology might not move those philosophers who take a cavalier attitude toward the ontology of commonsense. But for those who are willing to take commonsense at face value, it does not seem likely that their opposition to the package of (i)–(v) will proceed particularly well if they dig in their heels in opposing Plenitude.

2.2 Fundamentality

What of Pointy Object and Pointy Fact Fundamentality? Even if the plenitude of shorter and long-lived individuals recommended by Plenitude is embraced, that does not yet settle at all whether we ought to count point-sized individuals (or facts about them) as more fundamental than spatiotemporally larger material objects (or facts about the latter). Certainly we do not get immediate incentive from fundamental physics toward such a perspective. Taken at face value, it seems that physics counts long-lived particles rather than instantaneous segments of them as the targets of the fundamental physical laws. And isn't it prima facie natural – insofar as we have a grip on fundamentality at all – to think of the fundamental physical objects as the subject matter of the basic physical laws? So-called four-dimensionalists tend not to take the lead of physics or of physical law here. But on what grounds is this to be justified?

Notice that it is certainly not natural in general to think of a shorter-lived temporal part of an object as more fundamental than the object itself. Suppose that a statue is always made from the same lump but that the lump outlives the statue. The statue is a shorter-lived temporal part of the lump but is not intuitively more fundamental than it.[19] Similarly, if singing Socrates exists (an object that, of necessity, exists when and only when Socrates sings, being mereologically coincident with Socrates when he sings), it is not at all natural to think of it as more fundamental than Socrates.[20] One's first thought is that singing Socrates depends on Socrates but not vice versa.

On the side of four-dimensionalism, it may be tempting to posit the fundamentality of point-sized material parts vis-à-vis temporally extended particles by analogy with the relationship between spatial points and lines. Supposing that it is agreed that spatial points are more fundamental than the lines that they compose, isn't it natural to adopt the same account of the relation between zero-dimensional parts of a particle and the particle itself?

Even granting the fundamentality of points vis-à-vis lines (earlier, I made mention of the view, currently out of favor, that points exist derivatively, as the limits of lines), there seem to be some potentially significant points of disanalogy between this case and the case of long-lived particles. In the case of lines, it seems that all it takes for a line to exist is for spatiotemporal points to stand in appropriate spatiotemporal relations to each other. But in the case of particles, it does not seem that the existence of a particle is merely a matter of the appropriate spatiotemporal distribution of spatiotemporally point-sized bits of matter. Imagine a globe to spin around its north–south axis so that a point particle at the top and bottom remain stationary. In this case there is a particle throughout the process at each pole. Suppose instead that the globe is made to spin around a different axis. Assuming that there are instantaneous point-sized bits of matter everywhere that space is filled, there will, in this case be an instantaneous bit of matter at each pole at every instant. And assuming Universalism, there will be even in this case be an object composed of the instantaneous bits of matter that occupy, say, the North Pole, at each instant. But that object is not a particle, since, by hypothesis, no particle remains at the North Pole throughout the period. But compare the particle in the first case with the object that inhabits the North Pole in the second case. In each case, the spatiotemporal relations between the instantaneous bits of matter are the same. So it does not seem that the existence of a particle can consist merely in the appropriate spatiotemporal distribution of point-sized pieces of matter.[21] Given this insight, it is not altogether clear how to proceed. *Perhaps* one might still argue that the instantaneous pieces of matter are more fundamental than the particles and that the existence of a particle is derived from certain special relations that hold between certain instantaneous objects and not others.[22] But it is not at all clear that this is the correct picture – and in any case, the analogy with spatial points and lines provides no guidance whatsoever.

Another analogy that might be invoked in favor of the fundamentality of short-lived objects is with events. If one thinks of an event – say, a lightning storm – it seems that the various shorter stages of the storm are more fundamental than the storm itself; indeed, the storm would seem to consist merely in a spatiotemporal sequence of various shorter events. But here again the analogy may be misleading. For even supposing it is sufficient for the existence of a storm in an area that there be a temporal sequence of stormish episodes in the area,[23] we have just seen that it is not sufficient for the existence of a particle in an area that there be a temporal sequence of particle-ish episodes in that area.

Let me next turn to one well-known motivation for making facts about instantaneous objects fundamental, one that typically goes under the heading 'the argument from temporal intrinsics'.[24] Consider some long-lived particle that changes with respect to some pretty basic quality. Using colors as stand-ins for the relevant fundamental qualities, let us suppose that the particle is blue for a while and then red for a while. If we take the fundamental facts in the vicinity to concern the particle, we seem under pressure to relationalize them in a certain way: the fundamental facts would appear to consist in such facts as that the particle is red at such and such a time, and blue at such and such a time. The complaint underlying the argument from temporary intrinsics is that it is a bad thing for the fundamental facts to turn out relational in this way. Meanwhile, the line of thought runs, this untoward consequence can be avoided if we take the fundamental facts to concern instantaneous objects. Given that such objects do not persist and undergo change, there is no need to think of facts about *their* color as somehow relativized to times. We can think of the instantaneous things as having a certain color *simpliciter* – and the facts about the color of long-lived things as derivative from the color facts about the instantaneous things that make them up. There has been a great deal of discussion of this argument, and there is insufficient space to rehearse all the relevant moves here.[25] For now, let me simply record some skepticism about whether the case has really been made that it would be problematic were the fundamental facts to turn out relational in the way just adverted to. What is really so bad about making the fundamental facts about color relational? One bad answer is that we do not normally talk about something being red in relation to a certain time – we just say that it is red. This fails to notice the role of tense in the statement 'It is red' – the present tense serves, in effect, to tie the truth conditions of the statement to the time of utterance. Another kind of way of justifying the claim that color should not be fundamentally relational is more metaphysical: color seems to be an intrinsic quality – something about how a thing is in itself, not how it is in relation to things outside itself. The take-home lesson is supposed to be that intrinsic qualities of an object do not consist of relations to things external to them. According to this picture, then, it is acceptable to think that the color of a particle turns out to involve a relation to a temporal part of that object, but unacceptable to think that the color of a particle involves a relation to something – a time – which is not part of that object at all.

I have a number of concerns about the argument. For one thing, it seems to involve a kind of double standard. Very many philosophers are Platonists who believe that properties really exist which, while instantiated by objects, are not parts of objects. From such a perspective, it begins to look as if the fundamental facts about objects involve relations to things external to those objects – specifically instantiation relations to properties. But curiously, it is now generally thought an excessively 'scholastic' complaint to worry that this makes the qualitative character of an object depend on things external to that object. But if this complaint is not felt to be pressing, then it is no disaster, after all, to make the fundamental facts about color relational. Second, one wonders why we are entitled to be so confident in rejecting the view that all the fundamental facts underlying the qualitative manifold are relational. Why are we so confident that any of the fundamental properties are monadic? (Casual picture-thinking about colors will not justify any such contention.) Third, the argument assumes that particles change with respect to their absolutely fundamental monadic properties. An alternative perspective will treat, say, the fundamental properties underlying talk of mass as simple monadic properties and will attempt to *explain* the incapacity of a particle to change with respect to mass on this basis. According to this view, the fundamental properties of a particle – such as being an electron, or being negatively charged – hold of long-lived objects but do not involve a relation to times. Less fundamental facts are then explained in terms of those facts (e.g. a composite object is negatively charged at a time by virtue of being composed at that time by objects that are negatively charged *simpliciter* – where the objects that are negatively charged *simpliciter* are long-lived.)

In conclusion: self-proclaimed four-dimensionalists typically adopt a picture that reckons instantaneous objects to be more fundamental than long-lived ones and facts about instantaneous objects more fundamental than facts about long-lived ones. But the virtues of this picture are far from transparent.

2.3 Objects as wholly present

Let us turn finally to the three-dimensionalist slogan that persisting objects are always wholly present at whatever time they exist. I take it that in maintaining such a thesis, its advocate need not reject outright the thesis that objects have temporal parts. The slogan is not intended to rule out the hypothesis that the lump is currently coincident with a statue that will only ever be made of that lump and will pass out of existence before the lump. Similarly, the slogan is intended to be perfectly consistent with the thesis that objects can gain and lose parts: that I am wholly present now does not mean that if I will or did have a part, I have that part now. We are left with the task of saying in a positive way what the slogan is supposed to come to.

Philosophers often engage in picture-thinking when articulating metaphysical theses to themselves or others. And when it comes to issues about time and persistence, the most pervasive kind of picture-thinking involves imagery related to the drawing of a line.[26] Suppose someone wanted to think of himself as spread out in time. He draws a line and claims that it is a representation of himself in time. Just as the line is spread out in space with various parts, corresponding to the parts of space it occupies, so the object represented by the line is spread out in time, with various parts corresponding to the parts of time it occupies. Meanwhile, one who denies that he is spread out in time will adapt the line-drawing metaphor to his own ends. He will draw the line but think of himself now as the tip of the pen that produces the line. That tip moves along space as it produces a line but never occupies more than a single point – it is never spread out across the line. And it is the very same tip that is at various parts of the line at various times. Insofar as these kinds of debate operate at the level of picture-thinking, the four-dimensionalist thinks of his temporal reality on the model of line, while the three-dimensionalist proponent of wholly present objects adopts the model of a moving extensionless point that traces out the path of the line.

Insofar as the slogan of wholly present objects is motivated by such picture-thinking, the most plausible way to put flesh on its bones is to question the intelligibility (or at least the foundational status) of a tenseless language. We are all familiar and comfortable with statements involving the past, present, and future tense – "I was happy five minutes ago'"; "I will be going to the pub." But some philosophers prefer to present their views using a language in which tense disappears. Such philosophers tend to suppose that this tenseless view of reality is maximally perspicuous from a metaphysical point of view – that it allows us to move from the perspective of someone embedded into a particular locus in history to a God's-eye view of the world. One who takes tense seriously believes this is all a mistake – tense does not merely serve to encode our local perspective on the world, but provides the appropriate framework for the most revealing depiction of reality. There is thus, on this perspective, a deep disanalogy between space and time. There is no *deep* metaphysical contrast between what is here and what is not – my choice of 'here' is apt just because of where I happen to be, not because where I happen to be has grand metaphysical significance. Not so for what is, was, and will be.[27] (See also chapter 5 of this volume.)

Suppose we take tense seriously in this way. We will be happy to accept that I am spread out in space, but will question the idea of my being spread out in time. All the present places exist, so we can say perfectly well that I occupy them all. But for the serious tenser, the claim that I occupy each of a series of past present and future times is the sort of claim that is supposed to be understood in a tenseless language. After all, the idea is not that I *now* occupy each of those times, but that I do so from a God's-eye perspective. (Related worries beset such claims as that I am composed of

John Hawthorne

past, present, and future instantaneous objects, and that I exist by virtue of past, present, and future instantaneous objects existing.)[28] From this perspective, the claim that I am spread out in time has no more merit that the claim that I am spread out across many possible worlds: one should no more reconstrue what was and will be as a series of additional concrete realities that I inhabit than one should reconstrue what might happen to me as a series of additional concrete worlds that I inhabit.

Of course the serious tenser may be happy to accept that I am currently mereologically coincident with an instantaneous object, and that it will always be the case that there exists some instantaneous object or other that I am coincident with. One can thus see that the serious tenser could, if he wishes, accept suitably rewritten analogues of Plenitude. But such a philosopher could still use his commitment to a tensed metaphysic to question the picture according to which we are spread out in time in the way that we are in space and use the slogan that we are wholly present at the current time to convey his preferred perspective.

The perspective of the serious tenser promises to put flesh on bones of the picture-thinking described earlier. The reason why a line is a bad model for his temporal existence, one may say, is that, while all the points in the line concretely exist, one cannot coherently say this of all the points in time. And the reason why a moving point is a much better model is that, for any time during which the point is moving, it feels like the natural description of the state of the world is that the point exists at such and such a place but used to be and will be at such and such other places.

We have looked at one way of developing the slogan of being wholly present. But it is worth remembering that, unlike the serious tenser, many three-dimensionalists claim to be perfectly happy with the project of doing metaphysics in a tense-free language. What might *they* mean by claiming that we are wholly present at each time that we exist? Let me offer two ideas in this connection.

One attempt to give meaning to the slogan requires giving up a rather natural way of thinking of spatiotemporal location. On that natural way of thinking, there is just one spatiotemporal region that an object exactly occupies, one that is traced out by a space-time diagram that plots the life of the object. To simplify, let us suppose that there are four space-time points *a, b, c, d*, and the space-time diagram for a point particle depicts it as moving from *a* to *c*. Then, on this natural way of thinking, the space-time region that is exactly occupied by the particle is the sum of *a* and *c*. There are various derivative notions one can define. We can say that a region y is completely occupied by *x* iff *y* is part of the region exactly occupied by *x*. (Thus is the case described, the particle completely occupies the region consisting of *a*) And we can say that a region y is occupied by *x* iff *y* overlaps the region exactly occupied by *x*. (Thus, in the case described the particle occupies the region consisting of the sum of *c* and *d*.) And so on. On this way of thinking, one natural gloss on 'wholly occupies' is that a region *r* is wholly occupied by an object iff the region exactly occupied by the object is part of *r*, while another natural gloss identifies *exactly occupies* with *wholly occupies*. But on either gloss it falls out as obviously false that a persisting object wholly occupies any spatiotemporal region corresponding to a single instant of time.

Now an alternative and somewhat radical approach does not accept these ways of thinking about 'wholly occupies': assuming that we understand 'exactly occupies' as above, this radical view holds that facts about which region an object exactly occupies do not determine which regions an object wholly occupies. By way of analogy, let us pretend, as some philosophers have imagined possible, that an object can be bilocated – completely present in more than one place at the same time. Let us suppose, in particular, that a three-inch stick is bilocated so that it is end-to-end with itself. And let us contrast that with a state of affairs in which a six-inch stick is laid down. (Let us suppose, to simplify, that the stick is instantaneous so that there are no other times to worry about.) Now in each case, in the sense given, the region exactly occupied by the stick has exactly the same profile – an instantaneous six-inch sliver of space-time. But insofar as we can make sense of the bilocation story, we may think that there is a crucial difference between the two scenarios. In one, the stick exactly occupies a six-inch region by being bilocated in two three-inch regions, but in the other case not. Note that the notion of location that is being deployed in 'bilocation' cannot be understood in terms of any of the notions of location generated by space-time diagrams, since the diagram for the bilocated stick and the six-inch stick will be exactly the same. Those who can make sense of the relevant bilocation thesis will need a new notion of location – let us call that 'being wholly located'. Once one has that notion in hand, we will be well placed to at least make sense of the thesis that persisting objects are wholly located at different times. That will not be a trivial truth, of course. But at least it will be a thesis that is, on the one hand, substantial and interesting and, on the other, perfectly compatible with the facts displayed by the space-time diagrams for persisting objects. It may then be natural, moreover, to think of being wholly located as basic and exact location (glossed in the way we did earlier) as derivative. One is exactly located at the region that is the sum of all the regions at which one is wholly located; the facts of exact location hold by virtue of the facts of whole location.

Will such philosophers think that everything that exists at different times is wholly located at each time that it exists? Perhaps not. One might, for example, conjecture that a key metaphysical difference between events and persisting objects can be captured using the ideology of being wholly located: events are wholly located at the space-time region at which they are exactly located. But persisting objects are only wholly located at instantaneous regions. There are some epistemological puzzles here. How is one supposed to know which things are wholly located at the present and which things are not once it is conceded that the facts of exact occupation do not settle matters? But it is not clear that these are especially more pressing than other general epistemological concerns that arise within metaphysics.

A third, quite different, gloss on the idea of being wholly located is connected to intrinsicality. It is natural to distinguish facts that are intrinsic to a time – facts that have to do with how things are at that time, considered in itself – from what is extrinsic to that time. Now suppose I exist at a time. That does not yet settle whether it is intrinsic or extrinsic to that time that *I* exist at it. Let us say that an object is wholly located at a spatiotemporal region iff it is intrinsic to how things are at that region that that very object exists at it. On this gloss, someone who thinks that I am wholly located at each time that I exist maintains, as it were, that God could recognize me as present at any given time that I exist just by considering the world at that time, as it is in itself. (Such a person might convince himself that while God could

John Hawthorne

not recognize me as present in the world just by considering in itself a spatiotemporal region that included only my right arm, he could recognize me as present just by considering in itself the entire contents of any individual time at which I exist.) Of course this way of thinking not only makes heavy reliance on the intrinsic/extrinsic distinction, but also supposes that such a distinction is applicable to questions about individual essences – such as whether the property of containing Richard Nixon is intrinsic or extrinsic to this or that time. Many of those who are comfortable in general with questions of intrinsicality balk at questions of the latter form. Nevertheless, with the suitable ideology in place, an interesting gloss on being wholly located – of the sort just described – is available.

3 Conclusion

I have tried to identify a number of the key debates in the vicinity of current discussions about three- and four-dimensionalism. Those self-proclaimed three-dimensionalists who use 'four-dimensionalism' as a label for the doctrine of temporal parts and 'three-dimensionalism' as a label for its denial will find little comfort in the above remarks. But much of what self-described three-dimensionalists typically care about does not turn on that doctrine. Indeed, many of the key metaphysical leanings of such philosophers would be satisfied by some or all of (a) a denial of Uniqueness, (b) a denial of Pointy Object and Pointy Fact Fundamentality, and (c) some version of the doctrine that objects are wholly present at each time that they exist. As readers will discover for themselves, (a), (b), and (c) undermine much of the metaphysical picture-thinking that goes under the heading 'four-dimensionalist metaphysics'.

I have not paid attention to the ramifications of modern physics for the doctrines under consideration. In relativity, there is in general no objective fact of the matter as to whether two distant events are simultaneous or not.[29] Thus the notions of an extended object existing at a time and having various properties at a time are under-specified, because there is no objective fact of the matter as to which feature one end of an object has *at the same moment* as another end. Supposing no distinguished absolute simultaneity relations are countenanced, we need to consider carefully which of the ideas adumbrated above should be abandoned altogether, and which can be finessed in a way that preserves their original spirit but which no longer offends scientific sensibilities.

The impact of physics on the current disputes is not confined either to the metaphysics of space-time. On one fairly natural reading of the lessons of quantum mechanics (I have the phenomenon of superposition in mind), the occupation relation is not a simple two-place relation between objects and regions, but instead a scalar relation that allows that one object can occupy a number of regions to *some degree or other* without completely occupying any region.[30] Issues about the relative status and role of fields and particles provide a further example where physics can potentially impact the debates described here. In the case of fields, it seems highly unnatural to suppose that there are serious questions of identity over time. Questions such as 'Is the part of the field that is over here now the same as the part of the field that is over there then' are misconceived.[31] If we imagine two point particles to meet at a point and then diverge, it is natural to suppose there is a real question as to which went where. On the other hand, if we think of such a "collision" as fundamentally a matter of waves meeting each other (where the waves are not here conceived of as waves of some underlying moving substance), the field equations will unambiguously determine the evolution of a pattern of waves but will appear to render otiose the question 'Which went where?'. It is beyond the scope of this chapter to explore such issues.

I offer no final verdict here on which package, if any, will emerge as the best all-things-considered view about persisting material objects. But what does seem clear is that, even granting a plethora of temporal parts, there is a variety of promising theses in the vicinity of three-dimensionalism.[32]

Notes

1   My discussion of four-dimensionalism will thus have a somewhat different emphasis from that given by Sider in his *Four-Dimensionalism* (2001). In that work, Sider takes the doctrine of temporal parts to be the key to the four-dimensionalist's picture. As will become clear, I think the situation is more complicated. Themes similar to those explored here are discussed in my 'Three-Dimensionalism' (2006).

2   For useful background material on the logic of part and whole, see Simons (1997).

3   The intrinsic character of a thing is a matter of how a thing is in itself, as opposed to how it is with respect to the world outside itself. The intrinsic/extrinsic distinction is intuitive enough for most of us. It is a further question whether and how it can be defined (or whether it has to be accepted as a primitive distinction incapable of definition). For relevant discussion, see Lewis (1999: 111–15) and Langton and Lewis (1999).

4   One place that the last idea has potential application is in thinking about fields. On one fairly natural picture, the fields described in physics textbooks – including the gravitational, electric, and magnetic fields of Newtonian physics, the electromagnetic field of relativistic physics, and the electromagnetic, Dirac, Weyl-Neutrino, and Pi-Meson fields of quantum field theory – involve space-time itself taking on certain qualities. Insofar as facts about points are fundamental, the field-like quality of any region will be dependent on certain fundamental facts involving the values of fields at points.

5   See, for example, Quine (1991: 16) and Sider (2001: 110ff.).

6   It bears emphasizing that the posited identity is between the poached egg and a space-time region, not between the poached egg and a spatial region.

7   Note that it is not plausible at all that the oddity (1) is to be explained by the context-dependence of 'walks'.

8   For relevant discussion, see Lewis (1986a: 77).

9   I am grateful for discussions with Sarah Moss here.

10 To be precise, quantum field theory allows bosons (a category that includes photons, W-bosons and all other integer spin quanta) to be in identical states throughout history. Owing to technical reasons connected to so-called Fermi-Dirac statistics, this is not true of the other major category of particles, namely fermions.

11 As it happens, there is reason for the spatiotemporalist to be encouraged here. In so-called Boze-Einstein statistics in quantum field theory, the number of permutations of particle paths that can generate a particular spatiotemporal distribution of matter makes absolutely no difference regarding the probabilities of such distributions. For relevant discussion, see Huggett (1999).

12 One strategy for maintaining the identity claim in such a case is to say that the statue did not come into existence after the lump: the statue used to be a non-statue (just as a lord mayor used to be a non-lord mayor). But consider a case where the statue is not always made of exactly the same lump: here it is quite clear that the path of the statue is not the same as the lump that makes it up at a given time, and hence quite clear that the one is not identical to the other. Even here, we will happily say at that time that 'The statue is a lump of clay', putting considerable pressure on us to interpret such claims as other than claims of identity (for more, see note 14). I mention in passing that one, albeit radical, way to read such claims as identity claims, even in such a case, is Ted Sider's stage theory, which takes a given occurrence of 'That statue' and 'That lump' to refer to instantaneous objects, deploying deviant semantics for tensed claims to save commonsense. I shall not explore that view here. See Sider (1996).

13 The right diagnosis seems to be that the property expressed by 'well trained' when combined with the noun phrase 'That actress' is one that is hard to associate with that predicate in a setting when it is combined with 'That person'. For a much more sympathetic treatment of the Leibniz Law arguments from non-modal predicates than mine, see Fine (1993).

14 It is of course still incumbent upon such a view to explain what is in fact going on semantically when we say "The statue is a lump of clay," given that the relevant identity theses have been discredited. This challenge is, however, quite general: it arises for any view that allows for cases where some statue is not identical to a lump of clay but 'The statue is a lump of clay' is nevertheless felicitous. A promising starting point is to observe that there are good reasons for thinking that 'is' does not mean 'is identical to' in a claim like 'The statue is a lump of clay'. Suppose the statue is named 'David'. If 'The statue is a lump of clay' meant that the statue is identical to the lump of clay, then the further claim 'The statue is a lump of clay and David' ought to be felicitous. But it is not. Nevertheless, even granting that the claim is not an identity claim, there still remains the puzzle of how to make sense of the predication of 'lump of clay' of the statue given a view that no statue is identical to any lump of clay. There is no clear consensus on how the challenge is to be met. Some say that such sentences express an asymmetric relation of constitution between the statue and the lump (the statue is constituted by a lump, but not vice versa). This accounts for the felicity of 'That statue is a lump of clay.' But in certain contexts 'That lump of clay is a statue' is felicitous too, and this is not accounted for. One strategy that deserves investigation assimilates these sentences to a more general phenomenon whereby we take liberties in associating a kind or individual with a thing in a circumstance where the relevant thing does not belong to that kind or is not that individual, but which nevertheless has some appropriate relation to that individual or kind. To take an unsophisticated example: suppose some cars are going by, some of which contain actors, some politicians. I can point to one car and, taking the relevant liberty, felicitously say, "That is a politician" and then point to another and say "That is an actor" – cf. Nunberg (2004). Perhaps sentences such as 'That lump of clay is a statue' are a more subtle version of this phenomenon. (Further clues may be provided by cases where we predicate composites of a plurality. Suppose certain people comprise both the Warwickshire cricket club and the Coventry City football team. I can say, "They are the Warwichshire cricket club" and "They are the Coventry City football team," but will nevertheless be hesitant to identify the football team with the cricket club.) Further investigation is in order.

15 Here is Descartes in Meditation Six: "Hence the fact that I can clearly and distinctly understand one thing apart from another is enough to make me certain that the two things are distinct, since they are capable of being separated, at least by God" (2004: 54).

16 I am not claiming that Descartes would endorse this supposition.

17 This kind of argument is advanced by Sider (2001) and in his contribution to this volume (see chapter 6.1).

18 It is to be conceded that there are some views that come close to the liberalism endorsed by Plenitude, but which stop just short of it. Consider a material line. An alternative to the thesis that it is composed of point-sized parts is the thesis that it has parts smaller than any given finite size but that it has no parts of zero size. On this, so-called "gunky" picture of a line, every part of the line is composed of smaller parts but there are no ultimate parts of zero size. If one generalized this picture to four dimensions, one can easily imagine an alternative package to theses (i)–(v) that treats the spatial and temporal dimensions of objects (and even space-time itself) in analogous "gunky" ways. A second alternative – the spatiotemporal atom picture – generalizes to four dimensions the idea that a line is composed of incredibly small but extended minima. On this picture, matter (and even space-time itself) is composed of ultimate parts that have negligible – but still non-zero – extent along the temporal and spatial axes. In practice, philosophers who give voice to liberalism in ontology tend to care rather little about the contrast between Plenitude and those packages that result from combining either the atomic or the gunky picture (construed along the lines indicated) with universalism. When I speak in what follows about "opposing Plenitude," I mean those who opposes both Plenitude and these Plenitude-like views.

19 The claim that the statue is a temporal part of the lump under such circumstances is not tendentious – it follows straightforwardly so long as we mean by "temporal part" what Sider (chapter 6.1 in this volume) does.

20 For discussion of objects like singing Socrates, see Fine's Aristotle-inspired "Acts, Events and Things" (1981).

21 Thought experiments like this figure in some much-discussed unpublished lectures by Saul Kripke and in Armstrong (1980).

22 This is the strategy of those who posit a fundamental "genidentity" relation between point-sized pieces of matter; for discussion of this, see Hawley (2001). Alternatively, it may still be possible to argue that the existence of a particle consists merely in the right arrangement of point-sized bits of matter with the appropriate intrinsic character, so long as one has a rich enough conception of that character. For example, if it is coherent to think of the so-called stress energy tensor which characterizes the state of matter in relativistic physics as being constituted by properties that are intrinsic to points, then there will be a natural associated method for determining which aggregates of point-sized bits of matter count as particles on the basis of the relevant intrinsic properties (though not every stress energy tensor distribution can coherently be understood as corresponding to a colony of particles). I shall not pursue these issues further here, except to note that it is very tendentious to think of such tensor facts as intrinsic to points (just as in a non-relativistic setting, it is very tendentious to think of velocities as intrinsic).

23 In fact, things are a bit more complicated. The identity over time of this or that material object and/or various causal connections is often taken for granted when we classify something as an event. For some purposes, we may count ourselves under an illusion in thinking ourselves to have witnessed a single firework display in some region of the night sky if the evenings events before 9 p.m. were produced by one set of people and then those after 9 p.m. by a different set of people, with no unifying plan or intentions coordinating their activities. Similarly, if there was no causal thread at all between the stormy events before 9 p.m. and those after 9 p.m., it is not clear whether to classify the entire sequence as a single storm in the area or merely the results of two different storms passing through.

24 See, notably, Lewis (1986b: 202–4).

25 For helpful discussion, see Sider (2000) and relevant discussion in Sider (2001) and chapter 6.1, this volume.

26 In the *Critique of Pure Reason*, Kant wrote that, because our representation of time "yields no shape, we endeavour to make up for this want by analogies. We represent the time-sequence by a line progressing to infinity, in which the manifold constitutes a series of one dimension only; and we reason from the properties of this line to all the properties of time, with this one exception, that while the parts of the line are simultaneous the parts of time are always successive" (1978: 77).

27 With a commitment to the fundamentality of tense in place, one can argue for a deep contrast between genuine change and mere variation. Suppose I am now happy but used to be sad. It will be natural for the serious tenser to say that there is a proposition ascribing happiness to me which is true *simpliciter* (which instantiates the monadic property of truth) but which used to be false. But suppose it is raining over here and not over there. Then there is no proposition that is true *simpliciter* but which is false over there. This contrast disintegrates when one moves to a tenseless perspective on the world that treats spatial and temporal variation analogously. This provokes the common – and well-motivated – complaint that a tenseless perspective does not allow for genuine change. For relevant discussion, see Williamson (2002), which applies similar themes to the topic of contingency. Thanks to Ted Sider here.

28 There are some philosophers who think that all objects exist eternally. When an animal dies, it does not cease to exist. It ceases to become concrete. For sympathetic discussion, see Williamson (1999, 1998). Various ideas propounded in the text need to be rewritten once such a view is adopted. There are, for example, no objects that exist only for an instant, but there are objects that are concrete for an instant. And no object x exists by virtue of an object y, though perhaps x is concrete by virtue of y being concrete. (Thus it seems that for such a perspective metaphysical dependency relations hold between propositions, not objects.) Thus the thesis that I exist by virtue of various instantaneous objects existing will be rewritten as the thesis that I am concrete by virtue of various instantaneous objects being concrete. Such philosophers still have the option of being serious tensers. Supposing they are, such theses as the latter will be thrown into question.

29 Where 'distant' here means that no signal traveling at the speed of light or less can get from one event to the other event.

30 To be precise, the scalar is a complex scalar which designates the so-called ampliature with which the particle is present at a particular location. The phenomenon of superposition in this case merely means that what one would normally regard as a point-sized particle will typically have non-zero ampliatures at many locations at one time. There are awkward issues here for the four-dimensionalist who is insistent on taking point-sized instantaneous temporal parts of objects as fundamental, but I shall not pursue the matter here.

31 Standard formulations of particle mechanics are stated in terms of equations governing the evolution in time of the position (and other features) of given persisting particles. In field theory, however, the equations of motions are always stated as a set of equations governing the evolution of the entire configuration of the field over space at a given time. These equations make no reference whatsoever to persisting objects other than, possibly, the entire configuration of the field over space.

32 I am very grateful to Frank Arntzenius, Sarah Moss, Ted Sider, Timothy Williamson, and Dean Zimmerman for helpful discussion, and to Tamar Gendler, Ofra Magidor, and Ted Sider for comments on a draft of this paper.

References

Armstrong, D. 1980. "Identity Through Time," in P. van Inwagen, ed., *Time and Cause* (Dordrecht: D. Reidel), pp. 67–78.

Descartes, R. 1984. *The Philosophical Writings of Descartes*, vol. 2, ed. J. Cottingham, R. Stoothoff, and D. Murdock (Cambridge: Cambridge University Press), p. 54.

Fine, K. 1981. "Acts, Events and Things," in W. Leinfellner et al., *Language and Ontology*, Proceedings of the Sixth International Wittgenstein Symposium (Vienna: Hölder-Pichler-Tempsky), pp. 97–105.

——. 1993. "On the Non-Identity of Material Thing and Its Matter," *Mind* 40: 195–234.

Hawley, K. 2001. *How Things Persist* (Oxford: Oxford University Press).

Hawthorne, J. 2006. "Three-Dimensionalism," in Hawthorne, *Metaphysical Essays* (Oxford: Clarendon Press).

Huggett, N. 1999. "Atomic Metaphysics," *Journal of Philosophy* 96: 5–24.

Kant, I. 1978. *Critique of Pure Reason*, ed. Norman Kemp Smith (London: Macmillan), p. 77.

Langton, R. and Lewis, D. 1999. "Defining 'Intrinsic'," in Lewis, *Papers in Metaphysics and Epistemology* (Cambridge: Cambridge University Press).

Lewis, D. 1986a. "The Paradoxes of Time Travel," in Lewis, *Philosophical Papers*, vol. 2 (Oxford: Oxford University Press).

——. 1986b. *The Plurality of Worlds* (Oxford: Blackwell).

——. 1999. "Extrinsic Properties," in Lewis, *Papers in Metaphysics and Epistemology* (Cambridge: Cambridge University Press).

Nunberg, G. 2004. 'The Pragmatics of Deferred Reference," in L. Horn and G. Ward, eds., *The Handbook of Pragmatics* (Oxford: Blackwell).

Quine, W. V. 1991. "Things and Their Place in Theories," in Quine, *Theories and Things* (Cambridge, MA: Harvard University Press).

Sider, T. 1996. "All the World's a Stage," *Australasian Journal of Philosophy* 74: 433–53.

——. 2000. "The Stage View and Temporary Intrinsics," *Analysis* 60: 84–8.

——. 2001. *Four-Dimensionalism: An Ontology of Persistence and Time* (Oxford: Clarendon Press).

Simons, P. 1997. *Parts: A Study in Ontology* (Oxford: Clarendon Press).

Williamson, T. 1998. "Bare Possibilia," *Erkenntnis* 48: 257–73.

——. 1999. "Existence and Contingency," *Aristotelian Society*, suppl. vol. 73: 181–203.

——. 2002. "Necessary Existents," in A. O'Hear, ed., *Logic, Thought and Language* (Cambridge: Cambridge University Press), p. 233–51.

FREE WILL

Suppose that science could predict everything that happened in the world, down to the last motion of the last subatomic particle. Science could then predict exactly what a human being would do, in any circumstance. At first glance, this clashes with our ordinary picture of ourselves as *free*. Your choice to read a book on metaphysics was a free one; you could have spent the day watching television instead. Kadri Vihvelin argues that there is in fact no such clash. Given a proper understanding of what free will is, a person can be free even if she is determined to do what she does. Robert Kane disagrees. If we are to have free will, the laws of nature cannot be fully deterministic; they cannot fully specify how each and every object behaves.

Incompatibilism

Robert Kane

1 Determinism and the Garden of Forking Paths

The eighteenth-century philosopher, David Hume, called the free will issue "the most contentious question of metaphysics, the most contentious science" (1975: 95). The problem of free will has arisen in human history whenever people have been led to suspect that their actions might be determined or necessitated by factors unknown to them and beyond their control. That is why doctrines of *determinism* or *necessity* have been so important in the history of debates about free will.

Doctrines of determinism have taken many historical forms. People have wondered at various times whether their actions might be determined by fate or the decrees of God, by the laws of physics or the laws of logic, heredity or environment, unconscious motives, psychological or social conditioning, and so on. But there is a core idea running through all historical doctrines of determinism that shows why they are all a threat to free will. All doctrines of determinism imply that, given the past and the laws of nature at any given time, there is only one possible future. Whatever happens is therefore inevitable (it cannot but occur), given the past and the laws.

It is not difficult to see why people have thought that determinism so understood was a threat to free will. We believe we have free will when we view ourselves as agents capable of influencing the world in various ways. Open alternatives lie before is. We reason and deliberate among them and choose. We feel (i) it is "up to us" what we choose and how we act; and this means we could have chosen or acted otherwise. This "up-to-us-ness" also implies that (ii) the sources of our actions lie in us and not outside us in something beyond our control.

To illustrate: suppose Jane has just graduated from law school and she has a choice between joining a law firm in Chicago or a different firm in New York. If Jane believes her choice is a *free* choice (made "of her own free will"), she must believe both options are "open" to her while she is deliberating. She could choose either one. (If she did

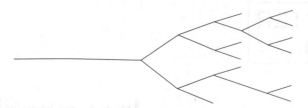

Figure 1

not believe this, what would be the point of deliberating?) But that means she believes there is more than one possible path into the future available to her and it is "up to her" which of these paths will be taken. Such a picture of an open future with forking paths – a garden of forking paths, we might call it (see figure 1) – is essential to our understanding of free will. This picture of different possible paths into the future is also essential, I believe, to what it means to be a person and to live a human life.

One can see why determinism would threaten this picture. If determinism is true, it seems there would not be more than one possible path into the future available to Jane, but only one. It would not be (i) "up to" her what she chose from an array of alternative possibilities, since only one alternative would be possible. It also seems that, if determinism were true, the (ii) sources or origins of her actions would not be in Jane herself but in something else outside her control that determined her choice (such as the decrees of fate, the foreordaining acts of God, her heredity and upbringing or social conditioning).

Described in this way, the conflict between free will and determinism appears self-evident to most people. It has always seemed so to me. But many philosophers and scientists, especially in modern times, have argued to the contrary that the supposed conflict between free will and determinism is not real. Determinism, they say, is really compatible with free will, despite the fact that most people naively think otherwise. This doctrine – *compatibilism* – has become popular among modern philosophers and scientists because it provides a neat and simple solution to the free will problem. If there is no conflict between free will and determinism, if they really are compatible, then the age-old problem of free will would be solved in one fell swoop. The free will problem would in fact be "dis-solved."

2 The Consequence Argument

Yet compatibilism is hard to believe for many people, myself included, despite the sophisticated arguments used in defense of it.[1] Eminent philosophers have found it hard to believe as well. Immanuel Kant called compatibilism a "wretched subterfuge" (1956: 189–90) and William James called it a "quagmire of evasion" (1956: 149). But the modern popularity of compatibilism among scientists and philosophers means it is no longer enough for those who believe in the incompatibility of free will and determinism ("incompatibilists," as they are called) to rely on intuitions and gut instincts to make their case. Sound arguments must be provided to show the incom-

Robert Kane

patibility of free will and determinism; and it turns out that new arguments for incompatibilism have indeed been proposed in modern philosophy.

We will begin with the most widely discussed of these new arguments for incompatibilism. It is called the "Consequence Argument" and is stated as follows by one of its proponents, Peter Van Inwagen:

> If determinism is true, then our acts are the consequences of the laws of nature and events in the remote past. But it is not up to us what went on before we were born; and neither is it up to us what the laws of nature are. Therefore the consequences of these things (including our own acts) are not up to us. (1983: 16)

To say it is not "up to us" what "went on before we were born," or "what the laws of nature are," is to say that there is nothing we can now do to change the past or alter the laws of nature (it is beyond our control). We can thus spell out this argument in the following steps.[2]

(1)   There is nothing we can now do to change the past.
(2)   There is nothing we can now do to change the laws of nature.
(3)   There is nothing we can now do to change the past and the laws of nature.
(4)   If determinism is true, our present actions are necessary consequences of the past and the laws of nature. (That is, it *must* be the case that, given the past and the laws of nature, our present actions occur.)
(5)   There is nothing we can now do to change the fact that our present actions occur.

In other words, we *cannot now do otherwise* than we actually do. Since this argument can be applied to any agents and actions at any times, we can infer from it that *if determinism is true, no one can ever do otherwise*; and if free will requires the power to do otherwise, then no one would have free will.

Defenders of the Consequence Argument, such as van Inwagen, think the first two premises are undeniable. We cannot now change the past (1) or the laws of nature (2). Step (3) states what appears to be a simple consequence of premises (1) and (2): if you can't change the past or the laws, then you can't change the conjunction of both of them. Premise (4) simply spells out what is implied by determinism. Some philosophers have questioned one or another of the first three steps of this argument. But most criticisms have focused on step (5). Step (5) follows from (3) and (4) by virtue of the following inference: if (3) there is nothing we can now do to change the past and laws of nature and (4) our present actions are necessary consequences of the past and laws, then (5) there is nothing we can now do to change the fact that our present actions occur. This inference is an instance of the following principle:

(TP)   If there is nothing anyone can do to change X, and if Y is a necessary consequence of X (if it must be that, if X occurs, Y occurs), then there is nothing anyone can do to change Y.

TP has been called a "Transfer of Powerlessness Principle," for it says in effect that if you are powerless to change something X, and something else Y is necessarily going to occur if X does, then you are also powerless to change Y. This makes sense. If we can't do anything to prevent X from occurring and Y cannot but occur if X does, then how could we do anything to prevent Y from occurring? Consider an example. Suppose the sun is going to explode in 2050 and there is nothing anyone can now do to change the fact that the sun will explode in 2050. Assume also that necessarily (given the laws of nature), if the sun explodes in 2050, all life on earth will end in 2050. If both these claims are true, it seems obvious that there is nothing anyone can now do to change the fact that all life on earth will end in 2050. Here is another example. If there is nothing anyone can now do to change the laws of nature, and the laws of nature entail that nothing goes faster than the speed of light, then there is nothing anyone can now do to change the fact that nothing goes faster than the speed of light.

But, despite the initial plausibility of this Transfer of Powerlessness Principle, critics of the Consequence Argument have challenged it. Everything depends, they say, on how you interpret the expression "There is nothing anyone can do to change...." Talking about what persons "can" (and "cannot") do is talking about their *powers*; and the notion of power is one of the most difficult in metaphysics, as John Locke pointed out three centuries ago. For example, many compatibilists interpret what it means to say that persons "can" or "have the power" to do things in the following way.[3] They say: "You can (or you have the power to do) something" simply means "If you wanted (or tried) to do it, you would do it." I can jump over this fence means I would jump over it, if I wanted to or tried to. If someone challenged my power to do it, the challenger would say: "I don't think you would manage to jump it *even if* you wanted or tried."

Now the interesting thing about this compatibilist interpretation of 'can' and 'power', is that, if it is correct, the Consequence Argument would fail. For on this interpretation, to say we can now change the past or the laws would mean that "*If* we now wanted or tried to change the past or the laws, we would change them." And this is false. No persons would change the past or the laws of nature, *even if* they wanted or tried to, because no one has the power to do it. But when we turn to ordinary actions like jumping over a fence, things are different. If you can jump over a fence that is in your path, it may well be true that you *would* jump over it, *if* you wanted to or tried, because jumping over fences is something you are capable of doing.

In other words, on the analysis of 'can' or 'power' that many compatibilists favor, the *premises* of the Consequence Argument come out *true* (you would *not* have changed the past or the laws, even if we wanted or tried to, because you are not capable of it). But the *conclusion* of the Consequence Argument comes out *false* (you would have jumped the fence, *if* you wanted or tried to, because jumping fences of this height is something you *are* capable of doing). Since the Consequence Argument would have true premises and a false conclusion on this analysis of 'can', it would be an invalid argument. What has happened to make it fail? The answer is that the transfer principle TP has failed. Your powerlessness to change the past and laws of nature does not *transfer* to your powerlessness to jump the fence. For you are not able to change the past and laws, but you are able to jump the fence – at least in this compatibilist sense.

But why should we accept the compatibilist account of 'can' or 'power'? Defenders of the Consequence Argument, such as van Inwagen, do not accept it. They respond

Robert Kane

as follows: "So the Consequence Argument fails on your compatibilist analysis of 'can' or 'power'. But that should not surprise us. For your compatibilist analysis was rigged in the first place to make freedom compatible with determinism. On your analysis, persons can jump the fence even though their doing so here and now is impossible, given the past and the laws of nature. That is not what we mean by 'can' in the Consequence Argument. We mean it is possible that you do it *here and now*, given all the facts that presently obtain. If your analysis allows you to say that persons can do otherwise, even though they can't change the past and the laws of nature and even though their actions are a necessary consequence of the past and the laws of nature, *then something must be wrong with your compatibilist analysis.* To us, the premises and rules of the Consequence Argument are far more plausible than any compatibilist analysis of 'can'."

At this point, arguments over the Consequence Argument tend to reach an impasse. Incompatibilist defenders of the argument claim that compatibilist critics are begging the question by interpreting 'can' in the Consequence Argument in a way that is compatible with determinism. But compatibilists respond by saying that defenders of the Consequence Argument are begging the question themselves by assuming that 'can' in the argument has an *incompatibilist* meaning rather than a compatibilist one.

3 Ultimate Responsibility

As a result of this impasse, debates have multiplied about just what 'can' and 'power' (and related expressions, such as "could have done otherwise") really mean.[4] We cannot follow all these complex debates here. But I do not think it matters. For I believe disagreements over the meaning of 'can' and 'power' are symptoms of a deeper problem in discussions about free will and determinism. The problem is that focusing on alternative possibilities or the power to do otherwise *alone*, as the Consequence Argument does, is *too thin a basis* on which to rest the case for the incompatibility of free will and determinism. One must look beyond debates about 'can', 'power', and 'could have done otherwise' to make the case for incompatibilism.

Fortunately, there is another place to look for reasons why free will might conflict with determinism. Recall that in section 1, I said that there were *two* reasons why people thought determinism must rule out free will. One was the condition of (i) alternative possibilities we have been considering: free will requires that we have both the power to do and to do otherwise (call this condition AP for alternative possibilities). But there was a second condition fueling incompatibilist intuitions: (ii) The sources of our actions must lie in us and not outside us in something beyond our control.

I call this second requirement for free will the condition of ultimate responsibility (or UR, for short); and I think it is even more important to free will debates than AP.[5] The basic idea of UR is this: To be ultimately responsible for an action, an agent must be responsible for anything that is a sufficient cause or motive for the action's occurring. If, for example, a choice issues from, and can be sufficiently explained by, an agent's character and motives (together with background conditions), then to be *ultimately* responsible for the choice, the agent must be at least in part responsible by virtue of choices or actions voluntarily performed in the past for having the character and motives he or she now has. Compare Aristotle's claim that if a man is responsible for the wicked acts that flow from his character, he must at some time in the past have been responsible for forming the wicked character from which these acts flow (1915: 1114a13–22).

This UR condition does not require that we can do otherwise (AP) for every act performed "of our own free wills." But UR does require that we could have done otherwise with respect to *some* acts in our past life histories by which we formed our present characters.[6] I call such character-forming actions "self-forming actions," or SFAs. To illustrate why some self-forming actions for which we could have done otherwise are required by UR, consider Daniel Dennett's example of Martin Luther (1984: 131–3). When Luther broke with the Church in Rome, initiating the Protestant Reformation, he said "Here I stand, I can do no other." Dennett asks us to suppose that Luther was literally right about himself at that moment. Given his character and motives at the time, he literally could not then have done otherwise. Does this mean Luther was not morally responsible? Not at all, says Dennett. In saying "I can do no other," Luther was not disowning responsibility for his act, but taking full responsibility for it. So Dennett concludes that "could have done otherwise," or AP, is not required for free will in a sense required by moral responsibility; and if free will does not require the power to do otherwise, then free will is compatible with determinism.

Dennett is a compatibilist and he is using this example to defend compatibilism. As an incompatibilist, my response to Dennett is to grant that Luther could have been responsible for this act, even *ultimately* responsible in the sense of UR, though he could not have done otherwise at that moment, even if his act was determined. But this would be so, I would argue, to the extent that Luther was responsible for his present motives and character by virtue of earlier struggles and SFAs that brought him to this point where he could do no other. Often we act from a will already formed, but it is "our own free will," by virtue of the fact that we formed our will by other choices or actions in the past (SFAs) for which we could have done otherwise (which did satisfy AP). If this were not so, there would have been nothing we could have *ever* done to make ourselves different from how we are – a consequence, I believe, that is incompatible with being (at least to some degree) ultimately responsible (UR) for what we are.

If the case for the incompatibility of free will and determinism cannot be made on AP alone, it can be made if UR is added. If agents must be responsible to some degree for anything that is a sufficient cause or motive of their actions, an impossible infinite regress of past actions would be required unless *some* actions in the agent's life history (SFAs) did not have sufficient causes or motives (and hence were not determined). What is noteworthy about this argument for incompatibilism, however, is that it focuses on the *sources* or *grounds* – causes and motives – of what we actually do rather than on the power to do otherwise. (Aristotle said that metaphysics is about the sources or grounds [*archai*] of things; and in that sense the free will issue is deeply metaphysical.) Where did our characters, motives, and purposes come from? Who produced them, and who is responsible for them? Was it we ourselves who are responsible for forming our characters and motives, or someone or something else – God, fate, heredity and environment, nature or upbringing, society or culture? Therein lies the core of the traditional "problem of free will." The problem of free *will* is not simply about the freedom to do what we want; it is about how we got to be the kinds of persons we are.

4 Can We Have Free Will?

Showing that free will is incompatible with determinism does not show that we have free will. One may be convinced that free will and determinism are incompatible and yet reject free will because one believes determinism is true. That is the position of *hard determinists*. They take the "hard" line that, since determinism is true and since free will is incompatible with determinism, no persons are ultimately responsible or blameworthy for their actions. But hard determinists are not the only ones who are skeptical about the existence of a free will that is incompatible with determinism. Many people (including many compatibilists) believe an incompatibilist free will is impossible *whether determinism is true or not.*

The reasons for believing this are related to an ancient dilemma: if free will is not compatible with determinism, it does not seem to be compatible with *indeterminism* either. An event that is undetermined might occur or not occur, given the entire past and laws of nature. So whether or not an undetermined event occurs would seem to be a matter of chance. But chance events are not under the control of anything, hence not under the control of agents. How then could they be free or responsible actions?

Suppose a choice occurred as the result of an undetermined event (say a quantum jump) in someone's brain. Would that be a free choice? Being undetermined, it would appear to be more of a fluke or accident than a responsible choice. Some twentieth-century scientists and philosophers have suggested that free will might be rescued by supposing that undetermined events in the brain, such as quantum jumps in atoms, might be amplified to have large-scale effects on choice or action.[7] Such a suggestion is highly controversial. But even if it was true, would it make any difference for free will? If a choice occurred as a result of an undetermined event in one's brain, such as a quantum jump, it would be unpredictable and uncontrollable – like the unexpected emergence of a thought or the uncontrolled jerking of an arm – quite the opposite of what we take free actions to be. It seems that undetermined events in the brain or body would occur spontaneously and would be more of a nuisance – or perhaps a curse, like epilepsy – rather than an enhancement of our freedom.

Here is another way of thinking about the problems that indeterminism poses for free will. Note that, if a choice or action is undetermined, it might occur otherwise, *given exactly the same past*, right up to the moment when it does occur. That is what indeterminism and probability mean: exactly the same past, different possible out-comes. (Recall the garden of forking paths.) Imagine, for example, that John has been deliberating about where to spend his vacation, in Hawaii or Colorado, and after much thought, has decided he prefers Hawaii and chooses it. If the choice was undetermined, then exactly the same deliberation, the same thought processes, the same beliefs, desires, and other motives – not a sliver of difference – that led up to John's favoring and choosing Hawaii over Colorado might by chance have issued in his choosing Colorado instead. That is very strange. If such a thing happened, it would seem a fluke or accident, like that quantum jump in the brain just mentioned, not a rational choice. Since John had come to favor Hawaii and was about to choose it, when by chance he chose Colorado, he would wonder what went wrong and perhaps consult a neurologist about the waywardness of his neural processes.

For reasons such as these, people have argued that undetermined choices would be "arbitrary," "capricious," "random," "irrational," "uncontrolled," "inexplicable," and mere matters of "luck" or "chance," rather than free and responsible choices.

In response to these objections, defenders of an incompatibilist or undetermined free will – they are often called *libertarians* in modern free will debates – have tended to reason as follows. Realizing that free will cannot *merely* be indeterminism or chance, libertarians have usually appealed to "extra factors," in the form of unusual or mysterious forms of agency or causation to make up the difference. For example, Immanuel Kant said that we cannot explain free will in scientific or psychological terms. To account for it, we have to appeal to the agency of what he called a "noumenal self" outside space and time that could not be studied in scientific terms (1958: 267). Other philosophers have claimed that only some sort of appeal to a mind or soul separate from a body could make sense of free will. Science might tell us there was indeterminacy or a place for causal gaps in the brain, but a non-material self, or what Nobel physiologist John Eccles calls a "transempirical power center" (1970: 87) would have to fill the causal gaps left in the brain by intervening in the natural order. Still other libertarians have appealed to a special kind of "agent-" or "immanent" causation that cannot be explained in terms of the ordinary modes of causation in terms of events familiar to the sciences.[8]

These "extra factor" strategies for making sense of free will have tended to reinforce the widespread criticism that incompatibilist notions of free will requiring indeterminism are mysterious and have no place in the modern scientific picture of the world. More important, as I see it, appeals to such extra factors do not solve the problems about indeterminism and chance they were designed to solve, while creating further mysteries of their own. They remind one of the Arkansas farmer when he first saw an automobile. After listening to how internal combustion engines worked, the farmer insisted on looking under the car's hood anyway because, as he said, "there must be a horse in there somewhere." To confront the deep problems that indeterminism and chance pose for free will, I believe we have to start over again and rethink issues about indeterminism and responsibility from the ground up, without relying on appeals to extra factors. What follows is my own attempt to do this. It is not the last word on the subject, but is meant to stimulate your thinking about the problem.[9]

5 Indeterminism and Responsibility

The first step in this rethinking is to note that indeterminism does not have to be involved in all acts done "of our own free wills" for which we are ultimately responsible, as argued earlier. Not all free acts have to be undetermined, but only those by which

Robert Kane

we made ourselves into the kinds of persons we are, namely "self-forming actions" or SFAs. Now I believe these undetermined SFAs occur at those difficult times of life when we are torn between competing visions of what we should do or become.

Perhaps we are torn between doing the moral thing and acting from ambition, or between powerful present desires and long-term goals, or we are faced with difficult tasks for which we have aversions. In all such cases, we are faced with competing motivations and have to make an effort to overcome temptation to do something else we also strongly want. There is tension and uncertainty in our minds about what to do at such times, I suggest, that is reflected in appropriate regions of our brains by movement away from thermodynamic equilibrium – in short, a kind of "stirring up of chaos" in the brain that makes it sensitive to micro-indeterminacies at the neuronal level. The uncertainty and inner tension we feel at such soul-searching moments of self-formation is thus reflected in the indeterminacy of our neural processes themselves. What is experienced internally as uncertainty then corresponds physically to the opening of a window of opportunity that temporarily screens off complete determination by influences of the past.

When we do decide under such conditions of uncertainty, the outcome is not determined because of the preceding indeterminacy – and yet it can be willed (and hence rational and voluntary) either way owing to the fact that, in such self-formation, the agents' prior wills are divided by conflicting motives. Consider a businesswoman who faces such a conflict. She is on her way to an important meeting when she observes an assault taking place in an alley. An inner struggle ensues between her conscience, to stop and call for help, and her career ambitions, which tell her she cannot miss this meeting. She has to make an effort of will to overcome the temptation to go on. If she overcomes this temptation, it will be the result of her effort, but if she fails, it will be because she did not *allow* her effort to succeed. And this is due to the fact that, while she willed to overcome temptation, she also willed to fail, for quite different and incommensurable reasons. When we, like the woman, decide in such circumstances, and the indeterminate efforts we are making become determinate choices, we *make* one set of competing reasons or motives prevail over the others then and there *by deciding*.

Now let us add a further piece to the puzzle. Just as indeterminism need not undermine rationality and voluntariness, so indeterminism in and of itself need not undermine control and responsibility. Suppose you are trying to think through a difficult problem, say a mathematical problem, and there is some indeterminacy in your neural processes complicating the task – a kind of chaotic background. It would be like trying to concentrate and solve a problem, say a mathematical problem, with background noise or distraction. Whether you are going to succeed in solving the problem is uncertain and undetermined because of the distracting neural noise. Yet, if you concentrate and solve the problem nonetheless, we have reason to say you did it and are responsible for it even though it was undetermined whether you would succeed. The indeterministic noise would have been an obstacle that you overcame by your effort.

There are numerous examples supporting this point, where indeterminism functions as an obstacle to success without precluding responsibility. Consider an assassin who is trying to shoot the prime minister, but might miss because of some undetermined events in his nervous system that may lead to a jerking or wavering of his arm. If the assassin does succeed in hitting his target, despite the indeterminism, can he be held responsible? The answer is clearly yes because he intentionally and voluntarily succeeded in doing what he was *trying* to do – kill the prime minister. Yet his action, killing the prime minister, was undetermined. Here is another example. A husband, while arguing with his wife, in a fit of rage swings his arm down on her favorite glass table-top intending to break it. Again, we suppose that some indeterminism in his outgoing neural pathways makes the momentum of his arm indeterminate so that it is undetermined whether the table will break right up to the moment when it is struck. Whether the husband breaks the table or not is undetermined and yet he is clearly responsible if he does break it. (It would be a poor excuse for him to say to his wife: "Chance did it, not me." Though indeterminism was involved, chance didn't do it: he did.)

Now these examples – of the mathematical problem, the assassin, and the husband – are not all we want since they do not amount to genuine exercises of (self-forming) free will in SFAs, like the businesswoman's, where the will is divided between conflicting motives. The woman wants to help the victim, but she also wants to go on to her meeting. By contrast, the assassin's will is not equally divided. He wants to kill the prime minister, but does not also want to fail. (If he fails therefore, it will be *merely* by chance.) Yet these examples of the assassin, the husband, and the like do provide some clues. To go further, we have to add some additional twists.

Imagine in cases of conflict characteristic of SFAs, like the businesswoman's, that the indeterministic noise which is providing an obstacle to her overcoming temptation is not coming from an external source, but has its source in her own will, since she also deeply desires to do the opposite. To understand how this could be, imagine that two crossing recurrent neural networks are involved, each influencing the other, and representing her conflicting motivations. (These are complex networks of interconnected neurons in the brain circulating impulses in feedback loops that are generally involved in higher-level cognitive processing.[10]) The input of one of these neural networks consists in the woman's reasons for acting morally and stopping to help the victim; the input of the other, her ambitious motives for going on to her meeting.

The two networks are connected so that the indeterminism that is an obstacle to her making one of the choices is present because of her simultaneous conflicting desire to make the other choice – the indeterminism thus arising from a tension-creating conflict in the will, as we said. This conflict, as noted earlier, would be reflected in appropriate regions of the brain by movement away from thermodynamic equilibrium. The result would be a stirring up of chaos in the neural networks involved. Chaos in physical systems is a phenomenon in which very small changes in initial conditions are magnified so that they lead to large and unpredictable changes in the subsequent behavior of a system. There is growing evidence that chaos plays a role in the information processing of the brain, providing some of the flexibility that the nervous system needs to adapt creatively – rather than in predictable or rigid ways – to an ever-changing environment.[11] The suggestion being made here is that, if chaotic behavior were enhanced in these neural networks by tension-creating conflict in the will, then minute quantum indeterminacies in the firings of individual neurons might be magnified so that these micro-indeterminacies would have large-scale indeterministic effects on the activity of the neural networks as a whole.[12] The result would be some significant indeterminism in the cognitive processing of each of the competing neural networks.

In such circumstances, when either of the competing networks "wins" (i.e. reaches an activation threshold, which amounts to choice), it would be like your solving the mathematical problem despite the indeterminism in your neural networks that made it uncertain you would succeed. And just as when you solved the mathematical problem despite the presence of this indeterminism, one could say you did it and were responsible for it, so one can say this as well, I would argue, in the present case, *whichever one is chosen*. The network through which the woman succeeds in reaching a choice threshold will have succeeded despite the indeterminism that was present because of the existence of the competing network.

Recall, as noted earlier, that under such conditions the choices, though undetermined, would not be "inadvertent," "accidental," "capricious," or "merely random" (as critics of indeterminism say), because they would be *willed* by the agents either way when they are made, and done for *reasons* either way – reasons that the agents then and there *endorse*. But these are the conditions usually required to say something is done "on purpose," rather than accidentally, capriciously, or merely by chance. Moreover, these conditions taken together, I argue, rule out each of the reasons we have for saying that agents act, but do not have *control* over their actions (compulsion, coercion, constraint, inadvertence, accident, control by others, etc.).[13] Of course, for undetermined SFAs, agents do not control or determine which choice outcome will occur *before* it occurs; but it does not follow, because one does control or determine which of a set of outcomes is going to occur before it occurs, that one does not control or determine which of them occurs, *when* it occurs.

When the above conditions for SFAs are satisfied, agents exercise control over their future lives *then and there* by deciding. Indeed, they have what I call "plural voluntary control" over the options in the following sense: They are able to bring about *whichever* of the options they will, *when* they will to do so, for the reasons they will to do so, on purpose rather than accidentally or by mistake, without being coerced or compelled in doing so or willing to do so, or otherwise controlled in doing or willing to do so by any other agents or mechanisms. Each of these conditions can be satisfied for SFAs as conceived above.[14] The conditions can be summed up by saying that the agents can choose either way *at will*.

Note also that this account of self-forming choices amounts to a kind of "doubling" of the mathematical problem. It is as if an agent faced with such a choice is *trying* or making an effort to solve *two* cognitive problems at once, or to complete two competing (deliberative) tasks at once – in our example, to make a moral choice and to make a conflicting self-interested choice (corresponding to the two competing neural networks involved). Each task is being thwarted by the indeterminism stirred up by the presence of the competing task, so it might fail. But if it succeeds, then the agents can be held responsible because, as in the case of solving the mathematical problem, the agents will have succeeded in doing what they were knowingly and willingly trying to do. Recall the assassin and the husband. Owing to indeterminacies in their neural pathways, the assassin might miss his target or the husband fail to break the table. But if they *succeed*, despite the probability of failure, they are responsible, because they will have succeeded in doing what they were trying to do.

And so it is, I suggest, with self-forming choices, except that in the case of self-forming choices, *whichever way the agents choose* they will have succeeded in doing what they were trying to do because they were simultaneously trying to make both choices, and one is going to succeed. Their failure to do one thing is not a *mere* failure, but a voluntary succeeding in doing the other.

Does it make sense to talk about the agent's trying to do two competing things at once in this way, or to solve two cognitive problems at once? Well, we now know that the brain is a parallel processor; it can simultaneously process different kinds of information relevant to tasks such as perception or recognition through different neural pathways. Such a capacity, I believe, is essential to the exercise of free will. In cases of self-formation (SFAs), agents are simultaneously trying to resolve plural and competing cognitive tasks. They are, as we say, of two minds. Yet they are not two separate persons. They are not dissociated from either task. The business-woman who wants to go back to help the victim is the same ambitious woman who wants to go to her meeting and make a sale. She is torn inside by different visions of who she is and what she wants to be, as we all are from time to time. But this is the kind of complexity needed for genuine self-formation and free will. And when she succeeds in doing one of the things she is trying to do, she will endorse that as her resolution of the conflict in her will, voluntarily and intentionally, not by accident or mistake.

6 Responsibility, Luck and Chance

You may find all this interesting and yet still find it hard to shake the intuition that if choices are undetermined, they *must* happen merely by chance – and so must be "random," "capricious," "uncontrolled," "irrational," and all the other things usually charged. Such intuitions are deeply ingrained. But if we are ever going to understand free will, I think we must break old habits of thought supporting such intuitions and learn to think in new ways.

The first step is to question the intuitive connection in people's minds between "indeterminism's being involved in something" and "its happening merely as a matter of chance or luck." 'Chance' and 'luck' are terms of ordinary language that carry the meaning of "its being out of my control." So using them already begs certain questions. Whereas 'indeterminism' is a technical term that merely precludes *deterministic* causation, though not causation altogether. Indeterminism is consistent with non-deterministic or probabilistic causation, where the outcome is not inevitable. It is therefore a mistake (alas, one of the most common in debates about free will) to assume that 'undetermined' means 'uncaused'.

Here is another source of misunderstanding. Since the outcome of the business-woman's effort (the choice) is undetermined up to the last minute, we may have the image of her first making an effort to overcome the temptation to go on to her meeting and then at the last instant "chance takes over" and decides the issue for her. But this is a mistaken image. On the view just presented, one cannot separate the indeterminism and the effort of will, so that *first* the effort occurs *followed* by chance or luck (or vice versa). One must think of the effort and the indeterminism as fused; the effort *is* indeterminate and the indeterminism is a property of the effort, not something separate that occurs after or before the effort. The fact that the effort has this property of being indeterminate does not make it any less the woman's *effort*. The complex recurrent neural network that realizes the effort in the brain is circulating impulses in feedback loops and there is some indeterminacy in these circulating impulses. But the whole process is her effort of will and it persists right up to the moment when the choice is made. There is no point at which the effort stops and chance "takes over." She chooses as a result of the effort, even though she might have failed. Similarly, the husband breaks the table as a result of his effort, even though he might have failed because of the indeterminacy. (That is why his excuse, "Chance broke the table, not me" is so lame.)[15]

Just as expressions like "she chose *by* chance" can mislead us in such contexts, so can expressions like "She got lucky." Recall that, with the assassin and husband, one might say "They got lucky" in killing the prime minister and breaking the table because their actions were undetermined. Yet they were responsible. So ask yourself this question: why does the inference "he got lucky, *so he was not responsible*" fail in the cases of the husband and the assassin? The first part of an answer has to do with the point made earlier that 'luck', like 'chance', has question-begging implications in ordinary language that are not necessarily implications of 'indeterminism' (which implies only the absence of deterministic causation). The core meaning of 'he got lucky' in the assassin and husband cases, which *is* implied by indeterminism, is that "he succeeded *despite the probability or chance of failure*"; and this core meaning does not imply lack of responsibility, *if he succeeds.*

If 'he got lucky' had other meanings in these cases that are often associated with 'luck' and 'chance' in ordinary usage (for example, the outcome was not his doing, or occurred by *mere* chance, or he was not responsible for it), the inference would not fail for the husband and assassin, as it clearly does. But the point is that these further meanings of 'luck' and 'chance' do not follow *from the mere presence of indeterminism*. The second reason why the inference "he got lucky, so he was not responsible" fails for the assassin and the husband is that *what* they succeeded in doing was what they were *trying* and *wanting* to do all along (kill the minister and break the table respectively). The third reason is that *when* they succeeded, their reaction was not "Oh dear, that was a mistake, an accident – something that *happened* to me, not something I *did*." Rather they *endorsed* the outcomes as something they were trying and wanting to do all along, knowingly and purposefully, not by mistake or accident.

But these conditions are satisfied in the businesswoman's case as well, *either way* she chooses. If she succeeds in choosing to return to help the victim (or in choosing to go on to her meeting) (i) she will have "succeeded *despite the probability or chance of failure*," (ii) she will have succeeded in doing what she was *trying* and *wanting* to do all along (she wanted both outcomes very much, but for different reasons, and was trying to make those reasons prevail in both cases), and (iii) when she succeeded (in choosing to return to help) her reaction was not "Oh dear, that was a mistake, an accident – something that happened to me, not something I did." Rather, she *endorsed* the outcome as something she was trying and wanting to do all along; she recognized it as her resolution of the conflict in her will. And if she had chosen to go on to her meeting she would have endorsed that outcome, recognizing it as her resolution of the conflict in her will.

But isn't it the case that the presence of indeterminism at least *diminishes* the control persons have over their choices and actions? Is it not the case that the assassin's control over whether the prime minister is killed (his ability to realize his purposes or what he is trying to do) is lessened by the undetermined impulses in his arm – and so also for the husband and his breaking the table? This limitation seems to be connected with a problem mentioned earlier that is often noted by critics of libertarian freedom – the problem that indeterminism, wherever it occurs, seems to be a *hindrance* or *obstacle* to our realizing our purposes and hence an obstacle to, rather than an *enhancement* of, our freedom.

There is something to this charge. But I think what is true in it reveals something important about free will. We should concede that indeterminism, wherever it occurs, *does* diminish control over what we are trying to do and *is* a hindrance or obstacle to the realization of our purposes. But recall that in the case of the businesswoman (and SFAs generally), the indeterminism that is admittedly diminishing her control over one thing she is trying to do (the moral act of helping the victim) *is coming from her own will* – the indeterminism is present because of her competing desire and effort to do the opposite (go to her business meeting). And the indeterminism that is diminishing her control over the other thing she is trying to do (act selfishly and go to her meeting) is likewise present because of her desire and effort to do the opposite (be a moral person and act on moral reasons). So, in each case, the indeterminism *is* functioning as a hindrance or obstacle to her realizing one of her purposes – a hindrance or obstacle in the form of resistance within her will which has to be overcome by effort.

If there were no such hindrance – if there were no resistance in her will – she would indeed in a sense have "complete control" over one of her options. There would no competing motives that would stand in the way of her choosing it. But then also she would not be free rationally and voluntarily to choose the other option because she would have no good competing reasons to do so. Thus, by *being* a hindrance to the realization of some of our purposes, indeterminism paradoxically opens up the genuine possibility of pursuing other purposes – of choosing or doing *otherwise* in accordance with, rather than against, our wills (voluntarily) and reasons (rationally). To be genuinely self-forming agents (creators of ourselves) – to have free will – there must at times in life be obstacles and hindrances in our wills of this sort that we must overcome.

Let me conclude with one final objection to this incompatibilist account of free will that is perhaps the most telling and has not yet been discussed. Even if one granted that persons, such as the businesswoman, could make genuine self-forming choices that were undetermined, isn't their something to the charge that such choices would be *arbitrary*? A residual arbitrariness seems to remain in all self-forming choices since the agents cannot in principle have sufficient or overriding *prior* reasons for making one option and one set of reasons prevail over the other.

There is some truth to this charge as well, but again I think it is a truth that tells us something important about free will. It tells us that every undetermined self-forming free choice is the initiation of what I have elsewhere called a "value experiment" whose justification lies in the future and is not fully explained by past reasons. In making such a choice, we say, in effect, "Let's try this. It is not required by my past, but it is consistent with my past and is one branching pathway in the garden of forking paths my life can now meaningfully take. Whether it is the right choice, only time will tell. Meanwhile, I am willing to take responsibility for it one way or the other" (Kane 1996: 145–6).

It is worth noting that the term 'arbitrary' comes from the Latin *arbitrium*, which means "judgment" – as in *liberum arbitrium voluntatis*, "free judgment of the will" (the medieval philosophers' designation for free will). Imagine a writer in the middle of a novel. The novel's heroine faces a crisis and the writer has not yet developed her character in sufficient detail to say exactly how she will act. The author makes a "judgment" about this that is not determined by the heroine's already formed past which does not give unique direction. In this sense, the judgment (*arbitrium*) of how she will react is "arbitrary," but not entirely so. It had input from the heroine's fictional past and in turn gave input to her projected future. In a similar way, agents who exercise free will are both authors of and characters in their own stories all at once. By virtue of "self-forming" judgments of the will (*arbitria voluntatis*) (SFAs), they are "arbiters" of their own lives, "making themselves" out of a past that, if they are truly free, does not limit their future pathways to a single one.

Suppose we were to say to such actors: "But look, you didn't have sufficient or *conclusive* prior reasons for choosing as you did, since you also had viable reasons for choosing the other way." They might reply: "True enough. But I did have *good* reasons for choosing as I did, which I'm willing to stand by *and take responsibility for.* If these reasons were not sufficient or conclusive reasons, that's because, like the heroine of the novel, I was not a fully formed person before I chose (and still am not, for that matter). Like the author of the novel, I am in the process of writing an unfinished story and forming an unfinished character who, in my case, is myself." That, I believe, is what free will is all about.

Notes

1   Arguments for and against compatibilism are discussed by Kadri Vihvelin in chapter 7.2 of this volume, "Compatibilism, Incompatibilism, and Impossibilism."

2   I have formulated the steps of the argument in my own terms, which are somewhat different from those of van Inwagen, though I believe they retain the spirit and essential steps of the argument.

3   See chapter 7.2 for further discussion of compatibilist interpretations of this kind.

4   Some of these debates about the meanings of 'can' and 'power' are discussed in chapter 7.2. For additional discussion of them, see the Suggested Further Reading at the end of this chapter.

5   This condition UR is discussed at length in my book *The Significance of Free Will* (1996: chs. 3, 5, and 7), where it plays an important role in my account of free will.

6   One might wonder why these character-forming actions or self-forming actions (SFAs) that are required at some time in the agent's life history by UR must be such that the agent "could have done otherwise." In other words, why must they satisfy AP? The two paragraphs that follow hint at why this must be so, but they do not give the full argument. A capsule version of the full argument – which appears in Kane (1996: ch. 7, and 2000)

– goes like this: UR requires that we must be responsible by virtue of our voluntary actions for anything that is a sufficient cause or motive for our acting as we do. We have a sufficient motive for doing something when our will is "set one way" on doing it before and when we act. For example, if an assassin is aiming a high-powered rifle at the prime minister intending to kill him, the assassin's will is set one way on (he has a sufficient motive for) killing his target. He might do something else than kill the prime minister. For example, he might miss his target or kill a bystander. But these other things will be done only by accident or mistake, unintentionally or unwillingly. Thus, his having a sufficient motive means that among the available things he might do, only one of them (killing the prime minister) would be voluntary and intentional. All the others would be unintentional or accidental. But UR says that if you have a sufficient motive for doing something in this sense – if your will is set one way on doing it, rather than doing anything else available to you – then to be ultimately responsible for your *will*, you must be to some degree responsible by virtue of past voluntary acts for your will's being set the way it is or for having the sufficient motive you do. This requirement is important because when we look at the responsibility of agents such as the assassin, we look to their motives and intentions. Those motives and intentions are the source of the assassin's guilt, whether he succeeds in killing the prime minister or fails and kills a bystander instead. So we need to know whether he (rather than someone or something else) is responsible for his will's being set one way on killing. But then we must look at those earlier voluntary acts by which he set his present will. And if it should turn out that his will was already set one way (had sufficient motives) when he performed those earlier voluntary actions by which he set his present will, then UR would require that he must have been responsible by virtue of still earlier voluntary actions for his will being set the way it was at the earlier time, and so on backwards indefinitely. We have a regress on our hands that can only be stopped by supposing that *some* actions in the agent's past lacked *sufficient* motives (as well as sufficient causes). Actions lacking sufficient motives would be actions in which the agents' wills were not already set one way before they performed the actions. Rather, the agents would set their wills voluntarily and intentionally *in one way or in another* in the performance of these "will-setting" actions themselves. But this means that, in performing such "will setting" actions, the agents would be able to act voluntarily and intentionally in *more than one way*, rather than only in one way voluntarily and intentionally, and in other ways merely by accident or mistake; and so these actions would satisfy AP. The agents could perform them and could do otherwise (either way voluntarily and intentionally). These will-setting actions are the SFAs required by UR. The idea is that we need to be able to perform such will-setting acts at *some* times in our life histories, if *we* are ever to be ultimately responsible for our wills' being set the way they are.

7   For example, Compton (1935: ch. 4), and Eccles (1970: ch. 5).

8   For discussion and defense of this "agent-causal" view, see the Suggested Further Reading at the end of this chapter.

9   The view I present in the following sections is defended in greater detail in Kane (1996: chs. 7–10).

10 Readable introductions for the non-specialist about the role of neural networks (including recurrent networks) in cognitive processing include Churchland (1996) and Spitzer (1999).

11 See, e.g. Skarda and Freeman (1987). Walter (2001: Part III) summarizes evidence that chaos plays a significant role in mental processing, though he takes a compatibilist view of free will. As Walter points out, it is a well-known fact that chaotic behavior, though unpredictable, is not itself indeterministic and is quite consistent with determinism. So chaos *alone* will not give us the genuine indeterminism we need for free will. But the

suggestion here is that some combination of chaos and quantum physics might provide the indeterminism needed for incompatibilist free will: Chaos in the brain might in certain circumstances magnify or amplify minute quantum indeterminacies involved in the timings of firings of individual neurons so that slight differences in when these neurons fire would have significant large-scale indeterministic effects on neural processing.

12 Of course there would have to *be* some significant quantum indeterminacy in the chemical activity of individual neurons that would be capable of being so chaotically amplified; and we do not know that such quantum indeterminacy is available. It is a matter for science to determine. But remember that the problem we are addressing is this: *If there was some significant indeterminism in the brain*, would it amount to just chance or could we make use of it to give a coherent incompatibilist account of free will? We cannot settle the empirical question of whether or not there is significant indeterminism in the brain, but we can try to say what might be done with the indeterminism to make sense of free will, *if* it was there.

13 See Kane (1996: ch. 8), where I show in greater detail that each of these conditions can be satisfied by SFAs.

14 Ibid.

15 We tend to think that if chance is involved in the deliberative process, chance must be the *cause* of the choice. But this does not follow if the role of indeterminism or chance in the deliberative process is to *hinder* the agents' efforts to make either of the competing choices they may want to make. This follows from a general point about probabilistic causation. A vaccination may hinder or lower the probability that I will get a certain disease, so it is causally relevant to the outcome. But if I get the disease despite it, the *vaccination* is a not a *cause* of my getting the disease, though it was causally relevant. The causes of my getting the disease are those causal factors (such as the infecting virus) that significantly *raised* the probability of its occurrence. Likewise, in the case of the choice the businesswoman makes (say, the moral choice), its causes are those factors that significantly raised the probability of her making *that* choice rather than the other, such as her *reasons* and motives for making the moral choice and her *effort* to overcome the temptation to make the opposing self-interested choice. This explains why the husband's excuse is so lame: "Chance broke the table, not me," he said. But while chance was involved, it was not the cause of the table's breaking. The cause was the husband's effort to break the table by swinging his arm as hard as he could, an act that significantly raised the probability that the table would break. The chance merely made it uncertain whether he would succeed.

References

Aristotle. 1915. *Nichomachean Ethics*. Vol. 9 of *The Works of Aristotle*, ed. W. D. Ross (London: Oxford University Press).

Churchland, P. M. 1996. *The Engine of Reason, the Seat of the Soul* (Cambridge MA: MIT Press).

Compton, A. H. 1935. *The Freedom of Man* (New Haven, CT: Yale University Press).

Dennett, D. 1984. *Elbow Room* (Cambridge MA: MIT Press).

Eccles, J. 1970. *Facing Reality* (New York: Springer-Verlag).

Hume, D. 1975 [1748]. *Enquiry Concerning Human Understanding* (Oxford: Oxford University Press).

James, W. 1956. "The Dilemma of Determinism," in *The Will to Believe and Other Essays in Popular Philosophy* (New York: Dover).

Kane, R. 1996. *The Significance of Free Will* (Oxford: Oxford University Press).

—. 2000. "The Dual Regress of Free Will," in *Philosophical Perspectives 14* (Oxford: Blackwell), pp. 57–80.

Kant, I. 1956 [1788]. *The Critique of Practical Reason*, trans. L. W. Beck (Indianapolis, IN: Bobbs-Merrill).

—. 1958. *Critique of Pure Reason* (London: Macmillan).

Skarda, C., and Freeman, W. 1987. "How Do Brains Make Chaos in Order to Make Sense of the World?" *Behavioral and Brain Sciences* 10: 161–95.

Spitzer, M. 1999. *The Mind Within the Net* (Cambridge MA: MIT Press, 1999).

van Inwagen, P. 1983. *An Essay on Free Will* (Oxford: Clarendon Press).

Walter, H. 2001. *Neurophilosophy of Free Will* (Cambridge MA: MIT Press).

Suggested further reading

The following collections of essays contain further readings on the issues about free will and incompatibilism discussed in this chapter:

Ekstrom, Laura, ed. 2001. *Agency and Responsibility: Essays on the Metaphysics of Freedom* (Boulder CO: Westview Press).

Kane, Robert, ed. 2002. *Free Will* (Oxford: Blackwell Publishers).

O'Connor, Timothy, ed. 1995. *Agents, Causes and Events*: *Essays on Free Will and Indeterminism* (Oxford: Oxford University Press).

Watson, Gary, ed. 2003. *Free Will* (Oxford: Oxford University Press).

For more advanced discussion of the issues, see the essays in Robert Kane, ed., *The Oxford Handbook of Free Will* (Oxford: Oxford University Press, 2002).

Compatibilism, Incompatibilism, and Impossibilism

Kadri Vihvelin

Debates that claim to be about the free will/determinism problem often aren't. Incompatibilism is usually understood as the claim that the truth of determinism entails the non-existence of free will: that there is no possible world where determinism is true and someone has free will. Compatibilism is the claim that the truth of determinism is compatible with the existence of free will: that there are possible worlds where determinism is true and someone has free will. So one would expect discussions of the free will/determinism problem to focus on determinism (and related questions about the metaphysics of laws, causation, and counterfactuals) and arguments about the relevance (or lack of relevance) of determinism to free will. But the literature is mostly preoccupied with other questions.

Perhaps the main reason for this is that incompatibilists and compatibilists tend, for the most part, to be free will believers, and therefore are quite properly concerned with more than just showing that free will is or isn't compatible with determinism. They also want to show that we in fact have (or at least might have) free will and they believe that they can show this only by providing an *analysis* of free will. And of course providing a philosophical analysis of anything is notoriously difficult. And in doing this, the energies of both sides get diverted away from the debate between them and towards a different debate, a debate with someone I will call the impossibilist.[1]

The impossibilist is someone who thinks that it is *metaphysically impossible* for us to have free will, either because she thinks that our concept of free will is incoherent or because she thinks that free will is incompatible with some necessarily true proposition. Neither the compatibilist nor the incompatibilist is an impossibilist (see below, for explanation), but some of the arguments that are presented as arguments for incompatibilism turn out, on closer inspection, to be arguments for impossibilism.

Another reason for the paucity of debate about determinism is that there are other apparent threats to free will which, though logically independent of determinism, tend to be associated with determinism – physicalism and the view that we are part of the natural order of things, subject without exception to the same kind of laws (deterministic or probabilistic) that govern everything else in the universe. Compatibilists typically think of themselves in the business of defending, not just the compatibility of free will with determinism, but also the compatibility of free will with physicalism and naturalism. Sometimes compatibilists assume that an incompatibilist *must* be someone who believes that free will is incompatible with physicalism and naturalism as well as with determinism. This is a mistake, but of course incompatibilists have traditionally embraced dualism and the doctrine of agent-causation (the view that we cause our actions in something like the way that God is supposed to cause things – by being "prime movers unmoved"). And arguments that are supposed to be arguments for incompatibilism often trade on intuitions that concern physicalism or naturalism rather than determinism; for instance, arguments that try to convince us that if determinism were true, we would not be different, in any relevant way, from *merely physical or merely mechanical* things – wind-up toys, simple robots, and so on.

My concern in this chapter is *only* with the free will/determinism problem; that is, only with the debate between the incompatibilist and the compatibilist. I will be defending compatibilism. But before I can do so, it is important to understand exactly what is at stake in this debate.

1 Defining the Problem

Let's begin with some definitions that are now standard in the literature. Determinism is a contingent and empirical claim: that the total state of the world at any time, together with all the laws, entails a unique future. Indeterminism is the negation of determinism. There is some dispute about the ways in which indeterminism might be true. Most people agree that indeterminism would be true if the fundamental laws turned out to be probabilistic; some people think that this is in fact the case. More controversially, some people think that the laws are somehow limited in scope, so they don't apply to some kinds of things (e.g. the non-physical minds of human beings) or they don't apply to all of the behaviors of some of the things (e.g. the freely willed actions of human beings). And perhaps there are other ways in which indeterminism might turn out to be true. These distinctions are important for incompatibilists, but do not matter for my purposes.

Since indeterminism is the negation of determinism, and determinism is a contingent thesis, we can divide the set of possible worlds into two non-overlapping subsets: worlds where determinism is true and worlds where indeterminism is true. Let's define the free will thesis as the claim that at least one human-like (non-godlike) creature has free will. We won't assume that the free will thesis is true, or even that it is possibly true.

We can now explain the difference between impossibilism, incompatibilism, and compatibilism.

The impossibilist says that free will is metaphysically impossible (or, perhaps, that it is metaphysically impossible for any non-godlike creature) and therefore the free will thesis is not only false, but *necessarily false*. That is, the impossibilist says that

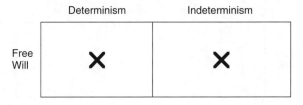

Figure 1   Impossibilism

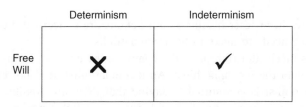

Figure 2   Incompatiblism

the free will thesis is false regardless of whether determinism is true or false, regardless of whether physicalism is true or false, and regardless of whether any other *contingent* claim about the world is true or false.

The incompatibilist may be a libertarian, who believes that determinism is in fact false, in the right kind of way, and that we have free will, or she may be a hard determinist, who believes that determinism is in fact true and so we don't have free will. However, she is not an impossibilist because she believes that the truth or falsity of determinism is *relevant* to the question of whether we have free will. She believes that there are possible worlds where human-like creatures have free will; that is, she believes that the free will thesis is at least *possibly true*. But she believes that the free will thesis and determinism *cannot* both be true. She believes that the *only* free will worlds are indeterministic worlds.

The compatibilist is someone who believes that the free will thesis and determinism can both be true; that is, she believes that the set of free will worlds is non-empty and includes deterministic worlds.

Figures 1–3 illustrate the fundamental differences between these three positions. If we understand each figure to circumscribe possible worlds, the crosses and checks represent the defining claims of each position. A cross asserts that the set of worlds is empty, a check that it is non-empty. The unfilled boxes are ones about which the position is neutral. The impossibilist's claims are represented by figure 1; the incompatibilist's claims are represented by figure 2.

The compatibilist and the incompatibilist disagree with the impossibilist and agree with one another that there are worlds where human-like creatures have free will. They disagree with one another about whether determinism is true at any of those worlds. The compatibilist's claims are represented by figure 3.

There have been compatibilists who have claimed more than this. R. E. Hobart (1934) famously argued that free will is not only compatible with determinism but

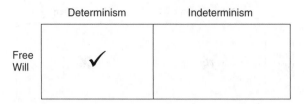

	Determinism	Indeterminism
Free Will	✓	

Figure 3 Compatibilism

positively requires it, at least insofar as our actions are concerned. But this claim is stronger than one needs to make to be a compatibilist.

The diagrams nicely illustrate how the compatibilist has less of an argumentative burden to bear than the incompatibilist. An incompatibilist need not be a libertarian but the incompatibilist is committed to saying that there are possible worlds where creatures more or less like us have free will. The compatibilist agrees with all that. It is the incompatibilist who must show something else; she must provide some argument that the worlds with free will all lie on the indeterministic side of the line.

2 Rules of Debate

Remember that there are objections to free will based on contingent claims independent of determinism (physicalism, naturalism) and there are arguments which claim that free will is metaphysically impossible. Because of this, the only way to provide a fully satisfactory defense of free will is to provide a positive account of what free will is. This is what compatibilists have traditionally tried to do. I agree that every compatibilist should have an account of free will (as should every incompatibilist). There is no other way of meeting the challenge of the impossibilist. However, debating the virtues of rival accounts of free will is not what the incompatibilist/compatibilist debate should be about.

The incompatibilist and compatibilist agree that free will is possible. They might even agree about a long list of necessary conditions for having free will. They might agree, for instance, that free will entails the ability to deliberate and make decisions on the basis of reasons, the ability to remember the past and to anticipate the future, the ability to learn from past experience and to use what one has learned as the basis of one's future deliberation and decision-making, the ability to "step back" from one's own character and to ask questions like "Is this the kind of person I really want to be?" And so on. The incompatibilist and compatibilist might even agree that many of the necessary conditions of free will are compatible with determinism. What they disagree about is whether *indeterminism* is a necessary condition. The incompatibilist needs an argument for this, an argument that has the basic structure:

(1)   Free will entails X.
(2)   X entails indeterminism.
(3)   Therefore free will entails indeterminism.

Kadri Vihvelin

Since the incompatibilist is not an impossibilist, X must be something that is metaphysically possible.

My defense of compatibilism will consist of a critique of the most important and influential arguments for incompatibilism. I will be arguing that the arguments either fail or turn out to be arguments for impossibilism. In order to lay the groundwork, let's begin by looking at one kind of impossibilist argument.

3 Fatalism

Impossibilism is the claim that there is no metaphysically possible world where any *non-godlike being* has free will. By "non-godlike" I mean someone who is not omniscient, omnipotent, infallible, infinite, the cause of its own existence, and so on.

There are two very different ways of arguing for impossibilism. The first kind of argument claims that our concept of free will is incoherent or entails something that cannot be satisfied by any non-godlike being. We will look at some examples of this kind of argument in the next section. The second kind of impossibilist argument claims that free will is incompatible with some necessarily true proposition or propositions. The fatalist's arguments fall into this category.

The fatalist is someone who argues, on the basis of claims about truth and time, to the conclusion that we don't have free will. What fatalist arguments have in common is a thesis about truth that I will call "Realism about the Future" (RF). RF says that the future is no less real than the past or present in this respect: there are detailed and specific truths about the future, including truths about our future actions. RF says that there are truths about what you will do in the future even if determinism is false and even if there is no way of knowing, ahead of time, what you will do. The fatalist accepts RF and argues from RF to the conclusion that we have no free will. The fatalist's arguments have nothing to do with the truth or falsity of determinism or any other contingent claim about the world; they are based only on RF together with other alleged necessary truths.

Some fatalist arguments are known to be invalid. For instance:

> It's either true that I will do X tomorrow or it's true that I won't do X tomorrow. Suppose it's true that I will do X tomorrow. Necessarily, if it's true that I will do X tomorrow, then I will do X tomorrow. (It would be a contradiction if it were true that I will do X tomorrow and I don't do X tomorrow.) Therefore, I *must* do X tomorrow. I have free will only if don't *have* to do what I do; that is, only if I can do otherwise. Therefore, I have no free will.

This argument, sometimes known as 'the fatalist fallacy', makes the mistake of reasoning from the necessity of a conditional to a claim of unconditional necessity. The fatalist's invalid argument has the form:

(1) P
(2) Necessarily, if P then Q.
(3) Therefore, it's necessary that Q. (Q must be the case; Q has to be the case; it cannot be otherwise than Q.)

An example:

(1) Jones raises his left hand.
(2) Necessarily, if Jones raises his left hand then Jones raises his hand.
(3) Therefore, it's necessary that Jones raises his hand. (Jones must raise his hand; Jones has to raise his hand; Jones cannot do otherwise.)

But not all fatalist arguments are invalid. For instance:

(1) I have free will only if I can do otherwise.
(2) I can do otherwise only if I can do otherwise given all the facts. (That is, only if my doing otherwise is *compossible with all the facts*.)
(3) All the facts include facts about the future, including facts about what I will do.
(4) Therefore I cannot do anything other than what I will actually do.
(5) Therefore I have no free will.

Note that here the fatalist's conclusion follows, not from RF alone – premise (3) – but from RF together with the fatalist's claim about what we mean, or should mean, when we say "I can do otherwise." If we want to deny the fatalist's conclusion while retaining RF, we must reject the fatalist's claim – premise (2) of the argument – that "I can do X" entails that I can do X, given *all the facts*.

Here's one more example of a fatalist argument:

(1) I have no control over the past.
(2) I have no control over the past because the past is "fixed" and "settled" in the following sense: there now exists a set of true propositions that completely describes the past.
(3) RF is true.
(4) Therefore, the future is "fixed" and "settled" in exactly the same sense that the past is: there now exists a set of true propositions that completely describes the future.
(5) Therefore I have no control over the future.
(6) I have free will only if I have at least some control over the future.
(7) Therefore I have no free will.

This argument draws its intuitive appeal from our commonsense way of thinking about truth and time.

We are all familiar with the idea that the past is "fixed" and not in our control. "What's done can't be undone." "There's no use crying over spilled milk." By contrast, we think that the future is at least partly "open," not "fixed," in our control, and up to us. We believe that we have free will with respect to the future, not with respect to the past.

There is an explanation for this contrast between our beliefs about the past and the future, an explanation that has to do with the fact that the direction of causation always runs from past to future, not future to past. Our choices and actions cause future events; they never cause past events. What we do makes a difference to the future; we cause the future to be what it would not have been had we not done what we did. But what we do makes no difference to the past; we don't cause the past to be what it would not have been had we acted differently.

The fatalist rejects this explanation. The fatalist says that we have no control over the past *because* there now exists a set of true propositions about everything that happened in the past – premise (2) of the argument. The fatalist thinks that we have the false belief that we have control over the future *because* we reject RF and therefore have the false belief that there are no truths about what we will do in the future. But we are wrong, says the fatalist. RF is true and it follows that there now exists a set of true propositions that completely describes the future – premise (4). Given this, *and given premise (2)*, it follows that I have no control over the future *for the same reason that I have no control over the past*. However, if we reject premise (2), the conclusion does not follow.

Most philosophers think that fatalist arguments are bad arguments because they conflate truth with necessity (either metaphysical necessity or the kind of relativized necessity we express when we say things like "I have no control over the past"). I agree, but this is not my point. Even if the fatalist had a good argument, it would be an argument for impossibilism, not incompatibilism. Neither determinism nor RF is part of our commonsense view, and commonsense tends to turn fatalist when forced to take seriously the idea that there are truths about our future actions. But if determinism is true, then there are truths about *all* our future actions. Given this, we need to be on guard, when looking at arguments for incompatibilism, to make sure that they are not fatalist arguments in disguise. And we must be very careful to make sure that the intuitions appealed to are not the same intuitions that support fatalism.

Fatalism is only one way of being an impossibilist. In the next section we will look at an argument that's usually thought to be an argument for incompatibilism. We will discover that it is in fact an argument for impossibilism.

4 The Clarence Darrow Argument

What has this boy to do with it? He was not his own father; he was not his own mother; he was not his own grandparents. All of this was handed to him. He did not surround himself with governesses and wealth. He did not make himself. And yet he is to be compelled to pay. (Darrow 1924)

The argument represented by this quote from Clarence Darrow is widely regarded as an argument for incompatibilism. More specifically, it is regarded as an argument for hard determinism – the thesis that determinism is true and *because of this* we lack free will (in the sense necessary to justify blame and punishment). But how are we supposed to understand the argument?

Here's one way:

(1) We have free will only if we make our selves – that is, only if we cause ourselves to be the kind of persons we are.
(2) We don't make our selves.
(3) Therefore we don't have free will.

But if we understand the argument in this way, then the second premise is false, even if determinism is true. We do make our selves, at least in the sense in which we make other things: we plant gardens, cook dinners, build boats, write books, and, over the course of our lives, we reinvent, recreate, and otherwise "make something of ourselves." We make ourselves by making choices and performing actions which include, among their consequences, changes in our selves. Insofar as we have the ability to make choices, and the ability to predict the consequences of these choices, and the ability to predict how these consequences will affect and change us, we have control over the kind of persons we turn out to be.

Second try:

(1) We have free will only if we are *entirely* self-made selves – that is, only if we have *complete control* over the kind of persons we are.
(2) We are not entirely self-made selves.
(3) Therefore we don't have free will.

In this reconstruction of the Darrow Argument, the second premise is true. But this is no longer an argument for hard determinism; it is an argument for impossibilism. The truth of the second premise has nothing to do with determinism; no human being (or any non-godlike being) is, or can be, an entirely self-made self. We all have to start from the raw materials given to us by our genes and early childhood environment; we make choices from a range of alternatives often fixed by circumstances outside our control; the causal upshots of our actions are often neither predictable nor in our control. To the extent that we succeed in remaking the self that was "handed" to us, this is only partly due to our efforts and abilities; luck *always* plays a role.[2]

Darrow's Argument counts as an argument for hard determinism, as opposed to impossibilism, only if we can find a way to understand his self-making requirement according to which selves cannot be self-made in deterministic worlds, but *can* be self-made in indeterministic worlds. If determinism is true, then the causes of our actions can always be traced back to earlier events and factors over which we had no control. If determinism is false, on the other hand, then it seems possible that some of our actions (our decisions, choices, and other mental acts) are caused by us, *and by nothing outside us*. This suggests the following way of understanding Darrrow's main premise. In order to have the kind of free will that's necessary for moral responsibility, we must have *ultimate* control over our selves in the following sense: we must be the causal initiators (first causes, "Prime Movers Unmoved") of the choices which cause us to be the adult selves we eventually are. On this reading, the argument goes like this:

(1) We have free will only if we are ultimately self-made selves – that is, only if *we* have *ultimate control* over the kind of person we are.
(2) We don't have ultimate control over the kind of persons we are.
(3) Therefore we don't have free will.

If determinism is true, the second premise is true. So the argument succeeds in showing that the kind of free will specified by premise (1) does not exist at any deterministic world.

To succeed as an argument for incompatibilism (as opposed to impossibilism), however, there must be indeterministic worlds where we (or other non-godlike creatures) have the kind of free will specified by premise (1). But there are no such worlds.

If it were possible to remake ourselves from scratch, in a way that gives *us* ultimate control over our later selves, it would be by way of reason. Imagine the most favorable scenario for doing this; suppose that we are literally presented with different types of characters, sets of values, and so on, and given a magic pill which will make us into whatever kind of person we want to be. How do we choose? We might flip a coin, but if we do this, then *we* are not the cause of our new persona, let alone the ultimate cause. If we want to be the cause of our new self, then we must choose on the basis of what we already are – our reasons, values, principles, together with our ability to deliberate, our ability critically to evaluate our own reasons, and so on. But this counts as ultimate (as opposed to garden-variety) self-making only if *we* caused ourselves to have the reasons (values, etc.) we already have. And this (on pain of infinite regress) is impossible. Our reasons (values, etc.) were ultimately just "handed" to us – it makes no difference whether the handing was by deterministic causation, chancy causation, or whether they popped into existence *ex nihilo*.

Even if determinism is false, we do not and *cannot* make our selves in the way that this reading of Darrow's Argument requires – by causing ourselves to have reasons for *all* our choices and reasons for *all* our reasons.

Historically, there have been two different ways of arguing for incompatibilism. One kind of argument is based on the idea that free will requires that we have ultimate control over our actions and thereby our selves. I have just argued that this kind of argument is an argument for impossibilism. The other kind of argument is based on the idea that free will requires that we have real (not just epistemic) options, that when we make a choice, we really have a choice, that what we actually do is not the only thing we can do.

There may be a link between the two arguments, insofar as someone might argue that we have ultimate control over our actions and thereby our selves only if we can do otherwise, and this entails indeterminism. But we don't need to assume this link. Our ordinary notion of free will includes the idea that we both make and *have* choices, that we have options, that we can do otherwise. If the incompatibilist can show that having options requires indeterminism, this would count as victory for the incompatibilist.

Some would deny this. They would say that the kind of free will that really matters – the kind that's necessary for moral responsibility – doesn't require options or "alternative possibilities," as they are sometimes called in the literature. I think this view mistaken. I am happy to grant that free will requires options. What's at issue is whether options require indeterminism.

Let's look at some arguments for the claim that determinism deprives us of options.

5 The Forking Paths Argument

(1) We have free will only if we can at least sometimes do otherwise.
(2) We can do otherwise only if choosing between actions is like choosing between forking paths: that is, only if more than one action is a lawful continuation of the actual past.

(3) If determinism is true, then only one action is a lawful continuation of the actual past.

(4) Therefore, if determinism is true, we can never do otherwise.

(5) Therefore, if determinism is true, we don't have free will.

Unlike the Clarence Darrow Argument, this is an argument for incompatibilism (as opposed to impossibilism).[3] The problem is that it's not much of an argument. Premise (2), once it is stripped of the forking paths metaphor, is an *assertion* of the incompatibilist thesis that we can do otherwise only at possible worlds where determinism is false.

Do we have any reasons independent of incompatibilism to accept premise (2)?

It's often claimed that our commonsense beliefs about what we can and cannot do support incompatibilism and that the incompatibilist sense of 'can' is just our ordinary sense and therefore does not need any further support or argument. Let's take a look at this claim.

Suppose that you have the ability to play the piano (you've taken lessons, you know how to play, your fingers are not broken or paralyzed), and you have the opportunity to do so, and you know you have the opportunity to do so; you are visiting me, and there is a piano in the living room where we are sitting. You have no reason to play the piano, and you don't take yourself to have any reason to play; however, if you had different reasons (if you wanted to show me how a tune goes, for instance, or if I asked you), you would play. Let's stipulate that you are not a victim of brain control, post-hypnotic suggestion, severe depression, or some other pathology that prevents you from forming the intention to play the piano or from acting on your intention. Let's also stipulate that there is no one standing behind the scenes ready to prevent you from playing the piano should you show any signs of wanting, intending, or trying to do so. Suppose, in other words, that this is a straight-forward ordinary case in which you fail to play the piano only because you prefer not to do so. This looks like a case where you *can play the piano*, and most people would agree. But premise (2) says that the facts, as described, do not suffice for the truth of the claim that you can play the piano. You can play the piano only if *more than this is true*; only if your action of playing the piano is a lawful continuation of past history. And the incompatibilist who defends premise (2) by appealing to our commonsense beliefs must claim that you have this additional belief if you believe that you can play the piano.

I don't think the incompatibilist's claim is very plausible. There is a much simpler explanation of what people believe, when they believe that they can play the piano in a situation like the one described above: They believe something they might express by saying: "I've got the ability to play the piano and there's a piano here and nothing stops me from playing it." Or: "I've got what it takes and the circumstances are right." Or, to put it yet another way, they believe that they have the ability and the opportunity to play the piano.

Of course, it is open to the incompatibilist to argue that this commonsense belief entails the falsity of determinism; that is, to argue that *if determinism is true, then we never have the ability to do anything we fail to do*, or to argue that *if determinism is true, then something always prevents us from doing anything we fail to do*. My

Kadri Vihvelin

point is that this alleged entailment is something that needs to be defended by argument; it cannot be simply "read off" our commonsense beliefs.

Is there any other way that the incompatibilist might argue that commonsense supports premise (2)? Well, she might appeal to another kind of case, a case that has sometimes been thought to be a paradigmatic example of the exercise of free will. Sometimes we are faced with a decision between possible actions in a case where we have equally strong or perhaps incommensurable reasons for doing each of the alternative actions. Perhaps we have two appealing job offers. Or perhaps we have to decide between a healthy dessert and a fattening but delicious dessert. Or perhaps we must decide between doing the right thing and doing what's in our best interest. Suppose your choice is between an apple and chocolate cake; you choose the cake, but believe that you could have chosen the apple instead. What you believe, according to the incompatibilist, is that you could have chosen the apple, given the laws and given all the facts about the past until just before you decided, *including all your reasons and your entire process of deliberation.*

Well, maybe. But I think that even this kind of case is one where we believe something *less* than what the incompatibilist claims. At some time before we make our decision, we believe that we 'have what it takes' to decide either way and we believe (if circumstances are favorable – we've got enough time to make up our minds, we are not depressed, in a panic, etc.) that nothing prevents us from making either choice. This appears to be neutral with respect to determinism. If we think about what we believe, *after the fact*, it's even clearer that we are not expressly committed to the belief that determinism is false. If we feel regret or blame ourselves for the choice we actually made, we don't just think: "I could have chosen the apple instead." We also think something along the lines of: "If only I had thought about it a bit longer or summoned up a bit more willpower, I would have chosen the apple instead." That is, even if the actual situation was one where our reasons were so equally balanced that we might as well have flipped a coin, we believe that *if* we had deliberated differently, or longer, we would have discovered stronger reasons for one of our options.

Of course, when we think this, we are also assuming that nothing prevented us from thinking a bit longer or exerting more willpower, and so on. The incompatibilist may argue that this belief entails the falsity of determinism; that is, she may argue that if determinism is true, then something *always* prevents us from doing anything we fail to do. My point, again, is that this alleged entailment is something that needs to be defended by argument.

Let's take stock. We have been considering the claim that commonsense supports the forking paths view of options – premise (2) of the argument. I have argued that this is far from obvious and that what commonsense believes may, for all we have been shown so far, be compatible with determinism.

What I am not saying: I'm not saying that commonsense believes that determinism is true, or that commonsense believes (even implicitly) that compatibilism is true. I think that commonsense has no opinion, one way or the other, about the truth of determinism, and therefore has never had to confront the question of what would be the case if determinism were true.

Nor am I making a kind of paradigm case argument for compatibilism. I'm not saying that these ordinary cases, where everyone believes that we have free will and options, are, by definition, cases where we have free will and options. I am not ruling out, *by stipulation*, the possibility of an argument that will show that incompatibilism is true.

Nor am I claiming that the correct analysis of 'can do otherwise' can be extracted from the claims that I have attributed to commonsense, and that this analysis is compatible with determinism. I think that this can in fact be shown, but I do not claim to have shown it here.

What I am saying is that the commonsense view does not clearly and obviously support incompatibilism in the way that is often claimed. The incompatibilist partial definition of 'can do otherwise' is global insofar as it says that a necessary condition of a person's being able to do otherwise is that there is a possible world with *exactly the same history and exactly the same laws where the person does otherwise*. The commitments of commonsense appear to be more restrictive than this; insofar as commonsense says that something must be held constant in any test of what a person can do, this is something about *the person* and her *surroundings*.

What the incompatibilist needs is an *argument* for the claim that we can do only those things that are a lawful continuation of past history. This brings us to the most important and influential incompatibilist argument in the literature: the Consequence Argument.

6 The Consequence Argument

The Consequence Argument is based on the claim that there is some sense in which the laws and the past are necessary, at least relative to us. Different forms of the argument express this necessity in different ways.[4] Some versions of the argument say that that the laws and the past are not up to us; some versions say that the laws and the past are not in our control or in our power; other versions say that they are something that we have no choice about. I will discuss a version of the argument similar to the one discussed by Robert Kane in this book (see chapter 7.1).

Assume determinism is true. If so:

(1) There is nothing I can do to change the remote past or the laws of nature.
(2) Necessarily, if the remote past and laws are what they are, my present actions occur.
(3) Therefore there is nothing I can do to change the fact that my present actions occur.
(4) Therefore I must do what I do; I cannot do otherwise.

This argument has strong intuitive appeal. The first premise seems undeniable. The second premise is entailed by the definition of determinism; it says that my present actions follow from facts about the past together with facts about the laws. But if I can't change the combination of the actual past together with the laws, then surely I can't change what follows from this – my present actions.

But remember the fatalist fallacy:

(1) It's true that I will do X tomorrow.
(2) Necessarily, if it's true that I will do X tomorrow, I will do X tomorrow.

Kadri Vihvelin

(3)   Therefore, it's necessary that I will do X tomorrow.

(4)   Therefore, I must do X tomorrow; I cannot do otherwise.

The only difference between the Consequence Argument and the fatalist fallacy is the claim about the necessity of the past and laws – that is, the claim that we can't change the past or the laws. Without this claim, the Consequence Argument would *be* the fatalist fallacy:

(1)   There are facts about the remote past and the laws of nature.

(2)   Necessarily, if these facts about the remote past and the laws are what they are, my present actions occur.

(3)   Therefore, there is nothing I can do to change the fact that my present actions occur.

(4)   Therefore, I must do what I do; I cannot do otherwise.

So it is very important for the incompatibilist to explain and defend the claim that the laws and the past are necessary; that is, to explain and defend the claim that we cannot change the past or laws.

Note, first, how the necessity of the laws and past cannot be defended. The incompatibilist cannot say that our inability to change the past is due to the fact that the past is already "fixed" or "settled" or consists in "facts carved in stone." For to say this is to invoke the fatalist's intuition that something is necessary simply because it is true or a fact. And the incompatibilist cannot say that deterministic laws are unchangeable simply because they entail universal generalizations which are true at all places and all times. Truth at every place and every time is still truth; only the fatalist claims that it is the same as necessity.

We need to be very careful when we talk about our ability or inability to change the facts. Since the Consequence Argument is supposed to be an argument for incompatibilism, not impossibilism, we must understand 'can change the fact that' in a way that does not make it *metaphysically impossible* to change a fact. Think of a fact about the present that you believe is up to you – a fact about one of your free actions, in a situation where you believe that you can do something else instead. Call this fact – the fact that you do X at time t – 'F'. Suppose that your beliefs are correct. You live at a world where there is free will (an indeterministic world, if you like) and you do X at time t and you really can do something else instead. Can you change F? Yes and no.

You *cannot* change F in the following way: you cannot change F from what it is originally to what it is after you change it. Suppose that F is the fact that you stay home on June 15, 2006 and suppose that you can go out that day. You *cannot* act so that the following is true: First F is the case (you stay home on June 15, 2006); then F is not the case (you don't stay home on June 15, 2006). That doesn't make any sense. If you could change facts in this way, you would be able to do something metaphysically impossible, and no one can do what is metaphysically impossible.

You *can* change F in the following way: there is something that you can do (go out) such that if you were to do it, then it would not be (and would never have been) the case that you stay home on June 15, 2006 and your act would be the event that makes this so. This is the sense in which it is metaphysically possible to change a fact; there is something that you can do such that if you do it, it would not be (and would never have been) the case that F and your act would either be the event that makes it not the case that F or would cause an event that makes it not the case that F. We need a name for this way of changing the facts; let's call it "causing the facts to be different."

Given this distinction, we can understand the first premise of the Consequence Argument as making the claim that we cannot change facts about the past and the laws in this second way; that is, as claiming that there is nothing that we can do that would *cause* facts about the past or the laws to be different. Should we accept this premise?

Let's begin with the past. It seems uncontroversial that we don't have causal power with respect to the past. Backwards causation (e.g. time travel) may be logically possible, but it's not something we are actually able to do. So we should agree that we can neither cause the past to be as it is nor cause the past to be different.

It's less clear what we should say about the laws. On the one hand, it seems that claims about the necessity of the laws need to be defended by defending a particular account of lawhood. If a Humean view of laws as "constant conjunctions" turned out to be correct, would we really be entitled to say that we cannot cause the laws to be different? On the other hand, it seems wildly implausible to think that we can run faster than the speed of light, walk on water, or perform other acts which entail the falsity of the actual laws. And if we were able to perform these law-breaking acts (or perform other acts which cause law-breaking events), then we would be able to cause the laws to be different. So let's agree that we cannot do or cause law-breaking events and for that reason cannot cause the laws to be different.

Now that we have figured out the sense in which we cannot change the past or the laws, we can return to the argument.

(1) There is nothing I can do to cause the remote past or the laws to be different.
(2) Necessarily, if the remote past and the laws are what they are, my present actions occur.
(3) Therefore, I cannot cause my present actions not to occur.
(4) Therefore I must do what I do; I cannot do otherwise.

We have agreed that the first premise is true, and the second premise is the definition of determinism. Here, finally, we have an argument that is not an impossibilist argument. But is it valid? If we accept the premises, must we also accept the conclusion?

Let's think it through by using a concrete example. Pretend that determinism is true and I just refrained from raising my hand. This is an ordinary case; no brain control, hypnosis, pathological conditions, and so on. As a compatibilist, I say that I could have done otherwise; I could have raised my hand. But the fact that I did not raise my hand is a logical consequence of facts about the remote past together with the laws. It therefore follows that if I had raised my hand, then either the remote past would have been different or the laws would have been different. The Consequence Argument succeeds if it is *also* true that if I had raised my hand, then my action would have *caused* the remote past or the laws to be different.

Kadri Vihvelin

Suppose, first, that the laws would have been the same and the past different. Consider one of the possible worlds where this is the case. This is a world where events happened differently in a way that provided me with some reason to raise my hand. Did my hand-raising cause these earlier events? Of course not. The direction of causation was the other way around; the earlier events caused me to have reasons that I did not in fact have, which caused me to raise my hand.

Suppose, second, that most of past history would have been the same, and the laws would have been slightly different. Consider one of the possible worlds where this is the case. This is a world where everything happened exactly as it actually did until shortly before the time when I did not raise my hand, at which point events happened differently in a way that provided me with some reason to raise my hand. The event whereby the history of this world diverged from the history of our world is an event that entails the falsity of *our* laws. Because of this law-breaking event, the laws at this world are slightly different from our laws. Did my hand-raising cause this law-breaking event and thereby cause the laws to be different? Of course not. The direction of causation was the other way around; the law-breaking event caused me to have reasons I did not in fact have, which caused me to raise my hand.

If I had raised my hand, either the past or the laws would have been different. But my action would not have *caused* either the past or the laws to be different. And since my action would not have caused the past or the laws to be different, I cannot cause either the past or the laws to be different.

This shows that the Consequence Argument is not valid. We can accept both premises, yet deny the conclusion. Even if determinism is true and it is true that we cannot cause either the past or the laws to be different, it does not follow that we cannot do otherwise.

7 Conclusion

My defense of compatibilism has been unorthodox. The standard compatibilist defense is to offer an account of free will but I have not attempted to provide even a sketch of an account. I have defended compatibilism by pointing out something that should be obvious but has gone unnoticed in the literature. The incompatibilist is not an impossibilist. Some impossibilists think that our concept of free will is incoherent or self-contradictory or impossible for any non-godlike being to satisfy, and I agree that a fully satisfactory defense of free will should meet these charges by saying enough about what free will is to make it plausible that a human-like being could have free will. The incompatibilist, however, is someone who agrees that free will is possible for human-like beings – but only at indeterministic worlds. Given this, the burden of proof lies with the incompatibilist. Not because the compatibilist claim needs no proof, but because the proof is so easily rendered.

To see this, reflect for a moment on the nature of the metaphysical dialectic. To show that something X is possible, all that is required is that we describe a possible world where X exists. Not only is this all that is required to prove that X is possible, it is all the proof and the only kind of proof there can possibly be of the possibility of X. On the other hand, someone who hopes to show that X is impossible must show that there is *no possible world* where X exists, by showing that the description of X entails some logical or metaphysical impossibility.

Accordingly, to show that free will and determinism are compatible we must describe a world at which there is free will and determinism. I have just now – in the preceding sentence – described it. That is all the *positive* argument the compatibilist can give or can be expected to give for her position.

Having given the best and only argument that can be given for compatibilism, it is now the burden of the incompatibilist to demonstrate how this description conceals some logical or metaphysical impossibility. In my view, in the long history of the free will debate, no incompatibilist has ever met this burden.[5]

Notes

1 Thanks to John Carroll, Theodore Sider, and Terrance Tomkow for helpful comments and discussion.
2 For discussion of the different ways in which our actions and judgments of moral responsibility are subject to luck, see Nagel (1979).
3 For discussion of versions of this argument, see Fischer (1994) and van Inwagen (2002).
4 The classic statement of the Consequence Argument is by Peter van Inwagen (1983). The secondary literature on this argument is immense; for a summary see Vihvelin (2003).
5 For defense of fatalism, see Taylor (1992). For defense of impossibilism, see Strawson (1986). For defense of compatibilism, see Dennett (1984), Lewis (1981), Vihvelin (2004), and Wolf (1990).

References

Darrow, Clarence. 1924, "The Plea of Clarence Darrow, in Defense of Richard Loeb and Nathan Leopold, Jr.," in S. Cahn, ed., *Philosophical Explorations: Freedom, God, and Goodness* (New York: Prometheus Books).

Dennett, Daniel. 1984. *Elbow Room: The Varieties of Free Will Worth Wanting* (Cambridge, MA: Bradford Book).

Fischer, John. 1994. *The Metaphysics of Free Will* (Oxford: Blackwell).

Hobart, R. E. 1934. "Free Will as Involving Determination and Inconceivable Without It," *Mind* 63: 1–27.

Lewis, David. 1981. "Are We Free to Break the Laws?" *Theoria* 47: 113–21.

Nagel, Thomas. 1979. "Moral Luck," in Nagel, *Mortal Questions* (Cambridge: Cambridge University Press), pp. 24–38.

Strawson, Galen. 1986. *Freedom and Belief* (Oxford: Clarendon Press).

Taylor, Richard. 1992. *Metaphysics* (Englewood Cliffs, NJ: Prentice-Hall).

van Inwagen, Peter. 1983. *An Essay on Free Will* (Oxford: Clarendon Press).

——. 2002. *Metaphysics* (Cambridge, MA: Westview Press).

Vihvelin, Kadri. 2003. "Arguments for Incompatibilism," Stanford Encyclopedia of Philosophy: <http://plato.stanford.edu/entries/incompatibilism-arguments/>.

——. 2004 "Free Will Demystified: A Dispositional Account," *Philosophical Topics* 32: *Agency*, ed. John Fischer, pp. 427–50.

Wolf, Susan. 1990. *Freedom Within Reason* (Oxford: Oxford University Press).

A house is made up of parts: bricks, wooden boards, wires, bathroom tiles, and so on. These bricks, boards, wires, and tiles are *parts* of the house; the house is a single object that is *composed* of them. After the house is torn down, and the bricks, boards, wires, and tiles have been carted off to various junkyards, they obviously no longer compose a *house*. But do they compose *something*? This something would, like a deck of cards or a galaxy, be a *scattered object*, since its parts would not be in close proximity to one another. James Van Cleve says "yes," the scattered bricks, boards, wires, and tiles do compose something. Indeed, *any* objects whatsoever compose a further object. Ned Markosian says "no." Although the bricks, boards, wires, and tiles composed something before they were scattered (namely, the house), after they were scattered they composed nothing at all.

The Moon and Sixpence: A Defense of Mereological Universalism

James Van Cleve

The thesis I am called upon to defend is this: given any collection of objects, no matter how disparate or widely scattered, there is a further object composed of them all. For example, there is an object composed of my left tennis shoe and the lace that is threaded through its eyelets – so far, perhaps, no surprise. But there are all of the following objects as well: the object composed of the lace threaded through my left shoe and the lace threaded through my right shoe; the object composed of the Eiffel Tower and the tip of my nose; the object composed of the moon and the six pennies scattered across my desktop. For any objects *a* through *z*, whatever and wherever they may be, there is an object having those objects as its parts. This thesis goes by several names: conjunctivism (Chisholm), unrestricted composition (Lewis), and mereological universalism (van Inwagen).[1] It is often thought to fly in the face of common sense, but it has won the allegiance of several philosophers, and it is a standard element in the formal theory of part and whole as it was developed in the twentieth century. In what follows I shall explain why I believe it to be true.

1 Classical Mereology

Mereology (from the Greek word *meros* for 'part') is the theory of part and whole. Lesniewski (1916), Tarski (1937), and Leonard and Goodman (1940) have all presented formal systems of mereology, with definitions, axioms, and proofs of theorems.[2] To give the flavor of these systems, I shall present some of their key definitions and axioms here.

Let us take as primitive the relation symbol '$x < y$' for 'x is part of y'. Other mereological notions can then be defined as follows, using 'iff' as an abbreviation for 'if and only if':

x is a *proper part* of *y* iff $x < y$ & $x \neq y$. (A proper part of something is a part of it that is distinct from the whole.)

x and *y* *overlap* (sometimes symbolized '*x* o *y*') iff for some object *z*, $z < x$ and $z < y$. (Things that overlap are things that have a part in common.)

x and *y* are *disjoint* iff *x* and *y* do not overlap. (Disjoint things are things with no part in common.)

Now for a notion that will be of special importance to us here, the notion of a mereological sum (or fusion). Tarski defines it thus:

x is a *sum* of set *A* iff $(y)(y$ is a member of $A \rightarrow y < x)$ & $(y)(y < x \rightarrow \exists z(z$ is a member of A & y o z). (In other words, every member of *A* is a part of *x*, and every part of *x* overlaps some member of *A*.)

For example, a sum of the set {the Eiffel Tower, JVC's nose} would be an entity that has each of the members of that set as parts and each of whose parts overlaps either the Eiffel Tower or JVC's nose. (Why don't we express the second clause of the *definiens* more simply by saying that every part of *x* is a member of *A*? The answer is that we wish to count as parts of the sum such things as the rivets and beams in the Eiffel Tower, which are not *members* of the doubleton set {the Eiffel Tower, JVC's nose}, but which do *overlap* one of the members.)

It is possible to define the notion of a sum without presupposing the existence of *sets*, so long as we use some other device to similar effect, such as plural variables. Van Inwagen (1990: 29) gives the following definition:

x is a sum of the *ys* = $_{df}$ the *ys* are all parts of *x* and every part of *x* overlaps at least one of the *ys*.[3]

Thus, a sum of all the pennies in the universe would be a thing of which all the pennies are parts and every part of which is (either a penny or) something overlapping a penny.[4]

Here is some alternative terminology: instead of saying that *x* is a sum of *A* (or of the *ys*), we could say that the various members of *A* (or the *ys*) *compose* *x*.[5] If the *ys* have been enumerated (say as *a* and *b*), we can use the expression '*a* + *b*' as a name for the sum of the *ys*.

I now proceed to Tarski's axioms, of which there are two. The first says that the relation *is part of* is transitive:

A1   If *x* is part of *y* and *y* is part of *z*, then *x* is part of *z*.

The second axiom pertains to the existence and uniqueness of sums:

A2 $\exists x(x$ is a member of A$) \rightarrow \exists x(x$ is a sum of A & $(y)(y$ is a sum of $A \rightarrow x = y))$

This axiom says that every non-empty set has a unique sum. It will be useful to divide the import of it in two. One half (the half that employs only the first conjunct in the

James Van Cleve

consequent) says that for any non-empty set of entities, there is *at least* one sum of that set, that is, at least one entity that the members of that set compose. The other half (the half that employs the second conjunct in the consequent) tells us that there is *at most* one such sum.

The uniqueness of sums is perhaps almost as controversial as their existence. It arguably implies that a statue and the clay of which it is made are one and the same, for they are both sums of exactly the same molecules. My main concern in what follows will be defending the existence half of the axiom, but at times I shall draw upon uniqueness as well.

There are other axiomatizations of classical mereology besides Tarski's, differing from his and from one another in what notions they take as primitive, in whether they presuppose the existence of sets, and in what principles they choose as axioms. For our purposes here, all these systems are equivalent. They all assume the same formal properties (transitivity and the like) for the part–whole relation, and they all have the same implications regarding the existence and uniqueness of sums.[6]

The view that every set has a sum, or that any objects whatsoever are parts composing a larger whole, has its mirror image in the doctrine that any objects whatsoever are wholes composed of smaller parts. The second view is a denial of the existence of mereological atoms, or simples, in favor of the view that everything has parts within parts *ad infinitum*.[7] To believe that matter is infinitely divisible in this way is to believe in what David Lewis calls *atomless gunk* (1991: 20). To believe in all the sums countenanced by the classical mereologist is to believe in what I shall call (without prejudice) *mereological junk*. Belief in junk and belief in gunk are independent of each other, and a commitment to gunk is not part of classical mereology. Nonetheless, the two views are to some extent mutually reinforcing (as I show below), and I myself accept a package of views in mereology that includes them both. To the question "When are objects parts?" I say "Always," and to the question "When are objects wholes?" I again say "Always."[8]

How did it come about that modern axiomatizations of mereology all take for granted an assumption that seemingly flies in the face of commonsense – that in addition to pebbles and houses and planets, there are such junky objects as the object allegedly composed of the moon and the pennies on my desk? I don't know, unless the answer is that the assumption is not so counterintuitive after all.[9] For my part, when I was first asked to entertain the idea that there are such wildly scattered and gerrymandered objects, my reaction was not "How crazy!" but "Why not?" In what follows, I shall do my best to get the reader to agree.

One word before we begin about what is at issue. If you accept that there is such a parcel or aggregate of matter as that composed of the moon and the pennies, you already agree with me, even if you don't consider that aggregate to be very thing-like. It need not be a *thing*, in any narrow sense of the term; it need only be *there*.

2 Against Real Coincidence

One of my reasons for believing in mereological universalism is that it affords a solution to what is sometimes called "the paradox of coincidence" or "the explosion of reality." I shall need to sketch some background before we can appreciate this problem. (See also chapter 6 in this volume.)

What is the ontological status of an everyday object like a desk or a snowball? Is it something over and above the matter of which it is composed? The broadly Aristotelian answer is "yes": the desk is distinct from the wooden pieces from which it was assembled, and the snowball is distinct from the snow from which it was crafted. The snowball is a compound of matter and essential form.[10] Its matter is a certain quantity of snow; its form is roundness together with separation from other snow. When the snow was formed into a ball, a genuinely new entity came into being. It is not identical with the snow for at least two reasons: first, the snow existed before the ball was created; second, the ball might survive the melting of some of the snow around its edges. It has an identity that transcends that of the particular matter of which it is made.

The Aristotelian position leads to a problem that Ernest Sosa has dubbed "the explosion of reality" (1993: 605–26).[11] To be drawn into the problem, ask yourself the following question: which aggregates of matter and which forms are such that when those aggregates come to exemplify those forms, a new entity is thereby created? It seems to me that an impartial Aristotelian ought to answer as follows: whenever *any* matter instantiates *any* form, a new entity thereby exists. Consider, for example, the entity Sosa calls a *snowdiscall*, which has as its matter a chunk of snow and as its form any shape between being round and being disc-shaped. If you take a snowball and flatten it, you destroy the snowball (having deprived it of its essential form), but you leave a snowdiscall in its place. Moreover, the snowdiscall you leave was there all along, sharing matter with the original snowball. Our own conceptual scheme may not recognize snowdiscalls, but that seems to be just a parochial failure to acknowledge entities that are ontologically on a par with snowballs.

From here it is but a short step to the recognition that an impartial Aristotelian (or "absolutist," as Sosa calls him) should admit that there are millions of entities inhering in any parcel of matter. Consider the following series of shapes: being round, being round or flattened up to degree 1, being round or flattened up to degree 2, and so on, until we reach the property of being round or flattened up to some degree including being squashed into a disc. We may distinguish infinitely many such shapes. From an impartial or absolute point of view, each of these shapes has as much claim as roundness to be regarded as the essential form of an entity of some type. An ordinary snowball, it would therefore seem, coincides with infinitely many other entities – snowdiscalls of all possible degrees.

Some may resist this result because they boggle at the sheer number of entities involved. I resist it myself because the entities involved would all share exactly the same place and exactly the same matter, thus violating two plausible philosophical principles: "Two or more things cannot be in the same place at the same time" and "There cannot be difference of entities without difference of content."[12]

How are we to avoid the endless proliferation of entities sharing exactly the same place and matter?[13] One way would be to eschew the Aristotelian line in favor of a logical atomist or eliminativist line. The eliminativist says that composite entities are really fictions or logical constructions. To say that a table exists is just shorthand for saying that some wooden legs and a top have been fastened together; it is not to

James Van Cleve

posit any new entity in addition to the parts. Similarly, to say that a snowball exists is just to say that some snow has been formed into a ball. We don't get the myriads of entities the absolutist recognizes because we don't even get as far as the table and the snowball. It is correct to say, of course, that there is a snowball in my hand, just as it is correct to say that the sun is now setting; but in either case, the truth underlying what it is correct to say is something different. Yes, the sun is setting, but that is simply to say that the earth is rotating so that the sun is disappearing from view. Yes, there is a snowball in my hand, but that is simply to say that some snow has been scooped up, made round, and placed in my hand. More generally, any statement asserting the existence of a composite entity or predicating something of it must be mere shorthand for some statement telling us how certain basic entities are configured.

The trouble for such eliminativism is that it does not go well with the possibility that perhaps there *are* no basic or simple entities.[14] As was said above, I am inclined to believe that all is gunk – that every entity has smaller parts, and that we never bottom out with the simple. If this is so much as possible, trouble arises for the eliminativist in the form of the following argument:

(1) Composite entities are (of necessity) *façons de parler*: to say that a composite exists is merely to say that its elements are arranged in a certain way.
(2) It is possible that there are no simples – that is, that everything is composite.
(3) Therefore, it is possible that everything that exists is a *façon de parler*.

The conclusion I take to be absurd – it cannot be that everything is a merely nominal existent. As a believer in the possibility of gunk, I reject Leibniz's maxim "if there are compounds, there must be simples," but I accept in its place "if there are nominal existents, there must be real existents."

We now have two problematic alternatives before us – unbridled Aristotelianism, which involves the incredible explosion of reality, and thoroughgoing eliminativism, which threatens to give us fictions unfounded in any facts. How are we to navigate between these extremes?

Sosa (1993) proposes to do so by espousing a view he calls *conceptual relativism*. (See also chapter 9 in this volume.) In Sosa's view, ascriptions of existence are always relative to conceptual schemes. What exists relative to one scheme may not exist relative to another, and nothing can be said to exist apart from all schemes. In order for an entity to exist relative to a scheme, the scheme must recognize the essential form of that entity as one of the approved forms whose union with appropriate matter generates a new object. The explosion is blocked, in Sosa's view, because we are not forced to say (and are indeed forbidden to say) that all the entities in the exploded universe exist absolutely speaking. Various of them exist relative to one or another scheme, but no scheme is privileged in a way that would enable us to say that the entities it recognizes are the entities that exist, period.

I have the following misgiving about the conceptual relativist's way out.[15] Is not absolutism itself one possible scheme? We abjured absolutism because it leads to an incredible explosion. But then shouldn't we also abjure any scheme that embraces absolutism? Yet that would go against the spirit of conceptual relativism, if conceptual relativism holds that all schemes are on a par. To put this question another way: how does conceptual relativism avoid the explosion if it bestows its blessing equally on all schemes, including schemes that set off the explosion? And at the other extreme: how does it avoid the absurdities of eliminativism if it countenances eliminativism as a possible scheme as well?

I prefer a route between Scylla and Charybdis that draws on the principles of classical mereology. As for Scylla (the explosion), classical mereology does admittedly involve an expansive proliferation of entities (for any n given initially, at least $2^n - 1$ altogether),[16] but it is more like a controlled nuclear reaction than an atomic blast. Moreover, classical mereology does not involve what seems to me the really serious objection to absolutism, namely, that it implies the existence of indefinitely many distinct entities sharing the same space and consisting of exactly the same matter as any given entity. This is because of the uniqueness axiom of classical mereology: if entities x and y have all the same parts (at some level of decomposition), they are really one and the same. You cannot have two entities, such as a snowball and a snowdiscall, that are composed of exactly the same H_2O molecules. For a given region of space, there will be at most one entity that exactly fills it, and, for a given tract of matter, there will be just one entity that is composed of exactly the matter in that tract.

Our Charybdis was the threat of total nihilism if we go eliminativist. For what if there are no simple or ultimate parts of matter? If all composite entities are merely nominal existents, it would then follow that everything is a merely nominal existent, which is absurd. But as a classical mereologist, I need not hold that *all* composites have merely nominal existence; I need only hold that composites of matter *and essential form* have nominal existence. Mereological sums are composite entities that are not constituted by any essential form – as far as their existence is concerned, nothing matters but their matter. Or, if you prefer, you could say that mereological sums are entities whose essential form is nothing more than the coexistence of the relevant parts. In any case, as sheer aggregates of matter, they exist just so long as their parts exist, no matter how radically rearranged, finely chopped, or widely scattered. So even if there are parts within parts all the way down, the threat of nihilism is averted. You can safely believe in gunk if you also believe in junk.

Here, then, is one philosophical advantage of classical mereology: it is one way of simultaneously avoiding the excesses of unbridled Aristotelianism and the austerities of thoroughgoing eliminativism.

3 Against Arbitrariness and Indeterminacy

Universalism is one answer to what van Inwagen calls the Special Composition Question: when do a number of objects form a whole? Or, as he states it using plural variables, when is there an object y such that the xs compose y (1990: 30–1)?[17] There are two extreme answers to this question: *always*, which is the answer given by universalists, and *never*, which is the answer given by the philosophers van Inwagen calls nihilists.[18] There are also various moderate or in-between answers, which give the answer "sometimes, but not always." In this section, I shall argue for universalism by elimination, exposing problems with nihilism and with all the likely in-between answers.

With nihilism, I can be brief. Nihilism says that no objects ever compose a whole – that there are no composite objects in the universe, but only mereological simples. There are no such things, then, as the Washington Monument or Clinton's desk or even a molecule of H_2O. That sounds drastic, but the force of the doctrine is mitigated somewhat if we accord a kind of nominal existence to composite objects. There are no desks, but there are atoms arranged desk-wise; no water molecules, but atoms of hydrogen and oxygen arranged H_2O-wise, and so on. (Actually, there are not even chemical atoms of hydrogen and oxygen, but there are mereological atoms arranged hydrogen-wise and oxygen-wise.) The reader will recognize nihilism as a very close relative of the eliminativism discussed in the previous section.[19]

It is close enough, indeed, to be subject to the same difficulty. Isn't it a possibility that there are no mereological atoms, that all is gunk? If so, nihilism becomes worthy of its name: it implies not just that there are no composite objects, but that there are no objects whatsoever that really exist. For this reason, I reject it.[20]

On, then, to the moderate answers, which hold that composition sometimes occurs, but not always – it is subject to restrictions.

If composition is restricted, it must presumably be restricted by some principle. The principle will look like this: the _x_s compose something iff the _x_s stand to one another in relation _R_. But what exactly would the principle be? The most obvious candidates are all open to criticism. Either they fail to gibe with the ordinary judgments they are supposed to codify, or they incur objectionable arbitrariness or vagueness, or both.

One restriction might be this: objects that compose something must exactly occupy some continuous region of space. Perhaps equivalently, they must be in contact: any two of them must either be in contact with each other or connected by a chain of contact relations running among the rest of them. That would rule out many of the more bizarre mereological sums, such as the sum of the Eiffel Tower and my nose. But it would also rule out many things that commonsense probably wishes to rule in: the land mass of the state of Michigan, tokens of the letter 'i', and, if physics is to be believed, almost all of the familiar objects around us. Even such a paradigm of continuity as my desk is really a scattered swarm of subatomic particles, separated from one another by comparatively vast distances.

Unless supplemented by some other principle, the continuity principle would also rule in many things that commonsense would prefer to rule out. Although tower + nose is ruled out (because disconnected), tower + nose + corridor of connecting air is ruled in – that object does occupy a continuous region of space.[21] If it is to be ruled out in the end, it must be because some other principle disqualifies the corridor of air as an eligible connecting part.[22]

Another principle that doubtless plays a role in everyday thought is that objects compose a whole if and only if they exhibit some degree of dynamical interconnectedness. This might be spelled out in various ways – for example, by saying that not many forces would separate the objects, or that they tend to move together as a unit. When I wiggle my nose, nothing much happens to the Eiffel Tower, but when I move the north end of my car into the garage, the south end usually comes along with it.

This principle might (or might not) be understood liberally enough so that the sun and the nine planets of our solar system, which tend to move together through the cosmos, compose an object.

The cohesion principle (as we may call it) does not tally any better than the contact principle with commonsense judgments about when objects make up a whole. A house built of carefully piled stones probably qualifies as a genuine whole for commonsense, even though one can move many of the stones without moving the rest of the house. Conversely, a mother cow and her newborn calf may move about together and exhibit a considerable degree of reluctance to be separated from one another without thereby being regarded as a whole.[23]

The two principles considered so far – that objects are parts of the same whole when they are in contact and when they move together in harness or share a common fate – are attributed to infants by some psychologists (Carey and Spelke 1994).[24] I must therefore be a very backward scholar, for it seems that I no longer recognize principles that were familiar to me before I was out of my cradle.

The principles of cohesion and contact are open to another criticism that has more general force, applying, as I suspect, to nearly any plausible moderate principle that the reader is likely to formulate.[25] It is this: if a principle invokes a relation whose holding is a matter of degree, then the principle is going to give rise either to objectionable arbitrariness or to objectionable vagueness.[26] There will be objectionable arbitrariness if some minute degree of cohesiveness (or whatever) makes the difference between forming a whole and not, and there will be objectionable vagueness if it is indeterminate at which point along some continuum of cohesiveness a new whole comes into being.

The objection I am raising has been elaborated by Ted Sider (2001: 121–32) in a form I will call the "Sider sorites."[27] There are three premises and a conclusion:

P1 If in some cases composition occurs and in other cases it does not, then there are cases in which composition occurs that are connected by a continuous series with cases in which composition does not occur.

P2 There is no sharp cut-off point in any such series. That is, there is no pair of adjacent cases such that composition (definitely) occurs in one and (definitely) does not occur in the other.

P3 It is always determinate whether composition occurs. That is, in every case, either composition (definitely) occurs or it (definitely) does not occur.

Conclusion: Either composition always occurs or it never occurs.

The argument is in effect an argument excluding all the moderate positions and forcing us to choose between the extremes. If we have already rejected the nihilist extreme, we are then left with universalism as the only game in town.

To see how Sider's conclusion follows from the premises, it may be useful to consider another instance of the same logical pattern in which we substitute 'baldness' for 'composition' to obtain a classical sorites.[28] The first premise then tells us that if baldness occurs on some heads but not others, then there are pairs of heads, one bald and the other not, between which there extends a continuous series of heads differing only slightly, say by one hair each. Of course, the heads need not lie next to each other along any spatial path, nor need the series be continuous in the mathematical sense implying that between any two heads there is a third. Sider's idea is just that we can construct a series in which adjacent members are as similar as we like in whatever respect is deemed relevant to the occurrence of baldness or composition. The second premise now tells us that a single hair never makes the difference between being bald and not being bald. The third premise tells us that every head must be either bald or not bald – *tertium non datur*. Sider actually says "definitely bald or definitely not bald," but these words, it seems to me, add nothing but emphasis.[29]

To extract our conclusion, note that P2 and P3 imply that the consequent of P1 is false. Suppose such a series of heads as P1 describes. The first head is bald; what about the second? It cannot be non-bald, or we would get a sharp cut-off, contrary to P2. Nor can it be indeterminate as to baldness or non-baldness, or we would violate P3. It must therefore be bald. We can repeat this reasoning for each successive head, proving eventually that the last head is bald, but that contradicts the description of the series. The antecedent of P1 must therefore be false, which is to say that the conclusion of the argument is true.

To illustrate what happens when we switch from baldness back to composition, imagine a hook, a line, and a pole that I buy in order to make a fishing rod. When the three components lie in separate bins at the hardware store, they do not (according to likely moderate principles) compose any further object. Side by side on my workbench, they still do not compose a new object. When the line is tied tightly enough around the hook at one end and the pole at the other, they *do* compose a new object. But what happens before the knots are tight? What if the diameter of the knots is several times that of the pole, so that lifting the pole leaves the line behind? What if the diameter is now one millimeter less? You get the idea: to avoid objectionable arbitrariness or indeterminacy, we must say that the three components *always* composed a further thing. (Of course, I am not saying that they always composed a fishing rod).

In the baldness version of the sorites, most will find the conclusion (that baldness occurs in all cases or none) absurd. They will therefore try to find a false premise. A commonly fingered culprit is P3: with vague predicates like 'bald', it may be said, we do get indeterminacy. There is a range of heads in the series that are neither bald nor not bald, and our sorites reasoning cannot traverse this region of indeterminacy.

That may be a good response to the baldness sorites,[30] but the parallel response is *not* a good response to the Sider sorites. We cannot treat composition on the model of baldness. The reason has been forcefully stated by David Lewis in a well-known passage:

> The only intelligible account of vagueness locates it in our thought and language. The reason it's vague where the outback begins is not that there's this thing, the outback, with imprecise borders; rather there are many things, with different borders, and nobody has been fool enough to try to enforce a choice of one of them as the official referent of the word 'outback'. Vagueness is semantic indecision. (1986: 212)

A Defense of Mereological Universalism | 329

It is a consequence of this thesis (often called the linguistic theory of vagueness) that whenever vagueness gives rise to indeterminacy about whether *P*, that is because some term occurring in '*P*' is vague – we haven't made up our minds what exactly it refers to. But then how can there be any indeterminacy about whether composition occurs? Lewis continues:

> But not all of language is vague. The truth-functional connectives aren't, for instance. Nor are the words for identity and difference, and for [mereological] overlap. Nor are the idioms of quantification, so long as they are unrestricted. How could any of these be vague? What would be the alternatives between which we haven't chosen?
>
> The question whether composition takes place in a given case, whether a given class does or does not have a mereological sum, can be stated in a part of language where nothing is vague. Therefore, it cannot have a vague answer. (Ibid.)

I believe Lewis's reasoning can be spelled out as follows. A correct answer to the Special Composition Question will take the form '∃*y*(the *x*s compose *y*) iff the *x*s stand to one another in relation *R*'. I have suggested that any candidate for '*R*' in a moderate answer will likely be vague, so that it will be vague or indeterminate whether the right-hand side of this biconditional holds, even when the *x*s have been perfectly delineated. In that case, it must also be vague or indeterminate whether the left-hand side holds. But how can that be? Recall that the left-hand side may be spelled out in mereological primitives thus: '∟*y*(the *x*s are all parts of *y* and every part of *y* has a part in common with at least one of the *x*s)'. The only terms occurring in that formula are variables, quantifiers, the logical connective 'and', and the mereological term 'is part of'. To which of those can we trace any indeterminacy?[31] Which of them have we not made up our minds about?

In this regard, contrast 'is part of' with 'is bald'. If we know exactly who James is and exactly how hair is distributed on his head, it may still be uncertain and indeterminate whether he is bald, because we have never decided exactly what property 'bald' expresses. But if we know exactly what objects *A* and *B* are, how can it be indeterminate whether one is part of the other? You draw the boundaries around any two objects, and I will tell you whether one is part of the other.

With the idioms of existence and quantification, it is again hard to find a source of indeterminacy in semantic indecision. 'Everything', 'something', 'there is' – is there really something here we haven't made up our minds about? As Lewis says, what would be the alternatives between which we haven't chosen?[32]

Lewis brings out a further reason for not assimilating existence to baldness, apparently connected with the dictum that existence is not a predicate. If it is vague whether someone is bald, there is someone whom we do not know how to classify – he sort of is, sort of isn't, and we just don't know what to say. But if it is vague whether there exists something composed of the *x*s, it is not that there sort of is and sort of isn't an entity composed by the *x*s and we just don't know whether to classify this entity as existent or non-existent. If the entity is there for us to equivocate over, it exists unequivocally. There is nothing that lies in the indeterminate zone between existing and not existing.[33]

Sider drives home the objection about vague existence engendered by vague composition in this way: a vague restriction on composition would make it indeterminate how many concrete objects there are in the universe, but there cannot be any indeterminacy in such a question about number, since it is stateable in purely logical vocabulary (2001: 126–30). One who is gung-ho on gunk (as I am) may not complete the argument in this way, since a gunky universe would contain an infinite number of objects even if there were vague restrictions on composition. Nonetheless, one may object to vague existence in particular cases even if it does not affect the total count of objects.

4 Souls and Brutes

There are two in-between answers to the Special Composition Question that deserve consideration before we finally settle in favor of universalism. One is van Inwagen's view that the *x*s compose something if and only if their activity constitutes a life – if and only if they are "ensouled" in the old-fashioned sense that connotes a mode of organization rather than an immaterial substance. The other is the "brute composition" view of Ned Markosian (1998), according to which it is simply a brute fact that some arrangements of objects compose things and others do not.

Let me begin by acknowledging a strong pressure pushing us away from the extremes and toward the middle. The David Lodge character Morris Zapp, a deconstructionist who had previously professed that the self is a fiction, was once jolted by the realization "I will die; therefore, I am." Zapp's realization, coupled with the assumption that what I am, if I exist, is some compound of particles, provides a basis for thinking that some in-between answer must be correct after all. If I am a composite object that presently exists, nihilism is false. If I am a composite object that will cease to exist upon the dispersal of its parts, universalism is false. So some in-between answer must be correct.

This is a powerful argument for a moderate answer. If it is to be resisted, it must apparently be on one of three grounds: that I don't really exist, that I won't really cease to exist, or that I am not a composite object. One who took the first option would presumably believe himself to be some sort of logical construct or nominal entity, like the particles arranged deskwise we considered above. One who took the second option would believe that he will not cease to exist upon his death, but will enjoy a Lucretian sort of immortality, no longer afflicted with consciousness but surviving as sundry particles scattered through the biosphere. One who took the third option would believe that he is an extended physical atom or a purely psychical monad. I leave the weighing of these options to the reader.[34]

Van Inwagen rejects all three options. He thinks that he and you and I are all composite objects. So what is special about the things making us up, but not about just any old things, that lets them compose something? Van Inwagen's answer is *life*: there is something that the *x*s compose iff the activity of the *x*s constitutes a life (1990: 82). In his view, living organisms are the only composite objects. If the *x*s are ever to amount to anything, they need to get a life.

As van Inwagen is at pains to acknowledge, it is often a vague matter whether the activity of a group of particles constitutes a life. There may be no definite point at which the activity of the cells in a growing embryonic mass comes to constitute a life, or at which the activity of a fatally damaged brain ceases to constitute a life. There may be no definite answer as to whether the activities associated with viruses and mitochondria ever constitute a life. On van Inwagen's view, then, composition is governed by a vague restriction. His view therefore incurs the objection of the previous section against theories that make it a vague matter whether composition occurs: they countenance a variety of vagueness that infects existence itself and cannot be traced to any terms whose meanings we have never made precise. In response, van Inwagen mounts a sustained challenge to the linguistic theory of vagueness (1990: chs. 17–19). I cannot hope to resolve the vagueness issue here, but must simply flag it as one of the matters on which the present debate turns.

The other in-between answer I want to consider is that of Ned Markosian (1998). In my objections above to moderate views, I took for granted that if composition is restricted, it must be restricted by some principle. That is precisely the assumption Markosian challenges. He advocates a position according to which some objects compose wholes, others do not, and there is no saying why. They just do or do not, as the case may be, and there is no deeper fact in virtue of which they do or do not. That certain objects compose wholes and others do not is simply a brute fact.

I cannot fault Markosian for his repudiation of principle, since in some matters, I myself am a man of no principle. Consider identity through time. If object *A* existing today is identical with object *B* that existed yesterday or last year, must there be some deeper fact in virtue of which that identity obtains? Not always. Imagine a perfectly homogeneous red fluid that fills an enclosed volume of space, perhaps remaining perfectly at rest or perhaps containing swirls and eddies within it. We distinguish these two possibilities even though in either case exactly the same qualities would be manifest at each time and place within the volume.[35] If there is movement within the fluid during an interval from t1 to t2, then some portion of the fluid occupying a region r2 at t2 is identical with some portion that was in a neighboring region r1 at t1. But what deeper facts does this identity fact derive from? None that are not themselves identity facts – for example, the fact that each sub-portion of the portion of fluid in r2 at t2 is identical with some sub-portion of the portion of fluid in r1 at t1. For that matter, the not further explicable identity of the regions r1 and r2 themselves must arguably be presupposed. I believe there are bound to be identity facts that do not hold in virtue of any further facts that are not themselves identity facts.[36]

Markosian's view enables him to sidestep the objections I raised to moderate views in the preceding section. I objected to certain obvious principles (of contact, cohesion, and the like) on the ground that they are either too strict or too lax to underwrite ordinary judgments about composition, and I intimated that a similar fate would befall any other moderate principles. Markosian can accept this in stride; it is part of his reason for declaring that no satisfactory principles governing composition are to be had. I also raised the objection that if composition is restricted, we can avoid objectionable indeterminacy only at the cost of objectionable arbitrariness, as shown in the Sider sorites. Markosian has a neat way around the sorites – he can say that there is nothing objectionable about sharp cut-off points between cases of composition and cases of non-composition. Consider a parallel he offers: we could line up a thousand individuals ranging in height from one to two meters in one-millimeter increments, the shorter 500 all left-handed and the taller 500 all right-handed. In this series there would be only a one-millimeter difference in height between the last of the lefties and the first of the righties. No problem, though, for who said height had anything to do with handedness? There is similarly no problem in a series where a minute difference in degree of cohesion (or whatnot) separates the cases where composition occurs from those in which it does not, for Markosian does not claim that cohesion or anything else is that in virtue of which composition obtains. Things would be otherwise for someone who thought cohesion was relevant and therefore had either to specify an exact degree of it or leave matters indeterminate.

Markosian's position is respectable and not easily refutable, but I have two qualms about it. First, although the view is advanced in defense of common sense, it is not entirely friendly to commonsense. The person on the street probably believes not only (i) that the beams and rivets of the Eiffel Tower compose an object while the Tower and the moon do not, but also (ii) that he has some idea why this is so, having to do with contact, cohesiveness, or the like. Markosian's view that composition is brute is consistent with point (i), but undermines point (ii). Second, although the view does not incur the same charge of arbitrariness as do intuitive principles of composition, it seems nonetheless to involve its own brand of arbitrariness. To see this, consider an analog of the brute composition view that might be advanced to solve the "explosion" problem of section 3. The problem was this: how can we admit that some objects are new entities over and above the matter of which they are composed without admitting that there are millions of objects co-inhabiting any lump of matter?[37] A believer in brute compounds of matter and form could deal with the problem by saying that only a few of all those millions exist, and it is a brute matter which. Perhaps when snow is formed into a ball, a new entity, a snowball, comes into being, but when snow is formed into a disk or an ellipsoid or an irregular lump, no new entity comes into being – the snow just becomes differently shaped. Why is that? It just is. I find that possibility hard to swallow, and brutal composition does not go down much easier.

5 Question or Pseudo-Question?

I expect that some readers of this chapter will be impatient with the entire issue. Is there or is there not an object composed of the pencil on my desk and the mug on the cabinet ten feet away? It makes no difference, these readers will say – there is really nothing here to argue about. I wish to close by discussing two grounds on which it might be urged that our question is a pseudo-question: that no empirical evidence or conceptual considerations will settle who is right, and that the difference between the two sides is merely verbal. (For more on this issue, see chapter 9.)

Gideon Rosen and Cian Dorr (2002) point out that the issue separating universalists and their opponents is neither straightforwardly empirical nor straightforwardly conceptual.[38] The issue is not straightforwardly empirical, for we cannot settle it simply by looking around or performing a test in a laboratory. Regardless of which side is right, the course of our experience will be the same. Nor is the issue straightforwardly conceptual, for we cannot settle it by an analysis of the meaning of 'part' (or other relevant terms) that shows the thesis propounded by one side to be analytic (and the opposed thesis therefore contradictory).

From this circumstance, the positivists of an older generation would have concluded that there is no genuine issue. If a thesis and an alleged rival of it are both consistent (so neither is analytic) and if they both tally equally well with the totality of observational data, then it cannot be the case that one of them is true and the other false. Perhaps both of them are true – both really say the same thing despite differences in verbal formulation. (That is what Reichenbach said about rival systems of geometry-cum-physics, such as Euclidean geometry coupled with a complex physics and non-Euclidean geometry coupled with a simple physics.) Perhaps neither of them is true – both are meaningless verbiage insofar as they go beyond what is supported by empirical data. (That is what Ayer said about the dispute between those who affirm and those who deny the existence of a transcendent God.) Either way, it is not the case that one thesis is true and its apparent rival false; there is nothing to debate about.

Positivism of that sort is no longer in vogue, and no wonder. What is the status of its leading principle – that one side in a debate cannot be awarded the palm unless it is either true on conceptual grounds or better supported than its rivals by the totality of observational data? As critics have often pointed out, the positivist's principle fails to measure up to its own standards. What empirical or conceptual considerations establish the positivist's own thesis, or at least give it an edge over the competing theses of metaphysical realists? None has ever been brought forth, and I doubt that any could be. The principle is therefore self-refuting, and cannot be used to discredit mereological debates.

Eli Hirsch takes the dispute among universalists, nihilists, and common-sense moderates to be a paradigm of a merely verbal dispute (2005: esp. p. 16; see also chapter 9.1 in this volume). In a dispute of this sort, there is a disputed sentence D and there are two undisputed sentences U1 and U2 such that everyone can agree that D is true if it is equivalent to U1 and everyone can agree that D is false if it is equivalent to U2. Moreover, one side is most charitably interpreted as meaning something with the same truth conditions as U1 by the disputed sentence and the other as meaning something with the same truth conditions as U2.[39] In the case at hand, one of the disputed sentences is 'There is an object x such that x is composed of the pencil on my desk and the mug on the cabinet', so let this be our D. Hirsch would say that everyone can agree that D is true if it has the same truth conditions as U1: there is a pencil on my desk *and* there is a mug on the cabinet. Everyone can also agree that D is false if it has the same truth conditions as U2: there is a *mass of matter* composed of the pencil on my desk and the mug on the cabinet. The only issue, Hirsch thinks, is whether U1 or U2 is what the disputed sentence means in English.[40]

For my part, I cannot see that the dispute is so easily shown to be verbal. To begin with, it is not obvious to me that U2 is false, for it is not clear to me that phrases like 'mass of matter' or 'portion of matter' in English do not apply to spatially disconnected objects. More seriously, I do not believe that U1, the supposedly charitable interpretation of the universalist's claim offered by Hirsch, is all I mean by D. I realize that unconverted members of my audience already assent to U1, and I am trying to convince them of something more. The something more, though *entailed* by U1 if I am right, is still something more, in the way in which a non-trivial theorem is something more than the axioms from which it follows. Perhaps my arguments in this chapter have fallen short of establishing universalism, but if so, that at least shows that there was something that needed to be established. Universalism is not merely a restatement of the obvious.[41]

Notes

1   Roderick Chisholm used the term 'conjunctivism' in his lectures. David Lewis (1986: 211–13) uses the term 'unrestricted composition', and Peter van Inwagen (1990: 74) uses the term 'universalism'. Of these three authors, only Lewis espouses universalism.

2   For a survey of various systems with references, see Simons (1987). One presentation of Tarski's system is Tarski (1956: 24–9). For the system of Nelson Goodman and Henry Leonard, see Goodman and Leonard (1940).

3   Van Inwagen (1990: 29); van Inwagen explains plural variables and plural quantification in his chapter 2. The device is explained and defended by David Lewis (1991: 62–71).

4   The phrase in parentheses is redundant, since every penny overlaps a penny.

5   Some authors, like van Inwagen, prefer to use the locution 'the ys compose x' only when there is no overlap among any of the ys. In this usage, New York City would be composed of its five boroughs, but not of the boroughs together with Central Park.

6   As an example, I present here an axiomatization of Leonard and Goodman's mereology due to Rolf Eberle, *Nominalistic Systems* (Dordrecht: D. Reidel, 1970). There are three axioms:

   A1 $x < y \leftrightarrow (z)(z \text{ o } x \rightarrow z \text{ o } y)$
   A2 $\exists x Fx \rightarrow \exists x(y)(y \text{ o } x \leftrightarrow \exists z(Fz \ \& \ y \text{ o } z))$
   A3 $(z)(z \text{ o } x \leftrightarrow z \text{ o } y) \rightarrow x = y$

   A1 does the work of Tarski's first axiom, for it implies that the part-of relation is transitive. (It also implies that the relation is reflexive.) A2 and A3 together do the work of Tarski's second axiom without taking for granted the existence of sets. A2 tells us that if there any Fs, then there is something that overlaps exactly those things that overlap an F. Since 'F' could be a disjunctive predicate like 'is identical either with the moon or with the Eiffel Tower', this axiom guarantees the existence of a sum of any two or more entities. A3 secures the uniqueness of sums. If x and y are composed of the same things, whatever overlaps either will overlap the other, and A3 tells us in that case that x and y are identical. (In the consequent of A3, I have put '$x = y$' where Eberle had a Leibnizian definition of it, '$A \rightarrow A[y//x]$'.)

7   Note that an atom in mereology is not the same as an atom in chemistry; it is a thing with absolutely no parts.

8   I have defended the gunk hypothesis (which is the Antithesis of Kant's Second Antinomy) from Kant's attempt to refute it in Van Cleve (1999: 63–5). For an argument in its favor, see Zimmerman (1996: 1–29).

9   Perhaps another reason is that some proponents of mereology wanted it to do some of the work of set theory, in which case a very catholic notion is needed of which objects make up wholes.

10   For discussion of the snowball as a paradigm composite of form and matter, see Sosa (1987: 155–87).

11   The key section of Sosa's article for present purposes, "Nonabsolute Existence and Conceptual Relativity," is reprinted along with an addendum in van Inwagen and Zimmerman

(1998: 399–410). I have developed the explosion problem independently (Van Cleve 1986: 141–56).

12 The first principle is often advanced under the name "the impenetrability of matter." The second is advanced by Nelson Goodman (1966: 36).

13 Ted Sider devotes a chapter of *Four-Dimensionalism* (2001) to "The Paradoxes of Coincidence," canvassing many more strategies than I consider here for avoiding the result that distinct objects can share the same parts and occupy the same location. The fact that such a plethora of strategies has been developed shows the extent and depth (at least among philosophers) of the intuition that real coincidence is something to be avoided if possible.

14 As noted by Sosa (1993).

15 For further discussion, see Van Cleve (2004).

16 If there are three atoms, *a*, *b*, and *c*, there will be seven entities altogether: *a*, *b*, *c*, *a* + *b*, *b* + *c*, *a* + *c*, and *a* + *b* + *c*. If *a*, *b*, and *c* have their own parts, there will be many more entities altogether.

17 Van Inwagen distinguishes this from the General Composition Question, which seeks an equivalent to 'the *x*s compose *y*' with the variable '*y*' free. For subtle reasons detailed in chapter 4 of *Material Beings*, he thinks the General Composition Question is much more difficult to answer than the Special Composition Question.

18 Actually, van Inwagen's nihilist says that there is never a *y* that the *x*s compose unless there is only one of the *x*s – the degenerate case of a thing composing itself.

19 Both doctrines imply that there are no composite objects, but they are not quite equivalent. One difference is that thoroughgoing eliminativism implies that there are no objects consisting of a single atom exemplifying a monadic form, while nihilism is silent on this point.

20 Ted Sider (1993) also raises this difficulty for nihilism.

21 I revert to the pretense that tower, nose, and air are themselves continuous.

22 For further objections to the principle of continuity or contact, see van Inwagen, (1990: ch. 3). For example, the principle would imply that a new thing comes into being when you and I shake hands.

23 The example is Ned Markosian's (1998).

24 Carey and Spelke find these principles (which they call the principles of contact and cohesion) guiding the reasoning even of 4-month-old infants. For example, an infant who sees two dumbbell heads moving together will be surprised when a screen obscuring the space between the heads is removed to reveal no connecting handle. This is supposed to show that the infant believes that if objects move together (cohesion), they are parts of one object, and if they are parts of one object, they are not separated by any gap (contact).

25 Actually, if the contact principle is understood strictly so that contact is not a matter of degree, it will not be open to the objection I am about to raise. It will, however, remain open to the objection that many of the objects recognized by commonsense are composed of parts that are not in strict contact.

26 I have voiced the complaint thus: "I doubt that we can find any principle for doing this [admitting just the wholes that commonsense normally admits] that is not either vague, arbitrary, or a matter of degree" (Van Cleve 1986: 145). I should perhaps have subordinated the first two disjuncts to the third: because the unity-making relations invoked in the principles are matters of degree, the principles will give rise either to arbitrariness or to vagueness.

27 I have adapted Sider's argument so that its conclusion is a disjunction – either universalism or nihilism – rather than universalism outright. See also chapter 6.1 in this volume.

28 The term 'sorites' is sometimes used broadly as a name for a chain of reasoning in which each intermediate conclusion is used as a premise to generate the next conclusion. It is also used more narrowly (as here) for instances of such reasoning involving vague predicates like 'is bald' and 'is a heap'. 'Soros' is the Greek word for 'heap'.

29 'Definitely F' and 'F' are arguably equivalent. Whatever is definitely F is F, and as for the converse, can there be anything that is F but not definitely so? We do not need to rely on this argument, however, for the original sorites reaches its conclusion just as well if 'F occurs or F does not occur' is substituted for 'F definitely occurs or F definitely does not occur' in P2 and P3.

30 Here is a reason for thinking otherwise, however: to block the argument from reaching the conclusion that the last head is bald, one must hold that somewhere along the series we pass from a head that is bald to a head with one more hair that is neither bald nor not bald, but simply indeterminate. Isn't a sharp divide between baldness and indeterminacy as bad as the already rejected sharp divide between baldness and non-baldness?

31 In actual instances of the formula, the plural variable 'the xs' will be replaced by a term referring to some concrete plurality of objects. We may suppose that there is nothing vague about what this term refers to, for we are investigating vagueness that arises even when the xs have been perfectly delineated.

32 A loophole in the argument of the last three paragraphs has occurred to me, but I do not know how seriously to take it. Could it be that we have left nothing unsettled about the meaning of the open sentence 'x is part of y' and nothing unsettled about the quantifier '$\exists y \ldots$', yet there is still indeterminacy in certain formulas constructed by putting these elements together, for example, '$\exists y(x$ is part of y & z is part of $y)$'?

33 Compare Lewis (1986: 212–13), and van Inwagen (1990: 233). This contrast between existence and baldness may in the end be spurious, however. In the final chapter of *Material Beings*, van Inwagen shows that it depends on the inference from 'it is indefinite whether $\exists x Fx$' to 'there is something such that it is indefinite whether *it* is F', and he sketches a logic in which this inference fails.

34 There is an important but hard-to-classify fourth option that we should also consider. In this option, one denies the premise that says 'if I am a composite object that will cease to exist upon the dispersal of its parts, universalism must be false'. The proponent of the option argues that this premise is false because 'universalism is true & I am a composite object & I will cease to exist upon the dispersal of my parts' is a possible combination. Let universalism be true (every set has a sum) and let me be a composite object in the sense that there is a certain set of objects of which I am a sum; it could still be true that I will cease to exist upon the dispersal of the parts in that set. Of course, a sum of those parts will still exist after their dispersal, but I am not and never was identical with that sum (says the proponent), even though I was formerly composed of the very parts that compose it. I was another sum, with essential properties (consciousness or life, perhaps) not possessed by the sum that exists after my demise. Assuming that the latter sum also existed while I did, this view rejects the uniqueness axiom of classical mereology.

In this view, some composite objects are "mere" mereological sums, while others are *supersums*: they satisfy the definition of a sum, but they also have persistence conditions or essential forms that go beyond those of a mere sum. Uniqueness is violated because a mere sum and a supersum may be sums of the same parts at the same time.

How shall we classify this view? It subscribes to the letter of universalism, but also has an air of moderation about it. We can raise something like the Special Composition Question all over again: when do the xs compose a supersum? If the answer is "only when their activity constitutes a life," then we are giving an answer that savors of moderation.

I believe that a position along the foregoing lines is the intended view of most of those who say that they wish to distinguish the 'is' of composition from the 'is' of identity. I am composed of the particles in a certain sum that coexists with me, they say, but I am not identical with that sum. They do not always realize that, for better or for worse, they are renouncing the uniqueness axiom. For a case in point, see Wiggins (1979: 297–315).

There is also a fifth view worthy of mention, advocated by Burke (1994). Burke would affirm three of the points that are part of the view described in the first paragraph of this note: that I am composed of a certain set of molecules at t1, that I will cease to exist upon the dispersal of these molecules at t2, and that the molecules will still compose something (have a sum) after their dispersal. Are there then *two* things composed of the same molecules at t1, a mere sum that will survive their dispersal and a person who will not? Burke says no – there is only one thing, the person. My scattered remains at t2 compose a *new* sum that did not exist previously. Burke thus upholds uniqueness *at* a time (there is only one thing composed of the members of a given set at a given time) by denying uniqueness *over* time (the same molecules may compose different things – now a person, now a sum – at different times).

35 This example comes from Broad (1925: 34–8). A similar example involving a rotating disk has been discussed by Kripke and others; see Sider (2001: 224–36).

36 Markosian says that his brutal composition view is compatible with the following supervenience thesis: worlds alike in their distribution of universals are alike in their compositional facts. The example of the fluid arguably shows that identity facts are not supervenient in this sense (determined by the distribution of universals).

37 Note that the existence principles of the Aristotelian go far beyond any composition principles – even the universalist's unrestricted composition principle. The unbridled Aristotelian believes not only that any *xs* compose something, but also that any *xs* compose indefinitely many things. The moon and the six pennies may compose not only their mereological sum, but also the configuration known as a full Monty, which exists just when the moon is full and the pennies all lie tails up. When we turn a penny over, we destroy the Monty but not the sum. Since these entities are distinct despite having the same parts, the Aristotelian implicitly rejects the uniqueness axiom of classical mereology.

38 See also what Hilary Putnam (1987: 18–19) has to say about the differences between the universalist (personified by "the Polish logician") and the atoms-only theorist (personified by Carnap).

39 The textbook example of a verbal dispute and its resolution was provided by William James in his report on a camping trip – quoted in Copi (1978: 127–8). One of the campers circled a tree in an effort to get a glimpse of a squirrel that was clinging to the trunk on the other side and always managing to keep the trunk between himself and his pursuer. A metaphysical dispute broke out among the rest of the campers: did the man go around the squirrel or not? Yes, James offered, if "going around" means being successively to the north, east, south, and west of him; no, if it means being successively to the front, left, rear, and right of him. James noted that most of the campers were satisfied with his solution, though some found it an evasion of the issue. Hirsch assimilates many disputes about the ontology of physical objects, such as the dispute between universalists and their opponents, to James's incident.

40 Hirsch applies this strategy to the dispute over *temporal* sums, such as the "first wood, then ceramic" object composed of the present temporal part of my pencil and a later temporal part of the mug, but I think he would apply it as well to the dispute over spatial sums of contemporaneous objects.

James Van Cleve

41 I wish to thank Derek Ettinger, Christopher Kane, Eli Hirsch, and Dean Zimmerman for their comments on earlier drafts.

References

Broad, C. D. 1925. *The Mind and its Place in Nature* (London: Kegan Paul).

Burke, Michael B. 1994. "Preserving the Principle of One Object to a Place: A Novel Account of the Relations among Objects, Sorts, Sortals, and Persistence Conditions," *Philosophy and Phenomenological Research* 54: 591–624.

Carey, Susan, and Spelke, Elizabeth. 1994. "Domain-Specific Knowledge and Conceptual Change," in *Mapping the Mind: Domain Specificity in Cognition and Culture* (Cambridge: Cambridge University Press), pp. 169–200.

Copi, Irving. 1978. *Introduction to Logic*, 5th edn. (New York: Macmillan).

Eberle, Rolf. 1970. *Nominalistic Systems* (Dordrecht: D. Reidel).

Goodman, Nelson. 1966. *The Structure of Appearance*, 2nd edn. (Indianapolis, IN: Bobbs-Merrill).

Goodman, Nelson, and Leonard, Henry. 1940. "The Calculus of Individuals and its Uses," *Journal of Symbolic Logic* 5: 45–55.

Hirsch, Eli. 2005. "Physical-Object Ontology, Verbal Disputes, and Commonsense," *Philosophy and Phenomenological Research* 70: 1–30.

Leśniewski, S. 1916, *Podstawy ogólnej teoryi mnogosci. I*, Moskow: Prace Polskiego Kola Naukowego w Moskwie, Sekcya matematyczno-przyrodnicza. (Trans. by D. I. Barnett as "Foundations of the General Theory of Sets. I," in S. Leśniewski, *Collected Works*, ed. S. J. Surma, J. Srzednicki, D. I. Barnett, and F. V. Rickey (Dordrecht: Kluwer, 1992; Vol. 1, pp. 129–73.)

Lewis, David. 1986. *On the Plurality of Worlds* (Oxford: Blackwell Publishing).

—. 1991. *Parts of Classes* (Oxford: Blackwell Publishing).

Markosian, Ned. 1998. "Brutal Composition," *Philosophical Studies* 92: 211–49.

Putnam, Hilary. 1987. *The Many Faces of Realism* (La Salle, ILL: Open Court).

Rosen, Gideon, and Dorr, Cian. 2002. "Composition as Fiction," in Richard M. Gale, ed., *The Blackwell Guide to Metaphysics* (Oxford: Blackwell Publishing), pp. 151–74.

Sider, Ted. 1993. "Van Inwagen and the Possibility of Gunk," *Analysis* 53: 285–9.

—. 2001. *Four-Dimensionalism* (Oxford: Oxford University Press).

Simons, Peter. 1987. *Parts: A Study in Ontology* (Oxford: Oxford University Press).

Sosa, Ernest. 1987. "Subjects Among Other Things," in James Tomberlin, ed., *Philosophical Perspectives*, vol. I (Atascadero, CA: Ridgeview Publishing Co.), pp. 155–87.

—. 1993. "Putnam's Pragmatic Realism," *The Journal of Philosophy* 90: 605–26.

Tarski, A. 1937. *Einführung in die mathematische Logik und in die Methodologie der Mathematik* (Vienna: Julius Springer). (Trans. with additions by O. Helmer as *Introduction to Logic and to the Methodology of Deductive Science* (New York: Oxford University Press, 1941.)

—. 1956. "Foundations of the Geometry of Solids," in *Logic, Semantics, and Metamathematics* (Oxford: Oxford University Press), pp. 24–9.

Van Cleve, James. 1986. "Mereological Essentialism, Mereological Conjunctivism, and Identity Through Time," *Midwest Studies in Philosophy* 11: 141–56.

—, James. 1999. *Problems from Kant* (Oxford: Oxford University Press).

—, James. 2004. "On What There is Now: Sosa on Two Forms of Relativity," in John Greco, ed., *Ernest Sosa and His Critics* (Oxford: Blackwell Publishing).

Van Inwagen, Peter. 1990. *Material Beings* (Ithaca, NY: Cornell University Press).

Van Inwagen, Peter, and Zimmerman, Dean W. 1998. *Metaphysics: The Big Questions*, (Oxford: Blackwell Publishing).

Wiggins, David. 1979. "Mereological Essentialism: Asymmetrical Essential Dependence and the Nature of Continuants," in Ernest Sosa, ed., *Essays on the Philosophy of Roderick M. Chisholm* (Amsterdam: Rodopi), pp. 297–315.

Zimmerman, Dean W. 1996. "Could Extended Objects Be Made Out of Simple Parts? An Argument for 'Atomless Gunk'," *Philosophy and Phenomenological Research* 56: 1–29.

Restricted Composition

Ned Markosian

1 Introduction

Consider two quarks: one near the tip of your nose, the other near the center of Alpha Centauri. Here's a question about these two subatomic particles: Is there an object that has these two quarks as its parts and that has no other parts? According to one view of the matter (a view endorsed, surprisingly, by a great many contemporary philosophers), the answer to this question is "yes." But according to commonsense, the answer to this question is really "no."

Here's a more general question. Under what circumstances do two or more objects compose a further object? According to one view of the matter (again, a view endorsed by a large number of contemporary philosophers), the answer to this question is that for any group of objects, no matter how disparate or spatially separated, there is an object composed of the members of that group. On this view, there are no restrictions on when "composition" occurs. If there are some objects, on this view, then there is automatically another object composed of those objects. But according to commonsense, it's not the case that for any group of objects, there is automatically an additional object composed of the members of that group. That is, according to commonsense, composition is restricted.

This chapter explores this commonsense view, together with its rival (the view that composition is unrestricted). It will be seen that, although the idea of restricting composition is intuitively very appealing, it proves to be more difficult than one might have thought to come up with a plausible proposal regarding just how composition is to be restricted. But I hope to show that, in the final analysis, it's better to accept the difficulties that go with restricting composition than it is to avoid them by leaving composition unrestricted.

2 The Special Composition Question

Recall the above example involving two quarks (one near the tip of your nose, the other near the center of Alpha Centauri). This is a clear case in which it seems that two objects fail to compose a further object. Now consider a different collection of subatomic particles: all the particles that make up your body right now. This is an equally clear case in which it seems that a bunch of objects do compose a further object. The existence of such cases gives rise to a very natural question: what is the general rule governing when composition occurs and when it doesn't occur?

Peter van Inwagen (1990) is responsible for this question's being widely discussed in contemporary metaphysics.[1] Here is a way of formulating the relevant question that is based on van Inwagen's work (1990: 28–9).[2]

x overlaps y = $_{df}$ there is a z such that z is a part of x and z is a part of y.

The *x*s *compose* y = $_{df}$ (i) the *x*s are all parts of y, (ii) no two of the *x*s overlap, and (iii) every part of y overlaps at least one of the *x*s.

The Special Composition Question (SCQ): What necessary and jointly sufficient conditions must any *x*s satisfy in order for it to be the case that there is an object composed of those *x*s?

Several preliminary matters need to be addressed before we begin considering answers to SCQ. First, note that SCQ is not asking for an analysis of the concept of composition. (To ask for such an analysis is to ask what van Inwagen calls the General Composition Question.) Second, we will, following van Inwagen, focus our attention here on physical objects (as opposed to non-physical objects), and on the problem of identifying the circumstances under which some physical objects compose an additional physical object.

Our third preliminary matter involves terminology. There's another notion related to the idea of composition that's also widely employed in discussions of mereology, namely, the notion of a "sum" or "fusion," which can be defined as follows.[3]

y is a *sum* (or *fusion*) of the *x*s = $_{df}$ every one of the *x*s is a part of y and every part of y overlaps at least one of the *x*s.

The difference between saying that y is composed of the *x*s and saying that y is a sum (or fusion) of the *x*s is that the former but not the latter entails that the *x*s do not overlap. So, for example, I'm a sum of my subatomic particles, and I'm also composed of them; but although I'm a sum of my subatomic particles and my brain, I'm not composed of my subatomic particles and my brain, since my subatomic particles and my brain overlap.[4] Thus an equivalent way of asking SCQ would be this: what necessary and jointly sufficient conditions must any *x*s satisfy in order for there to be an object that is a sum of those *x*s?

Our final preliminary matter involves a common presupposition that is shared by (virtually) all parties to the debate over restricted composition, namely, "anticonventionalism." This is the view that what exists is never a matter of human stipulation or convention. As van Inwagen says: "Let us always remember Abraham Lincoln's undeservedly neglected riddle: How many legs has a dog got if you call a tail a leg? The answer, said Lincoln, and he was right, is *four*, because calling a tail a leg doesn't make it one" (1990: 7–8).

3 Unrestricted Composition

We begin our consideration of responses to SCQ with the idea that the members of any collection objects whatsoever automatically form an additional object. Here's our main formulation of the view.

> Unrestricted Composition (UC): Necessarily, for any non-overlapping *x*s, there is a *y* such that *y* is composed of the *x*s.[5]

There are various considerations that count in favor of UC. To begin with, the early pioneers in the field of mereology assumed the truth of UC.[6] That should count for something. Furthermore, UC is a simple and elegant response to SCQ.

Another point in its favor is that, unlike some responses to SCQ that we will examine below, UC posits the existence of plenty of composite objects. Thus the proponent of UC will never have to deal with the problems that go with having a sparse ontology of composite objects.

Finally, a fourth point in its favor is that UC is consistent with the popular thesis that there can be no genuine vagueness in the world.[7] (According to this thesis, vagueness is merely a linguistic phenomenon, resulting from semantic indecision. No one has decided exactly where The Outback ends, but this does not mean that The Outback is a vague region with indeterminate boundaries.)

Despite the fact that UC has these four points in its favor, and is therefore an initially attractive theory, it must be noted that none of the above considerations actually entails that UC is true. And, as it turns out, there are some powerful considerations that count against UC. The main consideration against it is simply that UC has many very counterintuitive consequences. One of these involves the two quarks in the above example: according to UC, there is an object composed of that one quark near the tip of your nose and that other quark near the center of Alpha Centauri. But such an object, if it exists, is certainly not recognized by commonsense.

At least the two quarks in our example are similar to one another. Another type of counterintuitive consequence of UC has to do with cases involving very disparate items, such as your left shoe and our quark from the center of Alpha Centauri. According to UC, these objects also have a fusion (which is very much like a shoe, except for the fact that part of it is many light years from the rest and is extremely small).

These sorts of example could be multiplied endlessly. In general, the objection to UC is that it commits us to many bizarre objects that commonsense intuitions cannot countenance.

One possible response to this objection involves saying something along these lines:

Unrestricted composition is ontologically innocent. For the sum of some *x*s is nothing "over and above" the plurality of the *x*s. If you are committed to the plurality, then you are thereby committed to the sum.[8]

Unfortunately for the proponent of UC, it's fairly easy to see that this response to the objection fails. For although there's a sense in which it's true that UC is ontologically innocent, there's also an important sense in which it's false.

Here's the sense in which it's true that UC is ontologically innocent. If there are some *x*s, and if those *x*s have a sum, then the sum of the *x*s does not contain any new matter that's not already included in the matter that makes up the *x*s.

And here's the sense in which it's false that UC is ontologically innocent. If there are some *x*s, and if those *x*s have a sum, then the sum of the *x*s is something in addition to the *x*s. The easiest way to see this is to consider an example. Suppose we have two mereological simples[9] that are several miles apart in some space that's otherwise completely empty. And suppose we are asked, "How many objects are there in this space?" Well, there's clearly a difference between saying that there are two objects in the space, as commonsense tells us, and saying that there are three objects, as UC says. And the difference has to do with the number of objects that are said to exist.

This example makes it clear that, insofar as UC commits us to the existence of more objects than we are otherwise committed to, it is not ontologically innocent. UC may be philosophically respectable, and it may even be true. But ontologically innocent it is not.

A more promising response to the objection that UC has counterintuitive results involves admitting that UC commits us to a great many counterintuitive objects, but attempting to soften the blow by claiming that in ordinary contexts we restrict the domain of our quantifiers.[10]

Here's an example involving restricted quantifiers. At a party, the host says, "All the glasses are on the table." But he doesn't mean that all the glasses in the world are on the table. He means instead that all the glasses at the party are on the table. He is thus restricting the domain of his quantifiers to things at the party. And it should be clear that this sort of thing happens with great frequency in everyday discourse.

The proponent of UC can say, then, that we ordinarily restrict the domain of our quantifiers to objects composed of parts that are more or less in contact with one another and that tend to move around together. Thus, according to this line, a sentence like 'There is an object composed of Mia Hamm and the Taj Mahal' is false in ordinary contexts, because in those contexts we are restricting our quantifiers in a way that excludes such spatially scattered objects as the sum of Mia Hamm and the Taj Mahal. But still, according to this line, there nevertheless is an object composed of those two.

I think this is the most promising way for the proponent of UC to respond to the objection that UC has wildly counterintuitive consequences. But I don't think this response completely answers the objection. Here's why. The objection is not merely that if we accept UC then we shall have to say that many typical pronouncements of commonsense – such as that there's no object composed of Mia Hamm and the Taj Mahal – turn out to be false. (If that were all there is to the objection, then talking about how we often restrict the domain of our quantifiers would be a satisfactory way of replying to the objection.) Rather, the objection is that UC commits us to the existence of many strange objects that are never dreamt of by ordinary people. And talking about restricting the domain of our quantifiers does not address this problem. For suppose we are in a context in which we have explicitly stated that the domain of our quantifiers is completely unrestricted. ("I'm talking about absolutely everything there is, including whatever weird, not-recognized-by-commonsense objects there may be.") Then it's still very counterintuitive to say that there is an object composed of Mia Hamm and the Taj Mahal.

Now let's turn to a second objection to UC, namely, that it entails four-dimensionalism. (Four-dimensionalism, or 4D, is the thesis that objects persist through time by having different temporal parts at the different moments at which they are present. It is to be contrasted with Three-dimensionalism, or 3D, which is the thesis that objects persist through time by being wholly present at each moment at which they are present.[11])

Here's an argument to show that UC entails 4D.[12] To begin with, UC entails that there can be two distinct objects in the same place, and composed of the same parts, at the same time. To see why, think about yourself. You exist now, and you are currently composed of certain particles.[13] The particles that compose you now existed ten years ago, and were then widely scattered throughout the Earth's biosphere. According to UC, even though the particles in question were widely scattered throughout the Earth's biosphere ten years ago, they nevertheless composed something then. Since you were not widely scattered throughout the Earth's biosphere ten years ago, the object that the particles in question composed ten years ago was not you. Moreover, since, according to UC, the arrangement of some objects makes no difference to whether those objects compose something, the object that the particles in question composed ten years ago, and that was then distinct from you, still exists now.

But it's impossible for two objects (such as yourself and the scattered object composed of the particles in question ten years ago) to become one. Which means that, according to UC, there are now two distinct objects located where you are located, and composed of the exact same particles. One of these objects (namely, you) is what we might call "mereologically variable" – it's composed of different parts at different times. The other object in question (namely, the object that was composed of your current particles ten years ago, when they (and it) were widely scattered throughout the Earth's biosphere), is what we might call "mereologically constant" – it's always composed of the same parts.

Now, the only plausible way to allow that two distinct objects can be in the same place, and composed of the same parts, at the same time is to say that the relevant objects, like two roads that share a stretch of pavement, are extended things that share a segment or "stage" or "temporal part" (where a temporal part of an object, x, is, roughly, an object that exists for a shorter time than x and that perfectly overlaps x throughout its existence).[14] Thus the proponent of UC must say that you are a mereologically variable object that, at each moment of its existence, shares a temporal part with a mereologically constant object. (And does so with different mereologically constant objects at different times.) Similar remarks will be true with respect to virtually all other commonsense objects, including human beings, chairs, rocks, and stars.

The upshot is that UC entails 4D. But 4D is a highly controversial thesis. Hence this entailment is an important cost of UC.[15]

There is a third major disadvantage of UC, namely, that it entails a certain very radical thesis about identity over time for composite objects.[16] We have seen that UC entails that commonsense objects, like human beings and chairs, are mereologically variable objects that share temporal parts with various other mereologically constant objects. The existence of mereologically variable objects raises a question for the proponent of UC. The question concerns what it takes for an object that's composed of certain mereological simples at one time to be identical to an object composed of different simples at another time.[17]

Here is a closely related question. Given that the proponent of UC is committed to saying that, in some cases, an object composed of some xs at t1 is identical to an object composed of some ys (distinct from the xs) at t2, is there any way that he or she can restrict such "diachronic identity" for composite objects?

Theodore Sider (1990: ch. 4.9) has argued persuasively that the answer to this question is "no."[18] I don't have the space here to repeat Sider's argument, but the basic idea is that if we try to restrict diachronic identity for composite objects in a way that's supported by commonsense intuitions about individual cases, we'll have to accept either genuine vagueness in the world or else brute facts about diachronic identity for composite objects. And Sider takes both horns of this dilemma to be untenable.

Now, if Sider is right about these matters, the proponent of UC is also committed to the following, much more extreme, cross-time version of UC. (Note that I intend the domain of times in question to include both instants and extended periods of time.)

Unrestricted Composition with Unrestricted Diachronic Identity (UCUDI): Necessarily, for any non-overlapping xs, for any non-overlapping ys, and for any times, t1 and t2, such that the xs exist at t1 and the ys exist at t2, there is an object, z, such that z is composed of the xs at t1 and z is composed of the ys at t2.

One consequence of UCUDI is that there is an object that was composed of the shoes Abraham Lincoln was wearing at the time of his inauguration and is now composed of the players on the 2004 US Olympic soccer team. Another consequence is that there is an object that is composed of all your parts right now and that will, in ten minutes, be composed of all the eyeglasses in the world. In short, UCUDI entails the existence of all manner of strange persisting objects, including temporally gappy objects and objects that change radically over time in bizarre ways. In fact, considering the unusual nature of many of these putative objects, it is tempting to say that anyone who truly believes UCUDI does not understand by the words 'persisting object' what the rest of the world does. This is surely a very high price associated with UC.

4 Nihilism

I mentioned above that one advantage of UC is that it's a simple and elegant response to SCQ. UC shares this feature with a rival that's at the opposite end of the spectrum. I have in mind the view that there are no objects composed of two or more parts. Here is an official statement of the view.

Nihilism: Necessarily, for any non-overlapping *x*s, there is an object composed of the *x*s iff there is only one of the *x*s.[19]

In addition to simplicity and elegance, another characteristic that nihilism shares with UC is its consistency with the denial of vagueness in the world. Among its other virtues is that nihilism may allow one to avoid certain puzzles concerning composite objects, such as the ancient puzzle involving the ship of Theseus, the so-called paradox of undetached parts, and the problem of the many.[20]

Still, nihilism has its drawbacks. Chief among these is that there are not enough objects in the world, according to nihilism, to satisfy commonsense intuitions about what there is. For nihilism entails that there are no atoms, chairs, rocks, planets, or stars. It also entails that there are no cells, dogs, fish, or elephants. This complete lack of composite objects, given our ordinary beliefs in such things, is a general problem for nihilism. But there is also a particular version of this problem that concerns us: nihilism entails either that there are no people or that people are simples. And most of us would reject both of these alternatives.

One way for the nihilist to reply to the charge of having an impoverished ontology is to make use of a technique, developed by van Inwagen, that involves paraphrasing ordinary sentences that strike us as true – but that are false according to the nihilist – into sentences that, according to the nihilist, are in fact true.[21]

Here's the idea. Suppose we're in a situation in which ordinary people would say that there's a chair in the corner, but no ordinary person would say that there's an elephant in the corner. Consider these sentences.

(1) There is a chair in the corner.
(2) There is an elephant in the corner.

The nihilist says that in the imagined circumstances, (1) and (2) are both false. (For according to the nihilist there is neither a chair nor an elephant in the corner, but only some simples arranged in various ways.) But the nihilist wants to be able to capture the sense in which (1) is correct, as well as the sense in which (2) is incorrect. So consider the following paraphrases of (1) and (2).

(1a) There are some simples arranged chairwise in the corner.
(2a) There are some simples arranged elephantwise in the corner.

The nihilist can say that (1a) is true while (2a) is false, and that, moreover, the truth of (1a) corresponds to the sense in which (1) is correct (even though it is, strictly speaking, false); whereas the falsity of (2a) corresponds to the sense in which (2) is incorrect (in addition to being strictly speaking false).

More generally, the nihilist can say that sentences that entail the existence of composite objects, and that we would ordinarily take to be true, are literally false but nevertheless correct, because they correspond to literally true paraphrases like (1a); while sentences entailing the existence of composite objects that we would ordinarily take to be false are both literally false and incorrect, because they correspond to sentences like (2a).[22]

Unfortunately for the nihilist, however, not everyone will be convinced that the paraphrasing approach can do everything it's supposed to do. Here's why. Part of what the paraphrasing strategy is supposed to do is capture the sense in which it's correct, in certain situations, to say that there is a chair in the corner. So far, so good. But the other thing the paraphrasing approach is supposed to do for the nihilist is to soften the blow of having to say that there are no commonsense objects like chairs. And it's not clear that just being able to say that there are many cases of simples arranged chairwise makes up for having to say that there are not really any chairs. After all, the relevant intuition is not merely that in certain situations there's something correct about saying that there's a chair in the corner. The intuition is that it's literally true in those situations that there is a chair in the corner. To the extent that this intuition is right, the paraphrasing approach fails.

Moreover, recall from above the nihilist's problem of having to say either that there are no people or else that people are simples. Suppose the nihilist embraces the first horn of this dilemma. Then paraphrasing will only go so far toward solving the problem. For although we can say that there are some simples arranged personwise in the region where we take you to exist right now, what are we to say about the fact of your apparent consciousness? Suppose you are having the thought that would ordinarily be expressed by saying "I think, therefore I am." Then there seems to be consciousness going on in the region we take to be occupied by you, and it may or may not be possible to capture what is true about that with paraphrases like 'There are some simples arranged consciousnesswise in this region.' But either way, we will also need to account for the apparent fact that there is a single *subject* of that consciousness, which is the *same subject* that will be having a similar thought later on (when it will be different simples that are arranged consciousnesswise).[23] This is likely to be a difficult problem for the Nihilist to solve, which may be a good reason for the Nihilist to embrace the second horn of our current dilemma, and say that people are in fact mereological simples.[24]

5 Contact

UC and nihilism are both, in van Inwagen's terminology, "extreme answers" to SCQ. Let's consider some "moderate answers," according to which there are possible cases in which certain simples fail to compose an additional object, and possible cases in which certain other simples (or even the same simples arranged differently) do compose a further object. One such view is based on the idea that in order for some xs to compose something, they must not be spatially separated from one another, i.e., they must be in contact with one another. Here is an official formulation of this view.

> Contact: Necessarily, for any non-overlapping xs, there is an object composed of the xs iff the xs are in contact with one another.[25]

Although it's based on an intuitively appealing idea, contact nevertheless has some very counterintuitive consequences. Here's one: whenever I place a hand on my daughter's shoulder, a new composite object, with her and me as parts, comes into existence. Here's another: whenever two people stand in the same room, there is an object composed of the two people in question and the floor they are standing on. In general, contact seems to be far too liberal about the nature and number of composite objects in the world.

Or perhaps contact is really too conservative about the nature and number of composite objects in the world. For the different particles that make up an atom are presumably not, after all, in contact with one another. Which means that, according to contact, there may not actually be any atoms.[26]

6 Fastenation

A more promising idea is that in order for some objects to compose a further object, they must be somehow stuck together, so that they move around jointly. Here's a view based on this idea.

> Fastenation: Necessarily, for any non-overlapping xs, there is an object composed of the xs iff the xs are fastened together.[27]

In my experience, something like fastenation is the first thing that comes to mind among most non-philosophers when they initially consider SCQ. So I think the view probably has at least as much intuitive appeal as any other response to our question. But, unfortunately, fastenation is nevertheless subject to some serious objections. Here's one that comes from van Inwagen (1990: 57–8). Suppose two people, while shaking hands, become paralyzed so that they are unable to pull their hands apart. Then, according to fastenation, there is a new object in the world, composed of the two paralyzed handshakers. But that seems to be the wrong result.

Here's a second objection to fastenation.[28] The multigrade relation of being fastened together is a relation that comes in degrees. So we must ask, which degree of fastenation is relevant to bringing a new object into the world? The problem is that any particular answer to this question (such as .5 on a scale from 0 to 1, or .673621) seems intolerably arbitrary.

One possible reply to this objection is to say that any degree of fastenation at all is sufficient for there to be an object composed of the xs. Here's a view based on this idea.

> Weak Fastenation: Necessarily, for any non-overlapping xs, there is an object composed of the xs iff the xs are fastened together to some degree greater than zero.

But this view, besides being subject to the above paralyzed handshakers' objection to fastenation, also seems to give awkward results in cases involving some xs that are fastened together but to only a very small degree. In light of this, the proponent of fastenation may want to consider the following variation on the view.

> n-Fastenation: Necessarily, for any non-overlapping xs, it is true to degree n that there is an object composed of the xs iff the xs are fastened together to degree n.

But here we run into a different problem: n-fastenation presupposes that for any xs, there is a degree to which those xs are all fastened together; but no doubt this presupposition is false. Perhaps this problem can be solved, however, by declaring that the weakest degree of fastenation among any two of the xs determines the degree to which there's an object composed of those xs.

Still, n-fastenation entails that there can be genuine vagueness in the world and, as was noted above, many philosophers consider this idea untenable. Such philosophers will of course have no truck with n-fastenation.

A philosopher who does not mind positing vagueness in the world, on the other hand, may well want to embrace n-fastenation. Alternatively, she may want to combine elements of both weak fastenation and n-fastenation into the following view.

> Weak Fastenation With Degrees: (i) Necessarily, for any non-overlapping xs, there is an object composed of the xs iff the xs are fastened together to some degree greater than zero. (ii) Necessarily, for any non-overlapping xs that are fastened together to some degree greater than zero, and for any x among those xs, x is a part of the object composed of the xs to the degree to which x is fastened to the rest of the xs.

Here's a final problem for fastenation. How can we define the phrase 'the xs are fastened together'? It won't do, for example, to say that the xs are fastened together iff it's fairly difficult to move them away from one another without damaging them.[29] For on that definition, a newborn calf and its mother would count as being fastened together. And it turns out that other likely proposals seem to be equally problematic. So it looks like the proponent of Fastenation will be stuck with a view whose main concept must be taken as primitive.

7 Van Inwagen's Proposed Answer

In *Material Beings*, van Inwagen comes to the conclusion that there are no inanimate, composite objects. But, he reasons, if some simples function together in such a way that their activities constitute a life, then there's a composite object – a living thing – that they compose. On this view, the only objects in the world are simples and living organisms.

Before we look at an official formulation of this view, we need to get a bit clearer on two main concepts that the view is based on: the notion of the activities of some objects constituting a certain event, and the notion of a life. Van Inwagen doesn't offer a definition of 'the activities of the xs constitute event E', but he does offer several instructive examples, including the following: (i) the activities of the cattle constituted the stampede, and (ii) the activities of the water molecules in the pan constituted the cooling of the water in the pan (1990: 82). Although van Inwagen himself doesn't put it this way, I take it that the idea is roughly that the activities of some xs constitute an event, E, when E is a larger event that is a mereological sum of the events that are the activities of the xs.

What about the second main concept that van Inwagen's view is based on, that of a life? This too is a notion that van Inwagen does not attempt to define but, instead, one that he explains in various other ways (1990: sect. 9). Chief among the things he says in his explanation is that lives are events of a certain kind. At one point he imagines a disembodied intellect who has never heard of organic life and who is examining some earthly organism for the first time. He imagines this disembodied intellect saying the following.

> What I am observing is an unimaginably complex self-maintaining storm of atoms. This storm moves across the surface of the world, drawing swirls and clots of atoms into it and expelling others, always maintaining its overall structure. One might call it a homeo-dynamic event. (1990: 87)

Here's the view that van Inwagen proposes:

Van Inwagen's Proposed Answer (VIPA): Necessarily, for any non-overlapping xs, there is an object composed of the xs iff either (i) the activities of the xs constitute a life or (ii) there is only one of the xs.[30]

I mentioned above that the nihilist may be able to avoid certain traditional puzzles concerning composite objects, such as the puzzle involving the ship of Theseus, the paradox of undetached parts, and the problem of the many. Van Inwagen can make a similar claim about his view.[31] Another potential advantage of VIPA is that it, unlike nihilism, allows us to account for the single subject of a consciousness, as well as the persisting subject of a single consciousness over time, in a relatively straightforward way. For van Inwagen can plausibly say that the subject of a single consciousness is the organism that is conscious, and that the persisting subject of an extended consciousness is the enduring organism.

VIPA does have its disadvantages, however. Here's the main one. According to VIPA, the only composite objects in the world are organisms, and the only inanimate objects in the world are simples. This means that according to VIPA there are no atoms, rocks, bicycles, or stars. There are only simples and organisms. The main objection to the view that people are likely to have, then, is that there seem to be far more objects than VIPA allows. This is the reason that van Inwagen developed the strategy of paraphrasing, which was discussed above in connection with nihilism. I won't repeat here everything that was said above about the paraphrasing strategy as a way of dealing with the too-few-objects objection, but it should be clear that all the same considerations raised above will apply in the case of that objection and VIPA.

A second main objection to VIPA is that it (when combined with certain other plausible principles about the nature of lives) entails that there can be genuine vagueness in the world. For there appear to be indeterminate cases of an object's being "caught up" in a life. For instance, consider some simples that would ordinarily be taken to compose a carbon atom. Suppose those simples get ingested by a woman drinking tea, so that they're eventually absorbed into her bloodstream.[32] At precisely what instant does it come to be the case that those simples are caught up in that woman's life? Van Inwagen admits that there is no determinate answer to this question, that it follows from his view that there are times at which it is neither determinately true nor determinately false that those simples are parts of the relevant woman, and that it also follows that parthood and composition are both vague notions (1990: 217ff.). This is why VIPA entails that there can be genuine vagueness in the world.[33]

8 Brutal Composition

There is another conclusion that one could draw from consideration of all the disadvantages of the different answers to SCQ we have considered thus far. One could take all of this to show that there simply is no true answer to SCQ. That is, one could maintain that while some xs compose an object and others fail to do so, there is no systematic pattern to these phenomena. When some xs do compose an object, a person who reached this conclusion might say there is no further reason for the fact that those xs compose something. It's just a brute fact.

Before we can officially formulate this view, we need to address a preliminary matter. Suppose there is no rhyme or reason as to when composition occurs and when it doesn't, as the view in question suggests. There could still be a truth of the form "Necessarily, for any xs, there is an object composed of the xs iff −−." It would just have to be an infinitely long list of every possible situation involving some xs that compose a further object. But such a list would certainly be an uninformative "answer" to SCQ. In fact, it would really be no answer at all. Similarly, even such finitely long and true sentences as 'Necessarily, for any non-overlapping xs, there is an object composed of the xs iff the xs compose something' should not count as real answers to SCQ, since they are merely trivially true. So what the view we are currently considering must deny is that there is a finitely long, non-trivial answer to SCQ. Here then is the view.

> Brutal Composition (BC): There is no true, non-trivial, and finitely long answer to SCQ.[34]

BC has certain advantages (some of which it shares with other responses to SCQ). One important advantage of BC is that it's consistent with all of our commonsense intuitions about particular cases of composition. Another advantage of BC is that it's consistent with the idea that there cannot be genuine vagueness in the world. And a third advantage of BC (which it shares with nihilism) is that it seems to allow the 3Der (who denies that ordinary objects have temporal parts) to solve certain puzzles that fall under the heading of "problems of material constitution" in a relatively easy way.[35] (In fact, the proponent of BC can plausibly claim to have much more satisfying solutions to the problems of material constitution than the nihilist, since the BCer solves the problems without denying the existence of commonsense objects like ships and cats.) Moreover, despite the fact that BC shares each of these advantages with at least one other proposal mentioned in this essay, BC is the only proposal discussed here that enjoys all three of the relevant advantages.

Despite this fact, not everyone in the philosophical community has converted to BC (yet). And the view does admittedly have what seem to be several important dis- advantages. The first of these is simply that many people find it to be implausible. There is a general feeling, shared by many philosophers, that a question as intuitively graspable as SCQ must have an answer. A proponent of BC is likely to respond to this objection by agreeing that we should initially assume that any philosophical question as important and clear as SCQ has an answer, but also by claiming that in a case like this one, after careful consideration of all the likely answers has turned up nothing that seems to work, it's appropriate to conclude that there is in fact no answer.

A closely related objection that's likely to be raised against BC involves the idea that compositional facts are not the right sort of facts to be brute facts. Terence Horgan puts the objection this way.

> [A] good metaphysical theory or scientific theory should avoid positing a plethora of quite specific, disconnected, *sui generis*, compositional facts . . . if one bunch of physical simples compose a genuine physical object, but another bunch of simples do not compose any genuine object, then there must be some reason *why*; it couldn't be that these two facts are themselves at the explanatory bedrock of being. (1993: 695)[36]

I think a proponent of BC ought to insist, in response to this objection, that the concept of composition possesses the three main characteristics – (i) being relatively easy to grasp on an intuitive level, (ii) being such that there seem to be clear-cut cases of both instantiation and non-instantiation, and (iii) being such that no account of what it is in virtue of which some xs instantiate that concept seems to be forth- coming – that make a concept a suitable candidate for the status of brutality in our theorizing.

Another objection to BC comes from Theodore Sider (2001: 121–5).[37] Here's a modified version of Sider's argument. The proponent of BC has to say that there can be cases in which two or more objects compose an additional object and also cases in which two or more objects fail to compose an additional object.[38] So consider a pair of possible cases such that the simples in one case compose an object, and the simples in the other case do not. Now imagine further a series of cases that "connect" the two original cases, so that any two adjacent cases in the series are near-duplicates of each other in any respect that one might take to be relevant to the question of whether composition occurs: the number of simples involved, the spatial proximity of those simples to one another, the degree to which those simples are fastened together, etc. (Depending on how many cases you're willing to include, the series can be such that any two adjacent cases are arbitrarily close to being qualitative duplicates in the relevant respects.) Now, since we have at one end of the series a case of com- position, and at the other end a case of non-composition, it follows that somewhere in the series there will be a pair of adjacent cases such that in one case composition occurs and in the other case composition does not occur. Thus, there will be two cases that are near-duplicates of each other in all of the other respects, but that differ with respect to composition. And that seems implausible. Thus, this "continuum argument" seems to show that BC is false.

Here is how I think the BCer ought to reply to this argument.[39] It's true that we have intuitions according to which the factors that vary across the series are relevant to determining whether composition occurs. But it's also true that when you try to follow up those intuitions, and formulate answers to SCQ based on them, you end up with a set of incompatible moderate answers, each member of which has serious problems. So we know that those intuitions have to be given up. The upshot, according to this line of reasoning, is that you can't get a good argument based on the relevant intuitions, since we already know that those intuitions lead to implausible answers to SCQ.

According to this reply to the continuum argument, then, it's true that there is an "abrupt cut-off" in the relevant series of cases, but this does not pose a problem for the view. A BCer who makes this response to the argument might draw the following analogy. Suppose someone claims that people who are left-handed are not left-handed in virtue of being any particular height. And suppose someone else argues against this claim by pointing to a series of possible cases ranging from a five-foot-tall left-hander at one end of the series to a seven-foot-tall right-hander at the other end of the series. It would be implausible to argue that there could not be an "abrupt cut-off" in this series of people (i.e., a pair of adjacent cases in which two people who are near-duplicates with respect to height differ with respect to being left-handed), precisely because we don't think that a person's height determines whether that person is left-handed. Similarly, the BCer can say, once we accept that composition does not occur in virtue of the number of simples involved in a given case, or the spatial proximity of those simples to one another, or the degree to which those simples are fastened together, etc., then we will see that there is nothing implausible about an abrupt cut-off in the series of cases described in the continuum argument.

9 The Serial Response

It might be thought that the above responses to SCQ are all too simplistic, and that they go wrong in presupposing that there is a single "monolithic" answer to SCQ. Perhaps there is no one relation that any *x*s must stand in in order for it to be the case that there is an object composed of those *x*s. Perhaps the truth of the matter is that there are different types of "building blocks" in the world, and that for each such type, there is some unique relation such that whenever some *x*s of that type stand in that relation to one another, then there is an object composed of those *x*s.

Here is a sentence schema that will be useful in formulating a view based on this idea:

(SERIES) Necessarily, for any non-overlapping *x*s, there is an object composed of the *x*s iff *either* the *x*s are *F1*s and related by *R1*, *or* the *x*s are *F2*s and related by *R2*, *or*... the *x*s are *Fn*s and related by *Rn*.

And here is a response to SCQ that involves an appeal to SERIES:

The Serial Response to SCQ: The correct answer to SCQ is an instance of SERIES.[40]

One advantage of such a view is that it may allow us to avoid counterexamples to certain other answers to SCQ that involve a more narrow focus on just one particular factor that is said to be involved in composition, while at the same time yielding results that are consistent with commonsense intuitions about specific cases. Another advantage of the serial response is that some people have an intuition according to which different factors must be involved in different cases of composition, and this view fits that intuition.

There are two main objections to the serial response.[41] The first is simply that no one has yet formulated a plausible instance of SERIES. But perhaps someday someone will. The second objection is that, rather than avoiding the problems that afflict typical moderate answers to SCQ, the serial response seems to compound those problems. In general, the problem with moderate answers to SCQ is that they must identify some multigrade relation that is linked in the relevant way with the concept of composition; and, as our discussion so far has made clear, it's difficult to do this without generating counterintuitive consequences or presupposing the possibility of genuine vagueness in the world. In particular, it's difficult to specify conditions that can plausibly be said to be sufficient for composition without opening oneself up to a great many apparent counterexamples. The serial response apparently compounds the problem because it requires identifying not just one multigrade relation that's linked to the concept of composition in the relevant way, but several; and, moreover, the serial response also requires identifying several additional concepts (the referents of the expressions in place of 'F1', 'F2', etc.) that are also linked both to the concept of composition and to the relevant multigrade relations.

10 The Multi-Factor Approach

Some law schools employ an admissions policy that takes into account several different factors. For example, such a school might look at both a candidate's LSAT scores and her GPA. Moreover, the minimum LSAT score required for admission might vary inversely with respect to the minimum GPA. Thus, on such a system, candidates with relatively low LSAT scores need to have relatively high GPAs to get in, and those with relatively low GPAs need relatively high LSAT scores.

In many such cases, a particular law school's admissions policy can be captured by a formula. For example, the formula

$$[(LSAT \times 2) + (GPA \times 10)] \geq 695$$

means that if the sum of (the candidate's LSAT score times 2) plus (the candidate's GPA times 10) is greater than or equal to 695, then the candidate is admitted; and otherwise she is not. Such an admissions policy can also be captured equally well by a graph, such as the one in figure 1, with LSAT scores represented on its x axis, GPAs represented on its y axis, and a shaded area representing pairs of values for the two factors that correspond to positive admissions decisions.

A student of SCQ might think that composition works in a similar way. Perhaps there are several factors that determine whether composition occurs in a given case,

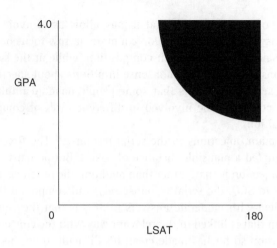

Figure 1

and perhaps, for each factor, the "minimum score" required for composition to take place varies inversely with respect to the other factors. Here's a simplistic theory to illustrate this idea. Suppose that for any xs, there are two factors relevant to whether those xs compose a further object: the degree of fastenation among the xs, and the degree to which the xs collectively contrast with their environment. Let each of these factors be quantifiable on a scale from 0 to 1. Then perhaps this formula,

(degree of fastenation + degree of contrast with environment) ≥ 1.5,

could represent the true answer to SCQ, which could be stated as follows:

The Fastenation + Contrast View: Necessarily, for any non-overlapping *x*s, there is an object composed of the *x*s iff the sum of the degree of fastenation among the *x*s and the degree of contrast between the *x*s and their environment is greater than or equal to 1.5.

And this answer to SCQ could also be represented by a graph like the one shown in figure 2.

I suspect that no actual philosopher will want to endorse the fastenation + contrast view. But this answer to SCQ illustrates a general approach to answering SCQ that has been undeservedly neglected. The general approach, which I will refer to as the Multi-Factor Approach (or MFA), involves saying that the correct answer to SCQ incorporates multiple, interdependent factors, on the model of the fastenation + contrast view. And although I have introduced the idea with a simplistic theory involving just two factors, it should be clear that MFA is consistent with there being any number of different, interdependent factors that are relevant to composition. Thus, for example, one who adopts MFA is free to say that for any non-overlapping *x*s, whether those *x*s compose a further object depends on (i) the degree of fastenation among the *x*s, (ii) the degree of contrast between the *x*s and their environment, (iii) the spatial

Ned Markosian

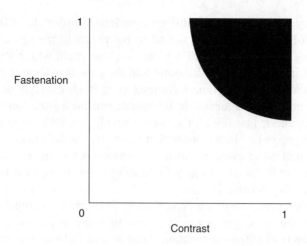

Figure 2

proximity of the *x*s to one another, (iv) the degree to which the activities of the *x*s constitute a life, (v) the degree of similarity among the *x*s, and (vi)–(xxxii) 27 other factors. Moreover, a philosopher who endorses MFA, and says that there are 32 factors relevant to whether composition occurs, can choose among a vast number of different possible ways of combining those 32 factors (such as adding all of the relevant numbers; or multiplying them; or adding some and multiplying others; or adding some, subtracting others, and dividing by another; and so on).

One important thing to notice about MFA is that, as the example of the fastenation + contrast view illustrates, each multi-factor answer to SCQ can be equally well represented by either a formula – such as: (degree of fastenation + degree of contrast with environment) ≥ 1.5) – or else a graph – such as the one in figure 2. The reason for this is that each multi-factor answer to SCQ corresponds to a function, and that function can be represented by (among other things) either a formula or a graph. Thus, for example, the fastenation + contrast view corresponds to a function from ordered pairs (each one consisting of a value for the degree of fastenation among the *x*s and a value for the degree of contrast between the *x*s and their environment) to Yes or No verdicts (indicating that the *x*s do or do not compose a further object). Similarly, any multi-factor answer to SCQ corresponds to a function from *n*-tuples (where each member of the *n*-tuple represents a possible score with respect to one factor that is relevant to composition) to Yes or No verdicts; and that function could be represented equally well by either a formula or a multi-dimensional graph.

In fact, these considerations bring to light a simple and intuitive way of representing any answer to SCQ that has heretofore gone unnoticed. Think of a many-dimensional space, with one dimension for each factor that anyone could possibly think is relevant to composition. Then each possible answer to SCQ can be thought of as a particular way of shading the regions of that multi-dimensional space. Nihilism, for example, corresponds to such a space with no points shaded anywhere in the multi-dimensional space; and unrestricted composition corresponds to such a space with every point shaded; and different moderate answers to SCQ correspond to different ways of shading some but not all of the points in the space.

Another thing to notice about MFA is that it's consistent with both the view that there is no genuine vagueness in the world and the view that there is genuine vagueness in the world. The fastenation + contrast view is an example of an MFA-style view that does not allow vagueness in the world; and for a variation that does allow ontological vagueness, just think of a similar graph, but with some points that are white (indicating cases in which composition determinately fails to occur), other points that are black (indicating cases in which composition determinately occurs), and still other points in varying shades of grey (indicating cases in which it is indeterminate whether composition occurs).

Why should we even consider an approach to SCQ that is as complicated as MFA? Well, I suspect that this approach will appeal to many people who feel that such monolithic answers to SCQ as fastenation, contact, and VIPA all fail precisely because composition is really a complicated matter involving various different, interdependent factors.

One advantage of MFA over brutal composition is that it preserves an intuition that many people have according to which there must be a correct answer to SCQ. Another advantage that MFA has over all of the other response to SCQ considered so far in the literature is that it preserves an intuition that many people have according to which various factors can be relevant to whether composition occurs in a given case. Another advantage the proponent of MFA can claim over at least some of its rivals is that it, like brutal composition, is consistent with commonsense intuitions regarding specific cases of some xs that may or may not compose an object. Another advantage proponents of MFA can tout is the consistency of their approach with every leading theory of vagueness. And, finally, it is worth noting that MFA appears not to be susceptible to arguments like Sider's continuum argument. (For the proponent of MFA can say that the true answer to SCQ is in fact sensitive to subtle differences in the different factors that are relevant to whether composition occurs, in a non-arbitrary way.)

Despite all of these appealing features of MFA, there are likely to be some objections. The main one I expect people to make is similar to an objection I mentioned above in connection with the serial response to SCQ: No one has yet come up with a promising theory that fits the approach. Another possible objection is that MFA requires that all the different factors allegedly relevant to whether composition occurs must be in some sense commensurable, whereas it's in fact plausible to think that many pairs of them will be incommensurable.[42]

11 The Mystery Response

Perhaps some readers will be tempted at this point to say that there must be a true answer to SCQ, but that it's just a mystery. Maybe the answer to the question is something that it's impossible for us to know. Or maybe it's something that is knowable, even to us, but is for whatever reason unknown to us so far. Either way, the various disadvantages of the theories we have considered to this point might seem to make this option at least worth considering.

One potential advantage of this mystery response to SCQ is that it allows us to preserve an intuition many people have according to which a question as straightforward as SCQ must have an answer. Another potential advantage of the mystery response is that it appears to be quite realistic about the fact that we don't seem to have discovered any completely satisfying answer to SCQ yet. A third advantage of the mystery response is that it's consistent with all our commonsense intuitions about particular cases of composition. And a fourth advantage is that it is consistent with the idea that there cannot be genuine vagueness in the world.

The main disadvantage of the mystery response, on the other hand, is that it seems to be something of a philosophical cop-out. (Although its proponents are likely to say, in response, "What can we do? We're completely convinced that there is an answer to SCQ, but equally convinced that we haven't seen it yet.")

12 Conclusion

Choosing among alternative philosophical theories always involves a cost-benefit analysis. To help the reader with our current choice, I have included a table summarizing the main benefits and costs of the different responses to SCQ we have considered here. As table 1 shows, each of the seven ways of restricting composition we have

Table 1   The main costs and benefits of various responses to SCQ

View	Main benefits	Main costs
UC	Traditional in mereology Simple, elegant Entails existence of plenty of objects Consistent with denial of vagueness in world	Counterintuitive results: far too many objects Entails 4D Entails UCUDI
Nihilism	Simple, elegant Consistent with denial of vagueness in world May allow one to avoid certain problems of material constitution	Counterintuitive results: too few objects Must say either that there are no people or else that people are simples
Fastenation	Satisfies many commonsense intuitions about particular cases	Counterintuitive results: paralyzed handshakers Problems with degrees (which may lead to positing vagueness in world) Difficulties with defining 'the xs are fastened together'

Table 1 *Continued*

View	Main benefits	Main costs
VIPA	May allow one to avoid certain problems of material constitution Can account for persisting subject of a single consciousness	Counterintuitive results: too few objects Entails genuine vagueness in world
Brutal composition	Consistent with commonsense intuitions about particular cases Consistent with denial of vagueness in world May allow 3Der to solve various problems of material constitution	Implausible to say that question like SCQ has no answer Implausible to say that compositional facts are brute facts Must admit that adjacent cases in Sider's continuum can differ with respect to composition
Serial response	May avoid counterexamples better than standard answers to SCQ Fits intuition that different factors are involved in different cases of composition	No one has yet come up with promising version Appears to multiply difficulties facing monolithic answers
Multi-factor approach	Preserves intuition that SCQ has an answer Preserves intuition that various factors can be relevant to composition Consistent with commonsense intuitions about particular cases Consistent with different theories of vagueness Avoids Sider's continuum argument	No one has yet come up with a promising version Possible problems with commensurability
The mystery response	Preserves intuition that SCQ has an answer Realistic about fact that we don't seem to have discovered one yet Consistent with commonsense intuitions about particular cases Consistent with denial of vagueness in world	Seems to be a philosophical cop-out

examined has its own costs. But to many of us, such costs as accepting brute compositional facts or admitting genuine vagueness into the world are relatively minor when compared to the triple whammy associated with UC. For the proponent of UC must first accept all of the many counterintuitive objects that the view entails; then he is forced to endorse the 4D view of persistence; and, finally, he must also accept UCUDI, with its radical and bizarre conception of persisting objects. In light of all of this, the choice for many of us will be clear: one way or another, composition must be restricted.[43]

360 | **Ned Markosian**

Notes

1 See also Hestevold (1980–1).

2 For an explanation of plural quantification, see van Inwagen (1990: sect. 2). Notice that 'part' is the only mereological term that is taken as primitive in van Inwagen's definitions.

3 See, for example, Goodman (1951), Leonard and Goodman (1940), Lesniewski (1983), Lewis (1986), and van Inwagen (1990).

4 Come to think of it, I may not even have a brain. For a discussion of the question of whether objects have "arbitrary undetached parts," see van Inwagen (1981).

5 The reason for the requirement that the *x*s be non-overlapping is simply that we have defined 'the *x*s compose *y*' in such a way that overlapping *x*s are prohibited from composing something. Here's an equivalent formulation of UC in terms of the notion of a mereological sum:

> Unrestricted Sums (US): Necessarily, for any *x*s, there is a y such that *y* is a sum of the *x*s.

For defenses of UC, see Lesniewski (1983), Leonard and Goodman (1940), Goodman (1951), Lewis (1986), Van Cleve (1986), Hudson (2001), and Sider (2001).

6 See Lesniewski (1983) and Leonard and Goodman (1940).

7 In fact, Lewis and Sider have argued that UC is entailed by the conjunction of the thesis that there can be no vagueness in the world and several uncontroversial theses about language. See Lewis (1986: 211–13); and Sider (2001: 120–39).

8 David Lewis (1991: 81–2) makes some remarks along these lines.

9 Mereological simples are objects that do not have proper parts (where a proper part is a part that's not identical to the whole). For a discussion of what characteristics an object must have in order to count as a mereological simple, see Markosian (1998b).

10 See, for example, Lewis (1986: 213). Quantifiers include phrases like 'all', 'every', and 'some'.

11 On the 3D and 4D views, see Sider 2001, and chapter 6 of this volume.

12 The argument that follows is adapted from an argument against UC presented by van Inwagen (1990: 74–80).

13 I'm assuming that you are identical to your body. If you disagree with that assumption, replace all references to you in the above argument with references to your body.

14 The above definition of 'temporal part' is loosely based on the definition given by Sider (2001: 59). But it is really a definition of 'proper temporal part'. A good definition of 'temporal part' would simply leave out the condition about existing for a shorter time than *x*.

15 In order to simplify the above argument, I have neglected to consider the several ways of resisting a commitment to 4D that are available to the proponent of UC. But since each of the relevant ways involves an appeal to some highly controversial thesis or other, the upshot remains the same: UC is a view with significant costs.

16 The argument that follows is adapted from an argument for 4D given by Sider (2001: ch. 4.9).

17 As I suggested above, the natural thing for the proponent of UC to say regarding identity over time in a case involving the same simples considered at two different times is that such a case always involves a single composite object persisting through time.

18 Sider actually argues for the conjunction of UC with the claim that diachronic identity for composite objects must be unrestricted. Note that, as Sider acknowledges, proponents of

brutal composition (see below) have a way of resisting his argument. So do those who are willing to admit genuine vagueness into the world.

19 'Iff' means *if and only if.* For a longer discussion of nihilism, see van Inwagen (1990: sect. 8).

20 For descriptions of these and other "problems of material constitution," see Rea (1997: Introduction).

21 See van Inwagen (1990: sect. 11). Van Inwagen develops the technique of paraphrasing as part of his defense of his own view (which is not nihilism, and which will be discussed below). It should be noted that van Inwagen uses the paraphrasing strategy in a way that differs slightly from the way in which it is used here. For according to van Inwagen, it's not that a sentence like (1) is strictly speaking false but, rather, that it's true because the proposition it expresses is the proposition expressed by (1a).

22 There is, however, a potential problem with this approach. See Sider (1993).

23 For a more careful presentation of a similar argument against Nihilism, on which the above argument is loosely based, see van Inwagen (1990: sect. 12).

24 Something like this may be what Roderick Chisholm (1978) ends up saying, although for somewhat different reasons.

25 See van Inwagen (1990: sect. 3).

26 Van Inwagen (1990: sect. 3) makes this point.

27 See van Inwagen (1990: 56), and Markosian (1998a). Van Inwagen calls the view in question "Fastening."

28 This and the remaining objections to fastenation-type views discussed below are presented in Markosian (1998a).

29 Compare the definition considered by van Inwagen (1990: 56–7).

30 Van Inwagen (1990: 82).

31 See van Inwagen (1990: sects. 13, 14, and 17).

32 The example is van Inwagen's (1990: 94–5, 217).

33 Van Inwagen also accepts as a consequence of his view that there can be genuine vagueness in the world about matters of identity – about, for example, whether this thing now is the same thing that was here earlier.

34 This view is defended in Markosian (1998a). In that paper I distinguish BC from the thesis that compositional facts are brute facts, although I say that the two theses naturally go together. (A brute fact is a fact that does not obtain in virtue of some other fact or facts.) Here, for the sake of simplicity and brevity, I will run these two claims together.

35 For more on how BC apparently allows the 3Der to solve these problems, see Markosian (1998a).

36 For a more detailed discussion of Horgan's objection see Markosian (1998a: 234–6).

37 Sider presents his version of the "continuum argument" as part of a larger argument for 4D, and the larger argument for 4D is based on Lewis's argument for UC. See Lewis (1986: 211–13).

38 Otherwise, either Nihilism or UC would be true.

39 The following reply to Sider's continuum argument against BC is adapted from Markosian (1998a: 237–240), which also contains a discussion of an alternative reply.

40 Cf. van Inwagen's (1990: sect. 7) discussion of "series-style" answers to SCQ. Compare also the view proposed by Rosenberg (1993), as well as the "Finite Serial Response" discussed in Markosian (1998a).

41 The objections that follow are adapted from Markosian (1998a: 230–2).

42 For the record, I think the best response to the second objection is to deny that the different factors must be commensurable. After all, there can be a function from ordered

pairs of values (for example) to Yes or No verdicts even if the values in question are incommensurable with one another.

43   I'm grateful to Hud Hudson, Shieva Kleinschmidt, and Dean Zimmerman for helpful comments on earlier drafts of this chapter.

References

Chisholm, Roderick. 1978. "Is There a Mind-Body Problem?" *The Philosophic Exchange* 2: 25–34.

Goodman, Nelson. 1951. *The Structure of Appearance* (Cambridge, MA: Harvard University Press).

Hestevold, H. Scott. 1980–1. "Conjoining," *Philosophy and Phenomenological Research* 41: 371–83.

Horgan, Terence, "On What There Isn't," *Philosophy and Phenomenological Research* 53 (1993), pp. 693–700.

Hudson, Hud. 2001. *A Materialist Metaphysics of the Human Person* (Ithaca: Cornell University Press).

Leonard, Henry S., and Goodman, Nelson. 1940. "The Calculus of Individuals and Its Uses," *Journal of Symbolic Logic* 5: 45–55.

Lesniewski, Stanislaw. 1983. "On the Foundations of Mathematics," *Topoi* 2: 3–52. (This is an abridged English translation of Lesniewski's 1927–31 pioneering papers on mereology; see Lewis (1991: 72n) for references to Lesniewski's Polish-language papers.)

Lewis, David. 1986. *On the Plurality of Worlds* (Oxford: Basil Blackwell).

——. 1991. *Parts of Classes* (Oxford: Basil Blackwell).

Markosian, Ned. 1998a. "Brutal Composition," *Philosophical Studies* 92: 211–49.

——. 1998b. "Simples," *Australasian Journal of Philosophy* 76: 213–26.

Rea, Michael. 1997. *Material Constitution* (Lanham, MD: Rowman & Littlefield).

Rosenberg, Jay F. 1993. "Comments on Peter van Inwagen's *Material Beings*," *Philosophy and Phenomenological Research* 53: 701–8.

Sider, Theodore. 1993. "Van Inwagen and the Possibility of Gunk," *Analysis* 53: 285–9.

——. 2001. *Four-Dimensionalism* (Oxford: Oxford University Press).

Van Cleve, James. 1986. "Mereological Essentialism, Mereological Conjunctivism, and Identity Through Time," *Midwest Studies in Philosophy* 11: 141–56.

Van Inwagen, Peter. 1981. "The Doctrine of Arbitrary Undetached Parts," *Pacific Philosophical Quarterly* 62: 123–37.

——. 1990. *Material Beings* (Ithaca: Cornell University Press).

CHAPTER NINE

METAONTOLOGY

9.1 "Ontological Arguments: Interpretive Charity and Quantifier Variance," Eli Hirsch

9.2 "The Picture of Reality as an Amorphous Lump," Matti Eklund

Metaphysicians often disagree about *ontology*, about *what exists*. They disagree over whether there exist abstract objects (chapter 1), possible worlds (chapter 3), past and future objects (chapter 5), temporal parts (chapter 6), composite objects (chapter 8), and other entities. But some find these disagreements baffling. Suppose philosopher X argues that holes exist. According to him, there exist holes in pieces of cheese, shirts, and so on. Philosopher Y disagrees. She says that all that exist are the pieces of cheese and the shirts; to say that "there are holes" in these objects is just a figure of speech. Now, a third philosopher, philosopher Z, is mystified by this debate. Nothing is really at issue in the debate between philosophers X and Y, thinks philosopher Z. They are merely using words differently. Eli Hirsch defends the outlook of philosopher Z (as applied to debates over temporal parts and composite objects); Matti Eklund argues against this outlook.

Ontological Arguments: Interpretive Charity and Quantifier Variance

Eli Hirsch

In the first section of this chapter, I introduce a certain kind of defense of common-sense ontology, one that derives from ordinary language considerations. The defense presupposes that quantifier expressions can have different meanings in different languages, and this idea is discussed in the second section.

1 Charity in the Philosophy Room

In philosophy we often operate at two levels. At one level we use the language of our community – English, in the present instance – to make assertions about various philosophical topics. At another level we may be thinking about the nature of language, in particular about how linguistic behavior determines meaning. The interaction between these two levels can become problematical when we find ourselves at the second level disagreeing about the meanings of our own assertions at the first level.

Let me try to illustrate the issue I'm driving at by considering the famous debate between Locke and Butler about the identity of a tree.[1] Locke held that we have to distinguish between a tree and the masses of matter that successively constitute it. A tree may lose a branch and still retain its identity as that same tree, though it is now made up of a different mass of matter. Butler insisted, on the contrary, that if we have a different mass of matter then, strictly speaking, we don't have the same tree. According to Butler, no object can persist through a change of parts.

Some philosophers (not all, by any means) will share my own immediate intuitive feeling that this dispute between Locke and Butler is not substantive, that it is in some sense merely verbal. Locke and Butler agree that we are faced with a situation in which some tree-composing masses of matter are related to each other in certain qualitative, spatiotemporal, and causal ways. They don't seem to disagree at all about what those relations are. (They are not, for example, disagreeing about "entelechies" or life-forces or anything like that, because their disagreement carries over to non-living things, such as rivers and ships.) It seems, therefore, that they are merely disagreeing about whether a situation in which masses of matter are interrelated in certain agreed-upon ways ought to be described in our language with the words "It's the same tree," or with the words "It's a different tree." Let "Lockean English" be an imagined version of English in which the semantic rules prescribe the former description, and "Butlerian English" an imagined version of English in which the semantic rules prescribe the latter description. Then it seems that all that these philosophers can be disagreeing about is whether the language we speak is in fact the first imagined language or the second.

Let's suppose provisionally that this really is their disagreement; I'll consider other alternatives later. If this is their disagreement, how can we try to resolve it? How can we determine whether the language we speak is Lockean English or Butlerian English?

We need to imagine, of course, that the semantic rules for Lockean and Butlerian English assign different truth conditions, not just for the mentioned sentences about trees, but for numerous sentences that imply identity through mereological change (i.e., change of parts).[2] Butlerian English is a "mereological essentialist" version of English, in which no sentence can count as true if it entails the sentence "Some objects persist through a change of parts."[3] Let me call this latter sentence "L" ("L" because it is accepted by Locke but not by Butler), and the "L-sentences" will be L together with the various particular identity sentences that entail it. I'm presently assuming that we can make intelligible to ourselves two versions of English: in Lockean English the L-sentences are true, whereas in Butlerian English they are false. Depending on which version of English we are speaking, we ought to either accept or reject the L-sentences. So which version are we speaking?

A highly influential principle of linguistic interpretation, sometimes called the *principle of charity*, says, roughly, that if we are trying to decide between two interpretations of a language, there is a presumption in favor of the one that succeeds better in making people's assertions come out true, or, if not true, at least reasonable.[4] The principle appeals to "ordinary use" in the sense of requiring us to interpret a language in the way that makes most rational sense out of how the language is used. If we apply the principle to the current linguistic behavior of our English-speaking community with respect to the L-sentences, it seems fairly obvious that we get a presumption in favor of the Lockean interpretation. Speakers of Butlerian English would treat the L-sentences as only loosely true but strictly false. This is clearly not the norm in our current community, where people would not hesitate to swear in court to the strict and literal truth of an L-sentence like "The tree that he banged into is the one that used to have more branches." (How odd that in Butler's famous passage he says that "when a man swears to" the identity through mereological change of a tree, he means it only loosely; surely the general presumption is that when people swear that something is so they mean it strictly.) But the appeal to charity doesn't end here. A central element of charity is what might be called *charity to retraction*. If the community retracts a set of sentences that were previously accepted, then considerations of charity must favor an interpretation which makes the sentences false.

Eli Hirsch

This is because there must surely be the presumption that people are more likely to get things right at the end of the day, after being able to examine more evidence or consider more arguments. Now the mereological essentialists are urging the community to retract its commitment to the strict and literal truth of the L-sentences. If the community agrees to retract, then it may follow by charity to retraction that, on the most plausible interpretation, the language being spoken is Butlerian English.

We seem, then, to have reached the following peculiar impasse. If we decide that we ought to retract the L-sentences, then the very fact of our having made that decision would establish the charitable presumption that we were speaking Butlerian English – in which case we were right to retract. If we decide that we ought not to retract, then the very fact of our having made that decision would establish the charitable presumption that we were speaking Lockean English – in which case we were right not to retract. It appears that, whichever way we decide, we are right just because we have so decided. There is an evident connection here to the "Wittgenstein paradox," which I'm not going to try to explore.[5] As regards the question whether our language is Lockean or Butlerian, I will, however, suggest an answer.

One route out of the impasse is to be clearer, and perhaps more modest, in our understanding of what the word 'we' means when it is said, "If we decide that we ought to retract, etc." If the linguistic community decides to retract, if retracting becomes the norm of the community, then it may indeed follow by charity to retraction that Butlerian English is the community's language. But if "we" are merely some philosophers who have decided to retract, that has virtually no effect on the interpretation of the language of the community. Even, therefore, if some philosophers find themselves at the first level inclined to follow Butler's urging to retract the L-sentences (even if this is their "intuition"), they must realize at the second level that it is a mistake to retract. They must acknowledge that, given the lack of authority that philosophers have in our culture, and given that, even if they were to have authority, they cannot agree amongst themselves on whether the L-sentences ought to be retracted (a fact that is not unrelated to their lack of authority), the community at large is going to stick with the L-sentences. Assuming that mereological essentialists intend to be speaking the language of the community – that is, plain, non-technical English – they must realize at the second level that this language is not Butlerian English. They must, therefore, stop being mereological essentialists. They must correct their first-level intuitions because of their second-level realization that these intuitions do not – and will not – reflect the linguistic practices of the community.

Of course there is nothing to prevent philosophers from knowingly adopting Butlerian English as a technical language that they believe serves some philosophical purpose (for example, the purpose of eliminating some of the vagueness that afflicts identity sentences in Lockean English). But these philosophers are not mereological essentialists in the sense that Butler was. They would not say, as he did, that when "we" – that is, we speakers of English – swear to its being the same tree we ought to mean this only loosely.

The focus of interpretive charity is not only on what people actually say, but on what they would say, especially what they would say "with their eyes wide open," as Sider has put it (2004: 680) That is indeed the rationale of charity to retraction. But ontological arguments of the sort given by mereological essentialists about the existence and identity of physical objects are not eye-opening in the relevant sense. They lead to irresolvably conflicting assertions or to ambivalence and confusion. The focus of interpretive charity must therefore be on the pre-philosophical assertions of commonsense. One has missed my point entirely if one is tempted to answer that it's necessary to be intellectually courageous and resolute and to continue to seek the ontological truth. Given my assumption that the conflicting ontological assertions are true or false depending on whether we speak Lockean or Butlerian English, the only truth we seek is which of these language is plain English. To find this out we have to learn to ignore the tower of Babel in the ontology room and focus our charity on what ordinary people say. Once we learn to do this, we are likely to find that our first-level philosophical intuitions gradually merge with the pre-philosophical convictions of commonsense. Even in ontology, one can learn to acquiesce to the language instead of battling it.

Let's imagine, however, a linguistic community in other ways like ours, but in which philosophers invariably agree that the L-sentences should be retracted. Everyone in this community, we may imagine, has the disposition to retract the L-sentences under the influence of philosophical reflection. Would it then follow by charity to retraction that the language of this community is Butlerian English, even though the vast majority of its members, having no knowledge of philosophy, persist in asserting the L-sentences with complete confidence? I am not sure how to answer this. For my immediate purposes it suffices to say that this imagined community is not ours. The role of philosophers in the imagined community should, however, be contrasted with the role of scientific experts in our actual community, for example, in getting people to retract the sentence "Whales are fish." There is a critical difference between the bearing of interpretive charity in scientific and philosophical examples. Apart from charity to retraction perhaps the most essential element of charity is what might be called *charity to understanding.* This is the presumption that members of the linguistic community generally understand what they are talking about to the extent at least that they do not make a priori (conceptual) mistakes about seemingly uncomplicated judgments. The scientists who claimed that people were mistaken about whales being fish did not imply that people were making a priori mistakes. The claim was rather that people were making empirical mistakes for relatively good reasons. It is in general a modest violation of interpretive charity – and certainly not a violation of charity to understanding – to suppose that people make reasonable empirical mistakes. My assumption throughout this chapter, however, is that issues of ontology are a priori. The mereological essentialists are claiming that ordinary people make innumerable a priori mistakes with respect to seemingly simple observational facts. This claim constitutes an overwhelming violation of charity to understanding. I doubt that this claim could stand even in the imagined community in which all philosophers agreed on it. It certainly cannot stand in our actual community.

Mereological essentialists have often followed Butler in granting to ordinary people that the L-sentences they assert about mereological change, while false in the "strict and philosophical sense," are true in some "loose and popular sense." Is that not sufficiently charitable to ordinary speech? The problem at this point, however, is not so much a matter of charity as the intelligibility of the distinction these philosophers want to make between "strict" and "loose" talk. A philosopher cannot simply announce from on high that some sentences generally accepted in the community are only "loosely true." This has to come out of an analysis of the use of these sentences in the community. One might as well say that ordinary people are just joking when they describe mereological change. (The reason why no one laughs is because the joke is old; small children, on the other hand, do have inexplicable laughing fits.) Butler seems to want to say that the statement "It's the same tree" is something like an *exaggeration*. But there are ordinary criteria for calling an utterance an exaggeration and these criteria are patently absent in assertions about mereological change. People, for instance, will not typically swear to an exaggeration, as already noted, and they will typically withdraw an exaggeration when challenged. Nothing like this happens in our linguistic community with respect to assertions about mereological change.

It must continually be borne in mind that our present assumption is that Butlerian and Lockean English are two possible languages. Mereological essentialists must therefore be able to explain by what criteria they take our community to differ from the possible community that speaks Lockean English, in which the L-sentences are (not exaggerations but) strictly true. It is not enough for these philosophers to rely on the strength of their private intuitions in the philosophy room. They have to explain why, all things taken into account, plain English is not Lockean English, as it superficially appears to be.

I should hope it is clear that what I have just been saying about the fallacy of mereological essentialism applies as well to every ontological position that wants the community to retract its ordinary assertions about the existence and identity of physical objects. I have in mind the plethora of currently popular positions that seem to fly in the face of commonsense. These include the doctrine of unrestricted mereological composition, according to which any two objects compose a third object;[6] the doctrine of temporal parts, according to which ordinary objects like trees have earlier and later parts;[7] ands sundry "nihilist" doctrines that deny the existence of all or most composite objects.[8] From my perspective, the philosophers who advance these various anti-commonsensical doctrines seem to be driven by an obsessive fascination with highly rarified general principles and philosophical riddles, which invariably override any pre-philosophical intuitions of commonsense. The intuitive sensibilities of these philosophers baffle me, but that is not my main point here. If these philosophers intend to use a technical language different from plain English, then they are required to stipulate what this technical language is (and to explain what interesting questions can arise once such a stipulation is made). If, however, they intend to speak plain English (which is what generally appears to be the case), then they seem to have failed drastically to interpret this language in a plausibly charitable manner. Their various doctrines seem to be trivially absurd in plain English, as charitably interpreted.

I don't mean to suggest that a sharp line can be drawn between the pre-philosophical intuitions of commonsense and the intuitions that philosophers profess to have in the philosophy room. What we have rather is a gradation of cases, going from the most unreflective perceptual judgments of ordinary people to the most esoteric judgments of professional philosophers. Consider the general principle, "Two things cannot occupy exactly the same place at the same time." Philosophers disagree about this principle. Locke had to deny it in order to distinguish between the tree and the mass of matter that makes it up. Mereological essentialists accept it, and often use it as an argument for their position. What should we say is the pre-philosophical intuition about this principle? Certainly people are initially inclined to accept it, but they are also often confused by it ("What about mixing wine and water?"), and they are taken by complete surprise when the principle is applied to an object and the matter that makes it up; that is clearly not the kind of case they had in the back of their minds when they wanted to accept the principle. Considerations of interpretive charity have to take all of this into account. To the extent that the principle seems attractive to the members of our linguistic community, charity would point to an interpretation of our language as being Butlerian English, in which the principle is true. On the other hand, to the extent that members of our community accept innumerable L-sentences such as, "That tree used to have more branches," charity points to an interpretation in terms of Lockean English. We seem to be faced with what might be called a "conflict of charity": we can choose an interpretation that is charitable to the principle or one that is charitable to the L-sentences. I think it's clear how this conflict needs to be resolved. The demands of charity in behalf of the L-sentences far outweigh those in behalf of the principle. The dominant tendency of our language is Lockean, not Butlerian.

There are several reasons for this. Most obviously, there is one principle contending with numerous L-sentences. Furthermore, people are almost always confused by the principle, whereas they frequently accept L-sentences with complete confidence and clarity. The last point is related to the fact that the principle is abstract, whereas the L-sentences are often rooted directly in perceptual experience. I've highlighted the importance of charity to understanding and retraction, but another central consideration is *charity to perception*, by which I mean the presumption that any language contains sentences used to make perceptual reports, and that these reports are generally accurate (to a fair degree of approximation). Charity to perception is central because of the undeniably close connection between perceptual experience and language learning. Although it need not be implausible to attribute some specific perceptual mistake to the community, such as the mistake of perceiving whales as fish, there must be a strong presumption against attributing to the community massive perceptual errors about the existence and identity of the objects typically encountered, especially errors that are alleged to be of an a priori conceptual nature. It is, all things considered, far more plausible to suppose that the members of our linguistic community are mistakenly attracted to a certain abstract principle than that they make innumerable mistakes about what they perceive in front of them. Philosophers ought to admit this, and ought therefore to admit that plain English is Lockean English, no matter what the strength might be of their own attraction to the principle.[9]

The generalities and riddles that often lead to anti-commonsensical ontology are not alien to ordinary thinking. If they were, they could not catch on even in the philosophy room. They reflect tendencies inherent in our language that are, however, defeated by other more predominant tendencies. Lockean English is certainly the dominant language of our community, but I think it need not be wrong to say that Butlerian English is in some sense contained germinally within plain English, as a kind of recessive undercurrent. Our ordinary concepts prepare us for Butlerian English, and may even push us in that direction, at least when we are engaged in thinking about certain kinds of questions.[10] In investigating the ontology of physical objects, part of our philosophical task is to try to understand these "dialectical tendencies" that I think can be viewed as in some sense implicit in what we ordinarily mean. What we must not allow to happen is that we are carried away into a language of our own creation without realizing it, identifying the predominant language with what is only an undercurrent in it.

(Definition of "ordinary language philosophers": philosophers who have been trained to monitor their first-level intuitions by paying attention to their second-level judgments about the demands of linguistic interpretation.)

2 Quantifier Variance

My provisional assumption has been that we can make intelligible to ourselves the two imagined versions of English, Lockean English and Butlerian English, but that assumption is by no means trivial. These languages would have to be viewed as differing not just in the meaning of such terms as "tree" and "ship," but also in the meaning of such quantifier expressions as "(some)thing" and "(there) exists." Consider, for example, the sentence, "In addition to masses of matter, there exist other material things." This sentence would qualify as true in Lockean English but, I assume, false in Butlerian English. (Butler implied, I think, that a tree or a ship is simply identical with a particular mass of matter.) The different semantic rules that would have the effect of rendering the sentence true in one language and false in the other must in some sense provide different rules for "counting what things there are in the world." If there could be these two languages they would have to embody in some sense different concepts of what it is for "there to exist something." Not all philosophers would admit that it makes sense to suppose that there could be different semantic rules with that effect.

Hilary Putnam has been a vigorous defender of the possibility of quantifier variance, that is, the possibility of quantifier expressions varying their meaning from one language to another. In two typical passages he says:

> [A]ll situations have many different correct descriptions, and ... even descriptions that, taken holistically, convey the same information may differ in what they take to be 'objects' ... [T]here are many usable extensions of the notion of an object. (1994: 304–5)

> [T]he logical primitives themselves, and in particular the notions of object and existence, have a multitude of different uses rather than one absolute 'meaning'. (1987: 71)

Putnam often calls his position "conceptual relativism," and he has often seen the overall import of this position as being in some significant sense anti-realist. Criticisms of Putnam have frequently centered on his anti-realism, and the specific doctrine of quantifier variance has therefore not often been properly isolated. In the present discussion I want to make sure that quantifier variance is clearly disassociated from anti-realism. It is only the former that interests me and that is presupposed in my discussion of Lockean and Butlerian English. The doctrine of quantifier variance, properly isolated, does not entail anti-realism. One should not say, "If the sentence 'In addition to masses of matter, there exist other material things' is true in Lockean

English but false in Butlerian English, then it is a matter of linguistic choice what exists in the world." It is rather a matter of linguistic choice what is meant by the expression 'what exists in the world'. Whether we speak Lockean or Butlerian English, the anti-realist statement "It is a matter of linguistic choice what exists in the world" can be – and, I think, ought to be – viewed as absurd. Anti-realism, therefore, is not at all what we are talking about here.

Once this point is understood, the temptation might be to make a mistake from the other side. "If all you're saying is that expressions like 'there exists (something)' can have different meanings in different languages, that's completely trivial. The expression might be used to mean 'Hello', for instance." The non-trivial question, however, is whether the expression can have different meanings in different languages while still retaining the general formal role of a *quantifier* expression, that is, roughly put, the formal role described in quantificational logic.[11] In Lockean and Butlerian English, the expression "there exists (something)" might be said to have the same "formal meaning," but, for these languages to function in the intended ways, the expression must have different meanings in the languages in the sense of contributing differently to the truth conditions of sentences in the languages.

If there could be the two languages, therefore, there must be an important sense in which the speakers "operate with different concepts of existence." It would be pointless to resist this formulation and to insist that, even if there could be the two languages, only one of them (at most) contains a "real quantifier" that expresses "the real concept of existence." This is pointless because the important question, for the argument in the last section and for related arguments, is whether it is possible for there to be languages that stand to each other in the manner of Lockean and Butlerian English. In what follows, therefore, I will make the quite natural stipulation that if there could be such languages then they could be said to contain quantifier expressions with different meanings, and these expressions would signify different concepts of existence. The important question is whether quantifier variance in this sense is an intelligible possibility.

Suppose it is not a possibility. Then the issue between Locke and Butler cannot be as I represented it in the last section. If quantifier variance is impossible, then we don't have two possible interpretations of English, the Lockean and the Butlerian, and the disagreement between Locke and Butler is not in any sense merely verbal. The impossibility of quantifier variance would make ontology seem far more substantive and profound. That may be a reason for philosophers to wish for it, but not a reason to accept it.

One thing we must not do is to allow the issue to degenerate into a battle of metaphors: "the world as containing ready-made objects" versus "the world as an amorphous lump divided up by language." These metaphors have had the effect in the literature of reinforcing the confusion that the issue is realism versus anti-realism. Once this confusion is put aside, the opponents of quantifier variance must squarely face the burden of showing why there could not possibly be languages related to each other in the manner of Lockean and Butlerian English.

I myself don't see how this burden can be met. Certainly I don't deny that there is something perplexing in the idea that the world might be described with different concepts of "there exists something." If we are realists, we are committed to the following formulation: "There exist things in the world independent of language, and language comes along and enables people to state truths about the things in the world." The difficulty is in seeing that this formulation does not entail "There exist things in the world independent of language, and any language that comes along must contain the same concept of 'the existence of things in the world' that I have just expressed." The doctrine of quantifier variance, in the realist sense that I'm assuming, accepts the first formulation but rejects the second. This is initially perplexing, but seems, on reflection, unavoidable.[12]

There are, I would agree, describable languages that strike us intuitively as being so bizarre that we can't take them seriously as being in some sense real possibilities. The imagined language in which 'grue' and 'bleen' replace 'green' and 'blue' certainly strike many people in this way.[13] As regards such "radically alien" languages, Kripke expresses the doubt whether we can in some sense make them really intelligible to ourselves ("from the inside") (1982: 98n78). That's a doubt I share. Some examples of quantifier variance may also generate this kind of doubt. Sider imagines a language in which "There exists something that is F" means that Quine says that there exists something that is F (2001b: xx). This language may indeed strike us as "too strange to be really intelligible." It seems in fact easier to cite a reason for the intuitive craziness of this language than it is for the grue-bleen language. It is well known that for any fact stateable in our language, there is an a priori necessarily equivalent fact stateable in the grue-bleen language. In this sense, the two languages have the same fact-stating power. The language with the intuitively crazy Quine-linked quantifier, however, would be drastically deficient in fact-stating power. That is one reason (I doubt it is the only one) why this example of quantifier variance may strike us as strange to the point of not being fully intelligible.

I assume that Butlerian and Lockean English have approximately the same fact-stating power. It's immediately clear that, for any sentence in Butlerian English, there is an a priori necessarily equivalent sentence in Lockean English. (Henceforth, I'll use "equivalent" as short for "a priori necessarily equivalent.") The point in the reverse direction is somewhat less clear. In order to find in Butlerian English a sentence equivalent to the true sentence of Lockean English, "A tree persisted while losing a branch." one would need to provide in terms of the former language an analysis of what counts in the latter as "the identity of a tree."[14] Such an analysis is, of course, hardly a trivial matter, but I think we can assume that there is in principle a sentence in Butlerian English that is at least more or less equivalent to the Lockean sentence.

It will help to bring into the discussion another possible language. I will take *four-dimensionalism* to be the highly popular position that combines the doctrine of temporal parts and the doctrine of unrestricted mereological compostion. Suppose that an ordinary tree, containing a trunk and some branches, stands in the yard. The doctrine of temporal parts implies that the tree is made up of daytime parts and nighttime parts; the same for the trunk. The doctrine of unrestricted mereological composition implies that there is an object composed of any combination of these parts, for example, the daytime parts of the tree and the nighttime parts of the trunk. According to four-dimensionalists, therefore, there is in the yard a highly visible brown wooden object that has branches during the day and has no branches during the night.

I would want to deal with four-dimensionalism in the same way I have dealt with mereological essentialism. We can imagine a language – let's call it 4D-English – in which all of the sentences asserted by the four-dimensionalists are true. The semantic rules for 4D-English permit one to describe any object in terms of "temporal parts," and any pair of objects in terms of their "sum." These rules allow one, therefore, to describe the ordinary situation of a tree standing in a yard with the words: "There is in the yard a highly visible brown wooden object that has branches during the day and has no branches during the night." From my point of view, we have three possible languages: Butlerian English, Lockean English, and 4D-English. These languages have essentially the same fact-stating power. In saying this, I'm assuming that all of these languages have the resources of set theory. So the 4D-English sentence just cited is equivalent in both Lockean and Butlerian English to the sentence, "There is a set containing pairs of objects and times, some of the times being during the day and some during the night, such that each object in a pair is brown, highly visible, and in the yard, and if the time in a pair is during the day the object in that pair has branches, and if the time in a pair is during the night the object in that pair does not have branches."

I can imagine a commonsense ontologist who holds that, while Butlerian and 4D-English have essentially the same fact-stating power as plain English, these languages are intuitively "too strange to be really intelligible." I'm not inclined to adopt that extreme position, though I do have a bit of sympathy for it. Since I take it that these are three possible languages, it seems that the only relevant question is which of them is plain English. Considerations of interpretive charity seem to indicate decisively that Lockean English is plain English. This is why the pre-philosophical assertions of commonsense are correct in plain English.[15]

The possibility of quantifier variance brings with it another possibility: quantifier vagueness. If the quantifiers in different languages can have different semantic functions, then it may be indeterminate (or unknowable because of vagueness) precisely how the quantifier functions in a given language.[16] Lewis and others have assumed that quantifier vagueness is not possible, and have argued against commonsense ontology on the grounds that, in this ontology, it must sometimes be indeterminate (or unknowable because of vagueness) how many objects exist in a given situation.[17] This argument has no force once quantifier variance is accepted.

The disagreement between mereological essentialists, four-dimensionalists, and defenders of commonsense is, on my view, merely verbal – merely a matter of language – in the following sense: Each side can charitably interpret each other side's position in terms of a language in which all the other side's assertions come out true.[18] I am not suggesting, however, that every ontological dispute is verbal in this sense. Suppose that a Platonist conjectures, "The set of bits of matter is in a one-to-one correspondence with the set of integers." A nominalist who rejects sets (and other abstract things) seems to have no way of making any charitable sense out of this conjecture. The reason for this is that nominalists apparently cannot make intelligible in terms acceptable to them a "Platonist language" which has essentially the same fact-stating power as their own "nominalist language." This point may not be clear if one focuses exclusively on sentences of pure set theory, that is, sentences that are either necessarily true or necessarily false. The Platonist conjecture just mentioned, however, which is intended to be true in some worlds and false in others, is, on the face of it, not equivalent to any sentence that nominalists can accept.[19]

Carnap's (1956) doctrine of "external questions" implies that the issue between Platonists and nominalists is merely a matter of language. There may be some intuitive sense in which this is correct, but nothing in the present chapter supports this position. As far as my argument goes, the relevance of quantifier variance to ontology is limited, roughly, to issues about the existence and identity of perceivable objects.

The position I'm defending here has been significantly challenged by Sider. His basic idea is that there is a constraint on linguistic interpretation requiring quantifiers to correspond to what he calls the world's "logical joints." Ontological arguments reveal where these joints are located. Since these arguments favor four-dimensionalism, as Sider believes, it follows that only the quantifiers of 4D-English correspond to the world's logical joints. The correct interpretation of plain English, therefore, must be 4-D English. Although charity to ordinary use counts against this interpretation, considerations of charity are trumped by the constraint binding the quantifier to the logical joints.[20]

Sider compares his quantifier constraint to Lewis's idea that there is a presumption in favor of interpreting general words as expressing (highly) natural properties (Lewis 1983: 370–7). The comparison seems, however, to work against him. Lewis's presumption is frequently defeated by considerations of charity to ordinary use. The word "game", for instance, would probably express a far more natural property if one-person games like solitaire were excluded, but ordinary use prevails. There are numerous examples of the same sort. To my knowledge, neither Lewis nor any other philosopher has presented an example of interpreting a general word in which clear-cut considerations of charity to ordinary use do not prevail. Why should it be different with words like "something" and "exists"? Even if there is a special interpretive presumption binding these words to the "logical joints," and even if this presumption is satisfied only by the 4D-quantifier, the use of these words in our community decisively trumps any such presumption and shows that 4D-English is not our language.[21]

There is a further move that Sider has recently made to which I am less sure how to respond (Sider 2004: 680–2).[22] He claims that even if it is agreed that plain English is not 4D-English, that need not bother four-dimensionalists. Granted, their assertions would then be false in plain English, but ontologists don't care about plain English. The tacit understanding amongst ontologists is that in the philosophy room they use an ontologically ideal language, whether or not it is plain English, in which the quantifiers correspond to the logical joints. Disagreements of ontology are disagreements about the logical joints, and therefore cannot be resolved by appealing to ordinary use.

One immediate point is that if philosophers who appear to be writing in plain English really aren't, that needs to be stipulated at the outset. It seems unclear, in any case, why it is necessary to switch to a new language, Ontologese (as Sider calls it), in order to argue about the logical joints. Why can't we simply add the technical expression "logical joints" to our language and then proceed in plain English? But this question leads to another one: Do we really have any good idea what is meant by the world's "logical joints"?

Let's be quite clear that, in the present argument, Sider agrees that plain English is not 4D-English. So the general picture is that ontologists like Sider start out in plain English, and they are able to discover, from within plain English, that the quantifiers of plain English fail to correspond to the world's logical joints. But how can we understand the nature of this failure? It is a trivial disquotational truth (in plain English) that the expression "everything that exists" refers to everything that exists. What could be better for a quantifier than to refer to everything that exists? Sider suggests that the ideal quantifier must express *existence* (in italics), and the plain English quantifier fails to do this. But the plain English word "existence" trivially expresses existence. It's clear that, for Sider, there is a distinction between existence (in the sense of plain English) and *existence*. The latter is evidently a technical concept that the ontologist must employ in order to explain what is wrong with plain English. There appears, however, to be no prospect within plain English of explaining what this technical concept means. The "logical joints" and "*existence*" must apparently be grasped in the philosophy room as undefined primitives.

Once again, the contrast with Lewis's naturalness presumption is important. When Lewis suggests that general words are linked to natural properties, he makes a serious effort to indicate in plain English what is meant by a "natural property." His most fundamental explanation, and the one that is widespread in the literature, is that a property is natural if the sharing of it makes for similarities. This explanation faces well-known difficulties of detail, but there is at least a definite intuitive connection between the technical notion of a natural property and the familiar notion of similarity. This intuitive connection is far-reaching, allowing naturalness to apply not just to monadic properties but also to relations, and even to the properties and relations of abstract things.[23] Lewis's notion of a natural property is not offered as an undefined primitive, as is Sider's notion of the world's logical joints. The latter notion seems, for this reason, far more obscure than the former. Moreover, given the notion of a natural property, Lewis's interpretive presumption makes immediate intuitive sense. The basic function of general words is to classify things, and there is a strong intuitive link between classifying things and bringing similar things together under a single word. This explains, at least in a rough intuitive way, the link between general words and natural properties. Sider has no comparable way of explaining the alleged link between quantifier expressions and the "logical joints."

I think that Sider's idea is that ontological arguments themselves reveal what the arguments are about. Those who have an aptitude for ontology become engaged with these arguments in a meaningful way. They thereby display their understanding of Ontologese and what is meant by the "logical joints," though they have no way to explain these matters in other terms. This is an intriguing idea, and, though I personally find it to be excessively obscure, I certainly cannot refute it.[24] I can only urge the practitioners of this form of ontology to make it abundantly clear that one thing they are not engaged in is debating in plain English about what exists.[25]

Notes

1 Locke (1690: bk. 2, ch. 27); Butler (1836).
2 I'm making the standard assumption that a language must contain some form of "truth condition" rules, i.e., rules that determine for the assertion of any sentence what conditions or states-of-affairs are required for the assertion to count as true.

3   Mereological essentialism is the view that an object cannot persist through a change of parts. Butler's mereological essentialism has been defended in the more recent literature by a number of philosophers, including Chisholm (1976: ch. 3); Van Cleve (1986).

4   Quine (1960: 59), Davidson (1984: esp. "Belief and the Basis of Meaning" and "Thought and Talk"); Lewis (1983a and 1983b: 370–7).

5   I refer to the paradox discussed in Kripke (1982). The paradox begins with the observation that our past use of an expression cannot determine a unique rule for correctly using it in the future.

6   See chapter 8 of this volume; also see Van Cleve (1986), Thomson (1983), Cartwright (1975), Lewis (1986: esp. 212–13), Sider (2001b: 120–32).

7   See chapter 6 of this volume; also see Lewis (1986: 202–4), Heller (1990; ch. 1 repr. in Kim and Sosa 1999), Sider (2001b).

8   See chapter 8 of this volume; also see Unger (1980), van Inwagen (1990), Merricks (2001).

9   For further discussion of "conflicts of charity," see Hirsch (2002a).

10 Compare with J. N. Findlay's notion of "logical dynamics" (1962: 76–7).

11 The formal role is illustrated by the principle that "This is F" entails "There exists something that is F," a principle that holds both in Lockean and Butlerian English.

12 One source of perplexity that I cannot go into here concerns the problematical effects of quantifier variance on referential semantics. For further discussion, see Hirsch (1999; 2002b; 2004; 2005). A novel referential argument against quantifier variance, which I will not be able to address here, is given by Matti Eklund in chapter 9.2 of this volume.

13 See Goodman (1973: 74), where the predicate "grue" is defined as applying to all things examined before a given time just in case they are green but to other things just in case they are blue. "Bleen" is defined in the corresponding manner.

14 Perhaps Butler himself gives us a too easy solution: we might translate the Lockean sentence into the Butlerian sentence, "A tree loosely persisted while losing a branch."

15 In associating plain English with Lockean English (that is, the version of English in which John Locke's assertions come out true), I have in mind only what Locke said about the identity and existence of physical objects. (I ignore his views about personal identity, modes, and various other matters.)

16 I intend this formulation to be neutral as between supervaluationist and epistemic views of vagueness. See Williamson (1994).

17 See Lewis (1986: 212–13); Sider (2001b: 120–32).

18 The relevant notion of a verbal dispute is clarified further in my "Physical-Object Ontology, Verbal Disputes, and Commonsense." (There may, of course, be other significant ways of defining what is meant by a verbal dispute.)

19 I make this remark with some reservations because I have no clear grasp of various linguistic resources nominalists sometimes allow themselves, such as, plural quantification, substitutional quantification, schemata, infinitary sentences, and fictions. One would have to examine whether such resources might allow nominalists to make charitable sense of the Platonists' assertions.

20 See Sider (2001a; 2001b: Introduction; 2004: 679–82).

21 Sider suggests that, in order for ordinary use to trump the presumption in favor of the 4D quantifier, roughly the following condition has to be satisfied: typical speakers, after being exposed to four-dimensionalist arguments, reject the four-dimensionalist claims, not just as false, but as "linguistically deviant" (2004: 680). No such extraordinary condition has, to my knowledge, ever been imposed on the interpretation of general words, and if it were, the effect, I think, would be to force us to reinterpret many words (including, probably, the word "game").

22 See also Dorr (2005).

23 Sider argues that, since Lewis's naturalness presumption must apply at abstract levels (e.g., in favoring "plus" to "quus"), this shows that property-naturalness cannot be straightforwardly explained in terms of similarity, any more than the logical joints can (2004: 682). I think, however, that it seems sufficiently straightforward to say that the triplets of numbers that are related by "plus" are all similar to each other – they have something in common – in the intuitive sense in which the triplets related by "quus" are not all similar to each other.

24 It would be instructive, I think, to compare and contrast Sider's position to that of an epistemologist who tries to fend off ordinary language critiques of the traditional claim that we do not perceive external objects, by insisting that the word "perceives," as used in the philosophy room, is not to be understood in plain English, but in a superior language of Epistemologese.

25 My thanks to Matti Eklund for comments on this paper.

References

Butler, Joseph. 1836. "Of Personal Identity," in *The Whole Works of Joseph Butler, LL.D.* (London: Thomas Tegg), pp. 263–70.

Carnap, Rudolph. 1956. "Empiricism, Semantics, and Ontology," in *Meaning and Necessity*, 2nd edn. (Chicago: University of Chicago Press).

Cartwright, Richard. 1975. "Scattered Objects," in K. Lehrer, ed., *Analysis and Metaphysics* (Dordrecht: Reidel); repr. in J. Kim and E. Sosa, eds., *Metaphysics: An Anthology* (Oxford: Blackwell Publishing, 1999).

Chisholm, Roderick. 1976 *Person and Object* (LaSalle, ILL: Open Court, 1976); repr. in J. Kim and E. Sosa, eds., *Metaphysics: An Anthology* (Oxford: Blackwell Publishing, 1999).

Davidson, Donald. 1984. *Inquiries into Truth and Interpretation* (Oxford: Oxford University Press).

Dorr, Cian. 2005. "What We Disagree About When We Disagree About Ontology," in Mark Kalderon, ed., *Fictionalism in Metaphysics* (Oxford: Oxford University Press), pp. 234–86.

Findlay, J. N. 1962. *Hegel: A Re-examination* (New York: Collier Books).

Goodman, Nelson. 1973. *Fact, Fiction, and Forecast*, 3rd edn. (Indianapolis and New York: Bobbs Merrill).

Heller, Mark. 1990. *The Ontology of Physical Objects: Four Dimensional Hunks of Matter* (Cambridge: Cambridge University Press).

Hirsch, Eli. 1999. "The Vagueness of Identity," *Philosophical Topics* 26.

—. 2002a. "Against Revisionary Ontology," *Philosophical Topics* 30.

—. 2002b. "Quantifier Variance and Realism," *Philosophical Issues* 12.

—. 2004. "Sosa's Existential Relativism," in J. Greco, ed., *Ernest Sosa and His Critics* (Oxford: Blackwell Publishing).

—. 2005. "Physical-Object Ontology, Verbal Disputes, and Commonsense," *Philosophy and Phenomenological Research* 70(1): 67–97.

Kripke, Saul A. 1982. *Wittgenstein on Rules and Private Languages* (Cambridge, MA: Harvard University Press).

Lewis, David. 1983a. "New Work for a Theory of Universals," *Australasian Journal of Philosophy* 61: 343–77.

—. 1983b. "Radical Interpretation," in *Philosophical Papers I* (New York: Oxford University Press).

—. 1986. *On the Plurality of Worlds* (Oxford: Blackwell Publishing).

Locke, John. 1690. *An Essay Concerning Human Understanding.*

Merricks, Trenton. 2001. *Objects and Persons* (Oxford: Oxford University Press).

Putnam, Hilary. 1987. "Truth and Convention: On Davidson's Refutation of Conceptual Relativism," *Dialectica* 41: 69–77.

—. 1994. "The Question of Realism," in *Words and Life* (Cambridge, MA: Harvard University Press).

Quine, W. V. 1960. *Word and Object* (Cambridge, MA: MIT Press).

Sider, Theodore. 2001a. "Criteria of Personal Identity and the Limits of Conceptual Analysis," *Philosophical Perspectives* 15: 188–209.

—. 2001b. *Four-Dimensionalism: An Ontology of Persistence and Time* (New York: Oxford University Press).

—. 2004. "Replies to Gallois, Hirsch, and Markosian," *Philosophy and Phenomenological Research* 68(3): 674–87.

Thomson, Judith Jarvis. 1983. "Parthood and Identity Across Time," *Journal of Philosophy* 80: 201–20; repr. in J. Kim and E. Sosa, eds., *Metaphysics: An Anthology* (Oxford: Blackwell Publishing, 1999).

Unger, Peter. 1980. "There Are No Ordinary Things," *Synthese* 41: 117–54.

Van Cleve, James. 1986. "Mereological Essentialism, Mereological Conjunctivism, and Identity Through Time," *Midwest Studies in Philosophy* 11: 141–56.

Van Inwagen, Peter. 1990. *Material Beings* (Ithaca, NY: Cornell University Press).

Williamson, Timothy. 1994. *Vagueness* (London: Routledge).

The Picture of Reality as an Amorphous Lump

Matti Eklund

1 Introduction

Ontology is the study of what there is. Here are some examples of disputes in modern analytic ontology:

(1) Abstract objects. The *nominalist* (as the label is used today) denies that there exist abstract objects. The *Platonist* holds that there are abstract objects. One example is numbers. The nominalist denies that there are numbers; the Platonist typically affirms it. (See chapter 1.)

(2) Ordinary objects. Consider ordinary objects – tables, chairs, animals, rocks, what have you. Commonsensically, we would hold that objects of all these types exist. But some philosophers deny this. Peter van Inwagen (1990) holds that organisms are the only macroscopic objects there are. Cian Dorr (2005) has argued that there are not any macroscopic objects at all.

(3) Extraordinary objects. Consider the purported object which is the sum of my nose and the Eiffel Tower. Consider "incars" which, if they exist, are exactly like cars, except that they only exist when or insofar as they are inside garages.[1] Do such objects exist? Commonsense arguably says no. But on a variety of philosophical views they do. (See chapter 8.)

Metaontology, which I will be concerned with, is about what ontology is. It is about the nature of questions like the ones mentioned. Specifically, I will be concerned with one particular dispute in metaontology, what I will call the dispute between robust ontologists and deflationists about ontology. On the *robust* conception of ontology, questions of ontology are real, genuine questions on a par with questions of science. On the *deflationary* conception of ontology, questions of ontology somehow fall short of this ideal. These characterizations are, to be sure, rough and impressionistic. But that is in the nature of the topic. The robust and deflationary conceptions of ontology are tendencies rather than full-fledged theses.

Sometimes the following imagery is employed to describe these two different views on ontology. The robust ontologist holds that there are real metaphysical joints in nature. The deflationary ontologist, by contrast, subscribes to the "picture of reality as an amorphous lump" as Michael Dummett puts it (e.g. 1981: 577). The deflationary conception is also sometimes described employing the "cookie-cutter metaphor," according to which reality considered in itself is like some amorphous dough and our concepts are like cookie-cutters, carving up reality into objects. It is worth stressing that these are mere pictures. A lot of philosophical work has to go into actually providing these pictures with definite content.

I will focus on the deflationary conception of ontology. Specifically, I will be concerned with what form an acceptable deflationism about ontology might take. The most well-known and important form of deflationism about ontology has historically been associated with William James and Rudolf Carnap, and among its most important current proponents are Hilary Putnam and Eli Hirsch.[2] (There are important differences between the views of these thinkers, but I will focus on the similarities.) Putnam calls his view the thesis of *conceptual relativity*. Hirsch calls his view the doctrine of *quantifier variance*. I will call this general type of deflationary view *ontological pluralism*. For most of the paper, I will critically discuss the ontological pluralist view. Then I will discuss whether there are other routes for the deflationist about ontology to take.

The ontological pluralist view on disputes such as the ones mentioned above is that the disputants can be seen simply as using 'exists', 'object', etc. – as we might say, *the ontological expressions* – differently. To this extent the disputants are simply speaking different languages. Whereas it might sound as if the disputes are really 'deep', there is nothing more deep going on than when you claim that the tomato is a vegetable and I claim it is a fruit. The dispute is in an important sense verbal. As in the tomato case, there is a genuine issue nearby: namely that of what is the correct thing to say *in English*. Maybe correct English is to say, for instance, that there are numbers. But nothing philosophically significant hinges on this, since we could equally well have spoken a language where "there are no numbers" is the correct thing to say. (Note that one naturally can take the ontological pluralist's line with respect to some of these disputes and not with respect to others. This I will, however, typically slide over. The reason is that the problems I will go on to raise for ontological pluralism are completely general.)

What ontological pluralists often say – below I will give, and discuss, some quotations – is that there are *different possible meanings for the ontological expressions*. Just as there can be different 'vegetable'-like expressions with slightly different meanings so that in some English-like languages "the tomato is a vegetable" is true and in some it is false, there can be different 'exists'-like expressions. In fact, this characterization also suggests one consideration in favor of ontological pluralism, one that seems to loom large in Hirsch's contribution to the present volume (chapter 9.1): according to the ontological pluralist, she only says about ontological expressions what is clearly right about other expressions, whereas the anti-pluralist unmotivatedly says that there is a difference between the two cases.

Another consideration motivating ontological pluralism is this. Ontological disputes like the ones briefly described above are notoriously *intractable*. It is easy to come to think that, for principled reasons, there is no way of settling these disputes. Now, of course, a dispute can be in this way intractable while not being empty or merely verbal in the way that the ontological pluralist says that many ontological disputes are. But the ontological pluralist can say that a good explanation of the intractability of ontological disputes is that the disputants are simply using ontological expressions with different meanings.

2 Ontological Pluralism

Putnam supports his "thesis of conceptual relativity" – the form of ontological pluralism that he defends – by a whole battery of arguments.[3] However, what normally takes center stage in Putnam's defense of ontological pluralism is a number of well-known examples. I will consider the two discussed prominently in Putnam (1987a) – and also in many other of his texts. The examples have to do with ontological questions of a rather special kind. One might agree on the pluralist's diagnosis of these examples, while holding that ontological questions of more traditional philosophical concern, like the ones listed above, are fully genuine. Still the examples both illustrate the issue well and promise to help motivate the pluralist's stance. Correspondingly, problems with these examples indicate general problems with pluralism.

One of Putnam's examples has to do with the different views of "Carnap" (not to be confused with the actual historical Carnap – Putnam uses the name just because the type of toy world considered is a type of world Carnap used to consider when discussing inductive logic) and "the Polish Logician" on the existence of *mereological sums*. The other has to do with different construals of what *points* are. I will argue both that neither example actually succeeds in supporting Putnam's ontological pluralism, and, more strongly, that Putnam's ontological pluralism is false.

Here is what we might call Putnam's mereology argument. Consider a world with three individuals: a, b, and c. How many *objects* are there in this world? We can imagine one philosopher ("Carnap") who says *three*; and another ("the Polish Logician") who accepts the existence of mereological sums, and says *seven* (a, b, c, a + b, a + c, b + c, and a + b + c).[4] Who is right? Putnam says that all we can say is that according to one conceptual scheme, three objects exist, and according to another, seven objects exist. There is no further question of which conceptual scheme gets matters right. There is, according to Putnam, no conceptual scheme-independent answer to the question of how many objects there are (1987a: 18ff.).

Putnam's other example motivating ontological pluralism departs from the observation that there are different ways of understanding talk of *points* in geometry. Let us call this the geometry argument.

> Think of the points in the plane. Are these parts of the plane, as Leibniz thought? Or are they "mere limits," as Kant said? . . . If you say, in this case, that these are "two ways of slicing the same dough," then you must admit that what is a *part* of space, in one version

of the facts, is an abstract entity (say, a set of convergent spheres – although there is not, of course, a unique way of construing points as limits) in the other version. But then you will have conceded that which entities are "abstract entities" and which are "concrete objects," at least, is version-relative. (1987a: 19)

As already mentioned, it may be tempting to express the ontological pluralist view by employing what is known as the "cookie cutter-metaphor." Expressed employing this metaphor, the view is that the world considered in itself is just like some amorphous dough, and the concepts employed are like cookie-cutters carving out cookies from the dough. The different conceptual schemes correspond to different sets of cookie-cutters. However, in the context of presenting the mereology argument, Putnam criticizes the metaphor:

> Take [the metaphor] seriously, and you are at once forced to answer the question, "What are the various parts of the dough?" If you answer, that (in the present case) the "atoms" of the dough are [the individuals] and the other parts are the mereological sums containing more than one "atom," then you have simply adopted [the Polish Logician's version]. Insisting that this is the correct view of the metaphysical situation is just another way of insisting that mereological sums *really* exist. (1987a: 33)

Insofar as there is a genuine argument here, it must be extracted from the text. For why, exactly, would one be forced to answer the question of what the parts of the dough are? Cannot the friend of the cookie-cutter metaphor say: when I say reality is like some dough, I mean precisely to deny that there is an objectively superior answer to the question of what the ultimate parts of reality are?

It seems Putnam's reasoning has to be the following. If the dough picture is right, it can be recognized as being so from any perspective; hence also from the perspective of "Carnap." But the dough picture says that it is possible to carve out seven objects from the dough. But that, in turn, is sufficient for there actually to be seven objects – for it is sufficient for a purported object to exist that a concept carving it out could exist. (Because otherwise we would be forced to say that objects are *created* by our carving them out.) Hence, the more ontologically decadent scheme – in this case, the Polish Logician's scheme – is the accurate one. But then the dough picture misfires. For there is a proper way to carve the dough after all: the way of carving it that yields as many objects as there can possibly be.

Let me now turn to criticism. Some of the criticisms will be directed only at Putnam's arguments for his brand of ontological pluralism. Other, more radical criticisms will be directed at ontological pluralism itself. My aim here is not wholly destructive. Later I will sketch the positive view suggested by these criticisms. I will begin by discussing Putnam's geometry argument.

The trouble with this argument is that Putnam simply omits to consider the following alternative possibility, which seems far more natural for someone inclined toward a conciliatory view: the two different perspectives on points can be represented as different possible theories, T_1 and T_2, such that 'point' means different things in the two different theories and is true of different things in the two theories. As characterized by one theory, 'points' are part of the plane, and as characterized by the other theory, 'points' are mere limits. But there is no conflict: for 'point' refers to different things in the two theories. Points$_1$ are parts of the plane; points$_2$ are mere limits. (If 'point' refers to different things in the two theories, the same holds of related predicates.)[5]

When using this case to argue for ontological pluralism, Putnam appears to assume that 'point' means the same in the two theories. Plausibly, what makes Putnam assume this is that both theories seem adequate for the purpose of representing what 'point' actually refers to. But this observation rather argues for the view that 'point' in ordinary language is *referentially indeterminate*, and can equally well be taken to be true of one type of entity as of the other. (A term is referentially indeterminate just in case, for all that has been determined with respect to its meaning, there are different possibilities concerning what it refers to that stand up equally well. The term is referentially indeterminate as between these candidate referents. Compare how a vague expression like 'heap' is arguably referentially indeterminate as between different candidate referents; or how Newton's term 'mass' is referentially indeterminate as between relativistic mass and rest mass.[6])

After the passage where the geometry example is presented, Putnam goes on to say: "My view is that God himself, if he consented to the question, 'Do points really exist or are they mere limits?', would say 'I don't know'; not because his Omniscience is limited, but because there is a limit to how far questions make sense" (1987a: 19). Clearly, Putnam takes this to be a metaphysical point. But there is a simpler interpretation of what is going on. The reason why there is not anything for God to know is the same as in the case of God's lack of knowledge of how many grains it takes to make a heap, or of whether Newton's term 'mass' is true of relativistic mass or rest mass.

The criticism of this argument of Putnam's is, in the first instance, only a criticism of the argument itself. The suggestion is that there is a natural way to understand the case which makes good in the sense that both views on points are somehow acceptable but which does not involve embracing ontological pluralism. Part of the interest of the rebuttal lies in its potential generalizability: maybe analogous moves can be made with respect to all cases Putnam might appeal to in support of his ontological pluralist view. But even so, nothing in this reply directly argues against the truth of ontological pluralism. In this respect, my discussion of Putnam's mereology argument, to which I will now turn, will be of more significance.[7]

Focus on the criticism that Putnam himself, in the context of presenting the mereology argument, levels at the cookie-cutter metaphor. An analogous argument is equally telling against Putnam's ontological pluralism. Here it goes. If ontological pluralism is true, its truth can be appreciated from any perspective. Hence also from that of, say, Putnam's Carnap. So already, from Carnap's perspective, the permissibility of saying that there are seven objects can be appreciated. But already, if it is permissible to say that there are seven objects, it is true to say that there are seven objects.

The crucial step is the last. This step may seem simply to beg the question against Putnam's ontological pluralism. But here is why this step can be taken. First, *ad hominem*: this is the same move that Putnam apparently makes in arguing against the cookie-cutter metaphor. (Already from the perspective of Putnam's Carnap, it can be seen that it is permissible to say that there are seven objects in the world under consideration.) Second, we can certainly, on the pluralist's view, think of Putnam's

Carnap and the Polish Logician as using two different languages, with different meanings assigned to the ontological expressions, including the existential quantifier. Consider then the Polish Logician's language, where, purportedly, the sentence that intuitively expresses that there are seven objects is true. Carnap can, we said, recognize that this language is as fine as Carnap's own language. What, then, should Carnap say about the truth value of a sentence of the Polish Logician's language the form 'F(t)', where 't' is a singular term of that language purporting to refer to an object Carnap officially does not recognize? Carnap should be able to recognize, on the assumption of the recognizable truth of ontological pluralism, that this sentence is true. But a sentence of this form is true only if 't' refers. In general, an atomic sentence, of any language, is true only if the predicate is true of the object referred to by the singular term.[8] But this presupposes that the singular term has a referent. The reasoning straightforwardly generalizes. For any two languages L and L', it holds that if the singular term 't' of L' is such that there are true atomic sentences of the form 'F(t)' in L', then 'F' is true of the object referred to by 't', and unless L is simply expressively impoverished, this is something which can be expressed in L.

Let me say a few words about what "expressively impoverished" means here. The notion will be of some importance in the discussion to follow. A language is expressively impoverished just in case there are facts which the language does not possess the means to express. Consider – to borrow an example from Dorr (2005), from which I have also taken the label "expressively impoverished" – a variant of English spoken by a community where the members have decided among themselves to speak a language in which, say for religious reasons, it is absolutely impossible to speak of anything that is at least a certain distance from Earth. There are some difficulties concerning how exactly to make the example work. For example, in this variant of English, the semantics of expressions of the form 'what x is thinking about' must be somewhat different from the semantics of the corresponding expressions of actual English: for what if x happens to be thinking of something too far from Earth? But there is no need to get into the details. The reason for bringing up the possibility of there being languages that are expressively impoverished in this sense is that what the ontological pluralist holds precisely is not simply that there are languages like this. What the ontological pluralist wishes to hold is that there are languages with significantly different sets of ontological expressions such that these languages are all maximally adequate for stating all the facts about the world.[9]

Turn now to how Hirsch argues for his version of ontological pluralism, in, for example, his contribution to this volume. Hirsch's argument proceeds in two steps. In the first, it is argued that for each coherent ontological position (within a certain class – Hirsch is never explicit on exactly how big the class is, but the scope of the proposal need not concern us), there is some possible language within which the position comes out true. In other words, there is some language where the ontological expressions have the right meanings for the position to come out true as stated in that language. In the second step, it is argued that, for example, appeal to the principle of charity militates in favor of taking us to speak a possible language where the commonsense view on what there is and is not comes out true.

On Hirsch's view, a sentence like "incars exist" comes out untrue in our language, but there is some other language where the corresponding sentence comes out true.

It is easy to modify my point about Putnam's mereology argument to refute this claim. Let 'Herbie' purport to name a car, and let 'Herbie*' purport to name the corresponding incar. By Hirsch's lights, the following holds. The term 'Herbie*' of our language does not refer (there is no referent for the term in the domain of the quantifiers of our language, even when the domain of quantification is absolutely unrestricted), but there is a language, call it L*, much like English such that the term 'Herbie*' of that language is in the extension of the predicate 'refers*' of that language, where 'refers*' is a counterpart of our predicate 'refers', and 'Herbie* exists*' is a true sentence of that language, where 'exists*' is a counterpart to our 'exists'.

By the same argument as one given against Putnam earlier, this is not a stable position. According to the view under consideration, there are true atomic sentences of L* of the form 'F(Herbie*)'; for example, "Herbie* is white." But is it not the case that for any atomic sentence of the form 'F(t)' of any language, that sentence is true only if the object referred to by 't' is in the extension of the predicate 'F'? This presupposes that 't' has a referent. Hence we should in the present case conclude that 'Herbie*' has a referent. So there exists something for 'Herbie*' to refer to.

Let me here also present a related argument against the pluralist view, departing from the same kind of idea as the argument just given. Consider the true sentence of L* "Herbie* is white" (1*) and the counterpart sentence "Herbie* is white" of our language augmented with the name 'Herbie*' purporting to refer to an incar (1). By the ontological pluralist's lights, (1) is untrue, but (1*) is true. But this, I submit, is impossible, given that the name 'Herbie*' of L* and the name 'Herbie*' of our language purport to refer to the same object.[10] By the pluralist's lights, (1) and (1*) differ in truth value. Hence they differ in meaning. If they differ in meaning, either they differ in composition or one or more constituents differ in meaning. The best candidate for a difference is clearly in the singular term, 'Herbie*'. But can it really plausibly be maintained that 'Herbie*' differs so in meaning between the two languages as for this to account for a difference in truth value between (1) and (1*)? These considerations suggest that the sentences (1) and (1*) cannot differ in truth value after all, and hence that ontological pluralism must be false.[11]

I have presented two arguments that purport to show that ontological pluralism must be false. The first, which we might call *the 'Tarskian' argument*, departs from the assumption that for any atomic sentence of the form 'F(t)' of any language, this sentence can be true only if there is something that 't' refers to, and this something is in the extension of 'F'; we might call this the Tarskian assumption.[12] The second, which we might call *the sameness argument*, departs from the fact that there is no way the ontological pluralist can make good on her claim that two sentence which stand in the relation to each other that 'F(Herbie*)' of our language and 'F(Herbie*)' of L* stand in truth value.

If *all* that could be said on behalf of the assumptions these arguments rely on is that they come out true *in English*, the arguments would not be successful against ontological pluralism. The ontological pluralist could say that all the arguments show is that we speak a possible language where all the different purported entities mentioned are truly said to exist. This does not vitiate the ontological pluralist's point that there are different possible languages, with different sets of ontological expressions, none of them "privileged." However, what I want to claim on behalf of the arguments that have been presented is that the assumptions they rely on are satisfied in all languages except ones that are expressively impoverished, in the sense earlier explained. What I claim on behalf of the Tarskian argument is that a language whose ontological expressions work in such a way that the Tarskian assumption (or the statement of that language which is its counterpart) fails to come out true is simply expressively impoverished: it fails to be able to state everything relevant to semantics. Maybe this claim can be resisted (although this would require some radical rethinking about the nature of semantic facts[13]).

However that may be, the sameness argument is in this respect safer. For this argument trades on nothing about what the language we are considering is itself able to express about truth and reference and existence. Rather, all that the sameness argument relies on is that we are employing a language where, for every term of another language that purports to refer to a specific object of a particular kind, there could be, in the language employed, a term purporting to refer to that same object. Certainly there are possible languages that fail to satisfy this condition. But such languages are obviously expressively impoverished: they are incapable of naming the purported objects in question.

3 A More Fundamental Worry

Thus far I have talked about ontological pluralism as if it were clear what the view comes to. But in fact it is not even clear whether there is a way to make adequate sense of the doctrine. Consider Putnam's formulations of the doctrine: "[T]he logical primitives themselves, and in particular the notions of object and existence, have a multitude of different uses rather than one absolute 'meaning'" (1987b: 71); "[T]here isn't one privileged sense of the word 'object'" (1994: 30); and, from Putnam's more recent book, "[W]hat logicians call 'the existential quantifier', the symbol '($\exists$x)', and its ordinary language counterparts, the expressions 'there are', 'there exist' and 'there exists a', 'some', etc., *do not have a single absolutely precise use but a whole family of uses*" (2004: 37); and, later, "conceptual relativity . . . holds that the question as to which of these ways of using 'exist' (and 'individual', 'object', etc.) is *right* is one that the meanings of the words in the natural language . . . simply leaves open" (2004: 43). Hirsch expresses his thesis as the denial of the claim that there is a "metaphysically privileged sense of the quantifier" (2002b: 61).

What might the claim that (say) 'object' and 'exist' do not have just one sense come to? There is a way of understanding it under which it is trivially true: these *strings of symbols*, or these *noises*, could be associated with different meanings. But this trivial claim cannot be what the ontological pluralist has in mind. No one would dream of denying it. If, by contrast, the claim is that 'object, 'exist', etc. do not just have one sense *while still meaning what they actually do*, the claim sounds patently false. Or, rather, it sounds patently false unless what is meant is that these expressions are somehow referentially indeterminate; and at least as far as Putnam is concerned, this really does seem to be the view. The idea would be that the ontological expressions are like vague expressions – or like what most theorists take vague expressions to be like – in that they have different semantic values under different acceptable assignments. This interpretation fits Putnam's formulations well. But there are two reasons for skepticism. First, ontological pluralism is clearly meant as a *metaphysical* thesis: a thesis about the nature of reality. But how can the truth of a metaphysical claim turn on (something as shallow as) the referential indeterminacy of some words we actually employ? Second, in order for the extension of any predicate to include some thing *a* under any acceptable assignment, *a* must exist. So, under the supposition that these ontological notions have different semantic values under different acceptable assignments, it turns out that the most generous assignment is the correct one. This contradicts the supposition. Reductio (cf. Sider 2001: 128).

It is better, perhaps, to fasten on the word "privileged" in Hirsch's formulation and in one of Putnam's formulations. On any reasonable view, there is a multitude of existence-like concepts – a number of different possible meanings for an 'exists'-like expression to have. Putnam's point can be taken to be that none is ontologically privileged: that none is determinately the best one for representing what the ontological facts actually are. This seems right as far as it goes: but it is still unclear what it might mean to say that one existence-like notion is ontologically superior to, or inferior to, or for that matter equally good as, another.

However, what the pluralist can be taken to mean is that two theories employing two different existence-like notions can be, in some important sense, *equivalent* to each other: despite differences in formulation, the theories somehow say *the same things* about the world. Compare how Hirsch, when outlining his version of ontological pluralism, says that there are "many possible perspectives on 'the existence of objects', which all are adequate for describing the same facts, the same 'way the world is'" (2004: 231). This can be seen as one way of cashing out the talk of 'privileged' concepts of existence. The concept of existence of one language L is superior to that of another language L′ just in case L′ is more expressively impoverished than L, and is so in virtue of the differences between the ontological expressions of the two languages. Ontological pluralism is then the view that there are languages with significantly different sets of ontological expressions, tied for maximal expressive richness.

This is better. But one problem here concerns what the nature of the equivalence between the theories is supposed to be. It would obviously be misguided to say that the theories, or statements therein, are *synonymous*. Synonymy is a matter of sameness of meaning, and even if some interesting equivalence relation obtains between the theories, or the statements therein, they do not actually mean the very same thing. And it would obviously not go far enough for the ontological pluralist's purposes to say that the theories are *necessarily equivalent*. This equivalence relation is too weak. The statements "2 + 2 = 4" and "nothing is both red and green all over" are both necessarily true and hence they are necessarily equivalent – they have the same truth values no matter what the world turns out to be like – but they do not describe the same facts, except on a radically coarse-grained conception of facts. What is needed is an equivalence relation intermediate in strength between these two. But it is quite unclear what equivalence relation this might be. Some of the counterexamples that can be used against identifying it as necessary equivalence can also be used against identifying it as a priori necessary equivalence. Another immediate suggestion is empirical equivalence (in the strong sense where it entails equivalence of theoretical virtues). But this is too weak: a realist of the kind Putnam attacks will feel comfortable in holding that theories can be empirically equivalent, yet one is true and the other false. Putnam (1978) proposed that two theories are "cognitively equivalent" if they explain the phenomena equally well and are mutually relatively interpretable.[14] But adding a relative interpretability clause does not get around the problem: the realist can comfortably say, of two theories which are equivalent in this sense, that one is true and the other false.

4 The Deflationary Conception of Ontology

I have at some length criticized ontological pluralism. Now let me turn to the consequences of the failure of ontological pluralism for deflationism about ontology.

In virtue of the influence of the views of theorists like Carnap, Putnam, and Hirsch, many would find it natural simply to equate deflationism about ontology with ontological pluralism. But remember the more fundamental thought of the deflationist: that *somehow* ontological disputes are non-disputes; and that *somehow* there is no privileged carving-up of the world into objects. There may be other ways to go for the deflationist besides taking the pluralist route. I will now turn to what else the deflationist might say about the nature of ontological questions.

For instance, the deflationist about ontology can embrace a maximally decadent ontology: *maximalism*, as I will call it. What maximalism says is that for any type of object such that there can be objects of that type given that the empirical facts are exactly what they are, there are such objects. The qualification about the empirical facts being exactly what they are is there to rule out that maximalism should be committed to the existence of phlogiston or Vulcan. The ontological decadence of maximalism consists in its willingness to countenance all sorts of metaphysically weird sorts of objects – like incars, or like unintuitive abstract objects – as existing.

This possibility that the deflationist about ontology should embrace maximalism is suggested by how the present criticisms of Putnam and Hirsch all point in one and the same direction: someone who accepts the assumptions from which Putnam and Hirsch start should end up accepting a decadent ontology. For example, the would-be ontological pluralist wants to say that sentence (1*) is true, and I have argued that she is thereby committed to taking also (1) to be true. Since the reasoning in no way trades on the specific case of incars, the following general point holds. For any type of object ϕ such that the would-be ontological pluralist holds that there are possible languages with a notion of existence such that Fs exist in the sense of this alternative notion of existence, the ontological pluralist will have to hold that some of these languages contain true atomic sentences of the form 'F(t)' where 't' purports to refer to a ϕ. By the same reasoning as earlier, the corresponding atomic sentence of English will also have to be true. (Maybe English does not contain the means for formulating a corresponding sentence, but in that case English is simply expressively impoverished.)

To embrace maximalism may seem to be to abandon deflationism. After all, maximalism constitutes a definite answer to the question of what objects there are. But I think maximalism can satisfy the deflationist's motivations. It is clear that deflationism, as a stance concerning metaphysical disputes, cannot be *identified* with maximalism: also a robust ontologist can adhere to maximalism. But this does not mean that the deflationist cannot embrace the view. Here, moreover, is why maximalism seems an attractive way for the ontological deflationist to go. Consider the following passage from Carl Ginet:

> But is it incoherent to suppose a type of *material* thing whose constitutive matter could completely change from one time to another in a nonpiecemeal fashion? Could I not introduce such a type of material thing by definition? I might stipulate that a *monewment* is a material object performing the same sort of function as a monument (commemorating something) and such that monewment x at t_2 is the same monewment as monewment y at t_1, if the matter constituting y at t_1 were subsequently destroyed all at once and thereafter new matter of pretty much the same sort and shape were put in the same place in order to restore the commemorating in the same fashion of whatever it was that monewment y at t_1 commemorated. (1985: 220)

In a well-known critical discussion, Peter van Inwagen (1990: 7) interprets Ginet as assuming that we are bringing objects into existence by our stipulations. But it is more natural to take Ginet to assume that, so long as the stipulation is logically coherent and the empirical facts cooperate (roughly: there are monuments), there are in fact monewments. (As I will put it, so long as *minimal conditions* are satisfied, there are monewments.) Generalizing the reasoning, we end up with a maximally decadent ontology, maximalism. The underlying reasoning can moreover be taken to rest on a deflationary assumption about ontology. Perhaps the best way to explain how this can be so is by employing some of the metaphors mentioned early on. The deflationist about ontology thinks of reality as an amorphous lump; the robust ontologist takes the world to have ontological "joints." If reality has joints then there can fail to be monewments even if the minimal conditions are satisfied. For the stipulation may fail to carve the world at its joints. But if, by contrast, reality is an amorphous lump, there is no way the stipulation can fail to carve the world at its joints: hence satisfaction of the minimal conditions is enough for the stipulation to be satisfied by something.[15] (Maximalism too faces serious problems. Let me briefly mention two. First, there is a problem about proper formulation: the above formulation in terms of consistency with the empirical facts being what they are at best fudges things. Second, there is a potential problem which we might call that of incompatible objects: one might argue that there are two kinds of purported objects, the Fs and the Gs, such that the Fs satisfy maximalism's conditions for existence and so do the Gs, but it is logically impossible for Fs and Gs to coexist. But discussion of those problems, and what we should take to be their upshot, falls outside the scope of this chapter.)

5 Conclusion

The criticisms of ontological pluralism have not been criticisms of deflationism about ontology in itself – except on the assumption that deflationism about ontology is inextricably tied to ontological pluralism. I have cast doubt on this assumption. Specifically, I have suggested that the deflationist might embrace what I have called maximalism. There are other possibilities as well. Let me end by briefly describing them. One is to embrace total *nihilism* – the view that there are no objects at all (cf. Dorr (2005)).[16] Another is to deny that questions about what there is have any literal content at all. Some theorists, prominently Stephen Yablo, have argued that normally when we utter ontologically committing sentences – sentences which require for their literal truth that certain objects exist, like "there is an even prime number" or "there are two tables in this room" – we really mean them only in a fictional spirit. We do not actually commit ourselves to the existence of these things. Rather, our utterances are only presented as true *on the assumption that the relevant objects exist*. This fictionalism in itself yields no deflationist conclusion about ontology. It leaves open that we can in principle leave the pretense behind and ask whether numbers or tables really exist. But Yablo at one point suggests (although does not even endorse this radical suggestion himself) that talk about what there is, like talk about "zillions," entirely lacks a literal meaning. There is no way to drop the pretense. This view, call it *absolute fictionalism*, would seem to be a kind of deflationism about ontology (Yablo 1998: 259). Third, even if all positive deflationist views that say something distinctive about the nature of ontological questions are found wanting, there is a fairly comfortable position for the would-be deflationist to fall back on. The would-be deflationist can say that even if ontological questions are genuine, there is no way to settle ontological questions, so the project of ontology is still futile. Call this agnosticism about ontology. The agnostic about ontology is perhaps not strictly a deflationist, since the agnostic acknowledges that ontological questions are genuine. But agnosticism may still be good enough for the purposes of the would-be deflationist: the criticism of the enterprise of ontology still stands. (Naturally, good skeptical questions can be raised also about the reasonableness of agnosticism. But consideration of those questions lies outside the scope of this paper. For discussion, see Bennett (forthcoming).)

I do not mean to push for nihilism, or absolute fictionalism, or agnosticism. In my view, maximalism is the most interesting, and promising, route for the deflationist to take. My purpose in bringing up these other views is only to emphasize how many other routes there are for the deflationist about ontology besides ontological pluralism.[17]

Notes

1 The incar example comes from Hirsch (1976: 361ff.).
2 See James (1907/46), Carnap (1950), Putnam (esp. 1987a, 1987b, 1994, 2004), and Hirsch (2002a, 2002b, 2004, and chapter 9.1 in this volume). Incidentally, I am somewhat doubtful about including James here, but often he is ascribed a view similar to these other theorists. See e.g. Pihlström (1996: 64–88) and Thayer (1968: 352–7).
3 Some of these arguments are: considerations about the "interpenetration" of convention and fact – see e.g. Putnam (1995: 58); the model-theoretic argument – see esp. Putnam (1980 and 1981: ch. 2); the semantic paradoxes – Putnam (1990: ch. 1); and quantum physics – Putnam (1990: ch. 1).
4 Here is a brief and not entirely untendentious characterization of what mereology is. Mereology is the study of the part–whole relation. An object which is a *mereological sum*

has other objects as parts, in the way described by mereology. An *individual* is an object that is not the sum of any other objects. For an overview of mereology, see e.g. Varzi (2003).

5   There are independent problems regarding taking any "conciliatory" view on the nature of points. What I argue in the text is only that even if we agree with Putnam that a conciliatory view should be adopted, it is not clear that Putnam's specific view should be.

6   The 'mass' example is from Field (1973). The point is that Newtonian physics spoke only of one quantity, 'mass', and, given what we know today, there is no quantity that satisfies all the assertions Newtonian physics made about mass, but there are two quantities that both come close – what we call relativistic mass and rest mass. What, then, does 'mass' as it occurs in Newtonian physics refer to? It does not seem plausible either that the term should lack reference altogether or that it should determinately refer to one or other of these quantities. Rather, it would appear that Newtonian 'mass' is referentially indeterminate as between relativistic mass and rest mass.

7   There are independent reasons to doubt whether the dispute over the nature of points is really properly understood as verbal. My argument is just that even if we agree with Putnam that in some sense the dispute is a non-dispute, his pluralist conclusion does not follow.

8   Some would argue this is an overgeneralization. They might say that, despite the fact that 'Vulcan' has no referent, sentences like "Vulcan = Vulcan" and "Vulcan is a planet" – roughly, sentences ascribing essential properties of the would-be referent – are true. In the main text I disregard this possibility. If you are inclined to think that the thesis assumed in the main text is an overgeneralization, just focus on atomic sentences not belonging to this special class.

9   Note that I say "maximally adequate" and not "perfectly adequate." The ontological pluralist might certainly hold that all languages are to some extent expressively impoverished. The core of the view is that among the different sets of ontological expressions a language might have, there is no set which makes for determinately more expressive richness.

10 One may ask: do terms of the alien language *purport to refer* at all (as opposed to *refer**), given a pluralist view? But the reason I am cavalier about talking about 'Herbie*' as purporting to refer is that even if it should not be strictly true that it does, the ontological pluralist must agree that there is some sort of very tight relation between the names 'Herbie*' of the two languages, and the most straightforward description of what the names have in common is that they purport to refer to the same object. Taking this description strictly and literally would be question-begging, but it need not be so taken for the argument.

11 I keep using atomic sentences of simple predicate-term form as my example. In principle, I could use other examples. But in the present argument the focus on simple atomic sentences has a point. The ontological pluralist wants to say that the ontological expressions have different meanings in the different languages she considers. But now we see how the supposed differences in meaning between the ontological expressions ramify: the ontological pluralist appears committed to saying that we cannot have a term in our language that purports to refer to the entities that are said to 'exist' in a language where the counterpart of the sentence "incars exist" comes out true.

12 Alfred Tarski (1935/83) was the first theorist clearly to lay out how the truth of a sentence depends on the reference of its constituents.

13 Notice just how radical the rethinking would have to be. Many would be attracted to the view that truth and reference should be dethroned from their status as central notions in semantics. I am not assigning to the notions of truth and reference any central or explana-

Matti Eklund

tory role. All I am relying on is that the Tarskian assumption is in fact true, not that it is central or explanatory.

14   Where a theory T1 is relatively interpretable into another, T2, iff the terms of T1 can be translated into the terms of T2 so that all theorems of T1 are theorems of T2. Two theories are mutually relatively interpretable iff they are relatively interpretable into each other.

15   There are also more theoretical ways that maximalism can be supported on deflationist grounds. See Matti (manuscript).

16   Nihilism in this sense must not be confused with the less radical doctrine of mereological nihilism, the view that there are no *composite* objects.

17   Many thanks to Eli Hirsch, Danny Korman, David Liebesman, Øystein Linnebo, Agustín Rayo, and Ted Sider for helpful conversations and comments. The title of this chapter is stolen from Dummett (1981: ch. 16), where Dummett keeps using this locution.

References

Bennett, Karen. Forthcoming. "Composition, Colocation, and Metaontology," in David Chalmers, David Manley, and Ryan Wasserman, eds., *Metametaphysics* (Oxford: Oxford University Press).

Carnap, Rudolf. 1950. "Empiricism, Semantics and Ontology," *Revue Internationale de Philosophie* 11: 20–40. Reprinted in Leonard Linsky, ed., *Semantics and the Philosophy of Language*, The University of Illinois Press at Urbana, 1952, pp. 208–28.

Dorr, Cian. 2005. "What we Disagree about when we Disagree about Ontology," in Mark Eli Kalderon, ed., *Fictionalism in Metaphysics* (Oxford: Oxford University Press), pp. 234–86.

Dummett, Michael. 1981. *Frege: Philosophy of Language*, 2nd edn. (Cambridge, MA: Harvard University Press).

Eklund, Matti. Manuscript. "The Deflationary Conception of Ontology."

Field, Hartry. 1973. "Theory Change and the Indeterminacy of Reference," *Journal of Philosophy* 70: 462–81.

Ginet, Carl. 1985. "Plantinga and the Philosophy of Mind," in James Tomberlin and Peter van Inwagen, eds., *Alvin Plantinga* (Dordrecht: Kluwer), pp. 199–223.

Hirsch, Eli. 1976. "Physical Identity," *Philosophical Review* 85: 357–89.

——. 1999. "The Vagueness of Identity," *Philosophical Topics* 26: 139–58.

——. 2002a. "Against Revisionary Ontology," *Philosophical Topics* 30: 103–27.

——. 2002b. "Quantifier Variance and Realism," in Ernest Sosa and Enrique Villanueva, eds., *Philosophical Issues 12: Realism and Relativism* (Oxford: Blackwell Publishing), pp. 51–73.

——. 2004. "Sosa's Existential Relativism," in J. Greco, ed., *Ernest Sosa and His Critics* (Oxford: Blackwell Publishing), pp. 224–32.

James, William. 1907/46. *Pragmatism: A New Name for Some Old Ways of Thinking* (New York: Longmans, Green and Co.).

Pihlström, Sami. 1996. *Structuring the World: The Issue of Realism and the Nature of Ontological Problems in Classical and Contemporary Pragmatism* (Helsinki: Acta Philosophica Fennica).

Putnam, Hilary. 1978. "Equivalence," in *Realism and Reason: Philosophical Papers*, vol. 3 (Cambridge: Cambridge University Press, 1983), pp. 26–45.

——. 1980. "Models and Reality," *Journal of Symbolic Logic* 45: 464–82; repr. in *Realism and Reason: Philosophical Papers*, vol. 3 (Cambridge: Cambridge University Press, 1983), pp. 1–25.

——. 1981. *Reason, Truth and History* (Cambridge: Cambridge University Press).

Putnam, Hilary. 1987a. *The Many Faces of Realism* (La Salle, ILL: Open Court).

—. 1987b. "Truth and Convention: On Davidson's Refutation of Conceptual Relativism," *Dialectica* 41: 69–77; repr. in *Realism with a Human Face* (Cambridge, MA: Harvard University Press, 1990), pp. 96–104.

—. 1990. *Realism with a Human Face* (Cambridge, MA: Harvard University Press).

—. 1994. "The Question of Realism," in *Words and Life* (Cambridge, MA: Harvard University Press), pp. 295–312.

—. 1995. *Pragmatism: An Open Question* (Oxford: Blackwell Publishing).

—. 2004. *Ethics Without Ontology* (Cambridge, MA: Harvard University Press).

Rosen, Gideon and Cian Dorr. 2002. "Composition as a Fiction," in Richard Gale, ed., *Blackwell Guide to Metaphysics* (Oxford: Blackwell Publishing).

Sider, Theodore. 2001. *Four-Dimensionalism* (Oxford: Oxford University Press).

Tarski, Alfred. 1935/83. "The Concept of Truth in Formalized Languages," in John Corcoran, ed., *Logic, Semantics, Metamathematics: Papers from 1923 to 1938*, 2nd edn. (Indianapolis: Hackett Publishing Company). English translation by J. H. Woodger of "Der Wahrheitsbegriff in Formalisierten Sprachen," *Studia Philosophica* 1 (1935).

Thayer, H. S. 1968. *Meaning and Action: A Critical History of Pragmatism*, (Indianapolis: Hackett Publishing Company).

Van Inwagen, Peter. 1990. *Material Beings* (Ithaca, NY: Cornell University Press).

Varzi, Achille. 2003. "Mereology," in Ed Zalta, ed., *Stanford Encyclopedia of Philosophy*, <http://plato.stanford.edu/entries/mereology/>.

Yablo, Stephen. 1998. "Does Ontology Rest on a Mistake?" *Proceedings of the Aristotelian Society*, suppl. vol. 72: 229–61.

Index

idealism 246–7
identity conditions 22–3
  diachronic 332
  unrestricted diachronic 346
impossibilism 303–5, 309, 310–11, 317–18
impossible worlds 56 n.28
'in virtue of': see grounding
incompatibilism 303, 317–18
indeterminism 291–2, 293–4; see also
  determinism
indexicals 226–7, 228–30, 243; see also
  actuality, as indexical
indispensibility arguments 38–40, 118–19
inference to the best explanation 26, 28, 30;
  see also explanation
innate ideas 15
instantiation 51–2, 273; see also properties
intentionality 121
intrinsicality 48–9, 88, 276–7, 278 n.3; see
  also properties, intrinsic
intuitions 95–6; see also commonsense

Jackson, F. 55 n.12
James, W. 286, 338 n.39, 383
Johnston, M. 174 n.3, 198
justification 21, 40–3, 76; see also knowledge

Kant, I. 54 n.2, 281 n.26, 286, 292, 335 n.8
knowledge 21, 23–4
  of abstracta: see abstracta, knowledge of
  of answers to ontological questions 393
  of causal relations 68, 89–91
  of laws of nature 76, 97
  see also justification
Kripke, S. 50, 55 n.16, 128–9, 131 n.2, 280
  n.21, 338 n.35, 375, 379 n.5

Lange, M. 72
Langton, R. 132 n.16, 278 n.3
language
  expressive power of 137–8; see also
    expressive impoverishment
  tenseless: see time, tenseless
laws of nature 67–80
  ability to break 287–8, 314–17
  anti-realism about 71, 100 n.6, 103 n.33
  meta- 96
  reduction of 81–100
  universalism 70–1
  see also causation

Le Poidevin, R. 60 n.67
Leibniz, G. 95, 325
Leibniz's Law 244, 248, 265, 268–9
Leonard, H. 321, 361 n.3, n.5, n.6
Lesniewski, S. 321, 361 n.3, n.5, n.6
Lewis, D. 37, 43, 46, 49, 54 n.3, 55 n.18, 58
  n.38, n.39, n.45, 59 n.51, n.59, 70, 82,
  93, 99, 100 n.1, 101 n.11, n.13, 105
  n.50, n.53, 111–31, 135–6, 138, 139–40,
  147–9, 169, 176 n.14, 246–7, 261 n.11,
  278 n.3, n.8, 281 n.24, 318 n.5, 321,
  329–31, 335 n.4, 337 n.33, 361 n.3, n.5,
  nn.7–8, n.10, 362 n.37, 377–8, 379 n.4,
  n.7, n.17, 380 n.23
libertarianism 292–6, 305
Lierse, C. 59 n.42
life: see organicism
Linsky, B. 150 n.4
location: see occupation
Locke, J. 15, 156, 174 n.1, 197–9, 203–5,
  288, 367–8, 379 n.15
Loewer, B. 100 n.5, 104 n.43, 105 n.53
Lowe, E. J. 100 n.4
luck 292–9
Lycan, W. 150 n.10

Mackie, J. L. 101 n.13
Maclaurin, J. 234
Markosian, N. 235–6, 331–3, 336 n.23
material coincidence 268, 323–6; see also
  material constitution
material constitution 194–6, 247–57; see
  also material coincidence
mathematical discourse 15, 19, 26
Maudlin, T. 103 n.34, 104 n.42
maximalism: see ontological maximalism
McDowell, J. 197, 199, 207 n.25
McGinn, C. 132 n.14
McTaggart, J. McT. E. 212, 214, 224 n.7,
  227, 231
Melia, J. 58 n.40
Mellor, D. H. 59 n.60, 101 n.13
Mendola, J. 176 n.20
mereological essentialism 250–1, 258–9,
  368
mereological junk 323
mereological nihilism 253–4, 259, 327,
  346–8
mereological simples 254; see also atomless
  gunk

possible worlds 11, 41–2, 43, 59 n.51, 111–31
  analysis of 115–18
  distinguishing 95
  ersatz 136–42
  reasons for believing in concrete 118–22
  see also modal realism
predicates
  observational 47
  physical 44–50
  structural 47–8
Price, H. H. 47–8, 237 n.2
Priest, G. 132 n.15, 133 n.26
Prior, A. N. 224 n.5, 229, 230–1, 233–5
projectivism 27
properties 1–3, 11–13, 24
  alien 46–7, 50–1, 137–8
  essential 127–8
  as ideas in God's mind 15
  intrinsic 246–7; *see also* intrinsicality
  natural 115, 131 n.12, 377–8
  qualitative 132 n.20
  relativized to times 245–6, 273; *see also*
    change
  structural 57 n.36, 58 n.38
  vs. concepts 124
propositional attitudes 15
propositions 11, 13, 141–2
Putnam, H. 38–9, 55 n.14, 338 n.38, 373,
    383, 384–7, 389–91

quantification
  existential 41–2
  plural 47–8, 322
  restricted 344
  universal 42–3
quantifier variance 373–8
quantum field theory 277–8, 278 n.10
Quine, W. V. O. 29, 38, 54 n.10, 103 n.30,
    118, 122, 131 n.3, n.11, 132 n.22, 278
    n.5, 379 n.4

Ramscar, M. 27
Ramsey, F. P. 59 nn.60–1, n.64, 105 n.53,
    148, 230
Rea, M. 261 n.8, 362 n.20
real definition 44–5, 47–8, 53; *see also*
    grounding
realism
  about abstracta 14
  about the future 307–9

recombination, Humean 85, 114–15
reduction 4, 83
  of causation 86–93
  of lawhood 68–71, 84–5
  of the modal to the occurrent 84–5
referential indeterminacy 386, 389
Reichenbach, H. 103 n.31, 228–9, 234, 236,
    237 n.2, 334
relations 11–13
relativism 30; *see also* indexicality
relativity, in physics: *see* time, relativity in
relevant alternatives 78
resemblance 1–2, 12–13, 45–53
resemblance nominalism 47–50, 53
responsibility 292–9
Roberts, J. 75–9, 105 n.48
Rodriguez-Pereyra, G. 59 n.48, n.49, n.51
Rosen, G. 39, 54 n.3, n.5, 55 n.14, 56 n.20,
    n.25, 333
Roy, T. 150 n.5
Russell, B. 26, 29, 54 n.6, 100 n.6, 103 n.30,
    n.33, 131, 247
Ryle, G. 86

Salmon, W. 103 n.31
Schaffer, J. 101 n.13, n.17, 102 n.19
Schiffer, S. 34, 43, 54 n.6
Schlesinger, G. 237 n.3
scientific practice 91–2, 95
sentences
  infinite 352
  superficial and fundamental uses of
    33–6
sets 11–12, 21–3
  structuralism about 149–50
Shalkwoski, S. 150 n.10
Shapiro, S. 56 n.26
Shoemaker, S. 59 n.42, 102 n.18, 174 n.2,
    176 n.15, 185
Sidelle, A. 59 n.42
Sider, T. 85, 101 n.12, 237 n.5, 278 n.1, n.5,
    279 n.12, 280 n.17, n.19, 281 n.25,
    328–31, 336 n.13, n.20, 338 n.35, 346,
    353, 361 n.5 , n.7, n.11, n.14, n.16,
    n.18, 362 n.22, 369, 375, 377–8, 379
    nn.6–7, n.17, nn.20–1, 380 nn.23–4,
    390
Sidgwick, H. 227
Simons, P. 278 n.2, 335 n.2
simplicity 29